TAKING SIDES

Clashing Views on Controversial
Issues in Anthropology
THIRD EDITION

D1542752

TAKING SIDES

Clashing Views on Controversial

Issues in Anthropology

THIRD EDITION

Selected, Edited, and with Introductions by

Kirk M. Endicott
Dartmouth College

and

Robert L. Welsch
Dartmouth College

McGraw-Hill/Dushkin
A Division of The McGraw-Hill Companies

For Karen and Sarah

Photo Acknowledgment
Cover image: © Geostock/Getty Images

Cover Art Acknowledgment
Maggie Nickles

Manufactured in the United States of America

Third Edition

123456789DOCDOC987654

Library of Congress Cataloging-in-Publication Data
Main entry under title:
Taking sides: clashing views on controversial issues in anthropology/selected, edited, and with introductions by Kirk M. Endicott and Robert L. Welsch.—3rd ed.
Includes bibliographical references and index.
1. Anthropology. I. Endicott, Kirk M., *comp.* II. Welsch, Robert L., *comp.*
306
0-07-310202-4
ISSN: 1530-0757

Printed on Recycled Paper

Preface

Many courses and textbooks present anthropology as a discipline that largely consists of well-established facts. In *Taking Sides: Clashing Views on Controversial Issues in Anthropology* we present the discipline in quite a different light. Here we focus on active controversies that remain unresolved. These issues represent the kind of arguments and debates that have characterized anthropology for more than a century. They show the varied ways that anthropologists approach the subject of their research and the kinds of anthropological evidence needed to bolster an academic argument.

Generally, we have chosen selections that express strongly worded positions on two sides of an issue. For most issues, several other reasonable positions are also possible, and we have suggested some of these in our introductions and postscripts that accompany each issue.

Taking Sides: Clashing Views on Controversial Issues in Anthropology is a tool to encourage and develop critical thinking about anthropological research questions, methods, and evidence. We have selected a range of readings and issues to illustrate the kinds of topics that anthropologists study. Another goal of this volume is to provide opportunities for students to explore how anthropologists frame and defend their interpretations of anthropological evidence. We have also chosen issues that raise questions about research methods and the quality or reliability of different kinds of data. All of these complex matters go into shaping the positions that anthropologists debate and defend in their writings. We hope that in discussing these issues students will find opportunities to explore how anthropologists think about the pressing theoretical issues of the day.

Plan of the book   This book is made up of 18 issues that deal with topics that have provoked starkly different positions by different anthropologists. We have divided the volume into five Parts reflecting the discipline's four main subfields (Biological Anthropology, Archaeology, Linguistic Anthropology, and Cultural Anthropology) as well as another Part dealing with Ethics in Anthropology. Each issue begins with an *introduction,* which sets the stage for the debate as argued in the YES and NO selections. Following these two selections is a *postscript* that makes some final observations and points the way to other questions related to the issue. In reading an issue and forming your own opinions, you should remember that there are often alternative perspectives that are not represented in either the YES or NO selections. Most issues have reasonable positions that might appear to be intermediate between the two more extreme viewpoints represented here in the readings. There are also reasonable positions that lie totally outside the scope of the debate presented in these selections, and students should consider all of these possible positions. Each postscript also contains *suggestions for further reading* that will help you find further resources to continue your study of any topic. Students researching any of these issues or related ones for a research paper will find these further readings (as well as their bibliographies) a useful place to begin a more intensive analysis. At the end of the book we have also included a list of all the *contributors to this volume,* which will give you information on the anthropologists and other commentators whose views are debated here. An *On the Internet* page accompanies each part opener. This page gives you Internet site addresses (URLs) that are relevant to the issues discussed in that part of the book. Many of these sites contain links to related sites and bibliographies for further study.

Changes to this edition   This edition has been updated to reflect several current and ongoing controversies that can help undergraduates understand the breadth and range of anthropological research within the four fields of the discipline. Four issues are new to this edition: "Did Prehistoric Native Americans Practice Cannibalism in the American Southwest?" (Issue 6), "Was Margaret Mead's Fieldwork on Samoan Adolescents Fundamentally Flawed?" (Issue 10), "Do Native Peoples Today Invent Their Traditions?" (Issue 11), and "Do Some Illnesses Exist Only Among Members of a Particular Culture?" (Issue 14). In addition, we have selected a new pair of readings to address "Did Napoleon Chagnon's Research Methods and Publications Harm the Yanomami Indians?" (Issue 17) that bring out the most salient point of the controversy raised by Patrick Tierney's critique of Napoleon Chagnon and his colleagues in *Darkness in El Dorado: How Scientists and Journalists Devastated the Amazon* (W. W. Norton, 2000). Finally, in response to requests from instructors who have used the first and second editions of Taking Sides *Anthropology,* we have brought back an issue dealing with concept of race in contemporary anthropological research: "Is Race a Useful Concept for Anthropologists?" (Issue 1).

A word to the instructor   An *Instructor's Manual With Test Questions* (multiplechoice and essay) is available through the publisher for the instructor using *Taking Sides* in the classroom. A general guidebook, called *Using Taking Sides in the Classroom,* which discusses methods and techniques for integrating the procon approach into any classroom setting, is also available. An online version of *Using Taking Sides in the Classroom* and a correspondence service for Taking Sides adopters can be found at http://www.dushkin.com/usingts/.

   Taking Sides: Clashing Views on Controversial Issues in Anthropology is only one of many titles in the Taking Sides series. If you are interested in seeing the table of contents for any of the other titles, please visit the Taking Sides Web site at http://www.dushkin.com/takingsides/.

Acknowledgments   We received many helpful comments and suggestions from many friends and colleagues, including Kamyar Abdi, Hoyt Alverson, Colin Calloway, Elizabeth Carpenter, Brian Didier, Dale Eickelman, Rachel Flemming, Jana Fortier, Laura Garzon, Rosemary Gianno, Paul Goldstein, Alberto Gomez, Robert Gordon, Allen Hockley, Judy Hunt, Peter Jenks, Sergei Kan, Steve Kangas, Katherine Keith, Kenneth Korey, Christine Kray, Laura Litton, Lynn MacGillivray, Deborah Martin, Deborah Nichols, Ventura Perez, Lynn Rainville, Kevin Reinhart, John Edward Terrell, Robert Tonkinson, John

Watanabe, and Lindsay Whaley. We also want to thank John Cocklin, Lucinda Hall, Francis X. Oscadal, Cindy Shirkey, Reinhart Sonnenberg, and Amy Witzel, members of the Baker-Berry Library Reference Department at Dartmouth College, all of whom helped track down many of the sources and background readings we have used in setting up these issues. We also want to thank our student research assistants Todd Rabkin Golden, Adam Slutsky, Whitney Wilking, and Rachel Yemeni and our Presidential Scholars/student research assistants Eric Goodman, Joseph Hanlon, Tate LeFebre, and Lauren Weldon. Ted Knight and Juliana Gribbins at McGraw-Hill/Dushkin offered useful advice, patience, and suggestions. We also want to thank Nichole Altman of McGraw-Hill in Dubuque, Iowa, for her help making this latest edition a reality. Finally, we wish to thank our wives, Karen L. Endicott and Sarah L. Welsch, for their support and encouragement during the preparation of this volume.

Kirk M. Endicott
Dartmouth College

Robert L. Welsch
Dartmouth College

Contents In Brief

Contents

Archaeologist João Zilhão discusses the recently found remains of a young child who was buried in a rock shelter in Portugal about 25,000 years ago. He concludes that the Lagar Velho child was a hybrid with mixed Neandertal and early modern human ancestry. Biological anthropologist Jean-Jacques Hublin maintains that the Lagar Velho child was merely one variant within the diverse early modern human population. He argues that there was some cultural influence from early modern humans to Neandertals but little or no interbreeding between them.

PART 2 ARCHAEOLOGY 57

Archaeologist Stuart J. Fiedel supports the traditional view that humans first reached the Americas from Siberia at the end of the last Ice Age (perhaps 14,000 years ago). He argues that there are currently no convincing sites dated before that time and is skeptical of statements by other archaeologists who date human occupation of sites such as Meadowcroft in Pennsylvania and Monte Verde in Chile significantly earlier. Archaeologist Thomas D. Dillehay asserts that the site he has excavated at Monte Verde, a complex site in Chile, proves that humans reached the New World well before the end of the last Ice Age, possibly as early as 30,000 years ago. He contends that those archaeologists who are skeptical about his carbon-14 dates and other findings are so entrenched in traditional thinking that they refuse to accept the solid evidence that Monte Verde provides.

Archaeologist Marija Gimbutas argues that the civilization of pre–Bronze Age "Old Europe" was matriarchal—ruled by women—and that the religion centered on the worship of a single great Goddess. Furthermore, this civilization was destroyed by patriarchal Kurgan pastoralists (the Indo-Europeans), who migrated into southeastern Europe from the Eurasian steppes in the fifth to third millennia B.C. Archaeologist Lynn Meskell considers the belief in a supreme Goddess and a matriarchal society in prehistoric Europe to be an unwarranted projection of some women's utopian longings onto the past. She regards Gimbutas's interpretation of the archaeological evidence as biased and speculative.

Archaeologists Brian Billman and Banks L. Leonard and bioarchaeologist Patricia Lambert argue that there is evidence of prehistoric cannibalism in the Mesa Verde region of southwestern Colorado. From their analysis of human skeletal remains and associated assemblages at Cowboy Wash, they conclude that the bodies of seven individuals were processed in ways that suggest that they were eaten by other humans. Archaeologists Kurt E. Dongoske and T.J. Ferguson and bioarchaeologist Debra L. Martin object that the analytical framework Billman et al. use assumes that cannibalism took place and does not adequately consider alternative hypotheses. Although Dongoske et al. feel that cannibalism was possible at Cowboy Wash, they contend that other interpretations of the same data are equally viable.

PART 3   LINGUISTIC ANTHROPOLOGY   125

Psychologist and primate specialist E. S. Savage-Rumbaugh argues that, since the 1960s, attempts to teach chimpanzees and other apes symbol systems similar to human language have resulted in the demonstration of a genuine ability to create new symbolic patterns. Linguist Joel Wallman counters that attempts to teach chimps and other apes sign language or other symbolic systems have demonstrated that apes are very intelligent animals, but up to now these attempts have not shown that apes have any innate capacity for language.

Sociolinguists John J. Gumperz and Stephen C. Levinson contend that recent studies of language and culture suggest that language structures human thought in a variety of ways that most linguists and anthropologists had not believed possible. Cognitive neuropsychologist Steven Pinker draws on recent studies in cognitive science and neuropsychology to support the notion that previous studies have examined language but have said little, if anything, about thought.

PART 4 CULTURAL ANTHROPOLOGY 167

YES: **Marvin Harris**, from "Cultural Materialism Is Alive and Well and Won't Go Away Until Something Better Comes Along," in Robert Borofsky, ed., *Assessing Cultural Anthropology* (McGraw-Hill, 1994) *170*

NO: **Clifford Geertz**, from *The Interpretation of Cultures: Selected Essays by Clifford Geertz* (Basic Books, 1973) *180*

Cultural anthropologist Marvin Harris argues that anthropology has always been a science and should continue to be scientific. He contends that the most scientific approach to culture is cultural materialism, which he has developed specifically to be a "science of culture." Anthropology's goal should be to discover general, verifiable laws as in the other natural sciences, concludes Harris. Cultural anthropologist Clifford Geertz views anthropology as a science of interpretation, and as such he argues that anthropology should never model itself on the natural sciences. He believes that anthropology's goal should be to generate deeper interpretations of diverse cultural phenomena, using what he calls "thick description," rather than attempting to prove or disprove scientific laws.

YES: **Derek Freeman**, from *Margaret Mead and Samoa: The Making and Unmaking of an Anthropological Myth* (Harvard University Press, 1983) *194*

NO: **Lowell D. Holmes and Ellen Rhoads Holmes**, from *Samoan Village: Then and Now,* 2d ed. (Harcourt Brace Jovanovich College Publishers, 1992) *204*

Social anthropologist Derek Freeman argues that Margaret Mead was wrong when she stated that Samoan adolescents had sexual freedom. He contends that Mead went to Samoa determined to prove anthropologist Franz Boas's cultural determinist agenda and states that Mead was so eager to believe in Samoan sexual freedom that she was consistently the victim of a hoax perpetrated by Samoan girls and young women who enjoyed tricking her. Cultural anthropologists Lowell D. Holmes and Ellen Rhoads Holmes contend that Margaret Mead had a very solid understanding of Samoan culture in general. During a restudy of Mead's research, they came to many of the same conclusions that Mead had reached about Samoan sexuality and adolescent experiences. Mead's description of Samoan culture exaggerates the amount of sexual freedom and the degree to which adolescence in Samoa is carefree but these differences, they argue, can be explained in terms of changes in Samoan culture since 1925 and in terms of Mead's relatively unsophisticated research methods as compared with field methods used today.

YES: **Roger M. Keesing**, from "Creating the Past: Custom and Identity in the Contemporary Pacific," *The Contemporary Pacific* (Spring/Fall 1989) *216*

Cultural anthropologist Roger M. Keesing argues that what native peoples in the Pacific now accept as "traditional culture" is largely an invented and idealized vision of their past. He contends that such fictional images emerge because native peoples are largely unfamiliar with what life was really like in pre-Western times and because such imagery distinguishes native communities from dominant Western culture. Hawaiian activist and scholar Haunani-Kay Trask asserts that Keesing's critique is fundamentally flawed because he only uses Western documents—and native peoples have oral traditions, genealogies, and other historical sources that are not reflected in Western historical documents. Anthropologists like Keesing, she maintains, are trying to hold on to their privileged position as experts in the face of growing numbers of educated native scholars.

Adoptee and adoption rights advocate Betty Jean Lifton argues that there is a natural need for human beings to know where they came from. Adoption is not a natural human state, she asserts, and it is surrounded by a secrecy that leads to severe social and psychological consequences for adoptees, adoptive parents, and birth parents. Anthropologists John Terrell and Judith Modell, who are each the parent of an adopted child, contend that the "need" to know one's birth parents is an American (or Western European) cultural construct. They conclude that in other parts of the world, where there is less emphasis placed on biology, adoptees have none of the problems said to be associated with being adopted in America.

Archaeologists James R. Denbow and Edwin N. Wilmsen argue that the San of the Kalahari Desert in southern Africa have been involved in pastoralism, agriculture, and regional trade networks since at least A.D. 800. They imply that the San, who were hunting and gathering in the twentieth century, were descendants of pastoralists who lost their herds due to subjugation by outsiders, drought, and livestock disease. Cultural anthropologist Richard B. Lee counters that evidence from oral history, archaeology, and ethnohistory shows that the Ju/'hoansi group of San living in the isolated Nyae Nyae-Dobe area of the Kalahari Desert were autonomous hunter-gatherers until the twentieth century. Although they carried on some trade with outsiders before then, it had minimal impact on their culture.

Physician Sangun Suwanlert from Thailand asks whether or not one particular illness he observed in northern Thai villages, called *phii pob,* corresponds to Western diagnostic categories or is restricted to Thailand. After documenting how this condition does not fit standard psychiatric diagnoses, he concludes that *phii pob* is indeed a "culture-bound syndrome" that can only occur among people who share rural Thai cultural values and beliefs. Medical anthropologist Robert A. Hahn counters that the very idea of the so-called culture-bound syndrome is flawed. He contends that culture-bound syndromes are reductionist explanations for certain complex illness conditions—that is, explanations that reduce complex phenomena to a single variable. Hahn suggests that such conditions are like any illness condition; they are not so much peculiar diseases but distinctive local cultural expressions of much more common illness conditions that can be found in any culture.

Indian social researcher Sudhir Kakar analyzes the origins of ethnic conflict from a psychological perspective to argue that ethnic differences are deeply held distinctions that from time to time will inevitably erupt as ethnic conflicts. He maintains that anxiety arises from preconscious fears about cultural differences. In his view, no amount of education or politically correct behavior will eradicate these fears and anxieties about people of differing ethnic backgrounds. American sociologist Anthony Oberschall considers the ethnic conflicts that have recently emerged in Bosnia and contends that primordial ethnic attachments are insufficient to explain the sudden emergence of violence among Bosnian ethnic groups. He adopts a complex explanation for this violence, identifying circumstances in which fears and anxieties were manipulated by politicians for self-serving ends. It was only in the context of these manipulations that ethnic violence could have erupted, concludes Oberschall.

PART 5   ETHICS IN ANTHROPOLOGY   321

Assistant professor of justice studies and member of the Pawnee tribe James Riding In argues that holding Native American skeletons in museums and other repositories represents a sacrilege against Native American dead and, thus, all Indian remains should be reburied. Professor of anthropology and archaeologist Clement W. Meighan believes that archaeologists have a moral and professional obligation to the archaeological data with which they work. Such data are held in the public good and must be protected from destruction, he concludes.

Anthropologist Terence Turner contends that journalist Patrick Tierney's book *Darkness in El Dorado* accurately depicts how anthropologist Napoleon Chagnon's research among the Yanomami Indians caused conflict between groups and how Chagnon's portrayal of the Yanomami as extremely violent aided gold miners trying to take over Yanomami land. Anthropologists Edward Hagen, Michael Price, and John Tooby counter that Tierney systematically distorts Chagnon's views on Yanomami violence and exaggerates the amount of disruption caused by Chagnon's activities compared to those of others such as missionaries and gold miners.

Postmodernist anthropologist James Clifford argues that the very act of removing objects from their ethnographic contexts distorts the meaning of objects held in museums. He contends that whether these objects are displayed in art museums or anthropological museums, exhibitions misrepresent ethnic communities by omitting important aspects of contemporary life, especially involvement with the colonial or Western world. Anthropologist Denis Dutton asserts that no exhibition can provide a complete context for ethnographic objects, but that does not mean that museum exhibitions are fundamentally flawed. Dutton suggests that postmodernists misunderstand traditional approaches to interpreting museum collections, and what they offer as a replacement actually minimizes what we can understand of ethnic communities from museum collections.

Introduction

Kirk M. Endicott

Robert L. Welsch

Anthropology is the study of humanity in all its biological, social, cultural, and linguistic diversity. Some of the founders of American anthropology, like Franz Boas, made important contributions to the understanding of human biology, culture, and language. But few such Renaissance men and women can be found today. To master the concepts, methods, and literatures involved in studying the different aspects of human variation, anthropologists have had to specialize. At times it may seem that no two anthropologists actually study the same things, yet they all are working toward a greater understanding of the commonalties and differences that define the human species.

Today, anthropology encompasses four major subdisciplines—biological anthropology, prehistoric archaeology, linguistic anthropology, and cultural anthropology—and several smaller subdisciplines. Controversial issues in each of these subfields are included in the first four parts of this volume.

Biological anthropology, also called *physical anthropology,* concerns the anatomy, physiology, mental capabilities, and genetics of humans and our nearest relatives, the primates. Traditionally, biological anthropologists, like other biologists, have understood human variation in evolutionary terms. Increasingly, as geneticists have introduced new ways of analyzing genetic data encoded in our DNA, biological anthropologists have described and explained human biological variation at the molecular level.

Fundamental questions for biological anthropologists include: How did our species evolve from early non-human primates? When did our species take on attributes that are associated with anatomically modern humans? Where did our species arise? What were the evolutionary forces that contributed to our anatomical and behavioral evolution? How and why did the hominids develop the capacity for culture—socially learned and transmitted patterns of behavior, thought, and feeling?

Paleoanthropologists (students of humankind's ancient ancestors) search for and excavate fossil bone fragments of long-dead primates, reconstruct their skeletons, and make inferences about their behavior patterns from bones, teeth, and other clues. They also use sophisticated dating techniques, computer models, and studies of living primates, both in the laboratory and in their natural environments, to create plausible models of human evolution and the relationships among the different branches of the primate order.

Archaeology, which is also referred to as *prehistory,* involves documenting, understanding, and explaining the history of human communities and civilizations that existed before written records. Unlike most historians who can turn to documents and papers to detail the life and times of their subjects, archaeologists must usually find evidence for their reconstructions of the past through excavations of sites where people formerly lived or worked.

One issue at the heart of most archaeological controversies is how we can or should interpret these varied kinds of data to reconstruct the ways of life of earlier times. Recurrent questions include: What is the use and meaning of an artifact? To what extent can we use current lifeways of tribal or foraging groups as analogies for how prehistoric communities lived?

A set of questions that archeologists continue to ask is when, why, and how people first settled different parts of the world. They also ask why innovations like agriculture developed at particular times and in particular places. Why did some societies develop into complex civilizations, while others remained village-based societies, free of centralized political authority?

A frequent point of debate among archaeologists concerns the dating of archaeological deposits. Accurate dating, even if only relative to other artifacts in a site, is clearly essential for accurate interpretations, although dating alone does not reveal the processes that led to particular changes in the archaeological record. Stratification—the principle that the lower layers of a deposit are older than the upper layers—is still the most reliable basis for relative dating within a site. Now archaeologists also draw on a wide battery of high-tech absolute dating methods—including carbon 14, potassium-argon, and thermoluminescence dating—which have varying degrees of accuracy for different time spans. Dating always requires interpretation because, for example, carbon samples may be contaminated by more recent organic material like tree roots, and scholars do not always agree on the correct interpretation.

Linguistic anthropology includes the study of language and languages, especially non-Western and unwritten languages, as well as the relationship between language and other aspects of culture. Language provides the categories within which culture is expressed. Some anthropologists regard linguistic anthropology as a subdivision of cultural anthropology because language is a part of culture and is the medium by which much of culture is transmitted from one generation to the next. A classic question for linguistic anthropologists has been: Do the categories of a language shape how humans perceive and understand the world? This question was first proposed by linguistic anthropologists Edward Sapir and Benjamin Whorf early in the twentieth century but continues to be one of the central questions of interest to linguistic anthropologists. Issue 8, "Does Language Determine How We Think?" addresses this question. Another question that linguistic anthropologists have debated for several decades concerns whether chimpanzees and other apes have the innate ability to use symbols in ways that resemble human language. This question is asked in Issue 7, "Can Apes Learn Language?" and is important because if apes are capable of complex symbolic activity, then language and culture are probably not the exclusive capabilities of humans but have their origins in our primate past.

Cultural anthropology, which is also called *social anthropology* in Great Britain or sometimes *sociocultural anthropology* in the United States, is concerned with the cultures and societies of living communities. Cultural anthropologists have proposed many different definitions of *culture.* Most emphasize that cultural behavior, thought, and feeling are socially created and learned, rather than generated by biologically transmitted instincts. Anthropologists differ considerably on the relative weight they assign to culture and instincts in explaining human behavior, as some of the issues in this volume show. Because cultures are human creations, they differ from one society to another.

Data for most cultural anthropologists come from observations, informal conversations, and interviews made while living within a study community. The hallmark of cultural anthropology is *fieldwork,* in which the anthropologist lives with another cultural group, learns their language, their customs, and their patterns of interaction. Anthropological fieldwork involves *participant observation*—observing while participating in the life of the community.

As in the other subfields of anthropology, cultural data must be interpreted. Interpretation begins with the creation of the research questions themselves. This reflects what investigators consider as being important to discover and directs their observations and questions in the field. At each step of data collection and analysis, the investigators' theories and interests shape their understanding of other cultures.

Much explanation in cultural anthropology is based on the comparison of cultural features in different societies. Some anthropologists explicitly make cross-cultural comparisons, using statistics to measure the significance of apparent correlations between such things as childrearing practices and adult personalities. Even anthropologists who concentrate on explaining or interpreting features of particular cultures use their knowledge of similar or different features in other societies as a basis for insights.

Like other anthropologists, cultural anthropologists look for uniformities in human behavior as well as variations. Understanding what patterns of human behavior are possible has been at the center of many controversies in cultural anthropology. Questions touched on in this book include: Is gender equality possible? Is violence inevitable? Can small-scale hunting and gathering societies live in contact with more powerful food-producing societies without being dominated by them?

Recently, cultural anthropologists have begun asking questions about possible biases in the ways anthropologists depict and represent other cultures through writing, films, and other media. This movement has been called *postmodern anthropology* or *critical anthropology.* Post-modernists ask, among other things: Do our theories and methods of representation inadvertently portray the people we study as exotic "Others," in exaggerated contrast with Western peoples? This is the question that lies behind Issue 18, "Do Museums Misrepresent Ethnic Communities Around the World?"

Ethics in anthropology Concerns about the ethics of research have become increasingly important in contemporary anthropology. The American Anthropological Association has developed a Code of Ethics covering both research and teaching (see the American Anthropological Association Web site at http://www.aaanet.org). It recognizes that researchers sometimes have conflicting obligations to the people and animals studied, host countries, the profession, and the public. One basic principle is that researchers should do nothing that could harm or distress the people or animals they study. Cultural anthropologists must be aware of the possibility of harming the living people with whom they work, but similar considerations also affect archaeologists and biological anthropologists because the artifacts of past communities often represent the ancestors of living communities. Here the interests of anthropologists and native peoples may diverge. For example, in Issue 16 we ask, "Should the Remains of Prehistoric Native Americans Be Reburied Rather Than Studied?" Similarly, in Issue 17 we consider the ethical responsibilities of individual field researchers by asking, "Did Napoleon Chagnon's Research Methods and Publications Harm the Yanomami Indians?" Issue 18, "Do Museums Misrepresent Ethnic Communities Around the World?" asks about the ethical obligations museums and anthropologists generally have toward the native peoples in our representations of these peoples and their ancestors.

Some Basic Questions

On the surface, the issues presented in this book are very diverse. Anthropologists from different subfields tend to focus on their own specialized problems and to work with different kinds of evidence. Most of the controversial issues we have chosen for this volume can be read as very narrow, focused debates within a subfield. But many of the issues that confront anthropologists in one subfield arise in other subfields as well. What has attracted us to the issues presented here is that each raises much broader questions that affect the entire discipline. In this section we briefly describe some of the basic questions lying behind specific issues.

Is Anthropology a Science or a Humanity?

Science is a set of ideas and methods intended to describe and explain phenomena in a naturalistic way, seeing individual things and events as the outcome of discoverable causes and as conforming to general laws. Anthropologists taking a scientific approach are concerned with developing broad theories about the processes that lead to observed patterns of variation in human biology, language, and culture. The humanities, on the other hand, are concerned with understanding people's cultural creations in terms of their meanings to their creators and the motivations behind their creation.

Biological anthropology seeks the reasons for human evolution and biological diversity largely in the processes of the natural world, and it uses the methods of the physical sciences for investigating those phenomena. Archaeology, too, uses natural science concepts and methods of investigation, but it also draws on understandings of human behavior that take account of culturally-influenced motivations, values, and meanings. Cultural anthropologists are divided over whether cultural anthropology should model itself on the natural sciences or on the humanities. Some cultural anthropologists try to discover the causes of particular cultural forms occurring at specific places and times, while others try to interpret the meanings (to the people themselves) of cultural forms in other societies in ways that are intelligible to Western readers. Issue 9, "Should Cultural Anthropology Model Itself on the Natural Sciences?" directly addresses the question of whether anthropology is part of the sciences or humanities.

Is Biology or Culture More Important in Shaping Human Behavior?

Most anthropologists accept that both genetically transmitted behavioral tendencies (instincts) and cultural ideas and norms influence human behavior, thought, and emotion. However, anthropologists diverge widely over the amount of weight that they assign to these two influences. *Biological determinists* believe that all human behavior is ultimately determined by the genes, and that culture merely lends distinctive coloration to our genetically driven behaviors. At the other extreme, *cultural determinists* believe that any instincts humans may have are so weak and malleable that cultural learning easily overcomes them. The conflict between supporters of the two extreme views, called the *nature-nurture debate,* has been going on for many years and shows no sign of being resolved soon.

Issue 10, "Was Margaret Mead's Fieldwork on Samoan Adolescents Fundamentally Flawed?", considers the Margaret Mead–Derrick Freeman controversy, which has its roots in the question of whether biology or culture is more important in shaping human behavior. From her research in Samoa, Mead claimed that nurture was most important, while some decades later Freeman concluded from his research in Samoa precisely the opposite. Other issues in this volume deal directly with the nature-nurture question, particularly Issue 2, "Are Humans Inherently Violent?"; Issue 6, "Did Prehistoric Native Americans Practice Cannibalism in the American Southwest?"; Issue 7, "Can Apes Learn Language?"; and Issue 14 "Do Some Illnesses Exist Only Among Members of a Particular Culture?"

Is the Local Development of Culture or Outside Influence More Important in Shaping Cultures?

In trying to explain the form a particular culture takes, different anthropologists place different amounts of emphasis on the local development of culture and on outside influence. Those who favor local development emphasize unique innovations and adaptations to the natural environment, while those favoring outside influences emphasize the borrowing of ideas from neighbors (*diffusion*) and changes forced upon a people by more powerful groups (*acculturation*). Most anthropologists recognize some influence from both sources, but some attribute overriding importance to one or the other.

The debate between proponents of local development of culture and proponents of outside influence plays a major role in two of the issues in this volume: Issue 11, "Do Native Peoples Today Invent Their Traditions?" and Issue 13, "Are San Hunter-Gatherers Basically Pastoralists Who Have Lost Their Herds?"

Some Theoretical Approaches

Anthropologists draw on many theories of widely varying scope and type. We present brief summaries of a number of theoretical approaches used by authors in this book so that you will recognize and understand them when you see them. We have arranged these theories in a rough continuum from most scientific in approach to most humanistic.

Biological evolution   Biological anthropology is based predominantly on the modem theory of biological evolution. This builds upon the ideas that Charles Darwin developed in the mid-nineteenth century. Darwin combined the idea of evolution—the development of species by means of incremental changes in previous species—with the concept of natural selection. Natural selection means that in a variable population those individuals best adapted to the environment are most likely to survive and reproduce, thus passing on their favorable characteristics (called *survival of the fittest*). The modem theory of biological evolution adds an understanding of genetics, including the concepts of *genetic drift* (random variation in gene frequencies) and *gene flow* (transmission of genes between populations). Most biological anthropologists today also subscribe to the notion of *punctuated equilibrium,* which states that evolutionary change takes place in fits and starts, rather than at an even pace.

Virtually all biological anthropologists use the modem theory of evolution, so their disagreements arise not over which theory to use, but over interpretations of evidence and questions of how the theory applies to specific cases.

Sociobiology   Sociobiology is a theory that attempts to use evolutionary principles to explain all behavior of animals, including humans. The best-known practitioner is biologist E. O. Wilson, whose book *Sociobiology: The New Synthesis* (Harvard University Press, 1975) sets out the basic concepts. Sociobiologists believe that human behavior is determined by inherited behavioral tendencies. The genes promoting behaviors that lead to survival and successful reproduction are favored by natural selection and thus tend to become more common in a population over the generations. For sociobiologists such behaviors as selfishness, altruism to close kin, violence, and certain patterns of marriage are evolutionarily and biologically determined. They see individual and cultural ideas as mere rationalizations of innate patterns of behavior. In their view, no culture will persist that goes against the "wisdom of the genes."

Cultural evolution   Drawing on an analogy with biological evolution, nineteenth-century cultural anthropologists developed the idea that complex societies evolve out of simpler ones. The unilineal schemes of such cultural evolutionists as Lewis Henry Morgan, E. B. Tylor, and James G. Fraser postulated that all societies pass through a fixed series of stages, from savagery to civilization. They regarded contemporary simple societies, like the tribal peoples of the Amazon, as "survivals" from earlier stages of cultural evolution.

Unilineal schemes of cultural evolution have now been discredited because they were speculative, ignored differences in patterns of culture change in different places, and were blatantly ethnocentric, regarding all non-Western cultures as inferior to those of Europe. But some archaeologists and cultural anthropologists still espouse more sophisticated versions of cultural evolution regarding at least some aspects of culture change.

Cultural ecology   The theory of cultural ecology was developed by cultural anthropologist Julian Steward in the 1930s as a corrective to the overly simple schemes of cultural evolution. Emphasizing the process of adaptation to the physical environment, he postulated that societies in different environments would develop different practices, though the general trend was toward higher levels of complexity, a process he called *multilinear evolution*. His idea of adaptation, like natural selection, explained why some societies and practices succeeded and were perpetuated, while other less well-adapted ones died out.

Many archaeologists and cultural anthropologists use versions of cultural ecology to explain why certain practices exist in certain environments. Marvin Harris's widely-used theory of *cultural materialism* is a further development of cultural ecology. The basic idea behind all versions of cultural ecology is that societies must fulfill their material needs if they are to survive. Therefore those institutions involved with making a living must be well adapted to the environment, while others, like religions, are less constrained by the environment.

Culture history   One of the founders of American cultural anthropology, Franz Boas, rejected the cultural evolution schemes of the nineteenth century, with their fixed stages of cultural development. He pointed out that all societies had unique histories, depending on local innovations and diffusion of ideas from neighboring societies. Also, change is not always toward greater complexity; civilizations crumble as well as rise. Boas advocated recording the particular events and influences that contributed to the makeup of each culture.

World system theory   The world system theory, which has gained great prominence in the social sciences in recent years, asserts that all societies, large and small, are—and long have been—integrated in a single worldwide political-economic system. This approach emphasizes the connections among societies, especially the influence of politically powerful societies over weak ones, as in colonialism, rather than local development of culture.

Cultural interpretation   Humanist anthropologists emphasize their role as interpreters, not explainers, of culture. They focus on the task of describing other cultures in ways that are intelligible to Western readers, making sense of customs that at first glance seem incomprehensible. The most prominent practitioner of cultural interpretation is Clifford Geertz, who coined the term *thick description* for this process. This approach is used especially for dealing with aspects of culture that are products of human imagination, like art and mythology, but even the institutions involved in physical survival, like families and economic processes, have dimensions of meaning that warrant interpretation.

Feminist anthropology   Feminist anthropology began in the 1970s as an approach meant to correct the lack of coverage of women and women's views in earlier anthropology. It has now developed into a thoroughgoing alternative approach to the study of culture and society. Its basic idea is that gender is a cultural construction affecting the roles and meanings of the sexes in particular societies. The aim of feminist anthropology is both to explain the position of women and to convey the meanings surrounding gender. Feminist anthropologists emphasize that all social relations have a gender dimension.

How Anthropologists Reach Conclusions

None of the issues considered in this volume have been resolved, and several are still the subject of heated, and at times, acrimonious debate. The most heated controversies typically arise from the most extreme points of view. When reading these selections students should bear in mind that only two positions are presented formally, although in the introductions and postscripts we raise questions that should guide you to consider other positions as well. We encourage you to question all of the positions offered before coming to any conclusions of your own. Remember, for more than a century anthropology has prided itself on revealing how our own views of the world are culturally biased. Try to be aware of how your own background, upbringing, ethnicity, religion, likes, and dislikes affect your assessments of the arguments presented here.

In our own teaching we have often used controversial issues as a way to help students understand how anthropologists think about research questions. We have found that five questions often help students focus on the most important points in these selections:

1. Who is the author?
2. What are the author's assumptions?
3. What methods and data does an author use?
4. What are the author's conclusions?
5. How does the author reach his or her conclusions from the data?

For each issue we suggest that you consider what school of thought, what sort of training, and what sort of research experience each author has. We often find it useful to ask why this particular author finds the topic worth writing about. Does one or the other author seem to have any sort of bias? What assumptions does each author hold? Do both authors hold the same assumptions?

For any anthropological debate, we also find it useful to ask what methods or analytical strategies each author has used to reach the conclusions he or she presents. For some of the issues presented in this book, authors share many of the same assumptions and are generally working with the same evidence, but disagree as to how this evidence should be analyzed. Some authors disagree most profoundly on what kinds of data are most suitable for answering a particular research question. Some even disagree about what kinds of questions anthropologists should be asking.

Finally, we suggest that you consider how the author has come to his or her conclusions from the available data. Would different data make any difference? Would a different kind of evidence be more appropriate? Would different data likely lead to different conclusions? Would different ways of analyzing the data suggest other conclusions?

If you can answer most of these questions about any pair of selections, you will be thinking about these problems anthropologically and will understand how anthropologists approach controversial research questions. After weighing the various possible positions on an issue you will be able to form sound opinions of your own.

On the Internet . . .

Human Origins and Evolution in Africa

Jeanne Sept, an anthropology professor at Indiana University who has done fieldwork on the question of human origins in Africa, created this Web site, which is entitled Human Origins and Evolution in Africa. The site contains much information and provides links to related Web sites.

http://www.indiana.edu/~origins/

Fossil Evidence for Human Evolution in China

The Fossil Evidence for Human Evolution in China Web site was created by the Center for the Study of Chinese Prehistory. This site includes a catalog of Chinese human fossil remains; provides links to other sites dealing with paleontology, human evolution, and Chinese prehistory; and includes other resources that may be useful for gaining a better understanding of China's role in the emergence of humankind.

http://www.chineseprehistory.org

Neandertal Origins

These sites have links to various articles about the relationship between Neandertal and modern humans as well as to other topics in human paleobiology.

http://archaeology.about.com/od/humanorigins/

http://www.handprint.com/LS/ANC/evol.html

Fossil Hominids: The Evidence for Human Evolution

Created by Jim Foley, this site is entitled Fossil Hominids: The Evidence for Human Evolution, and it provides links to recent articles about human evolution and the question of whether or not Neandertals and early modern humans interbred. A discussion of creationism and the Biblical interpretation of the origins of life is also presented.

http://www.talkorigins.org/faqs/homs/

PART 1

Biological Anthropology

*B*iological anthropologists, also called physical anthropologists, study the bodies, bones, and genetics of humans and of our nearest relatives, the other primates. Their basic goals are to understand human evolution scientifically and to explain contemporary human diversity. Fundamental questions include: How did our species evolve from early nonhuman primates? When did our species take on attributes that are associated with anatomically modern humans? Where did our species develop as a species, and what were the evolutionary forces that contributed to our anatomical evolution? These questions have traditionally required detailed comparisons of bones from living species and fossilized bones from extinct species. However, increasingly anthropologists asking these kinds of questions are developing new models about evolution from observing and studying living primates either in the laboratory or in their natural environment.

- Is Race a Useful Concept for Anthropologists?

- Are Humans Inherently Violent?

- Did Neandertals Interbreed With Modern Humans?

ISSUE 1

Is Race a Useful Concept for Anthropologists?

YES: George W. Gill, from "The Beauty of Race and Races," *Anthropology Newsletter* (March 1998)

NO: Jonathan Marks, from "Black, White, Other," *Natural History* (December 1994)

ISSUE SUMMARY

YES: Biological anthropologist Jonathan Marks argues that race is not a useful concept because there are no "natural" divisions of the human species. The popular idea of races as discrete categories of people who are similar to each other and different from all members of other races is a cultural—not a biological—concept, he concludes.

NO: Biological and forensic anthropologist George W. Gill contends that the concept of race remains a useful one. For him, races are conceived as populations originating in particular regions. He contends that because races can be distinguished both by external and skeletal features, the concept of race is especially useful in the forensic task of identifying human skeletons. Furthermore, the notion of race provides a vocabulary for discussing human biological variation and racism.

The European idea of humanity being divided into physically distinct types—races—developed after the Age of Exploration in the fifteenth and sixteenth centuries. Before the era of rapid transportation and mass population movements, most people were born, lived, and died without seeing anyone who looked appreciably different from themselves. But when European explorers reached Africa, East Asia, and the Americas, they were confronted with people who were very different from them in appearance and in their ways of life. Europeans tried to understand this unforeseen human diversity in terms of the religious worldview of the time. High councils of the Church debated whether or not particular peoples had souls that missionaries could save. Killing and enslaving colonized peoples was justified by the view that they were inherently inferior beings, not fully human.

By the nineteenth century the idea that populations looked and acted differently because of their different hereditary endowments was widely believed. Scholars viewed different groups as being at different stages of progress on the march to European-style civilization, and those that lagged behind were thought to have been held back by their inferior physical, mental, and moral endowments. The development of cultural evolutionary schemes in the second half of the century, inspired in part by Darwin's theory of the evolution of species, seemed to give a scientific basis for this view. In short, racism and the idea of race developed together. One of the founding figures in American anthropology, Franz Boas, fought a life-long battle against racism and the idea that cultural and psychological characteristics could be explained in terms of biology.

Toward the middle of the twentieth century, biological anthropologists tried to refine the concept of race by separating biological differences from cultural ones. They also began to focus on populations rather than individuals and on genetic variation instead of superficial physical differences such as head shape. One seemingly intractable problem emerged in the resulting analyses. Different sets of races appeared depending on the number and nature of the specific features considered. No matter how many races were distinguished, there were always some groups that did not fit.

Here, George W. Gill argues that races should be understood as populations derived from particular geographical regions. Such races can be distinguished not only through their external characteristics, such as skin color, but also by skeletal features. By using a combination of distinctive osteological characteristics, which are found in varying proportions in different geographical races, forensic anthropologists can make highly accurate guesses about the ancestry of persons whose bones they examine.

In his selection, Jonathan Marks distinguishes races as culturally defined categories—the popular usage known to most students and laypeople—from races as biological subspecies of human beings. Culturally defined races seem clear-cut because they are based on arbitrary criteria, such as the number of great-grandparents who came out of Africa. Marks concludes that there are no clusters of discrete characteristics that could unambiguously distinguish a member of one race from another. Therefore, race as a biological concepts is meaningless.

This issue touches on a number of thorny questions for anthropologists, some scientific and some ethical. What sorts of concepts are needed for discussing and analyzing human hereditary differences? Can geographical races be defined in terms of varying proportions of characteristics that together form a distinctive profile? What is the relationship between individuals and racial categories? Does the very idea of classifying humans into clear-cut categories inherently misrepresent the gradual nature of genetic variation and change? Is the term *race* so loaded with racist connotations that it must be replaced by a more neutral term before dispassionate discussion of human hereditary variation can proceed?

George W. Gill

 **YES**

The Beauty of Race and Races

What good is a worldview of race and races? To me the major races of humankind are among nature's most beautiful and fascinating creations. Biologically, they are our colorful symbol of success as an ecologically widely adapted species, and they are our hedge against extinction should one or more of these varied habitats disappear. Socially, race is a part of the source of ethnic pride and identity. Finally, forensically race forms one of the 4 cornerstones of personal identity (with sex, age and stature) and thus serves society as a means of reducing the residuum of the unidentified for law enforcement. This, in turn, often leads to the solution and reduction of many forms of serious crime.

Should We Scrap "Race"?

"Race differences," renowned geneticist Theodosius Dobzhansky once said, "are facts of nature which can, given sufficient study, be ascertained objectively." What did he mean by this, and was he correct?

At the time of Dobzhansky's writing, anthropology was at its peak in the revolutionary overhaul of the old typological race concept. Throughout anthropology, we were replacing it rapidly with a populational view, coupled with a realization that many of the curious physical differences among the world's peoples have (or had in the Pleistocene past) definite survival value. On the other hand, with all the new work at that time in blood factor analysis, and other serological trait studies (which seemed to be poorly explained by a "racial model"), the question was, should we just scrap the whole concept and move on?

Over the years, as I became involved in two separate kinds of anthropological activity (forensic anthropology research and casework, and teaching an undergraduate course on human variation), I decided that we should *not* scrap the race concept to describe and study human variation. First, the populational view of race and adaptive value of racial traits seemed to *disconnect race from racism*. After all, how could anyone be a racist as long as they realized that (1) the distinctive traits of each group have real "value" in a Darwinian sense and (2) each major population contains such a wide range of variation for almost any trait, that individuals cannot be judged by their group affinity? For three decades this idea was pervasive in anthropology. The assumption was that we were free to study any aspect of human variation without fearing misuse of the information, at least among educated people. We believed that increased knowledge and dialogue about race and races would help extinguish, not fan, the fires of racism. This position helped not only to breathe new life and vitality into human variation studies, but to promote open dialogue on both race and racism.

It was not until 1990 that the mere word *race* acquired such a social taboo that it could rarely be used in polite company, especially among anthropologists, those who ironically had just spent a century intensively studying the subject of race from practically every angle. The politically correct view has become the position that we should *not* study or even talk about race, first because there is no real biological validity to the concept and second because it clearly leads to racist thinking if we do talk about it. How true are these two assumptions? How does the first (the unreality of races) mesh with Dobzhansky's statements or with the experiences of modern forensic anthropologists? How does the second (that race thinking causes racism) mesh with the experiences of anthropology teachers?

Are Races Real?

For those truly interested in the degree of accuracy attained by human osteologists in determining geographic racial affinities by utilizing various new and traditional osteological methods, a number of pertinent articles are available. Many of these are well-conducted studies designed to test methods objectively for percentage of correct placement. In our 1990 handbook of new methods for forensic anthropologists (*Skeletal Attribution of Race*) Stanley Rhine and I compiled 14 contributions by a number of active forensic anthropologists that present new research. In a 1995 *Journal of Forensic Sciences* article (40(5):783) I also review a number of new methods for discerning American Indians from whites osteologically, as well as for evaluating skeletons of blacks and Polynesians.

These new methods are probably no better than many traditional non-metric approaches that utilize such things as alveolar prognathism, form of incisors and chin projection but simply have been quantitatively tested and reported in the literature. No osteologist would make a racial assessment in an actual case based on just *one* of these methods. That's why actual racial assessment results in real court cases or law enforcement reports run very close to 100% correct (as do assessments of sex, stature and age). If there is much doubt about any of these assessments, which can happen in the cases of very fragmentary skeletons or some that show a conflicting pattern of skeletal criteria, a board certified forensic anthropologist will not offer a conclusion.

My respected colleague C Loring Brace, who is as skilled as the leading forensic anthropologists at assessing ancestry from bones, does not subscribe to the concept of race. Neither does Norman Sauer, a board certified forensic anthropologist. Some of my students ask, how can these people, who can on a random sample of skeletons given to them out of context and who can

Figure 1

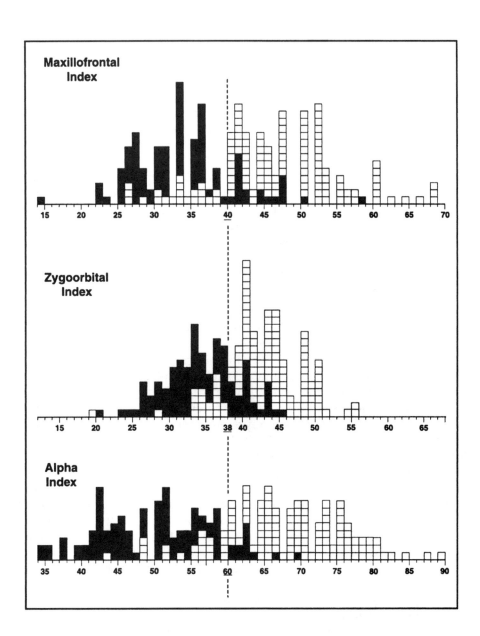

Plot values for black and white Americans, for each of three interorbital indexes. These indexes assess the degree of nasal projection. The same cutoff values (40-38-60) separate North American Indians from whites with approximately the same degree of accuracy. Initial samples in this study were 125 whites, 100 American blacks and 175 North American Indians. Percentages of correct placement are 88.8 for whites, 87.0 for blacks and 87.9 for Amerindians (using all three indexes together). (From G W Gill and B M Gilbert, "Racial Identification from the Mid-Facial Skeleton: American Blacks and Whites," G Gill and S Rhine, eds, *Skeletal Attribution of Race,* 1990)

classify them accurately by region (or "race" if forced to use this despised "social construct"), claim that they do not believe in race? My answer is that we can often *function* within systems that we do not believe in.

As a middle-aged American, for example, I am not sure that I believe any longer in the chronological "age" categories utilized by osteologists. Certainly some 40-year-olds have portions of their skeletons that look older than parts of some 50-year-olds. If called by law enforcement to provide "age" on a skeleton I can, however, provide an answer that will be proven sufficiently accurate should the decedent eventually be identified. I may not believe in society's "age" categories, but I can be very effective at "aging" skeletons. The next question of course is how "real" is age biologically? My answer is that if biological criteria can be used to assess age with reasonable accuracy, then it has *some* basis in biological reality even if the particular "social construct" that defines its limits might be imperfect. I find this true not only for age and stature estimations but for sex and race identifications.

The "reality of race" therefore depends more on the definition of *reality* than on the definition of *race*. If we choose to accept the system of racial taxonomy established traditionally by physical anthropologists, then human skeletons can be classified within it just as well as can living humans. The bony traits of the nose, mouth, femur and cranium are just as revealing to a good osteologist as skin color, hair form, nose form and lips to the perceptive observer of living humanity. I have been able to prove to myself over the years, in actual legal cases, that I am *more* accurate at assessing race from skeletal remains than from looking at living people standing before me. So those of us in forensic anthropology know that race, whether "real" or not, is just as well reflected (or better) by the skeleton as it is by the superficial soft tissue. The idea that race is "only skin deep," as any reputable forensic anthropologist will affirm, is simply not true.

Does Race Promote Racism?

Does teaching human variation, or discussing it in a framework of racial biology, promote or reduce racism? This is an important question, but one that does not have a simple answer. Most social scientists over the past decade have convinced themselves that it runs the risk of promoting racism in certain quarters. Anthropologists of the 1950s, 1960s and early 1970s, on the other hand, believed that they were *combating* racism by teaching courses on human races and racism. Which approach has worked best? What do the intellectuals among racial minorities believe? How do students react and respond?

Last spring when I served on a NOVA show panel in New York (Debates/Debates, June 1997) we were given the topic "Is There Such a Thing as Race?" Six of us were chosen, three proponents of the race concept and three antagonists. All had authored books or papers on race. Loring Brace and I were the two anthropologists "facing off" in the debate. The ethnic composition of the panel was three white and three black scholars.

Figure 2

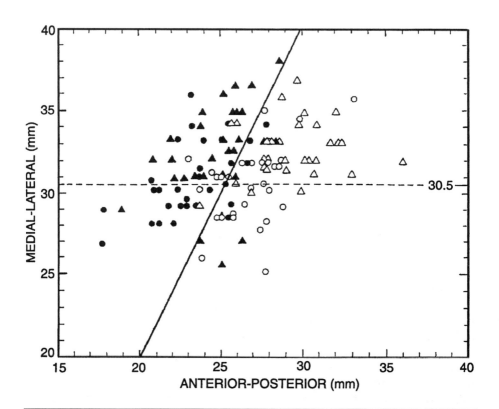

Plot points for North American Indian males and females and North American whites males and females, for two common measurements of the proximal femur. These measurements taken together reveal the degree of platymeria (flatness) of the proximal diaphysis. This method yields a percentage of correct placement of approximately 85% for both North American whites and North American Indians. (From G Gill and S Rhine, eds, *Skeletal Attribution of Race*, 1990)

As our conversations developed, I was struck by how similar many of my concerns regarding racism were to those of my two black teammates. Although recognizing that embracing the race concept can have risks attached, we were more fearful of the form of racism likely to emerge if race is denied and dialogue about it lessened. We three fear that the social taboo over the subject of race has served to suppress open discussion over a very important subject in need of dispassionate debate. One of my teammates, an affirmative action lawyer, is afraid that a denial that races exist also serves to encourage a denial that racism exists. He asked, how can we combat racism if no one is willing to talk about race?

My reasons for teaching at least part of my human variation course from the "racial perspective" are many. First, it seems easier to discuss and study the subject of biological variation with nomenclature and structure than without. Cultural anthropologists cannot discuss cultural diversity without names for specific cultures (no matter how arbitrary they might prove to be), nor can archaeologists deal with artifact assemblages without systems of classification. Along the same line, how can paleoanthropologists talk about hominid change through time without erecting taxonomic categories and creating names? Why is it that those who are more interested in the richness and beauty of biological variation among existing human populations (than past ones), or more interested in biological variation than cultural diversity, are denied the tools for communication and study granted all others? Has a focus on race caused more human suffering than a focus on culture or religion? Absolutely not. Infinitely more human suffering has been caused by religious persecution than racial bias, yet we are to celebrate human cultural diversity while carefully containing our enthusiasm for racial variation. I detect a bias based not on truth but on prejudice. Those of us (from all races and walks of life) fascinated by biological variation are greatly outnumbered by those more focused on cultural or "ethnic" variations. Are we a misunderstood minority in need of a political action group?

Who Will Benefit?

Students who have been the strongest supporters of my "racial perspective" on human variation have been almost invariably the minority students. The first black student in my human variation class several years ago came to me at the end of the course and said, "Dr Gill, I really want to thank you for changing my life with this course." He went on to explain that, "My whole life I have wondered about why I am black, and if that is good or bad. Now I know the reasons why I am the way I am and that these traits are useful and good." A human variation course with another perspective would probably have accomplished the same for this student *if* he had ever noticed it. The truth is, innocuous contemporary human variation classes with their politically correct titles and course descriptions do not attract attention of minorities or those other students who could most benefit.

Black, White, Other

While reading the Sunday edition of the *New York Times* one morning last February, my attention was drawn by an editorial inconsistency. The article I was reading was written by attorney Lani Guinier. (Guinier, you may remember, had been President Clinton's nominee to head the civil rights division at the Department of Justice in 1993. Her name was hastily withdrawn amid a blast of criticism over her views on political representation of minorities.) What had distracted me from the main point of the story was a photo caption that described Guinier as being "half-black." In the text of the article, Guinier had described herself simply as "black."

How can a person be black and half black at the same time? In algebraic terms, this would seem to describe a situation where $x = \frac{1}{2}x$, to which the only solution is $x = 0$.

The inconsistency in the *Times* was trivial, but revealing. It encapsulated a longstanding problem in our use of racial categories—namely, a confusion between biological and cultural heredity. When Guinier is described as "half-black," that is a statement of biological ancestry, for one of her two parents is black. And when Guinier describes herself as black, she is using a cultural category, according to which one can either be black or white, but not both.

Race—as the term is commonly used—is inherited, although not in a strictly biological fashion. It is passed down according to a system of folk heredity, an all-or-nothing system that is different from the quantifiable heredity of biology. But the incompatibility of the two notions of race is sometimes starkly evident—as when the state decides that racial differences are so important that interracial marriages must be regulated or outlawed entirely. Miscegenation laws in this country (which stayed on the books in many states through the 1960s) obliged the legal system to define who belonged in what category. The resulting formula stated that anyone with one-eighth or more black ancestry was a "negro." (A similar formula, defining Jews, was promulgated by the Germans in the Nuremberg Laws of the 1930s.)

Applying such formulas led to the biological absurdity that having one black great-grandparent was sufficient to define a person as black, but having seven white great grandparents was insufficient to define a person

From Jonathan Marks, "Black, White, Other," *Natural History* (December 1994). Copyright © 1994 by National History Magazine, Inc. Reprinted by permission of *Natural History*.

as white. Here, race and biology are demonstrably at odds. And the problem is not semantic but conceptual, for race is presented as a category of nature.

Human beings come in a wide variety of sizes, shapes, colors, and forms—or, because we are visually oriented primates, it certainly seems that way. We also come in larger packages called populations; and we are said to belong to even larger and more confusing units, which have long been known as races. The history of the study of human variation is to a large extent the pursuit of those human races—the attempt to identify the small number of fundamentally distinct kinds of people on earth.

This scientific goal stretches back two centuries, to Linnaeus, the father of biological systematics, who radically established *Homo sapiens* as one species within a group of animals he called Primates. Linnaeus's system of naming groups within groups logically implied further breakdown. He consequently sought to establish a number of subspecies within *Homo sapiens*. He identified five: four geographical species (from Europe, Asia, Africa, and America) and one grab-bag subspecies called *monstrosus*. This category was dropped by subsequent researchers (as was Linnaeus's use of criteria such as personality and dress to define his subspecies).

While Linnaeus was not the first to divide humans on the basis of the continents on which they lived, he had given the division a scientific stamp. But in attempting to determine the proper number of subspecies, the heirs of Linnaeus always seemed to find different answers, depending upon the criteria they applied. By the mid-twentieth century, scores of anthropologists—led by Harvard's Earnest Hooton—had expended enormous energy on the problem. But these scholars could not convince one another about the precise nature of the fundamental divisions of our species.

Part of the problem—as with the *Times's* identification of Lani Guinier—was that we humans have two constantly intersecting ways of thinking about the divisions among us. On the one hand, we like to think of "race"—as Linnaeus did—as an objective, biological category. In this sense, being a member of a race is supposed to be the equivalent of being a member of a species or of a phylum—except that race, on the analogy of subspecies, is an even narrower (and presumably more exclusive and precise) biological category.

The other kind of category into which we humans allocate ourselves—when we say "Serb" or "Hutu" or "Jew" or "Chicano" or "Republican" or "Red Sox fan"—is cultural. The label refers to little or nothing in the natural attributes of its members. These members may not live in the same region and may not even know many others like themselves. What they share is neither strictly nature nor strictly community. The groupings are constructions of human social history.

Membership in these *un*biological groupings may mean the difference between life and death, for they are the categories that allow us to be identified (and accepted or vilified) socially. While membership in (or allegiance to) these categories may be assigned or adopted from birth, the differentia that mark members from nonmembers are symbolic and abstract; they serve to distinguish people who cannot be readily distinguished by nature. So important are these symbolic distinctions that some of the strongest animosities are often expressed between very similar-looking peoples. Obvious examples are Bosnian Serbs and Muslims, Irish and English, Huron and Iroquois.

Obvious natural variation is rarely so important as cultural difference. One simply does not hear of a slaughter of the short people at the hands of the tall, the glabrous at the hands of the hairy, the red-haired at the hands of the brown-haired. When we do encounter genocidal violence between different looking peoples, the two groups are invariably socially or culturally distinct as well. Indeed, the tragic frequency of hatred and genocidal violence between biologically indistinguishable peoples implies that biological differences such as skin color are not motivations but, rather, excuses. They allow nature to be invoked to reinforce group identities and antagonisms that would exist without these physical distinctions. But are there any truly "racial" biological distinctions to be found in our species?

Obviously, if you compare two people from different parts of the world (or whose ancestors came from different parts of the world), they will differ physically, but one cannot therefore define three or four or five basically different kinds of people, as a biological notion of race would imply. The anatomical properties that distinguish people—such as pigmentation, eye form, body build—are not clumped in discrete groups, but distributed along geographical gradients, as are nearly all the genetically determined variants detectable in the human gene pool.

These gradients are produced by three forces. Natural selection adapts populations to local circumstances (like climate) and thereby differentiates them from other populations. Genetic drift (random fluctuations in a gene pool) also differentiates populations from one another, but in non-adaptive ways. And gene flow (via intermarriage and other child-producing unions) acts to homogenize neighboring populations.

In practice, the operations of these forces are difficult to discern. A few features, such as body build and the graduated distribution of the sickle cell anemia gene in populations from western Africa, southern Asia, and the Mediterranean can be plausibly related to the effects of selection. Others, such as the graduated distribution of a small deletion in the mitochondrial DNA of some East Asian, Oceanic, and Native American peoples, or the degree of flatness of the face, seem unlikely to be the result of selection and are probably the results of random biohistorical factors. The cause of the distribution of most features, from nose breadth to blood group, is simply unclear.

The overall result of these forces is evident, however. As Johann Friedrich Blumenbach noted in 1775, "you see that all do so run into one another, and that one variety of mankind does so sensibly pass into the other, that you cannot mark out the limits between them." (Posturing as an heir to Linnaeus, he nonetheless attempted to do so.) But from humanity's gradations in appearance, no defined groupings resembling races readily emerge. The racial categories with which we have become so familiar are the result of our imposing arbitrary cultural boundaries in order to partition gradual biological variation.

Unlike graduated biological distinctions, culturally constructed categories are ultrasharp. One can be French or German, but not both; Tutsi or Hutu, but not both; Jew or Catholic, but not both; Bosnian Muslim or Serb, but not both; black or white, but not both. Traditionally, people of "mixed race" have been obliged to choose one and thereby identify themselves unambiguously to census takers and administrative bookkeepers—a practice that is now being widely called into question.

A scientific definition of race would require considerable homogeneity within each group, and reasonably discrete differences between groups, but three kinds of data militate against this view: First, the groups traditionally described as races are not at all homogeneous. Africans and Europeans, for instance, are each a collection of biologically diverse populations. Anthropologists of the 1920s widely recognized *three* European races: Nordic, Alpine, and Mediterranean. This implied that races could exist within races. American anthropologist Carleton Coon identified *ten* European races in 1939. With such protean use, the term race came to have little value in describing actual biological entities within *Homo sapiens*. The scholars were not only grappling with a broad north-south gradient in human appearance across Europe, they were trying to bring the data into line with their belief in profound and fundamental constitutional differences between groups of people.

But there simply isn't one European race to contrast with an African race, nor three, nor ten: the question (as scientists long posed it) fails to recognize the actual patterning of diversity in the human species. Fieldwork revealed, and genetics later quantified, the existence of far more biological diversity within any group than between groups. Fatter and thinner people exist everywhere, as do people with type O and type A blood. What generally varies from one population to the next is the *proportion* of people in these groups expressing the trait or gene. Hair color varies strikingly among Europeans and native Australians, but little among other peoples. To focus on discovering differences between presumptive races, when the vast majority of detectable variants do not help differentiate them, was thus to define a very narrow—if not largely illusory—problem in human biology. (The fact that Africans are biologically more diverse than Europeans, but have rarely been split into so many races, attests to the cultural basis of these categorizations.)

Second, differences between human groups are only evident when contrasting geographical extremes. Noting these extremes, biologists of an earlier era sought to identify representatives of "pure," primordial races presumably located in Norway, Senegal, and Thailand. At no time, however, was our species composed of a few populations within which everyone looked pretty much the same. Ever since some of our ancestors left Africa to spread out through the Old World, we humans have always lived in the "in-between" places. And human populations have also always been in genetic contact with one another. Indeed, for tens of thousands of years, humans have had trade networks; and where goods flow, so do genes. Consequently, we have no basis for considering *extreme* human forms the most pure, or most representative, of some ancient primordial populations. Instead, they represent populations adapted to the most disparate environments.

And third, between each presumptive "major" race are unclassifiable populations and people. Some populations of India, for example, are darkly pigmented (or "black"), have Europeanlike ("Caucasoid") facial features, but inhabit the continent of Asia (which should make them "Asian"). Americans might tend to ignore these "exceptions" to the racial categories, since immigrants to the United States from West Africa, Southeast Asia, and northwest Europe far outnumber those from India. The very existence of unclassifiable peoples undermines the idea that there are just three human biological groups in the Old World. Yet acknowledging the biological distinctiveness of such groups leads to a rapid proliferation of categories. What about Australians? Polynesians? The Ainu of Japan?

Categorizing people is important to any society. It is, at some basic psychological level, probably necessary to have group identity about who and what you are, in contrast to who and what you are not. The concept of race, however, specifically involves the recruitment of biology to validate those categories of self-identity.

Mice don't have to worry about that the way humans do. Consequently, classifying them into subspecies entails less of a responsibility for a scientist than classifying humans into sub-species does. And by the 1960s, most anthropologists realized they could not defend any classification of *Homo sapiens* into biological subspecies or races that could be considered reasonably objective. They therefore stopped doing it, and stopped identifying the endeavor as a central goal of the field. It was a biologically intractable problem—the old square-peg-in-a-round-hole enterprise; and people's lives, or welfares, could well depend on the ostensibly scientific pronouncement. Reflecting on the social history of the twentieth century, that was a burden anthropologists would no longer bear.

This conceptual divorce in anthropology—of cultural from biological phenomena was one of the most fundamental scientific revolutions of our time. And since it affected assumptions so rooted in our everyday experience, and resulted in conclusions so counterintuitive—like the idea that the earth goes around the sun, and not vice-versa—it has been widely underappreciated.

Kurt Vonnegut, in *Slaughterhouse Five*, describes what he remembered being taught about human variation: "At that time, they were teaching that there was absolutely no difference between anybody. They may be teaching that still." Of course there are biological differences between people, and between populations. The question is: How are those differences patterned? And the answer seems to be: Not racially. Populations are the only readily identifiable units of humans, and even they are fairly fluid, biologically similar to populations nearby, and biologically different from populations far away.

In other words, the message of contemporary anthropology is: You may group humans into a small number of races if you want to, but you are denied biology as a support for it.

POSTSCRIPT

Is Race a Useful Concept for Anthropologists?

No one denies that variations in hereditary features between individuals and populations exist. The disagreement is over whether or not the concept of race, or subspecies, accurately expresses these variations. Marks argues that distinct races cannot be defined objectively on the basis of biological variations. Among other problems, differences among the members of any defined race are greater than those between races. Indeed, the average differences between traditional races represent only about 10 percent of our total species variation, while 90 percent of that variation is found within races. Gill contends, on the other hand, that combinations of characteristics cluster together, making it possible to distinguish geographical populations as separate races.

The majority of physical anthropologists today hold positions similar to Marks's. The American Anthropological Association (AAA) has created a "Statement on 'Race,'" which expresses the current view of most anthropologists on race and racism. It can be seen on the AAA Web site at www.aaanet.org/stmts/racepp.htm.

But, as Gill implies, the view that races do not exist seems nonsensical to the average American, who has grown up steeped in the idea that humanity is made up of different races. Racial categories are so ingrained in our vocabulary and thought that we identify people by race as readily as by sex or age. We are asked our race on official census forms, and many government policies, such as affirmative action, depend on the reality of race. What is needed, Marks would say, is recognition that this notion of race is a cultural—not a biological—construction.

The literature on race, including the concept of race, is enormous. Informative overviews of the concept of race in anthropology include Michael Banton's book *Racial Theories* (Cambridge University Press, 1987) and Eugenia Shanklin's short book *Anthropology and Race* (Wadsworth Publishing, 1994). Two landmark books in the development of anthropological views of race are Franz Boas's *Race, Language, and Culture* (The Free Press, 1940) and Ashley Montagu's *Man's Most Dangerous Myth: The Fallacy of Race* (Columbia University Press, 1945). Accessible books on forensic anthropology, which continues to use the concept of race, include Douglas Ubelaker and Henry Scammel's *Bones: A Forensic Detective's Casebook* (Edward Burlingame Books, 1992) and Stanley Rhine's *Bone Voyage: A Journey in Forensic Anthropology* (University of New Mexico Press, 1998).

ISSUE 2

Are Humans Inherently Violent?

YES: Richard Wrangham and Dale Peterson, from *Demonic Males: Apes and the Origins of Human Violence* (Houghton Mifflin Company, 1996)

NO: Robert W. Sussman, from "Exploring Our Basic Human Nature," *Anthro Notes* (Fall 1997)

ISSUE SUMMARY

YES: Biological anthropologist Richard Wrangham and science writer Dale Peterson maintain that male humans and chimpanzees, our closest nonhuman relatives, have an innate tendency to be aggressive and to defend their territory by violence. They state that sexual selection, a type of natural selection, has fostered an instinct for male aggression because males who are good fighters mate more frequently and sire more offspring than weaker and less aggressive ones.

NO: Biological anthropologist Robert W. Sussman rejects the theory that human aggression is an inherited propensity, arguing instead that violence is a product of culture and upbringing. He also rejects the contention that male chimpanzees routinely commit violent acts against other male chimps. Sussman regards the notion that human males are inherently violent as a Western cultural tradition, not a scientifically demonstrated fact.

Human history is rife with wars between groups of all types, from clans to nation-states, and interpersonal violence is common enough that all societies attempt to control it. But is violence a part of human nature, or is violence merely one of many human capabilities that may be either encouraged or discouraged by cultures?

The question of whether or not humans have an instinct for aggression has been around since the formative years of anthropology, and it is still being debated today. Some nineteenth-century scholars interpreted Darwin's concepts of "natural selection" and "survival of the fittest" to mean that the strong would kill off the weak. The strongest and most aggressive individuals, therefore, would have the most offspring, and their strength and instinct for aggression would gradually come to predominate in the population.

Most cultural anthropologists from the 1950s onward rejected the explanation of human aggression in terms of instincts, emphasizing instead the social and cultural causes of violence. They pointed out that the amount of aggression tolerated varies widely from one society to another and that individuals can become aggressive or peaceful depending on how they are raised. They held up such groups as the Semai of Malaysia (see Robert K. Dentan, *The Semai: A Nonviolent People of Malaya* [Holt, Rinehart & Winston, 1968]) as proof that culture could create a people who abhorred all forms of aggression and coercion. Whatever instinct for aggression humans might have, they argued, must be very weak indeed.

The question behind this issue concerns the nature of human nature. Have we a set of innate behavioral predispositions that, when set off by certain stimuli, are very likely to be expressed? Or, are any such predispositions at best weak tendencies that can be shaped or even negated by cultural conditioning? Many apparently innate behaviors in humans turn out to be highly variable in their strength and form. While the sucking instinct of babies operates predictably in all newborns, a hypothesized "mothering instinct" seems quite diverse in expression and variable in strength from one woman to another. The question, then, is whether the hypothesized aggression instinct is a powerful drive that all human males must express in one way or another or a weak and pliable tendency that some males may never act upon.

Richard Wrangham and Dale Peterson argue that human wars and interpersonal violence are driven by inherited behavioral tendencies that have evolved under pressure of sexual selection—natural selection of traits that enhance the reproductive success of one sex. Among both humans and chimpanzees, males who are aggressive use their fighting ability to dominate other males and to prevent them from mating with the available females. Therefore the genes causing aggression are passed on to succeeding generations in greater numbers than the genes causing nonaggressive behavior.

Robert W. Sussman rejects Wrangham and Peterson's assertion that natural selection favors aggressive human males and that aggressiveness is an inherited tendency rather than a result of environment and upbringing. He contends that human hunter-gatherers and most apes are remarkably non-aggressive, as were our earliest human ancestors, the australopithecines. He sees the evidence that chimpanzee males routinely attack other males as weak, and he questions the relevance of chimpanzee behavior for humans.

These selections raise a number of questions with regard to the nature and causes of human aggression. How can we determine whether a person's aggressive act is due to instinct, upbringing, or both? If male aggression in humans is based on instinct, how can scholars explain variations in the amount and type of aggression found in different individuals and cultures? If male aggression is not based on instinct, why is violence between men so widespread? What role did women have in the evolution of an instinct for male violence? To what extent can studies of animal behavior be applied to humans?

Richard Wrangham
and Dale Peterson

 **YES**

Demonic Males: Apes and the Origins of Human Violence

Paradise Lost

The killer ape has long been part of our popular culture: Tarzan had to escape from the bad apes, and King Kong was a murderous gorilla-like monster. But before the Kahama observations [in which males of one chimpanzee group killed the males of a neighboring group], few biologists took the idea seriously. The reason was simple. There was so little evidence of animals killing members of their own species that biologists used to think animals killed each other only when something went wrong—an accident, perhaps, or unnatural crowding in zoos. The idea fit with the theories of animal behavior then preeminent, theories that saw animal behavior as designed by evolution for mutual good. Darwinian natural selection was a filter supposed to eliminate murderous violence. Killer apes, like killers in any animal species, were merely a novelist's fantasy to most scientists before the 1970s.

And so the behavior of people seemed very, very different from that of other animals. Killing, of course, is a typical result of human war, so one had to presume that humans somehow broke the rules of nature. Still, war must have come from somewhere. It could have come, for example, from the evolution of brains that happened to be smart enough to think of using tools as weapons, as Konrad Lorenz argued in his famous book, *On Aggression,* published in 1963.

However it may have originated, more generally war was seen as one of the defining marks of humanity: To fight wars meant to be human and apart from nature. This larger presumption was true even of nonscientific theories, such as the biblical concept of an original sin taking humans out of Eden, or the notion that warfare was an idea implanted by aliens, as Arthur C. Clarke imagined in *2001: A Space Odyssey.* In science, in religion, in fiction, violence and humanity were twinned.

The Kahama killings were therefore both a shock and a stimulus to thought. They undermined the explanations for extreme violence in terms of uniquely human attributes, such as culture, brainpower, or the punishment of an angry god. They made credible the idea that our warring tendencies go back into our prehuman past. They made us a little less special.

And yet science has still not grappled closely with the ultimate questions raised by the Kahama killings: Where does human violence come from, and why? Of course, there have been great advances in the way we think about these things. Most importantly, in the 1970s, the same decade as the Kahama killings, a new evolutionary theory emerged, the selfish-gene theory of natural selection, variously called inclusive fitness theory, sociobiology, or more broadly, behavioral ecology. Sweeping through the halls of academe, it revolutionized Darwinian thinking by its insistence that the ultimate explanation of any individual's behavior considers only how the behavior tends to maximize genetic success: to pass that individual's genes into subsequent generations. The new theory, elegantly popularized in Richard Dawkins's *The Selfish Gene,* is now the conventional wisdom in biological science because it explains animal behavior so well. It accounts easily for selfishness, even killing. And it has come to be applied with increasing confidence to human behavior, though the debate is still hot and unsettled. In any case, the general principle that behavior evolves to serve selfish ends has been widely accepted, and the idea that humans might have been favored by natural selection to hate and to kill their enemies has become entirely, if tragically, reasonable.

Those are the general principles, and yet the specifics are lacking. Most animals are nowhere near as violent as humans, so why did such intensely violent behavior evolve particularly in the human line? Why kill the enemy, rather than simply drive him away? Why rape? Why torture and mutilate? Why do we see these patterns both in ourselves and chimpanzees? Those sorts of questions have barely been asked, much less addressed.

Because chimpanzees and humans are each other's closest relatives, such questions carry extraordinary implications, the more so because the study of early human ancestry, unfolding in a fervor as we approach the century's end, is bringing chimpanzees and humans even closer than we ever imagined. Three dramatic recent discoveries speak to the relationship between chimpanzees and humans, and all three point in the same direction: to a past, around 5 million years ago, when chimpanzee ancestors and human ancestors were indistinguishable.

First, fossils recently dug up in Ethiopia indicate that over 4.5 million years ago there walked across African lands a bipedal ancestor of humans with a head strikingly like a chimpanzee's.

Second, laboratories around the world have over the last decade demonstrated chimpanzees to be genetically closer to us than they are even to gorillas, despite the close physical resemblance between chimpanzees and gorillas.

And third, both in the field and in the laboratory, studies of chimpanzee behavior are producing numerous, increasingly clear parallels with human behavior. It's not just that these apes pat each other on the hand to show affection, or kiss each other, or embrace. Not just that they have menopause, develop lifelong friendships, and grieve for their dead babies by carrying them for days or weeks. Nor is it their ability to do sums like 5 plus 4, or to communicate with hand signs. Nor their tool use, or collaboration, or bartering for sexual favors. Nor even that they hold long-term grudges, deliberately hide their feelings, or bring rivals together to force them to make peace.

No, for us the single most gripping set of facts about chimpanzee behavior is what we have already touched on: the nature of their society. The social world of chimpanzees is a set of individuals who share a communal range; males live forever in the groups where they are born, while females move to neighboring groups at adolescence; and the range is defended, and sometimes extended with aggressive and potentially lethal violence, by groups of males related in a genetically patrilineal kin group.

What makes this social world so extraordinary is comparison. Very few animals live in patrilineal, male-bonded communities wherein females routinely reduce the risks of inbreeding by moving to neighboring groups to mate. And only two animal species are known to do so with a system of intense, male-initiated territorial aggression, including lethal raiding into neighboring communities in search of vulnerable enemies to attack and kill. Out of four thousand mammals and ten million or more other animal species, this suite of behaviors is known only among chimpanzees and humans.

Humans with male-bonded, patrilineal kin groups? Absolutely. *Male bonded* refers to males forming aggressive coalitions with each other in mutual support against others—Hatfields versus McCoys, Montagues versus Capulets, Palestinians versus Israelis, Americans versus Vietcong, Tutsis versus Hutus. Around the world, from the Balkans to the Yanomamö of Venezuela, from Pygmies of Central Africa to the T'ang Dynasty of China, from Australian aborigines to Hawaiian kingdoms, related men routinely fight in defense of their group. This is true even of the villages labeled by anthropologists as "matrilineal" and "matrilocal," where inheritance (from male to male) is figured out according to the mother's line, and where women stay in their natal villages to have children—such villages operate socially as subunits of a larger patrilineal whole. In short, the system of communities defended by related men is a human universal that crosses space and time, so established a pattern that even writers of science fiction rarely think to challenge it.

When it comes to social relationships involving females, chimpanzees and humans are very different. That's unsurprising. Discoveries in animal behavior since the 1960s strongly suggest that animal societies are adapted to their environments in exquisitely detailed ways, and obviously the environments of chimpanzees and humans are a study in contrast. But this just emphasizes our puzzle. Why should male chimpanzees and humans show such similar patterns?

Is it chance? Maybe our human ancestors lived in societies utterly unlike those of chimpanzees. Peaceful matriarchies, for example, somewhat like some of our distant monkey relatives. And then, by a remarkable quirk of evolutionary coincidence, at some time in prehistory human and chimpanzee social behaviors converged on their similar systems for different, unrelated reasons.

Or do they both depend on some other characteristic, like intelligence? Once brains reach a certain level of sophistication, is there some mysterious logic pushing a species toward male coalitionary violence? Perhaps, for instance, only chimpanzees and humans have enough brainpower to realize the advantages of removing the opposition.

Or is there a long-term evolutionary inertia? Perhaps humans have retained an old chimpanzee pattern which, though it was once adaptive, has now acquired a stability and life of its own, resistant even to new environments where other forms of society would be better.

Or are the similarities there, as we believe, because in spite of first appearances, similar evolutionary forces continue to be at work in chimpanzee and human lineages, maintaining and refining a system of intergroup hostility and personal violence that has existed since even before the ancestors of chimpanzees and humans mated for the last time in a drying forest of eastern Africa around 5 million years ago? If so, one must ask, what forces are they? What bred male bonding and lethal raiding in our forebears and keeps it now in chimpanzees and humans? What marks have those ancient evolutionary forces forged onto our twentieth-century psyches? And what do they say about our hopes and fears for the future? . . .

Sexual selection, the evolutionary process that produces sex differences, has a lot to answer for. Without it, males wouldn't possess dangerous bodily weapons and a mindset that sanctions violence. But males who are better fighters can stop other males from mating, and they mate more successfully themselves. Better fighters tend to have more babies. That's the simple, stupid, selfish logic of sexual selection. So, what about us? Is sexual selection ultimately the reason why men brawl in barrooms, form urban gangs, plot guerrilla attacks, and go to war? Has it indeed designed men to be especially aggressive?

Until we have carefully examined the evidence, our answer should be: not necessarily. Because the social, environmental, genetic, and historical circumstances for any single species are so extremely complex, we can't assume a priori that sexual selection has acted in any particular way for any single species. Among the 10 million or more animal species on earth, you can find interesting exceptions to almost every rule. On the one hand, you can find species like spotted hyenas, where such extraordinary ferocity has evolved among females that it outshines even the stark sexual aggression shown by males. And on the other, you will discover the pacifists. . . .

So there is no particular reason to think that human aggression is all cultural, or that our ancestors were as pacific as muriquis [nonaggressive monkeys of South America]. The only way to find out whether sexual selection has shaped human males for aggression is to leave the theory and go back to the evidence. There are two places to look for an answer. We can look at our bodies, and we can think about our minds. The easier part is our bodies.

·◦❀◦·

A biologist from Mars looking at a preserved human male laid out on a slab might find it hard to imagine our species as dangerous. Lined up next to male specimens from the other apes, or from virtually any other mammal species, human males don't look as if they are designed to fight at all. They are rather slender, their bones are light, and they appear to have no bodily weapons. People don't think of humans in the same way that they think of dangerous animals. That first impression is misleading, however. Humans are indeed designed to fight, although in a different way from most of the other primates.

Here's one clue. Men are a little larger and more heavily muscled than women. For other primate species, larger male size links strongly to male aggression. But with humans, that apparent evidence seems to conflict with the absence of fighting canine teeth. Could it be that humans break the general rule linking larger males to an evolved design for aggression?

Consider our teeth. The upper canines of most primates are longer and sharper than any other tooth. These long teeth are obvious weapons, bright daggers ground to a razor-sharp edge against a special honing surface on a pre-molar tooth in the lower jaw. Baboons, for example, have canines five to six centimeters long. Male baboons trying to impress each other grind their canines noisily, occasionally showing off their teeth in huge, gaping yawns. When male baboons make those display yawns, they are acting like cowboys twirling their revolvers.

By comparison, human canines seem tiny. They barely extend beyond the other teeth, and in males they are no longer than in females. Those canines may help us bite an apple, we love to imagine them elongated for the Halloween scare, and we unconsciously display them when we sneer, but our canines virtually never help us fight. In fact, the fossil record indicates that ever since the transition from rainforest ape to woodland ape, our ancestors' canines have been markedly smaller than they are in chimpanzees. In the woodlands, those teeth quickly became muriqui-like in appearance—one reason why some people wonder if woodland apes were as pacific as modern muriquis are.

But we should not allow ourselves to become misled by the evidence of canine teeth. The importance of a species' canines depends entirely on how it fights. . . .

Apes can fight with their fists because they have adapted to hanging from their arms, which means that their arms can swing all around their shoulders, the shoulder joint being a flexible multidirectional joint. So chimpanzees and gorillas often hit with their fists when they fight, and they can keep most canine-flashing opponents at bay because their arms are long. If chimpanzees and gorillas find punching effective, then surely the woodland apes, who were standing up high on hind legs, would have fought even better with their arms.

Fists can also grasp invented weapons. Chimpanzees today are close to using hand-held weapons. Throughout the continent, wild chimpanzees will tear off and throw great branches when they are angry or threatened, or they will pick up and throw rocks. Humphrey, when he was the alpha male at Gombe, almost killed me once by sending a melon-size rock whistling less than half a meter from my head. They also hit with big sticks. A celebrated film taken in Guinea shows wild chimpanzees pounding meter-long clubs down on the back of a leopard. (Scientists were able to get that film because the leopard was a stuffed one, placed there by a curious researcher. The chimpanzees were lucky to find a leopard so slow to fight back.) Chimpanzees in West Africa already have a primitive stone tool technology, and there could well be a community of chimpanzees today, waiting to be discovered, who are already using heavy sticks as clubs against each other. Certainly we can reasonably imagine that the woodland apes did some of these things.

. . . The shoulders of boys and girls are equally broad until adolescence; but at puberty, shoulder cartilage cells respond to testosterone, the male sex hormone newly produced by the testes, by growing. (In an equivalent way, pubertal girls get wider hips when their hip cartilage cells respond to estrogen, the female sex hormone.) The result is a sudden acceleration of shoulder width for boys around the age of fourteen, associated with relative enlargement of the upper arm muscles. In other words, the shoulders and arms of male humans—like the neck muscles of a red deer, the clasping hands of a xenopus frog, or the canine teeth of many other primates—look like the result of sexual selection for fighting. All these examples of male weaponry respond to testosterone by growing. They are specialized features that enlarge for the specific purpose of promoting fighting ability in competition against other males. Small wonder, then, that men show off to each other before fights by hunching their shoulders, expanding their muscles, and otherwise displaying their upper-body strength. . . .

If the bipedal woodland apes fought with fists and sometimes with weapons, those species should have had especially broad shoulders and wellmuscled arms, like modern men. We haven't enough fossils yet to know if that's true. Indeed, it is not yet absolutely certain that male woodland apes were larger than females, though most of the current fossil evidence suggests so. If they were, we can confidently imagine that the males were designed for aggression. Perhaps the early development of club-style weapons might also explain why the skulls of our ancestors became strikingly thicker, particularly with *Homo erectus* at 1.6 to 1.8 million years ago. That's a guess, but it's clear in any case that our present bodies carry the same legacy of sexual selection as other mammals whose males fight with their upper bodies. The broad shoulders and powerful, arching torso we so admire in Michelangelo's *David* are the human equivalent of antlers. The mark of Cain appears in our shoulders and arms, not in our teeth.

⋅⟨◉⟩⋅

What about our minds? Has sexual selection shaped our psyches also, in order to make us better fighters? Can sexual selection explain why men are so quick to bristle at insults, and, under the right circumstances, will readily kill? Can our evolutionary past account for modern war?

Inquiry about mental processes is difficult enough when we deal just with humans. Comparison with other species is harder still. The supposed problem is that animals fight with their hearts, so people say, whereas humans fight with their minds. Animal aggression is supposed to happen by instinct, or by emotion, and without reason. Wave a red rag in a bull's face and the bull charges thoughtlessly—that's the model. Human wars, on the other hand, seem to emerge, so Karl von Clausewitz declared, as "the continuation of policy with the admixture of other means." According to historian Michael Howard, human wars "begin with conscious and reasoned decisions based on the calculation, made by both parties, that they can achieve more by going to war than by remaining at peace." The principle seems as true for the measured deliberations on the top floor of the Pentagon as for the whispered councils among the Yanomamö, and it suggests a wholly different set of psychological processes from the supposedly rigid, instinctual, emotional drives of animals. The fact that we possess consciousness and reasoning ability, this theory says, takes us across a chasm into a new world, where the old instincts are no longer important. If there is no connection between these two systems, the rules for each cannot be the same. In other words, aggression based on "conscious and reasoned decisions" can no longer be explained in terms of such evolutionary forces as sexual selection.

The argument sounds fair enough, but it depends on oversimplified thinking, a false distinction between animals acting by emotion (or instinct) and humans acting by reason. Animal behavior is not purely emotional. Nor is human decision-making purely rational. In both cases, the event is a mixture. And new evidence suggests that even though we humans reason much more (analyze past and present context, consider a potential future, and so on) than nonhuman animals, our essential process for making a decision still relies on emotion. . . .

People have always accepted that animals act from emotions; humans . . . can never act without them. Suddenly the apparent chasm between the mental processes of chimpanzees and our species is reduced to a comprehensible difference. Humans can reason better, but reason and emotion are linked in parallel ways for both chimpanzees and humans. For both species, emotion sits in the driver's seat, and reason (or calculation) paves the road.

We are now ready to ask what causes aggression. If emotion is the ultimate arbiter of action for both species, then what kinds of emotions underlie violence for both? Clearly there are many. But one stands out. From the raids of chimpanzees at Gombe to wars among human nations, the same emotion looks extraordinarily important, one that we take for granted and describe most simply but that nonetheless takes us deeply back to our animal origins: pride.

Male chimpanzees compete much more aggressively for dominance than females do. If a lower-ranking male refuses to acknowledge his superior with one of the appropriate conventions, such as a soft grunt, the superior will become predictably angry. But females can let such insults pass. Females are certainly capable of being aggressive to each other, and they can be as politically adept as males in using coalitions to achieve a goal. But female chimpanzees act as if they just don't care about their status as much as males do.

By contrast, we exaggerate only barely in saying that a male chimpanzee in his prime organizes his whole life around issues of rank. His attempts to achieve and then maintain alpha status are cunning, persistent, energetic, and time-consuming. They affect whom he travels with, whom he grooms, where he glances, how often he scratches, where he goes, and what time he gets up in the morning. . . .

Eighteenth-century Englishmen used less dramatic tactics than wild chimpanzees, but that acute observer Samuel Johnson thought rank concerns were as pervasive: "No two people can be half an hour together, but one shall acquire an evident superiority over the other." Pride obviously serves as a stimulus for much interpersonal aggression in humans, and we can hypothesize confidently that this emotion evolved during countless generations in which males who achieved high status were able to turn their social success into extra reproduction. Male pride, the source of many a conflict, is reasonably seen as a mental equivalent of broad shoulders. Pride is another legacy of sexual selection. . . .

⚜

Our ape ancestors have passed to us a legacy, defined by the power of natural selection and written in the molecular chemistry of DNA. For the most part it is a wonderful inheritance, but one small edge contains destructive elements; and now that we have the weapons of mass destruction, that edge promotes the potential of our own demise. People have long known such things intuitively and so have built civilizations with laws and justice, diplomacy and mediation, ideally keeping always a step ahead of the old demonic principles. And we might hope that men will eventually realize that violence doesn't pay.

The problem is that males are demonic at unconscious and irrational levels. The motivation of a male chimpanzee who challenges another's rank is not that he foresees more matings or better food or a longer life. Those rewards explain why sexual selection has favored the desire for power, but the immediate reason he vies for status is simpler, deeper, and less subject to the vagaries of context. It is simply to dominate his peers. Unconscious of the evolutionary rationale that placed this prideful goal in his temperament, he devises strategies to achieve it that can be complex, original, and maybe conscious. In the same way, the motivation of male chimpanzees on a border patrol is not to gain land or win females. The temperamental goal is to intimidate the opposition, to beat them to a pulp, to erode their ability to challenge. Winning has become an end in itself.

It looks the same with men.

Exploring Our Basic Human Nature

Are human beings forever doomed to be violent? Is aggression fixed within our genetic code, an inborn action pattern that threatens to destroy us? Or, as asked by Richard Wrangham and Dale Peterson in their recent book, *Demonic Males: Apes and the Origins of Human Violence,* can we get beyond our genes, beyond our essential "human nature"?

Wrangham and Peterson's belief in the importance of violence in the evolution and nature of humans is based on new primate research that they assert demonstrates the continuity of aggression from our great ape ancestors. The authors argue that 20–25 years ago most scholars believed human aggression was unique. Research at that time had shown great apes to be basically non-aggressive gentle creatures. Furthermore, the separation of humans from our ape ancestors was thought to have occurred 15–20 million years ago (Mya). Although Raymond Dart, Sherwood Washburn, Robert Ardrey, E.O. Wilson and others had argued through much of the 20th century that hunting, killing, and extreme aggressive behaviors were biological traits inherited from our earliest hominid hunting ancestors, many anthropologists still believed that patterns of aggression were environmentally determined and culturally learned behaviors, not inherited characteristics.

Demonic Males discusses new evidence that killer instincts are not unique to humans, but rather shared with our nearest relative, the common chimpanzee. The authors argue that it is this inherited propensity for killing that allows hominids and chimps to be such good hunters.

According to Wrangham and Peterson, the split between humans and the common chimpanzee was only 6–8 Mya. Furthermore, humans may have split from the chimpanzee-bonobo line after gorillas, with bonobos *(pygmy chimps)* separating from chimps only 2.5 Mya. Because chimpanzees may be the modern ancestor of all these forms, and because the earliest australopithecines were quite chimpanzee-like, Wrangham speculates (in a separate article) that "chimpanzees are a conservative species and an amazingly good model for the ancestor of hominids" (1995, reprinted in Sussman 1997:106). If modern chimpanzees and modern humans share certain behavioral traits, these traits have "long evolutionary roots" and are likely to be fixed, biologically inherited parts of our basic human nature and not culturally determined.

Wrangham argues that chimpanzees are almost on the brink of humanness:

> Nut-smashing, root-eating, savannah-using chimpanzees, resembling our ancestors, and capable by the way of extensive bipedalism. Using ant-wands, and sandals, and bowls, meat-sharing, hunting cooperatively. Strange paradox . . . a species trembling on the verge of hominization, but so conservative that it has stayed on that edge. . . . (1997:107).

Wrangham and Peterson (1996:24) claim that only two animal species, chimpanzees and humans, live in patrilineal, male-bonded communities "with intense, male initiated territorial aggression, including lethal raiding into neighboring communities in search of vulnerable enemies to attack and kill." Wrangham asks:

> Does this mean chimpanzees are naturally violent? Ten years ago it wasn't clear. . . . In this cultural species, it may turn out that one of the least variable of all chimpanzee behaviors is the intense competition between males, the violent aggression they use against strangers, and their willingness to maim and kill those that frustrate their goals. . . . As the picture of chimpanzee society settles into focus, it now includes infanticide, rape and regular battering of females by males (1997:108).

Since humans and chimpanzees share these violent urges, the implication is that human violence has long evolutionary roots. "We are apes of nature, cursed over six million years or more with a rare inheritance, a Dostoyevskyan demon . . . The coincidence of demonic aggression in ourselves and our closest kin bespeaks its antiquity" (1997: 108–109).

Intellectual Antecedents

From the beginning of Western thought, the theme of human depravity runs deep, related to the idea of humankind's fall from grace and the emergence of original sin. This view continues to pervade modern "scientific" interpretations of the evolution of human behavior. Recognition of the close evolutionary relationship between humans and apes, from the time of Darwin's *Descent of Man* (1874) on, has encouraged theories that look to modern apes for evidence of parallel behaviors reflecting this relationship.

By the early 1950s, large numbers of australopithecine fossils and the discovery that the large-brained "fossil" ancestor from Piltdown, in England, was a fraud, led to the realization that our earliest ancestors were more like apes than like modern humans. Accordingly, our earliest ancestors must have behaved much like other non-human primates. This, in turn, led to a great interest in using primate behavior to understand human evolution and the evolutionary basis of human nature. The subdiscipline of primatology was born.

Raymond Dart, discoverer of the first australopithecine fossil some thirty years earlier, was also developing a different view of our earliest ancestors. At first Dart believed that australopithecines were scavengers barely eking out an existence in the harsh savanna environment. But from the fragmented and damaged bones found with the australopithecines, together with dents and holes in these early hominid skulls, Dart eventually concluded that this species had used bone, tooth and antler tools to kill, butcher and eat their prey, as well as to kill one another. This hunting hypothesis (Cartmill 1997:511) "was linked from the beginning with a bleak, pessimistic view of human beings and their ancestors as instinctively bloodthirsty and savage." To Dart, the australopithecines were:

> confirmed killers: carnivorous creatures that seized living quarries by violence, battered them to death, tore apart their broken bodies, dismembered them limb from limb, slaking their ravenous thirst with the hot blood of victims and greedily devouring livid writhing flesh (1953:209).

Cartmill, in a recent book (1993), shows that this interpretation of early human morality is reminiscent of earlier Greek and Christian views. Dart's (1953) own treatise begins with a 17th century quote from the Calvinist R. Baxter: "of all the beasts, the man-beast is the worst/ to others and himself the cruellest foe."

Between 1961–1976, Dart's view was picked up and extensively popularized by the playwright Robert Ardrey (*The Territorial Imperative, African Genesis*). Ardrey believed it was the human competitive and killer instinct, acted out in warfare, that made humans what they are today. "It is war and the instinct for territory that has led to the great accomplishments of Western Man. Dreams may have inspired our love of freedom, but only war and weapons have made it ours" (1961: 324).

Man the Hunter

In the 1968 volume *Man the Hunter,* Sherwood Washburn and Chet Lancaster presented a theory of "The evolution of hunting," emphasizing that it is this behavior that shaped human nature and separated early humans from their primate relatives.

> To assert the biological unity of mankind is to affirm the importance of the hunting way of life. . . . However much conditions and customs may have varied locally, the main selection pressures that forged the species were the same. The biology, psychology and customs that separate us from the apes . . . we owe to the hunters of time past . . . for those who would understand the origins and nature of human behavior there is no choice but to try to understand "Man the Hunter" (1968:303).

Rather than amassing evidence from modern hunters and gatherers to prove their theory, Washburn and Lancaster (1968:299) use the 19th-century concept of cultural "survivals": behaviors that persist as evidence of an earlier time but are no longer useful in society.

Men enjoy hunting and killing, and these activities are continued in sports even when they are no longer economically necessary. If a behavior is important to the survival of a species . . . then it must be both easily learned and pleasurable (Washburn & Lancaster, p. 299).

Man the Dancer

Using a similar logic for the survival of ancient "learned and pleasurable" behaviors, perhaps it could easily have been our propensity for dancing rather than our desire to hunt that can explain much of human behavior. After all, men and women love to dance; it is a behavior found in all cultures but has even less obvious function today than hunting. Our love of movement and dance might explain, for example, our propensity for face-to-face sex, and even the evolution of bipedalism and the movement of humans out of trees and onto the ground.

Could the first tool have been a stick to beat a dance drum, and the ancient Laetoli footprints evidence of two individuals going out to dance the "Afarensis shuffle"? Although it takes only two to tango, a variety of social interactions and systems might have been encouraged by the complex social dances known in human societies around the globe.

Sociobiology and E.O. Wilson

In the mid-1970s, E.O. Wilson and others described a number of traits as genetically based and therefore human universals, including territoriality, male–female bonds, male dominance over females, and extended maternal care leading to matrilineality. Wilson argued that the genetic basis of these traits was indicated by their relative constancy among our primate relatives and by their persistence throughout human evolution and in human societies. Elsewhere, I have shown that these characteristics are neither general primate traits nor human universals (Sussman 1995). Wilson, however, argued that these were a product of our evolutionary hunting past.

For at least a million years—probably more—Man engaged in a hunting way of life, giving up the practice a mere 10,000 years ago. . . . Our innate social responses have been fashioned through this life style. With caution, we can compare the most widespread hunter-gatherer qualities with similar behavior displayed by some of the non-human primates that are closely related to Man. Where the same pattern of traits occurs in . . . most or all of those primates—we can conclude that it has been subject to little evolution. (Wilson 1976, in Sussman 1997: 65–66).

Wilson's theory of sociobiology, the evolution of social behavior, argued that:

1. the goal of living organisms is to pass on one's genes at the expense of all others;
2. an organism should only cooperate with others if:
   (a) they carry some of his/her own genes (kin selection) or
   (b) if at some later date the others might aid you (reciprocal altruism).

To sociobiologists, evolutionary morality is based on an unconscious need to multiply our own genes, to build group cohesion in order to win wars. We should not look down on our warlike, cruel nature but rather understand its success when coupled with "making nice" with *some* other individuals or groups. The genetically driven "making nice" is the basis of human ethics and morality.

> Throughout recorded history the conduct of war has been common . . . some of the noblest traits of mankind, including team play, altruism, patriotism, bravery . . . and so forth are the genetic product of warfare (Wilson 1975:572–3).

The evidence for any of these universals or for the tenets of sociobiology is as weak as was the evidence for Dart's, Ardrey's and Washburn and Lancaster's theories of innate aggression. Not only are modern gatherer-hunters and most apes remarkably non-aggressive, but in the 1970s and 1980s studies of fossil bones and artifacts have shown that early humans were not hunters, and that weapons were a later addition to the human repertoire. In fact, C.K. Brain (1981) showed that the holes and dents in Dart's australopithecine skulls matched perfectly with fangs of leopards or with impressions of rocks pressing against the buried fossils. Australopithecines apparently were the hunted, not the hunters (Cartmill, 1993, 1997).

Beyond Our Genes

Wrangham and Peterson's book goes beyond the assertion of human inborn aggression and propensity towards violence. The authors ask the critical question: Are we doomed to be violent forever because this pattern is fixed within our genetic code or can we go beyond our past?—get out of our genes, so to speak.

The authors believe that we can look to the bonobo or pygmy chimpanzee as one potential savior, metaphorically speaking.

Bonobos, although even more closely related to the common chimpanzee than humans, have become a peace-loving, love-making alternative to chimpanzee-human violence. How did this happen? In chimpanzees and humans, females of the species select partners that are violent . . . "while men have evolved to be demonic males, it seems likely that women have evolved to prefer demonic males . . . as long as demonic males are the most successful reproducers, any female who mates with them is provided with sons who themselves will likely be good reproducers" (Wrangham and Peterson 1996:239). However, among pygmy chimpanzees females form alliances and have chosen to mate with less aggressive males. So, after all, it is not violent males that have caused humans and chimpanzees to be their inborn, immoral, dehumanized selves, it is rather, poor choices by human and chimpanzee females.

Like Dart, Washburn, and Wilson before them, Wrangham and Peterson believe that killing and violence is inherited from our ancient relatives of the past. However, unlike these earlier theorists, Wrangham and Peterson argue this is not a trait unique to hominids, nor is it a by-product of hunting. In fact, it is just this violent nature and a natural "blood lust" that makes both humans and chimpanzees such good hunters. It is the bonobos that help the authors come to this conclusion. Because bonobos have lost the desire to kill, they also have lost the desire to hunt.

> . . . do bonobos tell us that the suppression of personal violence carried with it the suppression of predatory aggression? The strongest hypothesis at the moment is that bonobos came from a chimpanzee-like ancestor that hunted monkeys and hunted one another. As they evolved into bonobos, males lost their demonism, becoming less aggressive to each other. In so doing they lost their lust for hunting monkeys, too . . . Murder and hunting may be more closely tied together than we are used to thinking (Wrangham and Peterson 1996:219).

The Selfish Gene Theory

Like Ardrey, Wrangham and Peterson believe that blood lust ties killing and hunting tightly together but it is the killing that drives hunting in the latter's argument. This lust to kill is based upon the sociobiological tenet of the selfish gene. "The general principle that behavior evolves to serve selfish ends has been widely accepted; and the idea that humans might have been favored by natural selection to hate and to kill their enemies has become entirely, if tragically, reasonable" (Wrangham and Peterson 1996:23).

As with many of the new sociobiological or evolutionary anthropology theories, I find problems with both the theory itself and with the evidence used to support it. Two arguments that humans and chimpanzees share biologically fixed behaviors are: (1) they are more closely related to each other than chimpanzees are to gorillas; (2) chimpanzees are a good model for our earliest ancestor and retain conservative traits that should be shared by both.

The first of these statements is still hotly debated and, using various genetic evidence, the chimp-gorilla-human triage is so close that it is difficult to tell exact divergence time or pattern among the three. The second statement is just not true. Chimpanzees have been evolving for as long as humans and gorillas, and there is no reason to believe ancestral chimps were similar to present-day chimps. The fossil evidence for the last 5–8 million years is extremely sparse, and it is likely that many forms of apes have become extinct just as have many hominids.

Furthermore, even if the chimpanzee were a good model for the ancestral hominid, and was a conservative representative of this phylogenetic group, this would not mean that humans would necessarily share specific behavioral traits. As even Wrangham and Peterson emphasize, chimps, gorillas, and bonobos all behave very differently from one another in their social behavior and in their willingness to kill conspecifics.

Evidence Against "Demonic Males"

The proof of the "Demonic Male" theory does not rest on any theoretical grounds but must rest solely on the evidence that violence and killing in chimpanzees and in humans are behaviors that are similar in pattern; have ancient, shared evolutionary roots; and are inherited. Besides killing of conspecifics, Wrangham "includes infanticide, rape, and regular battering of females by males" as a part of this inherited legacy of violent behaviors shared by humans and chimpanzees (1997:108).

Wrangham and Peterson state: "That chimpanzees and humans kill members of neighboring groups of their own species is . . . a startling exception to the normal rule for animals" (1996:63). "Fighting adults of almost all species normally stop at winning: They don't go on to kill" (1996:155). However, as Wrangham points out there are exceptions, such as lions, wolves, spotted hyenas, and I would add a number of other predators. In fact, most species do not have the weapons to kill one another as adults.

Just how common is conspecific killing in chimpanzees? This is where the real controversy may lie. Jane Goodall described the chimpanzee as a peaceful, non-aggressive species during the first 24 years of study at Gombe (1950–1974). During one year of concentrated study, Goodall observed 284 agonistic encounters: of these 66% were due to competition for introduced bananas, and only 34% "could be regarded as attacks occurring in 'normal' aggressive contexts" (1968:278). Only 10 percent of the 284 attacks were classified as 'violent', and "even attacks that appeared punishing to me often resulted in no discernable injury. . . . Other attacks consisted merely of brief pounding, hitting or rolling of the individual, after which the aggressor often touched or embraced the other immediately (1968:277).

Chimpanzee aggression before 1974 was considered no different from patterns of aggression seen in many other primate species. In fact, Goodall explains in her 1986 monograph, *The Chimpanzees of Gombe,* that she uses data mainly from after 1975 because the earlier years present a "very different picture of the Gombe chimpanzees" as being "far more peaceable than humans" (1986:3). Other early naturalists' descriptions of chimpanzee behavior were consistent with those of Goodall and confirmed her observations. Even different communities were observed to come together with peaceful, ritualized displays of greeting (Reynolds and Reynolds 1965; Suguyama 1972; Goodall 1968).

Then, between 1974 and 1977, five adult males from one subgroup were attacked and disappeared from the area, presumably dead. Why after 24 years did the patterns of aggression change? Was it because the stronger group saw the weakness of the other and decided to improve their genetic fitness? But surely there were stronger and weaker animals and subgroups before this time. Perhaps we can look to Goodall's own perturbations for an answer. In 1965, Goodall began to provide "restrictive human-controlled feeding." A few years later she realized that

> the constant feeding was having a marked effect on the behavior of the chimps. They were beginning to move about in large groups more often than they had ever done in the old days. Worst of all, the adult males were becoming increasingly aggressive. When we first offered the chimps bananas the males seldom fought over their food; . . . now . . . there was a great deal more fighting than ever before. . . . (Goodall 1971:143).

The possibility that human interference was a main cause of the unusual behavior of the Gombe chimps was the subject of an excellent, but generally ignored book by Margaret Power (1991). Wrangham and Peterson (1996:19) footnote this book, but as with many other controversies, they essentially ignore its findings, stating that yes, chimpanzee violence might have been unnatural behavior if it weren't for the evidence of similar behavior occurring since 1977 and "elsewhere in Africa" (1996:19).

Further Evidence

What is this evidence from elsewhere in Africa? Wrangham and Peterson provide only four brief examples, none of which is very convincing:

(1) Between 1979–1982, the Gombe group extended its range to the south and conflict with a southern group, Kalande, was suspected. In 1982, a "raiding" party of males reached Goodall's camp. The authors state: "Some of these raids may have been lethal" (1996:19). However, Goodall describes this "raid" as follows: One female "was chased by a Kalande male and mildly attacked. . . . Her four-year-old son . . . encountered a second male—but was only sniffed" (1986:516). Although Wrangham and Peterson imply that these encounters were similar to those between 1974–77, no violence was actually witnessed. The authors also refer to the discovery of the dead body of Humphrey; what they do not mention is Humphrey's age of 35 and that wild chimps rarely live past 33 years!

(2) From 1970 to 1982, six adult males from one community in the Japanese study site of Mahale disappeared, one by one over this 12 year period. None of the animals were observed being attacked or killed, and one was sighted later roaming as a solitary male (Nishida et al., 1985:287–289).

(3) In another site in West Africa, Wrangham and Peterson report that Boesch and Boesch believe "that violent aggression among the chimpanzees is as important as it is in Gombe" (1986:20). However, in the paper referred to, the Boesches simply state that encounters by neighboring chimpanzee communities are more common in their site than in Gombe (one per month vs. 1 every 4 months). There is no mention of violence during these encounters.

(4) At a site that Wrangham began studying in 1984, an adult male was found dead in 1991. Wrangham states: "In the second week of August, Ruizoni was killed. No human saw the big fight" (Wrangham & Peterson 1996:20). Wrangham gives us no indication of what has occurred at this site over the last 6 years.

In fact, this is the total amount of evidence of warfare and male-male killing among chimpanzees after 37 years of research!! The data for infanticide and rape among chimpanzees is even less impressive. In fact, data are so sparse for these behaviors among chimps that Wrangham and Peterson are forced to use examples from the other great apes, gorillas and orangutans. However, just as for killing among chimpanzees, both the evidence and the interpretations are suspect and controversial.

Can We Escape Our Genes?

What if Wrangham and Peterson are correct and we and our chimp cousins are inherently sinners? Are we doomed to be violent forever because this pattern is fixed within our genetic code?

After 5 million years of human evolution and 120,000 or so years of *Homo sapiens* existence, is there a way to rid ourselves of our inborn evils?

> What does it do for us, then, to know the behavior of our closest relatives? Chimpanzees and bonobos are an extraordinary pair. One, I suggest shows us some of the worst aspects of our past and our present; the other shows an escape from it. . . . Denial of our demons won't make them go away. But even if we're driven to accepting the evidence of a grisly past, we're not forced into thinking it condemns us to an unchanged future (Wrangham 1997:110).

In other words, we can learn how to behave by watching bonobos. But, if we can change our inherited behavior so simply, why haven't we been able to do this before *Demonic Males* enlightened us? Surely, there are variations in the amounts of violence in different human cultures and individuals. If we have the capacity and plasticity to change by learning from example, then our behavior is determined by socialization practices and by our cultural histories and not by our nature! This is true whether the examples come from benevolent bonobos or conscientious objectors.

Conclusion

The theory presented by Wrangham and Peterson, although it also includes chimpanzees as our murdering cousins, is very similar to "man the hunter" theories proposed in the past. It also does not differ greatly from early European and Christian beliefs about human ethics and morality. We are forced to ask:

Are these theories generated by good scientific fact, or are they just "good to think" because they reflect, reinforce, and reiterate our traditional cultural beliefs, our morality and our ethics? Is the theory generated by the data, or are the data manipulated to fit preconceived notions of human morality and ethics?

Since the data in support of these theories have been weak, and yet the stories created have been extremely similar, I am forced to believe that "Man the Hunter" is a myth, that humans are not necessarily prone to violence and aggression, but that this belief will continue to reappear in future writings on human nature. Meanwhile, primatologists must continue their field research, marshaling the actual evidence needed to answer many of the questions raised in Wrangham and Peterson's volume.

References

Ardrey, Robert. 1961. *African Genesis: A Personal Investigation into Animal Origins and Nature of Man.* Atheneum.
——. *The Territorial Imperative.* Atheneum, 1966.

Brain, C.K. 1981. *The Hunted or the Hunter? An Introduction to African Cave Taphonomy.* Univ. of Chicago.

Dart, Raymond. 1953. "The Predatory Transition from Ape to Man." *International Anthropological and Linguistic Review* 1:201–217.

Darwin, Charles. 1874. *The Descent of Man and Selection in Relation to Sex.* 2nd ed. The Henneberry Co.

Cartmill, Matt 1997. "Hunting Hypothesis of Human Origins." In *History of Physical Anthropology: An Encyclopedia,* ed. F. Spencer, pp. 508–512. Garland.

——. 1993. *A View to a Death in the Morning: Hunting and Nature Through History.* Harvard Univ.

Goodall, Jane. 1986. *The Chimpanzees of Gombe: Patterns of Behavior.* Belknap.

——. 1971. *In the Shadow of Man.* Houghton Mifflin.

Goodall, Jane. 1968. "The Behavior of Free-Living Chimpanzees in the Gombe Stream Reserve." *Animal Behavior Monographs* 1:165–311.

Nishida, T., Hiraiwa-Hasegawa, M., and Takahtat, Y. "Group Extinction and Female Transfer in Wild Chimpanzees in the Mahali Nation Park, Tanzania." *Zeitschrift für Tierpsychologie* 67:281–301.

Power, Margaret. 1991. *The Egalitarian Human and Chimpanzee: An Anthropological View of Social Organization.* Cambridge University.

Reynolds, V. and Reynolds, F. 1965. "Chimpanzees of Budongo Forest." In *Primate Behavior: Field Studies of Monkeys and Apes,* ed. I. DeVore, pp. 368–424. Holt, Rinehart, and Winston.

Suguyama, Y. 1972. "Social Characteristics and Socialization of Wild Chimpanzees." In *Primate Socialization,* ed. F.E. Poirier, pp. 145–163. Random House.

Sussman, R.W., ed. 1997. *The Biological Basis of Human Behavior.* Simon and Schuster.

Sussman, R.W. 1995. "The Nature of Human Universals." *Reviews in Anthropology* 24:1–11.

Washburn, S.L. and Lancaster, C. K. 1968. "The Evolution of Hunting." In *Man the Hunter,* eds. R. B. Lee and I. DeVore, pp. 293–303. Aldine.

Wilson, E. O. 1997. "Sociobiology: A New Approach to Understanding the Basis of Human Nature." *New Scientist* 70(1976):342–345. (Reprinted in R.W. Sussman, 1997.)

——. 1975. Sociobiology: *The New Synthesis.* Cambridge: Harvard University.

Wrangham, R.W. 1995. "Ape, Culture, and Missing Links." *Symbols* (Spring):2–9, 20. (Reprinted in R. W. Sussman, 1997.)

Wrangham, Richard and Peterson, Dale. 1996. *Demonic Males: Apes and the Origins of Human Violence.* Houghton Mifflin.

POSTSCRIPT

Are Humans Inherently Violent?

Wrangham and Peterson's argument that human males have an innate tendency toward aggressive behavior is a classic sociobiological explanation. Sociobiological explanations consist of two basic assertions: (1) that all human behavior is ultimately driven by instincts, and (2) that those instincts result from natural selection favoring the behaviors they cause. Sociobiology, which has become very popular in recent years, began in biology and ethology (the study of animal behavior) and spread to the social sciences, including psychology, where it is called "evolutionary psychology." Its popularity is probably due to its attempt to explain many confusing variations in behavior by using a few simple, scientific principles. Any human social behavior—from selfishness to altruism—can be explained by sociobiology. It's all in the genes. Why are human males aggressive? Sociobiology would say it is because natural selection favored our more aggressive ancestors, allowing them to have more children than less aggressive individuals, thus ensuring that the tendency for male aggression increased in our species.

To learn more about sociobiology in general, the best starting point is probably E. O. Wilson's seminal book *Sociobiology: The New Synthesis* (Harvard University Press, 1975). Works explaining the human propensity for violence in terms of instincts include—besides Wrangham and Peterson's book *Demonic Males* (Houghton Mifflin, 1996)—Konrad Lorenz's classic book *On Aggression* (Harcourt, Brace & World, 1967), Martin Daly and Margo Wilson's book *Homicide* (A de Gruyter, 1988), and Michael Ghiglieri's book *The Dark Side of Man: Tracing the Origins of Male Violence* (Perseus Books, 1999). Carrying sociobiological reasoning a step further, Randy Thornhill and Craig T. Palmer argue in their book *A Natural History of Rape: Biological Bases of Sexual Coercion* (MIT Press, 2000) that human males have an instinct for rape because in the evolution of hominids rape was an effective way for males to pass on their genes.

Sussman's argument that human violence is basically a product of social and cultural conditions comes from the tradition of cultural anthropology. He challenges Wrangham and Peterson's assumptions that human behaviors are driven by instincts. Sussman says that the behaviors that Wrangham and Peterson, following E. O. Wilson, attribute to instinct, such as territoriality and male dominance over females, are not in fact universal among humans and lower primates. He also rejects Wrangham and Peterson's contention that an instinct exists if a behavior is universal to the human species, is easy to learn, and is pleasurable to perform. By these criteria, Sussman says, dancing must also be caused by an instinct to

36

dance. Presumably a long list of similar activities, such as playing games and telling jokes, must also have their governing instincts. Sussman also rejects Wrangham and Peterson's contention that aggressive males would have been favored by natural (sexual) selection during hominid evolution. If this were so, he implies, why aren't all males equally aggressive today? How could the genes for nonaggressive behavior have survived countless generations of selection against them? Further, Sussman ridicules the notion that female hominids (or chimpanzees) would deliberately select aggressive males to father their offspring.

Important works challenging the sociobiological explanation of human violence include Ashley Montagu's book *The Nature of Human Aggression* (Oxford University Press, 1976), Richard Lewontin, Leon Kamin, and Stephen Rose's book *Not in Our Genes: Biology, Ideology, and Human Nature* (Pantheon Books, 1984), Kenneth Bock's book *Human Nature and History: A Response to Sociobiology* (Columbia University Press, 1980), and Matt Cartmill's book *A View to a Death in the Morning: Hunting and Nature Through History* (Harvard University Press, 1993). For descriptions and analyses of societies in which aggression is minimized, see Leslie E. Sponsel and Thomas A. Gregor's edited volume *The Anthropology of Peace and Nonviolence* (L. Rienner, 1994) and Signe Howell and Roy Willis's volume *Societies at Peace: Anthropological Perspectives* (Routledge, 1989).

ISSUE 3

Did Neandertals Interbreed With Modern Humans?

YES: João Zilhão, from "Fate of the Neandertals," *Archaeology* (July/August 2000)

NO: Jean-Jacques Hublin, from "Brothers or Cousins?" *Archaeology* (September/October 2000)

ISSUE SUMMARY

YES: Archaeologist João Zilhão discusses the recently found remains of a young child who was buried in a rock shelter in Portugal about 25,000 years ago. He concludes that the Lagar Velho child was a hybrid with mixed Neandertal and early modern human ancestry.

NO: Biological anthropologist Jean-Jacques Hublin maintains that the Lagar Velho child was merely one variant within the diverse early modern human population. He argues that there was some cultural influence from early modern humans to Neandertals but little or no interbreeding between them.

T he image of Neandertals (also spelled *Neanderthals*) has fluctuated widely since the mid-nineteenth century, when scholars first recognized that the fossil bones being unearthed in Europe were those of early humans and not just deformed individuals. The scientists who reconstructed the Neandertal skeletons were influenced by the theory of evolution introduced by Charles Darwin in his books *Origin of Species* (John Murray, 1859) and *Descent of Man* (John Murray, 1871). Some scientists pictured Neandertals as the "missing link" between humans and the apes. This view was exemplified by French scientist Marcellin Boule's 1909 analysis of a skeleton from Chapelle-aux-Saints, popularly known as the "Old Man." Classifying Neandertals as a separate species from humans, Boule illustrated the Chapelle-aux-Saints man in a slouching, bent-kneed posture, which he contrasted with the upright carriage of an Australian Aborigine, then thought to be the most primitive form of modern humans. Other scholars considered Neandertals the ancestors of Europeans or even of all humanity, positing a "Neandertal stage" of human evolution.

For example, the eminent anatomist Sir Arthur Keith analyzed the same Chapelle-aux-Saints remains and concluded that the Old Man was a full member of the human family. These sharply contrasting images express the enigmatic nature of Neandertals: they were both like us and not like us.

Evidence accumulated over the last 100 years has partially resolved the question of the status of the Neandertals. The notions of both a missing link and a global Neandertal stage of human evolution have been discarded. Today the predominant theories of recent human evolution are the "out of Africa" theory and the "multiregional evolution" theory. According to proponents of the out of Africa theory, Neandertals were a dead-end branch of humanity, which evolved out of *Homo erectus* in Europe and met its demise when modern humans arrived from Africa and outcompeted or killed the Neandertals off. Multiregionalists contend that Neandertals were descendants of part of the widespread *Homo erectus* population that evolved as a whole into modern humans. In their view Neandertals were local variants of the early human species who probably interbred with the incoming variants from Africa and whose genes were eventually mixed into the gene pool of modern Europe. Scientists are now seeking direct evidence of interbreeding in the bones, genes, stone tools, and behavior patterns of Neandertals and early modern humans in Europe.

João Zilhão discusses the recent find in Portugal of a fossil skeleton of a child, which appears to combine Neandertal features (e.g., short, thick limb bones) and modern human features (e.g., modern teeth and chin). He considers this child to be direct evidence that Neandertals interbred with the early modern humans who entered Europe after about 36,500 years ago. He argues that Neandertals created the sophisticated Châtelperronian stone tool industry before the arrival of modern humans, thus showing their intellectual similarity to the newcomers. Zilhâo maintains that the Neandertals disappeared by being absorbed into the larger early modern human population.

Jean-Jacques Hublin, on the other hand, doubts that the Lagar Velho child resulted from interbreeding between Neandertals and early modern humans, implying that it could have been just one variant of a diverse early modern population. He maintains that Neandertals borrowed ideas and exchanged products with early modern humans to a limited extent—thus accounting for the sophisticated Châtelperronian tool kit of the Neandertals— but that they remained biologically separate. He believes that Neandertals eventually died out because early modern humans outcompeted them for scarce resources during the last glacial period.

This dispute shows how scientists can draw opposing conclusions from the same evidence. How convincing do you find the writers' interpretations? Do you think it is likely that Neandertals borrowed tool-making techniques from early modern humans but did not interbreed with them? What kinds of evidence do you think scholars need to decisively answer the question of whether Neandertals and modern humans interbred? Are there other possible explanations for the disappearance of Neandertals that these authors do not consider? Does this question have any wider significance?

João Zilhão  **YES**

Fate of the Neandertals

The bones of a four-year-old child, buried for millennia in the rear of a rock-shelter in the Lapedo Valley 85 miles north of Lisbon, Portugal, comprised the first complete Palaeolithic skeleton ever dug in Iberia. Our November 28, 1998, find made national news, but an even greater surprise was in store when my colleague, Washington University anthropologist Erik Trinkaus, who measured the bones weeks after the discovery, reported that the child's anatomy could only have resulted from a mixed Neandertal-early modern human ancestry. Here, finally, was proof that Neandertals did not simply disappear from Europe 28,000 years ago. Instead, they interbred with modern humans and became part of our family.

The discovery was made by João Maurício and Pedro Souto, archaeology field assistants and members of a local archaeology group, who visited the valley at my request to check on reports that a student from a nearby village had found some prehistoric paintings. The reports turned out to be genuine. The student showed them a few small, red anthropomorphic figures in a style characteristic of the Copper Age (fourth and third millennia B.C.) painted on the back wall of a shallow rock-shelter on the north side of the valley.

While they were there, João and Pedro decided to inspect a larger shelter they saw on the opposite side of the valley. When they got there, the first thing they noticed was that archaeological deposits in the shelter had recently been destroyed; we later learned that in 1992 the landowner had bulldozed the upper six to nine feet of the shelter's fill to widen a rural trail used to reach property located farther up the valley. All that was left was a foot-and-a-half remnant of the original deposit in a fissure running along most of the length of the shelter's back wall. This remnant corresponds to a section of the original stratigraphic sequence lying between two and three feet below the former ground surface.

The remnant was extremely rich in charcoal, stone tools, and animal remains, including fossilized horse teeth, all suggesting an Upper Palaeolithic age (between 30,000 and 10,000 years ago) for the site. While collecting surface material that had fallen from the remnant, João and Pedro inspected a recess in the back wall. In the loose sediments they recovered several small bones stained with red ochre they thought could be human. Recognizing the potential significance of the discovery, they stopped investigating and reported their finds to me.

The following weekend, on December 6, I went to the site with my colleagues Cristina Araújo, a fellow archaeologist, and Cidália Duarte, a bioar-chaeologist specializing in burial taphonomy (how bodies are buried and preserved). João and Pedro presented their finds and two things almost imme-diately became clear. First, the bones they thought could be human were indeed the left forearm and hand bones of a young child. Second, stone tools found in the fissure dated the deposit to the Middle Solutrean and the Proto-Solutrean, that is, the period between 20,000 and 22,000 years ago. Since the juvenile human bones that lay some nine feet below this remnant belonged to a single individual and were very well preserved, the implication was obvious: a child had been buried at the site either in late Middle Palaeolithic or in early Upper Palaeolithic times, between 40,000 and 25,000 years ago. The ochre staining of the bones (a feature of all burials from the Gravettian period between 25,000 and 27,000 years ago) and rough estimates of the rate of sedi-mentation at the site led us to believe that a date closer to 25,000 years ago was more likely.

⋯⦿⋯

This conclusion prompted me to start a salvage excavation of the site, which we called the Lagar Velho rock-shelter after the ruin of an ancient olive-oil press at its entrance. The excavation began on December 12, 1998, continuing without interruption through Christmas and the New Year until January 7, 1999. Subsequently, in July and August, deep testing of the preserved deposits under the burial and in the central part of the shelter further documented the site's stratigraphy. The surface of the site was also excavated and extensively screened, enabling the recovery of many of the child's missing teeth and skull fragments. We realized the bulldozer had come within an inch or two of the skeleton, leaving it miraculously intact except for the skull, which had been crushed into more than 100 pieces. The presence of ancient fractures in the cranial fragments suggests that natural processes had collapsed it inward not long after burial, but fresh breaks show that further fragmentation occurred when the site was bulldozed, scattering skull fragments east of the burial.

The broken left side of the child's lower jaw, including the chin region, had been recovered at the outset in a very thin layer of disturbed deposits over-lying the burial. The chin featured the characteristic "snow-plow" shape found in Cro-Magnon people, the first anatomically modern humans, whose appear-ance on the European continent coincides with the disappearance of Neander-tals. The day after that lower jaw was recovered, discovery of a pierced marine shell of the species *Littorina obtusata,* the most common ornament in the Upper Palaeolithic of Portugal, reinforced the hypothesis that this was an early Upper Palaeolithic burial. The shell was found near the neck vertebrae, suggest-ing that the dead child was wearing it as a pendant when he was buried. As the excavation continued, we were able to uncover a nearly complete, *in situ* skele-ton (minus an intact skull), and establish that the body had been laid on its back, left side parallel to the cliff base, head to the east, feet crossed. Four red deer (*Cervus elaphus*) canines pierced through the root were found with the cranial remains. They suggest that the child was buried with some kind of decorated head wear. Pierced red deer canines have also been found on the skulls of Gravettian period people buried in Italy and Moravia.

The skeleton, especially the skull pieces, were heavily stained with red ochre as was the sediment in which the bones lay. This, and the fact that both the upper and the lower surfaces of the bones were stained, indicates that the body must have been wrapped in a shroud of ochre-painted skin, whose subsequent decay caused the transfer of the mineral pigment to the skeleton and sediment. The presence of a semi-rigid durable wrap around the body would also have provided the space for the post-mortem collapse of the child's ankle ligaments, evident in the position of the feet. At the base of the pit, immediately below and in contact with the child's legs, there was a thin black lens of charcoal, which belonged to a single branch of Scots pine. This suggests that a ritual fire was lit before the deposition of the body; the adjacent deposits contained no traces of charcoal.

Red deer bones found in association with the burial pit are distinct from those found in the surrounding and immediately underlying sediments. The latter present eroded surfaces, have a shine suggesting they were chewed and digested by carnivores, often display actual teeth punctures, and are associated with coprolites. In contrast, the deer bones found by the head and feet of the child's skeleton are well preserved, show no evidence of being mauled by carnivores, were in direct contact with the body, and provided a C14 date showing contemporaneity with the burial. Furthermore, no artifacts or other evidence of habitation were recovered at this level in this part of the shelter. The simplest explanation is that these bones belonged to parts of deer carcasses deposited in the grave as food offerings. The same may be true of the rabbit bones that overlay the child's right leg (three vertebrae, four ribs, and one sacrum fragment). They were also stained red, and two of the ribs were complete, suggesting that they were originally joined to the vertebrae.

Throughout the 1998–1999 salvage work we were able to count on the invaluable advice of Erik Trinkaus, to whom I e-mailed digital pictures of the excavation daily. Realizing the potential significance of the burial, Cidália Duarte and I invited him to the site to study the skeleton. An authority on Neandertals and early modern humans, Erik was already involved in analyzing Palaeolithic human material from Portugal.

While Cidália and I completed the fieldwork, Erik began to clean and reassemble the skeleton and work toward a preliminary anatomical description. After returning to the United States, he was able to compare the bones with his extensive data base on Neandertals and early modern humans. On January 25, I got a message from him which began with the ominous words: "The end of last week I made some quick comparisons of the Lagar Velho [child's] leg bone proportions with some data that I have, and it comes out looking like a Neandertal!" Other resemblances with Neandertals followed, but throughout this initial stage Cidália and I kept in mind Erik's cautionary remark in that first message: "unless I have made some silly mistake."

We decided to check and double check all the measurements ourselves, and eventually concluded that Erik had made no mistake—the child did present a mosaic of Neandertal and modern human features. Most prominent among the former, the arctic body proportions (with short limbs, especially the lower parts of the arms and legs), the robusticity of the limb bones and the angle at which the jaw bones meet at the chin; among the latter, the characteristic "snow-plow" chin and the size of the dentition. Body proportions are particularly important in this regard because the study of present-day populations has proved that they are genetically inherited and that the basic patterns of body shape are already established in the fetal stage of development. This makes it possible to compare the bones of the Lagar Velho child not only with those of other children but also with available adult skeletons from the same time period. Among the two possible ancestral populations of the group to which this child belonged, it is well-established that all Neandertals had arctic body proportions. On the contrary, all European early modern humans had tropical body proportions (long limbs), betraying their recent (in evolutionary time) African origin, in spite of the fact that they had been living for many millennia in the very cold steppe-tundra environments then present throughout the unglaciated parts of the continent located north of the Pyrenees.

⋅⊰❦⊱⋅

In the following months, after discussing our suspicions with human palaeontologists and primate biologists who study natural hybrids, we grew increasingly convinced: the child possessed an anatomy that could only be explained as the result of a mixed Neandertal-early modern human ancestry. Then, in early April, the first radiocarbon results started to arrive. Obtained from samples from the charcoal lens under the child's legs and from the animal bones associated with the grave, they confirmed our earlier estimates that the age of the burial was ca. 25,000 years old, some 3,000 years after Neandertals presumably disappeared from western Iberia. This made it clear that the mosaic of anatomical features in the Lagar Velho child could not have been the result of a rare, chance encounter producing a hybrid descendant from a Neandertal mother and a modern human father (or vice versa). On the contrary, it had to represent a mixture of populations. Put another way, Neandertals had not simply disappeared without descendants, they had been absorbed, through extensive interbreeding, into the modern human groups that had started to take over Iberia ca. 30,000 years ago. They had contributed to the gene pool of subsequent early Upper Palaeolithic populations of the peninsula and, therefore, had to be counted among our ancestors: they were family.

This conclusion contrasts with the prevailing view of the Neandertals as an evolutionary dead end, a side branch of the human tree, that has become so popular in the wake of the Eve hypothesis based on mitochondrial DNA (mtDNA). First proposed in 1987, this hypothesis states that Europeans descended entirely from anatomically modern human populations that gradually evolved in Africa from an ancestral *Homo erectus* stock after 250,000 years ago. Having begun to spread from there to the rest of the world some 50,000 years ago, these anatomically modern groups eventually replaced, without admixture, all indigenous anatomically archaic human forms of Eurasia. Thus, Neandertals became extinct with no descendants.

This view received strong support from the publication, in 1997, by Svante Päabo of the University of Munich and his colleagues, of a comparison between mtDNA extracted from the original Feldhofer Cave Neandertal type specimen found in 1856 and that of present-day human populations. It inferred that the difference was so significant as to put Neandertals outside the range of modern humanity, suggesting that they had belonged to an altogether different biological species and that interbreeding, although conceivable, could not have been significant. Possible support for this view comes from the mtDNA analysis of the rib of a 29,000-year-old fetal or neo-natal skeleton from Mezmaiskaya Cave, in the northern Caucasus, recently published in the journal *Nature*. The significance of the latter, however, remains to be seen. It is reported as a Neandertal infant, but its classification is in fact uncertain.

～◆◇～

Analysis of the Lagar Velho child's mtDNA would certainly help to test our interpretation. Unfortunately, this is likely to be impossible, due to the chemical weathering undergone by the child's fragile bones. However, as we prepared the preliminary publication of the burial and of our interpretation of the child's anatomy, the journal to which we had submitted it (*Proceedings of the National Academy of Sciences USA*) published a major paper on the variability of the DNA of African apes, our closest living relatives. This work showed that contemporary interbreeding populations of chimpanzees are genetically more diverse than modern humans and our Late Pleistocene fossil ancestors, including the one Neandertal specimen Päabo analyzed. By primate standards, therefore, the results obtained by Päabo's team indicated that present-day humans ought to be considered abnormally homogeneous. This low DNA variability is consistent with a single recent origin for modern humans (the Out-of-African model), but does not imply that Neandertals were a different species. It simply confirms, from genetic data, what palaeontologists have established for about a century on the basis of fossil bones: that Neandertals, as a separate, well-defined geographic variant of humanity that became differentiated during the Middle Pleistocene, are now extinct. That does not mean that they did not contribute to the gene pool of subsequent populations. The Lagar Velho child's anatomical mosaic suggests that they did, even if such a contribution eventually became so diluted as to become unrecognizable today.

Recent developments in the archaeology of the last Neandertals and the earliest modern humans in Europe point to a similar conclusion. Ever since the original Neander Valley fossil was discovered, most researchers have doubted that the Neandertals were capable of using symbols or manufacturing complex bone and ivory objects. While modern humans are thought to have created cave art and delicate carvings and to have engaged in specialized hunting, Neandertals have been viewed as scavengers or opportunistic hunters. When cultural remains found in late Neandertal sites suggested otherwise, the evidence was dismissed.

The earliest modern humans in Europe are associated with characteristic stone and bone tool-kits, called Aurignacian, whose first appearance in the archaeological record has been assumed for the last decade to date to ca. 40,000 years ago. In France and northern Spain, local Neandertals were thought to have copied some of the stone and bone tools of their new neighbors, the Aurignacian moderns, as well as their personal ornaments, giving rise to a new Neandertal cultural entity, the Châtelperronian. It was argued, however, that such an imitation would have been carried out with no real understanding of the underlying symbolic meaning of the objects.

Other kinds of explanations postulated post-depositional disturbance of sites to deny Neandertals any role in the manufacture of those items. Scholars such as Yvette Taborin of the University of Paris I and Randall White of New York University, for instance, suggested that the presence of personal ornaments and bone tools at the key site of Grotte du Renne, in Burgundy, France, would have been the result of a mixing of archaeological strata. Others, such as Jean-Jacques Hublin of Paris' Musée de l'Homme and Paul Mellars of Cambridge University suggested as an alternative explanation that such a presence might be due to Neandertals having collected or traded for objects manufactured by neighboring moderns.

The reassessment of the evidence from Grotte du Renne by Francesco d'Errico of the University of Bordeaux I, myself, and other colleagues showed that Châtelperronian Neandertals were indeed the makers of the personal ornaments and bone tools found there. Moreover, the grooved or perforated teeth of fox, wolf, bear, hyena, red deer, horse, marmot, bear, and reindeer recovered at the Grotte du Renne and other sites (such as Quinçay, in the Charente, France) were made with techniques different from those used by Aurignacian modern humans. The same is true of the different knapping techniques and tool types that appear among late Neandertals in various regions of Europe. These innovations everywhere fail to show any influence from the Aurignacian, while maintaining affinities with preceding Neandertal traditions.

D'Errico and I have also closely examined the archaeological record to verify whether the arrival of early modern humans in western Europe did indeed predate these Neandertal innovations, as had to be the case if the emergence of the innovations had been triggered by contact with the newcomers. We found, however, that wherever archaeological layers of both cultures are represented at the same sites, the Châtelperronian always underlies the Aurignacian. Similarly, research on hundreds of radiometric datings available for this period in Europe and the Near East shows that, wherever the context of the dated samples is well established, the first Aurignacian ones date to no earlier than ca. 36,500 years ago. The same radiometric data, however, indicate that, by then, Neandertals had already accomplished their own transition to behavioral modernity. In others words, there is no doubt that the Châtelperronian and other late

Neandertal cultures emerged in Europe well before any modern humans established themselves in neighboring areas.

This autonomous development included the manufacture and use of symbolic objects created for visual display on the body that reflected, as often observed in present-day traditional societies, different social roles. It is also at about 40,000 years ago that the earliest evidence for personal ornaments appears in the anatomically modern human populations of eastern and southern Africa. Thus, "modern" behavior seems to have appeared independently in different regions and among different groups of humans, much as would happen later in history with the invention of agriculture, writing, and social organization. On the strength of available data, our hypothesis that late Neandertal groups invented their own tools and ornaments is firmly supported. The notion that we were the only human type capable of developing a symbolic culture has collapsed.

If the two groups did not represent biologically different species and had attained a similar level of cultural achievement, why then did modern humans prevail? Why was it that the immigrants absorbed the locals and not the other way around? These are the really interesting questions for archaeologists and geneticists to ask. Biogeographic and demographic explanations may provide the answers. In the Pleistocene period, under climatic conditions much colder than today's, most of Eurasia was uninhabitable. The northernmost areas were covered by ice sheets and barren tundras, and population densities in the settled areas must have been much lower than in Africa. Erik Trinkaus' palaeodemographic analysis of Neandertal remains reveals those populations were highly unstable. Therefore, it is quite likely that between 100,000 and 40,000 years ago a large majority of all the planet's human beings lived in Africa, where the modern morphological form evolved.

If these African groups also had a higher fertility, as is commonly the case with warm climate populations of the same species when compared with those from colder climates, we can plausibly explain what happened. Africans started to disperse into the neighboring regions, a process that must have been hastened by a warming period between ca. 50,000 and ca. 30,000 years ago, during which the savannas of eastern Africa, and their faunas, spread into the Middle East. Given enough time, even a very small difference in fertility would put the much smaller and more scattered populations of Neandertals at a demographic disadvantage, especially if interbreeding were common.

Once modern humans became established throughout most of the European continent, their absorption of remnant Neandertal populations was just a matter of time. Radiometric data suggest that isolated Neandertal communities existed until quite late, not only in Iberia, where the evidence is the strongest, but also in Croatia and Crimea. In the case of southwestern Europe, the Ebro River in northern Spain seems to have represented some sort of biocultural "frontier" separating Aurignacian modern humans established north of the Cantabrian-Pyrenean mountains since ca. 36,500 years ago from Neandertals surviving south of them until ca. 28,000 years ago.

That Neandertals held on for so long shows just how well-adapted they must have been. No wonder that, when modern humans started to cross that "frontier," they saw them as fellow human beings and interbred, as demonstrated by the Lagar Velho child.

If, for our anatomically modern ancestors, Neandertals were just people—perhaps a little funny-looking, but people nonetheless—why should we believe otherwise and persist, against all available biological and cultural evidence, in trying to put them in an entirely different category?

Brothers or Cousins?

Meeting a male Neandertal face to face would be an unforgettable experience. He would have the bodily proportions of an Eskimo, with a long trunk and incredibly powerful shoulders and arms. He would weigh a muscular 200 pounds, and have a huge head with a long face, a big projecting nose, no chin, receding cheeks, and big eye sockets surmounted by a continuous browridge. Neandertal facial characteristics are so distinct that even primary school children can distinguish a Neandertal skull from a modern one.

Discovered more than a century-and-a-half ago, Neandertals are the most studied group of fossil hominids. The debate over the causes of their extinction and their relation to modern humans is one of the most passionate in the field of palaeoanthropology. Indeed, the Neandertals are not a remote species of extinct primates, but rather our closest neighbors in the hominid family tree. Discussing their biology and behavior means talking about our own. Interestingly, scholars and the public have viewed Neandertals differently over the years. While in the past Neandertals were often (but not always) imagined as ape-like hairy brutes, there is now a tendency to depict them as pacific, crafty hunter-gatherers just a shade stockier than modern humans but otherwise much like us. That Neandertals and early modern humans coexisted in Europe for 10,000 years and shared culture and technology while representing different species or sub-species of hominids is for some an uncomfortable fact. The present need among some researchers to integrate the Neandertals' behavior and biology with that of modern humans is a misguided response.

Debated Biology

Most palaeoanthropologists think Neandertals belong to a group clearly separate from modern humans. For more than 400,000 years in Europe, they adapted to their cool-to-cold climate, far from the majority of hominids living in tropical areas. Their physical uniqueness also resulted from geographical and genetic isolation. However, for more than a century some palaeoanthropologists argued that Neandertals were the ancestors of modern Europeans. When fully modern humans contemporary or even older than European Neandertals were discovered in the Near East and Africa, this hypothesis was abandoned. Today it is widely accepted that the sudden

From Jean-Jacques Hublin, "Brothers or Cousins?" *Archaeology*, vol. 53, no. 5 (September/October 2000). Copyright © 2000 by The Archaeological Institute of America. Reprinted by permission.

emergence in Europe of ancient modern humans, called Cro-Magnons, between 40,000 and 35,000 years ago resulted instead from their migration from warmer geographical areas. Most of the debate on the Neandertals now focuses on their exact biological relationship to us and on the possibility of genetic and behavioral exchange between them and the modern invaders.

The Neandertals' genetic signature has been revealed in DNA studies on individuals from the Feldhofer site in Germany, where Neandertals were first identified in the mid-nineteenth century, and from Mezmaskaya cave in the Caucasus, where a newborn Neandertal was found associated with Middle Palaeolithic artifacts. Genetic analysis of fossil hominids, however, is still in its infancy and very many questions remain. Only tiny samples of mitochondrial DNA can be analyzed, but the results from Feldhofer and Mezmaskaya are very similar even though the two individuals lived far apart. On average the Neandertal specimens differ more from those of modern humans around the world than they do from each other. This reinforces the view that the Neandertals have no close connection with modern European populations. At the moment it is very frustrating not to be able to compare Neandertal DNA with that of Cro-Magnons; Palaeolithic human DNA remains very difficult to find, and so far genetic evidence still does not provide us with a firm standard to decide whether Neandertals represented a distinct sub-species of *Homo sapiens,* or a very close sister species, *Homo neanderthalensis.*

Closer Encounters

Changes in stone-artifact production accompanied the replacement of Neandertals by modern invaders some 40,000 years ago. Mousterian tool kits produced by Neandertals were supplanted by new assemblages, but the most spectacular changes did not take place in stone technology. After millennia of very slow development, there was a burst of innovation: composite weapons made of bone, wood, and flint appeared; social organization evolved; and the structure of dwellings improved. Trade developed, as did the clear expression of symbolic thought revealed by arts and ornaments, and there was likely some sort of linguistic advancement. Recent studies of the Middle Stone Age (100,000 years B.P.) in south and central Africa suggest that some of these changes may in fact have begun a long time ago outside of Europe. The image we have of a disruptive "cultural revolution" in Europe may have resulted from an invasion by tropical hunter-gatherers who brought new techniques and behaviors with them.

While Neandertals and hominids display clear biological differences, the European archaeological record yields several "transitional" Neandertal assemblages between the Middle and Upper Palaeolithic. In the late 1970s, it was widely believed that European Neandertals had created only Mousterian (Middle Palaeolithic) artifacts predating 40,000 B.P. Later, Upper Palaeolithic assemblages, including the transitional ones, were all assigned to "Cro-Magnons," i.e., anatomically modern humans. Transitional tool kits such as the Châtelperronian in France and northern Spain, the Uluzzian in Italy, and the Szeletian in Central Europe, were considered early Upper

Palaeolithic assemblages. French and Spanish Châtelperronian assemblages are composed of truly Mousterian artifacts together with elongated blades for making knives and spearpoints. Their most indisputable "Upper Palaeolithic" feature is the rare but clear occurrence of decorated bone objects and body ornaments. Arcy-sur-Cure, 60 miles southeast of Paris, yielded a rather complete series of these artifacts on a floor stained with pigments where distinct huts had been located. In all respects this stratum contrasts dramatically with the amorphous underlying Mousterian floor.

For decades it was difficult to reconcile the almost total replacement of population in Europe 35,000 years ago with some kind of in situ cultural evolution. In the spring of 1979, the discovery of a new Neandertal specimen resolved the dilemma and completely changed our view of the last Neandertals. I still vividly remember those exciting weeks. My Ph.D. at the Science University Pierre and Marie Curie in Paris was just finished and a new and very unusual Neandertal skeleton was being examined on a large table in palaeoanthropologist Bernard Vandermeersch's office. In the following months Saint-Césaire, the cave site not far from the Cognac vineyards north of Bordeaux where the remains were discovered, would become world famous among palaeoanthropologists.

The Saint-Césaire Neandertal burial belonged to Châtelperronian strata and was well separated from the underlying Mousterian. Neandertals were thus the makers of the so-called transitional assemblages. The end of the Neandertals, we learned, did not coincide with the beginning of Upper Palaeolithic but was to be found within this transitional period. In the years following the Saint-Césaire discovery, several scholars, including myself, proposed a new explanation for these transitional industries. In our view, they resulted from interaction of the last Neandertals with the first modern Europeans over a significant period of time. While in some places Neandertals stayed away from the modern invaders and pursued their traditional way of life, they adopted new behaviors in areas of closer contact.

The first tool industry securely assigned to modern humans in Europe is the Aurignacian. One of its most remarkable features is the development of bone artifacts and especially standardized spearheads. The flint bladelets Cro-Magnon hunters produced were also likely part of bone and wood projectiles. The Aurignacians were the first European population to produce figurative art, and they did it in the most spectacular way, from stunning statues like the ivory figurines from Vogelherd, Germany, to the recently discovered painted images of animals at the Chauvet Cave in south-central France. The Chauvet Cave demonstrates that more than 31,000 years ago these groups had already mastered all rock-art techniques. Aurignacian assemblages are identified in eastern Europe before 40,000 B.P. and are also present in the West soon after.

Châtelperronian sites are centered in southwestern France and northern Spain. In some caves, at the periphery of this area, archaeologists have observed interstratifications between Châtelperronian and Aurignacian tools, suggesting that Neandertals and modern humans occupied the area at different times. Throughout the Palaeolithic, southwestern France was a favorable place to live, and when the first modern humans arrived, it was probably the European area most densely peopled by Neandertals. The last Châtelperronian assemblages are located in Quinçay in west-central France and at Arcy-sur-Cure. Palaeoanthropologists have even observed a longer persistence of Neandertals at the site of Zafarraya in Andalucia (Spain), where I excavated in the early 1990s. There, we dated Mousterian layers after 30,000 B.P., and several other sites have produced dates indicating that the southern Iberian peninsula was a refuge where late Neandertals survived apart from any Cro-Magnon cultural influence. Neandertals post-dating 30,000 B.P. have also been documented in the Balkans and Caucasus.

For some 10,000 years, Neandertals and modern humans shared a mosaic of territories in Europe though they didn't actually live in the same areas at the same time. The Palaeolithic world was an empty one and a Neandertal probably had little chance to meet the "aliens" within his or her lifetime. Very likely Neandertals and modern humans did not exploit their environment in the same way, encouraging the segregation of their territories. Researchers will have to write a different history for the disappearance of the Neandertals for each region of Europe. In some cases Neandertals were isolated from modern groups for thousands of years and were not influenced by them. In others, Neandertals adopted some innovations, maybe trading some objects. But on the whole these influences were rather limited and are mainly demonstrated by the Neandertals' use of bone objects and ornaments.

The exact age of the earliest Aurignacian sites, interpretation of sites where Châtelperronian and Aurignacian layers have been found, and the biological characteristics of the first Aurignacian modern humans have been the subject of all sorts of discussions. Although criticized, the "acculturation model," in which transitional industries result from the interaction between local Neandertals and modern invaders, is still the most widely accepted explanation for the cultural evolution of the last Neandertals. So far, only modern humans have been found associated with Aurignacian assemblages in Europe, and only Neandertals associated with Mousterian and Châtelperronian. The important points are that there is clearly a chronological overlap between the two groups of hominids, and after at least 400,000 years of separate evolution the Neandertals developed the use of decorated bone objects and body ornaments only at this time.

Recently Francesco D'Errico of the University of Bordeaux I and João Zilhão of the Instituto Português de Arqueologia have argued that the handful of pierced teeth and beads collected at some Châtelperronian sites could have been invented "independently" by Neandertals, just before the arrival of Aurignacians carrying thousands of virtually identical objects. This view seems to result from a strange political correctness toward our extinct cousins. They compare the Neandertals' supposed invention of these objects with the independent invention of agriculture in the Old World and Mesoamerica. This comparison is difficult to comprehend. If there were any indication that a Near Eastern group had sailed to the Americas in the Early Neolithic, long before farming appeared in the New World, nobody would dare claim Pre-columbian agriculture was invented "independently." More likely the meeting of modern humans and Neandertals in Europe spurred production of body ornaments, objects, and behavior related to individual and group identification.

Hybridization and Extinction

Were Neandertals a distinct sub-species of *Homo sapiens* or a very close but separate species? In either case, it is possible, even expected, that some interbreeding occurred between the two groups. In nature, close species such as coyotes and wolves interbreed when their ranges overlap. Among Neandertals and modern humans, there is little if any evidence of such a phenomenon. This is not surprising considering the rarity of specimens studied from the range of time when the two groups coexisted in Europe. In 1995, Fred Spoor of University College, London, Marc Braun of the University of Nancy, and I described morphological differences between the inner ear of Neandertals, modern humans, and fossil and extant hominoids such as gorillas and chimpanzees. The form of this organ in the skull base is set after six months of embryological development, and our findings suggested strong genetic differences between the groups. The inner ear of a baby from Arcy-sur-Cure's Châtelperronian layers was fully Neandertal with no hybrid characteristics. Some Aurignacian modern human remains display a high degree of robusticity, but no demonstrably Neandertal characteristics. If some genes were exchanged, they are not more visible in ancient modern human populations than a drop of milk in a cup of coffee.

The 25,000 year-old Lagar Velho child in Portugal, studied by Erik Trinkaus of Washington University in St. Louis, is said to show Neandertal features after the extinction of the group and thus is supposed to indicate earlier interbreeding (see ARCHAEOLOGY, July/August 2000, pp. 24–31). The issue is hotly debated and considering the anatomical variation in early modern humans and Neandertals, evaluating whether or not some physical characteristics are hybridized is a difficult task. In the case of the four-year-old Lagar Velho child, its youth makes this type of interpretation even more difficult. Between 40,000 and 30,000 years ago, there is not one well preserved specimen, Neandertal or Cro-Magnon, of the same age known in Europe that would allow us to evaluate how for example the body proportions of the Lagar Velho child compare with the variation of Upper Palaeolithic modern children. The comparisons that have been made have been restricted to some Neandertal specimens and to later or living modern humans. If the southern Iberian peninsula represented a long-lasting area of hybridization between Neandertals and modern humans, further discoveries will prove it. For now, across Europe, Neandertals and modern humans reveal themselves as two groups interacting in a limited way, exchanging even fewer genes than bone-carving techniques.

The Lagar Velho controversy presents another problem: the exact time and process of extinction of the last Neandertals. The long coexistence of

Neandertals and modern humans in Europe demonstrates that modern humans were not overwhelmingly superior. Indeed, Neandertals prospered in Europe for hundreds of millennia and initially were probably better adapted to local conditions than their warm-weather challengers. In fact, it took a long time for modern humans to adapt biologically to their new environment; it was only toward the end of the Upper Palaeolithic that their body proportions lost all the features (such as long limbs) reminiscent of their tropical origin. Their technical skills, however, were much better than those of the Neandertals. For the first time, humans were able to sustain themselves in periglacial environments at very high latitudes. The spectacular site of Sungir north of Moscow, dating to more than 22,000 years ago, is at a latitude where continuous Middle Palaeolithic settlements did not occur. Modern humans' technical innovations, such as the eyed needle, allowed them to make complex clothing that probably played a major role in this success, as did their establishment of social networks and new strategies for the appropriation and storage of food.

Several scenarios have been proposed to explain Neandertal extinction. Scholars have considered epidemic diseases resulting from contact with modern invaders, but nothing occurred like the decimation of Native Americans by viruses imported from Europe. Some kind of genocide has also been imagined. Although violence is difficult to demonstrate in the archaeological record, the interactions between the two groups may not always have been friendly. The extinction of the Neandertals was most likely a slow process that took some 10,000 years. Differences in mortality and fecundity rates between populations of small sizes also can lead to the replacement of one by the other. It is very possible there were several simultaneous causes.

I emphasize the role of climatic changes in the demise of the Neandertals. In the past 450,000 years, Europe periodically witnessed glacial episodes. Neandertals and their ancestors adapted biologically to the cool-to-cold environment but, because of their limited technical skills, mainly responded to these climatic changes by scaling back their geographic domain. At the peak of the last glacial era, some 20,000 to 18,000 years ago, even modern humans with their needles, sophisticated housing, and new social organization had to yield large portions of the territory they had settled in Europe, surviving in southern refuges. Previous glacial periods must have placed a greater strain on Neandertals, who suffered dramatic reductions of their territories and population, but always re-colonized the lost lands during milder periods.

Between 40,000 and 35,000 years ago, modern humans had invaded some parts of Europe during a long and unstable interglacial stage and co-existed with the Neandertals in a fragile environmental equilibrium. But in the freeze that accompanied the beginning of the last glacial age, habitable Europe shrunk again and competition for land increased between the groups. The equilibrium was subverted. Refuges where Neandertals survived during previous glacial crises were partly occupied by challengers who proved themselves better at responding to environmental change. In the more favorable refuges, Neandertals must have felt heavy pressure from their modern neighbors. Competition for natural resources, violent interactions, and differences in the ability to respond to the new environmental challenge all likely led to the extinction of the Neandertals. The age of the very last pockets of Neandertals recently documented at Zafarraya (Spain), possibly Vindjia (Croatia), and Mezmaskaya (Caucasus) matches the beginning of falling temperatures in western Europe, between 28,000 and 24,000 years ago. The places the Neandertals last gathered are significantly located in remote and mountainous areas that are natural refuges in southern Europe. It is in these places that the Neandertals' 400,000-year history came to an end.

POSTSCRIPT

Did Neandertals Interbreed With Modern Humans?

The debate rages on between those, like Zilhão, who believe that Neandertals interbred with early modern humans in Europe and those, like Hublin, who believe that Neandertals were a separate species or subspecies that became extinct. Resolving whether or not Neandertals and early modern humans interbred will probably require more direct evidence of how the two groups arose from *Homo erectus*—whether or not they formed separate species—and how they interacted when they met in Europe. Fortunately, new fossil and archaeological evidence is coming in fast. The discovery of the possibly mixed Lagar Velho child in Portugal in 1998 is just one especially dramatic example. A mitochondrial DNA test of Neandertal bones from central Europe proved similar to earlier results from the Neander Valley specimen, indicating that the earlier results were reliable and that Neandertals formed a closely related population. But resolving whether or not they were a separate species depends on obtaining mitochondrial DNA profiles of early modern humans from the same period for comparison.

There is a huge and rapidly growing literature on Neandertals. Because new evidence is coming in so fast, students should try to get the most recent possible sources. The Web site of the Neanderthal Museum in Germany, at `http://www.neanderthal.de`, is especially useful in this respect. It provides general information, the latest scholarly reports, and links to related sites. Because of the enormous public interest in Neandertals, most popular science magazines—including *Natural History, Archaeology,* and *Scientific American*—feature regular updates on the Neandertal controversy. An excellent recent overview of the controversy is Kate Wong's article "Who Were the Neanderthals?" *Scientific American* (April 2000). Recent books arguing against interbreeding theories include Christopher Stringer and Clive Gamble's *In Search of the Neanderthals* (Thames & Hudson, 1993), Ian Tattersall's *The Last Neanderthal* (Westview Press, 1999), and Ian Tattersall and Jeffrey H. Schwartz's *Extinct Humans* (Westview Press, 2000). Scholarly journals periodically devote parts of issues to the debate over the Neandertals. Recent examples include the *Current Anthropology* special supplement, "The Neanderthal Problem and the Evolution of Human Behavior" (vol. 39, 1998) and the *Current Anthropology* Forum on Theory in Anthropology, "The Neanderthal Problem Continued" (vol. 40, no. 3, 1999), in which anthropologists Paul Mellars, Marcel Otte, Laurence Straus, João Zilhão, and Francesco D'Errico present conflicting views of recent Neandertal evidence.

Archaeology Magazine

This is the Web site of *Archaeology* magazine. This site has a searchable database with links to various articles about recent issues in archaeology, including a number of articles on the goddess cult in Europe.

http://www.archaeology.org

Center for the Study of the First Americans

The Center for the Study of the First Americans works to promote interdisciplinary scholarly dialogue and to stimulate public interest concerning the colonization of the Americas. This Web site provides articles that describe several theories on how the Americas were first colonized.

http://www.centerfirstamericans.com/cat.html?c=4

On Monte Verde: Fiedel's Confusions and Misrepresentations

This site at the University of Kentucky, Tom Dillehay's home institution, outlines further criticisms of Stuart Fiedel's challenges to the research at Monte Verde.

http://www.uky.edu/Projects/MonteVerde/

Monte Verde Under Fire

This web page, which is from *Archaeology Magazine*, points out some of other criticisms of Tom Dillehay's research and conclusions at Monte Verde. It has links to other related sites.

http://www.archaeology.org/online/features/clovis/

PART 2

Archaeology

*A*rchaeologists are prehistorians concerned with questions about the unrecorded history of human communities and civilizations. Like other historians, archaeologists seek evidence about how people lived, what they subsisted on, and the kinds of social institutions they established. But, unlike most historians who can turn to documents and papers to detail the life and times of their subjects, archaeologists must find evidence in excavations. Over the past century, archaeologists have developed specialized methods for excavating and analyzing artifacts, stone tools, animal bones, shells, pollen, and carbon from old fires to determine a great deal about the environment, vegetation, subsistence patterns, living arrangements, and also when sites were occupied. At issue is how these varied kinds of data from ancient sources can be interpreted to reconstruct the lifeways of earlier times. A traditional set of questions that archeologists ask is when, why, and how did people first settle different parts of the world, such as the Americas. They also ask questions about the meaning and significance of certain kinds of artifacts, such as the goddess figures of ancient Europe and the Middle East. Archaeologists also ask questions about why complex civilizations rose and fell.

- Did People First Arrive in the New World After the Last Ice Age?

- Was There a Goddess Cult in Prehistoric Europe?

- Did Prehistoric Native Americans Practice Cannibalism in the American Southwest?

ISSUE 4

Did People First Arrive in the New World After the Last Ice Age?

YES: Stuart J. Fiedel, from *Prehistory of the Americas,* 2d ed. (Cambridge University Press, 1992)

NO: Thomas D. Dillehay, from "The Battle of Monte Verde," *The Sciences* (January/February 1997)

ISSUE SUMMARY

YES: Archaeologist Stuart J. Fiedel supports the traditional view that humans first reached the Americas from Siberia at the end of the last Ice Age (perhaps 14,000 years ago). He argues that there are currently no convincing sites dated before that time and is skeptical of statements by other archaeologists who date human occupation of sites such as Meadowcroft in Pennsylvania and Monte Verde in Chile significantly earlier.

NO: Archaeologist Thomas D. Dillehay asserts that the site he has excavated at Monte Verde, a complex site in Chile, proves that humans reached the New World well before the end of the last Ice Age, possibly as early as 30,000 years ago. He contends that those archaeologists who are skeptical about his carbon-14 dates and other findings are so entrenched in traditional thinking that they refuse to accept the solid evidence that Monte Verde provides.

$\mathbf{F}$or more than a century archaeologists have asked, When and how did human beings first arrive in the Americas? The conventional view is that humans arrived from Asia via an ancient land bridge across the Bering Strait, which connected Siberia and Alaska during the last Ice Age. This traditional view has several components that Stuart J. Fiedel analyzes in his selection. First, the land bridge existed because ocean water was trapped in glacial ice. But this same glacial ice would also have presented an impenetrable barrier to human passage until glacial ice began to recede at the very end of the Ice Age. A narrow corridor between two separate ice sheets appears to have opened up about 14,500 years ago. Second, once human populations had passed through this ice corridor, they found large populations of woolly mammoth, saber-toothed tiger, and other megafauna, and these species became extinct soon after the ice pack retreated. Third, the archaeological association of certain kinds of stone projectile points (called Clovis points) with the bones of several of these extinct species has suggested that humans hunted them for food. Some archaeologists have argued that excessive human hunting caused their extinction (the over-kill hypothesis).

Convincing radiocarbon dating of many sites on both continents suggests that if humankind first arrived in the Americas at the end of the Ice Age, they had spread throughout both continents within a thousand years or so. For many years, archaeologists have disputed whether or not this was enough time for this sort of human dispersal across many different ecological zones.

In his selection, Fiedel surveys the history of the search for the earliest Americans and focuses on two of the most promising candidates for acceptance as pre-Clovis sites: the Meadowcroft shelter in Pennsylvania and an upland coastal site in south-central Chile called Monte Verde. Fiedel is skeptical that either will prove unambiguously to be pre-Clovis, but he recognizes that, unlike most other sites thought to be early, neither of these can be firmly dismissed as postglacial, although for different reasons. His skepticism emerges from several angles simultaneously, and considers the question: If humans had settled the New World significantly before the last Ice Age, why have archaeologists not identified dozens of pre-Clovis sites before now?

Thomas D. Dillehay is probably best known for his archaeological excavations at Monte Verde, a site he has worked on for more than 20 years. He contends that this site is complex. One part fits what one might expect a genuine pre-Clovis site to look like: It was occupied for a relatively short time by a hunting-and-gathering group, and the tool kit is significantly simpler than that of most Clovis sites. But simple or not, this assemblage has now been dated to significantly earlier than the date that the corridor through the northern glacial ice pack appeared, which means that human settlement of the Americas must have occurred before the last glacial maximum.

Dillehay suggests that skeptics of the quality of his carbon-14 dates are largely reacting defensively to his findings because the findings would force archaeologists to abandon models about the early settlement of the Northern Hemisphere that they have held for many years. What one can see in these two selections is a clash of paradigms.

Fiedel and Dillehay raise a number of questions of general interest to archaeologists. Are the authors defending different theoretical models of New World settlement, or are the "facts of the case" genuinely problematic? Are early carbon-14 dates sufficient to establish the Monte Verde site as genuinely pre-Clovis, or do Dillehay and his colleagues need to work out the artifact sequences before we can accept their findings? As with other controversies in archaeology, the arguments here seem to be about the facts of Monte Verde, but are these archaeologists actually arguing about their own models? Would it be appropriate for a nonpartisan team of archaeologists to visit Monte Verde and assess Dillehay's findings either to demonstrate problems in the data or to establish the site as an early one once and for all?

Stuart J. Fiedel

 **YES**

The Paleo-Indians

Archaeological Evidence of the First Americans

In the latter part of the nineteenth century, American scholars and amateurs, inspired by Darwin's theories and the Stone Age discoveries made in Europe, sought evidence of early man in the New World. Sure enough, they turned up a great many stone tools. The crudeness of some of these suggested that they were very ancient, belonging either to the Pleistocene or even to some earlier epoch. In addition, human remains were found, and for these, too, great antiquity was claimed. However, the eminent Czech-born physical anthropologist, Aleš Hrdlička, ruthlessly demolished these claims, demonstrating that all the American skeletal finds represented humans of modern type. On the basis of this conclusion, Hrdlička asserted that Ice Age man had not lived in the Americas; he set the initial entry at about 3000 B.C. No one seems to have pointed out at the time that humans of modern type had lived during late glacial times in Europe, where their remains had been found at Cro-Magnon and elsewhere; so the absence of pre-*sapiens* fossils in the Americas did not preclude a Pleistocene occupation. Hrdlička's conservative view prevailed in scholarly circles until an astonishing discovery in 1927 rendered it untenable.

George McJunkin, a black cowhand, had noticed some bones protruding from the side of a gulley near Folsom, New Mexico. This find was brought to the attention of J. D. Figgins of the Denver Museum of Natural History, who excavated the site. The bones turned out to belong to a large, long-horned species of bison (*Bison antiquus*), which became extinct at the end of the Pleistocene. In 1926, Figgins found a stone spearpoint embedded in clay near the bones. This point was initially dismissed by other archaeologists as intrusive. But in 1927, Figgins came upon another point, this time lying between two bison ribs. He left the point in place, and invited several prestigious archaeologists to examine the new find. They agreed that the Folsom site presented an indisputable association of man-made artifacts with the remains of extinct Pleistocene animals. Initially, archaeologists could only guess the age of the Folsom remains; but, since 1950, a series of C14 dates for sites where stone points of the same type have been excavated place the Folsom culture at about 9000 to 8000 B.C.

Many more Folsom sites have been discovered since 1927. At a few of them, artifacts were recovered from geological strata lying *below* those that yielded Folsom points. The distinctive artifact type of these earlier assemblages is the Clovis point. Clovis points were first excavated at the Blackwater Draw site near Clovis, New Mexico; here, and at several other sites, they were found in association with the remains of mammoths. The Clovis or "Llano" culture of the western United States has been dated to about 9500 to 9000 B.C. Clovislike fluted points have a very wide geographic distribution, having been found throughout the United States and in Canada and Central America. The striking similarity of these points, found over such a vast area, has led many archaeologists to conclude that the points were made and used by closely related hunting bands.

We can envision one or several ancestral bands entering the northern Plains through the ice-free corridor, thus stumbling upon a hunter's paradise, teeming with game that had never experienced the terrible cunning and tenacity of the human predator. In such a favorable situation, the original human population would have grown rapidly: where growth is not constrained by food or space limitations, population can double or even triple in each successive generation. We can estimate, using some speculative yet reasonable calculations, the minimum length of time necessary for the Americas to have been filled to capacity with hunting bands. We start with figures derived from ethnographic studies of extant hunting and gathering groups. These studies indicate that, irrespective of environmental differences, the typical hunting band consists of 25 to 50 people. These studies also reveal a range of population densities, from 0.4 to 9.6 persons per 100 square km (1 to 25 persons per 100 square miles). Pleistocene densities may have exceeded the upper end of this range; we can use a figure of 0.4 persons per square km (one person per square mile). North and South America, south of the glacial margins at 10,000 B.C., contained roughly 26 million square km (10 million square miles). Ignoring for the moment environmental differences that made areas more or less suitable for human habitation, and applying the 0.4 per square km (one per square mile) density figure, we get 10,000,000 as the potential hunting population of the Americas. If we assume that a band of 25 people passed through the corridor into North America, and that this population doubled in each successive generation (every 30 years or so), we reach the 10,000,000 figure in about 500 years. In reality, judging from the scarcity of their typical artifacts, Paleo-Indian populations probably did not reach even one-tenth of this level. In any case, assuming an exponential growth rate, the difference is insignificant; the 1 million level could have been attained in about 350 years.

. . . It has sometimes been assumed that thousands of years must have elapsed between the initial entry of humans into North America and their arrival at Fell's Cave [in Patagonia]; however, our calculations have shown how rapidly population expansion could have occurred. The distance from the base of the corridor to Tierra del Fuego is about 13,000 km (8,000 miles). If the expansion of human population to the limits of the continents took as little as 500 years, we would have to assume that the rate of migration was about 26 km (16 miles) a year, or 780 km (480 miles) per generation. Such movement is quite feasible, particularly in light of evidence that Paleo-Indians sometimes made tools of flint that they had carried from sources located several hundred kilometers away (as, for example, at the Shoop site in Pennsylvania and the Wapanucket site in Massachusetts). The southward movement was probably wavelike, constantly widening on its southern front. The impact of this human wave on the herd animals of the Americas may well have contributed to their extinction. . . .

So, we see that the presence of man at "the end of the road," Tierra del Fuego, by about 9000 B.C., is consistent with an initial entry through the ice-free corridor as late as 9500 B.C. However, the widespread and easily recognized Clovis culture was not necessarily the earliest in the Americas. The archaeological record offers tantalizing hints of earlier occupation.

Over the years, thousands of crude stone tools have been found in North America. These closely resemble the chopper-chopping tools of East Asia; as you may recall, the latter were produced from hundreds of thousands of years ago until quite recently. Some archaeologists have suggested that the American choppers must be older than the Clovis points, that they in fact represent a "preprojectile point horizon." The absence of points in the supposedly pre-Clovis industries has been interpreted as evidence of a subsistence pattern involving less specialized hunting of large mammals and greater reliance on small game and plant foods.

However, claims for a preprojectile horizon must be regarded with skepticism. Most of the crude choppers have been surface finds, whose age cannot be determined. Others have been found in datable geological contexts, but they are so formless that they are almost certainly not artifacts at all. Still other choppers are definitely man-made, but are associated with relatively late, more delicate artifacts. Such choppers were probably used for tasks that did not require more finely made tools. Some crudely retouched bifaces found in North America superficially resemble the Acheulian handaxes of Europe and Africa; but the American pieces have been shown to be "blanks," stones retouched into rough form at a quarry site with a view toward later, finer modification into a desired tool. . . .

The most convincing evidence of pre-Clovis occupation in North America, south of the Pleistocene ice margins, comes from the Meadowcroft rockshelter in western Pennsylvania. Here, stone tools and waste flakes from the earliest culture-bearing layer (Stratum IIa) have been dated, by eight radiocarbon determinations, between 17,000 and 11,000 B.C. C14 dates for the overlying strata form a consistent sequence, and are appropriate for the Archaic and Woodland period cultural material with which they are associated. However, the geologist C. Vance Haynes has suggested that the early dates from the lowest level might be the result of contamination by old carbon from coal deposits in the vicinity of the site. This attempt to explain away the early dates has been vigorously disputed by the excavator of Meadowcroft, James Adovasio, and his colleagues. But there is other evidence that casts doubt on the dates for Stratum IIa. Flotation of soil samples from this layer yielded abundant remains of plants—pits, nutshells, and carbonized fragments. These remains clearly indicate that the prevailing environment at the time of the Stratum IIa occupation was the same as that which existed during later periods—a deciduous forest including oak, walnut, and hickory trees. But at the time indicated by the C14 dates for Stratum IIa, the front of the Laurentide ice sheet was only 83 km (50 miles) to the north of the rockshelter. It is almost certain that Meadowcroft lay within a band of tundra, bordered by forests of spruce and pine, at about 15,000 B.C. It was not until about 8500 B.C. that the tundra and boreal forest were replaced by deciduous forest, spreading up from the south. An earlier presence of deciduous forest around Meadowcroft at the height of the Wisconsin glaciation would be very surprising. The few animal bones from Stratum IIa do not resolve the apparent contradiction between the radio-carbon dates and the paleo-botanical evidence. Among the highly fragmented bones was a piece of antler that could be confidently assigned to the white-tailed deer. Other identified specimens represent passenger pigeon and southern flying squirrel. All three species usually inhabited temperate deciduous forests. No remains of extinct Pleistocene mammals such as horse, mastodon, or mammoth, nor remains of tundra-dwelling caribou, have been found at Meadowcroft.

The stone tools from the lowest levels of Meadowcroft rockshelter do not appear to be typical of eastern Paleo-Indian assemblages, but neither do they represent a preprojectile horizon. Small blades are common. Also found were a bifacially retouched flake knife (called "Mungai" by Adovasio) and a projectile point. This point is lanceolate in shape like a Clovis point, but it is neither fluted like Clovis points nor as finely retouched as they usually are. Haynes, who questions the pre-Clovis dating of this material, suggests that the point is basically similar to unfluted, post-Clovis Plano points. Adovasio, on the other hand, sees similarities to points from a few western sites, such as Fort Rock Cave, which may be earlier than 10,000 B.C. He suggests that the Meadowcroft point might represent the prototype from which Clovis and Plano points were derived.

The Upper Paleolithic character of the Meadowcroft lithic assemblage is obvious. This is not the first discovery of blades in an early context in North America; well-made blades were reported in 1963 from the Clovis site of Blackwater Draw in New Mexico. These had been detached from a cone-shaped core by striking a bone or antler punch, resting on the core's basal rim, with a stone hammer. The small blades from Meadowcroft were made in the same way. In the Old World, this technique probably developed out of Middle Paleolithic Levallois flaking from prepared cores; but blades, retouched into numerous tool types, first became dominant in Upper Paleolithic assemblages. But, as we have seen, some archaeologists have argued that the first Americans were exclusively users of crude chopper-chopping tools and broken bones; according to this view, they made neither bifacially flaked points nor blades. The development from these simple Lower Paleolithic tools to the elegantly made Clovis point would have been an indigenous process, unrelated to cultural developments in Eurasia. This seems to me a very unlikely course of events. Even if Clovis points were an American innovation—and to date, nothing like them has turned up in Asia—they were products of an Upper Paleolithic technological tradition, incorporating methods of blade production and retouching, which were developed in Eurasia. . . .

Two caves in the western United States may have been occupied before 10,000 B.C. In a deep level of a stratified sequence in Wilson Butte Cave, in southern Idaho, a bifacially worked, bipointed point and a blade have been C14 dated, using samples of associated bones, at about 12,500 B.C. It is conceivable that the dated bone was contaminated by older carbon in the surrounding soil, or that it was brought in from earlier deposits by rodents. At Fort Rock Cave in south-central Oregon, a charcoal concentration lying on Pleistocene lake gravels has been C14 dated at 11,200 B.C. Nearby were two projectile points, several scrapers and gravers, and some flakes, as well as a milling stone and a handstone fragment. These ground stone artifacts are suggestive of the processing of collected seeds, a subsistence activity that is well attested in the Desert Archaic culture of this region after about 8000 B.C. However, grinding stones do not occur at Paleo-Indian sites that are earlier than 8000 B.C. Therefore, some doubt exists as to the association of the dated charcoal and the lithic finds. But since an overlying level was C14 dated at 8200 B.C., it seems indisputable that the artifacts are at least that old.

Clovis

. . . The Clovis culture . . . appears distinctive in several important respects from known Siberian Paleolithic cultures. Cultural change and innovation must have occurred during the migration of the ancestral Paleo-Indians across Beringia and through the corridor. It seems, on present evidence, that the fluted point was invented in North America.

If we accept the evidence from Valsequillo, Meadowcroft, and the few other sites that indicate that man was present in the Americas as early as 20,000 B.C., the rapid spread of Clovis-style lithic industries around 9500–9000 B.C. becomes more difficult to explain. We must choose among several plausible models for Clovis expansion:

1. Pre-Clovis occupation was ultimately unsuccessful; earlier inhabitants vanished or were restricted to a few isolated areas before the Clovis point-makers arrived.
2. Pre-Clovis occupation was widespread and successful. Somewhere in North America, fluted points began to be made. Then, (a) this new technology spread quickly as it was adopted by local hunting groups, who found it useful in hunting big game, or (b) the fluted point gave its inventors such an adaptive advantage that they rapidly expanded, encroaching upon and replacing the original inhabitants of other areas.

Model 2(a) seems the least likely explanation. There are no significant regional distinctions among Clovis tool kits, such as would indicate the addition of point-making to ongoing local flint-working traditions. The known distribution of Clovis points causes problems for model 2(b). It seems unlikely that fluted points would have been decisively advantageous in all of the diverse environments—tundra, grassland, boreal and deciduous forests—that Paleo-Indians occupied at the end of the Pleistocene. Model 1 poses an obvious problem: Why should hunters equipped with a sophisticated Upper Paleolithic technology, including effective stone projectile points (found at most of the convincing pre-Clovis sites), and resourceful enough to have endured a trek through Beringia and the glacial corridor, have been any less successful than the Clovis hunters? The paleontologist Paul S. Martin has wryly suggested an answer to this problem: "Given the biology of the species, I can envision only one circumstance under which an ephemeral discovery of America might have occurred. It is that, sometime before 12,000 years ago, the earliest early man came over the Bering Strait without early woman."

Martin has proposed an elegant model of Paleo-Indian migration. His theory would account at once for the rapidity of occupation of North and South America, the uniformity of Clovis tool kits, and the extinction of many species of large mammals at the end of the Pleistocene. Discounting claims of earlier sites, Martin assumes that the makers of Clovis points were the first humans to pass through the ice-free corridor into North America. Here they encountered herds of animals that had no experience of human predation, and so had developed neither defensive nor reproductive strategies to deal with this new threat. Taking advantage of the seemingly limitless supply of game, the Clovis hunters multiplied rapidly, their numbers doubling with each generation. As their numbers grew, the hunters also pushed southward, their movement taking the form of a great wave of advance, with the greatest density of population at its front. After a brief bottleneck in Central America, the same sort of expansion occurred in South America. Martin calculates that the descendants of an original band of 100 people who emerged from the ice-free corridor could have finished off the large Pleistocene mammals in North America. He estimates that the maximum total animal biomass for unglaciated North America at the end of the Pleistocene was some 230 million metric tons. Human population in North America could have reached a maximum of 600,000, at a density of 0.4 per square km (one per square mile), in about 250 years. If, at the front of the wave of advance, one person did all of the hunting for himself and three others (as might the adult male in a small nuclear family), and if this hunter killed only one animal weighing 450 kilograms (or 992 pounds— about the weight of a young modern bison) per week, the animals at the front would have been wiped out in less than ten years. At this rate, all of the large mammals in the Americas could have been slaughtered in about 500 to 1,000 years—as long as it took for the Paleo-Indians to reach Tierra del Fuego.

Numerous objections have been raised against Martin's "overkill" hypothesis. However, scientists agree that there is a basic fact that requires explanation: at the end of the Pleistocene, some 32 genera of American mammals became extinct. These included the mammoth, the mastodon, the giant sloth, the armadillolike glyptodon, the camel, the horse, the saber-toothed "tiger" and the dire wolf. Clearly, these extinctions must be connected in some way with the major environmental and climatic changes that were caused by the retreat of the Wisconsin ice sheets. However, the ice sheets had retreated before, in previous interglacial episodes, but these events had not resulted in the extinction of so many species. As Martin points out, the unique factor present during the last glacial retreat was human hunting. . . .

Paleontologists have proposed several alternative explanations for the late Pleistocene extinctions. Most have seen climate change as the primary cause. Dramatic shifts in temperature and rainfall patterns led to contraction of the habitats of at least some Pleistocene mammals. Over-specialized animals could not adjust to the new environments, and large animals, with their greater food and space requirements, could not compete with smaller species for which readaptation was easier. But this theory does not account for the extinction of those mammals whose habitats changed very little as the ice sheets retreated. . . .

It has also been suggested that the late Pleistocene opening of the glacial corridor permitted not only human hunters but also an assortment of new parasites and disease organisms to invade North America. But epidemics did not cause widespread extinction during previous interglacials. Generally, after initial high fatality rates, populations became resistant, and more stable diseasehost relationships set in before extinction of the host. So diseases are unlikely to have been the critical factor in the Pleistocene extinctions.

The problem of Pleistocene extinctions is a challenging one, and none of the suggested solutions is entirely satisfactory. Many scientists would probably grant that Paleo-Indian hunters might have delivered the *coup de grâce* to several species, but would also emphasize that these and other mammals were already seriously weakened by climatic and environmental stress. . . .

Paleo-Indians in South America

Carbon dates from Fell's Cave in Patagonia indicate that man had reached the southernmost tip of South America by about 9000 or 8700 B.C. As we have seen, these dates are not inconsistent with an initial entry into South America only a few hundred years earlier. However, there have been claims that a few sites demonstrate occupation of the continent before 10,000 B.C. Clearly, if it can be proven that any South American sites are really that old, claims of pre-Clovis habitation of North American will gain credibility. . . .

An extraordinarily well-preserved and apparently very early site has been excavated at Monte Verde, in south central Chile. Twelve wooden structures, abundant plant remains, and bones of butchered mastodon and guanaco, all buried under a layer of peat, have been C14 dated to between 13,650 ± 250 and 11,790 ± 200 B.P. (ca. 11,700 to 9800 B.C.). A lower layer of the site yielded broken stones and charcoal that possibly represent remains of human activity more than 30,000 years ago. The long hiatus between this dubious occupation and the late Pleistocene reuse of the vicinity has not been convincingly explained. The houses, made of planks and small tree trunks, are thought to have been covered with hides. Clay-lined hearths had been excavated outside the houses. Wooden mortars and grinding stones were used to process plant food. Actual plant remains include wild potatoes, medicinal plants, and salt-rich plants that must have been brought from the coast, 30 km distant from the site. The stone tool kit is reported to be a very simple one, consisting mostly of split pebble choppers and flakes. Some roughened stones may have been tied together with leather thongs and used as bolas. Hunting devices of this sort would have been a necessity if stone spearpoints were unknown to this culture. In fact, however, two well-made, thin lanceolate spearpoints, chipped from basalt, have been found at Monte Verde. They bear some resemblance to the El Jobo points of Venezuela, which are associated with comparably early, but controversial, radiocarbon dates. At present, too little is known about the Monte Verde culture to compare it with any others. Apart from the mastodon remains, the lifeway represented seems more Archaic than Paleo-Indian. The 2,000-year range of the radiocarbon dates is surprisingly wide for a site that is thought to have been created during a single brief occupation. Acceptance of the most recent dates would take the site into the period of Clovis immigration. However, the predominantly simple stone tool kit attested at Monte Verde is not very similar to typical Clovis assemblages. Nevertheless, if the early C14 dates are verified by further research, Monte Verde will have provided irrefutable evidence of a human presence in the Americas about 1,000 years before the Clovis migration (or diffusion). If Monte Verde and other South American sites really do predate 10,000 B.C., archaeologists will have to explain the puzzling absence of proven sites of comparable antiquity in North America.

South America was occupied around 9000 B.C. by Paleo-Indians who made fluted points, stylistically distinctive from, yet obviously related to, the Clovis points of North America. In the 1930s, Junius Bird found "fishtail" points, many of them fluted, at Fell's Cave. Similar points have been discovered at El Inga, in the highlands of Ecuador. Unlike North American fluted points, these broadbodied points taper to markedly thinner stems, which take up more than a third of the points' length. However, some Clovis-like points from the southeastern United States have very similar fishtail-shaped bases, and are constricted just above the base so that they almost appear to have stems. A link between these northern and southern points is provided by several surface finds from Central America. Short, broad fishtail points of the type found at Fell's Cave, are known from Panama (Madden Lake) and Costa Rica (Turrialba). Somewhat thinner fishtail points, more similar to the Clovis-like points of eastern North America, have been found at the same sites, and also in western Costa Rica, Guatemala, and Durango, Mexico. Recently, a Clovis point like those found in the southwestern United States was collected from a site in the Quiche Basin, in the highlands of Guatemala; similar points are reported from recently excavated sites in Belize. Lacking firm chronological controls, we cannot be sure that the more slender of the Central American points represent a transitional phase in the stylistic evolution of fishtail points from North American Clovis prototypes; but this seems to be the best explanation of the existing evidence. The close resemblance of fishtail points from sites in Costa Rica and Patagonia, separated by more than 6,400 km (4,000 miles), implies a very rapid migration of Paleo-Indians along the mountainous spine of western South America. As in North America, such a rapid migration seems to imply that there was no previous human occupation of the region; alternatively, if the pre-10,000 B.C. dates are valid, the earlier population must have been so small and scattered that they could be easily replaced or absorbed by the makers of fluted points.

It should be noted that there have been finds in South America of leaf-shaped and lanceolate points that seem to be as old as the fishtail points. Some archaeologists argue that such points, of which the best known examples are the El Jobo points from Venezuela, may in fact be older than the fishtail type; however, this argument rests primarily on a few dubious radiocarbon dates. The closest North American parallels to the leaf-shaped points are the Lerma points of Texas and Mexico, and the San Dieguito points of California and the Great Basin; these types are dated to between 9000 and 6000 B.C.

Apart from fluted points, other items in the tool kit of the South American Paleo-Indians—scrapers, gravers, and knives—suggest a derivation from North American forms. The probable use of these tools in the processing of meat and hides further implies a continuation of the ancestral North American Paleo-Indians' pursuit of big game.

The South American Paleo-Indians' big game-hunting orientation is confirmed by associations of artifacts with remains of extinct Pleistocene mammals at several sites. There is evidence of the hunting of horse, mastodon, and giant ground sloth. The Paleo-Indians also hunted animals of modern species—deer and guanaco, various rodents, rabbits, and birds, particularly the ground-dwelling tinamou. The Paleo-Indians probably turned increasingly to such small game as the Pleistocene megafauna disappeared. Bones found at Los Toldos, Argentina, and Tagua Tagua in Chile hint at the early domestication of the dog, which would have been helpful in hunting the tinamou. In addition to small animals, plants became more important as a food source after 9000 B.C. There is evidence at Guitarrero Cave that beans and peppers were cultivated, and various tubers and fruits were collected, perhaps as early as 8500 B.C. and certainly before 7000 B.C. This dietary diversification in the Andean highlands is comparable to the broad spectrum adaptations that developed after the extinction of the Pleistocene megafauna in North America and Mesoamerica.

Thomas D. Dillehay

The Battle of Monte Verde

In archeology the simplest questions are often the hardest to answer. Two such questions—who were the first Americans and when did they reach the New World?—have tormented investigators for more than a century. Archaeologists have long believed that Asian immigrants, crossing the Bering land bridge in pursuit of big game, pioneered the New World about 11,000 years ago. Known as the Clovis people, after the site in New Mexico where their elaborate, fluted projectile points were first discovered, the immigrants gradually worked their way south. They were skilled hunters, and when their travels brought them to places teeming with an astonishing variety of prey, the result was a human population explosion. In a matter of centuries Clovis hunters moved throughout the Americas, helping to wipe out bison, woolly mammoths, camelids and other species in the so-called Pleistocene die-off.

Or perhaps not. In recent years a wave of discoveries outside North America has brought nearly every aspect of the migration theory under intense scrutiny. Fresh insights on the peopling of China, Japan and Siberia are redrawing the debate about the first Americans on a much broader canvas, framed by the entire Pacific Rim. And in South America a rash of controversial early dates has suggested that the Americas were settled even earlier than 11,000 years ago. Several sites in Tierra del Fuego, for instance, have been convincingly shown to be about 11,000 years old.

How could people have arrived in North America and at the southern tip of South America at approximately the same time? Did they journey through Alaska before the Clovis hunters, or did they sail across the seas to reach South America just as Clovis hunters were crossing the Bering land bridge? Faced with such questions, New World archaeologists have divided into Clovis and pre-Clovis camps. The dispute between the two has become so emotionally charged that one archaeologist has likened it to the debate between creationists and evolutionists.

Twenty years ago I was drawn into the fray when I began excavating Monte Verde, a site near the town of Puerto Montt, in south-central Chile. Monte Verde had been discovered accidentally in 1976 by some local lumbermen clearing paths for their ox carts. They had been cutting back the banks of a small creek in a marshy area when they literally stumbled on some large bones and buried wood. The bones were later determined to be the remains of mastodons. In 1977, when the find was brought to my attention, I was head of the anthropology department at the Southern University of Chile in Valdivia. That year I formed an international interdisciplinary team, which eventually grew to eighty members, and we began to excavate the site.

Early on, we knew that Monte Verde was an exceptional site. But we also knew that our finds would provoke a barrage of skepticism, not least because of their age. According to firm radiocarbon dates, the most impressive remains date from 1,500 years before Clovis hunters are said to have discovered North America. The possible remains of human habitation in Monte Verde's deepest levels are nearly 20,000 years older than that.

⋘◉⋙

Archaeologists are, by necessity, masters of inference. From the meanest, most innocuous of things—discarded oyster shells, broken pots, the subtle bands of color and texture in an excavation wall—we try to re-create an entire world and its inhabitants. To the uninitiated, the process may seem as occult as counting the angels on the head of a pin. How does this standing stone signify religion? Why is that "chopper" not just a rock? How can so much be made of so little?

Thanks to some happy accidents of nature, the remains at Monte Verde are of a far more evocative kind. Some 12,500 years ago the site was an openair settlement on the banks of what is now Chinchihuapi Creek. All around were sandy knolls, small bogs and a cool, damp forest. As the bogs spread into the adjacent creek bed, they buried the abandoned settlement under a layer of fibrous peat, preserving it like an exotic specimen pickled in formaldehyde. The water protected the remains from the wear and tear of changing humidity. It also prevented oxygen from reaching the remains, thereby keeping bacteria from digesting them.

Once it was carefully drained and stripped of its layers of protective peat, the site revealed much more than the usual cache of bones and stone tools. From wood structures to medicinal plants to hunks of meat, it held a wealth of organic debris that normally disappears from the archaeological record. More than any other early site in the Americas, Monte Verde would enable us to reconstruct life in the Ice Age.

⋘◉⋙

At the beginning of the project, we put together a team that included geologists, botanists, forestry scientists and zoologists to study the fauna and flora preserved at the site. Our digging uncovered the remains of a sixty-foot-long tentlike structure sturdy enough to house twenty or thirty people, some of them year-round. The frame was made of logs and planks anchored by stakes, and the walls consisted of poles covered with hides (from mastodons and paleo-llamas, judging by the bones we excavated). The entire structure was bound together with cordage and string made of junco reed. Inside the tent, planks and poles apparently set off individual living spaces, each of which had a brazier pit lined with clay. Hundreds of microscopic flecks of hide, embedded in the dirt, suggest that the floor was probably covered with skins.

Outside the tent we found two large communal hearths, a supply of firewood, and wooden mortars with their grinding stones. Near the hearths, we uncovered two brown, sopping hunks of meat next to some mastodon bones. The most dramatic remains, however, are of a more delicate variety. About 12,000 years ago one of the Monte Verdeans walked across some soft, wet clay brought to the site for refurbishing the hearths. As the clay hardened, it preserved three footprints for posterity. In one print the toes, heel and arch of a foot were clearly visible. On the basis of the print's size and shape, specialists from our team of forensic anthropologists think it was made by a small adult or a large adolescent.

West of the main building, we found a wishbone-shaped structure made of wooden uprights set into a foundation of sand and gravel hardened with animal fat. Mastodon carcasses were butchered inside the structure, hides were prepared and tools were manufactured. Because the medicinal parts of certain plants were found next to those remains, we think the Monte Verdeans may have also gone there to practice healing.

In southern Chile today the Mapuche people use medicinal plants to treat rheumatism, stomach aches, dysentery, infected cuts and pulmonary problems, among other ailments, as well as to induce abortions. The twenty-three kinds of medicinal plants found at Monte Verde are all still used to treat various problems. Boldo leaf (*Peumus boldus*), for instance, is used for intestinal ailments and hallucinations, natre leaf (*Solanum crispum*) reduces fever, and *Lycopodium* (a kind of club moss) gives a natural talcum powder that soothes skin infections. Some of the plants are native to the area, but about half come from the coast, and one is found only in arid regions to the north.

To modern sensibilities, the most intriguing plants preserved at the site are the ones that now seem most commonplace: potatoes. Many explorers and scientists, Charles Darwin among them, have noted the wide variety and abundance of wild potatoes in southern Chile. On the basis of studies done on wild potatoes in the region, Soviet botanists in the 1930s speculated that potatoes originally came from that area and from Peru. The presence of the tuber at Monte Verde, in the cracks and pits of wooden mortars and in food storage pits in the corners of shelters, confirms the Soviet hypothesis and underlines the importance of southern Chile in the evolution of the potato.

The smorgasbord of food scraps the Monte Verdeans left behind suggests that the bulk of their diet was made up of meat from mastodons, paleo-llamas, small animals and freshwater mollusks, together with aquatic plants from freshwater marshes and other areas. Most of those foods are found in ecological zones thirty-five miles from Monte Verde, along the Pacific shoreline and in the Andean mountains. Three varieties of seaweed—a rare occurrence on the southern coast—were probably scavenged some fifty miles to the west or received in trade. Salt, pebbles worn flat and round by ocean waves (ideal for polishing animal hides or grinding food), and bitumen used to attach stone tools to wooden hafts were also found at the site, demonstrating that the Monte Verdeans brought back more than food from the coast.

To make use of so many resources from so many ecological zones, the Monte Verdeans devised a sophisticated division of labor. Residential areas are separate from non-residential areas at the site, and certain areas are associated with specific tools and food remains. In one living space, for instance, quartz artifacts for cutting and scraping were found with the remains of fruits and tubers that grow only in brackish estuaries, which suggests that the occupants specialized in collecting resources from the coast. In another area of the tent, stone scrapers and pieces of skin indicate that people worked animal hides there.

·◈·

Our excavations at Monte Verde have revealed a much more complex social and economic organization than archeologists have come to expect of early New World cultures. The excavations also call into question the commonly accepted idea that all Ice Age bands were nomadic. Our evidence shows that some of the people at the site's younger settlement remained there year-round, living off a wide variety of plants and animals. Although few sites contemporaneous with Monte Verde have been found so far, we think the Monte Verdeans probably belonged to a scattered group of colonizers accustomed to temperate wetlands and forests. The fact that they used many river resources suggest that they came from the Maullín River basin, seven miles to the north, into which Chinchihuapi Creek discharges.

For all their surprising sophistication, the Monte Verdeans had fairly crude tools. True, our excavations uncovered some artifacts made of wood, such as digging sticks, as well as some bone artifacts, such as a baton for striking flakes off stones and gouges made of mastodon tusks. But many of the tools we found were simply pebbles from the creek bed or distant ocean beaches. Their damaged edges, coated with residues from food plants, identify them as tools that were picked up, used and then discarded. Other stones were simply split or struck to remove a few flakes. Only a few stone specimens, such as bifacially flaked projectile points and chopping tools, grooved sling stones and grinding stones, would be universally accepted as human tools even if they had been discovered in a different setting with no corroborating evidence.

Our findings should serve as a cautionary tale for archaeologists seeking indisputable artifacts in ancient sites. If, as it sometimes seems, we deceive ourselves by thinking that rocks are tools, we may just as often mistake tools for rocks. The oldest, deepest levels at Monte Verde are a case in point. Four feet below the latest settlement, in another area of the site, we found twenty-four fractured pebbles and three shallow depressions, lined with clay, containing burned wood and seeds. Seven of the pebbles were probably flaked by people; four of the twenty-four pebbles show polish or striations on their sharp edges from the cutting and scraping of meat, hides and plants. Charcoal from two of the depressions has been radiocarbon-dated to about 33,000 years ago.

Were the charcoal and the pebbles around it made by people? The evidence is inconclusive. But if the answer is yes, the faint traces the early Monte Verdeans left behind suggest that they were probably transient explorers. The paleo-ecological evidence indicates that 33,000 years ago the region was going through an interglacial period. As the climate warmed up and moors and beech forests began to appear, southern Chile would have grown increasingly hospitable to colonists.

⌐◦⌐

[In] January [1997] a multidisciplinary research team will be at the University of Kentucky for two days to inspect the Monte Verde artifacts and to discuss the site in greater detail. The team will then travel to Chile for a three-day visit to examine the site setting and the stratigraphy. I have mixed feelings about the visit. Although we have been calling for a site visit since 1979, no one has accepted our offer. Given that the military government of General Augusto Pinochet was in power throughout the 1970s and 1980s, some archaeologists were understandably reluctant to visit us. Even more of them, however, were put off by the late Junius B. Bird of the American Museum of Natural History.

Dean of paleo-Indian research in South America, Bird was sent to inspect the site in 1979, when the National Geographic Society was funding our excavations. He arrived at the site early, when we were still establishing our base camp and grid system. Bird stayed for just two days, during which time we screened dirt only from the site's sterile upper layers. He later told colleagues in the United States and Chile that he did not see any cultural materials at Monte Verde and that the site was still of questionable value.

As far as artifacts were concerned, Bird spoke the truth. If he had stayed just two more weeks at the site, however, he would have seen us uncover the dramatic 12,500-year-old remains. As a result of that visit, unfortunately, the archaeological community—particularly Thomas F. Lynch of Cornell University in Ithaca, New York, and other strong advocates of the Clovis paradigm—joined Bird in dismissing the site.

⌐◦⌐

Much of the debate about the existence of pre-Clovis peoples in the Americas hinges on standards of archaeological evidence. Clovis advocates maintain, with some justification, that most pre-Clovis sites are nothing more than jumbled deposits of old soil and much younger artifacts and plant remains. Pre-Clovis advocates counter that their opponents are isolationists and chauvinists, that they too often reject sites without proper evidence of disproof. If the same standards were applied to Clovis sites, they go on to say, many of those sites would not be accepted either.

In the years since Bird's visit, Clovis proponents, led by Lynch, have criticized Monte Verde on nearly every count. The site's 12,500-year-old layers, they say, must be contaminated by younger artifacts that worked their way down with burrowing animals, tree roots or through cracks in the ground. The material that was radiocarbon-dated must be contaminated by petroleum. The wood and bone artifacts must have been picked up from another site and washed into Monte Verde by floods.

None of those claims have been backed up by any geological or archaeological evidence. In the fifteen years that our team worked at the site, we did not find a single artifact above the 12,500-year-old level. There is one Archaic site, between 8,000 and 5,000 years old, about a third of a mile upstream from Monte Verde. But those deposits are buried several hundred yards inland, in an intact stratum not subject to erosion or flooding. The artifacts from that site, in any case, are made of raw materials entirely different from those at Monte Verde. Moreover, there is no geological, archaeological or other evidence to indicate that the younger Monte Verde remains were ever disturbed. The footprints, house floors, tied and knotted strings and other materials we found—all of them intact—verify the site's high archaeological integrity.

In recent years, as we have published more data on the site, much of the criticism of it has subsided. Even Lynch, to his credit, has conceded that the younger level of the site is valid, though he and others reserve final judgement until all the archaeological data is published. I can only hope that my second volume of findings from Monte Verde, due to be published by Smithsonian Institution Press [in] February [1997], will put their remaining doubts to rest.

⋅⊰❦⊱⋅

Support for pre-Clovis colonization of the Americas is starting to come from other disciplines as well, though each new theory brings its own guesses, loose ends and inconsistencies. The linguist Richard A. Rogers of the University of Kansas in Lawrence thinks native North American languages are too various to have evolved only in the past 11,000 years. Given the rate at which languages diversify, he suggests that people were living in southern parts of the continent substantially more than 18,000 years ago, when the Pleistocene ice sheets had reached their greatest extent.

The bioanthropologist Christy G. Turner II of Arizona State University in Tempe has proposed an alternate scenario. On the basis of a comparison of teeth from 9,000 skeletons discovered in Eurasia and in America, he has proposed that the first immigrants entered Alaska from northern China more than 12,000 years ago. Their descendants then rapidly colonized the Americas, all the way to Tierra del Fuego. Other biological evidence, such as the high incidence of shovel-shaped incisors, the absence of blood group B and the rarity of group A, shows that all Native Americans except the recently arrived Eskimos and Aleuts are closely related to one another and clearly distinct from their Asiatic ancestors.

Some biological anthropologists suggest that Native Americans are genetically similar because the first colonizers were few in number—perhaps only a single band of hunters and foragers. But the diverse lineages indicated by the genetic data also suggests that people arrived in the Americas more than 11,000 years ago, and that more genetic variability exists among members of the Native American population than anyone had previously estimated. It may be that instead of a massive migration of big-game hunters at the end of the Ice Age, between 12,000 and 11,000 years ago, several small bands walked from Siberia to Alaska much earlier. To avoid the massive ice sheets that mantled Alaska until about 13,000 years ago, they may have skirted the Pacific coast on foot or by boat.

The migration to the Americas represents the last step in a worldwide human dispersion. Recent findings of fossil skeletons and genetic data indicate that people physically identical to ourselves lived in Africa and the Near East at least 90,000 years ago. From there they spread out across the face of Europe and Asia in slowly advancing waves, reaching China, Japan and Australia about 30,000 years ago. Many archaeologists believe that only fully modern humans had the skills and tools necessary to adapt successfully to the harsh, arid grasslands of Siberia and, later, to push into the coldest reaches of North America.

The big picture of modern human origins has become clearer, but the debate about allegedly pre-Clovis peoples remains as contentious as it was when the first Ice Age sites were discovered more than fifty years ago. Monte Verde demonstrates conclusively that people were living in the Americas more than 12,000 years ago. But archaeologists still have little solid evidence to suggest that people made it to the New World before 15,000 years ago.

⋅◆⋅

Although I was braced for some criticism when we first began excavating Monte Verde, I was taken aback by how quickly our work was cast into the middle of the pre-Clovis controversy. Every few months, it seems, a new instant analysis of Monte Verde and other pre-Clovis sites appeared, all without a site visit or a review of all the evidence. Given that many good archaeologists, including the late Ruth Simpson and Louis S. B. Leakey, have lost some of their standing as "objective" scientists by championing failed pre-Clovis sites, the skepticism is understandable. And to be honest, I have been guilty of some instant analysis of my own—for example, when questioning finds at the Pedra Furada site in Brazil, which are said to be between 15,000 and 45,000 years old. Instant-opinion-hurling has become something of a sport in the study of the first Americans—a sport that reveals our arbitrary understanding of little-known sites and of the peopling of the Americas.

Much of the bickering, I believe, has served only to trivialize the processes of scientific proof, criticism and debate. In the case of many early sites, it has distracted archaeologists from the cultural value of their findings and from the interdisciplinary research methods they have employed. More important, it has led to a neglect of questions such as, Why did people migrate to the New World in the first place? And how did they adapt so quickly to environments ranging from the frozen wastes of Alaska to the equatorial rain forests of South America? In archaeology, it sometimes seems, a single priority—the omnipotent radiocarbon date—still overshadows any other information about a site.

Admittedly, the date that people first arrived in the New World is a key to how they managed to do so. Depending on when they arrived, the first Americans might have had to navigate an ocean or traverse glaciers, build snow shelters against the cold or thatched huts against the tropical rains. Yet the dating game has little importance if one cannot assign wider cultural and historical meaning to an archaeological site.

Archaeologists will probably never find the remains of the very first Americans. Even if they do, they may not recognize those remains for what they are. Like the Mapuche's ancestors, those of us who study them are bound to go down many long paths that lead nowhere, and sometimes to turn on one another in frustration. But if we give as much attention to the pattern and process of human dispersion as we do to its timing, perhaps we can get better at choosing the good paths—and at making the journey a joyful one.

POSTSCRIPT

Did People First Arrive in the New World After the Last Ice Age?

Even if one accepts Monte Verde as a genuine pre-Clovis site, how wide-spread across the hemisphere were such pre-Clovis settlements? Were the Monte Verde settlers with their simple technologies in use 14,000 years ago ancestors of peoples living in the region who had a more sophisticated Clovis technology? Do Monte Verde and Clovis sites represent two distinct migrations into the New World or the rapid cultural evolution of a single people? More-over, dating Monte Verde to 14,000 years ago does not explain where the Monte Verde people came from, how long they had been in the Americas, or how they got there.

The debate over Monte Verde raises many questions that will continue to challenge archaeologists for many years to come. It will continue to raise issues about the limits of carbon-14 dating and more generally about the standards of archaeological evidence. But it also raises questions about archaeological models. Why have early sites been so difficult to locate? Are archaeologists looking for the right kinds of artifacts? Do we have reason-able models of human settlement patterns that would allow us to find occupation sites used by people 30,000 years ago?

Those interested in the early debate about Monte Verde and the question of whether any preglacial sites exist in the New World should consult Dillehay's first report, "Early Rainforest Archaeology in Southwestern South America: Research Context, Design, and Data at Monte Verde," in B. A. Purdy, ed., *Wet Site Archaeology* (Telford Press, 1988), together with Thomas Lynch's assessment, "Glacial-Age Man in South America? A Critical Review," *American Antiquity* (vol. 55, 1990); Dillehay and Michael B. Collins's "Monte Verde, Chile: A Comment on Lynch," *American Antiquity* (vol. 56, 1991); Ruth Gruhn and Alan L. Bryan's "A Review of Lynch's Descriptions of South American Pleistocene Sites," *American Antiquity* (vol. 56, 1991); and Lynch's "Lack of Evidence for Glacial-Age Settlement of South America: Reply to Dillehay and Collins and to Gruhn and Bryan," *American Antiquity* (vol. 56, 1991).

Students may also find two recent popular articles about the first Americans of interest: *Archaeology* (November/December 1999) published a book review essay by Mark Rose, which outlines the current debate, and *Scientific American's Discovering Archaeology* (February 2000) devoted a special section to "The Puzzle of the First Americans," dealing with a variety of current research problems and theoretical concerns.

ISSUE 5

Was There a Goddess Cult in Prehistoric Europe?

YES: Marija Gimbutas, from "Old Europe in the Fifth Millennium B.C.: The European Situation on the Arrival of Indo-Europeans," in Edgar C. Polomé, ed., *The Indo-Europeans in the Fourth and Third Millennia* (Karoma Publishers, 1982)

NO: Lynn Meskell, from "Goddesses, Gimbutas, and 'New Age' Archaeology," *Antiquity* (March 1995)

ISSUE SUMMARY

YES: Archaeologist Marija Gimbutas argues that the civilization of pre–Bronze Age "Old Europe" was matriarchal—ruled by women—and that the religion centered on the worship of a single great Goddess. Furthermore, this civilization was destroyed by patriarchal Kurgan pastoralists (the Indo-Europeans), who migrated into southeastern Europe from the Eurasian steppes in the fifth to third millennia B.C.

NO: Archaeologist Lynn Meskell considers the belief in a supreme Goddess and a matriarchal society in prehistoric Europe to be an unwarranted projection of some women's utopian longings onto the past. She regards Gimbutas's interpretation of the archaeological evidence as biased and speculative.

The idea that prehistoric societies were matriarchal and worshiped a supreme Goddess has deep roots in European thought. The Greeks, like the Babylonians, regarded the earth as feminine and associated it with goddesses, a notion preserved in our expressions "Mother Earth" and "Mother Nature." In the nineteenth century some cultural evolutionists, like J. J. Bachofen (*Das Mutterrecht*, Benno Schwabe, 1861) and John Ferguson MacLellan (*Primitive Marriage: An Inquiry Into the Origin of the Form of Capture in Marriage Ceremonies,* 1865), postulated that the earliest human societies were woman-centered, but they became patriarchal ("male-governed") before the beginning of written records. Coincidentally some classicists began to see a single great Goddess lying behind the goddesses of classical

Greece, and they linked this Goddess to the female figurines ("Venus figures") being turned up in archaeological sites in the Balkans and southeastern Europe. In 1903 the prominent classicist Jane Ellen Harrison drew the threads together, postulating that in prehistoric southeastern Europe there existed a peaceful, woman-centered civilization where people lived in harmony with nature and worshiped a single female deity. This civilization was later destroyed by patriarchal invaders from the north, who brought war and male deities. By the 1950s most archaeologists specializing in Europe accepted the view that a Goddess religion and matriarchal social system had spread throughout Europe before being replaced by the male-centered societies of the Bronze Age. But in the 1960s a young archaeologist, Peter Ucko, challenged this view on the basis of extensive analyses of figurines from throughout eastern Europe and the eastern Mediterranean. He saw that there was great variation among figurines in time and space, and far from all were female. This led the archaeological establishment to retreat to a more agnostic view, once again reserving judgment over the nature of the earliest European religions.

One archaeologist who retained and even elaborated on the theory of the ancient matriarchal society and the Goddess, however, was the late Marija Gimbutas. In the following selection, Gimbutas presents her version of the theory and some of the evidence for it. She bases her interpretation on a large body of archaeological materials, especially the remains of buildings, clay models of buildings, and figurines. She contends that this matrifocal ("woman-focused") culture was destroyed by the invasions of patriarchal, nomadic pastoralists from the steppes of southern Russia, but traces of the earlier culture linger among the non–Indo-European peoples of Europe, like the Basques, and were mixed into the later patriarchal culture.

Lynn Meskell, however, criticizes Gimbutas and her followers for adopting a highly speculative gynocentric ("female-centered") interpretation of the evidence, one that she believes consistently ignores contrary evidence and other possible interpretations. Meskell argues that Gimbutas has allowed her desire to affirm the existence of an ancient feminist utopia to color and distort her interpretation of the archaeological record, leading her, for example, to overlook the large numbers of figurines that are male or ambiguous in gender. She suggests that the current popularity of Gimbutas's view is due to "New Age" feminists hoping to ground their utopian visions in a past that they see as having been unfairly destroyed by men.

These selections raise a number of questions that are important not only for our understanding of the prehistory of Europe, but for archaeological interpretation in general. Are any other interpretations of this evidence possible? If so, how can we choose among the different possible readings? Can archaeologists insulate themselves from social and political currents of their day and provide "objective" interpretations of their findings? What is the proper role of imagination in creating a comprehensive picture of a vanished way of life from the small set of clues that have survived the vicissitudes of time?

Marija Gimbutas  **YES**

Old Europe in the Fifth Millennium B.C.

With the growing realization of the necessity to distinguish the Neolithic and Copper Age pre-Indo-European civilization from the "Indo-Europeanized" Europe of the Bronze Age, I coined, ten years ago, the new term "Old Europe." This term covers, in a broad sense, all Europe west of the Pontic Steppe before the series of incursions of the steppe (or "Kurgan") pastoralists in the second half of the fifth, of the fourth, and the beginning of the third millennium B.C., for in my view Europe is not the homeland of the Indo-European speakers. In a narrower sense, the term Old Europe applies to Europe's first civilization, i.e., the highest Neolithic and Copper Age culture focused in the southeast and the Danubian basin, gradually destroyed by repeated Kurgan infiltrations. . . .

The two cultural systems are very different: the first is sedentary, matrifocal, peaceful, art-loving, earth- and sea-bound; the second is patrifocal, mobile, warlike, ideologically sky-oriented, and indifferent to art. The two systems can best be understood if studied before the period of their clash and mélange, i.e., before ca. 4500–4000 B.C. . . .

Social Organization

Theocratic monarchies? Old European societies were unstratified: there were no contrasting classes of rulers and laborers, but there was a rich middle class which rose as a consequence of metallurgy and expansion of trade. Neither royal tombs, distinct in burial rites from those of the rest of the population, nor royal quarters, distinguished by extravagance, have been discovered. I see no evidence of the existence of a patriarchal chieftain system with pronounced ranking of the Indo-European type. Instead, there are in Old Europe a multitude of temples with accumulations of wealth—gold, copper, marble, shells, and exquisite ceramics. The goods of highest quality, produced by the best craftsmen, belonged not to the chief, as is customary in chiefdoms, but to the Goddess and to her representative, the queen-priestess. The social organization represented by the rise of temples was a primary centrifugal social force.

From Marija Gimbutas, "Old Europe in the Fifth Millennium B.C.: The European Situation on the Arrival of Indo-Europeans," in Edgar C. Polomé, ed., *The Indo-Europeans in the Fourth and Third Millennia* (Karoma Publishers, 1982). Copyright © 1982 by Karoma Publishers, Inc. Reprinted by permission of The Estate of Marija Gimbutas. Notes omitted.

The question of government organization is as yet difficult to answer. Central areas and secondary provinces can be observed in each culture group. Some of the foci were clearly more influential than others, but whether centralized government existed we do not know. I favor the theory of small theocratic kingdoms or city-states, analogous to Etruscan *lucomonies* and Minoan palaces, with a queen-priestess as ruler, and her brother or husband as supervisor of agriculture and trade. The basis of such a structure was more social and religious in character than civil, political, or military.

The matrilinear society.   There is absolutely no indication that Old European society was patrilinear or patriarchal. Evidence from the cemeteries does not indicate a subordinate position of women. There was no ranking along a patriarchal masculine-feminine value scale as there was in Europe after the infiltration of steppe pastoralists who introduced the patriarchal and the patrilinear systems. The study of grave equipment in each culture group suggests an egalitarian society. A division of labor between the sexes is demonstrated by grave goods, but not a superiority of either. The richest graves belong to both men and women. Age was a determining factor; children had the lowest number of objects.

A strong support for the existence of matrilinearity in Old Europe is the historic continuity of matrilinear succession in the non-Indo-European societies of Europe and Asia Minor, such as the Etruscan, Pelasgian, Lydian, Carian, and Basque. Even in Rome during the monarchy, royal office passed regularly through the female line—clearly a non-Indo-European tradition most probably inherited from Old Europe, Polybius, in the second century B.C., speaking of the Greek colony, Lokroi, on the toe of Italy, says, "all their ancestral honors are traced through women." Furthermore, we hear from Greek historians that the Etruscans and prehistoric Athenians had "wives in common" and "their children did not know their own fathers." The woman in such a system is free to marry the man of her choice, and as many as she pleases (there is no question of adultery—that was a male invention), and she retains control of her children with regard to their paternity. This evidence led George Thomson to the assumption that group marriage was combined with common ownership in prehistoric Aegean societies. Matrilinear succession on some Aegean islands (e.g., Lesbos, Skyros) is reported by written records in the eighteenth century and continues in partial form to this very day. Matrilinear succession to real property and prenuptial promiscuity were practiced in isolated mountainous regions of southwestern Yugoslavia up to the twentieth century. Such customs are certainly unthinkable in present patriarchal society; only a very deeply rooted tradition could have survived for millennia the counter-influence of the patrilinearity of surrounding tribes.

A matrifocal society is reflected by the types of Old European goddesses and their worship. It is obvious that goddesses, not gods, dominated the Old European pantheon. Goddesses ruled absolutely over human, animal, and plant life. Goddesses, not male gods, spontaneously generated the life-force and created the universe. As demonstrated by the thousands of figurines and temples from the Neolithic through the Copper Ages, the male god was an adjunct of the female goddess, as consort or son. In the models of house-shrines and temples, and in actual temple remains, females are shown as supervising the preparation and performance of rituals dedicated to the various aspects and functions of the Goddess. Enormous energy was expended in the production of cult equipment and votive gifts. Some temple models show the grinding of grain and the baking of sacred bread. The routine acts of daily existence were religious rituals by virtue of replicating the sacred models. In the temple workshops, which usually constitute half the building or occupy the floor below the temple proper, females made and decorated quantities of the various pots appropriate to different rites. Next to the altar of the temple stood a vertical loom on which were probably woven the sacred garments and temple appurtenances. The most sophisticated creations of Old Europe—the most exquisite vases, sculptures, etc., now extant—were women's work (the equipment for decoration of vases so far is known only from female graves). Since the requirements of the temple were of primary importance, production for the temple must have doubled or tripled the general level of productivity, both stimulating and maintaining the level of feminine craftsmanship.

Religion

Temples.   The tradition of temple buildings begins in the seventh millennium B.C. A remarkable series of temple models and actual rectangular temples from the sixth and fifth millennia B.C. bear witness to a great architectural tradition.

At present about 50 models from various culture groups and phases are known. They are more informative than the actual temple remains, since they present details of architecture, decoration, and furnishings otherwise unavailable to prehistoric archaeology. Actual remains of sanctuaries suggest that miniature models in clay were replicas of the real temples. They almost always were found at the altars, probably as gifts to the goddess.

The seventh and sixth millennia temple models seemed to have conceived of the temple as literally the body or the house of the deity. Shrine models from Porodin near Bitola in Macedonia, for instance, have a cylindrical "chimney" in the middle of the roof upon which is modeled the masked features of a largeeyed Bird Goddess, a necklace encircling her neck ("chimney"). Other models have round openings fit for the goddess to enter in the shape of a bird or are made in the form of a bird's nest. . . .

The figurines portrayed (in clay models) and found in actual shrines are shown to perform various cult activities—ritual grinding, baking of sacred bread, attending sacrifices—or are seated on the altar, apparently used for the reenactment of a particular religious ceremony. In the mid-fifth millennium Cucuteni (Early Tripolye) shrine at Sabatinivka in the valley of Southern Bug in the Ukraine, 16 figurines were sitting on chairs on the altar, all with snake-shaped heads and massive thighs. One held a baby snake. The other group of 15 were in action—baking, grinding, or standing at the dish containing remains of a bull sacrifice. In the corner next to the altar stood a life-size clay throne with horned back support, perhaps for a priestess to supervise the ceremony. At Ovčarovo near Trgovište, northeastern Bulgaria, 26 miniature cult objects were found within the remains of a burned shrine. They included four figurines with upraised arms, three altar screens (or temple facades) decorated with symbols, nine chairs, three tables, three lidded vessels, three drums, and several dishes larger than figurines. Such objects vividly suggest ceremonies with music and dances, lustrations, and offerings.

The production of an enormous variety of cult paraphernalia—exquisite anthropomorphic, zoomorphic, and ornithomorphic vases, sacrificial containers, lamps, ladles, etc.—is one of the very characteristic features of this culture and may be viewed as a response to the demands of a theo-centric culture where most production centered around the temple. The consideration of these creations is unfortunately beyond the scope of this article. Regarding the technological and aesthetic skills, nothing similar was created in the millennia that followed the demise of Old Europe.

Ceremonial costume and mask.   A wealth of costume details is preserved on the clay figurines. Deep incisions encrusted with white paste or red ochre affirm the presence of hip-belts, fringe, aprons, narrow skirts, blouses, stoles, a variety of hair styles, and the use of caps, necklaces, bracelets, and medallions. Whether these fashions were commonly worn, or were traditional garb for priestesses or other participants in ritual celebrations, can only be conjectured. The latter was probably the case; most of the figurines seem to have been characters in tableaux of ritual. But, ritual or not, the costumes reflect stylistic conventions of dress and taste characteristic of the period.

In the female costume several dress combinations recur persistently: partly dressed figures wear only a hip-belt, or a hip-belt from which hangs an apron or panels of an entire skirt of fringe, resembling a hula skirt; others wear a tight skirt with shoulder straps or a blouse.

A number of figurines show incised or painted stoles over the shoulders and in front and back. The skirt, which generally begins below the waist and hugs the hips, has a decorative texture of white encrusted incisions, showing net-pattern, zigzags, checkerboard, or dots. The skirt narrows below the knees, and on some figurines wrappings around the legs are indicated. It may be that the skirt was slit in front below the knees and fastened between the legs with woven bands. This type of skirt gives the impression of con-straining movement and quite likely had a ritualistic purpose.

The figurines tell little about male attire; males are usually portrayed nude, except for a large V-shaped collar and a belt. In the last phase of the Cucuteni culture male figures wear a hip-belt and a strap passing diagonally across the chest and back over one of the shoulders. . . .

Special attention to coiffure and headgear is evidenced. The Bird and Snake Goddess in particular, or devotees associated with their images, had beautiful coiffures, a crown, or decorative headbands. VinCa and Butmir figurines have hair neatly combed and divided symmetrically in the center, the two panels perhaps separated by a central ribbon. Late Cucutenian figurines, primarily nude, but some wearing hip-belt and necklace, have a long, thick coil of hair hanging down the back and ending in a large, circular bun or with an attached disc, reminiscent of the style favored by Egyptian ritual dancers of the third millennium B.C. A typical item of dress is a conical cap on which radial or horizontal parallel incisions perhaps represent its construction of narrow ribbon-like bands.

Figurines were portrayed wearing masks representing certain goddesses, gods, or their sacred animals, or else they were simply shown as bird-headed (with beaked faces on a cylindrical neck), snake-headed (with a long mouth, round eyes, and no nose), or ram- or other animal-headed. Frequently-occurring perforations of the mask were obviously intended to carry some sort of organic attachment. Plumes, flowers, fruits, and other materials could have been employed in this way. . . .

Deities worshipped.   In the literature on prehistoric religion the female figures of clay, bone, and stone are usually considered to be the "Mother Goddess." Is she indeed nothing more than an image of motherhood? The term is not entirely a misnomer if we understand her as a creatress or as a cosmogenic woman. It must be emphasized that from the Upper Paleolithic onward the persona of the Goddess splintered the response to the developing economy, and the images of deities portray not only the single maternal metaphor of the deity. Study of the several stereotypical shapes and postures of the figurines and of the associated symbolism of the signs incised upon them clearly shows that the figurines intend to project a multiplicity of divine aspects and a variety of divine functions.

There are, in my opinion, two primary aspects of the Goddess (not necessarily two Goddesses) presented by the effigies. The first is, "She who is the Giver of All"—Giver of Life, Giver of Moisture, of Food, of Happiness; she is also "Taker of All," i.e., Death. The second aspect of the Goddess is connected with the periodic awakening of nature: she is springtime, the new moon, rebirth, regeneration, and metamorphosis. Both go back to the Upper Paleolithic. The significance of each aspect is visually supported on the figurines by appropriate symbols and signs. The first aspect of the Goddess as Giver and Taker of All, that is, as both beginning and end of life, is accompanied by aquatic symbols—water birds, snakes, fish, frogs, all animals associated with water—and representations of water itself in the form of zigzag bands, groups of parallel lines, meanders, nets, checkerboards, and running spirals. The second aspect of the Goddess as Rebirth, Renewal, and Transcendance is accompanied by the symbols of "becoming": eggs, uteri, phalluses, whirls, crescents, and horns which resemble cornucopias. The Goddess often appears in the form of a bee, a butterfly, or a caterpillar. This second group involves male animals such as bulls and dogs.

The Giver of All, the Fish, Water Bird, and Snake Goddess

Hybrids of the human female with bird or snake dominated mythical imagery throughout the Upper Paleolithic, Neolithic, Chalcolithic, and Copper Ages from ca. 26,000 to the end of Old Europe at ca. 3000 B.C., but lingered in the Aegean and Mediterranean regions through the Bronze Age and later—at least 40 percent of the total number of figurines belong to this type. The Fish, Bird, and Snake Goddesses were interrelated in meaning and function. Each is Creatress and Giver. They are, therefore, inseparable from cosmogonic and cosmogenic myths such as water birds carrying cosmic eggs. She as the Mother or *Source* is the giver of rain, water, milk, and meat (sheep, their skin and wool). Her portrayals usually show exaggerated breasts marked with parallel lines, or a wide-open beak or round hole for a mouth. Her large eyes are a magical source, and are surrounded by aquatic symbolism (usually groups of parallel lines). Beginning in the Neolithic, the ram (the earliest domesticated animal, a vital source of food and clothing) became her sacred animal. The symbols of this goddess on spindle whorls and loom weights suggest that she was the originator or guardian of the crafts of spinning and weaving. Metaphorically, as "the spinner and weaver of human life," she became the Goddess of Fate.

Along with the life-giving aspect of the Goddess, her life-taking or death-giving aspect must have developed in preagricultural times. The images of vultures and owls are known from the Upper Paleolithic and from the earliest Neolithic (in the frescoes of Çatal Hüyük, in central Anatolia, vultures appear above headless human beings). The figurine type of the nude goddess with large pubic triangle, folded arms, and face of an owl, well known from Old European graves, may be representative of the Goddess in the aspect of night and death.

In early agricultural times, the Giver of All developed another function, a function vital to tillers of the soil—namely, that of "Giver of Bread." Her images were deposited in grain silos or in egg-shaped vases, where they were indispensable insurance for the resurgence of plant life. She also appears as a pregnant woman, her ripe body a metaphor of the fertile field. She was worshipped with her sacred animal, the pig. The fattening of the pig encouraged the growth and ripening of crops or fertility in general.

Richly represented throughout the Neolithic, Chalcolithic, and Copper Ages, still another aspect of the Goddess is, by natural association, that of "Birth-giving Goddess." She is portrayed with outstretched legs and upraised arms in a naturalistic birth-giving posture. This stereotypic image appears in relief on large vases and on temple walls; carved in black and green stone or alabaster, it was worn as an amulet.

The "Periodic Regeneration" aspect of the Goddess may be as ancient as the Giver of All aspect, since symbols of "becoming" are present in the Upper Paleolithic: crescents and horns appear in association with Paleolithic nudes. To regenerate the life-force was her main function; therefore, the Goddess was flanked by male animals noted for physical strength—bulls, he-goats, dogs. In her incarnation as a crescent, caterpillar, bee, or butterfly, she was a symbol of new life; she emerged from the body or horns of the bull as a bee or butterfly.

The female principle was conceived as creative and eternal, the male as spontaneous and ephemeral. The male principle was represented symbolically by male animals and by phalluses and ithyphallic animal-masked men—goatmen or bull-men. They appear as adjuncts of the Goddess. The figurines of ecstatic dancers, goat- or bull-masked, may represent worshippers of the Goddess in rituals enacting the dance of life. . . .

Conclusion: The Kurgan Penetration

Old Europe was rapidly developing into an urban culture, but its growth was interrupted and eventually stopped by destructive forces from the east—the steadily increasing infiltration of the semi-nomadic, horse-riding pastoralists from the Pontic steppes. Periodic waves of infiltration into civilized Europe effected the disintegration of the first European civilization. Only on the islands, like Crete, Thera, and Malta, did the traditions of Old Europe survive for almost two millennia. The Bronze Age culture that followed north of the Aegean was an amalgam of the substrate and totally different elements of an eastern culture.

Thanks to a growing number of radiocarbon dates, archaeologists can ascertain the periods of Kurgan penetration into Europe. There was no single massive invasion, but a series of repeated incursions concentrated into three major thrusts:

- Wave No. 1, ca. 4400–4200 B.C.
- Wave No. 2, ca. 3400–3200 B.C.
- Wave No. 3, ca. 3000–2800 B.C.

The steppe (or "Kurgan") people were, above all, pastoralists. As such, their social system was composed of small patrilinear units that were socially stratified according to the strategic services performed by its male members. The grazing of large herds over vast expanses of land necessitated a living pattern of seasonal settlements or small villages affording sufficient pasturage for animals. The chief tasks of a pastoral economy were executed by men, not by women as was characteristic of the indigenous agricultural system.

It was inevitable that an economy based on farming and another which relied on stock breeding would produce unrelated ideologies. The upheaval of the Old European civilization is registered in the abrupt cessation of painted pottery and figurines, the disappearance of shrines, the termination of symbols and signs.

Old European ceramics are readily identified with the rich symbolic signs and decorative motifs that reflect an ideology concerned with cosmogony, generation, birth, and regeneration. Symbols were compartmentalized or interwoven in a myriad combination—meanders and spirals, chevrons and zigzags, circles, eggs, horns, etc. There were a multitude of pictorial and sculptural representations of goddesses and gods, of worshippers, and sacred animals. Kurgan pottery is devoid of symbolic language and of aesthetic treatment in general because it obviously did not serve the same ceremonial purposes as that of Old Europe. The stabbing and impressing technique is quite primitive and seems to focus on only one symbol, the sun. Occasionally, a schematized fir tree occurs which may symbolize a "tree-of-life."

Mythical images that were in existence on the Eurasiatic steppe dispersed now over a large part of Europe, and continued to the beginning of Christianity and beyond. The new ideology was an apotheosis of the horseman and warrior. The principal gods carry weapons and ride horses or chariots; they are figures of inexhaustible energy, physical power, and fecundity. In contrast to the pre-Indo-European cultures whose myths centered around the moon, water, and the female, the religion of pastoral, semi-sedentary Indo-European peoples was oriented toward the rotating sky, the sun, stars, planets, and other sky phenomena such as thunder and lightning. Their sky and sun gods were shining, "bright as the sky"; they wore starry cloaks adorned with glittering gold, copper, or amber pendants, torques, chest plates, belts. They carried shining daggers, swords, and shields. The Indo-Europeans glorified the magical swiftness of arrow and javelin and the sharpness of the blade. Throughout the millennia, the Indo-Europeans exulted in the making of weapons, not pottery or sculpture. The touch of the ax blade awakened the powers of nature and transmitted the fecundity of the Thunder God; by the touch of his spear tip, the god of war and the underworld marked the hero for glorious death.

Goddesses, Gimbutas, and 'New Age' Archaeology

For a century a notion of a prehistoric Mother Goddess has infused some perceptions of ancient Europe, whatever the realities of developing archaeological knowledge. With the reverent respect now being given to Marija Gimbutas, and her special vision of a perfect matriarchy in Old Europe, a daughter-goddess is now being made, bearer of a holy spirit in our own time to be set alongside the wise mother of old.

Introduction

The field of archaeology, like many others, is prone to fads and fictions within the academic community and general public alike. A recurrent interest since the 19th century has been the notion of an omnipotent Mother Goddess, whose worship symbolizes a cultural continuity from the Palaeolithic era to modern times. The principle advocate for this theory over the past two decades, Marija Gimbutas, is seen to offer archaeological validity to these claims as a result of her recognized academic standing and long history of fieldwork in southeast European sites. From the material particulars of archaeology in her earlier work she moved toward an ideal vision of prehistory (compare Gimbutas 1965; 1970; 1971a; 1973 with interpretations in 1974; 1981; Gimbutas *et al.* 1989; 1989a; 1989b; 1991; 1992). Her widely published theories appeal to those committed to ecofeminism and the 'New Age' range of esoteric concerns, which include ancient religion and mythology. Whilst this vision of the past appears to embrace aspects of cognitive, gender and even feminist archaeologies, the interpretations it presents are simply hopeful and idealistic creations reflecting the contemporary search for a social utopia.

The concept of The Goddess is entangled within a larger, more complex, political phenomenon that involves regional and nationalist struggles (Chapman 1994; Anthony in press), linguistic aetiology (Renfrew 1987; Mallory 1989: 81), contemporary gender struggles and the feminist cause (Hallett 1993; Passman 1993). However, the revisionist histories on offer (Eisler 1987; Gimbutas 1974; 1989a; 1989b; 1991; 1992; Orenstein 1990;

Spretnak 1992; etc.) do not aim for a more complete understanding of ancient societies *in toto*. Rather, they provide altogether alternative historical projections of what certain groups see as desirable. Re-writing the past from an engendered perspective is certainly long overdue, yet re-weaving a fictional past with claims of scientific proofs (e.g. Gimbutas 1992) is simply irresponsible. Such 'new and improved' histories are more telling of contemporary socio-sexual concerns rather than their ancient antecedents.

Why the Goddess and Why Now?

Why has there been a proliferation of studies devoted to the concept of a Mother Goddess in recent years? Why has this appeal been so persistent, particularly to the general public? Whereas the academic study of figurines is usually integrated within regional culture studies, the notion of the Goddess has assumed larger proportions to the wider community. As a result, the literature of the Goddess lies at the interface where academic scholarship meets New Age gynocentric, mythologized interpretations of the past (Eisler 1987; Gimbutas 1974; 1989a; 1992; Spretnak 1992). This is a radically burgeoning field in women's studies and New Age literature, and its books must far outsell their scholarly counterparts. Since achieving icon status, The Goddess has been linked with movements and disciplines as diverse as christianity, feminism and ecofeminism, environmentalism, witchcraft and archaeology. In each of these the Goddess phenomenon is taken as a given rather than one speculative interpretation to be considered with alternative hypotheses. The past is being used in the present as an historical authority for contemporary efforts to secure gender equality (or superiority?) in spiritual and social domains.

. . . The current interest in the Goddess is not purely academic, but stems from a desire to remedy the results of millennia of misogyny and marginalization (Frymer-Kensky 1992: vii) in both religious and secular spheres. My contention is that the connection has materialized in response to female disempowerment in our own recent history, particularly within religious power bases. The Goddess serves as a vehicle for women's groups and activists to reinforce legitimization of their position by means of an ancient antecedent. Contrary to the bloodied, materialist history and overt androcentrism of the Church, she is earth-centered, offering refuge and a counterbalance to the remote, punitive male god of western religions (Frymer-Kensky 1992; Spretnak 1992).

. . . Many of these initial gynocentric theories of prehistory share a fundamental commonality to prior androcentric premises since they both employ 'sexist' paradigms in re-constru(ct)ing the past. Thus they do not promote credibility: rather they damage and delimit the positive attributes of gender-based research, due to their poor scholarship, ahistorical interpretations, fictional elements and reverse sexism. I see no detriment to current quests if we acknowledge that inequality was operative in the past, as it was in the historic cultures of the Near East and Mediterranean.

The Figurines as Archaeological Data

Figurines collectively termed Mother Goddesses or Venuses emanate from various regions and span an immense time-depth from the Palaeolithic to the Bronze Age and into historical periods, with considerable variability in form, style, decoration and context. This class of artefact—if that is an appropriate term—appears throughout much of Europe and southwest Asia, primarily southeast Europe and the Mediterranean islands from the Cyclades to Crete, Malta and Majorca (Ehrenberg 1989: 65; Malone *et al.* 1992: 76). The figures are generally accorded the status of 'art', although ethnographic evidence suggests that they do not form a distinct category. In a further tendency to project 20th-century biases of what constitutes 'good art', it has been suggested that carefully made sculptures were produced for important occasions by priestesses or mother figures (Gimbutas *et al.* 1989: 220). Conversely, the simple, schematic examples could have been made by any member of the community (male?). Figurines have been objectified, taken as devoid of spatial and cultural specificity; yet objects do not have inherent meaning divorced from their historically specific context of production and use (Hodder 1991; Dobres 1992a; 1992b).

For many figurines, provenience and context are lost due to poor excavation or non-archaeological recovery (for Cycladic figures see Gill & Chippindale 1993). Runnels (1990) and McPherron (1991) have noted the limits of excavation and recording by Gimbutas for her own site at Achilleion (Gimbutas *et al.* 1989), on which much of the larger picture is reliant. Dating, methodology, testing, typological and statistical analyses have all come under fire, not to mention artistic licence and over-interpretation. Weaknesses in scholarship have prevented Gimbutas' attempts, and the question of gender studies, to be taken seriously in archaeological circles (Tringham 1991: 97; 1993).

As part of a gynocentric agenda, female figurines have been considered largely to the exclusion of male and sexless examples (Gimbutas 1971b; 1974; 1986; 1989a; 1989b; 1992; Gimbutas *et al.* 1989), this selection shaping the vision of a single, omnipresent female deity. Her position is clear: male divinities were not prominent before the Indo-European invasion (see van Leuven 1993: 84). Many are undeniably female. Many are also male, androgynous, zoomorphic or indeterminate (see Marinescu-Bîlcu 1981; Hodder 1990; Milojkovic 1990; Pavlovic 1990; Talalay 1993); these are dismissed.

To her credit, Gimbutas assembled a large corpus of southeast European figurines in English publications, with copious photographs and illustrations. She aimed to investigate figurine attributes such as raw materials, production and form to some degree. However, studies of production have been undertaken more systematically by other scholars (Murray 1970), coupled with analyses of decorative motifs and positioning (Ucko 1968; Marinescu Bîlcu 1981; Pogozheva 1983) and patterns of breakage. It is unfortunate that Gimbutas did not incorporate findings from these studies into her later publications.

Mediterranean Matriculture and the Indo-European Debate

One key debate in 19th-century anthropology, currently experiencing a revival, hinges on the traditional matriarchal view of cultural evolution. Eminent scholars such as Morgan, Engels and Bachofen led the early debate, influenced by their own socio-intellectual biases, though failing to make the distinction between matriarchy, matrilinearity and matrilocality. Bachofen's evolutionist interpretations, long since discredited within academia, have now resurfaced in the Goddess literature. . . .

It has become popular in the past decade to view Neolithic cultures as matriarchal or matrifocal (Hayden 1986: 17), and to depict them as peaceful, harmonious and artistic in contrast to the more aggressive, destructive patriarchal societies that followed (Chapman 1991; Tringham 1991; Conkey & Tringham in press): the overthrowing of matriarchy by patriarchial society was the real Fall which has beleaguered Europe ever since. Childe raised a powerful analogue, arguing that using female figurines to substantiate matriarchal or matrilineal society was as accurate an indicator as the image of the Virgin Mary in the modern patriarchy (Childe 1951: 65). We should not ignore the possibility of matriarchy; rather we are not clear what form such evidence would take.

This line of reasoning ties directly into the polemic debate surrounding Indo-European archaeology and linguistics, in which Gimbutas was a major player (see Renfrew 1987: xiii; Mallory 1989: 182). Briefly, her view of Old Europe in the Neolithic period was characterized by its unfortified settlements (*contra* Marinescu Bîlcu 1981; Anthony in press) where a peaceful existence prevailed without threat of violence or fear of death itself. Within the matriarchy there were no husbands, yet men fulfilled important roles in construction, crafts and trade. Women's lives were liberal, socially and sexually, and inextricably bound to the rich religious system which ensured their prominence (Gimbutas 1992). Old Europe is portrayed as culturally homogeneous (*contra* Pavlovic 1988: 33; Mallory 1989: 22), socially egalitarian (*contra* Tringham 1990: 605; Anthony in press), devoid of human or animal sacrifice (*contra* Marinescu Bîlcu 1981; Anthony in press). Accordingly, this utopian existence was abruptly destroyed by Indo-European invasions: more specifically by the equocentric Kurgan culture from the Russian steppe. . . .

There is a striking congruence between Gimbutas' own life and her perception of Old Europe. Born in Lithuania, she witnessed two foreign occupations by 'barbarian invaders'; however, those from the East stayed. This prompted her immigration to the United States during which time the Soviet occupation of the Baltic states continued almost up until her death in 1994. In her own words, 'history is showing us between eight and ten million women had to die for her [the Goddess] . . . the wise people of the time . . . so it reminds me of the same [*sic*] what happened in Stalin's Europe when the cream of the society had to be removed and only fools were left to live. What happened in the twentieth century is the greatest shame of human history' (Gimbutas 1992). This strongly mirrors her view of Old Europe, a creative, matriarchal and *good* society which was invaded by men with weapons from the East.

Other writers (see Eisler 1987; Passman 1993) have run with Gimbutas' theories by stressing the superiority of assumed matristic cultures in Old Europe, Anatolia, Egypt and Minoan Crete on the basis of their peaceful, egalitarian, non-fortified communities and even their predisposition to vegetarianism (?) (Passman 1993: 187). Such a scenario is not borne out archaeologically. Walls and ditches at Nea Nikomedia, Dimini and Sesklo may have defensive functions. Both Neolithic and Chalcolithic sites like Tîrpesti, Ovcharovo, Polyanitsa and Tripolye clearly demonstrate fortification (Marinescu-Bîlcu 1981; Anthony in press: 20). Sites such as Dimini and Agia Sophia (Demoule & Perlès 1993) suggests status differentiation within communities, as does Selevac (Tringham & Krstic 1990: 206), with more evidence of social hierarchy from the cemeteries at Varna, Durankulak and other East Balkan sites (Anthony in press: 20). In addition, there is evidence of human sacrifice at Traian-Dealui, Fîntînilor (Marinescu-Bîlcu 1981: 135) and later from Knossos (Wall *et al.* 1986); animal sacrifices are attested at Poiana în Pisc and Anza. Artefactual evidence from Egypt indicates that weapons, in addition to items displaying battle scenes, were amongst the most common in the predynastic repertoire (see Davis 1992).

Even without the overwhelming archaeological data, historical evidence from Greece (Humphreys 1983; Hallett 1993), Egypt (Robins 1993) and Mesopotamia (Frymer-Kensky 1992) plus numerous ethnographic accounts suggest that cultures with strong female deities—if indeed they are deities—may still regard women in the profane world as a low-status group. The romanticized view of antiquity many feminists and pseudo-feminists present has more to do with creating an idealized past to contrast with our own secular, impersonal and industrialized present than with archaeological facts (Hays 1993: 84). Their visionary work links notions of 'ancient' and 'future', so enabling a richly figured heritage, once lived and lost, to be experienced again (Passman 1993: 182). This political reconstruction of a matristic past furnishes the seed for a return to Edenic conditions, ecological balance, healing the planet and matriculture itself, in opposition to the forecasts of Armageddon and the second coming (Starhawk 1982; Orenstein 1990; Passman 1993).

Cultic Figurines From a Sexist Perspective

Although proponents of post-processualism (e.g. Hodder 1987; 1990; 1991; Shanks & Tilley 1987) aim to understand symbolic systems, they still regard the archaeological record as a polysemous text that can be read (Hays 1993). Some have taken their position as reader to the extreme. Herein lies Gimbutas' attraction for a New Age audience, since she adopts the role of translator (channeller?) for a symbolic language stretching back millennia into the Neolithic mindset. In answer to Onians' claim that figurines represent ancient erotica, Gimbutas argues that 'love-making is clearly far from the thoughts of the ancient artist' (1981: 32). Knowing 'our European prehistoric forefathers were more philosophical than we seem to think' (1981: 39), she understands how they would be stunned to hear these new hypotheses. She further claims that the Achilleion figurines 'represent deities and their sacred animals, witness to continuous ritual performances in temples and at ovens in courtyards' (Gimbutas *et al.* 1989: 335). Her typological analysis was narrowed to fit these criteria, without mention of other functional interpretations. Similarly, she dismissed alternative explanations of Cycladic figures from mortuary contexts in favour of the Great Goddess (or stiff White Goddess) from a deeply rooted European tradition (1974: 158; 1992).

From the 1970s onwards Gimbutas presented arguments, with increasing fervour, to challenge a balanced and complementary view of the sexes in sacred and profane spheres (Hayden 1986; Chapman 1991). Her publications, including site reports (where one expects some attempt to discuss the data without a charged interpretation), were devoted to the Goddess and her manifestations; the gods are overlooked. At Anza 'only one [figurine] can possibly be male' (1976: 200), at Sitagroi 'only 1% can be considered as possibly portraying men' (1986: 226), at Achilleion the divine creatrix does not require male fecundity since 'her divine bisexuality stresses her absolute power' (Gimbutas *et al.* 1989: 196). In these reports every figure that is not phallic—and some that clearly are—are taken as symbols of the Goddess. This includes parallel lines, lozenges, zigzags, spirals, double axes, butterflies, pigs and pillars. Why this miscellany are self-evidently emblems of a female, much less a deity, is never explained. And indeed even the *male* may be symbolically *female*: 'although the male element is attached, these figurines remain essentially female' (1989a: 232). Gimbutas denied that phallicism was symbolic of procreation since Neolithic peoples did not understand the nature of biological conception (1974: 237).

Gimbutas was emphatic that Neolithic mythology was not polarized into male and female, due to the supremacy of the Mother. From this assumption she extrapolated, concomitantly, the role of women was not subordinate to men (Gimbutas 1974: 237; see Chapman 1991; Tringham 1991). Yet male, sexless and zoomorphic figures do exist, which makes the notion of an omnipotent Mother Goddess difficult to support. Ucko's examination of the later Knossos figurines demonstrated that androgynous examples were equal in number to the identifiable female statuettes (1968: 316; see Conkey & Tringham in press). Ucko (1968: 417) further concluded that most scholars treat male figures as exceptions, dismiss the sexless examples and regard female figurines as a singular deity without convincing explanation for their obvious variation.

The Goddess Contextualized

In addressing the archaeological context of finds at Anza, Sitagroi and Achilleion, Gimbutas interpreted partially excavated dwellings as 'house-shrines' and 'cult-places', and benches as 'altars' (1981; 1986; Gimbutas *et al.* 1989). She concluded human activities like grinding grain, baking bread, weaving and spinning were inseparable from divine participation (Gimbutas *et al.* 1989: 213–15). To Gimbutas it was 'obvious that the Goddess ruled over human, animal and plant life' (Gimbutas *et al.* 1989: 220). Perhaps these areas represented dwellings or workshops in view of associated finds like spindle whorls, a needle, awl and pottery discs? Indeed, few artefacts and features from these sites are assigned a mundane status (1981: 198–200; Gimbutas *et al.* 1989: 36–46, 213–15).

. . . Evidence from Anza, Selevac, Tîrpesti and Achilleion (see Gimbutas 1981; Gimbutas *et al.* 1989; Marinescu-Bîlcu 1981; Hodder 1990; Tringham 1990) indicates that figurines are found in every kind of context—refuse pits included. This would signify, as Gimbutas prefers, that the sacred is everywhere. Conversely, it could demonstrate that these figures are not sacred at all; or they may have multiple meanings which change as a figure is made, used and discarded.

Alternative Hypotheses

Recent work in Kephala (northern Greece) uncovered figurines near graves, which would indicate a possible function as territorial markers to reinforce ancestral ties in the Neolithic period (Talalay 1991: 49). Ethnographic reports from Africa over the past 200 years also suggest this kind of placement may be associated to ancestor cults. Further functions proposed include dolls, toys, tokens of identification, primitive contracts, communication or as part of birthing rituals (Talalay 1993: 40–43). Other plausible interpretations include teaching devices, tools of sorcery, magic, healing or initiation (Ehrenberg 1989: 75). Talalay proposes that clay legs from the northern Peloponnese served to symbolize social and economic bonds among communities like those of marriage contracts or identification of trading partners (1987: 161–2). These alternatives, as opposed to a universal deity, may explain the practice of discard. To assume *a priori* that there is a Goddess behind every figurine is tantamount to interpreting plastic figures of Virgin Mary and of 'Barbie' as having identical ideological significance. . . .

Conclusion: The Goddess, Pseudo-Feminism and Future Research

Whilst the concept of gender as a structuring principle is relatively new to archaeology, many progressive and scholarly studies have emerged in the last few years (e.g. Gero & Conkey 1991; Wylie 1991; Dobres 1992a; 1992b; Bacus *et al.* 1993; Brown 1993; Conkey & Tringham in press). However, many feminists feel that the establishment of an originary myth of the basis of scientific historical reality will facilitate the restoration of women's power. It then follows that the patriarchy will be dismantled and the lost pre-patriarchal culture can be regained (Passman 1993: 187). Matriculture is seen to give feminism the legitimacy the system demands.

Contrary to this position I argue, as feminist and archaeologist, that the approaches of Gimbutas and her advocates contrast markedly to many feminists (Brown 1993: 254), especially those involved in archaeo-logical discourse. This is not to say that Gimbutas claimed to do feminist archaeology; rather that she has been adopted as an icon within the movement, more ardently outside archaeological circles. However, some feminists do not accept her methodology, since she was so steeped within the 'establishment' epistemological framework of polar opposites, rigid gender roles, barbarian invaders and cultural stages (Fagan 1992; Brown 1993) which are now regarded as outmoded. It is unfortunate that many archaeologists interested in gender are drawn to historical fiction and emotional narratives, which either replace or accompany serious archaeo-logical dialogues. At this juncture sound feminist scholarship needs to be divorced from methodological shortcomings, reverse sexism, conflated data and pure fantasy, since this will only impede the feminist cause and draw attention away from the positive contribution offered by gender and feminist archaeologies. Gero & Conkey (1991: 5) assert that we are now in a position to draw from and contribute to emergent theoretical develop-ments within archaeology, particularly post-processual directions that see social and symbolic theories as central. Gender, however, cannot be sepa-rated from other archaeological considerations and become the type of speciality area Gimbutas created.

In future studies we should not expect to delineate a rigid and unitary code which holds for all contexts (Hodder 1987), but rather to identify the dimensions of meaning pertaining to particular societies and to compre-hend their social locus. It may prove more informative to ask 'how did the social production of this object contribute to its meanings and uses?', 'how did these meaningful objects enhance people's understanding of their lives?' and 'what other associated activities were operative that can inform us about social context?' (Dobres 1992a: 17–18). Naturally the multiplicity of manifestations relative to their archaeological contexts must be considered, coupled with the socioeconomic concerns of their manufacturers.

To conclude, academic and popular audiences alike need to review criti-cally the evidence for a solitary universal Mother Goddess, along with other plausible interpretations. Although the post-processualists have stressed notions of pluralism, most now advocate that not *all* pasts are equal. The gynocentric narratives discussed above reveal more about our relationship(s) with the past and certain contemporary ideologies (Conkey 1992) than how these figurines were deployed in antiquity.

The Mother Goddess metanarrative presents a possible challenge to feminist archaeologies in that solidarity can often prevent us from con-testing theories presented by women which seem to espouse pro-female notions: even if the evidence would suggest otherwise. Loyalty to a mis-represented picture of the past and our human heritage by dismissing or misconstruing the archaeological record cannot be supported under the guise of any political standpoint. Needless to say, many men feel that they are not in a position to engage in these issues and that only other women can do so. This exclusivity is not conducive to scholarly development; neither is failing to counter claims of a gendered superiority supported by 'scientific' archaeology that ultimately has filtered into mainstream society. An engendered re-balancing of the scales is long overdue and critically important to the trajectory of the discipline. However, emphasis on one sex to the exclusion of the other is not only detrimental to serious gender/feminist studies, but threatens the interpretative integrity of archaeology.

References

Anthony, D. W. In press. Nazi and ecofeminist prehistories: ideology and empiricism in Indo-European archaeology, in P. Kohl & C. Fawcett (ed.), *Nationalism, politics and the practice of archaeology:* 1–32. Cambridge: Cambridge University Press.

Bacus, E.A. *et al.* 1993. *A gendered past: a critical review of gender in archaeology.* Ann Arbor (MI): University of Michigan Press.

Brown, S. 1993. Feminist research in archaeology. What does it mean? Why is it taking so long?, in Rabinowitz & Richlin (ed.): 238–71.

Chapman, J. 1991. The creation of social arenas in the Neolithic and copper age of SE Europe: the case of Varna, in P. Garwood *et al* (ed.). *Sacred and profane:* 152–71. Oxford: Oxford University Committee for Archaeology, Monograph 32.

—— 1994. Destruction of a common heritage: the archaeology of war in Croatia. Bosnia and Hercegovina, *Antiquity* 68: 120–26.

Childe, V. G. 1951. *Social evolution.* London: Watts.

Conkey, M. W. 1992. Mobilising ideologies: the archaeologics of Paleolithic 'art'. Paper delivered to the American Anthropological Association, San Francisco.

Conkey, M. W. & R. E. Tringham. In press. Archaeology and the Goddess: exploring the contours of feminist archaeology, in A. Stewart & D. Stanton (ed.), *Feminism in the academy: rethinking the disciplines.* Ann Arbor (MI): University of Michigan Press.

Davis, W. 1992. *Masking the blow: the scene of representation in late prehistoric Egyptian art.* Berkeley (CA): University of California Press.

Demoule, J.-P. & C. Perles. 1993. The Greek Neolithic: a new review, *Journal of World Prehistory* 7(4): 355–416.

Dobres, M.-A. 1992a. Re-presentations of Palaeolithic visual imagery: simulacra and their alternatives, *Kroeber Anthroplogical Society Papers* 73–4: 1–25.

Ehrenberg, M. 1989. *Women in prehistory.* London: British Museum Publications.

Eisler, R. 1987. *The chalice and the blade: our history, our future.* San Francisco (CA): Harper Row.

Fagan, B. M. 1992. A sexist view of prehistory, *Archaeology* 45(2): 14–16, 18, 66.

Frymer-Kensky, T. 1992. *In the wake of the goddess: women, culture and the biblical transformation of pagan myth.* New York (NY): Ballantine.

Gero, J. M. & M. W. Conkey. 1991. Tensions, pluralities and engendering archaeology: an introduction to women and prehistory, in Gero & Conkey (ed.): 2–29.

Gero, J. M. & M. W. Conkey (ed.). 1991. *Engendering archaeology: women and prehistory.* Oxford: Basil Blackwell.

Gill, D. W. J. & C. Chippindale. 1993. Material and intellectual consequences of esteem for Cycladic figures, *American Journal of Archaeology* 97: 601–59.

Gimbutas, M. 1965. *The Bronze Age cultures in central and eastern Europe.* The Hague: Mouton.

—— 1970. Proto-Indo-European culture: the Kurgan culture during the 5th, 4th and 3rd millennium BC in G. Cardona *et al.* (ed.), *Indo-European and Indo-Europeans:* 155–97. Philadelphia (PA): University of Pennsylvania Press.

—— 1971a. *The Slavs.* London: Thames & Hudson.

—— 1971b (ed). *Neolithic Macedonia: as reflected by excavations at Anza, southeast Yugoslavia.* Los Angeles (CA): UCLA Institute of Archaeology. Monumenta Archaeologica 1.

—— 1973. The beginning of the Bronze Age in Europe and the Indo-Europeans—3500–2500 BC, *Journal of Indo-European Studies* 1(2): 163–214.

—— 1974. *Gods and goddesses of old Europe.* London: Thames & Hudson.

—— 1981. Vulvas, breasts and buttocks of the Goddess Creatress: commentary on the origins of art, in G. Buccellati & C. Speroni (ed.), *The shape of the past. Studies in honour of Franklin D. Murphy:* 19–40. Los Angeles (CA): UCLA Institute of Archaeology.

—— 1986. Mythical imagery of Sitagroi society, in Renfrew *et al.* (ed.): 225–301.

—— 1989a. *The language of the Goddess: unearthing hidden symbols of western civilisation.* London: Thames and Hudson.

—— 1989b. Women and culture in Goddess-oriented Old Europe, in J. Plaskow & C. C. Christ (ed.), *Weaving the visions:* 63–71. San Francisco (CA): Harpers.

—— 1991. *The civilization of the Goddess: the world of Old Europe.* San Francisco (CA): Harpers.

—— 1992. *The age of the Goddess: ancient roots of the emerging feminine consciousness.* Boulder (CO): Sounds True Recordings. Audio tape #A192.

Gimbutas, M., S. Winn & D. Shimabuku. 1989. *Achilleion: a Neolithic settlement in Thessaly, Greece 6400–5600 BC.* Los Angeles (CA): UCLA Institute of Archaeology.

Hallett, J. P. 1993. Feminist theory, historical periods, literary canons, and the study of Greco-Roman antiquity, in Rabinowitz & Richlin (ed.): 44–72.

Hayden, B. 1986. Old Europe: sacred matriarchy or complimentary opposition in A. Bonanno (ed.), *Archaeology and fertility cult in the Mediterranean:* 17–41. Amsterdam: B. R. Grunner.

Hays, K. A. 1993. When is a symbol archaeologically meaningful?: meaning, function and prehistoric visual arts, in N. Yoffee and S. Sherratt (ed.), *Archaeological theory: who sets the agenda?:* 81–92. Cambridge: Cambridge University Press.

Hodder, I. R. 1987. Contextual archaeology: an interpretation of Çatal Hüyük and a discussion of the origins of agriculture. *University of London Institute of Archaeology Bulletin* 24: 43–56.

—— 1990. *The domestication of Europe: structure and contingency in Neolithic societies.* Oxford: Basil Blackwell.

Humphreys, S. C. 1983. *The family, women and death: comparative studies.* London: Routledge & Kegan Paul.

Mcpherron, A. 1991. Review of Gimbutas *et al.* (1989), *American Antiquity* 56(3): 567–8.

Mallory, J. P. 1989. *In search of the Indo-Europeans.* London: Thames & Hudson.

Malone, C., A. Bonanno, T. Goulder, S. Stoddart & D. Trump. 1993. The death cults of prehistoric Malta. *Scientific American* (December): 76–83.

Marinescu-Bilcu. 1981. *Tirpesti: from prehistory to history in eastern Romania.* Oxford: British Archaeological Reports. International series 107.

Milojkovic, J. 1990. The anthropomorphic and zoomorphic figurines, in Tringham & Krstic (ed.): 397–436.

Murray, J. 1970. *The first European agriculture, a study of the osteological and botanical evidence until 2000 BC.* Edinburgh: Edinburgh University Press.

Orenstein, G. F. 1990. *The reflowering of the Goddess.* New York (NY): Pergamon Press.

Pavlovic, M. 1990. The aesthetics of Neolithic figurines, in *Vinca and its world: international symposium. The Danubian region from 6000 to 3000 BC. Belgrade, Smederevska Palanka, October 1988:* 33–4. Belgrade: Academy of Arts and Sciences.

Passman, T. 1993. Out of the closet and into the field: matriculture, lesbian perspective and feminist classics, in Rabinowitz & Richlin (ed.): 181–208.

Pogozheva, A. P. 1983. *Antropomorfnaya plastika Tripol'ya.* Novosibirsk: Akademiia Nauk, Sibirskoe Otdelenie.

Renfrew, C. 1987. *Archaeology and language: the puzzle of Indo-European origins.* London: Jonathan Cape.

Robins, G. 1993. *Women in ancient Egypt.* London: British Museum Press.

Runnels, C. 1990. Review of Gimbutas *et al.* (1989), *Journal of Field Archaeology* 17: 341–5.

Shanks, M. & C. Tilley. 1987. *Re-constructing archaeology: theory and practice.* Cambridge: Cambridge University Press.

Spretnak, C. 1992. *Lost goddesses of early Greece.* Boston (MA): Beacon Press.

Starhawk. 1982. *Dreaming the dark: magic, sex and politics.* Boston (MA): Beacon Press.

Talalay, L. E. 1991. Body imagery of the ancient Aegean. *Archaeology* 44(4): 46–9.

—— 1993. *Dolls, deities and devices. Neolithic figurines from Franthchi cave, Greece.* Bloomington (IN): Indiana University Press. Excavations at Franchthi Cave, Greece 9.

Tringham, R. E. 1991. Households with faces: the challenge of gender in prehistoric architectural remains, in Gero & Conkey (ed.): 93–131.

—— 1993. Review of Gimbutas (1991). *American Anthropologist* 95: 196–7.

Tringham, R. E. & D. Krstic (ed.). 1990. *Selevac: a Neolithic village in Yugoslavia.* Los Angeles (CA): UCLA Institute of Archaeology Monumenta Archaeologica 15.

Ucko, P. J. 1968. *Anthropomorphic figures of predynastic Egypt and Neolithic Crete with comparative material from the prehistoric Near East and Mainland Greece.* London: Andrew Szmidla.

Van Leuven, J. 1993. Review of Gimbutas (1991). *Journal of Prehistoric Religion* 7: 83–4.

Wall, S. M., J. H. Musgrave & P. M. Warren. 1986. Human bones from a late Minoan 1b house at Knossos. *Annual of the British School at Athens* 81: 333–88.

Wylie, M. A. 1991. Gender theory and the archaeological record: why is there no archaeology of gender?, in Gero & Conkey (ed.): 31–47.

POSTSCRIPT

Was There a Goddess Cult in Prehistoric Europe?

Over the past 20 years a popular women's movement, the "Goddess Movement," has grown up, especially in the United States, around the idea that the earliest organized religion was based on worship of a supreme Goddess. This is largely a reaction against the perceived androcentrism and antifemale bias of Christianity, Judaism, Islam, and other world religions and of the civilizations they underpin. Proponents believe that by reviving this religion, they can undo the cultural and psychological harm inflicted on women (and men) by our long history of patriarchal religions and cultures.

Many feminist archaeologists are ambivalent toward the Goddess Movement and Gimbutas's contribution to it. They believe, on the one hand, that Gimbutas's work helps to correct the imbalance in conventional presentations of human prehistory, in which women are usually portrayed as minor bit players. But they are concerned about the quality of her methodology and theories. Feminist archaeologists also worry that Gimbutas's "old-fashioned" ideas, such as the notion of universal stages of cultural evolution and her static view of gender relations, do not contribute to an archaeology in which feminist views are an integral part.

For background on the Goddess Movement's roots in European thought, see Ronald Hutton's "The Neolithic Great Goddess: A Study in Modern Tradition," *Antiquity* (vol. 71, 1997). Also see Jane Ellen Harrison's *Prolegomena to the Study of Greek Religion* (Cambridge University Press, 1903).

For elaboration of Gimbutas's views, see her books *The Language of the Goddess* (Harper & Row, 1989), *The Civilization of the Goddess* (Harper & Row, 1991), and *The Living Goddesses* (University of California Press, 1999).

For critiques of the Goddess theory see Peter Ucko's works: his article "The Interpretation of Prehistoric Anthropomorphic Figurines," *Journal of the Royal Anthropological Institute* (vol. 92, 1962) and his monograph *Anthropomorphic Figurines of Predynastic Egypt and Neolithic Crete With Comparative Material From the Prehistoric Near East and Mainland Greece* (Royal Anthropological Institute, 1968). Also see Anne Baring and Jules Cashford's *The Myth of the Goddess* (Viking Press, 1991) and Margaret Conkey and Ruth Tringham's "Archaeology and the Goddess: Exploring the Contours of Feminist Archaeology," in D. C. Stanton and A. J. Stewart, eds., *Feminisms in the Academy* (University of Michigan Press, 1995). Conkey and Tringham's article also gives an excellent overview of the controversy and discussion of its significance for feminist archaeology.

ISSUE 6

Did Prehistoric Native Americans Practice Cannibalism in the American Southwest?

YES: Brian R. Billman, Patricia M. Lambert, and Banks L. Leonard, from "Cannibalism, Warfare, and Drought in the Mesa Verde Region During the Twelfth Century A.D.," *American Antiquity* (January 2000)

NO: Kurt E. Dongoske, Debra L. Martin, and T.J. Ferguson, from "Critique of the Claim of Cannibalism at Cowboy Wash," *American Antiquity* (January 2000)

ISSUE SUMMARY

YES: Archaeologists Brian Billman and Banks L. Leonard and bio-archaeologist Patricia Lambert argue that there is evidence of prehistoric cannibalism in the Mesa Verde region of southwestern Colorado. From their analysis of human skeletal remains and associated assemblages at Cowboy Wash, they conclude that the bodies of seven individuals were processed in ways that suggest that they were eaten by other humans.

NO: Archaeologists Kurt E. Dongoske and T.J. Ferguson and bioarchaeologist Debra L. Martin object that the analytical framework Billman et al. use assumes that cannibalism took place and does not adequately consider alternative hypotheses. Although Dongoske et al. feel that cannibalism was possible at Cowboy Wash, they contend that other interpretations of the same data are equally viable.

The idea that "primitive" people are prone to cannibalism has a long history in Western thought. During the Age of Exploration, European explorers eagerly sought and readily accepted reports that the tribal people they encountered were cannibals, and they used such claims as a justification for conquering, converting, enslaving, or exterminating them. Many societies around the world—including contemporary Pueblo peoples of the American Southwest—regard cannibalism as a sign of utter depravity and attribute it to enemy groups, despised minorities (such as Jews in medieval Europe), witches, or monsters. Until recently most cultural anthropologists believed that some tribal peoples had practiced cannibalism for various reasons, ranging from revenge against enemies to reverence for deceased relatives, but these practices ceased soon after European contact. Thus, cultural anthropologist William Arens caused a major sensation in 1979 when he wrote in his book *The Man-Eating Myth: Anthropology and Anthropophagy* (Oxford University Press) that he was highly skeptical that any people had ever practiced cannibalism as a socially approved institution. Most evidence of cannibalism, he said, was circumstantial or based on second- or thirdhand reports, often reports in which members of one group accused a neighboring, enemy group of the horrible deed.

Many archaeologists believe that some prehistoric peoples practiced cannibalism, and they have tried to specify the kinds of evidence that would indicate cannibalism in the archaeological record. Although archaeologists deal with hard evidence, such as bones and stone tools, that evidence must be interpreted. They try to imagine the most likely sequence of human behaviors and other events that could have produced the assemblage of bones and artifacts actually found, the process termed "taphonomy." Archaeologists have often invoked cannibalism when they find human bones that were apparently treated in the same fashion as the bones of game animals found at the same site. Biological anthropologist Christie Turner and others have developed lists of characteristics of bones and their context that they believe unequivocally indicate cannibalism, at least when found in combination. These include such features as cut marks on bones, split open long bones (as if the marrow was extracted), and burned bones (as if the flesh was cooked). Using these criteria, Turner has concluded that at least 38 archaeological sites in the American Southwest show evidence of cannibalism. Other archaeologists and biological anthropologists have objected that the evidence is inconclusive, as the same combination of characteristics could be due to other causes, such as revenge massacres, secondary burial practices, or deliberate mutilation of the bodies of suspected witches.

In the first selection, Billman, Lambert, and Leonard argue that a massacre and episode of cannibalism is the most plausible explanation for the assemblage of bone fragments and artifacts found at site 5MT10010 at Cowboy Wash. They examine cut marks on the bones, patterns of fractures, traces of blood on stone tools, and a coprolite (fossilized piece of excrement) for evidence supporting their hypothesis. They also point to indications that the site was abandoned immediately after the apparent episode of cannibalism. They go on to suggest that the attack and cannibalism were due to extreme drought and food shortages, which caused some groups to attempt to eliminate or drive off other groups that were competing for the limited resources.

In response, Dongoske, Martin, and Ferguson criticize Billman et al. for prematurely concluding that cannibalism took place at Cowboy Wash and for only adducing evidence that supports that conclusion. They point out that Billman et al.'s explanation ignores about 75 percent of the bone fragments found at the site, and they offer alternative possible explanations for the bone fragmentation, bone burning, blood traces on stone tools, and the coprolite containing human proteins.

Brian R. Billman, Patricia
M. Lambert, and Banks L. Leonard  **YES**

Cannibalism, Warfare, and Drought in the Mesa Verde Region during the Twelfth Century A.D.

Around A.D. 1150, a violent sequence of events took place at a small Puebloan habitation site (5MT10010) in southwestern Colorado. Seven individuals—men, women, and children—were systematically dismembered and defleshed. Body parts of at least three individuals were placed on a fire and roasted. After processing and discarding these remains, the perpetrators walked away, leaving human remains and tools scattered on the floors of two pithouses.

The possible existence of cannibalism has emerged as one of the most controversial issues in southwestern archaeology. Disarticulated, broken, and cut-marked human bone assemblages have been reported in the northern Southwest for nearly 100 years. Many investigators have proposed that at least some of those assemblages resulted from cannibalism. Turner and Turner have reviewed data from 40 sites in the American Southwest with disarticulated assemblages, and concluded that 32 sites meet their proposed criteria for the presence of cannibalism. Explanations for the occurrence of cannibalistic behavior in the American Southwest include starvation, pathological acts by deranged individuals, or social control. In contrast, others have proposed that these assemblages may have resulted from extreme violence or mutilation of the dead, the disturbance of secondary burials, or the destruction of witches.

Resolution of this controversial issue requires investigations at three scales of analysis. At the site level, fine-grained analyses of the condition and distribution of human remains and associated artifacts and ecofacts are required to reconstruct the formation processes that created and modified the assemblages. Next, settlement pattern data drawn from local surveys and the excavation of nearby contemporary sites are needed to examine the social context of the occurrences at the community level. Finally, regional analysis of the spatial and temporal distribution of similar assemblages is required to understand the historical development of the phenomenon. Both fine-grained studies of individual assemblages and reviews of their regional occurrence have been conducted. However, information on the local social context of these finds has been lacking, even though such data are essential for bridging the gap between site-specific and regional scales.

In this paper, we examine this issue by presenting the results of our investigation of 5MT10010 (a small Early Pueblo III habitation site in southwestern Colorado), the local settlement context of that site, and distribution of similar possible incidences of cannibalism in the Mesa Verde region. The results of our analysis of the battered, broken remains of seven individuals and associated artifacts recovered from the site implicate humans in the disarticulation and reduction of those bodies. Evidence of cooking of the human remains, blood residue found on associated tools, and analysis of an associated coprolite [piece of excrement] support our interpretation that people prepared and consumed human body parts. Local settlement pattern data indicate that 5MT10010 was part of a small community that may have been extinguished in a single, violent episode of raiding and cannibalism. Further, our review of well-documented cases of disarticulated and modified human remains in the Mesa Verde region points to a sharp increase in cannibalism around A.D. 1150, a time of drought and the collapse of the Chaco system. We propose that, faced with severe environmental stress, food scarcity, and sociopolitical upheaval in the mid A.D. 1100s, certain groups in the Mesa Verde region used violence to terrorize or even eliminate neighboring villages, and that cannibalism was part of this pattern of violence. This apparent outbreak of cannibalism subsided as rapidly as it began. No possible cases of cannibalism postdating A.D. 1200 have been reported in the Mesa Verde region, and few cases have been documented anywhere in the American Southwest after that date.

Numerous cases of cannibalism have been documented over the last 200 years in many different cultures throughout the world. Reasons for the occurrence of this practice range from ancestor worship, starvation, deviant acts by deranged individuals, or political terrorism. Although cannibalism apparently holds a macabre fascination with a wide segment of contemporary European and North American society—note the amount of media attention garnered by this issue in recent years—the occurrence of cannibalism in the American Southwest prior to European contact is not necessarily an issue of great importance in anthropology. However, the documentation of an outbreak of cannibalism and violence in the Mesa Verde region in the mid A.D. 1100s and the subsequent suppression of that behavior does raise questions of profound anthropological importance. Under what circumstances do groups of individuals turn to terroristic, violent, or genocidal; and under what circumstances do they turn away from it? In this paper we hope to move the debate from the issue of whether or not cannibalism occurred in the prehistoric Southwest to questions of broader anthropological significance. . . .

The Osteological Evidence for Cannibalism at 5MT10010

The osteological evidence for cannibalism at 5MT10010 is essentially the same as that described for an increasing number of sites in the American Southwest and elsewhere in the world. Turner and Turner summarize the taphonomic features used to identify cannibalism in the archaeological record to include "breakage, cutting, anvil or hammerstone abrasions, burning, missing vertebrae, and fragment polishing." . . . Other common characteristics of these assemblages, as summarized by Turner, include occurrence during "a single, short-term depositional episode, . . . good to excellent bone preservation, . . . nearly complete disarticulation of elements, . . . almost universal breakage of the head, face, long bones, [animal] gnawing on fewer than 5 percent of all specimens . . . ," and a high ratio of breakage to burning and cut marks. In addition, Villa notes the lack of evidence for even the most basic attempt at formal burial as an important criterion for distinguishing cannibalistic activities. . . . Collectively, these criteria indicate that human remains were treated like those of food animals found in archaeological contexts.

The evidence from 5MT10010 is consistent with these criteria. First, these remains were not intentionally buried, nor is there any indication that they were accorded respectful treatment. The treatment of the disarticulated remains at 5MT10010 was dramatically different from the treatment of most of the Puebloan period human remains recovered during the UMUILAP [Ute Mountain Ute Irrigated Lands Archaeological Project]. As elsewhere in the northern Southwest, individuals were interred in a flexed position with vessels and other burial goods, indicating concerned treatment of the dead. Although valuable artifacts were present in the pithouses at 5MT10010, their distribution did not correlate with that of the human remains, and they did not obviously constitute burial goods. . . . The mutilation and haphazard distribution of body parts preclude any notion of respectful treatment of the dead in pithouses at 5MT10010.

Second, evidence of perimortem dismemberment and bone breakage was abundant at 5MT10010, and included the disarticulation of bones at joints and heavy fracturing of skeletal elements. Almost no skeletal elements remained articulated, and perimortem breakage was apparent in many, including the cranial vault bones, ribs, marrow-rich long bones, and fat-laden vertebrae. According to Turner and Turner, the underrepresentation of vertebrae in particular may be attributable to their having been "smashed to extract their oily content by boiling."

Direct evidence of the use of tools to process the remains provides a third critical line of evidence. Following criteria detailed in White, marks identified as evidence for tool use included cut marks from sharp-edged knives, and chop marks, percussion pits, and percussion striae from chopping tools and hammerstones. In the 5MT10010 assemblage, cut marks were particularly apparent on the ribs, clavicles, humeri, and femora in proximity to sites of major muscle and connective tissue attachment, and provide evidence that bodies were processed while still covered with flesh. . . .

Notably, no canine puncture marks or other signs of carnivore involvement were observed in these remains, despite the presence of such damage on human remains from other sites in Cowboy Wash. In other words, carnivores were around and scavenged human corpses when they could, but they obviously did not have access to the bodies (at least, while fleshed) in this case.

Their condition therefore cannot reasonably be attributed to the activities of nonhuman scavengers.

Up to this point, a reasonable argument could still be made for mutilation without intent to consume the remains. However, the light color and excellent surface condition of the bones in this assemblage suggests that the flesh was removed from the bones, perhaps through stewing or boiling, rather than left to rot away over time. Even more compelling osteological evidence for the consumption of human remains at 5MT10010, however, is the distinct pattern of burning. Many, if not most, of the burned bones in this assemblage were exposed to fire while still covered with flesh, as the patchy distribution of scorch marks favoring exposed broken ends and thinly fleshed expanses clearly indicates. The absence of burn marks on the internal surfaces of many fire-affected cranial and limb elements further indicates that a second phase of disarticulation and breakage took place after rather than before cooking. It is difficult to argue that disposal was the ultimate goal of fire processing. None of the three pithouses was burned, nor were any of the bones from these structures calcined, as usually occurs with at least a portion of the skeleton in cremation. Rather, the browning and occasional blackening apparent in some of these remains is more consistent with limited, controlled exposure to fire for purposes of cooking the flesh. . . .

Although these lines of evidence indicate that seven people at 5MT10010 were mutilated and processed as though for consumption, the actual cause of death of each individual is obscured by subsequent activities. No projectiles or other weapons were found in association with the remains. Any one of a number of observed blows could have caused death. Establishing if any of the traumatic injuries was the cause of death was not possible. . . .

Cannibalism at 5MT10010: The Evidence from Ancient Feces

Although various lines of osteological evidence demonstrate that human body parts were butchered and cooked in the same manner that people prepared food animals for consumption, the bones from 5MT10010 do not document the actual ingestion of human flesh. The only scientific evidence that has the potential to bridge the gap between preparation and consumption is preserved human waste. Such evidence was previously lacking in contexts from which "cannibalized" human remains have been recovered. Thus, the human coprolite found in the hearth of Feature 15 provided a rare opportunity to establish such a link.

Analyses of the coprolite detected absolutely no macroscopic plant remains and found that starch granules and phytoliths were virtually absent. The absence of starch granules is a strong indication that maize kernels were not present in the meal or meals represented in the coprolite. The absence of macroscopic plant remains is extremely unusual for an Anasazi coprolite. The only pollen present was from Cheno-am, low-spine Compositae, and trace amounts of Poaceae, all of which could have derived from windblown, ambient pollen during spring. Characteristics of texture, color, and odor in a reconstituted sample of the coprolite indicated that the meal or meals it represented were probably entirely composed of meat. The size and shape of the coprolite demonstrate that it was of human origin.

Analysis of the coprolite by ELISA (enzyme immunosorbent assay) revealed the presence of human myoglobin in the coprolite. . . . Myoglobin is an oxygen-carrying molecule that transports oxygen from the surface of the muscle to the energy generating apparatus within the muscle. Myoglobin is found only in skeletal muscles and cardiac muscle cells. Importantly, it is not found in the smooth muscles of the digestive system, in blood, or in vascular tissue. Control tests were conducted to determine if human myoglobin is present in normal individuals (25 samples), individuals with blood in their stools (10 samples), or individuals that had consumed cooked beef within 24 hours (4 samples). None of these samples tested positive for human myoglobin. The stool samples from people who had eaten beef did test positive for bovine myoglobin, which demonstrates that myoglobin can survive the process of cooking and digestion and can be detected in human fecal material. In sum, results of the analysis of the human coprolite are consistent with osteological and artifactual evidence of cannibalism at 5MT10010 and demonstrate that human flesh was not only processed but also consumed at the site. This is the first direct evidence of the consumption of human flesh in the prehistoric Southwest.

Cannibalism on the Southern Piedmont of Ute Mountain

If we are to understand the butchering and consumption of human remains at 5MT10010, we must first understand the local social context of those acts. Fortunately, we are in a unique position to reconstruct the social history and organization of the community associated with the site. After several years of archaeological investigations conducted in the area, the Puebloan occupation of the southern piedmont of Ute Mountain is well documented. . . .

Investigations indicate that during the Puebloan era there were five separate occupations of the southern piedmont between A.D. 600 and 1280. During that period, the piedmont was abandoned more than it was occupied (approximately 380 years of abandonment and 300 years of occupation), a fact that attests to the marginal nature of the area. . . .

The focus of this paper is the occupation between A.D. 1075 and the early A.D. 1150s. At the start of that period, the pattern of settlement on the southern piedmont changed dramatically. In contrast to the dispersed pattern of occupation in late Basketmaker III (A.D. 600–725) and middle-to-late Pueblo II (A.D. 1050–1075), there was a significant influx of population and three communities were founded. The formation of these communities represents a third attempted colonization of the southern piedmont and a new colonization strategy. In this period, horticulturalists attempted to colonize the piedmont by establishing communities in the most productive areas of floodwater agriculture. Establishing integrated communities may have provided a means of sharing risk among households. . . .

The pattern of abandonment at these three sites . . . is remarkably similar to that of 5MT10010. The processing of human remains appears to have occurred at abandonment. Numerous artifacts, including whole ceramic vessels, ground and flaked stone tools, a rabbit blanket, a woven mat, and baskets, were left in the pithouses. Blood residue analysis indicates that some of the stone tools left behind at abandonment were used to butcher human remains. Like 5MT10010, contexts associated with the final use of the three sites—*in situ* hearth deposits, floors, and single event trash dumps near the time of abandonment—contained almost no cultivated plant remains. . . .

In summary, all of the excavated sites, and perhaps the entire early Pueblo III Cowboy Wash community, were abandoned suddenly just after the processing and consumption of humans. Community residents left behind large quantities of high-quality, valuable artifacts, many of which were light-weight and easily transportable. A significant portion of the community appears to be represented in the total assemblage of butchered human remains. Finally, the occurrence of cannibalism on the southern piedmont of Ute Mountain was temporally limited. Despite the excavation of 71 sites, including 29 habitation sites from all of the episodes of Puebloan occupation of the pied-mont, only one other possible incident of cannibalism has been found that does not clearly date to around A.D. 1150. . . .

The abandonment of the Cowboy Wash community around A.D. 1150 corresponds to a period of extreme drought from A.D. 1145 to 1193. Based on tree ring data, Burns has proposed that this was the second worst prolonged shortfall of corn yields in the period from A.D. 652 to 1968. Ethnobotanical evidence from the four sites likewise confirms that crop yields were probably very low and that stored domesticated foods probably were severely diminished at abandonment. The correlation of this outbreak of cannibalism at Cowboy Wash with the second worst regional drought in the tree-ring record surely is more than mere coincidence.

Cannibalism in the Mesa Verde Region

If the events at Cowboy Wash were isolated occurrences in the northern South-west, it would be easy to dismiss them as the pathological acts of a small group of demented individuals or a rare case of starvation induced cannibalism. How-ever, these sites are but four of 32 sites in the northern Southwest that have yielded similar assemblages of cut, battered, disarticulated, and partially burned human remains. In order to place the Cowboy Wash sites in the context of the prehistory of the Mesa Verde region, a subset of Turner's 32 possible cannibal-ism sites was reviewed. This review was limited to sites in the Mesa Verde region that are well documented and well dated, thus reducing the number of sites from 32 to 18.

Our review of primary sources on those 18 sites revealed two interesting patterns relevant to understanding the events that occurred at the aban-donment of the Cowboy Wash sites. First, there is a cluster of occurrences of cannibalism in the Mesa Verde region around A.D. 1150, the time of abandonment of the Cowboy Wash sites. . . . What these data suggest is that half of the well-documented, well-dated disarticulated assemblages from the 1,300-year Puebloan occupation of the Mesa Verde region occurred during a 25-year period between A.D. 1150 and 1175. The other nine sites date to between A.D. 850 and 1125. Although there apparently was a severe outbreak of cannibalism between A.D. 1150 and 1175, cannibalism may have occurred periodically for several hundred years prior to that outbreak. In other words, these data suggest that, although occurrences were rare prior to A.D. 1150, there may have been an existing local precedent for cannibalism in the Mesa Verde region.

The second pattern revealed by the review of literature relates to the types of sites where cannibalized assemblages were found. In the Southwest, sites with these kinds of human remains can be divided into three distinct types: isolated assemblages found away from habitation sites, habitation sites with dumped secondary deposits, and habitation sites with *in situ* floor deposits. Isolated assemblages have been reported from a few locations in the Southwest, including one of the 18 sites in the Mesa Verde region.

At sites with secondary deposits, butchered human remains are located in pits, trash deposits, or the fill of abandoned rooms, but not on the floors or other use surfaces of structures. This pattern suggests that human bodies were processed at the site, after which the butchering areas were cleaned and the remains dumped elsewhere on the site with no effort at formal burial. Of the 18 Mesa Verde sites, only 5MTUMR2346 in Mancos Canyon may fit this pattern. . . .

As the name suggests, sites with *in situ* floor deposits have scatters of human remains on the floors of structures. Human remains were deposited at the time of abandonment and apparently resulted from the *in situ* processing of human beings. Numerous artifacts were left behind in association with the human remains, including butchering tools, personal ornaments, and typical domestic artifacts such as metates, manos, and whole ceramic vessels. Eight of the nine sites dating between A.D. 1125 and 1175 have these characteristics. In contrast to the secondary deposit sites, assemblages at these sites appear to have resulted from a single, intense episode of cannibalism, rather than several episodes spread over the duration of the occupation of the site.

Explaining Cannibalism in the American Southwest

Many explanations have been offered for these assemblages of broken, battered, and sometimes partially burned human remains. Andrew Darling and others have proposed that disarticulated remains found at prehistoric Puebloan sites were the result of executions of individuals, families, or even villages suspected of practicing witchcraft and cannibalism. Based on a review of ethnographic literature on historic pueblos, Darling argues that witchcraft was so closely associated with acts of human sacrifice and cannibalism in Puebloan traditions that the concepts of witch and cannibal became virtually synonymous. Further, he notes that the physical destruction of witches played a large role in ridding the community of evil influences and preventing sickness. His reconstructed model of witch execution involves a trial of the suspect followed by death, dismemberment, defleshing, and burning.

Darling's argument has several shortcomings, as do similar reconstructions. First, Darling unintentionally provides evidence for the existence of cannibalism, albeit couched in terms of witchcraft. Many of his accounts specifically mention cannibalism or suspected cannibals, suggesting that the practice existed even if it was not socially sanctioned. Second, his argument is limited by a lack of historic or ethnographic evidence of dismemberment, defleshing, and burning of witches. His compiled research on 24 Zuni witch trials suggests that witch executions might have occurred in the historic period, but he does not present accounts of what happens to the bodies of witches after execution. Perhaps because of this lack of historical evidence, Darling is unable to propose a set of material correlates for distinguishing cannibalism from witch execution in the archaeological record. Instead he offers a hypothetical reconstruction of the disposal of bodies that follows exactly the same steps as cannibalism except for the final consumption of flesh.

One possible distinguishing trait between witch destruction and cannibalism is the degree of burning of the bodies of suspected witches. Darling emphasizes the importance of burning for purification. However, at 5MT10010 and similar sites, many bones show no signs of direct fire exposure and those that do generally exhibit a patchy distribution of browning and occasional blackening more consistent with cooking than with incineration.

In contrast, Turner and Turner have argued that these assemblages are clearly the remains of cannibalism, a finding that has been supported by our analysis and independent analyses such as White, Dice, and Minturn. . . .

A third possible explanation for the occurrence of these disarticulated human remains in the region is hunger-induced cannibalism, as is documented in France and Germany during the Middle Ages, during Euroamerican expeditions to the Canadian Arctic, during the settlement of the western American frontier, and during World War II when Japanese troops on the Kokoda trail of New Guinea were isolated from supplies. Indeed, the low incidence of cultigens at the Cowboy Wash sites and the date of their abandonment in a period of regional drought are consistent with simple food shortage as an explanation.

Several aspects of the evidence at sites like 5MT10010 do not resemble historic accounts of simple, hunger-induced cannibalism. First, such incidents typically occurred within groups that were trapped by severe winter conditions, held prisoner, or cut off during military campaigns. In those cases, escape was impossible, and all other food resources were depleted or unreachable. The Cowboy Wash area is low in elevation and lacks insurmountable barriers to movement even in winter. Thus, dispersal from the sites to other areas may have been possible. Numerous instances of population movement at both local and regional levels are known for prehistoric and historic Puebloan groups, and immigration clearly was an important strategy for coping with environmental and social stress.

Second, all of the people in these assemblages appear to have been processed, if not consumed, in one incident. There is no evidence that people were consumed slowly over a period of weeks or months as individuals gradually succumbed to hunger, disease, or ongoing military action.

Finally, as previously noted, the demographic profile of the Cowboy Wash assemblage differs in important respects from natural death profiles. Infants and young children—the age group most susceptible to malnutrition and disease—are present but are significantly underrepresented. Older children and adolescents, on the other hand, are more common than in natural death profiles from the region.

Osteological data from the other Puebloan habitation sites excavated during the UMUILAP shed light on the social context of events at 5MT10010. Traumatic injuries likely to have resulted from interpersonal conflict were common in the individuals recovered during the course of the UMUILAP. . . .

These data are evidence that the cannibalistic events that culminated in the abandonment of the southern piedmont took place in a climate of violence. The death of many of the inhabitants of Cowboy Wash in a single incident and the apparent sudden and complete abandonment of the community following that incident is consistent with a successful attack by an outside group. Because the Cowboy Wash community was relatively small and isolated compared to other communities in the region, it was vulnerable to attack. Further, the presence of large quantities of Chuskan ceramics demonstrates that the community either consisted of Chuskan immigrants or had closer ties with groups outside the Mesa Verde region than with groups within the region. Such a situation would have made the community more susceptible to aggression by other local groups.

Whereas the present data strongly suggest that site inhabitants were the victims in Cowboy Wash, and perhaps in the majority of cases in the Mesa Verde region, the identity of the perpetrators is less clear. Although it seems likely that another Anasazi group or groups were involved, the data are insufficient on this point. . . .

The outbreak of violence around A.D. 1150 may have been caused by severe drought and possibly the social and ideological breakdown that followed the abandonment of Chaco Canyon and the collapse of the Chaco system. The reshuffling of the population in the San Juan basin and Mesa Verde region introduced outsiders into new areas, perhaps upsetting local intercommunity alliances that had maintained peace. The search for diminishing resources in the face of drought also would have heightened competition and increased psychological stress. Violence, raiding, and warfare have been documented as one response to environmental stress and resource scarcity in the American Southwest and elsewhere in the world. Mutilation and consumption of individuals killed in conflict is a potential strategy for instilling fear in opposing groups. In the mid A.D. 1100s, certain groups in the Mesa Verde region may have used just such a practice to terrorize, intimidate, or even eliminate neighboring villages, especially those composed of recent immigrants to the region or whose primary alliances were with groups outside the region. In that time of severe drought, human flesh also could have constituted an important spoil of war.

Whatever the root cause, the outbreak of cannibalism apparently stopped as suddenly as it began. Tree-ring and regional settlement pattern data indicate that by the end of A.D. 1100s, much of the Mesa Verde region was abandoned, possibly due to the worsening environmental and social conditions. When climatic conditions improved in the early A.D. 1200s, the area was reoccupied by Puebloan groups until the final abandonment of the region around A.D. 1280. Although osteological evidence from Cowboy Wash and archaeological data from elsewhere in the northern southwest demonstrate that lethal violence continued in late Pueblo III times, no incidents of cannibalism have been reported in the Mesa Verde region after A.D. 1200. The occurrence of an even more severe drought in the Mesa Verde region in the late A.D. 1200s may not have resulted in any incidents of cannibalism. Beyond the Mesa Verde region, only two cases of disarticulated, modified human remains associated with Puebloan sites has been documented in the entire northern Southwest after A.D. 1200. The reason for the sudden demise of this one- or two-generation outbreak of cannibalism and violence remains even more mysterious than its origins. . . .

Kurt E. Dongoske, Debra L. Martin,
and T. J. Ferguson

 **NO**

Critique of the Claim of Cannibalism at Cowboy Wash

The article by Billman et al. contributes to a growing body of data that demonstrates the complex variability of the Pueblo world during the twelfth century. Although the article's title promises a comprehensive review of major cultural and environmental processes (drought, warfare, cannibalism, regional interactions), relatively little theory regarding these processes informs their research design, and much of their interpretation is based on weak inferences. The empirical data they present are not used to test alternative hypotheses or rigorously examine expectations derived from modeling. Dynamic aspects of cultural patterns relating to migration, settlement, environment, abandonment, mortuary behaviors, conflict and group identity are implicated in their research but are not adequately contextualized.

The conclusion that cannibalism occurred at Cowboy Wash is founded, like the majority of other recent claims of cannibalism, on the assumption that perimortem modification of human bone (i.e., breakage, cutmarks, percussion striae, burning, missing vertebrae, and fragment end "polishing") in *every case* is due to cannibalism. Billman et al. draw primarily on Turner's accounts of alleged cannibalism in the Southwest for their methodology. The authors argue that if human bones are processed and deposited in a manner thought to be similar to the bones of game animals, then the only possible conclusion is that human flesh was consumed. At Cowboy Wash, the claim for cannibalism is specifically said to be based on 1) human involvement in the disarticulation and reduction of seven bodies, 2) evidence of cooking of the human remains, 3) blood residue found on associated tools, and 4) analysis of a coprolite.

Our response to the study by Billman et al. is intended to provide a critical yet constructive commentary, propose fresh ways of thinking about what assemblages of disarticulated and broken bones might mean, and reformulate how research questions are being asked. We believe that the research approach used in the Cowboy Wash study, and other studies that narrow the focus to cannibalism, is ultimately too limited to address the full range of variability that exists in disarticulated and broken bone assemblages. In many ways, this approach lacks a rigorous scientific approach that uses hypothesis testing and strong inferences to deduce patterns and interpretations about complex human behaviors. There is a tendency to assume that there is just one means to an end, and to force data to fit preconceived notions about past cultural and formation processes.

In our comments, we seek to generate a dialogue regarding the method and theory used to study disarticulated bone assemblages and conflict in the American Southwest. In so doing, we consider the variation and ambiguities in the data, and suggest avenues for a more rigorous approach in future research. We begin with a few general comments, and then specifically address the four lines of evidence advanced by Billman et al. as support for their interpretation that people prepared and consumed human body parts.

General Comments about Cowboy Wash Archaeology and the Study of Cannibalism

The article by Billman et al. is essentially a site report that focuses on the categories of data the authors think support their conclusion. Cannibalism is invoked in the title and sets the tone for the study. In pre-emptive strikes, the authors provide what we think is superficial denouncement of alternative hypotheses such as witch execution, secondary burial, ritualized dismemberment, and massacre. As archaeologists, we can generate any number of interesting and even fantastical hypotheses, but because we work with a particular kind of empirical data, these hypotheses need to be framed in such a way that evidence can be used to either reject or fail to reject them. In contrast, the Cowboy Wash study essentially asserts that cannibalism has been found and presents the data in particular ways that bolster rather than tests that assertion.

As anthropologists, we are concerned with the indiscriminate use of the word cannibalism. Cannibalism has many meanings, all of which have loaded cultural connotations, and carries some very heavy historical and emotional baggage. The word was concocted by Columbus to label the people he first encountered (the Tainos). He referred to all of the groups on the islands as "caribes," who he believed were flesh-eaters, and this term helped to ideologically pave the way for the eventual campaign of conquest, Christianization, and genocide that followed. Any characterization of Indians as "cannibals" dredges up a long history of oppression and racism, and we have to realize that this may generate ill-will and negative emotions about archaeology in many descendant communities.

The anthropological discourse on cannibalism has been used in the past to establish differences and construct racial boundaries dividing "civilized" people from the "other." Anthropological accounts of cannibalism are part of a "we/they" dichotomy that legitimizes treating the "other" as inferior. This has implications for how archaeological studies are used in a larger social context. As Kilgour has observed, cannibalism is gaining force as a symbol associated with the tools of oppression used by a guilty imperial past and fears about the present. Much of the anthropological literature on cannibalism is a meta-myth used as a means of boundary definition in the construction of Western identity. Historically, the conceptualization of cannibalism has been used both as a foil for emerging Western identity and as a legitimization of cultural appropriation.

We raise this point not out of an attempt to be politically correct but to simply draw attention to the larger discourse in which our archaeological findings are used. Archaeologists need to think about the broad social and cultural implications of their research. With respect to cannibalism, this does not mean that it is a forbidden subject for investigation but that its investigation must meet the most rigorous scientific standards possible. Since much rides on claims of cannibalism, the standards of proof must be high. Our work will be appropriated by the popular press so our research must be unassailable, and we must be precise in what we mean when we use the term cannibalism.

In the literature that documents cultures where cannibalism is said to have been practiced, a wide range of behaviors fall into that category. These include exocannibalism (eating those outside your group), endocannibalism (eating those within our group), ceremonial cannibalism (eating small token amounts), ritualized cannibalism (more ritual than gastronomical), vengeance cannibalism (more symbolic than gastronomic), and psychopathic cannibalism (Jeffrey Dahmer comes to mind). Some may argue that it would be too difficult to tease apart these various kinds of behaviors from the present data. However, we believe that a discussion of the variability in the possible motivations for cannibalism would be useful and necessary to generate more complex and multifaceted theories.

Arens has challenged virtually all ethnographic and historical accounts of cannibalism as a cultural practice (as opposed to survival cannibalism, e.g., a plane crash in the Andes), claiming they rest upon embarrassing and unsupported empirical grounds. According to Arens, ethnographic investigations of cannibalism have tended to document the existence of cannibalism after the cessation of the presumed activity, rather than observing and describing it in the present tense. Arens argues that the good anthropology involves the description of custom prior to its interpretation. Arens' thesis is controversial, of course, and has been challenged by many critics who question the methods and data used in his historical analysis.

We think archaeology has a vital role to play in the investigation of cannibalism. As White has pointed out, "Cannibalism is a globally claimed but sparsely documented human behavior. Its spatial and temporal dimensions, situational contexts, and archaeological signatures are poorly understood." Given the absence of uncontested ethnographic documentation of cannibalistic behavior, we think that archaeology may offer the best, and perhaps only, means to scientifically verify the occurrence of anthropophagy as a cultural practice. Like Arens, we do not argue that customary cannibalism did not exist in the past, only that the current evidence for it is weak. If it existed in the past, there should be incontrovertible archaeological evidence of its existence. . . .

Osteology and Taphonomy: Evidence for Cannibalism?

We have methodological concerns about the use of taphonomy in the Cowboy Wash study. Our experience with disarticulated and broken bones is that stratigraphy and depositional history is crucial for understanding these bone assemblages. Bone by bone placement vis-à-vis other artifacts in horizontal and stratigraphic profile are key elements in unraveling the sequence and ordering of the various processes that effected where the bones ended up, how they came to be broken and burned, and what kinds of processes mimic each other. Taphonomic analysis is difficult and complex, particularly when assemblages have had multiple steps involved in their modification and interment. The categories of bone changes used by Billman and colleagues are very narrowly conceived (i.e., breakage, tool marks, burning). Accounting for the presence and absence of these observations artificially reduces them in scope and meaning.

For example, to understand how a bone came to have a spiral fracture, it is crucial to know its placement, impact, size of area affected, and relationship to other indicators such as percussion pits, adherent flakes, incipient fracture lines, conchoidal scars, percussive striae, flaking, and peeling. In other words, not all spiral fractures are created equal. These variables can provide crucial data about how the bone came to be broken with a high degree of specificity and this can define a number of taphonomic processes at work. Burning is likewise a very broad, diverse, and problematic category to describe as simply a present or absent phenomenon because there are literally a dozen or so factors involved in how burning affects bone surfaces. Burning is extremely difficult to detect and differentiate when it alters the bone slightly and mimics normal weathering. Dry or wet bone, high or low heat, and short or long exposure all differentially affect bone surfaces. In short, these categories of bone changes are complex, multifaceted, and important to document using as fine-grained analysis as possible. The behaviors that led to the events examined by the authors are obviously complex and possibly not singular.

We are disappointed that the reporting of osteology and taphonomy in the Cowboy Wash study does not present the data in the detail needed to meaningfully compare this assemblage with other assemblages. White recommends procedures for the recovery and analysis of broken and scattered human bone from archaeological and forensic contexts. He identifies 17 variables of bone modification that are relevant to claims of cannibalism. Only 4 variables (perimortem breaks, cut marks, chop marks, burning) are reported in the Cowboy Wash study, thus masking the variability that is essential to understanding human behavior and formation processes.

Furthermore, the Cowboy Wash study does not adequately account for all the bone specimens (individual pieces of bone). For instance, the Feature 3 assemblage contained 1,150 bone specimens, yet only 287 minimum number of elements (MNE) are tabulated; the Feature 13 assemblage contained 479 bone specimens, yet only 86 MNE are tabulated. How conjoinable bones were handled in the analysis is not adequately described. Presumably the remaining bones in the assemblages were unidentifiable but these are not accounted for in the tables. As White demonstrates, indeterminate bones can be grouped into meaningful categories, including indeterminate cranial fragments, various types of indeterminate long bones, and completely indeterminate bone groups. Understanding the human modification of these indeterminate categories of bone is essential to unraveling the taphonomic processes of the assemblage. As far as we can determine, in the Cowboy Wash study these indeterminate bones apparently constitute about 75 percent of the total assemblage. . . .

For too long, skeletal and mortuary analyses in the Southwest have focused on normative assumptions. This practice has greatly hampered our ability to see the abundance of variability in mortuary behavior both within and among sites and regions. There have not been any good studies of what the "rules" are for disposal of the dead in Ancestral Pueblo communities. Even the ethnohistoric information on preparation and disposal of the dead is not well known. It is possible that in the ancient Southwest there were cultural norms about the proper curation of some bones in some contexts at some sites that involved bone reduction, modification, and secondary burial. Why not? We simply do not know at this point what constitutes normal mortuary behavior. Therefore, it is difficult to consider all of the disarticulated remains that have been recovered over the years to be abnormal and the result of cannibalism or even violence. And it is even more problematic to lump all of the disarticulated remains together under a single cause.

We provide one cautionary example here. There were three disarticulated bone assemblages from the La Plata Highway project examined by a team of osteologists (led by Martin) in conjunction with archaeologists at the Museum of New Mexico. Turner and Turner also analyzed these remains but mistakenly concluded that all of the bone deposits were the result of cannibalism. A detailed taphonomic analysis conducted by Akins demonstrated quite conclusively that one of the assemblages was due to carnivore damage and recent (trenching) damage, one was due to ancient movement of remains and secondary burial, and one was likely due to some human activity involving dismemberment and intentional arrangement. The La Plata study demonstrates that three seemingly similar bone assemblages upon closer inspection using a more fine-grained taphonomic and contextualized analysis are actually dissimilar, and the products of several very different processes.

Evidence for Cooking Human Remains?

Billman et al. assert that "evidence of cooking of human remains" supports their interpretation of cannibalism. The only direct evidence that might indicate cooking is burned bones, and, in fact, Billman et al. assert these burned bones indicate parts of two individuals were "roasted." This raises a question about how the body parts of the other five individuals were cooked. . . .

There are other questions about the patterning of burned bones in the site assemblage. Billman et al. state that, "Many, if not most, of the burned bones in this assemblage were exposed to fire while still covered with flesh, as the patchy distribution of scorch marks favoring exposed broken ends and thinly fleshed expanses clearly indicates." As discussed above, the tabulation of burning as a presence/absence variable makes this difficult to evaluate. The elements tabulated for the two bone assemblages also exhibit different patterns of burning that remained unexplained with respect to possible consumption. Billman et al. add that the burning patterns indicate "a second phase of disarticulation and breakage took place after rather than before burning," yet the explanation of this postburning breakage is not adequately addressed. While these patterns are certainly intriguing, we do not think in and of themselves they are evidence of cooking. The behaviors that would produce these patterns are not described, and an alternate explanation (as offered below) is possible.

Indirect evidence of cooking might include breakage of marrow-rich long bones and breakage of bones into small pieces that could fit into stew pots. In this regard, however, no "pot polishing" was observed in the assemblage. Billman et al. state that the pale color of bones "could" have resulted from processing for fat extraction and "may" provide a line of evidence for stewing. They suggest that the reduction strategy "may" have served the specific purpose of producing pot-sized fragments. Billman et al. assert that "the remains resembled refuse from animal foods consumed by Cowboy Wash inhabitants" but do not present the comparative data needed to assess this claim. All in all, we find the evidence for cooking to be suggestive but equivocal.

Blood Residue Analysis: Evidence for Cannibalism?

Billman et al. contend that the identification of human blood on two sharp lithic flakes is supporting evidence that these tools were used in the process of defleshing human remains. We believe that this is circumstantial evidence and does not corroborate a conclusion that human remains were processed for consumption. An alternative explanation for the appearance of human blood residue on lithic flakes, as any flintknapper can attest to, is the frequency that one experiences cuts on the hands during the knapping process. Therefore, it would not be unreasonable to expect blood residue on these artifacts as a result of a prehistoric "accident" in tool manufacture or resharpening. An equally valid alternative explanation is that these artifacts could contain human blood residue as a result of low-level contamination produced during the handling of the artifacts during excavation. Thus, Billman et al.'s conclusion that the blood residue analysis indicates that some of the identified tool kits were used to butcher the human remains is at best premature, but more probably an unreliable conjectural conclusion. . . .

Fecal Evidence for Cannibalism?

The article presents the analysis of fecal material as the "smoking gun" proving cannibalism. This is hard to accept based solely on three paragraphs of discussion. We are left with the perception that the authors are asking us to "trust" their conclusion, without offering us an in-depth discussion of the analytical process used to derive the data used in their conclusion. We note that the techniques used to analyze the fecal data offered as conclusive evidence for cannibalism are as yet unsupported, unverified, and unreplicated by other scientists in different laboratories. The mere citation of a letter on file from a microbiologist is not satisfactory.

While the actualistic studies reported by Billman et al. indicate that bovine myoglobin can survive cooking and digestion for 24 hours, blood proteins are known to degrade with time. Whether or not human myoglobin survives in analytically traceable amounts for 800 years or more has yet to be determined. With ELISA, problems with degradation of blood proteins may result in antigen binding that produce nonspecific results.

While ELISA is a standard technique for these kinds of assays, we need to know that the small coprolite retrieved was never directly handled by any humans because this could contaminate the material by introducing foreign proteins (found in abundance on everyone's hands). This sort of contamination is known to affect immunological methods in molecular paleontology.

Because the fecal data are so sketchy, the authors out of necessity focused on Reinhard's process of elimination method in which the absence of macroscopic plant remains suggests that the coprolite did contain meat. This line of reasoning using negative evidence is weak and unconvincing. We do not accept the authors' conclusion that the fecal data "... is the first direct evidence of the consumption of human flesh in the prehistoric southwest." We have to ask the question: Isn't anyone else bothered by the fact that there were virtually *no* plant remains in the fecal material? Is this even possible in humans? Although Reinhard says this is surely a human piece of feces, we would like other scientists (faunal specialists) to verify that this is not in fact a carnivore coprolite.

We are not microbiologists, and therefore before accepting the claim that the coprolite contains human myoglobin, we await peer review and publication of the fecal study by *Science* or another scientific journal specializing in biomolecular research. As presented in the Cowboy Wash study, the fecal evidence is suggestive but not convincing. More work pursuing this line of evidence is warranted in future studies.

Aspects of Archaeological Context

In part, a mode of "abandonment" described as "catastrophic" is used as a line of evidence supporting the claim of cannibalism. In the Feature 3 pithouse, the inference of rapid abandonment is based on *in situ* artifacts and disarticulated human remains found on the floor and in the southern chamber. However, the bone pile in the southern chamber is reported to "lay on top of a layer of trash that was deposited well before abandonment." At the same time, Billman et al. infer that "evidently the bone in this pile was dumped down the ventilator shaft from the ground surface at the time of site abandonment." Apparently, the authors think the trash in the southern chamber was either dumped down the ventilator shaft or dragged into the chamber during the occupation of the pithouse. Whether or not this pattern of trash deposition would foul the air drawn down the ventilator shaft is not addressed by the authors, yet this is a relevant issue to their reconstruction of the occupational history of the structure. We have questions but no answers as to what this means in terms of their argument. Trash deposition in a occupied structure seems to be an anomaly. . . .

Finally, Billman et al. suggest there was a "ritual" placement of scapulae on either side of the deflector in the Feature 3 pithouse. This sort of ritual behavior seems somewhat contradictory to the dominant theme of the paper that violent cannibalism was a form of disrespect. After a brief mention of the possible ritual placement of human remains, the authors never return to considering what this means in terms of their interpretation of cannibalism, or in terms of distinguishing between different kinds of cannibalism.

Alternative Explanations

One can easily develop alternative explanations for the disarticulated and broken bone found at Cowboy Wash. In their discussion of disarticulated, butchered, burned, and commingled human remains recovered from two puebloan sites in northwestern New Mexico, Oglivie and Hilton offer warfare and secondary mortuary practices as alternative explanations to cannibalism. In their discussion, Oglivie and Hilton cite Willey's Crow Creek Massacre as an example of prehistoric warfare that resulted in the disarticulated and butchered human remains in the archaeological record. This mass interment contained the modified remains of at least 486 men, women, and children from the Plains site in South Dakota. The osteological evidence of warfare consisted of mutilations including scalping, blows to the head, evulsions, decapitation, burning, and dismemberment. Interestingly, Willey noted that the bone damage patterns resulting from warfare mimicked those patterns seen in butchered faunal assemblages.

For the sake of argument, we offer the following alternative hypothesis that accounts for the osteological data. The small community was attacked by unknown perpetrators. Many of the community members escaped but some were captured and killed. As was done in Kosovo and Rwanda in recent times, individuals were hacked repeatedly. Some bodies fell near fires or in fires and were subjected to burning. Perpetrators ransacked the site and took what they wanted. The perpetrators left. Carnivores dragged off key pieces of the bodies. Later, the survivors returned and gathered up all remaining body parts and deposited them in two pitstructures as a form of burial and last rites, and quickly relinquished use of the site for habitation.

Breakage associated with violent death, ritualized dismemberment, and movement of cadavers in varying states of decomposition by carnivores or humans can account for all the bone damage reported by Billman et al.. What we thus have are plausible but mutually exclusive explanations for the same archaeological assemblage. As scientists, we think the fact that one or the other of the hypotheses can't be proven false with the existing data indicates we simply don't yet know enough about the phenomena. The need for more study is indicated before conclusions about cannibalism are made.

Theoretical Considerations

In writing about what he considered to be an incident of cannibalism in the Mesa Verde region, White cautioned that "Just as no person characterizes all American pioneers of the last century as cannibals on the basis of cannibalism of the Donner Party, no person should characterize all Anasazi as cannibals." Yet this is essentially what Billman et al. do in developing a theoretical perspective on the purported "outbreak of cannibalism" they say characterized the twelfth century in the Mesa Verde region.

In offering an explanation for cannibalism, Billman et al. leap from 5MT10010 to all of Cowboy Wash and the Mesa Verde region. They assert there are similarities in processing of disarticulated human remains throughout the region but no data describing these similarities are presented or analyzed. In considering the regional context, Billman et al. refer to 18 *"possible* cannibalism sites" and then in the next paragraph promptly describe these sites as a "severe outbreak of cannibalism." Why the authors move from discussion of "possible" cannibalism sites to writing about them as if they were all confirmed incidents of cannibalism begs explanation. These things bring to mind Arens' admonition that we need to describe a custom prior to its interpretation.

Billman et al. speculate that "correlation of this outbreak of cannibalism at Cowboy Wash with the second worst drought in the tree-ring record surely is more than mere coincidence." However, only half of the disarticulated assemblages in the Mesa Verde region temporally coincide with the Cowboy Wash sites, so the authors conclude that cannibalism may have occurred periodically for several hundred years prior to the Cowboy Wash "outbreak." At the same time, they suggest cannibalism occurred over two centuries, they claim that cannibalism never became a multigenerational or institutionalized practice. They seem to want it both ways—a phenomenon spanning centuries and an "outbreak" concomitant with people leaving the sites they dug.

While Billman et al. suggest the low incidence of cultigens and the abandonment of the Cowboy Wash sites in a period of drought are consistent with hunger-induced cannibalism, they note that other aspects of the situation are not, i.e., the Cowboy Wash residents were free to migrate to other areas, and the incidence of purported cannibalism occurred in one brief episode rather than over a long period, as is found in historical cases of starvation cannibalism. A climatic explanation for cannibalism as a way to obtain a source of food in hard times ultimately fails because the purported behavior apparently occurred in both good and bad climatic regimes.

Billman et al. then suggest that cannibalism is related to terrorism used to control scarce resources in a time characterized by severe drought and, possibly, a social and ideological breakdown that accompanied the collapse of the Chaco regional system. Again, however, the occurrence of disarticulated and broken bone assemblages over a period of 200 years seems to argue against this as an explanation. Turner and Turner's thesis that cannibalism was a terroristic behavior introduced by cannibal warriors from Mexico led by a psychopath like Charles Manson does not seem to apply to Cowboy Wash because a lack of Chacoan outliers seems to indicate the area did not directly participate in the Chacoan system. Furthermore, the violence at Cowboy Wash occurred after the occupation of Chaco, and no mechanism for diffusion of this form of social behavior is offered.

A smorsgabord of theoretical variables and explanations is offered in the Cowboy Wash study to explain mutilation and consumption of human beings.

In the end, however, this pastiche of notions is unsatisfying, and the authors acknowledge they haven't really explained cannibalism by beginning their concluding paragraph with the statement, "Whatever the root cause . . ." The study ends by noting that the weather in the Mesa Verde region improved, and while lethal violence continued elsewhere in the northern Southwest, there are no more incidents of cannibalism in Mesa Verde, even though a more severe drought occurred. The authors conclude, "The reason for the sudden demise of this one- or two-generation outbreak of cannibalism and violence remains even more mysterious than its origins."

Unless and until archaeologists can offer a theory that accounts for cannibalism over many generations, and during varying climatic regimes, we do not think cannibalism is the best or only explanation for assemblages with disarticulated and broken bones. We are also concerned about a theory that only explains a portion of the total variability in disarticulated assemblages. Turner and Turner list 76 sites with disarticulated and broken bones, only 38 of which are reputed to evidence cannibalism. What about the other half of the variability? We think we need a model that explains the full range of variability, not just a portion of it.

Given the relative rarity of sites with assemblages of disarticulated and commingled human remains, and the long time span that applies to these assemblages, we think it is probable that there are multiple explanations for their occurrence. As White concluded, "It is premature to offer comprehensive regional explanations for the assemblages . . . and there is no reason to conclude that the reasons behind them will not be multiple and independent." Assemblages of disarticulated and commingled human remains in the northern Southwest are phenomena that span at least 800 years and tens of thousands of square kilometers of space. These assemblages occur in a variety of archaeological contexts, including rock shelters, crypts, open sites, pit structures, kivas, and pueblo rooms. Patterns of perimortem modification of the human remains in these assemblages vary, and there are thus a number of different possible explanations to account for their presence in archaeological sites.

In the final analysis, we think the statement that the entire early Pueblo III Cowboy Wash community was perhaps "abandoned suddenly after the processing and consumption of humans" remains a supposition rather than a demonstrated fact. If nothing else, the Cowboy Wash study indicates that the theory of cannibalism in the Southwest is weak and in need of further development. . . .

POSTSCRIPT

Did Prehistoric Native Americans Practice Cannibalism in the American Southwest?

Billman, Lambert, and Leonard see the evidence that cannibalism took place at site 5MT10010 at Cowboy Wash as so compelling that they quickly dismiss all alternative possible explanations of the assemblage. They regard the presence of human myoglobin in a coprolite (piece of excrement) as conclusive proof that humans ate other humans there. Dongoske, Martin, and Ferguson respond that the evidence lends itself to several possible interpretations, of which cannibalism is only one. In their view, Billman et al.'s classification of the cut marks on the bones, for example, is too crude to distinguish whether the bodies were dismembered for food or as part of some mortuary practice. They also argue that the coprolite should be tested by other independent labs, and they ask whether it might have been produced by a carnivorous animal, rather than a human being.

This controversy centers on one of the fundamental problems in archaeology, namely that the physical remains in archaeological sites do not speak for themselves. They must be interpreted. The analyst must engage in a process of deduction that goes from the physical evidence to an account of the probable human actions and natural processes that produced the existing pattern of remains. More adventurous scholars then go on to speculate about *why* the people carried out those actions. Some archaeologists believe that physical remains are a better route to the "truth" about a culture than what living people say they do and believe. In a famous study, archaeologist William Rathje and his colleagues at the University of Arizona showed, by analyzing people's garbage, that middle class suburbanites in Tucson, Arizona, inaccurately describe their patterns of consumption to researchers, for example, by understating the amount of beer they consume at home. On the question of whether the ancestors of the Pueblo Indians practiced cannibalism, bioarchaeologist Christy Turner has been quoted as saying that "we can't trust the ethnographic record. When the Spanish arrived, they dictated to the Puebloans what they should and shouldn't do" (Constance Holden, "Witches or *Cannibals*," *Science*, January 29, 1999). Archaeologists of this persuasion seem to see the actions and statements of living peoples as merely obscuring what really happened. Similarly, some argue that we should not depend too much on the "ethnographic analogy"—the reconstruction of behavior at an archaeological site by comparison with the documented behavior of recent societies of a similar type in a similar environment—as this precludes our recognition of prehistoric behaviors that were completely different from recent ones. This consideration is particularly important when dealing with our prehuman ancestors, who might or might not have behaved like fully modern humans. Thus, even if we believe that most if not all people today view a practice such as cannibalism with horror and disgust, how can we know that people in prehistoric times didn't see it as perfectly normal and reasonable?

Other archaeologists, however, view archaeological remains as inherently ambiguous, contending that we can seldom know for certain the nature of the human actions that produced an assemblage of material remains, much less the reasons for and meanings of those actions. They argue, therefore, that we must consider clues from the ethnographic record, ethnohistorical records, and the cultures of the still-living descendants of the people who produced the remains. For those archaeologists, the attitude of modern and historically documented Pueblo Indians toward cannibalism *is* relevant to the interpretation of Anasazi remains, as it helps to assess the likelihood of the various actions that could have produced the remains, including cannibalism, mortuary practices, and witch execution. They argue that those who ignore the influence of the cultures of the producers are in danger of interpreting the evidence on the basis of their own unexamined cultural assumptions, including assumptions about human nature. For them the question of whether cannibalism was actually widely practiced during historical times, or whether it was falsely attributed to tribal peoples by European explorers, is relevant to the interpretation of archaeological evidence, as it gives an idea of how common it would have been prehistorically.

The literature on the issue of prehistoric cannibalism is growing rapidly. Useful overviews of the question of whether cannibalism occurred in the American Southwest include Stephen Plog's article "Social Conflict, Social Structure and Processes of Culture Change" (*American Antiquity* 68(1), 2003) and Randall H. McGuire's article "Stories of Power, Powerful Tales: A Commentary on Ancient Pueblo Violence" (*The Dynamics of Power*, Maria O'Donovan, ed., Center for Archaeological Investigations, Southern Illinois University, Occasional Paper No. 30, 2002). Important works supporting the occurrence of cannibalism in the American Southwest include Tim White's book *Prehistoric Cannibalism at Mancos* (Princeton University Press, 1992), a detailed analysis of the evidence from one site; Christy and Jacqueline Turner's book *Man Corn: Cannibalism and Violence in the Prehistoric American Southwest* (University of Utah Press, 1999), which summarizes evidence for the region as a whole; and Sharon Hurlbut's article "The Taphonomy of Cannibalism: A Review of Anthropogenic Bone Modification in the American Southwest" (*International Journal of Osteoarchaeology* volume 10, 2000), which includes a comparison of a variety of postmortem bone modifications found worldwide. Billman et al. offer their rebuttal of Dongoske et al. in P.M. Lambert et al.'s article "Response to Critique of the Claim of Cannibalism at Cowboy Wash" (*American Antiquity* 65, 2000). Tim White reports on recent research in Europe, claiming that cannibalism was practiced by *Homo antecessor* about 800,000 years ago and by Neanderthals about 100,000 years ago in his article "Once Were Cannibals" (*Scientific American*, special edition, July 2003).

The Chimpanzee and Human Communication Institute Home Page

The Chimpanzee and Human Communication Institute provides information on this site about current research on teaching American Sign Language to chimpanzees. The site includes information about experiments with chimps as well as links to other sites dealing with the question of whether apes can learn a language.

http://www.cwu.edu/~cwuchci/

UsingEnglish.com

UsingEnglish.com contains a page that has information on the Sapir-Wharf hypothesis. Also on this page is a link to a discussion on this topic. Numerous links to sites on the subject from various sides can also be found on this page.

http://www.usingenglish.com/speaking-out/
linguistic-whorfare.html

The Language of Thought Hypothesis

The Language of Thought Hypothesis site provides a description of the hypothesis, which proposes that thought and thinking take place in a mental language. This site also contains a summary of arguments that support and refute this hypothesis.

http://www.seop.leeds.ac.uk/entries/
language-thought/

PART 3

Linguistic Anthropology

*L*inguistic anthropologists study languages, particularly non-Western and unwritten languages. They also investigate the complex relationship between language and other aspects of culture. Language provides the categories within which culture is expressed and is the medium by which much of culture is transmitted from one generation to the next. Here we consider two classic questions that have confronted linguistic anthropologists for several decades. The first concerns whether chimpanzees and other apes have the innate ability to use symbols in ways that resemble human language. This question is important because if apes are capable of complex symbolic activity, then language and culture are probably not the exclusive capabilities of humans but have their origins in our primate past. The second question concerns whether categories of a language shape how humans perceive and understand the world. Although first proposed early in the twentieth century, this issue continues to be one of the central questions in linguistic anthropology.

- Can Apes Learn Language?

- Does Language Determine How We Think?

ISSUE 7

Can Apes Learn Language?

YES: E. S. Savage-Rumbaugh, from "Language Training of Apes," in Steve Jones, Robert Martin, and David Pilbeam, eds., *The Cambridge Encyclopedia of Human Evolution* (Cambridge University Press, 1999)

NO: Joel Wallman, from *Aping Language* (Cambridge University Press, 1992)

ISSUE SUMMARY

YES: Psychologist and primate specialist E. S. Savage-Rumbaugh argues that, since the 1960s, attempts to teach chimpanzees and other apes symbol systems similar to human language have resulted in the demonstration of a genuine ability to create new symbolic patterns.

NO: Linguist Joel Wallman counters that attempts to teach chimps and other apes sign language or other symbolic systems have demonstrated that apes are very intelligent animals, but up to now these attempts have not shown that apes have any innate capacity for language.

For more than a century anthropologists have generally assumed that humankind's ability to make tools and use language are two characteristics that distinguish humans from other animals. In the 1960s and 1970s Jane Goodall and other primatologists convincingly demonstrated that chimpanzees, our nearest biological relatives, made simple tools, thus narrowing the gap between apes and humans. Beginning in the 1940s a series of other scientists have worked with gorillas, chimps, and most recently the bonobo (or pygmy chimp), attempting to teach these apes simple forms of human-like language.

In the 1950s psychologist B. F. Skinner argued that human children learn natural language through conditioning, such that positive responses to utterances from proud parents and other adults essentially train children to recognize both grammatical patterns and vocabulary. But in the 1960s linguist Noam Chomsky disproved Skinner's theory, showing that human language is so highly complex that it must require some innate biological capability, which he called a "language acquisition device." In several respects, all of the ape-language experiments since then have sought to understand when this biological capacity for language learning evolved in primates.

The early years of the ape-language projects encountered one major difficulty. Try as they might, trainers could not get apes to vocalize human words reliably. This difficulty was a consequence of the fact that a chimp's vocal apparatus simply does not allow the possibility of human utterances.

Since Chomsky's studies of human language, linguists have generally accepted that the manipulation of symbols in systematic grammatical ways, rather than the ability to make utterances, is the most important and complex aspect of human language. Thus, if apes could manipulate symbols in linguistic ways, researchers hoped they could demonstrate that the ability to acquire language is a biological trait shared by at least certain species of the apes and humans.

If true, the ability to learn and use language, the last barrier that separates human beings from our nonhuman primate relatives, has fallen away. This view has its supporters and detractors, many of whom—largely on political or religious grounds—would either like to see humans as just another of the great apes or would prefer to view human beings as unique in the animal kingdom. But at issue is whether or not the long series of ape-language projects has demonstrated that apes can learn to manipulate signs and symbols.

E. S. Savage-Rumbaugh and her husband Duane Rumbaugh have been among the most innovative researchers in their field at the intersection of anthropology, linguistics, and cognitive psychology. They argue that of all the great apes a certain species of pygmy chimps, the bonobo, is biologically closest to *Homo sapiens.* Their recent work with a bonobo named Kanzi has been among the most successful of these ape-language projects. After tracing the history of these projects, Savage-Rumbaugh concludes that Kanzi's ability to use symbols closely resembles similar abilities observed among young human children.

Joel Wallman interprets the evidence very differently from Savage-Rumbaugh. He acknowledges that the various gorillas, chimps, and bonobos are clever animals, which have learned to respond to their trainers. But he argues that these animals have not learned anything resembling human language. However, chimps and bonobos are clever animals, and while they do not have full linguistic abilities, their abilities to use mental abstractions suggest that at least modest versions of these mental processes arose before our branch of the hominoid lineage split off from the lineage of the great apes.

These selections raise a number of questions about the similarities and differences between apes and humans. What kind of linguistic ability do these ape learners exhibit? Do their symbolic strings genuinely parallel early childhood language acquisition? Most importantly, do these ape-language studies show that apes and human beings genuinely share a common ability for language? What are the minimal features that make up any natural language?

Language Training of Apes

Can apes learn to communicate with human beings? Scientists have been attempting to answer this question since the late 1960s when it was first reported that a young chimpanzee named Washoe in Reno, Nevada had been taught to produce hand signs similar to those used by deaf humans.

Washoe was reared much like a human child. People made signs to her throughout the day and she was given freedom to move about the caravan where she lived. She could even go outdoors to play. She was taught how to make different signs by teachers who moved her hands through the motions of each sign while showing her the object she was learning to 'name'. If she began to make a portion of the hand movement on her own she was quickly rewarded, either with food or with something appropriate to the sign. For example, if she was being taught the sign for 'tickle' her reward was a tickling game.

This training method was termed 'moulding' because it involved the physical placement of Washoe's hands. Little by little, Washoe became able to produce more and more signs on her own. As she grew older, she occasionally even learned to make new signs without moulding. Once Washoe had learned several signs she quickly began to link them together to produce strings of signs such as 'you me out'. Such sequences appeared to her teachers to be simple sentences.

Many biologists were sceptical of the claims made for Washoe. While they agreed that Washoe was able to produce different gestures, they doubted that such signs really served as names. Perhaps, to Washoe, the gestures were just tricks to be used to get the experimenter to give her things she wanted; even though Washoe knew how and when to make signs, she really did not know what words meant in the sense that people do.

The disagreement was more than a scholarly debate among scientists. Decades of previous work had demonstrated that many animals could learn to do complex things to obtain food, without understanding what they were doing. For example, pigeons had been taught to bat a ball back and forth in what looked like a game of ping pong. They were also taught to peck keys with such words as 'Please', 'Thank you', 'Red' and 'Green' printed on them. They did this in a way that made it appear that they were

From E. S. Savage-Rumbaugh, "Language Training of Apes," in Steve Jones, Robert Martin, and David Pilbeam, eds., *The Cambridge Encyclopedia of Human Evolution* (Cambridge University Press, 1999). Copyright © 1999 by Cambridge University Press. Reprinted by permission.

communicating, but they were not; they had simply learned to peck each key when a special signal was given.

This type of learning is called *conditioned discrimination* learning, a term that simply means that an animal can learn to make one set of responses in one group of circumstances and another in different circumstances. Although some aspects of human language can be explained in this way, such as 'Hello', 'Goodbye', 'Please' and 'Thank you', most cannot. Human beings learn more than what to say when: they learn what words stand for.

If Washoe had simply signed 'drink' when someone held up a bottle of soda, there would be little reason to conclude that she was doing anything different from other animals. If, however, Washoe used the sign 'drink' to represent any liquid beverage, then she was doing something very different—something that everyone had previously thought only humans could do.

It was difficult to determine which of these possibilities charcterised her behaviour, as the question of how to distinguish between the 'conditioned response' and a 'word' had not arisen. Before Washoe, the only organisms that used words were human beings, and to determine if a person knew what a word stood for was easy: one simply asked. This was impossible with Washoe, because her use of symbols was not advanced enough to allow her to comprehend complex questions. One- and two-year-old children are also unable to answer questions such as these. However, because children are able to answer such questions later on, the issue of determining how and when a child knows that words have meanings had not until then been seen as critical.

Teaching Syntax

Several scientists attempted to solve this problem by focusing on sentences instead of words. Linguists argue that the essence of human language lies not in learning to use individual words, but rather in an ability to form a large number of word combinations that follow the same set of specific rules. These rules are seen as a genetic endowment unique to humans. If it could be shown that apes learn syntactical rules, then it must be true that they were using symbols to represent things, not just perform tricks.

Three psychologists in the 1970s each used a different method in an attempt to teach apes syntax. One group followed the method used with Washoe and began teaching another chimpanzee, Nim, sign language. Another opted for the use of plastic symbols with the chimpanzee Sarah. Still another used geometric symbols, linked to a computer keyboard, with a chimpanzee named Lana. Both Lana and Sarah were taught a simple syntax, which required them to fill in one blank at a time in a string of words. The number of blanks was slowly increased until the chimpanzee was forming a complete 'sentence'. Nim was asked to produce syntactically correct strings by making signs along with his teacher.

Without help from his teachers, Nim was unable to form sentences that displayed the kind of syntactical rules used by humans. Nim's sign usage could best be interpreted as a series of 'conditioned discriminations' similar to, albeit more complex than, behaviours seen in many less-intelligent animals. This work suggested that Nim, like circus animals but unlike human children, was using words only to obtain rewards.

However, the other attempts to teach sentences to apes arrived at a different conclusion, perhaps because a different training method was used. Both Sarah and Lana learned to fill in the blanks in sentences in ways that suggested they had learned the rules that govern simple sentence construction. Moreover, 6 per cent of Lana's sentences were 'novel' in that they differed from the ones that she had been taught. Many of these sentences, such as 'Please you move coke in cup into room', followed syntactical rules and were appropriate and meaningful communications. Other sentences followed the syntactical rules that Lana had learned, but did not make sense; for example, 'Question you give beancake shut-open'. Thus, apes appeared to be able to learn rules for sentence construction, but they did not generalise these rules in a way that suggested full comprehension of the words.

By 1980, Washoe had matured and given birth. At this time there was great interest in whether or not she would teach her offspring to sign. Unfortunately, her infant died. However, another infant was obtained and given to Washoe. This infant, Loulis, began to imitate many of the hand gestures that Washoe used, though the imitations were often quite imprecise. Washoe made few explicit attempts to mould Loulis's hands. Although Loulis began to make signs, it was not easy to determine why he was making them or what, if anything, he meant. Loulis has not yet received any tests like those that were given to Washoe to determine if he can make the correct sign when shown an object. It is clear that he learned to imitate Washoe, but it is not clear that he learned what the signs meant.

The question of whether or not apes understand words caused many developmental psychologists to study earlier and earlier aspects of language acquisition in children. Their work gave, for the first time, a detailed insight into how children use words during the 'one-word' stage of language learning and showed that children usually learn to understand words before they begin to use them. At the same time, there was a new approach to the investigation of ape language. Instead of teaching names by pairing an object with its sign or symbol and rewarding correct responses, there was a new emphasis on the communicative aspect of symbols. For example, to teach a symbol such as 'key', a desirable item was locked in a box that was given to the chimpanzee. When the chimpanzee failed to open it, he was shown how to ask for and how to use a key. On other occasions, the chimpanzee was asked to retrieve a key for the teacher, so that she might open the box.

This new approach was first used with two chimpanzees named Sherman and Austin. It resulted in a clearer symbolic use of words than that found in animals trained by other methods. In addition, because these chimpanzees were taught comprehension skills, they were able to communicate with one another and not just with the experimenters. Sherman and Austin could use their symbols to tell each other things that could not be conveyed by simple glances or by pointing. For example, they could describe foods they had seen in another room, or the types of tools they needed to solve a problem. Although other apes had been reported to sign in each other's presence, there was no evidence that they were intentionally signing to each other or that they responded to each other's signs.

Most important, Sherman and Austin began to show an aspect of symbol usage that they had not been taught; they used symbols to say what they were going to do *before* they did it. Symbol use by other apes had not included descriptions of intended actions; rather, communications had been begun by a teacher, or limited to simple requests.

Sherman and Austin also began to use symbols to share information about objects that were not present and they passed a particularly demanding test, which required them to look at symbols and answer questions that could be answered only if they knew what each symbol represented. For example, they could look at printed lexigram symbol such as 'key', 'lever', 'stick', 'wrench', 'apple', 'banana', 'pineapple' and 'juice', and state whether each lexigram belonged to the class of 'food' words or 'tool' words. They could do this without ever being told whether these lexigram symbols should be classified as foods or tools. These findings were important, because they revealed that by using symbols an ape can describe what it is about to do.

How Similar Is Ape Language to Human Language?

Even though it was generally agreed that apes could do something far more complex than most other animals, there still remained much disagreement as to whether ape's symbols were identical to human symbols. This uncertainty arose for two reasons: apes did not acquire words in the same manner as children—that is, by observing others use them; and apes did not appear to use true syntactical rules to construct multiple-word utterances.

The first of these differences between ape and child has recently been challenged by a young pygmy chimpanzee or bonobo named Kanzi. Most previous studies had focused on common chimpanzees because pygmy chimpanzees are very rare (they are in great danger of having their habitat destroyed in the coming decade and have no protected parks).

In contrast to other apes, Kanzi learned symbols simply by observing human beings point to them while speaking to him. He did not need to have his arms placed in position, or to be rewarded for using a correct symbol. More important, he did not need to be taught to comprehend symbols or taught that symbols could be used for absent objects as well as those present. Kanzi spontaneously used symbols to announce his actions or intentions and, if his meaning was ambiguous, he often invented gestures to clarify it, as young children do.

Kanzi learned words by listening to speech. He first comprehended certain spoken words, then learned to read the lexigram symbols. This was possible because his caretakers pointed to these symbols as they spoke. For example, Kanzi learned 'strawberries' as he heard people mention the word when they ran across wild strawberries growing in the woods. He soon became able to lead people to strawberries whenever they asked him to do so. He similarly learned the spoken names of many other foods that grew outdoors, such as wild grapes, honeysuckle, privet berries, blackberries and mushrooms, and could take people to any of these foods upon spoken request.

Unlike previous apes reared as human children, Kanzi was reared in a semi-natural woodland. Although he could not produce speech, he understood much of what was said to him. He could appropriately carry out novel spoken requests such as 'Will you take some hamburger to Austin?', 'Can you show your new toy to Kelly?' and 'Would you give Panzee some of your melon?'. There appeared to be no limit to the number of sentences that Kanzi could understand as long as the words in the sentences were in his vocabulary.

During the first 3 or 4 years of his life, Kanzi's comprehension of spoken sentences was limited to things that he heard often. However, when he was 5 years old, he began to respond to novel sentences upon first hearing them. For example, the first time he heard someone talk about throwing a ball in the river, he suddenly turned and threw his ball right in the water, even though he had never done this before. Similarly, when someone suggested, for fun, that he might then try to throw a potato at a turtle that was nearby, he found a potato and tossed it at the turtle. To be certain that Kanzi was not being somehow 'cued' inadvertently by people, he was tested with headphones. In this test he had to listen to a word and point to a picture of the word that he heard. Kanzi did this easily, the first time he took the test.

About this time, Kanzi also began to combine symbols. Unlike other apes, he did not combine symbols ungrammatically to get the experimenter to give something that was purposefully being held back. Kanzi's combinations had a primitive English word order and conveyed novel information. For example, he formed utterances such as 'Ball go group room' to say that he wanted to play with a specific ball—the one he had seen in the group room on the previous day. Because the experimenter was not attempting to get Kanzi to say this, and was indeed far from the group room, such a sentence conveyed something that only Kanzi—not the experimenter—knew before Kanzi spoke.

Thus Kanzi's combinations differed from those of other apes in that they often referred to things or events that were absent and were known only to Kanzi, they contained a primitive grammar and were not imitations of the experimenter. Nor did the experimenter ask rhetorical questions such as 'What is this?' to elicit them, Kanzi's combinations include sentences such as 'Tickle bite', 'Keep-way balloon' and 'Coke chase'. As almost nothing is yet known of how pygmy chimpanzees communicate, they could use a form of simple language in the wild. Kanzi understands spoken English words, so the ability that is reflected in language comprehension is probably an older evolutionary adaptation than is the ability to talk.

Studying ape language presents a serious challenge to the long-held view that only humans can talk and think. Certainly, there is now no doubt that apes communicate in much more complex and abstract ways than dogs, cats and other familiar animals. Similarly, apes that have learned some language skills are also able to do some remarkable non-linguistic tasks. For example, they can recognise themselves on television and even determine whether an image is taped or live. They can also play video games, using a joystick to catch and trap a video villain.

Scientists have only just begun to discover ways of tapping the hidden talents for language and communication of our closest relatives. Sharing 98 per cent of their DNA with human beings, it has long been wondered why African apes seem so much like us at a biological level, but so different when it comes to behaviour. Ape-language studies continue to reveal that apes are more like us than we ever imagined.

Joel Wallman  **NO**

Aping Language

Experiments carried out over the past two decades . . . attempted to impart a language, either natural or invented, to an ape. The debate engendered by these projects has been of interest—consuming for some, passing for others— to all of those whose concerns include the enduring questions of human nature, among them anthropologists, psychologists, linguists, biologists, and philosophers.

An adequate treatment of the linguistic capabilities of apes entails consideration of a number of related issues, each of which is an interesting problem in its own right. Continuities in primate mentality, the relationship between language and thought in the individual and in the species, and the origin of language . . . are themes that . . . recur throughout this [debate].

. . . [N]one of the ape-language projects succeeded, despite employing years of tutelage far more intense than that experienced by most children, in implanting in an ape a capacity for language equal to that of a young child, let alone an adult. . . .

Why the Ape-Language Controversy Is a Controversy

All scientific arguments have in common at least these elements: (1) a minimum of two positions regarding the subject in dispute, positions generally held to be irreconcilable, and (2) an intensification of the normal emotional investment of the scientist in his or her position, due in some measure to the contending itself but perhaps also related to the ideological significance of the subject within the larger society. If, in addition, the argument includes suggestions of fraudulent or quasi-fraudulent procedures, the disagreement becomes a controversy. To the extent that this is an accurate characterization of scientific controversies, the ape-language debate is an exemplary one.

The radical opposition of opinion about the achievement of the various ape-language projects is well conveyed by the following quotations:

> [Washoe] learned a natural human language and her early utterances were highly similar to, perhaps indistinguishable from the early utterances of human children. (Gardner and Gardner 1978, p. 73)

The evidence we have makes it clear that even the brightest ape can acquire not even so much as the weak grammatical system exhibited by very young children. (Premack and Premack 1983, p. 115)

On measures of sign performance (form), sign order (structure), semantic relations (meaning), sign acts (function) and sign acquisition (development), apes appear to be very similar to 2 to 3 year old human children learning sign . . . Apes also appear to be very similar to 2 to 3 year old human children learning to speak. (Miles 1978, p. 114)

[The experimental chimpanzees] show, after years of training and exposure to signing, not the slightest trace of homological development parallel to that of human children. (Leiber 1984, p. 84)

After years of gentle teaching Koko has learned to use American Sign Language—the very same sign language used by the deaf. With her new-found vocabulary, Koko is now providing us with an astounding wealth of knowledge about the way animals view the world. (Patterson 1985a, p. 1) . . .

There are several sources of the stridency of the debate.

. . . [L]anguage, at least in the European intellectual tradition, is the quintessential human attribute, at once evidence and source of most that is transcendent in us, distinguishing ours from the merely mechanical nature of the beast. Language is regarded as the *sine qua non* of culture, and its presence in our species is the most salient behavioral difference between us and the other hominoids—with the relinquishing of tool use and, more recently, tool making (Goodall 1971; Beck 1980) as uniquely human capabilities, the significance of language as a separator has grown. And resistance to losing our quintessential attributes is, arguably, itself one of those uniquely human traits. Hence, some ape partisans (Linden 1974; Gysens-Gosselin 1979) have argued, the prevalent reluctance to accord the talking apes their due. An occasional variant of this interpretation is the accusation that those who refuse to recognize ape language are insufficiently committed to the Darwinian perspective or, worse, are anti-Darwinian. Thus Linden (1987) depicts those who question the likelihood of ape–human linguistic continuities as latter-day Wilberforces, averse to investigating "creatures who threaten to paralyze us by shedding light on the true nature and origins of our abilities" (p. 8).

A countervailing vector of our ideology, perhaps peculiar to our culture but possibly pancultural, consists of careless anthropomorphic projection and an irrepressively attractive vision of communication between our own and other species. In fact, it seems correct to observe that, at least until recently in the debate and probably up to the present, the majority opinion, both lay and scientific, regarding the linguistic capabilities of the apes has been positive. People seem not only accepting but positively desirous of the possibility of ape language.

Even if language did not have the sacrosanct status it does in our conception of human nature, the question of its presence in other species would still promote argument, for we are lacking any universally accepted, unassailable diagnostic criteria for language. There is no shortage of candidates for the indispensable attribute of language. For Katz (1976) and Limber

(1977), the projective capability is crucial, the provision of language for the articulation of any conceivable new proposition through a novel combination of words. Savage-Rumbaugh (1981) holds the referential nature of individual symbols to be the essence of language, while Premack (1984) and Marshall (1971) see the capacity for representation of real-world situations to be paramount, and so on. The property most commonly invoked as definitive of language is its predication on a system of abstract rules for the production and interpretation of utterances—in other words, grammar. Hockett's (1959, 1960, 1963; Hockett and Altmann 1968) famous list of so-called design features of language—including rapid fading, duality of patterning, and displacement—has provided a useful orientation for those trying to capture the differences between human and nonhuman natural systems of communication. What is wanting, nonetheless, is consensus on what the necessary and sufficient, as distinguished from inessential, property or properties of language are and hence on how we might unequivocally identify language in another species.

This problem of defining features is more severe where the language of the young child is concerned, and it is the child's language that is taken by most parties to the debate to be the proper material for comparison with the apes. If the young child is not, in fact, capable of linguistically encoding anything she can think of, if her production and understanding of utterances do not suggest abstract grammatical constituents and processes, then can it be said that the child has language? Limber (1977) and Lightfoot (1982), at least, would say no.

This is a defensible position, its major problem found in the fact that the young child's language, which may not yet be language, will eventually become language. How is this discontinuity in development to be bridged? The difficulty is not the existence of a discontinuity per se—there are a number of others in human development. The physiological transition from prepubescence to pubescence, for example, poses a similar problem—the two developmental phases are identifiably distinct, yet there are no two adjacent points in time about which it could be said that the child was prepubescent in the first but pubescent in the second.

What makes the transition from "nonlanguage" (. . . early language) to language more problematic is that, unlike the case of puberty, in which the first phase is defined largely by the absence of characteristics of the later one, early language has its own, very salient features. Moreover, there are some striking functional and possibly structural similarities between these features and those of adult language. . . . And, contrary to those who would deny language to the young child, there is extensive evidence for grammatical structure in the earliest word combinations (Bloom 1970; Brown 1973), and, some have suggested (De Laguna 1927; McNeill 1970), in single-word utterances as well. (The proper characterization of this structure, however, is the subject of ongoing debate in developmental psycholinguistics—in fact, this may be the dominant concern of the field. . . .

Language, in summary, is central to our self-definition as a species, even though we have yet to derive an adequate definition of language itself, one that includes the essential but excludes the merely contingent.

Behaviorist Roots of the Ape-Language Experiments

There is an additional source of the contention surrounding the ape-language question. The issues in the debate tend to resonate along the longstanding cleavage within the behavioral sciences between those who advocate study of cognition and/or innately determined behavior, on the one hand, and those, on the other, who are behaviorist in method and theory.

Behaviorism, or stimulus–response psychology, came into being in the early decades of this century as an avowed antidote to the introspectionist trend in turn-of-the-century psychological investigation. Knowledge, thought, intention, affect, and all other unobservable mental phenomena were banished in favor of overt behavior as the only proper subject of a scientific psychology. To explain the behavior of animals, behaviorism, like the eighteenth-century empiricism from which it descends, posits a bare minimum of cognitive apparatus: (1) perception, (2) a capacity to represent in durable format the results of perception, and (3) the ability to form associations among those representations. In the behaviorist paradigm, the acquisition and strengthening of such associations constitute learning.

An association may be formed between a perceptual stimulus and an inborn response if that stimulus consistently accompanies another one that is innately connected to the response, as in the celebrated conjunction of the ticking of a metronome, food, and salivation in Pavlov's dogs. Or an animal may form an association between one of its own actions and a subsequent stimulus, as when a pigeon comes reliably to peck a button because its activation results in the dispensing of food. In this process, an association is created between an action and a following stimulus that "reinforces" that action. To qualify as a reinforcing stimulus, a consequence need not be one that we would regard a priori as satisfying or pleasant—in fact, any stimulus that increases the probability of the organism emitting the behavior that preceded it is, by definition, reinforcing.

In the behaviorist conception, all behavior is determined either by current stimuli or by past consequences. Language is verbal behavior; words function both as responses to stimuli and as stimuli themselves, eliciting further responses. Thus a sentence can be interpreted as a chain of stimulus–response events, each word a response to the preceding one and also a stimulus evoking the next, with the first word elicited by an environmental stimulus or an internal one, a "private event." Or, in some formulations, the entire sentence is regarded as one complex response to a stimulus.

The orthodox behaviorist account of learning has little use for traditional distinctions among types of behavior. Nor are species differences in behavioral mechanisms acknowledged. Although sometimes touted as such, the latter attitude is not an appreciation of evolutionary continuity, with the selectively and historically wrought similarities and divergences in behavior that such a theoretical affirmation entails. Rather, it reflects a commitment to cross-species *homogeneity,* a rejection of the notion that there are important differences across species in the processes that underlie the development and causation of behavior. . . .

Like other contemporary adherents of behaviorism, the ape-language experimenters embraced the various concessions to reality that the most primitive versions of behaviorism were forced to make over the years. The Gardners, for example, acknowledge that some parts of the innate behavioral repertoire of a species are more plastic and hence more readily conditioned than others, and also that species differ in their intrinsic propensities for various behaviors. Thus the chimpanzee's inborn motivation to communicate obviates conditioning as laborious as another behavior might require. That language acquisition in the chimpanzee and in the child are similarly dependent on extensive molding, shaping, and imitation, however, is an assumption that is fundamental to their research, and fundamentally erroneous. Indeed, their suggestion that the linguistic performance of the preschool child requires "intensive training" (1971, p. 188) is the *opposite* of one of the few claims to which virtually all language-acquisition researchers would assent. . . .

Lastly, it may be worth observing that the potential personal rewards of the ape projects have been substantial and emotional commitment commensurately high—the first person or team to give language to another species would certainly attain scientific immortality.

⋅⟨❀⟩⋅

. . . In describing their aspirations for Washoe, the first of the modern apelanguage pupils, the Gardners expressed pessimism about a direct assault on the question "Can an ape talk?" and . . . adopted instead an unabashedly behavioristic goal: "We wanted to develop behavior that could be called conversation" (1969, p. 665). And critics . . . have maintained that Washoe and her peers, though they may have simulated conversation, acquired neither a human language nor something crucially like one, but rather a system of habits that are crude facsimiles of the features of language.

Refuting the claim that apes have the ability to learn a language logically entails proving that they do *not* have it. This [selection] has not succeeded in doing something that cannot be achieved: proving that something does not exist. The relevant refutable claim, rather, is that one or more of the animals featured in these pages learned a language. Refuting this unequivocally, however, presupposes a set of definitive criteria for language and a demonstration that at least one of them was not met by each of the animals in question. . . . [S]uch criteria do not yet exist, either for adult forms or for children's forms of language. So it is not possible in principle to show that no ape *could* learn a language, and it is not possible in practice to show that none *has* learned a language. . . .

The ape-language experiments confirmed what students dating back at least as far as the gestalt psychologist Wolfgang Kohler have repeatedly demonstrated, which is that apes are highly intelligent creatures, probably second only to us, on measures of human intelligence. We may wonder how the evolutionary process engendered such a powerful mentality in the midst of the African rain forests, asking, like Humphrey (1976), of what use "conditional oddity discrimination" is to an ape in the jungle. But the cognitive prowess of the apes is a fact regardless of our inability to account for it.

That the apes, too, are reflexive and capable of impressively abstract mentation suggests that at least modest versions of these faculties arose before the ancestral hominoid lineage diversified into the African apes on the one hand and us on the other. Consider a modest assertion: a capacity for culture requires at least ape-level powers of abstraction. And a case could be made for self-awareness, too, as prerequisite to culture. To the extent that Freud's understanding of humanity's cultural creations as "immortality projects" is sound, an ego is presupposed. If the capacity for language, too, had arisen prior to that last hominoid divergence, then linguistics might have been a branch of comparative psychology, the ape-language experiments would never have been conceived, and this [selection] would have been about something else, say patterns of interspecies marriage. But, for that matter, had language arisen prior to the split that produced them and us—had we all spoken the same language—there might not have been a them and an us.

POSTSCRIPT

Can Apes Learn Language?

The two sides on the issue of ape-language ability remain widely separated. At the heart of the issue are several questions about (1) the biological nature of human beings and their nearest primate relatives; (2) the character of language and cognition, particularly among children who are just beginning to acquire language; and (3) the best and most unbiased methods for investigating apelanguage abilities.

One of the strongest critics of the ape-language experiments is the cognitive psychologist Steven Pinker, who outlines his arguments in his book *The Language Instinct* (HarperCollins, 1994). Pinker argues that ape trainers have inadvertently used very subtle conditioning to train their primates. The sequences of symbols produced by even the most talented of the apes are far simpler than normal children's linguistic abilities. His view is that Savage-Rumbaugh and other trainers have overinterpreted the primate symbolic sequences and ignored numerous random "utterances." Chimps and bonobos may be clever animals, he concedes, but their cleverness is conditioned along the lines that Skinner had proposed; it is not linguistic behavior as understood by Chomsky and most linguists. If true, Pinker's criticism suggests that all of the ape-language projects have been failures, and at best trainers have tricked themselves into believing that apes can use symbols in linguistic ways.

Do the ape-language experiments introduce bias by interpreting symbolic strings too broadly and ambiguously? Are detractors of these experiments themselves biased, refusing to believe that apes are capable of any human-like linguistic or cognitive processes? And even if these experiments do not demonstrate an ability to use symbols in ways that precisely parallel child language use, can they not tell us a great deal about general patterns of cognition relevant to both humans and primates?

If Pinker is correct that humans use a different part of the brain for language than do apes when making natural vocalizations, then the efforts to demonstrate language ability in even the brightest of the great apes may ultimately be unsuccessful. Nevertheless, as Wallman and Savage-Rumbaugh suggest, however primitive apes' use of symbols may be, researchers may still learn a great deal about certain kinds of cognitive processes. If research does convincingly show that apes have some kind of language capability, there is still much to be learned about ape cognition in several of the areas that Savage-Rumbaugh has suggested.

Such advances are possible only if ape-language researchers can develop research methods that are completely free from bias and inadvertent human conditioning of their ape subjects. While Savage-Rumbaugh and the other researchers have tried to minimize the possibility of conditioning on their subject animals, as Pinker suggests, the context of the training makes it difficult to exclude the possibility of conditioning.

Up to now none of the ape-language projects have been able to tell us much, if anything, about ape communication in natural settings because all of the projects were conducted in laboratory settings. Even though no languagelike communication has been identified among wild chimps or bonobos, there is still much to be learned about how these species communicate. Such studies, particularly if they can be linked to the ape-language experiments, may have a great deal to offer about primate cognition, and they may ultimately offer insights about the process of language acquisition in human children.

For a discussion of Washoe and other early ape-language projects, see R. Allen Gardner and Beatrice T. Gardner's essay "Communication With a Young Chimpanzee: Washoe's Vocabulary," in Rémy Chauvin, ed., *Modèles Animaux du Comportement Humain* (Centre National de la Recherche Scientifique), Herbert S. Terrace's *Nim* (Knopf, 1979), and David Premack and Ann Premack's *The Mind of an Ape* (W. W. Norton, 1983). On Kanzi, see Savage-Rumbaugh and Roger Lewin's *Kanzi: The Ape at the Brink of the Human Mind* (Wiley, 1994). On child language acquisition, see Pinker's *Language Learnability and Language Development* (Harvard University Press, 1984). For Skinner's original behavorist model of language learning, see his *Verbal Behavior* (Appleton-Century-Crofts, 1957) and Chomsky's critique *Syntactic Structures* (Mouton, 1957). Students may also enjoy Pinker's most recent analysis of what defines language in *Words and Rules: The Ingredients of Language* (Basic Books, 1999). For recent views about the state of ape-language experiments, see Savage-Rumbaugh, Stuart G. Shaker, and Talbot J. Taylor's *Apes, Language, and the Human Mind* (Oxford University Press, 1998), Barbara J. King, ed., *The Origins of Language: What Nonhuman Primates Can Tell Us* (SAR Press, 1999), and Barbara J. King's *The Information Continuum: Evolution of Social Information Transfer in Monkeys, Apes, and Hominids* (SAR Press, 1994).

ISSUE 8

Does Language Determine How We Think?

YES: John J. Gumperz and Stephen C. Levinson, from "Introduction: Linguistic Relativity Re-examined" and "Introduction to Part 1," in John J. Gumperz and Stephen C. Levinson, eds., *Rethinking Linguistic Relativity* (Cambridge University Press, 1996)

NO: Steven Pinker, from *The Language Instinct: How the Mind Creates Language* (Perennial Classics, 2000)

ISSUE SUMMARY

YES: Sociolinguists John J. Gumperz and Stephen C. Levinson contend that recent studies of language and culture suggest that language structures human thought in a variety of ways that most linguists and anthropologists had not believed possible.

NO: Cognitive neuropsychologist Steven Pinker draws on recent studies in cognitive science and neuropsychology to support the notion that previous studies have examined language but have said little, if anything, about thought.

For more than a century, anthropologists and linguists have observed that the world's languages differ in a number of significant ways. While some languages, such as French or Spanish, require speakers to mark the gender of most nouns, English does not. Some languages in Africa, New Guinea, and Latin America have only two, three, or four basic color terms, while English has eleven. Some languages are rich in cover terms such as tree, bird, or animal, while others have many terms for the different species but may lack any single term that would include all kinds of trees, birds, or animals. Do such differences among the world's languages have any effect on how different people think about the world in which they live?

The idea that human thought changes with different languages has come to be known as the question of linguistic relativity. It is most widely associated with the linguistic anthropologist Edward Sapir and his sometime student Benjamin Lee Whorf. Early in the twentieth century Sapir had drawn on his studies of Native American languages to suggest that different lexical (vocabulary) items and different grammatical features did lead various Indian groups to view the world differently from white English-speaking Americans. By the 1950s the idea that the language people spoke shaped the way they were inclined to think about the world had become known as the Sapir-Whorf hypothesis.

Although the Sapir-Whorf hypothesis had been generally accepted by most American anthropologists, few accepted the hypothesis in its strongest and most deterministic form. Derived from Whorf's writings, the strong version implied that humans were prisoners of their native language and could only think in terms of that language's grammatical and lexical categories. Since most anthropologists learned these exotic languages and with training were themselves able to understand both the words and the exotic worldviews, most anthropologists recognized that language could not be so deterministic. On the other hand, most anthropologists recognized that their informants approached the world quite differently from themselves.

The first formal test of linguistic relativity came in 1969 when cognitive anthropologist Brent Berlin and Paul Kay published *Basic Color Terms* (Berkeley, University of California Press). Examining the color terminologies of more than 100 languages from around the world, they concluded that the number of key or basic color terms a language might have is highly variable, from as few as two to as many as twelve. But the particular hues that would be coded was highly predictable and not at all random. Berlin and Kay suggested that all people perceive colors the same, but how they assign particular color chips to different color terms is anything but arbitrary.

In the 1970s these and other studies of how different people classified their natural, biological, and social worlds suggested to most anthropologists that language's role in culture was primarily limited to prescribing how people classified the world they inhabited rather than on people's thought processes. Thus, for about two decades the Sapir-Whorf hypothesis was relegated to the dustbin of bad anthropological theories. But in the 1990s a growing number of linguists and linguistic anthropologists began to reevaluate the hypothesis, and a growing number has come to see the relationship between language and thought in a variety of new ways.

The first selection, by John J. Gumperz and Stephen C. Levinson, examines some new studies, suggesting that new findings on the issue of linguistic relativity are emerging from many quarters in linguistics and anthropology. Accepting a nondeterministic reading of Sapir and Whorf, they explore some of the directions this new research is taking.

As anthropologists and linguists began to reexamine Sapir-Whorf, new criticisms have arisen from the new field of cognitive neuroscience. Here, Steven Pinker evaluates the linguistic relativity question, drawing on recent studies by cognitive neuroscience. He tends to view the relativity problem in more determinist terms than do Gumperz and Levinson, as well as most of the anthropologists who are currently working on this problem.

John J. Gumperz and
Stephen C. Levinson

 **YES**

Rethinking Linguistic Relativity

Introduction: Linguistic Relativity Re-Examined

Language, Thinking, and Reality

Every student of language or society should be familiar with the essential idea of linguistic relativity, the idea that culture, *through* language, affects the way we think, especially perhaps our classification of the experienced world. Much of our experience seems to support some such idea, for example the phenomenology of struggling with a second language, where we find that the summit of competence is forever over the next horizon, the obvious absence of definitive or even accurate translation (let alone the ludicrous failure of phrasebooks), even the wreck of diplomatic efforts on linguistic and rhetorical rocks.

On the other hand, there is a strand of robust common sense that insists that a stone is a stone whatever you call it, that the world is a recalcitrant reality that imposes its structure on our thinking and our speaking and that the veil of linguistic difference can be ripped aside with relative ease. Plenty of subjective experiences and objective facts can be marshalled to support this view: the delight of foreign friendships, our ability to "read" the military or economic strategies of alien rivals, the very existence of comparative sciences of language, psychology, and society.

These two opposing strands of "common sense" have surfaced in academic controversies and intellectual positions over many centuries of Western thought. If St. Augustine (354–430) took the view that language is a mere nomenclature for antecedently existing concepts, Roger Bacon (1220–92) insisted, despite strong views on the universal basis of grammar, that the mismatch between semantic fields in different languages made accurate translation impossible. The Port Royal grammarians of the seventeenth century found universal logic thinly disguised behind linguistic difference, while the German romantics in a tradition leading through to Humboldt in the nineteenth century found a unique *Weltanschauung*, "world view," in each language. The first half of our own century was characterized by the presumption of radical linguistic and cultural difference reflecting profound cognitive differences, a presumption to be found in anthropology, linguistics

144

and behaviourist psychologies, not to mention philosophical emphasis on meaning as use. The second half of the century has been dominated by the rise of the cognitive sciences, with their treatment of mind as inbuilt capacities for information processing, and their associated universalist and rationalist presuppositions. St. Augustine would probably recognize the faint echoes of his views in much modern theorizing about how children acquire language through prior knowledge of the structure of the world.

There is surely some spiral ascent in the swing of this pendulum. Nevertheless it is important to appreciate how little real scientific progress there has been in the study of lexical or morphosyntactic meaning—most progress in linguistics has been in the study of syntax and sound systems, together with rather general ideas about how the meaning of phrases might be composed out of the meaning of their constituents. Thus there is still much more opinion (often ill-informed) than solid fact in modern attitudes to "linguistic relativity."

There are three terms in the relation: language, thought, and culture. Each of these are global cover terms, not notions of any precision. When one tries to make anything definite out of the idea of linguistic relativity, one inevitably has to focus on particular aspects of each of these terms in the relation. This [selection] will show how each can be differently construed and, as a consequence, the relation reconsidered. In addition the connecting links can be variously conceived. Thus by the end of the [selection] the reader will find that the aspects of language and thinking that are focused on are selective, but also that the very relation between culture and community has become complex. Readers will find the original idea of linguistic relativity still live, but functioning in a way that differs from how it was originally conceived.

Linguistic Relativity Re-Examined

The original idea, variously attributable to [Wilhelm von] Humboldt, [Franz] Boas, [Edward] Sapir, [and Benjamin Lee] Whorf, was that the semantic structures of different languages might be fundamentally incommensurable, with consequences for the way in which speakers of specific languages might think and act. On this view, language, thought, and culture are deeply interlocked, so that each language might be claimed to have associated with it a distinctive worldview.

These ideas captured the imagination of a generation of anthropologists, psychologists, and linguists, as well as members of the general public. They had deep implications for the way anthropologists should conduct their business, suggesting that translational difficulties might lie at the heart of their discipline. However, the ideas seemed entirely and abruptly discredited by the rise of the cognitive sciences in the 1960s, which favoured a strong emphasis on the commonality of human cognition and its basis in human genetic endowment. This emphasis was strengthened by developments within linguistic anthropology, with the discovery of significant semantic universals in color terms, the structure of ethnobotanical nomenclature, and (arguably) kinship terms.

However, there has been a recent change of intellectual climate in psychology, linguistics, and other disciplines surrounding anthropology, as well as within linguistic anthropology, towards an intermediate position, in which more attention is paid to linguistic and cultural difference, such diversity being viewed within the context of what we have learned about universals (features shared by all languages and cultures). New work in developmental psychology, while acknowledging underlying universal bases, emphasizes the importance of the socio-cultural context of human development. Within sociolinguistics and linguistic anthropology there has also been increasing attention to meaning and discourse, and concomitantly a growing appreciation of how interpretive differences can be rooted as much in the systematic uses of language as in its structure.

. . .[T]he ideas we associate today so especially with Whorf and Sapir have a long and distinguished lineage on the one hand, while perhaps being no more than one of two opposing perennial strands of thought, universalism vs. relativism, on the other. Nevertheless, they crystallized in a particular fashion in American intellectual life of the 1940s. The idea of a close link between linguistic and conceptual categories took on a new meaning in the context of three further background assumptions characteristic of the first half of the century. One was the presumption of a (sometimes tempered) empiricist epistemology, that is, the view that all knowledge is acquired primarily through experience. The other was the structuralist assumption that language forms a system of oppositions, such that formal distinctions directly reflect meaning distinctions. The third was the idea of an unconscious mental life, and thus the possibility of linguistic effects beyond conscious awareness. It was the conjunction of these background ideas together with the specific formulation of the" linguistic relativity" hypothesis that gave the hypothesis its particular character in the history of ideas.

Sapir may have originated the phrase, but the *locus classicus* (though by no means the most careful statement) of the concept of linguistic relativity is the popular articles by Whorf, where the following oft-quoted passages may be found which illustrate all the central themes.

Epistemology

> We dissect nature along lines laid down by our native languages. The categories and types that we isolate from the world of phenomena we do not find there because they stare every observer in the face; on the contrary, the world is presented in a kaleidoscopic flux of impressions which has to be organized by our minds—and this means largely by the linguistic systems of our minds.

> — (1956:213) . . .

Unconscious Thought

> [T]he phenomena of language are to its own speakers largely of a background character and so are outside the critical consciousness and control of the speaker.

> — (1956:211)

Linguistic Relativity

> The phenomena of language are background phenomena, of which the talkers are unaware or, at most, dimly aware . . . These automatic, involuntary patterns of language are not the same for all men but are specific for each language and constitute the formalized side of the language, or its "grammar" . . .
>
> From this fact proceeds what I have called the "linguistic relativity principle," which means, in informal terms, that users of markedly different grammars are pointed by their grammars toward different types of observations and different evaluations of externally similar acts of observation, and hence are not equivalent as observers, but must arrive at somewhat different views of the world.
>
> — (1956:221) . . .

The boldness of Whorf's formulation prompted a succession of empirical studies in America in the 1950s and early 1960s aimed at elucidating and testing what now became known as the Sapir–Whorf hypothesis. Anthropological and linguistic studies by Trager, Hoijer, Lee, Casagrande, and others have been well reviewed elsewhere. These studies hardly touched on cognition, but in the same period a few psychologists (notably Lenneberg, Brown, Stefflre) did try to investigate the relation between lexical coding and memory, especially in the domain of color, and found some significant correlations. This line of work culminated, however, in the celebrated demonstration by Berlin & Kay of the language-independent saliency of "basic colors," which was taken as a decisive anti-relativist finding, and effectively terminated this tradition of investigations into the Sapir-Whorf hypothesis. There followed a period in which Whorf's own views in particular became the butt of extensive criticism.

It is clear from this background that the "Sapir-Whorf" hypothesis in its classical form arose from deep historical roots but in a particular intellectual climate. Even though (it has been closely argued by Lucy the original hypothesis has never been thoroughly tested, the intellectual milieu had by the 1960s entirely changed. Instead of empiricism, we now have rationalistic assumptions. Instead of the basic tenets of structuralism, in which each linguistic or social system must be understood first in internal terms before comparison is possible, modern comparative work (especially in linguistics) tends to presume that one can isolate particular aspects or traits of a system (e.g. aspect or subjecthood) for comparison. The justification, such as it is, is that we now have the outlines of a universal structure for language and perhaps cognition, which provides the terms for comparison. It is true that the assumption of unconscious processes continues, but now the emphasis is on the unconscious nature of nearly all systematic information processing, so that the distinctive character of Whorf's habitual thought has been submerged.

In this changed intellectual climate, and in the light of the much greater knowledge that we now have about both language and mental processing, it would be pointless to attempt to revive ideas about linguistic relativity in their original form. Nevertheless, there have been a whole range of recent intellectual shifts that make the ground more fertile for some of the original seeds to grow into new saplings. It is the purpose of this [selection] to explore the implications of some of these shifts in a number of different disciplines for our overall view of the relations between language, thinking, and society.

The Idea Behind the Present [Selection]

This [selection] explores one chain of reasoning that is prompted by these recent changes in ideas. The line of argument runs in the following way.

Linguistic relativity is a theory primarily about the nature of meaning, the classic view focusing on the lexical and grammatical coding of language-specific distinctions. In this theory, two languages may "code" the same state of affairs utilizing semantic concepts or distinctions peculiar to each language; as a result the two linguistic descriptions reflect different construals of the same bit of reality. These semantic distinctions are held to reflect cultural distinctions and at the same time to influence cognitive categorizations, an issue re-examined . . . below.

Assuming that there is such a link between linguistic structure and conceptual categories, the possibility of conceptual relativity would seem at first sight to depend on whether linguistic codings are significantly different across languages. Very little, however, is actually known about substantive semantic or conceptual universals. It is true that there are demonstrations of universal semantic principles in a few domains like color terminology, ethnobiological taxonomies, perhaps also in systems of kinship terminology. However, these demonstrations carry no necessary general implications, and the same holds for studies of grammatical meaning. . . .

Yet, on further reflection, distinctive linguistic (grammatical or lexical) codings are not the only ways in which "meanings" or interpretations can vary systematically across cultures. This is brought out by recent developments in the theory of meaning. These developments show that "meaning" is not fully encapsulated in lexicon and grammar, which provide only schematic constraints on what the speaker will be taken to have meant in a particular utterance. . . .

A large part of the burden of interpretation is thus shifted from theories of context-free lexical and grammatical meaning to theories of use in context. Some important principles of the use of language may plausibly be argued to be universal. . . . Yet others seem much more clearly culture-specific. For example, the ethnography of speaking has shown how diverse can be the principles governing the production and interpretation of utterances in specific speech events—court proceedings, formal greetings, religious rituals, councils, and the like. . . .

This [selection] therefore spans a large terrain, from the classic Whorfian issues of the relation of grammar to thought on the one hand to consideration of language use in sociolinguistic perspective on the other. One key idea that supports this span is the notion of indexicality, conceived not just in terms of the contextual dependence of deictic items, but also in the broader Peircean sense, as a broad relationship between interpreters, signals, and the context of interpretation. Indexicality necessarily anchors meaning and interpretation to the context of language use and thus to wider social organization. Issues of linguistic relativity are in this way directly related to the variable cultural structuring of contexts. . . .

Introduction to Part I . . .

The Very Idea: Causal Links Between Language and Thinking

Might the language we speak affect the way we think? Generations of thinkers have been intrigued by this idea. Aarsleff summarized Humboldt's influential views thus: "Humboldt's entire view of the nature of language is founded on the conviction that thinking and speaking, thought and language form so close a union that we must think of them as being identical, in spite of the fact that we can separate them artificially. Owing to this identity, access to one of the two will open nearly equal access to the other."

Whorf, as we saw [earlier], brought to the idea a new and heady mix of an empiricist epistemology, an insistence on the underlying systematicity of language as a structured semantical system, and an emphasis on the unconscious influence of language on habitual thought. . . .

The phrase "linguistic determinism" has come to stand for these views that there is a causal influence from linguistic patterning to cognition. Despite phrases like "linguistic conditioning," "linguistic legislation," "inexorable control," etc., Whorf's own considered position seems to have been that language influences unconscious habitual thought, rather than limiting thought potential. Thus the phrase "linguistic determinism" should be understood to imply that there is *at least some* causal influence from language categories to nonverbal cognition; it was not intended to denote an exclusive causal vector in one direction—probably no proponent has held the view that what cannot be said cannot be thought.

The idea that language could determine (however weakly) the nature of our thinking nowadays carries more than a faint whiff of anachronism; rather it seems to belong to an altogether different age, prior to the serious study of mind as an information processing device. That device, in the predominant metaphor of our time, is instantiated in "wetware," whose properties are in turn dictated by the genetic code of the species. Although those properties are only dimly understood, still it is generally presumed, as Fodor has influentially put it, that the mind is "modular," composed of subsystems specialized to the automatic unconscious processing of particular kinds of information, visual, auditory, haptic, and so on. Since we can, for example, talk about what we see, the output of these specialized systems must, it seems, be available to some central information processing system, where "thinking," in the sense of ratiocination and deliberation, occurs. This picture (a close analogy of course to the computers of the day) of a single generalized central processor with specialized input/output devices is beginning to give way to a more complex version: each specialized input/output device is itself a system of modules, while "central processes" may themselves be differentiated into different "languages of thought" (propositional, imagistic, and so on). . . . Nevertheless the essentials of the Fodorean view are very generally held.

Thus, on this widespread view, we can expect thinking in all essentials to have universal properties, to be couched in an inner language structurally the same for all members of the species, and to be quite unrelated to the facts of linguistic diversity. The tenor of the anti-Whorfian assumptions can be gauged from the following quotations: "For the vocabulary of the language, in and of its self, to be a moulder of thought, lexical dissections and categorizations of nature would have to be almost accidentally formed, rather as though some Johnny Appleseed had scattered named categories capriciously over the earth"; "Whorf's hypothesis [of linguistic determinism] has engendered much confusion, and many circular arguments. Its converse often seems more plausible" and "there is no evidence for the strong version of the hypothesis—that language imposes upon its speakers a particular way of thinking about the world"; "The discussions that assume that language determines thought carry on only by a collective suspension of disbelief."

In short, many authors find the thesis of linguistic determinism wildly adventurous or even ridiculous. On the other hand, others have recently claimed to find it sober and plausible. It is therefore useful to attempt to clarify the issues by dissecting the relativity hypothesis into its component parts, and in particular by isolating the "determinism" hypothesis from other linked ideas. Clearly, the hypothesis of linguistic relativity relies on the presumption of linguistic difference. Thus the discovery of universals may have a bearing on that hypothesis. But the hypothesis that linguistic categories might determine aspects of non-linguistic thinking is quite independent of facts about linguistic difference. Let us therefore spell out the nexus of interlinked hypotheses (where the numbers *[1]* and *[2]* refer to the premises and the number *[3]* to an implied conclusion).

[1] Linguistic Difference
Languages differ substantially in their semantic structure: both the intensions (the senses) and extensions (the denotations) of lexical and morpho-syntactic categories may differ across languages (and may do so independently).

[2] Linguistic Determinism
Linguistic categorizations, implicit or explicit, may determine or codetermine or influence aspects of non-linguistic categorization, memory, perception or thinking in general.

This is often said to have a "strong" and a "weak" form: under the strong claim, linguistically uncoded concepts would be unattainable; under the weak form, concepts which happen to be linguistically coded would be facilitated or favored (e.g. would be more accessible, easier to remember, or the default coding for non-linguistic cognition).

✎◈✎

The mechanisms whereby semantic distinctions may have an influence on cognition can be left open; a prior task is to show that there is indeed some correlation. Whorf himself of course held the view that the unconscious "compulsive patterning" of grammatical oppositions would play a special role in habitual unreflective patterns of thought.

Linguistic Relativity

Given that:

(1) differences exist in linguistic categories across languages;
(2) linguistic categories determine aspects of individuals' thinking;

then:

(3) aspects of individuals' thinking differ across linguistic communities according to the language they speak.

Note that the conclusion here will hold even under the weakest versions of (1) and (2). Thus if there is *at least some* aspect of semantic structure that is not universal, *and at least some* cognitive effect of such distinctive semantic properties, then there must be *at least some* systematic cognitive variation in line with linguistic difference. That would seem . . . to be as trivially true as the strongest version of linguistic relativity (that one's semantic inventory of concepts provides one's total vocabulary of thoughts) is trivially false. Thus the central problem is to illuminate the degrees of language difference, and the ways in which semantics and cognitive categories and processes interact.

Now notice that modern views complicate this picture by apparently subscribing to various aspects of these propositions while robustly denying the conclusion in the syllogism above. For example, a common modern stance is:

(1') languages differ in semantic structure, but only at a molecular level—at an atomic level, the conceptual "atoms" (e.g. "male," "adult," etc.) are identical, and are merely assembled into some culture-specific notion like "uncle";
(2') "determinism" between semantic categories and conceptual categories is in a sense trivially complete, since they are one and the same—the meanings of words are expressed in a "language" that is identical to the "language of thought." . . .

Thus although the identity of linguistic and conceptual categories in (2') alone might be thought to entail linguistic relativity, it is in fact usually associated with some claim (often implicit) like that in (1'), allowing subscribers to presume that the "language of thought" (alias: system of semantic representations) is universal. Then the conclusion in (3) no longer follows. In schematic form we may now oppose the two views thus:

The Whorfian Syllogism

(1) Different languages utilize different semantic representation systems which are informationally non-equivalent (at least in the sense that they employ different lexical concepts);

(2) semantic representations determine aspects of conceptual representations;
>   *therefore*
(3) users of different languages utilize different conceptual representations.

The Anti-Whorfian Syllogism

(1′) Different languages utilize the same semantic representation system (if not at the molecular then at least at the atomic level of semantic primes);
(2′) universal conceptual representations determine semantic systems, indeed THE semantic representation system just is identical to THE propositional conceptual system (the innate "language of thought");
>   *therefore*
(3′) users of different languages utilize the identical conceptual representation system.

Despite the fact that the doctrines appear diametrically opposed, they are nevertheless, on suitable interpretations, *entirely compatible*, as long as one subscribes to the distinction between atomic and molecular levels of semantic representation. Then, on an atomic level, semantic representations, and their corresponding conceptual representations, are drawn from a universal language of thought, while on the molecular level there are language-specific combinations of universal atomic primitives, which make up lexical meanings (and meanings associated with morpho-syntactic distinctions) and which may have specific conceptual effects.

Most semantic analysts in practice work with an assumption of such "semantic decomposition" of linguistic expressions. But it is worth pointing out that there are in fact fundamental problems with that assumption which have long been recognized, and some of those who subscribe enthusiastically to (2′) might lose some of their enthusiasm if they realized that without (1′), (2′) implies the strongest version of linguistic relativity.

Let us take stock. Proposition (1) is evidently true, in the sense that languages clearly employ distinct lexical meanings. (1′) may or may not be tenable, but is in fact compatible with (1). Likewise (2) and (2′) are compatible if we make a distinction between atomic and molecular concepts: the inventory of concepts in the language of thought could determine the range of possible lexical concepts, but such lexical concepts once selected could in turn determine the concepts we employ when solving non-linguistic problems. (3) would be the conclusion from (1) and (2). All thus hinges on (2). Is it even remotely plausible?

Although the thesis of linguistic determinism seems at first sight to have an anachronistic flavor, it can easily be brought to bear on modern theorizing in a way that makes it look anything but silly. First, note that there is considerable psychological evidence that our working memory is restricted to about half a dozen chunks of information, but is indifferent to the underlying complexity of those chunks. Thus mental operations are facilitated by grouping elementary concepts into larger chunks. And this is just what lexical items do for us. Thus there is every reason to think that such chunks might play an important role in our thinking. . . .

Within such a framework, it is quite easy to show that in certain respects and for certain phenomena linguistic determinism *beyond* thinking-for-speaking is not only plausible, but must be correct. The reasoning can be exemplified as follows. Consider a language that has no words for *'in front,' 'behind,' 'left,' 'right,'* and so on, preferring instead to designate all such relations, however microscopic in scale, in terms of notions like 'North,' 'South,' 'East,' 'West,' etc. Now a speaker of such a language cannot remember arrays of objects in the same way as you or I, in terms of their relative location from a particular viewing angle. If I think of the visual array currently in front of me, I think of it as, say, "boy in front of tree, dog to left of tree." Later I can so describe it. But that will not do for the speaker of the language with 'North'/ 'South'/'East'/'West' notions: remembering the array in terms of notions like 'front' and 'left' will not allow him to reconstruct the cardinal directions. So if he remembers it that way, he will not be able to describe it later; while if he remembers the array in a way congruent with the linguistic coding (in terms of 'North' and 'East', etc.), then he will be able to code it linguistically. So it seems *prima facie* quite clear that the speaker of such a language and I simply MUST code our experiences differently for memory in order to speak our different languages. In short, thinking in a special way for speaking will not be enough: we must mentally encode experiences in such a way that we can describe them later, in the terms required by our language.

There are in fact just such languages that require the use of cardinal directions. Furthermore, this *prima facie* argument about the cognitive consequences of speaking such different languages can be backed up by empirical investigation: it turns out that in non-linguistic tasks speakers of languages that use 'North'/'South'/'East'/'West' systems instead of 'front'/'back'/'left'/ 'right' systems do indeed remember spatial arrays differently, in ways that can be demonstrated experimentally and observationally.

Is this a peculiar case? One needs to think afresh to assess the possibilities. From the perspective of speech production, there are three different kinds of ways in which a particular language might determine how we think. First, the grammatical or lexical categories may force a specific way of thinking at the time of speaking (the "regimentation" of thoughts described above). Second, such thinking-for-speaking may itself require the coding of situations in specific forms at the time that they are experienced. This is clearly so in the North/South/East/West case above. It is also clearly so in many other cases: for example, obligatory coding of number in languages with plural marking will require noticing for all possible referents whether or not they are singletons—some languages without plural marking will let one say in effect "I saw bird on the lawn," but in English I must say either a *bird* or *birds* and must therefore have remembered how many relevant birds there were; or in systems of honorifics based on relative age, I must have ascertained before speaking whether the referent is senior or junior to me; or in systems of aspect requiring distinctions between perfective and imperfective, I must attend to the exact nature of event-overlap. These are language-specific distinctions that seem to require noticing special properties of the world so that one is ready to encode them linguistically should the need arise. Such examples suggest that those theorists who reluctantly subscribe to a relativity in thinking-for-speaking, will have also to subscribe to a consequent relativity in thinking at the time at which events are experienced. Thirdly, one may also go on to consider the consequences, or after-effects, of thinking-for-speaking in a particular way. There may for example be memory effects: it may be easier to remember aspects of events that have been coded for speaking during prior verbalization (hence we may indulge in speaking-for-thinking). Since some languages will enforce particular codings (e.g. in systems of aspect, honorifics, number-marking, etc.), they may ensure that their speakers recall certain features of situations better than others.

NO

Steven Pinker

Mentalese

Is thought dependent on words? Do people literally think in English, Cherokee, [or] Kivunjo . . . ? Or are our thoughts couched in some silent medium of the brain—a language of thought, or "mentalese"—and merely clothed in words whenever we need to communicate them to a listener? No question could be more central to understanding the language instinct.

In much of our social and political discourse, people simply assume that words determine thoughts. Inspired by [George] Orwell's essay "Politics and the English Language," pundits accuse governments of manipulating our minds with euphemisms like *pacification* (bombing), *revenue enhancement* (taxes), and *nonretention* (firing). Philosophers argue that since animals lack language, they must also lack consciousness—[Ludwig] Wittgenstein wrote, "A dog could not have the thought 'perhaps it will rain tomorrow'"—and therefore they do not possess the rights of conscious beings. Some feminists blame sexist thinking on sexist language, like the use of *he* to refer to a generic person. Inevitably, reform movements have sprung up. Many replacements for *he* have been suggested over the years, including *E, hesh, po, tey, co, jhe, ve, xe, he'er, thon,* and *na*. The most extreme of these movements is General Semantics, begun in 1933 by the engineer Count Alfred Korzybski and popularized in long-time best-sellers by his disciples Stuart Chase and S. I. Hayakawa. (This is the same Hayakawa who later achieved notoriety as the protest-defying college president and snoozing U.S. senator.) General Semantics lays the blame for human folly on insidious "semantic damage" to thought perpetrated by the structure of language. Keeping a forty-year-old in prison for a theft he committed as a teenager assumes that the forty-year-old John and the eighteen-year-old John are "the same person," a cruel logical error that would be avoided if we referred to them not as *John* but as $John_{1972}$ and $John_{1994}$, respectively. The verb *to be* is a particular source of illogic, because it identifies individuals with abstractions, as in *Mary is a woman*, and licenses evasions of responsibility, like Ronald Reagan's famous nonconfession *Mistakes were made*. One faction seeks to eradicate the verb altogether.

And supposedly there is a scientific basis for these assumptions: the famous Sapir-Whorf hypothesis of linguistic determinism, stating that people's thoughts are determined by the categories made available by their language, and its weaker version, linguistic relativity, stating that differences among languages cause differences in the thoughts of their speakers. People who remember little else from their college education can rattle off the factoids: the languages that carve the spectrum into color words at different places, the fundamentally different Hopi concept of time, the dozens of Eskimo words for snow. The implication is heavy: the foundational categories of reality are not "in" the world but are imposed by one's culture (and hence can be challenged, perhaps accounting for the perennial appeal of the hypothesis to undergraduate sensibilities).

But it is wrong, all wrong. The idea that thought is the same thing as language is an example of what can be called a conventional absurdity: a statement that goes against all common sense but that everyone believes because they dimly recall having heard it somewhere and because it is so pregnant with implications. (The "fact" that we use only five percent of our brains, that lemmings commit mass suicide, that the *Boy Scout Manual* annually outsells all other books, and that we can be coerced into buying by subliminal messages are other examples.) Think about it. We have all had the experience of uttering or writing a sentence, then stopping and realizing that it wasn't exactly what we meant to say. To have that feeling, there has to be a "what we meant to say" that is different from what we said. Sometimes it is not easy to find *any* words that properly convey a thought. When we hear or read, we usually remember the gist, not the exact words, so there has to be such a thing as a gist that is not the same as a bunch of words. And if thoughts depended on words, how could a new word ever be coined? How could a child learn a word to begin with? How could translation from one language to another be possible?

The discussions that assume that language determines thought carry on only by a collective suspension of disbelief. . . .

As we shall see in this [selection], there is no scientific evidence that languages dramatically shape their speakers' ways of thinking. But I want to do more than review the unintentionally comical history of attempts to prove that they do. The idea that language shapes thinking seemed plausible when scientists were in the dark about how thinking works or even how to study it. Now that cognitive scientists know how to think about thinking, there is less of a temptation to equate it with language just because words are more palpable than thoughts. By understanding *why* linguistic determinism is wrong, we will be in a better position to understand how language itself works. . . .

The linguistic determinism hypothesis is closely linked to the names Edward Sapir and Benjamin Lee Whorf. Sapir, a brilliant linguist, was a student of the anthropologist Franz Boas. Boas and his students (who also include Ruth Benedict and Margaret Mead) were important intellectual figures in this century, because they argued that nonindustrial peoples were not primitive savages but had systems of language, knowledge, and culture as complex and valid in their world view as our own. In his study of Native American languages Sapir noted that speakers of different languages have to pay attention to different aspects of reality simply to put words together into grammatical sentences. For example, when English speakers decide whether or not to put *-ed* onto the end of a verb, they must pay attention to tense, the relative time of occurrence of the event they are referring to and the moment of speaking. Wintu speakers need not bother with tense, but when they decide which suffix to put on their verbs, they must pay attention to whether the knowledge they are conveying was learned through direct observation or by hearsay.

Sapir's interesting observation was soon taken much farther. Whorf was an inspector for the Hartford Fire Insurance Company and an amateur scholar of Native American languages, which led him to take courses from Sapir at Yale. In a much-quoted passage, he wrote:

> We dissect nature along lines laid down by our native languages. The categories and types that we isolate from the world of phenomena we do not find there because they stare every observer in the face; on the contrary, the world is presented in a kaleidoscopic flux of impressions which has to be organized by our minds—and this means largely by the linguistic systems in our minds. We cut nature up, organize it into concepts, and ascribe significances as we do, largely because we are parties to an agreement to organize it in this way—an agreement that holds throughout our speech community and is codified in the patterns of our language. The agreement is, of course, an implicit and unstated one, *but its terms are absolutely obligatory*; we cannot talk at all except by subscribing to the organization and classification of data which the agreement decrees.

What led Whorf to this radical position? He wrote that the idea first occurred to him in his work as a fire prevention engineer when he was struck by how language led workers to misconstrue dangerous situations. For example, one worker caused a serious explosion by tossing a cigarette into an "empty" drum that in fact was full of gasoline vapor. Another lit a blowtorch near a "pool of water" that was really a basin of decomposing tannery waste, which, far from being "watery," was releasing inflammable gases. Whorf's studies of American languages strengthened his conviction. For example, in Apache, *It is a dripping spring* must be expressed "As water, or springs, whiteness moves downward." "How utterly unlike our way of thinking!" he wrote.

But the more you examine Whorf's arguments, the less sense they make. Take the story about the worker and the "empty" drum. The seeds of disaster supposedly lay in the semantics of *empty*, which, Whorf claimed, means both "without its usual contents" and "null and void, empty, inert." The hapless worker, his conception of reality molded by his linguistic categories, did not distinguish between the "drained" and "inert" senses, hence, flick . . . boom! But wait. Gasoline vapor is invisible. A drum with nothing but vapor in it looks just like a drum with nothing in it at all. Surely this walking catastrophe was fooled by his eyes, not by the English language.

The example of whiteness moving downward is supposed to show that the Apache mind does not cut up events into distinct objects and actions. Whorf presented many such examples from Native American languages. The Apache equivalent of *The boat is grounded on the beach* is "It is on the beach pointwise as an event of canoe motion." *He invites people to a feast* becomes

"He, or somebody, goes for eaters of cooked food." *He cleans a gun with a ramrod* is translated as "He directs a hollow moving dry spot by movement of tool." All this, to be sure, is utterly unlike our way of talking. But do we know that it is utterly unlike our way of thinking?

As soon as Whorf's articles appeared, the psycholinguists Eric Lenneberg and Roger Brown pointed out two non sequiturs in his argument. First, Whorf did not actually study any Apaches; it is not clear that he ever met one. His assertions about Apache psychology are based entirely on Apache grammar— making his argument circular. Apaches speak differently, so they must think differently. How do we know that they think differently? Just listen to the way they speak.

Second, Whorf rendered the sentences as clumsy, word-for-word translations, designed to make the literal meanings seem as odd as possible. But looking at the actual glosses that Whorf provided, I could, with equal grammatical justification, render the first sentence as the mundane "Clear stuff—water—is falling." Turning the tables, I could take the English sentence "He walks" and render it "As solitary masculinity, leggedness proceeds." Brown illustrates how strange the German mind must be, according to Whorf's logic, by reproducing Mark Twain's own translation of a speech he delivered in flawless German to the Vienna Press Club:

> I am indeed the truest friend of the German language—and not only now, but from long since—yes, before twenty years already. . . . I would only some changes effect. I would only the language method—the luxurious, elaborate construction compress, the eternal parenthesis suppress, do away with, annihilate; the introduction of more than thirteen subjects in one sentence forbid; the verb so far to the front pull that one it without a telescope discover can. With one word, my gentlemen, I would your beloved language simplify so that, my gentlemen, when you her for prayer need, One her yonder-up understands.
>
> . . . I might gladly the separable verb also a little bit reform. I might none do let what Schiller did: he has the whole history of the Thirty Years' War between the two members of a separate verb inpushed. That has even Germany itself aroused, and one has Schiller the permission refused the History of the Hundred Years' War to compose—God be it thanked! After all these reforms established be will, will the German language the noblest and the prettiest on the world be.

Among Whorf's "kaleidoscopic flux of impressions," color is surely the most eye-catching. He noted that we see objects in different hues, depending on the wavelengths of the light they reflect, but that physicists tell us that wavelength is a continuous dimension with nothing delineating red, yellow, green, blue, and so on. Languages differ in their inventory of color words: Latin lacks generic "gray" and "brown"; Navajo collapses blue and green into one word; Russian has distinct words for dark blue and sky blue; Shona speakers use one word for the yellower greens and the greener yellows, and a different one for the bluer greens and the nonpurplish blues. You can fill in the rest of the argument. It is language that puts the frets in the spectrum; Julius Caesar would not know shale from Shinola.

But although physicists see no basis for color boundaries, physiologists do. Eyes do not register wavelength the way a thermometer registers temperature. They contain three kinds of cones, each with a different pigment, and the cones are wired to neurons in a way that makes the neurons respond best to red patches against a green background or vice versa, blue against yellow, black against white. No matter how influential language might be, it would seem preposterous to a physiologist that it could reach down into the retina and rewire the ganglion cells.

Indeed, humans the world over (and babies and monkeys, for that matter) color their perceptual worlds using the same palette, and this constrains the vocabularies they develop. Although languages may disagree about the wrappers in the sixty-four crayon box—the burnt umbers, the turquoises, the fuchsias—they agree much more on the wrappers in the eight-crayon box—the fire-engine reds, grass greens, lemon yellows. Speakers of different languages unanimously pick these shades as the best examples of their color words, as long as the language has a color word in that general part of the spectrum. And where languages do differ in their color words, they differ predictably, not according to the idiosyncratic taste of some word-coiner. Languages are organized a bit like the Crayola product line, the fancier ones adding colors to the more basic ones. If a language has only two color words, they are for black and white (usually encompassing dark and light, respectively). If it has three, they are for black, white, and red; if four, black, white, red, and either yellow or green. Five adds in both yellow and green; six, blue; seven, brown; more than seven, purple, pink, orange, or gray. But the clinching experiment was carried out in the New Guinea highlands with the Grand Valley Dani, a people speaking one of the black-and-white languages. The psychologist Eleanor Rosch found that the Dani were quicker at learning a new color category that was based on fire-engine red than a category based on an off-red. The way we see colors determines how we learn words for them, not vice versa.

The fundamentally different Hopi concept of time is one of the more startling claims about how minds can vary. Whorf wrote that the Hopi language contains "no words, grammatical forms, constructions, or expressions that refer directly to what we call 'time,' or to past, or future, or to enduring or lasting." He suggested, too, that the Hopi had "no general notion or intuition of TIME as a smooth flowing continuum in which everything in the universe proceeds at an equal rate, out of a future, through a present, into a past." According to Whorf, they did not conceptualize events as being like points, or lengths of time like days as countable things. Rather, they seemed to focus on change and process itself, and on psychological distinctions between presently known, mythical, and conjecturally distant. The Hopi also had little interest in "exact sequences, dating, calendars, chronology."

What, then, are we to make of the following sentence translated from Hopi?

> Then indeed, the following day, quite early in the morning at the hour when people pray to the sun, around that time then he woke up the girl again.

Perhaps the Hopi are not as oblivious to time as Whorf made them out to be. In his extensive study of the Hopi, the anthropologist Ekkehart Malotki, who reported this sentence, also showed that Hopi speech contains tense, metaphors for time, units of time (including days, numbers of days, parts of the day, yesterday and tomorrow, days of the week, weeks, months, lunar phases, seasons, and the year), ways to quantify units of time, and words like "ancient," "quick," "long time," and "finished." Their culture keeps records with sophisticated methods of dating, including a horizon-based sun calendar, exact ceremonial day sequences, knotted calendar strings, notched calendar sticks, and several devices for timekeeping using the principle of the sundial. No one is really sure how Whorf came up with his outlandish claims, but his limited, badly analyzed sample of Hopi speech and his long-time leanings toward mysticism must have contributed.

Speaking of anthropological canards, no discussion of language and thought would be complete without the Great Eskimo Vocabulary Hoax. Contrary to popular belief, the Eskimos do not have more words for snow than do speakers of English. They do not have four hundred words for snow, as it has been claimed in print, or two hundred, or one hundred, or forty-eight, or even nine. One dictionary puts the figure at two. Counting generously, experts can come up with about a dozen, but by such standards English would not be far behind, with *snow, sleet, slush, blizzard, avalanche, hail, hardpack, powder, flurry, dusting,* and a coinage of Boston's WBZ-TV meteorologist Bruce Schwoegler, *snizzling.*

Where did the myth come from? Not from anyone who has actually studied the Yupik and Inuit-Inupiaq families of polysynthetic languages spoken from Siberia to Greenland. The anthropologist Laura Martin has documented how the story grew like an urban legend, exaggerated with each retelling. In 1911 Boas casually mentioned that Eskimos used four unrelated word roots for snow. Whorf embellished the count to seven and implied that there were more. His article was widely reprinted, then cited in textbooks and popular books on language, which led to successively inflated estimates in other textbooks, articles, and newspaper columns of Amazing Facts.

The linguist Geoffrey Pullum, who popularized Martin's article in his essay "The Great Eskimo Vocabulary Hoax," speculates about why the story got so out of control: "The alleged lexical extravagance of the Eskimos comports so well with the many other facets of their polysynthetic perversity: rubbing noses; lending their wives to strangers; eating raw seal blubber; throwing Grandma out to be eaten by polar bears." It is an ironic twist. Linguistic relativity came out of the Boas school, as part of a campaign to show that nonliterate cultures were as complex and sophisticated as European ones. But the supposedly mind-broadening anecdotes owe their appeal to a patronizing willingness to treat other cultures' psychologies as weird and exotic compared to our own. As Pullum notes,

> Among the many depressing things about this credulous transmission and elaboration of a false claim is that even if there *were* a large number of roots for different snow types in some Arctic language, this would *not*, objectively, be intellectually interesting; it would be a most mundane and unremarkable

fact. Horsebreeders have various names for breeds, sizes, and ages of horses; botanists have names for leaf shapes; interior decorators have names for shades of mauve; printers have many different names for fonts (Carlson, Garamond, Helvetica, Times Roman, and so on), naturally enough. . . . Would anyone think of writing about printers the same kind of slop we find written about Eskimos in bad linguistics textbooks? Take [the following] random textbook . . . , with its earnest assertion "It is quite obvious that in the culture of the Eskimos . . . snow is of great enough importance to split up the conceptual sphere that corresponds to one word and one thought in English into several distinct classes . . ." Imagine reading: "It is quite obvious that in the culture of printers . . . fonts are of great enough importance to split up the conceptual sphere that corresponds to one word and one thought among non-printers into several distinct classes . . ." Utterly boring, even if true. Only the link to those legendary, promiscuous, blubber-gnawing hunters of the ice-packs could permit something this trite to be presented to us for contemplation.

If the anthropological anecdotes are bunk, what about controlled studies? The thirty-five years of research from the psychology laboratory is distinguished by how little it has shown. Most of the experiments have tested banal "weak" versions of the Whorfian hypothesis, namely that words can have some effect on memory or categorization. Some of these experiments have actually worked, but that is hardly surprising. In a typical experiment, subjects have to commit paint chips to memory and are tested with a multiple-choice procedure. In some of these studies, the subjects show slightly better memory for colors that have readily available names in their language. But even colors without names are remembered fairly well, so the experiment does not show that the colors are remembered by verbal labels alone. All it shows is that subjects remembered the chips in two forms, a nonverbal visual image and a verbal label, presumably because two kinds of memory, each one fallible, are better than one. In another type of experiment subjects have to say which two out of three color chips go together; they often put the ones together that have the same name in their language. Again, no surprise. I can imagine the subjects thinking to themselves, "Now how on earth does this guy expect me to pick two chips to put together? He didn't give me any hints, and they're all pretty similar. Well, I'd probably call those two 'green' and that one 'blue,' and that seems as good a reason to put them together as any." In these experiments, language is, technically speaking, influencing a form of thought in some way, but so what? It is hardly an example of incommensurable world views, or of concepts that are nameless and therefore unimaginable, or of dissecting nature along lines laid down by our native languages according to terms that are absolutely obligatory . . .

※⟨◉⟩※

People can be forgiven for overrating language. Words make noise, or sit on a page, for all to hear and see. Thoughts are trapped inside the head of the thinker. To know what someone else is thinking, or to talk to each other about the nature of thinking, we have to use—what else, words! It is no wonder that many commentators have trouble even conceiving of thought without words—or is it that they just don't have the language to talk about it?

As a cognitive scientist I can afford to be smug about common sense being true (thought is different from language) and linguistic determinism being a conventional absurdity. For two sets of tools now make it easier to think clearly about the whole problem. One is a body of experimental studies that break the word barrier and assess many kinds of nonverbal thought. The other is a theory of how thinking might work that formulates the questions in a satisfyingly precise way . . . .

•◦◉◦•

Now we are in a position to pose the Whorfian question in a precise way. Remember that a representation does not have to look like English or any other language; it just has to use symbols to represent concepts, and arrangements of symbols to represent the logical relations among them, according to some consistent scheme. But though internal representations in an English speaker's mind don't *have* to look like English, they *could*, in principle, look like English—or like whatever language the person happens to speak. So here is the question: Do they in fact? For example, if we know that Socrates is a man, is it because we have neural patterns that correspond one-to-one to the English words *Socrates, is, a,* and *man,* and groups of neurons in the brain that correspond to the subject of an English sentence, the verb, and the object, laid out in that order? Or do we use some other code for representing concepts and their relations in our heads, a language of thought or mentalese that is not the same as any of the world's languages? We can answer this question by seeing whether English sentences embody the information that a processor would need to perform valid sequences of reasoning—without requiring any fully intelligent homunculus inside doing the "understanding."

The answer is a clear no. English (or any other language people speak) is hopelessly unsuited to serve as our internal medium of computation. Consider some of the problems.

The first is ambiguity. These headlines actually appeared in newspapers:

- Child's Stool Great for Use in Garden
- Stud Tires Out
- Stiff Opposition Expected to Casketless Funeral Plan
- Drunk Gets Nine Months in Violin Case
- Iraqi Head Seeks Arms . . .

Each headline contains a word that is ambiguous. But surely the thought underlying the word is *not* ambiguous; the writers of the headlines surely knew which of the two senses of the words *stool, stud,* and *stiff* they themselves had in mind. And if there can be two thoughts corresponding to one word, thoughts can't be words.

The second problem with English is its lack of logical explicitness. Consider the following example, devised by the computer scientist Drew McDermott:

Ralph is an elephant.
Elephants live in Africa.
Elephants have tusks.

Our inference-making device, with some minor modifications to handle the English grammar of the sentences, would deduce "Ralph lives in Africa" and "Ralph has tusks." This sounds fine but isn't. Intelligent you, the reader, knows that the Africa that Ralph lives in is the same Africa that all the other elephants live in, but that Ralph's tusks are his own. . . .

A third problem is called "co-reference." Say you start talking about an individual by referring to him as *the tall blond man with one black shoe*. The second time you refer to him in the conversation you are likely to call him *the man;* the third time, just *him*. But the three expressions do not refer to three people or even to three ways of thinking about a single person; the second and third are just ways of saving breath. Something in the brain must treat them as the same thing, English isn't doing it.

A fourth, related problem comes from those aspects of language that can only be interpreted in the context of a conversation or text—what linguists call "deixis." Consider articles like *a* and *the*. What is the difference between *killed a policeman* and *killed the policeman?* Only that in the second sentence, it is assumed that some specific policeman was mentioned earlier or is salient in the context. Thus in isolation the two phrases are synonymous, but in the following contexts (the first from an actual newspaper article) their meanings are completely different:

- A policeman's 14-year-old son, apparently enraged after being disciplined for a bad grade, opened fire from his house, *killing a policeman* and wounding three people before he was shot dead.
- A policeman's 14-year-old son, apparently enraged after being disciplined for a bad grade, opened fire from his house, *killing the policeman* and wounding three people before he was shot dead.

Outside of a particular conversation or text, then, the words *a* and *the* are quite meaningless. They have no place in one's permanent mental database. Other conversation-specific words like *here, there, this, that, now, then, I, me, my, here, we,* and *you* pose the same problems, as the following old joke illustrates:

First guy   I didn't sleep with my wife before we were married, did you?

Second guy   I don't know. What was her maiden name? . . .

These examples (and there are many more) illustrate a single important point. The representations underlying thinking, on the one hand, and the sentences in a language, on the other, are in many ways at cross-purposes. Any particular thought in our head embraces a vast amount of information. But when it comes to communicating a thought to someone else, attention spans are short and mouths are slow. To get information into a listener's head in a reasonable amount of time, a speaker can encode only a fraction of the message into words and must count on the listener to fill in the rest. But *inside a single head*, the demands are different. Air time is not a limited resource: different parts of the brain are connected to one another directly with thick cables that can transfer huge amounts of information quickly. Nothing can be left to the imagination, though, because the internal representations *are* the imagination.

We end up with the following picture. People do not think in English or Chinese or Apache; they think in a language of thought. This language of thought probably looks a bit like all these languages; presumably it has symbols for concepts, and arrangements of symbols that correspond to who did what to whom. . . . But compared with any given language, mentalese must be richer in some ways and simpler in others. It must be richer, for example, in that several concept symbols must correspond to a given English word like *stool* or *stud*. There must be extra paraphernalia that differentiate logically distinct kinds of concepts, like Ralph's tusks versus tusks in general, and that link different symbols that refer to the same thing, like *the tall blond man with one black shoe* and *the man*. On the other hand, mentalese must be simpler than spoken languages; conversation-specific words and constructions (like *a* and *the*) are absent, and information about pronouncing words, or even ordering them, is unnecessary. Now, it could be that English speakers think in some kind of simplified and annotated quasi-English, with the design I have just described, and that Apache speakers think in a simplified and annotated quasi-Apache. But to get these languages of thought to subserve reasoning properly, they would have to look much more like each other than either one does to its spoken counterpart, and it is likely that they are the same: a universal mentalese.

Knowing a language, then, is knowing how to translate mentalese into strings of words and vice versa. People without a language would still have mentalese, and babies and many nonhuman animals presumably have simpler dialects. Indeed, if babies did not have a mentalese to translate to and from English, it is not clear how learning English could take place, or even what learning English would mean.

POSTSCRIPT

Does Language Determine How We Think?

In many respects the two positions on linguistic relativity differ largely on whether they accept the "strong" version of Sapir-Whorf or the more widely held "weaker" version in which language provides people with the concepts with which they can view the world. It is not clear that anyone, including Whorf, ever accepted the most deterministic position that has often been attributed to him. Sapir's writings on the subject are ambiguous but have generally been interpreted as a weaker formulation. Pinker and other critics from neuropsychology typically frame the question in its strongest and most deterministic reading. See Paul Kay and Willett Kempton's 1984 article "What Is the Sapir-Whorf Hypothesis?" *American Anthropologist* (vol. 86) for a similar view by anthropologists. Cognitive psychologist Jerry A. Fodor takes a similar point of view in *The Language of Thought* (Harvard University Press, 1975). Such differences in approach raise the question of whether or not these two groups of scholars are actually talking past one another. Since the strong version of the hypothesis is rarely accepted, would it not be more productive to explore the limits of the weaker version?

In mainstream anthropology the relativity question has often been framed in terms of language's effect on a people's worldview, which is another version of the weak hypothesis. See, for example, Jane Hill and Bruce Mannheim's "Language and World View," *Reviews in Anthropology* (vol. 21, 1992). Two books by linguists suggest ways in which the weak version of linguistic relativity can help us understand the relationship between language and culture even in our own language: George Lakoff's *Women, Fire and Dangerous Things* (University of Chicago Press, 1987) and George Lakoff and Mark Johnson's *The Metaphors We Live By* (University of Chicago Press, 1980).

The most important early statements by Whorf are to be found in a volume of his papers from the 1930s, collected in 1956 by John B. Carroll in *Language, Thought, and Reality: Selected Writings* (Technology Press). For a more recent and detailed survey of anthropological approaches to the Sapir-Whorf hypothesis, see John A. Lucy's review article, "Linguistic Relativity," *Reviews in Anthropology* (vol. 26, 1997).

Cultural Materialism

The Cultural Materialism Web site, created by Dr. M. D. Murphy of the University of Alabama, features an explanation of cultural materialism, a summary of the history of cultural materialism, and a list of pertinent scholars. This site also gives links to other relevant Web sites.

```
http://www.as.ua.edu/ant/Faculty/murphy/
               cultmat.htm
```

Margaret Mead's Anthropological Work

This site, created by the American Museum of Natural History, explores Margaret Mead's life and provides a history of her anthropological work. It also includes links to articles that discuss Mead's influence on anthropology.

```
http://www.amnh.org/exhibitions/expeditions/
treasure_fossil/Treasures/Margaret_Mead/mead.html
```

The following site has Margaret Mead's biography with lots of details.

```
http://www.interculturalstudies.org/IIS/Mead/
               index.html
```

This site considers Margaret Mead's centennial and its significance.

```
http://www.interculturalstudies.org/IIS/Mead/
            2001centennial.html
```

The !Kung of the Kalahari Desert

The !Kung of the Kalahari Desert Web site contains general information about this group of people who are now called the Ju/'hoansi by most scholars.

```
http://www.ucc.uconn.edu/~epsadm03/Kung.html
```

Islam for Today

Islam for Today is a Web site that provides basic information about Islam for non-Muslims. Explore the links to basic Islamic beliefs, Muslim history and civilizations, and articles on Islam.

```
http://www.islamfortoday.com
```

Collisions of Religions and Violence: Redux

Collisions of Religions and Violence: Redux is a Web site that contains a special issue of the journal *Cross Currents* and deals specifically with the question of whether or not conflict and violence emerge from immutable religious and ethnic differences.

```
http://www.crosscurrents.org/violencespecial.htm
```

PART 4

Cultural Anthropology

*C*ultural anthropologists study the culture and society of living communities. Like other anthropologists, cultural anthropologists are concerned with developing and testing models about the human condition and the range of human possibilities, such as whether gender inequality or violence are inevitable in human societies. Some anthropologists have asked whether the lives of small hunting-gathering bands resemble the lifeways of early human groups with similar technologies. Other anthropologists have asked about the strength of other people's religious beliefs. But at the heart of anthropological debate today is whether anthropology should model itself on the natural sciences or whether anthropologists should see their role more as interpreters of human cultures.

- Should Cultural Anthropology Model Itself on the Natural Sciences?

- Was Margaret Mead's Fieldwork on Samoan Adolescents Fundamentally Flawed?

- Do Native Peoples Today Invent Their Traditions?

- Is It Natural for Adopted Children to Want to Find Out About Their Birth Parents?

- Are San Hunter-Gatherers Basically Pastoralists Who Have Lost Their Herds?

- Do Some Illnesses Exist Only Among Members of a Particular Culture?

- Is Ethnic Conflict Inevitable?

ISSUE 9

Should Cultural Anthropology Model Itself on the Natural Sciences?

YES: Marvin Harris, from "Cultural Materialism Is Alive and Well and Won't Go Away Until Something Better Comes Along," in Robert Borofsky, ed., *Assessing Cultural Anthropology* (McGraw-Hill, 1994)

NO: Clifford Geertz, from *The Interpretation of Cultures: Selected Essays by Clifford Geertz* (Basic Books, 1973)

ISSUE SUMMARY

YES: Cultural anthropologist Marvin Harris argues that anthropology has always been a science and should continue to be scientific. He contends that the most scientific approach to culture is cultural materialism, which he has developed specifically to be a "science of culture." Anthropology's goal should be to discover general, verifiable laws as in the other natural sciences, concludes Harris.

NO: Cultural anthropologist Clifford Geertz views anthropology as a science of interpretation, and as such he argues that anthropology should never model itself on the natural sciences. He believes that anthropology's goal should be to generate deeper interpretations of diverse cultural phenomena, using what he calls "thick description," rather than attempting to prove or disprove scientific laws.

For more than a century, anthropologists have viewed their discipline as a science of humankind or as a science of culture. But not all anthropologists agree about what being a science should mean. At issue has been the question: Just what kind of science is anthropology?

Nineteenth- and early-twentieth-century anthropologists generally viewed anthropology as one of the natural sciences, and most early theorists, such as Edward Tylor, James Fraser, and Lewis Henry Morgan, saw anthropology as an extension of biology. Like biology, anthropology is a comparative discipline, and ethnographic descriptions of particular societies resemble the systematic descriptions that biologists provide about different species. Most early anthropologists were also attracted to the theories of the naturalist Charles Darwin, whose theory of natural selection attempted to explain how natural species evolved. For anthropologists evolution meant explaining how one social form evolved into another, how one kind of society developed into another.

With the rise of functionalism in the 1920s, evolutionary models became much less important as sociocultural anthropologists made detailed studies of individual societies, conducting ethnographic fieldwork lasting a year or two. Research became a total immersion into the culture, and anthropologists were expected to learn the local language, conduct participant observation, and try to understand the indigenous culture from the "native's point of view."

Although many anthropologists abandoned evolutionary questions in the 1920s, several new kinds of evolutionary models emerged after the Second World War. Leslie White proposed a unilineal model, arguing that cultural evolution could be explained in terms of how much energy a people could capture with their technology. Julian Steward proposed a rather different multilinear model to explain how societies in widely scattered parts of the world respond similarly to environmental and ecological constraints.

Building on these kinds of evolutionary models, Marvin Harris developed an approach he has called "cultural materialism." For Harris cultural materialism makes anthropology a science that parallels the evolutionary and biological sciences. But whereas biologists try to explain the physical evolution of species through natural selection, Harris argues that anthropologists should explain cultural evolution by understanding "cultural selection." Some cultural practices, whether actual behaviors or ideas, directly influence the community's successful adaptation to its material environment. Harris contends that anthropology's research agenda should be to establish regular, predictable, and verifiable laws just as scientists in other scientific fields do.

In his selection, Clifford Geertz argues that anthropologists should not attempt any kind of positivist science at all and that it is futile to seek scientific laws to explain human behavior. He contends that such laws would be either so general as to be meaningless, so obvious as to be trivial, or so specific to particular cultural settings as to have no relevance to other communities. The interpretation of cultures requires "thick description," in which the anthropologist is sensitive to cultural meanings and can provide a nuanced understanding of what he or she has observed, heard, and experienced in the field. Thus, for Geertz, anthropology should develop as a science of interpretation, and by definition such a science of interpretation cannot consist of verifiable laws; instead, it depends on the personal interpretive abilities of each individual anthropologist.

These selections pose several questions that lie at the heart of all sociocultural anthropology. Should anthropologists focus their attention on developing evolutionary theories, such as the kinds of cultural materialist explanations Harris seeks? Or, should anthropology primarily seek a more modest role in the multicultural world of today, attempting to translate and make sense of other people's cultural practices? And finally, is anthropology big enough to hold both of these perspectives and others as well?

Marvin Harris

 **YES**

Cultural Materialism Is Alive and Well and Won't Go Away Until Something Better Comes Along

Cultural materialism is a paradigm whose principles are relevant to the conduct of research and the development of theory in virtually all of the fields and subfields of anthropology. Indeed, it has been guesstimated (Thomas 1989:115) that half of the archaeologists in the United States consider themselves to be cultural materialist to some degree. For cultural materialists, whether they be cultural anthropologists, archaeologists, biological anthropologists, or linguists, the central intellectual experience of anthropology is not enthnography but the exchange of data and theories among different fields and subfields concerned with the global, comparative, diachronic, and synchronic study of humankind: the origin of the hominids, the emergence of language and culture, the evolution of cultural differences and similarities, and the ways in which biocultural, mental, behavioral, demographic, environmental and other nomothetic processes have shaped and continue to shape the human world.

Culture

. . . The culture in cultural materialism refers to the socially conditioned repertories of activities and thoughts that are associated with particular social groups or populations. This definition of culture stands opposed to the fixed, "essentialist" notions that inspire those who define culture as a realm of pure and uniform ideas hovering over the hub-bub of the daily life of specific individuals. For cultural materialists, culture elements are constructed (more specifically, abstracted) from the bedrock of the immensely variable thoughts and behavior of specific individuals (Harris 1964a). . . . [C]ultural materialists have long argued that culture is at bottom an unfolding material process (*viz.* the concept of "behavior stream") rather than an emanation of a platonic archetype. . . . Yet, it would be completely self-defeating to limit the definition of culture and the scope of the social sciences . . . to the bedrock of individual thought and activity. Although we cannot see or touch entities such as a mode of production or a transnational corporation or a sociocultural system, to the extent that these

From Marvin Harris, "Cultural Materialism Is Alive and Well and Won't Go Away Until Something Better Comes Along," in Robert Borofsky, ed., *Assessing Cultural Anthropology* (McGraw-Hill, 1994). Copyright © 1994 by McGraw-Hill, Inc. Reprinted by permission of Robert Borofsky. Notes and references omitted.

are logical and empirical abstractions built up out of the observation of individual-level events, they possess a reality that is not inferior to any other reality. Indeed, it is imperative for human survival and well-being that we learn to rise above individual thoughts and actions to the level at which we can begin to examine the aggregate effects of social life and the behavior of such higher-order entities as institutions and whole sociocultural systems. Political economies are as real as the individuals who fall under their sway, and a lot more powerful.

Paradigms

Paradigms stipulate the principles which govern the conduct of research. Principles fall into two classes: rules for acquiring, testing, and validating knowledge (i.e., epistemological principles) and rules for generating and evaluating theories (i.e., theoretical principles). A widely misunderstood aspect of scientific paradigms is that neither the epistemological or theoretical principles nor the paradigm as a whole has the status of a scientific theory. Principles such as creationism, natural selection, or the priority of infrastructure are not falsifiable. This does not mean however that paradigms are "ships that pass in the night." Paradigms can be compared with each other and evaluated from two standpoints: (1) their logical structure and internal coherence and (2) their respective abilities to produce scientific theories in conformity with the criteria discussed below. From this vantage point, the alternatives to cultural materialism presented in this [selection] offer slight hope of safe passage. I see a lot of sunken ships in the muddy waters of post-postmodernism—ships built out of flawed accounts of the history of anthropological theory, parochial agendas, inchoate conceptions of the nature of human society and human cultures, and a lack of well-formed epistemological and theoretical principles or useful substantive achievements that might justify a future— any future—for anthropology.

Epistemological Principles: Science

Cultural materialism is based on certain epistemological principles which are held in common by all disciplines which claim to have scientific knowledge. Scientific knowledge is obtained by public, replicable operations (observations and logical transformations). The aim of scientific research is to formulate explanatory theories which are (1) predictive (or retrodictive), (2) testable (or falsifiable), (3) parsimonious, (4) of broad scope, and (5) integratable or cumulative within a coherent and expanding corpus of theories.

The same criteria distinguish scientific theories which are more acceptable from those which are less acceptable. Scientific theories find acceptance in accordance with their relative powers of predictability, testability, parsimony, scope, and integratability as compared with rival theories about the same phenomena. Since one can only approach, but never completely reach, perfection in this regard, scientific theories are held as tentative approximations, never as "facts."

This view of science derives from the logical positivist and empiricist philosophical traditions. . . . Note that it makes no claim to being "value free." Rather it proposes to overcome the inevitable biases of all forms of knowledge by methodological rules that insist upon opening to public scrutiny the operations by which particular facts and theories come to be constructed. The oftrepeated charge by postmodernist science-bashers that there is no community of observers who can or do scrutinize anthropological, especially ethnographic operations . . . is belied by the intense criticisms to which crucial facts and theories are regularly subjected in the pages of anthropology's principal journals. Challenges by other observers to the ethnographic accuracy of the work of Boas, Mead, Benedict, Redfield, Evans-Pritchard, Malinowski, Lee, Vayda, and Chagnon just for starters, whether based on fresh fieldwork or written sources, clearly do fulfill the scientific model for independent testing by other observers. . . . It may take awhile, but ethnographers working in the same region if not the same village do help to keep each other in touch with basic ethnographic facts. However, I certainly agree . . . that the future of ethnography lies in greatly expanding the use of field teams and the number of restudies rather than, as Marcus proposes . . . increasing the number of experimental, personalistic, and idiosyncratic field studies carried out by untrained wouldbe novelists and ego-tripping narcissists afflicted with congenital logo-diarrhea.

. . . The reason that cultural materialists favor knowledge produced in conformity with the epistemological principles of science is not because science guarantees absolute truth free of subjective bias, error, untruths, lies, and frauds. It is because science is the best system yet devised for reducing subjective bias, error, untruths, lies, and frauds. . . .

Following the lead of Clifford Geertz and under the direct influence of postmodern philosophers and literary critics such as Paul De Man, Jacques Derrida, and Michel Foucault, interpretationist anthropologists have adopted an increasingly arrogant and intolerant rhetoric aimed at ridding anthropology of all vestiges of scientific "totalizing" paradigms. According to Stephen Tyler, for example, sociocultural anthropologists should abandon

> the inappropriate mode of scientific rhetoric that entails "objects," "facts," "descriptions," "inductions," "generalizations," "verification," "experiment," "truth," and like concepts that, except as empty invocations, have no parallels either in the experience of ethnographic fieldwork or in the writing of ethnographies. The urge to conform to the canons of scientific rhetoric has made the easy realism of natural history the dominant mode of ethnographic prose, but it has been an illusory realism, promoting, on the one hand, the absurdity of "describing" nonentities such as "culture" or "society" as if they were fully observable, though somewhat ungainly, bugs, and, on the other, the equally ridiculous behaviorist pretense of "describing" repetitive patterns in isolation from the discourse that actors use in constituting and situating their action, and all in simpleminded surety that the observers' grounding discourse is itself an objective form sufficient to the task of describing acts. (1986:130)

Tyler's totalizing renunciation of the search for objects, facts, descriptions, inductions, generalizations, verification, experiment, truth, and "like concepts"(!)

in human affairs mocks itself so effectively that any attempt at rebuttal would be anticlimactic. I do think it may be useful, however, to point out that the "simpleminded surety" with which positivists and behaviorists are alleged to view human social life flagrantly distorts the entire history of science in general, during which all sureties, simpleminded or not, have been subject to relentless skepticism, and the history of logical positivism in particular, during which the struggle to create objective data languages has constituted the central focus of a vast and continuing philosophical effort.

Anthropology's dedicated science-bashers are not mollified by the assurance that cultural materialists seek probabilities rather than certainties, generalizations rather than laws. . . .

Questions and Answers

The fallacies that embolden these queries are so transparent that one must wonder if the interlocutors really intend to be taken seriously. . . .

Question   Just how often does something have to recur in order for it to serve as the basis for a generalization?

Answer   The more times the better.

Question   If generalizations cannot be expected to be applicable to any specific case, what good are they?

Answer   The better the generalization, the more *probable* its applicability to the particular case, the more useful it is. (It is definitely useful to know that a particular person who smokes four packs of cigarettes a day is ten times more likely to get lung cancer than one who doesn't smoke, even though not all heavy smokers get lung cancer.)

Question   Why must science be equated with generalizing?

Answer   Because science is by definition a generalizing form of knowledge.

Question   Is the mandate to generalize nothing but a "procedural rule"?

Answer   Of course. And anyone is free to ignore the rule but to do so is to cease doing science. (It is also likely to get you killed the next time you step off the curb against the light, or the next time you strike a match to look inside your gas tank.)

Last question   Instead of generalizing, why not consider "all the particularity of the individual case"?

Answer   Because there are no limits to particularity. Any project that proposes to deliver *all* the particularities of any macrophysical event, human or not human, therefore makes a preposterous claim on our time and resources. For this reason, in science endless particularity is the exact equivalent of endless ignorance.

Epistemological Principles: Emics and Etics

In addition to the general epistemological principles shared with other scientific disciplines, cultural materialism is also based on epistemological principles which are specific to the study of human sociocultural systems. These involve: (1) the separation of mental events (thoughts) from behavior (actions of body parts and their environmental effects) and (2) the separation of emic from etic views of thoughts and behavior . . . The reason for the epistemological distinction between mental and behavioral events is that the operations (observational procedures) used to obtain knowledge of mental events are categorically distinct from those needed to obtain knowledge of behavioral events. In the former, observers depend directly or indirectly on participants to communicate what is going on inside their heads; in the latter observers are not dependent on actors to identify the actor's body motions and the environmental effects of those motions. The reason for the further distinction between emic and etic events is that the separation of mental from behavioral events does not exhaustively specify the epistemological status of the categories (data language) employed in the identification of mental or behavioral events. Observers have the option of describing both kinds of events in terms of categories that are defined, identified, and validated by the community of participants (emics) or by the community of observers (etics). Four types of knowledge stem from these distinctions: (1) emics of thought; (2) emics of behavior; (3) etics of behavior; (4) etics of thought.

To illustrate, consider the practice of indirect infanticide in northeast Brazil: (1) A sample of economically and socially deprived mothers condemns and abhors infanticide. (2) These mothers insist that their own behavior has been devoted to sustaining the life of their infants. (3) Observers note, however, that some of these mothers actually withhold food and drink from certain infants, especially from infants that are first and last born. (4) On the basis of the observed occurrence of maternal neglect and high infant mortality, it can be inferred that these disadvantaged women have thoughts that are contrary to or that modify their elicited emics of thought and behavior. . . . Emic and etic versions of social life are often but not necessarily contradictory. . . . But failure to distinguish between emic and etic and between mental and behavior data renders much of the sociocultural literature of cultural anthropology useless by literally preventing researchers from understanding the referential significance of their descriptive discourse (Harris 1968; Marano 1982; Headland, Pike, and Harris 1990).

Despite a persistent barrage of uninformed or malicious assertions to the contrary, cultural materialists insist that the proper study of humankind is both emics and etics and both thought and behavior. . . .

While no cultural materialist has ever advocated making the subject matter of cultural anthropology exclusively etic or behavioral, the postmodernists and their idealist predecessors have relentlessly advocated essentialist exclusions with regard to what cultural anthropologists ought to study. . . .

Theoretical Principles

These rest on the assumption that certain categories of behavioral and mental responses are more directly important to the survival and well-being of human individuals than others and that it is possible to measure the efficiency with which such responses contribute to the achievement of an individual's survival and well-being. This assumption lies at the basis of the "costing" of alternative patterns of behavior which in turn is essential for identifying optimizing behavior and thought . . . and the development of materialist theories of the causes of sociocultural differences and similarities.

The categories of responses whose costs and benefits underwrite cultural selection and cultural evolution are empirically derived from the biological and psychological sciences that deal with the genetically given needs, drives, aversions, and behavioral tendencies of *Homo sapiens*: sex, hunger, thirst, sleep, language acquisition, need for affective nurturance, nutritional and metabolic processes, vulnerability to mental and physical disease and to stress by darkness, cold, heat, altitude, moisture, lack of air, and other environmental hazards. This list is obviously not intended to encapsulate the whole of human nature. It remains open-ended and responsive to new discoveries about the human biogram and population-specific genetic differences. . . .

Infrastructure, Structure, and Superstructure

The components of social life which most directly mediate and facilitate the satisfaction of biogram needs, drives, aversions, and behavioral tendencies constitute the causal center of sociocultural systems. The burden of this mediation is borne by the conjunction of demographic, technological, economic, and ecological processes—the modes of production and reproduction—found in every socio-cultural system. More precisely, it is the etic behavioral aspect of the demo-techno-econo-environmental conjunction that is salient. . . . Infrastructure constitutes the interface between nature in the form of unalterable physical, chemical, biological, and psychological constraints on the one hand, and culture which is *Homo sapiens*'s primary means of optimizing health and well-being, on the other. . . . Cultural optimizations and adaptations must in the first and last instance conform to the restraints and opportunities of the environment and of human nature.

In addition to infrastructure, every human sociocultural system consists of two other major subsystems: structure and superstructure, each with its mental/behavioral and emic/etic aspects. Structure denotes the domestic and political subsystems, while superstructure denotes the realm of values, aesthetics, rules, beliefs, symbols, rituals, religions, philosophies, and other forms of knowledge including science itself.

The basic theoretical principles of cultural materialism can now be stated: (1) optimizations of the cost/benefits of satisfying biogram needs probabilistically (i.e. with more than chance significance) determine (or select for) changes in the etic behavioral infrastructure; (2) changes in the etic behavioral infrastructure probabilistically select for changes in the rest of the sociocultural system. The combination of 1 and 2 is the principle of the primacy of infrastructure.

As a guide to theory-making, the primacy of infrastructure enjoins anthropological researchers concerned with the explanation of sociocultural differences and similarities to concentrate on and to give priority to the formulation of hypotheses and theories in which components of the etic behavioral infrastructure are treated as independent variables while components of structure and superstructure are treated as dependent variables. The practical consequence of such a commitment of research effort is that the search for causal infrastructural variables will be conducted with decisively greater persistence and in greater detail than is likely under the auspices of alternative paradigms. The history of anthropological theory demonstrates that those who lack a paradigmatic commitment inevitably "quit early" when confronted with difficult, puzzling phenomena. . . .

Another aspect of the principle of the primacy of infrastructure that is surrounded by misinformation is the feedback between infrastructure and structure or superstructure. It would be convenient for materialist-bashers if the principle of the primacy of infrastructure meant that cultural materialists regard the mental, emic, and symbolic-ideational aspects of sociocultural systems as mere mechanical reflexes or epiphenomena of infrastructure. ("Harris thinks ideas, symbols, values, art, and religion are unimportant aspects of human life. Ugh!") Again I quote from Murphy's paper: "As for the materialists, they fail to recognize that cultural forms have lives of their own and are not mere epiphenomena of underlying 'infrastructures'" (page 57). The attempt by Murphy and others to portray cultural materialism as a paradigm in which "the ideas by which men [sic] live have no importance for their action" (Bloch 1985b:134) is totally at variance with the prominence of the phrase "sociocultural system" in the specification of cultural materialist principles. Why does one bother to talk about the systemic role of structure and superstructure if infrastructure alone has importance for action? Do cultural materialists propose that people go about producing and reproducing at random and without an idea in their heads? Could sociocultural life as we know it exist if there was nothing but infrastructure? Certainly not. No more than one can imagine people living without an infrastructure, i.e., living on ideas alone. . . . The issue is not whether thought is important for action, but whether thoughts and actions are equally important in the explanation of the evolution of sociocultural systems. Cultural materialism—indeed any genuinely materialist paradigm in the social sciences—says no. The system is asymmetrical. Infrastructural variables are more determinative of the evolution of the system. But this does not mean that the infrastructure can do without its superstructure. . . .

To illustrate, consider the changes in U.S. family life since World War II with reference to the disappearance of the male breadwinner role, the demise of the multiparous stay-at-home housewife, and the rise of feminist ideologies emphasizing the value of sexual, economic, and intellectual independence for women. As I have proposed elsewhere (Harris 1981a), these structural and superstructural transformations are the determined outcome of a shift from goods-producing industrialism to service-and-information-producing industrialism, mediated by the call-up of a reserve army of housewives into low-paying service-and-information nonunion jobs. The infrastructural transformations themselves were related to the use of electronic technologies and to declining productivity in the unionized smokestack industries which had created and sustained the male-breadwinner-stay-at-home-housewife families. The rise of a feminist ideology which glamorized the wage labor market and the intellectual, sexual, and emotional independence of women was the determined outcome of the same infrastructural force. However, it is clear that both the structural and superstructural changes have exerted and continue to exert an amplifying, positive-feedback effect on the infrastructural transformations. As the consequences of the call-up of the female labor force manifest themselves in higher divorce rates, lower first marriage rates, and historically low fertility rates, service-and-information industrialism is in turn amplified into an ever-more dominant mode of production and reproduction. Similarly, as feminist ideologies continue to raise consciousness against the vestiges of male breadwinner sexism, men and women find themselves locked into the labor force as competitors, wages for both are driven down, unions are driven out, and the profitability of the service-and-information industries rises, encouraging more diversion of capital from goods-producing enterprises into service-and-information production. . . .

Power and Cultural Materialist Theories

For proposing that changes in sociocultural systems are selected for in conformity with optimizing principles, cultural materialism has been caricatured as a form of functionalism in which all is for the best in the best of all possible worlds (Diener, Nonini, and Robkin 1978). This accusation cannot be reconciled with cultural materialism's long-standing focus on problems of class, caste, racial, and sexual inequality and exploitation. . . .

The fact that modes of production and reproduction are selected for in conformity with optimizing principles does not mean that every member of a society benefits equally from this selection process. Where marked differences of power have evolved as between sexes and stratified groups, the benefits may be distributed in a completely lopsided and exploitative fashion. Under such circumstances, the costs and benefits must be reckoned not only with respect to individuals in their infrastructural context but with respect to the political-economic decisions of power holders. This does not mean that all changes which benefit ruling-class interests necessarily have adverse effects on everyone else, as Marxists have wanted us to believe. For example, as indicated above, the rise of the service and information sectors in hyperindustrial mixed economies reflects the higher rates of profit to be obtained from unorganized labor. Thus, an increasing portion of the industrial labor force consists of women who have to some extent risen above their previous condition as unpaid housewife-mothers dominated by blue-collar male chauvinist husbands. There is no contradiction involved in holding that the greater advantages accruing to U.S. capitalist interests are facilitated by a lesser but still favorable balance of benefits over costs accruing to women. The behavior of both strata exhibits the predicted optimizations even though one might hold that the gain for most women, especially for minority women, is slight by comparison.

Cultural materialism is thus no less emphatic about the importance of political-economic inequality as a modifier of optimization process than are various Marxist theoreticians who claim to have a monopoly on the defense of the oppressed (Harris 1991). . . . One can never escape the question of benefits for whom or of costs for whom. Far from neglecting or "covering up" the effects of political factors on optimizations, cultural materialists recognize regular systemic feedbacks from the structural to the infrastructural level which give rise to political economy, political demography, political technology, and political ecology. One cannot for example explain the adoption and spread of technological devices such as shotguns, of new varieties of wheat and rice, tractors, or solar cell generators apart from the interests of trading companies, agribusiness, and petrochemical transnational corporations, local landowners, banks, etc. . . .

Where Is Cultural Anthropology Going?

A popular myth among interpretationist science-bashers is that positive anthropology deservedly collapsed because of its failure to produce a coherent body of scientific theories about society and culture. Marcus and Fischer for example assert that there is a crisis in anthropology and related fields because of the "disarray" in the "attempt to build general and comprehensive theories that would subsume all piecemeal research" (1986:118). This implies that the postmodernists have made a systematic study of the positivist corpus of theories that deal with the parallel and convergent evolution of sociocultural systems. But they have not done this. It was only after World War II that nonbiological, positivist cultural and archaeological paradigms gained acceptance among anthropologists. In the ensuing years unprecedented strides have been made in solving the puzzles of sociocultural evolution through a genuinely cumulative and broadening corpus of sophisticated and powerful theories based on vastly improved and expanded research methods. The cumulative expansion of knowledge has been especially marked within archaeology and at the interface between archaeology and cultural anthropology (see e.g. Johnson and Earle 1987). It is ironic, then, that at the very moment when anthropology is achieving its greatest scientific successes, anthropologists who have never tested the positivist theoretical corpus which they condemn hail the death of positivist anthropology and the birth of a "new" humanistic paradigm. Only those who know little about the history of anthropological theories could hail such a paradigm as "new," much less as "a refiguration of social thought" (Darnell 1984:271).

This raises the question of why antipositivistic humanism has become so attractive to a new generation of anthropologists (and other practitioners of social "science"). One reason may be that the generation of students reared during the 1960s and early 1970s believes that positivist social science is responsible for such twentieth-century scourges as fascism, Stalinism, U.S. imperialism, corpocracies, and the educational-industrial-military complex. No doubt hyperindustrialism, high tech, and the "technological fix" lead to feelings of dehumanization and alienation. But the association between all of this and positivist social science is spurious. The problem is not that we have had too much of positivist social science but that we have had too little (Harris 1974:264ff). The atrocities of the twentieth century have been carried out precisely by people who were ignorant of or vehemently opposed to positivist social science (e.g., Lenin, Stalin, Hitler, Mussolini). Too many anthropologists seem to have forgotten that there is a flip side to relativism, phenomenology, and antipositivism—the side on which relativists who denounce reason and scientific knowledge construct the world in their own image.

Clifford Geertz  **NO**

Thick Description: Toward an Interpretive Theory of Culture

I

[Here I argue] for a narrowed, specialized, and, so I imagine, theoretically more powerful concept of culture to replace E. B. Tylor's famous "most complex whole," which, its originative power not denied, seems to me to have reached the point where it obscures a good deal more than it reveals.

The conceptual morass into which the Tylorean kind of *pot-au-feu* theorizing about culture can lead, is evident in what is still one of the better general introductions to anthropology, Clyde Kluckhohn's *Mirror for Man*. In some twenty-seven pages of his chapter on the concept, Kluckhohn managed to define culture in turn as: (1) "the total way of life of a people"; (2) "the social legacy the individual acquires from his group"; (3) "a way of thinking, feeling, and believing"; (4) "an abstraction from behavior"; (5) a theory on the part of the anthropologist about the way in which a group of people in fact behave; (6) a "storehouse of pooled learning"; (7) "a set of standardized orientations to recurrent problems"; (8) "learned behavior"; (9) a mechanism for the normative regulation of behavior; (10) "a set of techniques for adjusting both to the external environment and to other men"; (11) "a precipitate of history"; and turning, perhaps in desperation, to similes, as a map, as a sieve, and as a matrix. In the face of this sort of theoretical diffusion, even a somewhat constricted and not entirely standard concept of culture, which is at least internally coherent and, more important, which has a definable argument to make is (as, to be fair, Kluckhohn himself keenly realized) an improvement. Eclecticism is self-defeating not because there is only one direction in which it is useful to move, but because there are so many: it is necessary to choose.

The concept of culture I espouse . . . is essentially a semiotic one. Believing, with [German sociologist and political economist] Max Weber, that man is an animal suspended in webs of significance he himself has spun, I take culture to be those webs, and the analysis of it to be therefore not an experimental science in search of law but an interpretive one in search of meaning. It is explication I am after, construing social expressions on their surface enigmatical. But this pronouncement, a doctrine in a clause, demands itself some explication.

II

. . . [I]f you want to understand what a science is, you should look in the first instance not at its theories or its findings, and certainly not at what its apologists say about it; you should look at what the practitioners of it do.

In anthropology, or anyway social anthropology, what the practitioners do is ethnography [the study of human cultures]. And it is in understanding what ethnography is, or more exactly *what doing ethnography is,* that a start can be made toward grasping what anthropological analysis amounts to as a form of knowledge. This, it must immediately be said, is not a matter of methods. From one point of view, that of the textbook, doing ethnography is establishing rapport, selecting informants, transcribing texts, taking genealogies, mapping fields, keeping a diary, and so on. But it is not these things, techniques and received procedures, that define the enterprise. What defines it is the kind of intellectual effort it is: an elaborate venture in, to borrow a notion from [British philosopher] Gilbert Ryle, "thick description."

Ryle's discussion of "thick description" appears in two recent essays of his (now reprinted in the second volume of his *Collected Papers*) addressed to the general question of what, as he puts it, *"Le Penseur"* is doing: "Thinking and Reflecting" and "The Thinking of Thoughts." Consider, he says, two boys rapidly contracting the eyelids of their right eyes. In one, this is an involuntary twitch; in the other, a conspiratorial signal to a friend. The two movements are, as movements, identical; from an I-am-a-camera, "phenomentalistic" observation of them alone, one could not tell which was twitch and which was wink, or indeed whether both or either was twitch or wink. Yet the difference, however unphotographable, between a twitch or wink is vast; as anyone unfortunate enough to have had the first taken for the second knows. The winker is communicating, and indeed communicating in a quite precise and special way: (1) deliberately, (2) to someone in particular, (3) to impart a particular message, (4) according to a socially established code, and (5) without cognizance of the rest of the company. As Ryle points out, the winker has now done two things, contracted his eyelids and winked, while the twitcher has done only one, contracted his eyelids. Contracting your eyelids on purpose when there exists a public code in which so doing counts as a conspiratorial signal *is* winking. That's all there is to it: a speck of behavior, a fleck of culture, and— *voilà!*—a gesture.

That, however, is just the beginning. Suppose, he continues, there is a third boy, who, "to give malicious amusement to his cronies," parodies the first boy's wink, as amateurish, clumsy, obvious, and so on. He, of course, does this in the same way the second boy winked and the first twitched: by contracting his right eyelids. Only this boy is neither winking nor twitching, he is parodying someone else's, as he takes it, laughable, attempt at winking. Here, too, a socially established code exists (he will "wink" laboriously, overobviously, perhaps adding a grimace—the usual artifices of the clown); and so also does a message. Only now it is not conspiracy but ridicule that is in the air. If the others think he is actually winking, his whole project misfires as completely, though with somewhat different results, as if they think he is twitching. One can go further: uncertain of his mimicking abilities, the would-be satirist may practice at home before the mirror, in which case he is not twitching, winking, or parodying, but rehearsing; though so far as what a camera, a radical behaviorist, or a believer in protocol sentences would record he is just rapidly contracting his right eyelids like all the others. Complexities are possible, if not practically without end, at least logically so. The original winker might, for example, actually have been fake-winking, say, to mislead outsiders into imagining there was a conspiracy afoot when there in fact was not, in which case our descriptions of what the parodist is parodying and the rehearser rehearsing of course shift accordingly. But the point is that between what Ryle calls the "thin description" of what the rehearser (parodist, winker, twitcher . . .) is doing ("rapidly contracting his right eyelids") and the "thick description" of what he is doing ("practicing a burlesque of a friend faking a wink to deceive an innocent into thinking a conspiracy is in motion") lies the object of ethnography: a stratified hierarchy of meaningful structures in terms of which twitches, winks, fake-winks, parodies, rehearsals of parodies are produced, perceived, and interpreted, and without which they would not (not even the zero-form twitches, which, *as a cultural category,* are as much nonwinks as winks are nontwitches) in fact exist, no matter what anyone did or didn't do with his eyelids.

Like so many of the little stories Oxford philosophers like to make up for themselves, all this winking, fake-winking, burlesque-fake-winking, rehearsed-burlesque-fake-winking, may seem a bit artificial.

. . . In finished anthropological writings, . . . this fact—that what we call our data are really our own constructions of other people's constructions of what they and their compatriots are up to—is obscured because most of what we need to comprehend a particular event, ritual, custom, idea, or whatever is insinuated as background information before the thing itself is directly examined. . . . There is nothing particularly wrong with this, and it is in any case inevitable. But it does lead to a view of anthropological research as rather more of an observational and rather less of an interpretive activity than it really is. Right down at the factual base, the hard rock, insofar as there is any, of the whole enterprise, we are already explicating: and worse, explicating explications. Winks upon winks upon winks.

. . . The point for now is only that ethnography is thick description. What the ethnographer is in fact faced with—except when (as, of course, he must do) he is pursuing the more automatized routines of data collection—is a multiplicity of complex conceptual structures, many of them superimposed upon or knotted into one another, which are at once strange, irregular, and inexplicit, and which he must contrive somehow first to grasp and then to render. And this is true at the most down-to-earth, jungle field work levels of his activity: interviewing informants, observing rituals, eliciting kin terms, tracing property lines, censusing households . . . writing his journal. Doing ethnography is like trying to read (in the sense of "construct a reading of") a manuscript—foreign, faded, full of ellipses, incoherencies, suspicious emendations, and tendentious commentaries, but written not in conventionalized graphs of sound but in transient examples of shaped behavior.

III

Culture, this acted document, thus is public, like a burlesqued wink or a mock sheep raid. Though ideational, it does not exist in someone's head; though unphysical, it is not an occult entity. The interminable, because unterminable, debate within anthropology as to whether culture is "subjective" or "objective," together with the mutual exchange of intellectual insults ("idealist!"— "materialist!"; "mentalist!"—"behaviorist!"; "impressionist!"—"positivist!") which accompanies it, is wholly misconceived. Once human behavior is seen as (most of the time; there *are* true twitches) symbolic action—action which, like phonation in speech, pigment in painting, line in writing, or sonance in music, signifies—the question as to whether culture is patterned conduct or a frame of mind, or even the two somehow mixed together, loses sense. The thing to ask about a burlesqued wink or a mock sheep raid is not what their ontological status is. It is the same as that of rocks on the one hand and dreams on the other—they are things of this world. The thing to ask is what their import is: what it is, ridicule or challenge, irony or anger, snobbery or pride, that, in their occurrence and through their agency, is getting said.

This may seem like an obvious truth, but there are a number of ways to obscure it. One is to imagine that culture is a self-contained "super-organic" reality with forces and purposes of its own; that is, to reify it. Another is to claim that it consists in the brute pattern of behavioral events we observe in fact to occur in some identifiable community or other; that is, to reduce it. But though both these confusions still exist, and doubtless will be always with us, the main source of theoretical muddlement in contemporary anthropology is a view which developed in reaction to them and is right now very widely held— namely, that, to quote [anthropologist] Ward Goodenough, perhaps its leading proponent, "culture [is located] in the minds and hearts of men."

Variously called ethnoscience, componential analysis, or cognitive anthropology (a terminological wavering which reflects a deeper uncertainty), this school of thought holds that culture is composed of psychological structures by means of which individuals or groups of individuals guide their behavior. "A society's culture," to quote Goodenough again, this time in a passage which has become the *locus classicus* of the whole movement, "consists of whatever it is one has to know or believe in order to operate in a manner acceptable to its members." And from this view of what culture is follows a view, equally assured, of what describing it is—the writing out of systematic rules, an ethnographic algorithm, which, if followed, would make it possible so to operate, to pass (physical appearance aside) for a native. In such a way, extreme subjectivism is married to extreme formalism, with the expected result: an explosion of debate as to whether particular analyses (which come in the form of taxonomies, paradigms, tables, trees, and other ingenuities) reflect what the natives "really" think or are merely clever simulations, logically equivalent but substantively different, of what they think.

As, on first glance, this approach may look close enough to the one being developed here to be mistaken for it, it is useful to be explicit as to what divides them. If, leaving our winks and sheep behind for the moment, we take, say, a

Beethoven quartet as an, admittedly rather special but, for these purposes, nicely illustrative, sample of culture, no one would, I think, identify it with its score, with the skills and knowledge needed to play it, with the understanding of it possessed by its performers or auditors, nor, to take care, *en passant*, of the reductionists and reifiers, with a particular performance of it or with some mysterious entity transcending material existence. The "no one" is perhaps too strong here, for there are always incorrigibles. But that a Beethoven quartet is a temporarily developed tonal structure, a coherent sequence of modeled sound—in a word, music—and not anybody's knowledge of or belief about anything, including how to play it, is a proposition to which most people are, upon reflection, likely to assent.

To play the violin it is necessary to possess certain habits, skills, knowledge, and talents, to be in the mood to play, and (as the old joke goes) to have a violin. But violin playing is neither the habits, skills, knowledge, and so on, nor the mood, nor (the notion believers in "material culture" apparently embrace) the violin. To make a trade pact in Morocco, you have to do certain things in certain ways (among others, cut, while chanting Quranic Arabic, the throat of a lamb before the assembled, undeformed, adult male members of your tribe) and to be possessed of certain psychological characteristics (among others, a desire for distant things). But a trade pact is neither the throat cutting nor the desire. . . .

Culture is public because meaning is. You can't wink (or burlesque one) without knowing what counts as winking or how, physically, to contract your eyelids, and you can't conduct a sheep raid (or mimic one) without knowing what it is to steal a sheep and how practically to go about it. But to draw from such truths the conclusion that knowing how to wink is winking and knowing how to steal a sheep is sheep raiding is to betray as deep a confusion as, taking thin descriptions for thick, to identify winking with eyelid contractions or sheep raiding with chasing woolly animals out of pastures. The cognitivist fallacy—that culture consists (to quote another spokesman for the movement, [anthropologist] Stephen Tyler) of "mental phenomena which can [he means "should"]—be analyzed by formal methods similar to those of mathematics and logic"—is as destructive of an effective use of the concept as are the behaviorist and idealist fallacies to which it is a misdrawn correction. Perhaps, as its errors are more sophisticated and its distortions subtler, it is even more so.

The generalized attack on privacy theories of meaning is, since early [Edmund] Husserl and late [Ludwig] Wittgenstein, so much a part of modern thought that it need not be developed once more here. What is necessary is to see to it that the news of it reaches anthropology; and in particular that it is made clear that to say that culture consists of socially established structures of meaning in terms of which people do such things as signal conspiracies and join them or perceive insults and answer them, is no more to say that it is a psychological phenomenon, a characteristic of someone's mind, personality, cognitive structure, or whatever, than to say that Tantrism, genetics, the progressive form of the verb, the classification of wines, the Common Law, or the notion of "a conditional curse" . . . is. What, in a place like Morocco, most prevents those of us who grew up winking other winks or attending other sheep from grasping what people are up to is not ignorance as to how cognition works . . . as a lack of familiarity with the imaginative universe within which their acts are signs. . . .

IV

. . . [T]he aim of anthropology is the enlargement of the universe of human discourse. That is not, of course, its only aim—instruction, amusement, practical counsel, moral advance, and the discovery of natural order in human behavior are others; nor is anthropology the only discipline which pursues it. But it is an aim to which a semiotic concept of culture is peculiarly well adapted. As interworked systems of construable signs (what, ignoring provincial usages, I would call symbols), culture is not a power, something to which social events, behaviors, institutions, or processes can be causally attributed; it is a context, something within which they can be intelligibly—that is, thickly—described. . . .

In short, anthropological writings are themselves interpretations, and second and third order ones to boot. (By definition, only a "native" makes first order ones: it's *his* culture.) They are, thus, fictions; fictions, in the sense that they are "something made," "something fashioned"—the original meaning of *fictiō*—not that they are false, unfactual, or merely "as if" thought experiments. . . .

V

Now, this proposition, that it is not in our interest to bleach human behavior of the very properties that interest us before we begin to examine it, has sometimes been escalated into a larger claim: namely, that as it is only those properties that interest us, we need not attend, save cursorily, to behavior at all. Culture is most effectively treated, the argument goes, purely as a symbolic system (the catch phrase is, "in its own terms"), by isolating its elements, specifying the internal relationships among those elements, and then characterizing the whole system in some general way—according to the core symbols around which it is organized, the underlying structures of which it is a surface expression, or the ideological principles upon which it is based. Though a distinct improvement over "learned behavior" and "mental phenomena" notions of what culture is, and the source of some of the most powerful theoretical ideas in contemporary anthropology, this hermetical approach to things seems to me to run the danger (and increasingly to have been overtaken by it) of locking cultural analysis away from its proper object, the informed logic of actual life. There is little profit in extricating a concept from the defects of psychologism only to plunge it immediately into those of schematicism.

Behavior must be attended to, and with some exactness, because it is through the flow of behavior—or, more precisely, social action—that cultural forms find articulation. They find it as well, of course, in various sorts of artifacts, and various states of consciousness; but these draw their meaning from the role they play (Wittgenstein would say their "use") in an ongoing pattern of life, not from any intrinsic relationships they bear to one another. . . .

A further implication of this is that coherence cannot be the major test of validity for a cultural description. Cultural systems must have a minimal degree of coherence, else we would not call them systems; and, by observation, they normally have a great deal more. But there is nothing so coherent as a paranoid's delusion or a swindler's story. The force of our interpretations cannot rest, as they are now so often made to do, on the tightness with which they hold together, or the assurance with which they are argued. Nothing has done more, I think, to discredit cultural analysis than the construction of impeccable depictions of formal order in whose actual existence nobody can quite believe.

If anthropological interpretation is constructing a reading of what happens, then to divorce it from what happens—from what, in this time or that place, specific people say, what they do, what is done to them, from the whole vast business of the world—is to divorce it from its applications and render it vacant. A good interpretation of anything—a poem, a person, a history, a ritual, an institution, a society—takes us into the heart of that of which it is the interpretation. When it does not do that, but leads us instead somewhere else—into an admiration of its own elegance, of its author's cleverness, or of the beauties of Euclidean order—it may have its intrinsic charms; but it is something else than what the task at hand—figuring out what all that rigamarole with the sheep is about—calls for. . . .

The ethnographer "inscribes" social discourse; *he writes it down.* In so doing, he turns it from a passing event, which exists only in its own moment of occurrence, into an account, which exists in its inscriptions and can be reconsulted. . . .

The situation is even more delicate, because, as already noted, what we inscribe (or try to) is not raw social discourse, to which, because, save very marginally or very specially, we are not actors, we do not have direct access, but only that small part of it which our informants can lead us into understanding. . . .

VI

So, there are three characteristics of ethnographic description: it is interpretive; what it is interpretive of is the flow of social discourse; and the interpreting involved consists in trying to rescue the "said" of such discourse from its perishing occasions and fix it in perusable terms. The *kula* is gone or altered; but, for better or worse, *The Argonauts of the Western Pacific* remains. But there is, in addition, a fourth characteristic of such description, at least as I practice it: it is microscopic.

This is not to say that there are no large-scale anthropological interpretations of whole societies, civilizations, world events, and so on. Indeed, it is such extension of our analyses to wider contexts that, along with their theoretical implications, recommends them to general attention and justifies our constructing them. . . .

It is merely to say that the anthropologist characteristically approaches such broader interpretations and more abstract analyses from the direction of exceedingly extended acquaintances with extremely small matters. He confronts the same grand realities that others—historians, economists, political scientists, sociologists—confront in more fateful settings: Power, Change, Faith, Oppression, Work, Passion, Authority, Beauty, Violence, Love, Prestige; but he confronts them in contexts obscure enough . . . to take the capital letters off them. These all-too-human constancies, "those big words that make us all afraid," take a homely form in such homely contexts. But that is exactly the advantage. There are enough profundities in the world already.

Yet, the problem of how to get from a collection of ethnographic miniatures— . . . an assortment of remarks and anecdotes—to wall-sized culturescapes of the nation, the epoch, the continent, or the civilization is not so easily passed over with vague allusions to the virtues of concreteness and the down-to-earth mind. For a science born in Indian tribes, Pacific islands, and African lineages and subsequently seized with grander ambitions, this has come to be a major methodological problem, and for the most part a badly handled one. The models that anthropologists have themselves worked out to justify their moving from local truths to general visions have been, in fact, as responsible for undermining the effort as anything their critics—sociologists obsessed with sample sizes, psychologists with measures, or economists with aggregates—have been able to devise against them.

Of these, the two main ones have been: the Jonesville-is-the-USA "microcosmic" model; and the Easter-Island-is-a-testing-case "natural experiment" model. Either heaven in a grain of sand, or the farther shores of possibility.

The Jonesville-is-America writ small (or America-is-Jonesville writ large) fallacy is so obviously one that the only thing that needs explanation is how people have managed to believe it and expected others to believe it. The notion that one can find the essence of national societies, civilizations, great religions, or whatever summed up and simplified in so-called "typical" small towns and villages is palpable nonsense. What one finds in small towns and villages is (alas) small-town or village life. If localized, microscopic studies were really dependent for their greater relevance upon such a premise—that they captured the great world in the little—they wouldn't have any relevance.

But, of course, they are not. The locus of study is not the object of study. Anthropologists don't study villages (tribes, towns, neighborhoods . . .); they study *in* villages. You can study different things in different places, and some things—for example, what colonial domination does to established frames of moral expectation—you can best study in confined localities. But that doesn't make the place what it is you are studying. . . .

The "natural laboratory" notion has been equally pernicious, not only because the analogy is false—what kind of a laboratory is it where *none* of the parameters are manipulable?—but because it leads to a notion that the data derived from ethnographic studies are purer, or more fundamental, or more solid, or less conditioned (the most favored word is "elementary") than those derived from other sorts of social inquiry. The great natural variation of cultural forms is, of course, not only anthropology's great (and wasting) resource, but the ground of its deepest theoretical dilemma: how is such variation to be squared with the biological unity of the human species? But it is not, even metaphorically, experimental variation, because the context in which it occurs varies along with it, and it is not possible (though there are those who try) to isolate the *y*'s from *x*'s to write a proper function. . . .

The methodological problem which the microscopic nature of ethnography presents is both real and critical. But it is not to be resolved by regarding a remote locality as the world in a teacup or as the sociological equivalent of a cloud chamber. It is to be resolved—or, anyway, decently kept at bay—by realizing that social actions are comments on more than themselves; that where an interpretation comes from does not determine where it can be impelled to go. Small facts speak to large issues, winks to epistemology, or sheep raids to revolution, because they are made to.

VII

There is an Indian story—at least I heard it as an Indian story—about an Englishman who, having been told that the world rested on a platform which rested on the back of an elephant which rested in turn on the back of a turtle, asked (perhaps he was an ethnographer; it is the way they behave), what did the turtle rest on? Another turtle. And that turtle? "Ah, Sahib, after that it is turtles all the way down."

. . . Cultural analysis is intrinsically incomplete. And, worse than that, the more deeply it goes the less complete it is. It is a strange science whose most telling assertions are its most tremulously based, in which to get somewhere with the matter at hand is to intensify the suspicion, both your own and that of others, that you are not quite getting it right. But that, along with plaguing subtle people with obtuse questions, is what being an ethnographer is like.

There are a number of ways to escape this—turning culture into folklore and collecting it, turning it into traits and counting it, turning it into institutions and classifying it, turning it into structures and toying with it. But they *are* escapes. The fact is that to commit oneself to a semiotic concept of culture and an interpretive approach to the study of it is to commit oneself to a view of ethnographic assertion as, to borrow W. B. Gallie's by now famous phrase, "essentially contestable." Anthropology, or at least interpretive anthropology, is a science whose progress is marked less by a perfection of consensus than by a refinement of debate. What gets better is the precision with which we vex each other. . . .

My own position in the midst of all this has been to try to resist subjectivism on the one hand and cabbalism on the other, to try to keep the analysis of symbolic forms as closely tied as I could to concrete social events and occasions, the public world of common life, and to organize it in such a way that the connections between theoretical formulations and descriptive interpretations were unobscured by appeals to dark sciences. I have never been impressed by the argument that, as complete objectivity is impossible in these matters (as, of course, it is), one might as well let one's sentiments run loose. As [economist] Robert Solow has remarked, that is like saying that as a perfectly aseptic environment is impossible, one might as well conduct surgery in a sewer. Nor, on the other hand, have I been impressed with claims that structural linguistics, computer engineering, or some other advanced form of thought is going to enable us to understand men without knowing them. Nothing will discredit a semiotic approach to culture more quickly than allowing it to drift into a combination of intuitionism and alchemy, no matter how elegantly the intuitions are expressed or how modern the alchemy is made to look.

The danger that cultural analysis, in search of all-too-deep-lying turtles, will lose touch with the hard surfaces of life—with the political, economic, stratificatory realities within which men are everywhere contained—and with the biological and physical necessities on which those surfaces rest, is an ever-present one. The only defense against it, and against, thus, turning cultural analysis into a kind of sociological aestheticism, is to train such analysis on such realities and such necessities in the first place. It is thus that I have written about nationalism, about violence, about identity, about human nature, about legitimacy, about revolution, about ethnicity, about urbanization, about status, about death, about time, and most of all about particular attempts by particular peoples to place these things in some sort of comprehensible, meaningful frame.

To look at the symbolic dimensions of social action—art, religion, ideology, science, law, morality, common sense—is not to turn away from the existential dilemmas of life for some empyrean realm of de-emotionalized forms; it is to plunge into the midst of them. The essential vocation of interpretive anthropology is not to answer our deepest questions, but to make available to us answers that others . . . have given, and thus to include them in the consultable record of what man has said.

POSTSCRIPT

Should Cultural Anthropology Model Itself on the Natural Sciences?

Cultural anthropology is often viewed as a big tent capable of embracing many diverse points of view, as the selections by Harris and Geertz suggest. One can see a number of parallels between anthropology and biology in this respect as well. Biology has always included those who provide systematic descriptions of natural species as well as theoretical biologists who develop and test evolutionary models. Some view anthropology in a similar way, arguing that Geertz's interpretive anthropology is merely the descriptive side of anthropology, while Harris's cultural materialism together with other evolutionary and ecological approaches provide the theoretical grounding. As Harris notes, most biological anthropologists and archaeologists either explicitly or implicitly draw on some form of cultural materialist theory, and it is this shared evolutionary theory that unifies the three main subfields of anthropology.

Geertz strongly disagrees with this view of anthropology, arguing that any positivist, nomothetic anthropology misses the nuance and subtlety that makes human cultures worth studying in the first place. But while Geertz is the most prominent champion of this viewpoint, he is not the harshest critic of efforts to turn anthropology into a law-based science. A number of younger scholars, such as James Clifford, George Marcus, and Stephen Tylor, have been much more vocal in their attacks on positivism in anthropology. Many of their arguments have origins in the interpretive approach developed by Geertz in the 1960s, but they have urged anthropology to become a self-reflective social science, which is often referred to as "critical theory." For these scholars, anthropologists should illuminate the implicit, underlying assumptions that have motivated anthropologists. Sometimes called "postmodernism," this perspective encourages anthropologists to deconstruct the assumptions of Western cultures. Some have suggested that critical theorists are more concerned with studying the culture of anthropology than with understanding anthropology's traditional subjects. In this sense, positivism in anthropology has become one of their most visible targets.

Cultural materialism is one direction for an evolutionary science of culture to develop, but it is not the only kind of "scientific" anthropology that has been proposed. Another evolutionary anthropology is "sociobiology," which takes a somewhat different approach from Harris. Sociobiologists argue that humans, like all animals, are genetically programmed to respond in certain ways, and cultural practices are just an external manifestation of inner biological drives. For example, sociobiologists argue that, like other species, humans are internally driven to pass on their genes to the next generation.

Thus, they expect individuals to be altruistic toward their offspring as well as others who are closely related to them and therefore share some of the same genetic material. Increasingly, sociobiologists have developed theories that they maintain are both testable and verifiable.

Must all anthropologists have the same perspective, or is the discipline strengthened by having diverse theoretical points of view? Is there some middle ground between cultural materialism and an interpretive (or even a critical) anthropology?

For an extended treatment of Harris's views, see his *Cultural Materialism: The Struggle for a Science of Culture* (Random House, 1979). Two of Harris's other books put his theories into practice: *Cows, Pigs, Wars, and Witches* (Random House, 1974) and *Cannibals and Kings: The Origins of Cultures* (Random House, 1977).

Geertz's *The Interpretation of Cultures* (Basic Books, 1973), for which his selection was written, is the most coherent statement outlining the breadth and scope of an interpretive anthropology. It contains what is probably his best-known interpretive essay, "Deep Play: Notes on the Balinese Cockfight." Students should also consult his *Local Knowledge: Further Essays in Interpretive Anthropology* (Basic Books, 1983) and *Works and Lives: The Anthropologist as Author* (Stanford University Press, 1988). Michael Fisher's review essay "Interpretive Anthropology," *Reviews in Anthropology* (vol. 4, no. 4, 1977) offers a useful overview.

For background on sociobiology, see Edmund O. Wilson's *Sociobiology: The New Synthesis* (Belknap Press, 1975), Daniel G. Freedman's *Human Sociobiology: a Holistic Approach* (Free Press, 1979), and Georg Breuer's *Sociobiology and the Human Dimension* (Cambridge University Press, 1992). For an alternative view, see Marshall Sahlins's critique *The Use and Abuse of Biology: An Anthropological Critique of Sociobiology* (University of Michigan Press, 1976).

Important essays from a critical perspective are contained in two edited volumes: George E. Marcus and Michael M. J. Fisher's *Anthropology as Cultural Critique: An Experimental Moment in the Human Sciences* (University of Chicago Press, 1986) and James Clifford and George E. Marcus's *Writing Culture: The Poetics and the Politics of Anthropology* (University of California Press, 1986).

ISSUE 10

Was Margaret Mead's Fieldwork on Samoan Adolescents Fundamentally Flawed?

YES: Derek Freeman, from *Margaret Mead and Samoa: The Making and Unmaking of an Anthropological Myth* (Harvard University Press, 1983)

NO: Lowell D. Holmes and Ellen Rhoads Holmes, from *Samoan Village: Then and Now,* 2d ed. (Harcourt Brace Jovanovich College Publishers, 1992)

ISSUE SUMMARY

YES: Social anthropologist Derek Freeman argues that Margaret Mead was wrong when she stated that Samoan adolescents had sexual freedom. He contends that Mead went to Samoa determined to prove anthropologist Franz Boas's cultural determinist agenda and states that Mead was so eager to believe in Samoan sexual freedom that she was consistently the victim of a hoax perpetrated by Samoan girls and young women who enjoyed tricking her.

NO: Cultural anthropologists Lowell D. Holmes and Ellen Rhoads Holmes contend that Margaret Mead had a very solid understanding of Samoan culture in general. During a restudy of Mead's research, they came to many of the same conclusions that Mead had reached about Samoan sexuality and adolescent experiences. Mead's description of Samoan culture exaggerates the amount of sexual freedom and the degree to which adolescence in Samoa is carefree but these differences, they argue, can be explained in terms of changes in Samoan culture since 1925 and in terms of Mead's relatively unsophisticated research methods as compared with field methods used today.

In 1925 a student of anthropologist Franz Boas named Margaret Mead set off for a nine-month study of adolescent women in Samoa. At only 23 years old, Mead was just barely beyond adolescence herself. Concerned about Mead's safety in a remote and distant place, Boas arranged for her to stay with an

American family. Here she could live in a European-style house and her physical safety would be ensured. For the next several months she studied the culture and lives of young Samoan women by visiting their village.

On her return to New York in 1925, she wrote up her dissertation for Boas, revising this volume for publication in 1928. She titled the book *Coming of Age in Samoa: A Psychological Study of Primitive Youth for Western Civilization*. Mead concluded that because Samoan culture was so much more relaxed about sexuality than Western culture, Samoan adolescents had a much more tranquil transition from childhood to adulthood than was observed in America and other Western countries. *Coming of Age in Samoa* was an immediate best-seller and it earned Mead renown as a scientist.

In 1983 Derek Freeman published his book entitled *Margaret Mead and Samoa: The Making and Unmaking of an Anthropological Myth* (Harvard University Press), an excerpt of which is provided as the Yes-side selection. Freeman argues that Mead was so eager to find support for her model that she blatantly biased her Samoan fieldwork findings and in effect falsified her data.

Freeman had worked in Western Samoa from 1940 to 1943, returning for further fieldwork from 1965 to 1967. During his research he found evidence that challenges some of Mead's published field data as well as a number of her conclusions regarding Samoan adolescence. He contends that his findings call into question Mead's entire project. He also contends that Mead's young Samoan informants perpetrated a hoax on her by making up stories about their promiscuity.

Freeman's selection is countered by a selection written by Lowell D. Holmes and Ellen Rhoads Holmes, who, in the 1950s, had conducted a restudy of the same community that Mead had visited. Holmes and Holmes had expressly intended to test the reliability and validity of Mead's findings. They conclude that while Mead's characterizations of Samoans are in some ways exaggerated, the characterizations are by no means fundamentally wrong.

These selections allow us to ask a number of questions about Mead's research: Did Mead unintentionally exaggerate her findings about sexual freedom? Or did she intentionally falsify her field data, specifically so that she could support Boas's model of cultural determinism? Could Mead's excesses be explained as the consequence of her being a youthful and inexperienced field researcher? Or can differences between Mead's findings and those of the selection authors be explained in other ways?

These selections raise a number of questions about the replicability of anthropological fieldwork, as well. Is it possible to conduct a systematic restudy of another anthropologist's field subjects? Can an anthropologist working in another village or on another island reliably challenge the findings of another anthropologist?

This issue also raises questions about the adequacy of Freeman's ethnographic data and his conclusions. Did Freeman also have biases that fundamentally affect his conclusions and should encourage us to challenge his assertions? Do either Mead or Freeman provide data that could resolve the nature-nurture question?

Margaret Mead and Samoa

Preface

By far the most widely known of Margaret Mead's numerous books is *Coming of Age in Samoa,* based on fieldwork on which she embarked in 1925 at the instigation of Franz Boas, her professor at Columbia University. Boas had sent the 23-year-old Mead to Samoa to study adolescence, and she returned with a startling conclusion. Adolescence was known in America and Europe as a time of emotional stresses and conflicts. If, Mead argued, these problems were caused by the biological processes of maturation, then they would necessarily be found in all human societies. But in Samoa, she reported, life was easy and casual, and adolescence was the easiest and most pleasant time of life. Thus in anthropological terms, according to Mead, Samoa was a "negative instance"— and the existence of this one counterexample demonstrated that the disturbances associated with adolescence in the United States and elsewhere had cultural and not biological causes. In the controversy between the adherents of biological determinism and those of cultural determinism, a controversy that was at its height in the 1920s, Mead's negative instance appeared to be a triumphant outcome for believers in the sovereignty of culture.

When *Coming of Age in Samoa* was published in 1928 it attracted immense attention, and its apparently conclusive finding swiftly entered anthropological lore as a jewel of a case. Since that time Mead's finding has been recounted in scores of textbooks, and through the vast popularity of *Coming of Age in Samoa,* the best-selling of all anthropological books, it has influenced the thinking of millions of people throughout the world. It is with the critical examination of this very widely accepted conclusion that I am concerned [here].

Scientific knowledge, as Karl Popper has shown, is principally advanced through the conscious adoption of "the critical method of error elimination." In other words, within science, propositions and theories are systematically tested by attempts to refute them, and they remain acceptable only as long as they withstand these attempts at refutation. In Popper's view, "in so far as a scientific statement speaks about reality it must be falsifiable," and rational criticism entails the testing of any particular statement in terms of its correspondence with the facts. Mead's classing of Samoa as a negative instance obviously depends on the adequacy of the account of Samoan culture on which it is based. It is thus very much a scientific proposition, for it is fully open to testing against the relevant empirical evidence.

While the systematic testing of the conclusions of a science is always desirable, this testing is plainly imperative when serious doubts have been expressed about some particular finding. Students of Samoan culture have long voiced such doubts about Mead's findings of 1928. . . . I adduce detailed empirical evidence to demonstrate that Mead's account of Samoan culture and character is fundamentally in error. I would emphasize that I am not intent on constructing an alternative ethnography of Samoa. Rather, the evidence I shall present has the specific purpose of scientifically refuting the proposition that Samoa is a negative instance by demonstrating that the depictions on which Mead based this assertion are, in varying degree, mistaken.

In undertaking this refutation I shall limit my scrutiny to those sections of Mead's writings which have stemmed from, or refer to, her researches on Samoa. My concern, moreover, is with the scientific import of these actual researches and *not* with Margaret Mead personally, or with any aspect of her ideas or activities that lies beyond the ambit of her writings on Samoa. I would emphasize also that I hold in high regard many of the personal achievements of Margaret Mead, Franz Boas, and the other individuals certain of whose assertions and ideas I necessarily must question in the pages that follow.

. . . When I reached Western Samoa in April 1940, I was very much a cultural determinist. *Coming of Age in Samoa* had been unreservedly commended to me by [Ernest] Beaglehole, and my credence in Mead's findings was complete.

After two years of study, during which I came to know all the islands of Western Samoa, I could speak Samoan well enough to converse in the company of chiefs with the punctilio that Samoan etiquette demands, and the time had come to select a local polity for intensive investigation. My choice was Sa'anapu, a settlement of 400 inhabitants on the south coast of Upolu. On my first visit to Sa'anapu I had become friendly with Lauvi Vainu'u, a senior talking chief. . . . I was to become his adopted son. From that time onward I lived as one of the Lauvi family whenever I was in Sa'anapu.

In my early work I had, in my unquestioning acceptance of Mead's writings, tended to dismiss all evidence that ran counter to her findings. By the end of 1942, however, it had become apparent to me that much of what she had written about the inhabitants of Manu'a in eastern Samoa did not apply to the people of western Samoa. After I had been assured by Samoans who had lived in Manu'a that life there was essentially the same as in the western islands, I realized that I would have to make one of the objectives of my research the systematic testing of Mead's depiction of Samoan culture.

Soon after I returned to Sa'anapu its chiefs forgathered one morning at Lauvi's house to confer on me one of the chiefly titles of their polity. I was thus able to attend all *fono*, or chiefly assemblies, as of right, and I soon came to be accepted by the community at large. From this time onward I was in an exceptionally favorable position to pursue my researches into the realities of Samoan life.

By the time I left Samoa in November 1943 I knew that I would one day face the responsibility of writing a refutation of Mead's Samoan findings. This would involve much research into the history of early Samoa. This task I began in 1945 in the manuscript holdings of the Mitchell Library in Sydney and later continued in England, where I thoroughly studied the Samoan archives of the London Missionary Society.

During 1946–1948, while studying anthropology at the University of London, I wrote a dissertation on Samoan social organization. . . . There then came, however, the opportunity to spend some years among the Iban of Borneo. With this diversion, . . . the continuation of my Samoan researches was long delayed.

I finally returned to Western Samoa, accompanied by my wife and daughters, at the end of 1965. Sa'anapu, now linked Apia by road, was once again my center of research. The chiefs of Sa'anapu immediately recognized the title they had conferred on me in 1943, and I became once again an active member of the Sa'anapu *fono*. My family and I remained in Samoa for just over two years, making frequent visits elsewhere in the district to which Sa'anapu belongs, as also to numerous other parts of the archipelago, from Saua in the east to Falealupo in the west.

Many educated Samoans, especially those who had attended college in New Zealand, had become familiar with Mead's writings about their culture. A number of them entreated me, as an anthropologist, to correct her mistaken depiction of the Samoan ethos. Accordingly, early in 1966 I set about the systematic examination of the entire range of Mead's writings on Samoa, seeking to test her assertions by detailed investigation of the particulars of the behavior or custom to which they referred. . . .

[I]n 1967 organized a formal traveling party to [the island of] Ta'ū. We visitors were received as long-lost kinsmen, and in the company of chiefs from both Ta'ū and Sa'anapu I was able to review all those facets of Mead's depiction of Samoa which were then still at issue. In Ta'ū I also recorded the testimony of men and women who remembered the period to which Mead's writings refer. In many instances these recollections were vivid and specific; as one of my informants remarked, the happenings of the mid 1920s were still fresh in their memories.

As my inquiries progressed it became evident that my critical scrutiny of Mead's conclusions would have to extend to the anthropological paradigm of which *Coming of Age in Samoa* was a part. . . .

My researches were not completed until 1981, when I finally gained access to the archives of the High Court of American Samoa for the 1920s. Thus my refutation of Mead's depiction of Samoa appears some years after her death. In November 1964, however, when Dr. Mead visited the Australian National University, I informed her very fully, during a long private conversation, of the empirical basis of my disagreement with her depiction of Samoa. From that time onward we were in correspondence, and in August 1978, upon its first completion, I offered to send her an early draft of my refutation of the conclusions she had reached in *Coming of Age in Samoa*. I received no reply to this offer before Dr. Mead's death in November of that year.

In September 1981 I returned to Western Samoa with the specific purpose of submitting a draft of [my] book to the critical scrutiny of Samoan scholars. . . . In the course of the refutation of Mead's misleading account of their culture, which many Samoans encouraged me to undertake, I have had to deal realistically with the darker side of Samoan life. During my visit of 1981 I found among contemporary Samoans both a mature appreciation of the need to face these realities and a clear-headed pride in the virtues and strengths of the Samoan way of life. . . .

Mead's Misconstruing of Samoa

. . . [The] notion that cultural determinism was absolute was "so obvious" to Mead that . . . she also avowed it in *Coming of Age in Samoa,* in respect of adolescent behavior.

That this doctrine of the absoluteness of cultural determinism should have seemed "so obvious" to Mead is understandable. Anthropology, when she began its study in 1922, was dominated by Boas' "compelling idea," as Leslie Spier has called it, of "the complete moulding of every human expression—inner thought and external behavior—by social conditioning," and by the time she left for Samoa in 1925 she had become a fervent devotee of the notion that human behavior could be explained in purely cultural terms. Further, although by the time of Mead's recruitment to its ranks cultural anthropology had achieved its independence, it had done so at the cost of becoming an ideology that, in an actively unscientific way, sought totally to exclude biology from the explanation of human behavior. Thus as, [Alfred] Kroeber declared, "the important thing about anthropology is not the science but an attitude of mind"—an attitude of mind, that is, committed to the doctrine of culture as a superorganic entity which incessantly shapes human behavior, "conditioning all responses." It was of this attitude of mind that Mead became a leading proponent, with (as Marvin Harris has observed) her anthropological mission, set for her by Boas, being to defeat the notion of a "panhuman hereditary human nature." She pursued this objective by tirelessly stressing, in publication after publication, "the absence of maturational regularities."

In her own account of this mission, Mead describes it as a battle which she and other Boasians had had to fight with the whole battery at their command, using the most fantastic and startling examples they could muster. It is thus evident that her writings during this period, about Samoa as about other South Seas cultures, had the explicit aim of confuting biological explanations of human behavior and vindicating the doctrines of the Boasian school. By 1939 this battle, according to Mead, had been won. . . .

For Mead's readers in North America and elsewhere in the Western world, there could be no more plausible location for the idyllic society of which she wrote than in the South Seas, a region that since the days of Bougainville has figured in the fantasies of Europeans and Americans as a place of preternatural contentment and sensual delight. So, as Mead reports, her announcement in 1925 that she was going to Samoa caused the same breathless stir as if she had been "setting off for heaven." Indeed, there were many in the 1920s, according to Mead, who longed to go to the South Sea islands "to escape to a kind of divine nothingness in which life would be reduced to the simplest physical terms, to sunshine and the moving shadows of palm trees, to bronze-bodied girls and bronze-bodied boys, food for the asking, no work to do, no obligations to meet."

. . . How did the young Margaret Mead come so to miscronstrue ethos and ethnography of Samoa? The fervency of her belief in cultural determinism and her tendency to view the South Seas as an earthly paradise go some way in accounting for what happened, but manifestly more was involved.

The Ph.D. topic that Boas assigned to Mead was the comparative study of canoe-building, house-building, and tattooing in the Polynesian culture area. During 1924 she gathered information on these activities from the available literature on the Hawaiians, the Marquesans, the Maori, the Tahitians, and the Samoans. These doctoral studies did not have any direct relevance to the quite separate problem of adolescence in Samoa that Boas set her in 1925, and, indeed, the fact that her reading was mainly on Eastern rather than Western Polynesia concealed from her the marked extent to which the traditional culture and values of Samoa differ from those of Tahiti. Again, during the spring of 1925 she had little time for systematic preparation for her Samoan researches. Indeed, the counsel she received from Boas about these researches prior to her departure for Pago Pago lasted, she tells us, for only half an hour. During this brief meeting Boas' principal instruction was that she should concentrate on the problem he had set her and not waste time doing ethnography. Accordingly, when in the second week of November 1925 Mead reached Manu'a, she at once launched into the study of adolescence without first acquiring, either by observation or from inquiry with adult informants, a thorough understanding of the traditional values and customs of the Manu'ans. This, without doubt, was an ill-advised way to proceed, for it meant that Mead was in no position to check the statements of the girls she was studying against a well-informed knowledge of the fa'aSamoa [Samoan way of life].

It is also evident that Mead greatly underestimated the complexity of the culture, society, history, and psychology of the people among whom she was to study adolescence. Samoan society, so Mead would have it, is "very simple," and Samoan culture "uncomplex." . . .

As any one who cares to consult Augustin Krämer's *Die Samoa-Inseln,* Robert Louis Stevenson's *A Footnote to History,* or J. W. Davidson's *Samoa mo Samoa* will quickly discover, Samoan society and culture are by no means simple and uncomplex; they are marked by particularities, intricacies, and subtleties quite as daunting as those which face students of Europe and Asia. Indeed, the fa'aSamoa is so sinuously complex that, as Stevenson's step-daughter, Isobel Strong, once remarked, "one may live long in Samoa without understanding the whys and wherefores." Mead, however, spent not even a few months on the systematic study of Manu'a before launching upon the study of adolescence immediately upon her arrival in Ta'ū in accordance with Boas' instructions. Thus, she has noted that while on her later field trips she had "the more satisfactory task of learning the culture first and only afterwards working on a special problem" in Samoa this was "not necessary."

. . . Another problem was that of being able to communicate adequately with the people she was to study. Mead had arrived in Pago Pago without any knowledge of the Samoan language. . . . In this situation Mead was plainly at some hazard pursuing her inquiries in Manu'a, for Samoans, when diverted by the stumbling efforts of outsiders to speak their demanding language, are inclined not to take them seriously.

Mead, then, began her inquiries with her girl informants with a far from perfect command of the vernacular, and without systematic prior investigation of Manu'an society and values. Added to this, she elected to live not in a Samoan household but with the handful of expatriate Americans who were the local representatives of the naval government of American Samoa, from which in 1925 many Manu'ans were radically disaffected. . . . Of the immense advantage that an ethnographer gains by living among the people whose values and behavior he is intent on understanding there can be not the slightest doubt. Mead, however, within six weeks of her arrival in Pago Pago, and before she had spent any time actually staying in a traditional household, had come to feel that the food she would have to eat would be too starchy, and the conditions of living she would have to endure too nerve-racking to make residence with a Samoan family bearable. In Ta'ū, she told Boas, she would be able to live "in a white household" and yet be in the midst of one of the villages from which she would be drawing her adolescent subjects. This arrangement to live not in a Samoan household but with the Holt family in their European-style house, which was also the location of the government radio station and medical dispensary, decisively determined the form her researches were to take.

According to Mead her residence in these government quarters furnished her with an absolutely essential neutral base from which she could study all of the individuals in the surrounding village while at the same time remaining "aloof from native feuds and lines of demarcation." Against this exiguous advantage she was, however, depriving herself of the close contacts that speedily develop in Samoa between an ethnographer and the members of the extended family in which he or she lives. Such contacts are essential for the gaining of a thorough understanding of the Samoan language and, most important of all, for the independent verification, by the continuous observation of actual behavior, of the statements being derived from informants. Thus, by living with the Holts, Mead was trapping herself in a situation in which she was forced to rely not on observations of the behavior of Samoans as they lived their lives beyond the precincts of the government station on Ta'ū, but on such hearsay information as she was able to extract from her adolescent subjects. . . .

It is evident then that although, as Mead records, she could "wander freely about the village or go on fishing trips or stop at a house where a woman was weaving" when she was away from the dispensary, her account of adolescence in Samoa was, in the main, derived from the young informants who came to talk with her away from their homes in the villages of Lumā, Si'ufaga, and Faleasao. So, as Mead states, for these three villages, from which all her adolescent informants were drawn, she saw the life that went on "through the eyes" of the group of girls on the details of whose lives she was concentrating. This situation is of crucial significance for the assessment of Mead's researches in Manu'a, for we are clearly faced with the question of the extent to which the lens she fashioned from what she was being told by her adolescent informants and through which she saw Samoan life was a true and accurate lens.

. . . [M]any of the assertions appearing in Mead's depiction of Samoa are fundamentally in error, and some of them preposterously false. How are we to account for the presence of errors of this magnitude? Some Samoans who have read *Coming of Age in Samoa* react, as Shore reports, with anger and the insistence "that Mead lied." This, however, is an interpretation that I have no hesitation in dismissing. The succession of prefaces to *Coming of Age* in Samoa published by Mead in 1949, 1953, 1961, and 1973 indicate clearly, in my judgment, that she did give genuine credence to the view of Samoan life with which she returned to New York in 1926. Moreover, in the 1969 edition of *Social Organization of Manu'a* she freely conceded that there was a serious problem in reconciling the "contradictions" between her own depiction of Samoa and that contained in "other records of historical and contemporary behavior." . . .

Mead's depiction of Samoan culture, as I have shown, is marked by major errors, and her account of the sexual behavior of Samoans by a mind-boggling contradiction, for she asserts that the Samoans have a culture in which female virginity is very highly valued, with a virginity-testing ceremony being "theoretically observed at weddings of all ranks," while at the same time adolescence among females is regarded as a period "appropriate for love-making," with promiscuity before marriage being both permitted and "expected." And, indeed, she actually describes the Samoans as making the "demand" that a female should be "both receptive to the advances of many lovers and yet capable of showing the tokens of virginity at marriage." Something, it becomes plain at this juncture, is emphatically amiss, for surely no human population could be so cognitively disoriented as to conduct their lives in such a schizophrenic way. Nor are the Samoans remotely like this, for . . . they are, in fact, a people who traditionally value virginity highly and so disapprove of premarital promiscuity as to exercise a strict surveillance over the comings and goings of adolescent girls. That these values and this regime were in force in Manu'a in the mid 1920s is, furthermore, clearly established by the testimony of the Manu'ans themselves who, when I discussed this period with those who well remembered it, confirmed that the fa'aSamoa in these matters was operative then as it was both before and after Mead's brief sojourn in Ta'ū. What then can have been the source of Mead's erroneous statement that in Samoa there is great premarital freedom, with promiscuity before marriage among adolescent girls, being both permitted and expected?

The explanation most consistently advanced by the Samoans themselves for the magnitude of the errors in her depiction of their culture and in particular of their sexual morality is, as [Eleanor Ruth] Gerber has reported, "that Mead's informants must have been telling lies in order to tease her." Those Samoans who offer this explanation, which I have heard in Manu'a as well as in other parts of Samoa, are referring to the behavior called *tau fa'ase'e*, to which Samoans are much prone. *Fa'ase'e* (literally "to cause to slip") means "to dupe," as in the example given by Milner, *"e fa'ase'e gofie le teine*, the girl is easily duped"; and the phrase *tau fa'ase'e* refers to the action of deliberately duping someone, a pastime that greatly appeals to the Samoans as a respite from the severities of their authoritarian society.

Because of their strict morality, Samoans show a decided reluctance to discuss sexual matters with outsiders or those in authority, a reticence that is especially marked among female adolescents. Thus, Holmes reports that when he and his wife lived in Manu'a and Tutuila in 1954 "it was never possible to obtain details of sexual experience from unmarried informants, though several of these people were constant companions and part of the household." Further, as Lauifi Ili, Holmes's principal assistant, observes, when it comes to imparting information about sexual activities, Samoan girls are "very close-mouthed and ashamed." Yet it was precisely information of this kind that Mead, a liberated young American newly arrived from New York and resident in the government station at Ta'ū, sought to extract from the adolescent girls she had been sent to study. And when she persisted in this unprecedented probing of a highly embarrassing topic, it is likely that these girls resorted, as Gerber's Samoan informants have averred, to *tau fa'ase'e,* regaling their inquisitor with counterfeit tales of casual love under the palm trees.

This, then, is the explanation that Samoans give for the highly inaccurate portrayal of their sexual morality in Mead's writings. It is an explanation that accounts for how it was that this erroneous portrayal came to be made, as well as for Mead's sincere credence in the account she has given in *Coming of Age* in Samoa, for she was indeed reporting what she had been told by her adolescent informants. The Manu'ans emphasize, however, that the girls who, they claim, plied Mead with these counterfeit tales were only amusing themselves, and had no inkling that their tales would ever find their way into a book.

While we cannot, in the absence of detailed corroborative evidence [but see addendum following], be sure about the truth of this Samoan claim that Mead was mischievously duped by her adolescent informants, we can be certain that she did return to New York in 1926 with tales running directly counter to all other ethnographic accounts of Samoa, from which she constructed her picture of Manu'a as a paradise of free love, and of Samoa as a negative instance, which, so she claimed, validated Boasian doctrine. It was this negative instance that she duly presented to Boas as the ideologically gratifying result of her inquiries in Manu'a. . . .

We are thus confronted in the case of Margaret Mead's Samoan researches with an instructive example of how, as evidence is sought to substantiate a cherished doctrine, the deeply held beliefs of those involved may lead them unwittingly into error. The danger of such an outcome is inherent, it would seem, in the very process of belief formation. . . .

In the case of Mead's Samoan researches, certainly, there is the clearest evidence that it was her deeply convinced belief in the doctrine of extreme cultural determinism, for which she was prepared to fight with the whole battery at her command, that led her to construct an account of Samoa that appeared to substantiate this very doctrine. There is, however, conclusive empirical evidence to demonstrate that Samoa, in numerous respects, is not at all as Mead depicted it to be.

A crucial issue that arises from this historic case for the discipline of anthropology, which has tended to accept the reports of ethnographers as entirely empirical statements, is the extent to which other ethnographic accounts may have been distorted by doctrinal convictions, as well as the methodological question of how such distortion can best be avoided. These are no small problems. I would merely comment that as we look back on Mead's Samoan researches we are able to appreciate anew the wisdom of Karl Popper's admonition that in both science and scholarship it is, above all else, indefatigable rational criticism of our suppositions that is of decisive importance, for such criticism by "bringing out our mistakes . . . makes us understand the difficulties of the problem we are trying to solve," and so saves us from the allure of the "obvious truth" of received doctrine.

Addendum: New Evidence of the Hoaxing of Margaret Mead

In my book *The Fateful Hoaxing of Margaret Mead* (1998) there is an account, based on the sworn testimony of Fa'apua'a, of how Margaret Mead in March of 1926 on the island of Ofu in American Samoa was hoaxed about the sexual mores of the Samoans by her two Samoan traveling companions, Fa'apua'a and Fofoa.

I [have recently discovered] direct evidence, from Mead's own papers, that Margaret Mead was indeed taken in by the "whispered confidences" (as she called them) of Fa'apua'a and Fofoa. This incontrovertible historical evidence finally brings to closure the long-running controversy over Margaret Mead's Samoan fieldwork. . . .

The crucially important direct evidence in question is contained in a little known book entitled *All True! The Record of Actual Adventures That Have Happened To Ten Women of Today* that was published in New York in 1931 by Brewer, Warren and Putnam. The "adventure" by Dr. Margaret Mead is entitled "Life as a Samoan Girl". It begins with a wistful reference to "the group of reverend scientists" who in 1925 sent her to study (Mead, 1925) "the problem of which phenomena of adolescence are culturally and which physiologically determined" among the adolescent girls of Samoa, with "no very clear idea" of how she was "to do this." It ends with an account of her journey to the islands of Ofu and Olosega in March of 1926 with the "two Samoan girls," as she calls them, Fa'apua'a and Fofoa. In fact, Fa'apua'a and Fofoa were both twenty-four years of age and slightly older than Dr. Mead herself. Dr. Mead continues her account of her visit to the islands of Ofu and Olosega with Fa'apua'a and Fofoa by stating: "In all things I had behaved as a Samoan, for only so, only by losing my identity, as far as possible, had I been able to become acquainted with the Samoan girls receive their whispered confidences and learn at the same time the answer to the scientists' questions."

This account, by Mead herself, is fully confirmed by the sworn testimony of Fa'apua'a (cf. Freeman, 1998, Chapter 11). It can be found on p. 141 of the second and paperback edition (1999) of my book *The Fateful Hoaxing of Margaret Mead: A historical analysis of her Samoan research.* It is definitive historical evidence that establishes that Martin Orans is in outright error in asserting (1996:92) that it is "demonstrably false that Mead was taken in by Fa'apua'a and Fofoa." It is also evidence that establishes that *Coming of Age in Samoa,* far from being a "scientific classic" (as Mead herself supposed) is, in certain vitally significant respects (as in its dream-like second chapter), a work of anthropological fiction.

References

Freeman, Derek, 1999, *The Fateful Hoaxing of Margaret Mead,* Boulder: Westview, 2nd edition.

Mead, Margaret, 1925, Plan of Research Submitted to the National Research Council of the U.S.A. (Archives of the National Academy of Sciences).

Mead, Margaret, 1928, *Coming of Age in Samoa.* New York: Morrow.

Mead, Margaret, 1931, "Life as a Samoan Girl," in *All True! The Record of Actual Adventures That Happened to Ten Women of Today.* New York: Brewer, Warren and Putnam.

Orans, Martin, 1996, *Not Even Wrong: Margaret Mead, Derek Freeman and the Samoans,* Novato: Chandler and Sharp.

Lowell D. Holmes and
Ellen Rhoads Holmes

 **NO**

Samoan Character and
the Academic World

On January 31, 1983, the *New York Times* carried a front-page article, the headline of which read, "New Samoa Book Challenges Margaret Mead's Conclusions." The book that precipitated this somewhat unexpected turn of events was *Margaret Mead and Samoa: The Making and Unmaking of an Anthropological Myth* by Derek Freeman, an emeritus professor of anthropology at Australian National University in Canberra. This work, which some claim set off the most heated controversy in sociocultural anthropology in one hundred years, is described by its author as a "refutation of Mead's misleading account" of Samoan culture and personality as presented in her 1928 ethnography, *Coming of Age in Samoa.*

The *New York Times* article was of special interest to me because, in 1954, I had conducted a year-long methodological restudy of the Mead data under attack. I had lived in Ta'ū village, where Mead had worked twenty-nine years earlier, and had used many of her informants in a systematic and detailed evaluation of every observation and interpretation she had made about the lifestyle of the people in that Samoan village. A methodological restudy, incidentally, involves a second anthropologist going into the field with the *express purpose* of testing the reliability and validity of the findings of a former investigator. This restudy is made in order to establish what kinds of errors of data collection or interpretation might have been made by certain kinds of people, in certain kinds of field research situations, researching certain kinds of problems. For example, Margaret Mead was a twenty-three-year-old woman investigating a male-dominated society that venerates age. She was a student of Franz Boas and, therefore, went equipped with a particular theoretical frame of reference. She was also on her first field trip—at a time when research methods were crude. My task in this methodological restudy was not only to analyze how my findings might be different from hers (if that would be the case), but I would also attempt to speculate on how differences in the status of the investigators (for example, sex, age, family situation, education) and other personal factors might affect the collection and interpretation of data.

My critique of Margaret Mead's study was presented in my doctoral dissertation, *The Restudy of Manu'an Culture. A Problem in Methodology,* which by 1983 had been collecting dust on a Northwestern University library shelf for some twenty-seven years. I was therefore eager to obtain a copy of Freeman's new evaluation of Mead's work from its publisher, Harvard University Press. In reading the book this is what I found.

In *Margaret Mead and Samoa: The Making and Unmaking of an Anthropological Myth* (1983), Derek Freeman argues that Mead perpetuated a hoax comparable in consequence to that of Piltdown Man when, in 1928, she described Samoa as a paradise where competition, sexual inhibition, and guilt were virtually absent. Refusing to believe that adolescents in all societies inevitably experience emotional crises—storm and stress—because of biological changes associated with puberty (as hypothesized in *Adolescence* in 1904 by psychologist G. Stanley Hall), Mead set out to discover a society where the passage to adulthood was smooth and without trauma. She described such a society in *Coming of Age in Samoa*. In delineating this "negative instance" (which challenged Hall's theory of universal adolescent rebellion and strife), Margaret Mead had in effect established that nurture (culture) is more critical than nature (biology) in accounting for adolescent maturation behavior in the human species. Derek Freeman, on the other hand, rejects the idea that human behavior is largely shaped by culture and believes that Mead and her mentor, Franz Boas (commonly called the "Father of American Anthropology"), were guilty of *totally* ignoring the influence of biological heredity. He believes that Mead's "negative instance" results entirely from faulty data collection and that Mead's Samoan findings have led anthropology, psychology, and education down the primrose path of pseudoscience. Freeman's book, therefore, is an attempt to set the record straight through his own, more accurate, observations of Samoa and Samoans—although his observations of Samoan behavior were in another village, on another island, in another country, and fourteen years later.

Freeman's main theoretical approach in this evaluation of Mead's work derives from the German philosopher of science, Karl Popper, who maintains that science should be deductive, not inductive, and that progress in scientific research should consist essentially of attempts to refute established theories. Thus, Derek Freeman is out to destroy the credibility of what he interprets as the "absolute cultural determinism" to be found in the work of Margaret Mead as well as in much of the work of Boas and his other students. This claim is, of course, spurious, as any student of American anthropological theory knows. For example, in Melville J. Herskovits' biography of Franz Boas, we find the statement that, because of his "rounded view of the problem Boas could perceive so clearly the fallacy of the eugenicist theory, which held the destiny of men to be determined by biological endowment, with little regard for the learned, cultural determinants of behavior." By the same token, he "refused to accept the counter-dogma that man is born with a completely blank slate, on which can be written whatever is willed. He saw both innate endowment and learning—or, as it was called popularly, heredity and environment—as significant factors in the making of the mature individual" (1953:28). Herskovits also points out that "numerous examples can be found, in reports on the various studies he conducted, of how skillfully Boas was able to weave cultural and biological factors into a single fabric" (*Ibid.*).

Marvin Harris concurs: "American anthropology has always been concerned with the relationships between nature (in the guise of habitat and genic programming) and culture (in the guise of traditions encoded in the brain, not in the genes). Neither Boas nor his students ever denied that *Homo sapiens* has a species-specific nature" (1983:26). In his book, *The Rise of Anthropological Theory*, Harris writes, "Boas systematically rejected almost every conceivable form of cultural determinism" (1968:283).

Evaluation of the Mead Data

My restudy experience in Ta'ū village in 1954 led me to conclude that Margaret Mead often overgeneralized; that, in many cases, we interpreted data differently; and that, because of her age and sex, some avenues of investigation apparently were closed to her—particularly those having to do with the more formal aspects of village political organization and ceremonial life. However, her overall characterization of the nature and dynamics of the culture were, in my judgment, quite valid and her contention that it was easier to come of age in Samoa than in America in 1925–1926 was undoubtedly correct. In spite of the greater possibilities for error in a pioneer study, Mead's age (only 23), her sex (in a male-dominated society), and her inexperience, I believe the reliability and validity of the Ta'ū village research is remarkably high.

I look upon an ethnographic account as a kind of map to be used in finding one's way about in a culture—in comprehending and anticipating behavior. Mead's account never left me lost or bewildered in my interactions with Samoan islanders, but I also felt that if one were to come to a decision about the comparative difficulties of coming of age in Samoa and the United States, it would be necessary to know something about what life was like for adolescents in America in 1925–1926. Joseph Folsom's book, *The Family*, published in 1934, but researched about the time Mead was writing *Coming of Age in Samoa*, provided that information. Folsom describes the social environment in which children came of age at that time as follows:

> Children are disciplined and trained with the ideal of absolute obedience to parents. Corporal punishment is used, ideally in cold blood. . . . All sexual behavior on the part of children is prevented by all means at the parents' disposal. . . . For the sake of prevention it has been usual to cultivate in the child, especially the girl, an attitude of horror or disgust toward all aspects of sex. . . . Premarital intercourse is immoral though not abhorrent. . . . Violations are supposedly prevented by the supervision of the girl's parents. . . . Illegitimate children are socially stigmatized. . . . The chief stigma falls upon the unmarried mother, because she has broken an important sex taboo (1934:10–25). . . .

While Freeman contends that Mead was absolutely wrong about nearly everything (partly, he maintains, because the teenage girls she used as informants consistently lied to her), I found discrepancies mainly in such areas as the degree of sexual freedom Samoan young people enjoy, the competitive nature of the society, the aggressiveness of Samoan behavior, and the degree of genuine affection and commitment between lovers and spouses.

I saw Samoan culture as considerably more competitive than Mead, although I never considered it as inflexible or aggressive as Freeman does. I observed a great preoccupation with status, power, and prestige among men of rank and, on more than one occasion, was present at fierce verbal duels between Talking Chiefs trying to enhance their own prestige and, incidentally, that of their village. . . .

I also found that Samoan culture was not as simple as Margaret Mead claimed, nor was Ta'ū village the paradise she would have us believe. She often romanticized, overgeneralized, and, on some occasions, took literary license in her descriptions of Samoan lifeways. For example, her very dramatic chapter, "A Day in Samoa," crowds typical activities (some of which occur only at particular times of the year) into a typical day and thereby presents a village scene that was much more vibrant, bustling, and picturesque than I ever encountered in any twenty-four hour period. Mead's chapter is good prose, but is it good anthropology? . . .

I also did not agree with Mead on the degree of sexual freedom supposedly enjoyed by her informants, but I believe her characterization comes closer to the truth than that of Freeman. Samoans have a very natural and healthy attitude toward sex. Judging by the number of illegitimate children in Ta'ū village when I was there and by the fact that divorce frequently involved claims of adultery, I would conclude that, while Samoans are far from promiscuous, they are not the puritanical prudes Freeman paints them to be. However, I must admit that it was difficult to investigate anything of a sexual nature, primarily because of pressure from the London Missionary Society church. Even today, older Samoans seem more distressed over Mead's claims that they are sexually active than Freeman's claims that they are aggressive with strong passions, even psychopathological tendencies. I would assume, however, that Mead was better able to identify with, and therefore establish rapport with, adolescents and young adults on issues of sexuality than either I (at age 29—married with a wife and child) or Freeman, ten years my senior.

Freeman maintains that Mead imposed her own liberated ideas of sexuality onto the Samoans and that her teenage informants consistently lied to her about these matters solely out of mischief. He has recently made contact with one of Mead's informants, Fa'apua'a Fa'amu, who lived in Fitiuta while Mead was working in Ta'ū village. Freeman believes this informant when she says that she consistently lied to Mead (while also identifying her as a good friend), but Freeman does not seem to consider the possibility that she may be lying to him. The possibility of Mead's informants being successful at such long-term deception is simply not credible considering the fact that Mead was an extremely intelligent, well-trained Ph.D. who constantly cross-checked her data with many informants. Anyone who has studied her field notes in the Library of Congress, as I have, must be impressed with her savvy and sophistication.

I must also disagree with Mead's statements that all love affairs are casual and fleeting, and no one plays for very heavy emotional stakes. Custom dictates that displays of affection between spouses and between lovers not take place in public. However, expressions of love and affection were often observed in the families of my informants. . . .

Although I differed with Margaret Mead on many interpretations, the most important fact that emerged from my methodological restudy of her Samoan research is that, without doubt, Samoan adolescents have a less difficult time negotiating the transition from childhood to adulthood than American adolescents. . . .

Critique of the Freeman Refutation

My objections to Derek Freeman's picture of Samoa are much more substantial than to the picture presented by Margaret Mead. Basically, I question Freeman's objectivity and believe he is guilty of an age-old temptation in science, which was recognized as early as 1787 by Thomas Jefferson—no slouch of a scientist himself. In a letter to his friend Charles Thomson, Jefferson wrote, "The moment a person forms a theory, his imagination sees, in every object, only the traits which favor that theory" (Martin 1952:33).

Not only does Freeman ignore counterevidence, he also ignores time and space and assumes that it is legitimate to assess data obtained by Mead in Manu'a in 1925–1926 in terms of the data he collected in Western Samoa in the 1940s, 1960s, and 1980s.

Time differences.   Freeman plays down the fact that Mead did her study of Ta'ū village in the Manu'a Island group of American Samoa fourteen years before he arrived as a teacher (not as an anthropologist) in Western Samoa and that he did not return to Samoa with the express purpose of refuting Mead's study until forty-three years after her visit. Minimizing this time gap, he arbitrarily states that "there is no . . . reason to suppose that Samoan society and behavior changed in any fundamental way during the fourteen years between 1926, the year of the completion of Mead's inquiries, and 1940, when I began my own observation of Samoan behavior" (1983:120).

However, Freeman did not visit Ta'ū village, the site of Mead's research, until 1968. Having established to his satisfaction that there had been few changes in Samoan culture during this long period of time, Freeman went on to state that he would "draw on evidence of my own research in the 1940s, the years 1965 to 1968, and 1981" (1983:120). I might add that he would draw upon historical sources, some of which go back as far as the early eighteenth century, to prove his points. My own analysis of Samoan cultural change, as published in *Ta'ū, Stability and Change in a Samoan Village* (1958), indicates, however, that while there was relative stability in the culture from 1850 to 1925 and from 1925 to 1954, change definitely did take place, particularly in the twentieth century. There is absolutely no basis for Freeman's dealing with Samoa as though it existed in a totally static condition despite its long history of contact with explorers, whalers, missionaries, colonial officials and bureaucrats, entrepreneurs, anthropologists, and, more recently, educators with Western-style curricula and television networks.

Place differences.   It also must be kept in mind that Sa'anapu (where Freeman observed Samoan culture) is not Ta'ū village (where Mead did her study). They are different villages, on different islands, in different countries, and there are great historical and political differences between the island of Upolu in Western Samoa and Ta'ū island in the isolated Manu'a Group of American Samoa. Western Samoa has experienced a long and often oppressive history of colonialism under Germany and New Zealand, while the Manu'a Group and American Samoa in general have been spared this. The U.S. Navy administration (1900–1951) exerted little influence outside the Pago Pago Bay area on the island of Tutuila, and the Department of the Interior, which took over from the Navy, has been an ethnocentric—but still benevolent—force in the political history of the territory. While Sa'anapu is on the opposite side of Upolu from Apia, it has daily bus communication with that port town, with all of its banks, supermarkets, department stores, theaters, bookstores, and nightclubs. Cash cropping has always been more important in Western Samoa than in American Samoa, and today, the economies of the two Samoas are vastly different. . . . On five separate research trips to Manu'a, I have never witnessed a single physical assault or serious argument that threatened to get out of hand. However, urban centers such as Apia in Western Samoa and Pago Pago in American Samoa have a very different character. As early as 1962, there were delinquency problems in the Pago Pago Bay area involving drunkenness, burglary, assaults, and rapes. Young people who migrate to urban areas such as Pago Pago and Apia are no longer under the close supervision and control of their *matai* [chief of the family] and often behave in very nontraditional ways. It is difficult, indeed, to make a blanket statement that all villages in Samoa are the same and that all behavior within the two Samoas is comparable. I have studied several villages during my thirty-seven-year contact with Samoa, and I find each unique in numerous, social, ceremonial, economic, and political respects.

Freeman's subjective use of literature.   A serious scientist considers all the literature relating to his or her research problem. One does not select data that supportive and ignore that which is not. Freeman violates that principle repeatedly. . . . When [Ronald Rose's book, *South Seas Magic* (1959)] can be used to corroborate or advance Freeman's position, he is quoted; however, where Rose's statements concerning Samoan sexual behavior run contrary to Freeman's claims, and fall in line with Mead's observations, his work is ignored. For example, while Freeman insists that Samoans are puritanical and sexually inhibited, Rose writes that "sexual adventures begin at an early age. Although virginity is prized, it is insisted on only with the taupo. . . . If a girl hasn't had a succession of lovers by the time she is seventeen or eighteen, she feels she is 'on the shelf' and becomes the laughing stock among her companions" (1959:61).

   With regard to the matter that Freeman believes was Mead's spurious example of a "negative instance"—a culture where coming of age is relatively less stressful—Rose writes (but understandably is not quoted by Freeman) as follows:

> Mental disturbances, stresses and conflicts occur at puberty but, as might be expected. these are not quite as common as in our society where taboos associated with sex abound (*Ibid.*: 164).

One can question the objectivity of a scientist who describes Samoans as "an unusually bellicose people" (1983:157) and attempts to substantiate the claim with citations from the eighteenth century, but fails to quote the favorable impressions of the very first European to come in contact with Samoan islanders from the village of Ta'ū, the very village Mead studied. In 1722, Commodore Jacob Roggeveen anchored his vessel off the village of Ta'ū and allowed a number of the islanders to come aboard. After a two-hour visit, the Commodore wrote in his log:

> They appeared to be a good people, lively in their manner of conversing, gentle in their deportment towards each other, and in their manners nothing was perceived of the savage. . . . It must be acknowledged that this was the nation the most civilized and honest of any that we had seen among the Islands of the South Sea. They were charmed with our arrival amongst them, and received us as divinities. And when they saw us preparing to depart, they testified much regret (Bumey 1816:576).

Rather than quote Roggeveen, Freeman chooses to discuss, as an example of Samoan bellicosity, the La Perouse expedition's visitation at Tutuila in 1787 that ended in tragedy. It is true that Samoans in the village of A'asu attacked a shore party, killing several crew members, but what Freeman fails to mention is that the attack occurred only after crew members punished a Samoan for pilfering by hanging him by his thumbs from the top of the longboat mast. . . .

It also should be noted that the eminent writer, Robert Louis Stevenson, who lived among Samoans the last four years of his life, recorded in his chronicle of Samoan events, *A Footnote to History,* that Samoans were "easy, merry, and pleasure loving; the gayest, though by no means the most capable or the most beautiful of Polynesians" (1892:148) and that their religious sentiment toward conflict was "peace at any price" (*Ibid.*: 147).

Observers contemporary with Mead in Samoa also record descriptions of Samoan chararacter that do not square with Freeman's allegations or his citations from early literature. For example, William Green, the principal of the government school in American Samoa in the 1920s writes:

> Personal combats and fist fights are rather rare today. I believe there has been no murder case in American Samoa since our flag was raised in 1900. Natives will suffer indignities for a long time before resorting to a fight but they remain good fighters. Boxing contests are held occasionally. . . . Respect for elders and magistrates has, I suppose, tended to discourage frequent combats. Life is easy, and one's habitual tendencies and desires are seldom blocked (1924:134).

Professional Reactions

. . . It is questionable whether any anthropology book to date has created such a media circus or produced such a media hero as *Margaret Mead and Samoa, The Making and Unmaking of an Anthropological Myth*. It is also doubtful whether any academic press ever mounted such a campaign of Madison Avenue hype to market a book as did Harvard University Press. The early reviews of the book and feature articles about the controversy were primarily penned by journalists and tended to be highly supportive of Freeman's critique, but once the anthropologists began evaluating the Freeman book, the tide took a definite turn. George Marcus of Rice University called the book a "work of great mischief," the mischief being that Freeman was attempting to reestablish "the importance of biological factors in explanations of human behavior" (1983:2). . . . Marvin Harris observed in his review that Freeman "seems obsessed with the notion that to discredit Mead's Samoan material is to discredit any social scientist who holds that 'nurture' is a more important determinant of the differences and similarities in human social life than nature" (1983:26).

It is only fair to point out that Derek Freeman had, and continues to have, a cadre of anthropological supporters, mostly in Europe and Australia, and the Samoans are mixed in their support of Mead or Freeman. . . .

Like most American anthropologists, and a few scholarly Samoans, we believe the Freeman book has done a disservice to Samoans and to the memory of Margaret Mead. *Margaret Mead and Samoa* is not an objective analysis of Mead's work in Manu'a, but an admitted refutation aimed at discrediting not only Margaret Mead, but Franz Boas and American cultural anthropology in general. Anthropology has often been referred to as a "soft science" throughout much of this rhubarb over Samoa and nature/nurture. It is little wonder, since Freeman's diatribe, published by a supposedly scholarly press, has been accepted by the media, by a select group of anthropologists, and by a number of distinguished ethologists and sociobiologists as legitimate anthropology. Margaret Mead would have loved to have debated the issues with Derek Freeman, but unfortunately, the book was not published while she was alive. It would have been great sport and good for the science of anthropology. As a friend wrote immediately after the publication of Freeman's book, "Whatever else she was, Margaret was a feisty old gal and would have put up a spirited defense which would quickly have turned into a snotty offense." We would have put our money on the plump little lady with the no-nonsense attitude and the compulsion to "get on with it."

References

Burney, James. 1816. *A chronological history of the voyages and discoveries in the South Seas or Pacific Ocean*. London: Luke Hansard and Sons.

Folsom, Joseph K. 1934. *The family: Its sociology and psychiatry*. New York: J. Wiley and Sons.

Freeman, Derek. 1983. *Margaret Mead and Samoa: The making and unmaking of an anthropological myth*. Cambridge, MA: Harvard University Press.

Green, William M. 1924. "Social traits of Samoans." *Journal of Applied Sociology* 9:129 135.

Hall, G. Stanley. 1904. *Adolescence: Its psychology and its relations to physiology, anthropology, sociology, sex, crime, religion and education.* New York: D. Appleton and Company.

Harris, Marvin. 1968. *The rise of anthropological theory.* New York: Thomas Y. Crowell Company.

———. 1983. "The sleep-crawling question." *Psychology Today* May:24–27.

Herskovits, Melville J. 1953. *Franz Boas.* New York: Charles Scribner's Sons.

Holmes, Lowell D. 1958. *Ta'ū: Stability and change in a Samoan village.* Reprint No. 7, Wellington, New Zealand: Polynesian Society.

Marcus, George, 1983. "One man's Mead." *New York Times Book Review* March 27, 1983:2–3, 22–23.

Martin, Edwin T. 1952. *Thomas Jefferson: Scientist.* New York: Henry Schuman.

Rose, Ronald. 1959. *South Seas magic.* London: Hale.

Stevenson, Robert Louis. 1892. *Vailima papers and A footnote to history.* New York: Charles Scribner's Sons.

POSTSCRIPT

Was Margaret Mead's Fieldwork on Samoan Adolescents Fundamentally Flawed?

The response to Freeman's *Margaret Mead and Samoa* was quite extraordinary and included books, journal articles, editorials, and conference papers. Special sessions at the annual meetings of the American Anthropological Association were devoted exclusively to the Mead-Freeman debate. The first reaction was largely defensive. But as the initial shock of Freeman's assertions wore off, scholars began to address some of the specific points of criticism. A representative sample of these would include Lowell D. Holmes's *Quest for the Real Samoa: The Mead/Freeman Controversy and Beyond* (Bergin and Garvey, 1987) and Hiram Caton's edited volume, *The Samoa Reader: Anthropologists Take Stock* (University Press of America, 1990).

A number of scholars have pointed out that Samoan life has changed significantly since Mead's fieldwork. The Christian Church now exerts a much stronger pressure over the very same women that Mead had interviewed. Another point is that Mead's informants themselves have become much more puritanical as old women than they were as girls. These women now have reputations of social propriety to uphold that would not have concerned them in their youth. Can we believe that they had the same views so many years ago?

In the 1980s Freeman returned to Ta'u with an Australian documentary film crew, specifically to interview some of Mead's now elderly informants. When asked what they had told Mead 60 years earlier, the women stated that they fibbed continuously and explained that it is a cherished Samoan custom to trick people in these ways. Freeman and the film crew take such statements as incontrovertible evidence that Mead was hoaxed. But if it is Samoan custom to trick others, how can Freeman and his film crew be certain that they are not victims of a similar hoax?

Another Samoa specialist, Martin Orans, approaches the controversy in his book *Not Even Wrong: Margaret Mead, Derek Freeman, and the Samoans* (Chandler & Sharp, 1996). Orans contends that neither Mead nor Freeman framed their research questions about cultural determinism in ways that can be tested. Arguing that anthropologists must frame their conclusions as testable hypotheses, Orans asserts that Mead and Freeman are so vague that neither makes their case, and both are so ambiguous that they are "not even wrong." But if Orans is correct, how can anthropologists frame the nature-versus-nurture debate in more specific and testable ways in specific field settings?

ISSUE 11

Do Native Peoples Today Invent Their Traditions?

YES: Roger M. Keesing, from "Creating the Past: Custom and Identity in the Contemporary Pacific," *The Contemporary Pacific* (Spring/Fall 1989)

NO: Haunani-Kay Trask, from "Natives and Anthropologists: The Colonial Struggle," *The Contemporary Pacific* (Spring 1991)

ISSUE SUMMARY

YES: Cultural anthropologist Roger M. Keesing argues that what native peoples in the Pacific now accept as "traditional culture" is largely an invented and idealized vision of their past. He contends that such fictional images emerge because native peoples are largely unfamiliar with what life was really like in pre-Western times and because such imagery distinguishes native communities from dominant Western culture.

NO: Hawaiian activist and scholar Haunani-Kay Trask asserts that Keesing's critique is fundamentally flawed because he only uses Western documents—and native peoples have oral traditions, genealogies, and other historical sources that are not reflected in Western historical documents. Anthropologists like Keesing, she maintains, are trying to hold on to their privileged position as experts in the face of growing numbers of educated native scholars.

In 1983 Eric Hobsbawm and Terence Ranger published a collection of essays entitled *The Invention of Tradition* (Cambridge University Press). For many anthropologists trained in a structural-functionalist style of research, this volume was striking because it suggested two points that seemed to fly in the face of many cherished anthropological ideas. First, they argued that traditions in all societies change as a response to the political, economic, and social needs of the community. Second, they contended that the "historical" traditions societies celebrated were often invented in the recent past as a way of distinguishing one indigenous group from a dominant one. By 1983 most anthropologists had accepted the axiom that all societies change over time. Culture and social institutions may work to inhibit changes and keep society functioning as it had in the previous generation, but innovations inevitably occurred. What made Hobsbawm and Ranger's book so important was that it used several Western examples to demonstrate that even in Western countries with rich historical documentation, institutions such as Scottish tartans could become routinized and accepted as a traditional and essential marker of Scottish ethnicity, even though the custom had existed for barely a century. They argued that the idea that tartans had ancient origins was particularly appealing to the Scots because it distinguished them from the dominant English culture that had long oppressed them.

In the following selection, Roger M. Keesing builds on Hobsbawm and Ranger's argument by turning his attention to the "invention of tradition" in Pacific countries. Throughout the Pacific, people now accept as historical traditions and customs practices that could only have emerged following the invasion and conquest of their islands by Western people. Keesing contends that because colonial intrusion has been so comprehensive, Pacific islanders know almost nothing about what their precolonial societies were really like. As a result, islanders have grasped onto certain idealized images of their past as themes and motifs to celebrate the distinctiveness of their cultures from dominant Western society. These idealized and largely fictional images have great political power for oppressed people, and they have often become a rallying point for various social movements. Nevertheless, concludes Keesing, these images of Pacific traditions find little support in historical documents and should largely be understood as modern mythmaking for the political ends of modern Pacific elites.

Hawaiian activist Haunani-Kay Trask attempts to turn Keesing's argument on its head by suggesting that Keesing's assertions about the "inventions" of Hawaiian traditions are yet another example of colonialism, racism, and white presumptions of superiority. She contends that Keesing only accepts Western historical sources, completely ignoring oral tradition, local mythologies, genealogies, and even rituals. Historical documents were biased by Western culture, argues Trask, and often represented an inaccurate understanding of native culture and social institutions. She questions whether or not white anthropologists have a privileged view of native customs, suggesting that most of Keesing's claims are racist attempts to further belittle native understanding and appreciation of the past.

Do native peoples or Western anthropologists have a better understanding of the native past? Have native traditions changed as much as Keesing would have us believe? Have these changes been the direct result of Western colonialism or have native peoples been active agents in such changes? Are Western historical sources biased and inaccurate when describing native practices? Are native oral traditions today accurate and authentic visions of traditional ways of life? Is there an authentic cultural tradition in any society, or, as Keesing suggests, are there different traditions for chiefs and for commoners, for men and for women? And, finally, are these "traditions" powerful as tools to fight oppression?

Roger M. Keesing  **YES**

Creating the Past: Custom and Identity in the Contemporary Pacific

Across the Pacific, from Hawai'i to New Zealand, in New Caledonia, Aboriginal Australia, Vanuatu, the Solomon Islands, and Papua New Guinea, Pacific peoples are creating pasts, myths of ancestral ways of life that serve as powerful political symbols. In the rhetoric of postcolonial nationalism (and sometimes separatism) and the struggles of indigenous Fourth World peoples, now minorities in their own homelands, visions of the past are being created and evoked.

Scholars of Pacific cultures and history who are sympathetic to these political struggles and quests for identity are in a curious and contradiction-ridden position in relation to these emerging ideologies of the past. The ancestral ways of life being evoked rhetorically may bear little relation to those documented historically, recorded ethnographically, and reconstructed archaeologically—yet their symbolic power and political force are undeniable.

Perhaps it does not matter whether the pasts being recreated and invoked are mythical or "real," in the sense of representing closely what actual people did in actual times and places. Political symbols radically condense and simplify "reality," and are to some extent devoid of content: that is how and why they work. Perhaps it matters only whether such political ideologies are used for just causes, whether they are instruments of liberation or of oppression. In the contemporary Pacific they are being used both to recapture just rights and to deny them. The question is less simple than that.

The process of recapturing the past, of reconstructing, of questioning Western scholarship—historical and anthropological—is important and essential. My intention is neither to defend established versions of the past from a standpoint of vested scholarly interest, nor to debunk emerging political myths by comparing them to actual pasts to which I claim privileged access. Rather, in showing contradictions in this process of political mythmaking and in showing how in many ways the contemporary discourses of cultural identity derive from Western discourses, I seek to promote a more genuinely radical stance in relation to both the more distant and the more recent past—and to Western domination, of minds as well as societies.

From Roger M. Keesing, "Creating the Past: Custom and Identity in the Contemporary Pacific," *The Contemporary Pacific*, vol. 1, nos. 1 & 2 (Spring/Fall 1989). Copyright © 1989 by University of Hawaii Press. Reprinted by permission. Notes and references omitted.

The discourse of identity, legitimacy, and historical origins—the political mythmaking of our time—is not as different from the political mythmaking of the pre-European Pacific as it might seem.

The "invention of tradition" has been extensively explored in recent years . . . , in relation to theoretical issues of ideology and representation, questions of political economy (such as the invention and evocation of a symbolically constructed Scottish Highlands culture, replete with woollen kilts from British mills as well as bagpipes . . . , and the dynamics of national-identity construction in postcolonial nation states. These phenomena have not been extensively explored for the Pacific. Nonetheless, they have occurred in other times and places and are going on at present in other settings. Contemporary Malaysia, where a mythic "Malay culture," a conflation of indigenous (but heavily Indianized) court traditions and Islam, is being used to persecute and disenfranchise Chinese and Indian minorities and indigenous ethnic groups, is a case in point.

Modern Mythmaking in the Pacific

Before I turn to some of the important theoretical issues raised by contemporary movements and ideologies of cultural identity, let me sketch briefly the range of phenomena I am concerned with.

Beginning with ideologies of *kastom* in contemporary Melanesia, I will illustrate four variants, or levels, mainly with reference to the Solomon Islands. These phenomena have counterparts in Vanuatu and Papua New Guinea.

First, at a national and regional level, are rhetorical appeals to "The Melanesian Way," and idealizations of custom (most often emanating from a Westernized elite). In Vanuatu in particular, the ideologies and charters of the postcolonial state enshrine customary law and institutions.

Second, are ritualized celebrations of custom in the form of the arts—music, dance, "traditional" dress—as dramatically enacted in art festivals, tourist events, and rituals of state.

Third, the rhetoric of custom is invoked with reference to a particular region or island or province within a postcolonial state. This may take the form of competition for state resources and political power, regional separatism, or even secessionist demands. . . . In the emergence of Papua New Guinea, secessionist claims by North Solomons and East New Britain were cast partly in terms of customary unity. . . .

Fourth, if the field of view is narrowed to particular language groups, particularly on islands like Malaita (or Tanna) where the commitment to "traditional" culture remains strong, we find ideologies of *kastom* used to resolve the contradictions between ancestral ways and Christianity. As Burt has documented, the Kwara'ae of central Malaita have produced origin myths that trace their ancestors back to wandering tribes of Israelites and codify ancestral rules in the style of Biblical commandments. The creation of mythical customs has been encouraged and even demanded by institutions of the postcolonial state that empower and legitimize "paramount chiefs" or other "traditional" leaders: contemporary Melanesia is now filled with "paramount chiefs" in areas that in precolonial times had no systems of chiefly authority or hereditary rank. . . .

In Australia, idealized representations of the pre-European past are used to proclaim Aboriginal identity and the attachment of indigenous peoples to the land, and are being deployed in environmentalist as well as Aboriginal political struggles. In New Zealand, increasingly powerful and successful Maori political movements incorporate idealized and mythicized versions of a precolonial Golden Age, the mystical wisdom of Aotearoa.

Hawai'i and New Caledonia exhibit further variants on the themes of Fourth World political struggle, with idealized representations of precolonial society deployed to assert common identity and to advance and legitimate political demands. In the Hawaiian case, a cultural tradition largely destroyed many decades ago must be reconstituted, reclaimed, revived, reinvented. A denial that so much has been destroyed and lost is achieved by political mythology and the sanctification of what survives, however, altered its forms. In New Caledonia, the issues are not simply the desperate struggle for political power and freedom from colonial oppression, but also the creation of both common bonds and common cultural identity among peoples whose ancestors were deeply divided, culturally and linguistically, into warring tribes speaking mutually unintelligible languages.

Some Theoretical Themes

These discourses of cultural identity in the contemporary Pacific, although they depict the precolonial past and claim to produce countercolonial images, are in many ways derived from Western ideologies.

... [C]ontemporary Third World (and Fourth World) representations of their own cultures have been shaped by colonial domination and the perception of Western culture through a less direct reactive process, a dialectic in which elements of indigenous culture are selected and valorized (at the levels of both ideology and practice) as *counters to* or *commentaries on* the intrusive and dominant colonial culture. That is, colonized peoples have distanced themselves from (as well as modeling their conceptual structures on) the culture of domination, selecting and shaping and celebrating the elements of their own traditions that most strikingly differentiate them from Europeans.

... Pacific Island elites, and Aboriginal Australians, Maori, and Hawaiians in a position to gain leadership roles and become ideologues, have been heavily exposed, through the educational process, to Western ideologies that idealize primitivity and the wisdom and ecological reverence of those who live close to Nature. Idealizations of the precolonial past in the contemporary Pacific have often been derivatives of Western critiques of modern technology and progress; ironically, those in the Pacific who in their rhetorical moments espouse these idealized views of the past are mainly (in their political actions and life-styles) hell-bent on technology, progress, materialism, and "development."

In the process of objectification, a culture is (at the level of ideology) imagined to consist of "traditional" music, dances, costumes, or artifacts. Periodically performing or exhibiting these fetishized representations of their cultures, the elites of the new Pacific ritually affirm (to themselves, the tourists, the village voters) that the ancestral cultural heritage lives on.

. . . [A]ssertions of identity based on idealizations of the ancestral past draw heavily on anthropological concepts—particularly ideas about "culture"—as they have entered Western popular thought. It is ironic that cultural nationalist rhetoric often depicts anthropologists as villains who appropriate and exploit, although that anti-anthropological rhetoric is itself squarely shaped by anthropology's concepts and categories. . . .

European scholars are implicated in a more direct way in some of the misrepresentations of ancestral cultures. Some of the classic accounts and generalizations about the cultures of Polynesia and Melanesia by expatriate scholars—to which Islanders have been exposed through books and other media—are misleading. Western scholars' own misrenderings and stereotypes have fed back into contemporary (mis)representations of the Pacific past.

In questioning the political myths of our time, I am not defending the authority of anthropological representations of the Pacific past, or the hegemonic position of scholarly discourse in relation to the aspirations of indigenous peoples to recapture their own pasts. The past . . . is contested ground. I am urging that in contesting it, Pacific Islanders be more relentlessly radical and skeptical—not that they relinquish it to the "experts." (We who claim expertise, too, can well reflect on the politics and epistemology of our privileged authority.)

Finally (and critically), if I seem to imply a gulf between the authenticity of actual precolonial societies and cultures and the inauthenticity of the mythic pasts now being invented in the Pacific, such a characterization in fact perpetuates some of anthropology's own myths. The present political contexts in which talk of custom and ancestral ways goes on are of course very different from precolonial contexts. Nonetheless, such mystification is inherent in political processes, in all times and places. Spurious pasts and false histories were being promulgated in the Pacific long before Europeans arrived, as warrior leaders draped veils of legitimacy over acts of conquest, as leaders sought to validate, reinforce, [and] institutionalize, . . . and as factions battled for dominance. Ironically, then, the "true" and "authentic" cultures of the Pacific past, overlain and distorted by today's political myths, represent, in part at least, cumulations of the political myths of the ancestors.

In Pacific communities on the eve of European invasion, there were multiple "realities"—for commoners and for chiefs, for men and for women, for young and for old, for free persons and for captives or slaves, for victors and for vanquished. Genealogies, cosmologies, rituals were themselves contested spheres. The "authentic" past was never a simple, unambiguous reality. The social worlds of the Pacific prior to European invasion were, like the worlds of the present, multifaceted and complex.

Moreover, however the past may be constructed as a symbol, and however critical it may be for historically dominated peoples to recapture this ground, a people's cultural heritage poses a challenge to radical questioning. We are all to some degree prisoners of "real" pasts as they survive into the present—in the form of patriarchal values and institutions, of patterns of thought, of structures of power. A deeply radical discourse (one that questions basic assumptions) would aspire to liberate us from pasts, both those of our ancestors and those of (colonial or other) domination, as well as to use them as political symbols.

Let me develop these arguments. . . .

The Fetishization of "Culture"

Not only in the Pacific are dramatizations and ritual enactments of cultural traditions being celebrated—in the form of dress, music, dance, handicrafts— while actual cultural traditions are vanishing. The two processes—the celebration of fossilized or fetishized cultures and the destruction of cultures as ways of life and thought—are going on in the Soviet Union, eastern Europe, and China and also in the Andean states, Brazil, Malaysia, and Indonesia. Perhaps it is an essential element in the process of nation building, where populations are ethnically diverse. Most often, a dominant national population imposes its language and cultural tradition on minority groups while appearing to value and preserve minority cultures: they are preserved like specimens in jars. . . . What greater alienation than watching those who dominate and rule you perform symbolically central elements of your cultural heritage: selling *your* culture?

What makes the Pacific distinctive here is the way, particularly in the Melanesian countries, the specimens in the jars are the cultures those with political power have themselves left behind. Members of the Westernized elites are likely to be separated by gulfs of life experience and education from village communities where they have never lived: their ancestral cultures are symbols rather than experienced realities. Bringing the specimens out of the jars on special occasions—cultural festivals, rituals of state—is a denial of alienation at a personal level, and a denial that cultural traditions are being eroded and destroyed in the village hinterlands. . . .

By the same logic, the "cultures" so commoditized and packaged can be sold to tourists. I have commented elsewhere on the way this commoditization shapes Pacific cultures to fit Western fantasies:

> Mass tourism and the media have created a new Pacific in which what is left or reconstructed from the ruins of cultural destruction of earlier decades is commoditized and packaged as exoticism for the tourists. The Pacific [is] Fantasy Land for Europe and the United States (and now for Japan) . . . to be symbolically constructed—and consumed by a consumerist society, to serve its pleasures and needs.
>
> The commoditization of their cultures has left tens of thousands of Pacific Islanders as aliens in their own lands, reduced to tawdry commercialized representations of their ancestors, histories and cultures. Beneath the veneer of fantasy, the Islanders are pauperized in village hinterlands or themselves commoditized as menial employees. Serving the comforts as well as the fantasies of rich tourists, they are constrained to smile and "be happy," because that is part of their symbolic image.

We need only think of tourism in Fiji. There, at least, the elements of culture enacted for tourists represent a version, if an edited and Christianized one (no strangling of widows in the hotel dining rooms), of a past that actually existed. The representations of "Hawaiian culture" for tourists, with hula dances, ukuleles, and pineapples, illustrate that where there is a gulf between historical realities and the expectations of tourists, the fantasies will be packaged and sold.

Invented Pasts and Anthropology

The objectification of a way of life, the reification of the customs of ancestors into a symbol to which a political stance is taken—whether of rejection or idealization—is not new in the Pacific, and is not confined to Islanders who have learned the Western concept of "culture." The so-called Vailala Madness of the Gulf Division of Papua in 1919, where villagers destroyed cult objects in a wave of iconoclasm, and proclaimed their rejection of the ways of ancestors who had withheld material riches from them, is but one example. Other classic "cargo cults" echoed the same theme.

The political stances being taken toward the ways of the ancestors in the contemporary Pacific reflect some of the same mechanisms. When massively confronted with an engulfing or technologically dominating force—whether early colonial invaders or more recently the world capitalist system and late-twentieth-century technology and wealth—one is led to take an objectified, externalized view of one's way of life that would hardly be possible if one were simply *living* it. Land, and spiritual connection to it, *could not* have, other than in a context of invasion and displacement and alienation, the ideological significance it acquires in such a context.

The ideologies of our time, unlike cargo cult ideologies, are phrased in terms of "culture" and other anthropological concepts, as they have passed into Western popular thought and intellectual discourse. This is hardly surprising, given the educational experiences of Pacific Island leaders, but it is problematic nonetheless, because the concepts that have been borrowed oversimplify in ways that have bedeviled anthropology for decades. First, "culture" represents a reification. A complex system of ideas and customs, attributed a false concreteness, is turned into a causal agent. Cultures are viewed as doing things, causing things to happen (or not happen).

In the framework of functionalist anthropology, societies and cultures have been attributed a spurious coherence and integration and portrayed in a timeless equilibrium. The timelessness and integration of the ideologically constructed Pacific pasts represent in part a projection of anthropology's own conceptual simplifications into contemporary political myths.

. . . Pacific Island peoples asserting their identity and their continuity with the past are led to seek, characterize, and proclaim an "essence" that has endured despite a century or more of change and Westernization.

In a different and older anthropological tradition—one that lives on in anthropology museums, hence is represented in the contemporary Pacific—a culture is metonymically represented by its material artifacts. This museological tradition, which has old roots in the nineteenth-century folklorism of Europe, has fed as well into the discourse on cultural identity, as I have noted. From it derives the view that in preserving the material forms and performance genres of a people, one preserves their culture.

In borrowing from anthropological discourse, ideologies of cultural identity in the contemporary Pacific have not only acquired conceptual oversimplifications but have incorporated some empirical distortions and misinterpretations for which anthropologists (and other European scholars) are ultimately responsible.

It is not that Aboriginal or Maori activists, or contemporary Samoans or Trobriand Islanders, are uncritical in their acceptance of what anthropologists have written about them. In Aboriginal struggles for land rights, for example, one of the battles has been waged against orthodox views, deriving ultimately from Radcliffe-Brown, of the patrilineality of local territorial groups—views incorporated into federal land rights legislation. The ironies and contradictions of Aboriginal peoples being denied rights they believe are culturally legitimate on grounds that they do not fit an anthropological model have chilling implications for those of us who would claim privileged authority for our "expertise" or *our* constructions of the past.

There is a further twist of irony when scholarly interpretations that may be faulty, or at least misleadingly oversimplified or overgeneralized, have been incorporated by Pacific Islanders into their conceptions of their own pasts. Let me illustrate with the concept of *mana* in Oceanic religion. . . . When I was at the University of South Pacific in 1984 and spoke on *mana*, I discovered that Polynesian students and faculty had been articulating an ideology of a common Polynesian cultural heritage and identity in which *mana* was central. Yet, as I pointed out, in many languages in Western Polynesia *mana* is used as a noun only to describe thunder, lightning, or other meteorological phenomena. Where *mana is* used as a noun to refer to spiritual power, in a number of Polynesian languages, it seems to be a secondary usage, less common than its usage as a stative verb ('be effective', 'be potent', 'be sacred').

Mana in the sense it has acquired in anthropology seems centrally important only in a few languages of eastern Polynesia, notably Maori and Hawaiian. . . .

The imputation of mystical wisdom to Polynesians (who in the process were distinguished from their dark-skinned, savage, cannibal neighbors to the west) has roots in European theories of race. The construction of the Polynesians in European thought, a process going back to the early explorers, has been brilliantly examined by Bernard Smith. Most striking has been the construction of Maori culture in European imagination. . . . The cosmic philosophy of the Maori, the mystical worldview, is as much a European as a Polynesian creation. Even though contemporary Maori ideologues attempt to discredit some aspects of the representation of Maori culture by Western scholars, the counterrepresentation advanced as authentic seems deeply infused by early Western romanticizations of the Maori. . . .

Political Mythology and Cultural "Authenticity": A Wider View

So far, I have implied that there is a wide gulf between the authentic past—the real ways of life that prevailed in the Pacific on the eve of European invasion—and the representations of the past in contemporary ideologies of cultural identity. This gulf requires a closer look.

. . . My point is . . . that the real past was itself highly political. Pacific societies, in pre-European times, were far from stable and static . . . : they were, as the archaeological record makes very clear, marked by political expansions and contractions, regional systems, warfare, trade—and change. Anthropological models have by and large failed to capture the dynamics of cultural production and change. Cultures are often imagined to be like coral reefs, the gradual accumulation of countless "polyps." . . . To the contrary, . . . cultural production is a highly political process. The symbolic material of cultures—rules imputed to ancestors, rituals, myths—serves ideological ends, reinforcing the power of some, the subordination of others.

From such a viewpoint, the authentic ancestral cultures of the past begin to appear in a different light. The rituals, the myths, the ideologies of hierarchy and the sanctity of chiefs, served political purposes. Conquering chiefs—or their priestly retinues—invented genealogies connecting them to the gods, and discrediting fallen rivals. Those individuals or classes acquiring sufficient political power to control symbolic production could bend cultural rules and roles to their own ends, reinforcing and legitimating their power. (The old Polynesian process whereby ascendant chiefly factions produce and impose versions of the past that legitimate their ascendancy in cosmic and genealogical terms has clearly continued into the latter twentieth century, notably in Tonga.) "Ancestral cultures" themselves represented legitimations of political power and aspirations; cultures were contested spheres. In this sense, the political myths of the contemporary Pacific that refashion the past to advance the interests of the present are not so different from the political myths of the past, dutifully recorded by the early ethnographers.

There are political contexts where it is important for an idealized vision of the past to be used as counter to the present: to the world capitalist system as it incorporates poor Third World countries on its margins as primary producers and consumers; to mindless materialism, disintegration of bonds of kinship and community, narcissistic individualism, destruction of environments for short-term profit. There is a place for pastoral visions, in the West and in the Pacific.

And there is certainly a place for discourses of resistance cast in terms of cultural identity. For Fourth World indigenous minorities in the Pacific—Maori, Aboriginal Australians, Kanaks, Hawaiians—a reverence for what survives of the cultural past (however altered its forms), and for a lost heritage, is a necessary counterpoint to deep anger over the generations of destruction.

But such ideologies become self-delusory if they are not interspersed with visions of "real" pasts that cast into relief not simply their idealized virtues, but their cracks of contradictions. . . . European scholars of the Pacific have been complicit in legitimating and producing male-oriented and elitist representations of societies that were themselves male- and (in many cases) elite-dominated. A critical skepticism with regard to pasts and power, and a critical deconstruction of conceptualizations of "a culture" that hide and neutralize subaltern voices and perspectives, should, I think, dialectically confront idealizations of the past. I am encouraged by the emergence, in the last several years, of critical writings in this vein by Pacific Islanders, including Epeli Hau'ofa and a number of feminist critics.

This is not the time to leave the past to the "experts," whether of the present generation or their predecessors. . . .

A more radical Pacific discourse would also be more deeply self-reflexive about the hegemonic force of Western education, of Christianity (an integral part of the colonial-imperialist project), of Western pastoral myths as appropriations of Otherness. . . .

A similar self-reflexivity is a continuing challenge for scholars working in the Pacific. Both the political implications and epistemology of our projects and representations are deeply problematic. The frame of certainty that surrounds scholarly expertise—like mythical history—is less solid than it seems: it dissolves in the right mixture of astute skepticism and self-reflexivity. But specialists on the Pacific do not best serve the interests of a less hegemonic scholarship or best support the political struggles of decolonizing and internally colonized Pacific peoples by suspending their critical judgment or maintaining silence—whether out of liberal guilt or political commitment—regarding mythic pasts evoked in cultural nationalist rhetoric. Our constructions of real pasts are not sacrosanct, but they are important elements in a continuing dialogue and dialectic.

Natives and Anthropologists: The Colonial Struggle

As a Hawaiian, a long-time outspoken defender of my people's claim to nation-hood, a scholar, and a Native who knows her history and people, I found Roger Keesing's article . . . a gem of academic colonialism. Knowing oldfashioned racism too crude to defend but bitterly clinging to his sense of white superiority, Keesing plows the complaining path of the unappreciated missionary who, when confronted by ungrateful, decolonizing Natives, thinly veils his hurt and anger by the high road of lamentation: Alas, poor, bedeviled Natives "invent" their culture in reaction to colonialism, and all in the service of grimy politics!

Keesing's peevishness has a predictably familiar target: Native nationalists—from Australia and New Zealand through the Solomons and New Caledonia to Hawai'i. The problem? These disillusioned souls idealize their pasts for the purpose of political mythmaking in the present. Worse, they are so unoriginal (and, by implication, unfamiliar with what Keesing calls their "real" pasts) as to concoct their myths out of Western categories and values despite their virulent opposition to same. Thus the romanticization of pre-European Native pasts (the "Golden Age" allegedly claimed by the Maori); the assertion of a common Native identity (eg, Fijian "culture"); the "ideology" of land as spiritually significant (supposedly argued by Hawaiians, Solomon Islanders, Kanaks, and Aborigines). The gospel, according to Keesing, is that these claims are "invented." To be specific, there never was a "Golden Age," a common identity, or a spiritual attachment to the land.

Proof? Keesing supplies none, either on the charge that Native nationalists have made such claims or that their claims are false. He merely asserts fabrication then proceeds to belabor, through the mumbo jumbo of academic "discourse," the crying need for Natives (and academics) to face "our" pasts with "skepticism," while pursuing a "critical deconstruction of conceptualizations" to achieve "dialectical confrontation." The final intention should be to "liberate us" from our pasts.

Well, my answer to Keesing has been said by modern-day Natives to would-be White Fathers many times: What do you mean "us," white man?

Among Hawaiians, people like Keesing are described as *maha'oi haole*, that is, rude, intrusive white people who go where they do not belong. In Keesing's case, his factual errors, cultural and political ignorance, and dismissive attitude qualify him perfectly as *maha'oi*. Unlike Keesing; I cannot speak for other Natives. But regarding Hawaiian nationalists, Keesing neither knows whereof he speaks, nor given his *maha'oi* attitude, does he care.

Example.   Keesing only cites works by *haole* academics on the current situation in Hawai'i. Obviously, he hasn't bothered to read our Native nationalists and scholars, including those, like myself, who have been very critical of these same *haole* academics. Indeed, most of his comments on Hawaiian nationalists come from one problematic and contested article (contested by Natives, that is) by anthropologist Jocelyn Linnekin, hardly a sound evidentiary base for sweeping claims that we invent our past.

Beyond his poverty of sources, there is Keesing's willful ignorance of solid evidence from Native forms of history—genealogy—which reveal that in pre-*haole* Hawai'i our people looked on land as a mother, enjoyed a familial relationship with her and other living things, and practiced an economically wise, spiritually based ethic of caring for the land, called *mālama 'āina*.

Contrary to Linnekin's claims, and Keesing's uncritical acceptance of them, the value of *mālama 'āina* has been "documented historically," and "recorded ethnographically," (as Keesing might learn if he read Native sources), two of the criteria Keesing cites as central to any judgment of the accuracy of "ancestral ways of life being evoked rhetorically" by Native nationalists today.[1] If Natives must be held to Keesing's criteria, why should he be allowed to escape them?

The answer is that Keesing, with many Western academics, shares a common assumption: Natives don't know very much, even about their own life-ways, thus there is no need to read them. (The only "real" sources are *haole* sources, hegemony recognizing and reinforcing hegemony).

Keesing's racism is exposed here. Not only has he refused to read what we Native nationalists write and say, he has refused to look at our sources of knowledge. But then, Keesing believes, Natives are so colonized, why bother?

Example.   Keesing has also failed to distinguish between what Hawaiian national-ists say about our ways of life and what the mammoth tourist industry adver-tises "Hawaiian culture" to be, including "hula dances, ukuleles, and pineapples." Because he is totally ignorant of modern Hawaiian resistance, he is also totally ignorant of the Native criticism of the tourist industry, including the myth of happy Natives waiting to share their "culture" with tourists. In fact, after years of Native resistance to tourism, the churches in Hawai'i (with the push of Native nationalists and international ecumenical groups) sponsored a confer-ence on the impact of tourism on Hawaiian people and culture in 1989. At that conference, Hawaiians from each of our major islands spoke eloquently of tourism's damage to Hawaiian sites, dance, language, economics, land, and way of life. The declaration issued from that conference listed ways to halt this damage, including a ban on all resorts in Hawaiian communities. Keesing should be reading this kind of primary evidence if he wants to learn what Hawaiian nationalists think about tourism and our culture.

Example.   Keesing claims that Native nationalists hark back to an "authentic," "simple, unambiguous reality," when, in fact, "there were multiple 'realities'— for commoners and chiefs, for men and for women . . ." in cultures where "genealogies, cosmologies, rituals were themselves contested spheres."

As usual, the critical reader finds not a single reference here to a single Native nationalist statement. More *haole* sources follow, especially Keesing on Keesing. But where are the Natives?

In the dark, naturally.

The truth is that Keesing has made a false charge. Those of us in the current Hawaiian nationalist movement know that genealogies are claimed and contested all the time. Some of the chiefly lineages have legal claims on lands taken by the United States government at the American annexation of Hawai'i in 1898, which means that genealogies have an impact beyond the Hawaiian community. Cosmologies are also contested, with nationalists citing and arguing over accuracy and preferability.[2]

Finally, at the Center for Hawaiian Studies—which generates nationalist positions, sponsors nationalist conferences, and teaches the historical background and political substance of nationalist arguments—students are required to take a course on genealogies.

Given Roger Keesing's shameless claims about us Hawaiian nationalists, I invite him to take this course, or any other offered at our center. We Natives might teach him something.

Example.   Keesing asserts that "cultural nationalist rhetoric often depicts anthropologists as villains who appropriate and exploit." In a note, he adds that anthropologists are "imagined to be appropriating and profiting from other people's cultures. . . ."

In Hawai'i, contract work is a major source of funding for archaeologists and anthropologists. These people are hired by investors and state or private institutions to survey areas and deem them ready for use. In highly controversial cases regarding removal of Hawaiian bones and destruction of Hawaiian temple and house sites, many archaeologists and anthropologists have argued *for* development and *against* preservation while receiving substantial sums of money. At its worst, these controversies have exposed the racist paternalism of anthropologists who pit (in their own words) *emotional* Hawaiians who try to stop disinterment and development against *scientific* anthropologists who try to increase the store of (Western) knowledge.

Of course, these *haole* anthropologists would be outraged were we Hawaiians to dig up *their* relatives for osteological analysis, search for evidence of tuberculosis and other diseases, and, not coincidentally, get paid handsomely for our troubles. To my knowledge, no anthropologist has ever dug up missionary bones, despite their plentiful presence. Nor has any haole "expert" ever argued that missionary skeletons should be subjected to osteological analysis, despite historical evidence that missionaries did bring certain diseases to Hawai'i. White colonialism in Hawai'i ensures that it is the colonizers who determine disinterment. Since we are the colonized, we have no power to disinter the bones of the colonizer. Thus, Native remains are dug up and studied. Missionary and explorer remains are sacrosanct.

Apart from contract work, anthropologists make academic careers and employment off Native cultures. Keesing may not think this is "profiting," but anthropologists who secure tenure by studying, publishing, and lecturing about Native peoples are clearly "profiting" through a guaranteed lifetime income. Of course, Keesing is disingenuous, at best. He knows as well as Native nationalists that anthropologists without Natives are like entomologists without insects.

For Hawaiians, anthropologists in general (and Keesing in particular) are part of the colonizing horde because they seek to take away from us the power to define who and what we are, and how we should behave politically and culturally.[3] This theft testifies to the stranglehold of colonialism and explains why self-identity by Natives elicits such strenuous and sometimes vicious denials by members of the dominant culture.

These denials are made in order to undermine the legitimacy of Native nationalists by attacking their motives in asserting their values and institutions. But motivation is laid bare through the struggle for cultural expression. Nationalists offer explanations at every turn: in writing, in public forums, in acts of resistance. To Natives, the burst of creative outpouring that accompanies cultural nationalism is self-explanatory: a choice has been made for things Native over things non-Native. Politically, the choice is one of decolonization.

The direct links between mental and political decolonization are clearly observable to representatives of the dominant culture, like Keesing, who find their status as "experts" on Natives suddenly repudiated by Natives themselves. This is why thinking and acting like a native is a highly politicized reality, one filled with intimate oppositions and psychological tensions. But it is not Natives who create politicization. *That* was begun at the moment of colonization.

In the Hawaiian case, the "invention" criticism has been thrown into the public arena precisely at a time when Hawaiian cultural and political assertion has been both vigorous and strong willed. Since 1970, Hawaiians have been organizing for land rights, including claims to restitution for the American overthrow of our government in 1893 and for forced annexation in 1898. Two decades of struggle have resulted in the contemporary push for Hawaiian sovereignty, with arguments ranging from complete secession to legally incorporated land-based units managed by Hawaiians, to a "nation-within-a-nation" government akin to Native American Indian nations. The US government has issued two reports on the status of Hawaiian trust lands, which encompass nearly half the State of Hawai'i. And finally, a quasi-governmental agency—the Office of Hawaiian Affairs—was created in 1978, partly in response to Hawaiian demands.

This kind of political activity has been accompanied by a flourishing of Hawaiian dance, a move for Hawaiian language immersion schools, and a larger public sensitivity to the destructive Western relationship to the land compared to the indigenous Hawaiian way of caring for the land.

Non-Native response to this Hawaiian resistance has varied from humor, through mild denial that any wrong has been committed against the Hawaiian people and government, to organized counteraction, especially from threatened agencies and actors who hold power over Hawaiian resources. Indeed, representatives of the dominant culture—from historians and anthropologists to bureaucrats and politicians—are quick to feel and perceive danger because, in the colonial context, all Native cultural resistance is political: it challenges hegemony, including that of people like Keesing who claim to encourage a more "radical stance" toward our past by liberating us from it.

But Keesing obviously knows nothing about Hawaiians. He has failed to distinguish land claims from cultural resurgence, although both have nationalist origins. And he has little or no background regarding the theft of Hawaiian domain and dominion by the American government in the nineteenth century. Given this kind of ignorance of both our recent and distant past, Keesing would do better to take a "radical" look at the racism and arrogance of *his* culture which originated anthropology and its "search for the primitive."

As for nationalist Hawaiians, we know our future lies in the ways of our ancestors, not in the colonial world of *haole* experts. Our efforts at "liberation" are directed against the colonizers, whether they be political agencies, like the American government, or academics, like Keesing himself. We do not need, nor do we want to be "liberated" from our past because it is the source of our understanding of the cosmos and of our *mana*.

In our language, the past (*ka wā mamua*) is the time in front or before; the future (*ka wā mahope*) is the time that comes after. In the words of one of our best living Native historians, Lilikalā Kameʻeleihiwa (whom Keesing did not read), "The Hawaiian stands firmly in the present, with his back to the future, and his eyes fixed upon the past, seeking historical answers for present-day dilemmas. Such an orientation is to the Hawaiian an eminently practical one, for the future is always unknown whereas the past is rich in glory and knowledge."

Notes

1. In her article, Linnekin writes, "For Hawaiʻi, 'traditional' properly refers to the precontact era, before Cook's arrival in 1778." But later on the same page, she admits that "tradition is fluid . . ." Despite this confusion she criticizes Hawaiians for a "reconstruction of traditional Hawaiian society" in the present.

   But what constitutes "tradition" to a people is ever-changing. Culture is not static, nor is it frozen in objectified moments in time. Without doubt, Hawaiians were transformed drastically and irreparably after contact, but remnants of earlier lifeways, including values and symbols, have persisted. One of these values is the Hawaiian responsibility to care for the land, to make it flourish, called *mālama ʻāina* or *aloha ʻāina*. To Linnekin, this value has been invented by modern Hawaiians to protest degradation of the land by developers, the military, and others. What Linnekin has missed here—partly because she has an incomplete grasp of "traditional" values but also because she doesn't understand and thus misapprehends Hawaiian cultural nationalism—is simply this: the Hawaiian relationship to land has persisted into the present. What has changed is ownership and use of the land (from collective use by Hawaiians for subsistence to private use by whites and other non-Natives for profit). Asserting the Hawaiian relationship in this changed context results in politicization. Thus, Hawaiians assert a "traditional" relationship to the land *not* for political ends, as Linnekin (and Keesing) argue, but because they continue to believe in the cultural value of caring for the land. That land use is now contested makes such a belief political. This distinction is crucial because the Hawaiian cultural motivation reveals the persistence of traditional values, the very thing Linnekin (and Keesing) allege modern Hawaiians to have "invented."

2. In Hawai'i the Kawananakoa line contests the loss of governance, since they were heirs to the throne at the time of the American military-backed overthrow of Hawaiian Queen Lili'uokalani. The Salazar family lays claim to part of the Crown lands for similar reasons. Regarding land issues, the Ka'awa family occupied Makapu'u Point in 1988 in protest over its current use. Their argument revolved around their claim to ownership because of their genealogical connection to the Kamehameha line. Among nationalist organizations, 'Ohana o Hawai'i, led by Peggy Ha'o Ross, argues claims to leadership based on genealogy. These examples illustrate the continuity of genealogy as profoundly significant to Hawaiians in establishing mana and, thus, the power to command recognition and leadership. Keesing obviously knows nothing about any of these families or their claims.

3. The United States government defines Native Hawaiians as those with 50 percent or more Hawaiian blood quantum. Those with less than 50 percent Hawaiian blood are not considered to be "Native" and are thus not entitled to lands and monies set aside for 50 percent bloods. Hawaiians are the only human beings in the State of Hawai'i who are categorized by blood quantum, rather like Blacks in South Africa.

While bureaucrats are happily dividing up who is and is not Native, the substance of *what* constitutes things Hawaiian is constantly asserted by anthropologists against Native nationalists. Of course, the claim to knowledge by anthropologists is their academic training applied to the field. Native nationalists' claim to knowledge is their life experience as Natives.

The problem is more serious than epistemology, however. In a colonial world, the work of anthropologists and other Western-trained "experts" is used to disparage and exploit Natives. What Linnekin or Keesing or any other anthropologist writes about Hawaiians has more potential power than what Hawaiians write about themselves. Proof of this rests in the use of Linnekin's argument by the US Navy that Hawaiian nationalists have invented the sacred meaning of Kaho'olawe Island (which the US Navy has controlled and bombed since the Second World War) because nationalists need a "political and cultural symbol of protest" in the modern period. Here, the connection between anthropology and the colonial enterprise is explicit. When Natives accuse Western scholars of exploiting them, they have in mind the exact kind of situation I am describing. In fact, the Navy's study was done by an anthropologist who, of course, cited fellow anthropologists, including Linnekin, to argue that the Hawaiian assertion of love and sacredness regarding Kaho'olawe was "fakery." Far from overstating their case, Native nationalists acutely comprehend the structure of their oppression, including that perpetuated by anthropologists.

POSTSCRIPT

Do Native Peoples Today Invent Their Traditions?

Building on Hobsbawm and Ranger's notion of the "invention of traditon," Keesing makes the case that in most—if not all—Pacific societies, the history and cultural traditions that are regarded as authentic are substantially different from the events and practices that actually occurred. In his mind, there can also be little doubt that controlling what is accepted as tradition has become politically important. How does Trask's concern over professional bias impact Keesing's other arguments? What criteria would Trask suggest as a substitute as a way of judging which practices are authentic traditions and which are modern innovations?

Many other anthropologists have addressed the question of the invention of tradition. In Hawaii, the best-known work is by Jocelyn Linnekin, especially her 1983 essay "Defining Tradition: Variations on the Hawaiian Identity," *American Ethnologist* (vol. 10) and her book *Children of the Land* (Rutgers University Press, 1985). See also Trask's review of the latter in the *Hawaiian Journal of History* (vol. 20, 1986).

Questions about the invention of traditions have become important in North America as well. In 1997 Brian D. Haley and Larry R. Wilcoxon published an essay in *Current Anthropology* (vol. 38) entitled "Anthropology and the Making of Chumash Tradition." They argued that anthropologists and environmentalists had encouraged Chumash Indians to exaggerate claims that a site proposed for industrial development was traditionally sacred. The following year, archaeologist John McVey Erlandson published a reply to Haley and Wilcoxon in *Current Anthropology* (vol. 39). Like Keesing, Erlandson drew on historical (white American) sources to defend his position that the site was held to be sacred.

Another anthropologist, Alan Hanson, wrote a similar but more focused argument about the invention of tradition among the Maori of New Zealand in "The Making of the Maori: Culture Invention and Its Logic," *American Anthropologist* (vol. 91, no. 4, 1989). This essay prompted a vigorous and at times hostile debate within New Zealand, and at one point some Maori threatened to censure the American Anthropological Association because of this article, which some considered racist and anti-Maori. Stephen Webster discusses this topic in light of the so-called Maori renaissance, a revival of Maori cultural values within the modern bicultural state of New Zealand in his book, *Patrons of Maori Culture: Power, Theory and Ideology in the Maori Renaissance* (University of Otago Press, 1998).

ISSUE 12

Is It Natural for Adopted Children to Want to Find Out About Their Birth Parents?

YES: Betty Jean Lifton, from *Journey of the Adopted Self: A Quest for Wholeness* (Basic Books, 1994)

NO: John Terrell and Judith Modell, from "Anthropology and Adoption," *American Anthropologist* (March 1994)

ISSUE SUMMARY

YES: Adoptee and adoption rights advocate Betty Jean Lifton argues that there is a natural need for human beings to know where they came from. Adoption is not a natural human state, she asserts, and it is surrounded by a secrecy that leads to severe social and psychological consequences for adoptees, adoptive parents, and birth parents.

NO: Anthropologists John Terrell and Judith Modell, who are each the parent of an adopted child, contend that the "need" to know one's birth parents is an American (or Western European) cultural construct. They conclude that in other parts of the world, where there is less emphasis placed on biology, adoptees have none of the problems said to be associated with being adopted in America.

T he 1976 television miniseries *Roots*, based on the book by Alex Haley, led many Americans to try to search out their own family stories, to find their own "roots." For most the effort merely meant asking grandparents about their ancestors. But for adopted children in America, information about their forebears was sealed by court order, and there was rarely any knowledge about their birth parents available to them from their adopted parents. Information about birth parents was usually kept secret to protect the birth parents from public scandal, since most adopted children were conceived out of wedlock and quietly put up for adoption with the understanding that the child and the public would never be able to link the birth parents with the adoptee. As social mores have changed in the United States, relatively little stigma now surrounds being an unwed mother or a single parent. But court records for most adoptions remain sealed, leading to a growing movement advocating open adoption records.

For several decades, adoptees' attempts to find their birth parents have become a growing social movement, with advocacy organizations, support groups, and self-help groups all attempting to help adoptees find their birth parents and which often help birth parents find the children they put up for adoption in their youth. Many of these groups insist that there is an inherent human right for adoptees to know their biological parents and for parents to know their natural children. These groups contend that there is a natural bond between parents and children that has been severed by adoption.

In the following selection, Betty Jean Lifton considers the psychological factors at play when children are put up for adoption, where knowledge of their birth parents is denied them. Drawing on her personal experiences as an adoptee as well as on interviews with dozens of other adoptees, Lifton considers how psychologically damaging this veil of secrecy is on adoptees, both as children and as adults. For her, people have a natural need to know where they came from. It is unnatural to grow up separated from and without knowledge of one's natural clan, she argues. The lack of such knowledge of one's roots has a negative impact on the child's psyche and leads them to seek out their roots, concludes Lifton.

Anthropologists John Terrell and Judith Modell counter that the "natural" need to know one's parents, as so often discussed by the adoption rights movement, is an American cultural construct. American and Western European culture emphasizes the difference between biological and adoptive families, viewing adoptive relationships as less real than biological ones. In most non-Western societies, people have very different views of adoption, typically viewing adoptive relationships as equal to biological ones. Citing examples from Hawaii and other parts of Oceania, they challenge the primacy of blood relationships over all other kinds of kinship ties. They argue that in America open adoptions would probably be healthier for all concerned parties but that it would be better still if Americans had a better understanding of the diverse ways other peoples have for understanding and dealing with adoption.

Are kin relations based on biology stronger than relationships based on other ties? Is there something in our genes that makes us have a more important relationship with our biological or birth parents than with others? Are adoptees likely to have stronger bonds with their adopted parents than with their birth parents? What do the experiences of Hawaiians and other Pacific Islanders say about how natural it is to want to know one's birth parents? Is the adoption rights movement in America a social phenomenon that could only emerge in America or does it touch on universal values and psychological needs?

 **YES**

Betwixt and Between

> "Then I shan't be exactly human?" Peter asked.
> "No."
> "What shall I be?"
> "You will be Betwixt-and-Between," Solomon said, and certainly he was a
> wise old fellow, for that is exactly how it turned out.
>
> — James Barrie, *Peter Pan in Kensington Gardens*

Many people identify with the familiar condition of being Betwixt and Between, just as they identify with Peter Pan, the boy who did not want to grow up and face the responsibilities of the real world.

Peter, James Barrie tells us, is "ever so old," but really always the same age: one week. Though he was born "so long ago," he never had a birthday, nor is there the slightest chance of his having one. He escaped from his home when he was seven days old by flying out the window to Kensington Gardens.

Barrie doesn't tell us what was going on in Peter's family that after only seven days he knew he had to take off. But adoptees recognize Peter Pan as a brother. They, too, became lost children when they separated as babies from their natural families and disappeared into a place very much like never-never land. Like Peter, they are fantasy people. Denied the right to see their real birth certificates and the names of those who brought them into the world, they can't be sure they ever had a real *birth* day. They can never grow up because they are always referred to as an "adopted child."

I didn't realize that, like Peter, I wasn't "exactly human" until I was seven *years* old. It was the moment my mother told me I was adopted. Like most adoptive parents faced with breaking such bleak news, she tried to make adoption sound special, but I could feel the penetrating chill of its message. I was not really her child. I had come from somewhere else, a place shrouded in mystery, a place that, like myself, was Betwixt and Between.

As I listened, I could feel a part of myself being pulled into the darkness of that mystery—a place already carved out by Peter and the lost children. I would never be the same again.

This was to be our secret, my mother said. Hers and mine. I was not to share it with anyone—not even my father. It would break his heart if he suspected

I knew. In this way I learned that secrecy and adoption were inextricably mixed, as in a witch's brew. By becoming a keeper of the secret, I was to collaborate in the family conspiracy of silence.

I didn't know then that our little family secret was connected to the *big* secret in the closed adoption system, just as our little conspiracy was connected to the larger social conspiracy around adoption. My mother and father had been assured that my birth records would be sealed forever, that I would never be able to learn the identity of my original family. Secrecy was the magic ingredient that would give our adoptive family the aura of a blood-related one. Secrecy was the magic broom that would sweep away all feelings of grief and loss on the part of any of the parties involved.

As I played my role of the good daughter—repressing a natural need to know where I came from—I was unaware that the secrecy inherent in the adoption system was shaping and constricting the self through which I organized my perception of reality. By denying my natural curiosity about where I came from, and my grief for my lost birth parents and for the child I might have been, I was shrinking my emotional space to the size permitted by that system. So, too, were my adoptive parents forced by the secrecy to shrink their emotional space as they denied their need to grieve for the natural child they might have had.

We were trapped in a closed family system where secrecy cut off real communication. We were not unlike those families who keep secrets around alcoholism, divorce, incest, and all the other things that family members are prone to hide from their neighbors and from one another.

I had no idea of this as a child. Having repressed my real feelings, I was not consciously aware of my pain. And as a consequence, I was not consciously aware of myself, except as someone unreal pretending to be real. I did things that my human friends did, even looked real in my high school and college graduation pictures, and in the photographs taken at my wedding, before I flew off with my husband to the Far East.

Perhaps I might have never been in touch with my feelings if, shortly after my return from Japan, a relative, recently married into my adoptive family, had not remarked about something she heard—that my natural parents had been killed in a car accident. Her statement was like a Zen slap, knocking me into another state of consciousness. I had been told my parents were dead, but I had not been told this story. When I tried to clear up the mystery of how they died, I was shocked to learn that they had been very much alive at the time of my adoption—and might still be.

Much that had lain repressed in me now began stirring. I started to wonder how my mind had been able to cut off the primal subject of who my parents were. Even if it were true that they were dead, why had I not asked any questions about them? After all, dead people have names; they have relatives they have left behind; they have graves. Why had I behaved as if death had wiped out all traces of their existence? It was my first conscious brush with the psychological mystery that forms the core of this [selection]: How does a child's mind close down when it senses danger, and stay closed until some life event or crisis inadvertently jars it open? And what traumatic effects does this have on the child's growing sense of self?

‧⟨❂⟩‧

As a writer, I set out to explore the psychological complexities of being adopted in my book *Twice Born: Memoirs of an Adopted Daughter.* I was amazed, even alarmed, at what surfaced. The compliant adopted child within, as elusive as ever, was in many ways a stranger to the adult I had become. The anger, barely contained under what passed as irony and wit, could no longer be disguised as I dredged up memories of that child's helplessness in the face of mysteries too dark to comprehend. Even as I wrote about my search and reunion, I felt burdened with guilt, as if it were a disloyalty to my deceased adoptive parents. Nor had I fully absorbed the depths of what I had been through. I found a birth mother who had tried to hold on to me but, as an unmarried seventeen-year-old with no emotional or financial support, finally had to let go. Once she was defeated, she put on the scarlet letter—S for secrecy and shame—and did not tell either of her two husbands or her son about me. We met secretly twice before I had to leave for a summer in Japan. The psychic chaos I felt during those two months in Tokyo—as if I had fallen into a black hole—was so great that when I returned to the States I did not call her for fear of falling back into that dark place: a place, as we will see, that is not unfamiliar to many adoptees who have internalized the taboos of the closed adoption system. At the time of my reunion, there were no books to sanction my search for my mother or to prepare me for what I might experience.

My next book, *Lost and Found, the Adoption Experience,* was an attempt to write such a book and, in so doing, to illuminate the existential condition of being adopted. I explored the psychological pitfalls that await adoptees all through the life cycle when they are forced to close off their real feelings and live *as if* their families of origin were not an inherent part of their identity. I laid out the difficult stages of awakening that adoptees experience before they dare to set out in search of the missing pieces in their lives.

As the search phenomenon was still relatively new at that time, the last part of the book gave an overview of the varieties of reunion experience and the psychological growth and accommodation that everyone—adoptee, adoptive parents, and birth parents—has to make. . . .

‧⟨❂⟩‧

[Looking at my own life,] I found an adopted woman waiting there, one who was more sensitive than ever to the lack of respect for the rights of adopted children to know who they are, and who was still absorbed with the psychological mysteries inherent in adoption. Once again I was faced with the same questions I had been grappling with earlier: Why do adopted people feel so alienated? Why do they feel unreal, invisible to themselves and others? Why do they feel unborn? Now, however, I had a new question that I felt would shed light on the others: How do adopted people form a sense of self in the closed adoption system?

The psychoanalyst Karen Horney defined the real self as the alive, unique, personal center of ourselves that wants to grow. When the real self is prevented from free, healthy growth because of abandoning its needs to others, one can become alienated from it. She quotes Kierkegaard on the alienation and loss of self as "sickness unto death." Adoptees, who often say they feel they have no self, can be seen as expressing this despair. Having abandoned their need to know their origins for the sake of their adoptive parents, they are left with a hole in the center of their being. They feel they don't exist.

Of course, everyone has some kind of self. The adoptee born psychologically into the closed adoption system and shaped by its myths, secrets, and taboos from first conscious memory, and even before, has a unique self, an adopted self. But this fragile self has a basic inner division brought about by the need for denial that is built into the closed adoption system.

When I began research for this [selection], I was primarily interested in how secrecy affects the formation of the adopted self. I saw it as emotional abuse (of which adoptive parents are unaware) because it distorts the child's psychic reality. In the course of interviewing adoptees, however, I realized that it is not just secrecy that affects their sense of self but rather a series of traumas. This "cumulative adoption trauma" begins when they are separated from the mother at birth; builds when they learn that they were not born to the people they call mother and father; and is further compounded when they are denied knowledge of the mother and father to whom they were born.

I was not unfamiliar with the literature on trauma. My husband, Robert Jay Lifton, has been preoccupied with trauma on a massive scale. As a journalist, I have reported on the war-wounded, orphaned, and traumatized children of Hiroshima, Korea, Vietnam, and the Holocaust. Still, as an adopted person, loyal to my adoptive parents, I didn't allow myself to see that closed adoption is also a form of trauma—an invisible and subtle one—until years later when I began noticing parallels between adopted children and children of alcoholics, children of survivors (even survivors themselves), and children who have been abused.

There has already been some misunderstanding about the linking of adoption to trauma. Far from being regarded as traumatic, adoption is still widely viewed as fortunate for the child who is rescued from homelessness, and for the adoptive parents who are rescued from childlessness. And in most cases it is. Yet the word *trauma* has been slipping into the psychological literature on adoption with increasing frequency in the last decade as clinicians come to realize the high psychic cost that both parent and child pay when they repress their grief and loss.

I have come to believe in the course of my research that it is unnatural for members of the human species to grow up separated from and without knowledge of their natural clan, that such a lack has a negative influence on a child's psychic reality and relationship with the adoptive parents. By enveloping their origins with secrecy, the closed adoption system asks children to disavow reality, to live *as if* they were born to the parents who raise them. They grow up feeling like anonymous people cut off from the genetic and social heritage that gives everyone else roots.

·⟨◉⟩·

As I write this, we are Betwixt and Between change and stasis in the adoption field. We are between two systems: the traditional closed one that for almost half a century has cut adopted children off from their heritage, and an open one in which birth mothers choose the adoptive parents of their baby and maintain some contact with the family. It is a time when the best interests of the child, for which the adoption system was originally created, have become subordinate to the best interests of the adults, as fierce custody battles are waged over the few available healthy white infants.

Meanwhile, adoption records remain sealed in all but two states due to the influence of a conservative lobby group, the National Council for Adoption, that has managed to polarize the field by labeling those who seek reform as "anti-adoption." Reformers who are working to open the system, as well as the records, however, are not anti-adoption but rather anti–closed adoption and pro–adopted children.

While no amount of openness can take away the child's trauma of being separated from his mother, or save the child from the trauma of learning she was not born into the adoptive family, we can remove the secrecy that compounds those two traumas. We can begin to demystify the adoptive family and to see it with much of the strengths and weaknesses of other families. The conservatives argue for the myth of the happy adoptive family that has no problems because love conquers all. But we will see that something more is expected of the adopted family: an excess of happiness that is meant to make up for the excess of loss that everyone in the triad experiences, and an excess of denial to cover that loss. Exposing the myths of the adoptive family while still holding on to the very real need and love that parents and child have for each other has been the challenge facing me. . . .

The adoptees [I studied] are mostly successful people in that they are productive in their work and their private lives. But, . . . much of their psychic energy has been taken up with adjusting to the mystery of their origins by disavowing their need to have some knowledge of and contact with their blood kin. . . .

The adoptive family has managed to "pass" until now; it remains, for the most part, an unexplored constellation that has escaped psychological detection. Many professionals regard its psychodynamics as being the same as that of other families, overlooking the trauma that the parents as well as the child experience due to the conspiracy of silence built into the closed system.

Because it is a social rather than a natural construct, we can see the strengths and malfunctions of the adoptive family as a laboratory to illuminate some of the most fundamental issues around mothering and mother loss, attachment and bonding, separation and loss, denial and dissociation, and the human need for origins. We can see the deep need that parents and child fill for each other, but we can also see the problems that occur between parents and child when secrets prevent open communication between them.

In *Lost and Found* I spoke of what I called the Adoption Game, a family system that operates by unspoken rules that require everyone in it to live a double life. While seeming to exist in the real world with their adoptive family, the children are at the same time inhabiting an underground world of fantasies and fears which they can share with no one. The adoptive parents also live a double life. Believing themselves to be doing everything for their children, they withhold from them the very knowledge they need to develop into healthy adults. This double role of savior/withholder eventually works against the adoptive parents, estranging them from their children. So, too, the birth mother is forced to live a double life from the moment she surrenders her baby. Advised to go on as if nothing has happened, she keeps secret what is probably the most important and traumatic event of her life.

In [*Journey of the Adopted Self: A Quest for Wholeness*], I speak not of adoption games but of adoption ghosts. In many ways [the] book is a ghost story, for it tells of the ghosts that haunt the dark crevices of the unconscious and trail each member of the adoption triangle (parents and child alike) wherever they go. Unless one is aware of these ghosts, one will never be able to understand or to help the child who is adopted, the parents who adopt, or the parents who give up a child to adoption.

Who are these ghosts?

The adopted child is always accompanied by the ghost of the child he might have been had he stayed with his birth mother and by the ghost of the fantasy child his adoptive parents might have had. He is also accompanied by the ghost of the birth mother, from whom he has never completely disconnected, and the ghost of the birth father, hidden behind her.

The adoptive mother and father are accompanied by the ghost of the perfect biological child they might have had, who walks beside the adopted child who is taking its place.

The birth mother (and father, to a lesser extent) is accompanied by a retinue of ghosts. The ghost of the baby she gave up. The ghost of her lost lover, whom she connects with the baby. The ghost of the mother she might have been. And the ghosts of the baby's adoptive parents.

All of these ghosts are members of the extended adoptive family, which includes the birth family. . . .

[The] book, then, is about the search for the adopted self. It is not about the literal search in the material world, where one sifts through records and archives for real people with real names and addresses; but rather about the internal search in which one sifts through the pieces of the psyche in an attempt to understand who one was so that one can have some sense of who one is and who one can become. It is the quest for all the missing pieces of the self so that one can become whole.

It is the search for the answer to that universal question—Who am I?—behind which, for the adoptee, lurks: Who is the mother who brought me into this mysterious world?

John Terrell and
Judith Modell

 **NO**

Anthropology and Adoption

Anthropologists, we believe, are likely to forget that "what every anthropologist knows" is not necessarily what everyone else knows. In the quest for tenure, professional visibility, and academic achievement, anthropologists may also overlook the possibility that what they know could be important to people who are not anthropologists, too, if only they know. Here is one example.

Adoption in America

In North America, most children grow up living with at least one of the parents they were born to; most children grow up assuming they will live with children born to them. Consequently, perhaps, many people in our society think of adoption as a second-best way of becoming a family (Schaffer and Lindstrom 1989:15). The psychological and social ties binding an adoptive family together are looked on as weaker than "natural" ties of blood. And adoption is seen as difficult and risky. The risk is held to be especially great when a child does not "match"—look like or share the background of—its adoptive parents (Bates 1993). This is preeminently true of transracial and international adoptions, in which a child, who has no say in the matter, is severed not only from its "real" family but also from ethnic roots and cultural heritage: in a word, from its true identity.

Recently, advocates of adoption have been emphasizing the difference between adoptive and biological families (e.g., Melina 1986; Register 1991; Schaffer and Lindstrom 1989), often as a way of helping parents through such "alternative parenthood" (Kirk 1984). Adoptive families are different, for one thing, because adoption is not typical in American society. They are more profoundly different because, it is said, all parties in the "adoption triad" (birth parents, adoptees, and adoptive parents) must cope with psychological pain and feelings of loss. Adoptive parents "lose" the chance to have a biological child and the perpetuation of their blood line. An adopted child loses its natural heritage. And birth parents lose their children.

Moreover, it is presumed that adoptive parents must deal with feelings of inadequacy, and birth parents with feelings of incompetence or frustration. Adoptees, in this argument, suffer throughout their lives because "adoption cuts off people from a part of themselves" (Brodzinsky et al. 1992:3). Even children who were adopted in the first days or weeks of life "grieve not only for the parents they never knew, but for the other aspects of themselves that have been lost through adoption: the loss of origins, of a completed sense of self, of genealogical continuity" (Brodzinsky et al. 1992:11–12). Because they have not been raised by those who gave them life, even the most well-adjusted adoptees, we are told, go through predictable ups and downs of psychological adaptation that distinguish them as a recognizable class of persons who may need special counseling and professional help (Brodzinsky et al. 1992; Samuels 1990:87–113).

Adoption in Oceania

Anthropologists know that what is problematic or self-evident in one society may not be so in another. Oceanic societies—Hawaii among them—are well known in anthropological literature for the frequency and apparent casualness of adoption. What most Americans know about our 50th state, however, does not usually include the information that the last reigning monarch was an adopted, or *hanai,* child. Moreover, this was a crucial fact in her story and remains significant in the interpretations Hawaiians make of their culture and history. In her autobiography, Queen Liliuokalani wrote:

> Immediately after my birth I was wrapped in the finest soft tapa cloth, and taken to the house of another chief, by whom I was adopted. Konia, my foster-mother, was a granddaughter of Kamehameha I., and was married to Paki, also a high chief; their only daughter, Bernice Pauahi, afterwards Mrs. Charles R. Bishop, was therefore my foster-sister. In speaking of our relationship, I have adopted the term customarily used in the English language, but there was no such modification recognized in my native land. I knew no other father or mother than my foster-parents, no other sister than Bernice. [Liliuokalani 1990:4]

She goes on to say that Paki treated her exactly as any other father would treat his child, and that when she would meet her biological parents, she would respond with perhaps more interest, but always with the same demeanor that was due all strangers who noticed her.

Liliuokalani adds that her biological mother and father had other children, ten in all. Most of them were adopted into other chiefs' families. She says it is difficult to explain to outsiders why these adoptions seem perfectly natural to Hawaiians. "As intelligible a reason as can be given is that this alliance by adoption cemented the ties of friendship between chiefs. It spread to the common people, and it has doubtless fostered a community of interest and harmony" (Liliuokalani 1990:4).

Given what anthropologists know about adoption throughout Oceania, (for example, Brady 1976; Carrol 1970; Howard 1990; Levy 1973; Mandeville 1981; Webster 1975), what this royal informant says about the place and popularity of adoption in her native land is not peculiar. For her—and not uniquely—adoption was a loving and generous transaction, not a response to need or crisis. Furthermore, such a loving and generous gesture benefited the whole society as well as the particular individuals involved.

The point of view represented by Queen Liliuokalani—and by other people in Pacific Island societies who share her experiences (Modell 1994a)—ought to be a lesson for Americans, with our quite different story of adoption. As Bartholet (1993) argues, birth parents, adoptive parents, and adoptees should know that people elsewhere in the world may look on adoption in a variety of ways that do not resemble our assumptions and biases about this form of kinship. They need to know that what adoption means, and what it signifies for participants, is malleable, contingent, pragmatic: a "social construction," not a natural fact or a universal cultural given.

Anthropology and Adoption

Anthropologists are likely to find this observation self-evident; adoption is made—*fictio*—by those who practice this mode of child having and child rearing. But, with some exceptions (e.g., Modell 1994b), anthropologists have not been drawn to study the politics and practice of adoption in Western societies: apparently what anthropologists find interesting elsewhere may be less interesting, or deeply private, at home. A glance over the abundant published literature on kinship, in fact, suggests that studying adoption generally plays a peripheral role in anthropology: as a way of illuminating a kinship system, as a mechanism of social mobility, or as a way of transmitting property. Little disciplinary attention has been paid to the diverse ways people think about, react to, and represent the meaning of adoption.

This is not to say that nothing exists on the subject. In the early 20th century, Lowie remarked on the frequency of adoption in Pacific Island societies, forgetting his cultural relativism to claim that child exchange in such societies went "well beyond the rational" (Lowie 1933). His surprise prompted others to inquire into the consequences of the unfamiliar behavior of moving large numbers of children from household to household. Three decades later, in the early 1960s, Levy discovered in a small village in Tahiti that more than 25 percent of children were adopted; this was not untypical for Polynesian societies. Levy went on to analyze the impact of this generous "transaction in parenthood" in his path-breaking account of Tahitian culture and personality (Levy 1973).

Anthropologists such as Marshall picked up other threads in the (slowly) growing tapestry on adoption in the Pacific. In an article examining created kin in Trukese society, Marshall concludes that what is common to kinship is a notion of sharing, differently enacted and represented in different contexts (1977:656–657). To analyze kinship cross-culturally and without bias, he argues, one must explore the nature of nurture and of sharing. His article demonstrates the significance of creating kin through constructed sibling and parent-child bonds for revealing the meanings of kinship. To act like kin is to be kin; to care for reciprocally is to have a relationship. Conduct and performance make (and unmake) kin, with a fluidity that differs from "biogenetic" notions of kinship characteristic of American society (Marshall 1977).

Marshall's article confirms the extent to which kinship is not "natural" but "cultural," representing an intense experience of love and of obligation between individuals. Moreover, these experiences may change over the course of a person's life, depending on circumstances and on perceptions of the "usefulness" and rewards of being related.

Two volumes on adoption in Oceania underscored the importance of created kinship in Pacific Island societies: [Vern] Carroll's *Adoption in Oceania* (1970) and [Ivan] Brady's *Transactions in Kinship* (1976). In both volumes the contributing anthropologists explore the structure and the functions of adoption, with varying degrees of attention to Carroll's initial warning about applying the single term *adoption* to diverse arrangements across cultures. The goal of challenging the universality of a definition of *adoption* is, as Ward Goodenough concludes in the epilogue to the 1970 volume, only imperfectly met. Treating adoption largely as a social institution, the articles in these volumes tended not to explore the meanings of the experience for the individuals involved or to establish a framework for interpretive analysis of the cultural and personal significance of "child exchange" wherever, and however, it occurs.

Silk offers an alternative to the conventional treatment of adoption in anthropological literature. In a 1980 article, she notes the frequency of adoption in Pacific Island societies compared with almost all others in the world, and asks why. Her answer draws on sociobiological theory. Silk argues that as a way of modifying extreme family size, adoption is adaptive for the group, though it may be a risk for the individual child. Following her theoretical premise, the risk lies in the tendency of parents to treat their biological—more *closely related*—children differently from the way they treat an adopted child (Silk 1980:803). She further suggests that, consequently (and necessarily), biological parents retain an interest in the child they have given away; thus, bonds are maintained, not severed, by adoption. In offering a sociobiological explanation, Silk does not mean to exclude the social and cultural factors that affect the transaction; her primary aim is to distinguish societies in which adoption occurs frequently from those in which it occurs rarely (Silk 1980:816). She does not question the concept of adoption itself.

Frequency has continued to be a feature that brings adoption to the attention of anthropologists, most of whom come from a society in which adoption affects "only" about 2 or 3 percent of children in any one year (Adamec and Peirce 1991). Anthropologists of Eskimo (Inuit) societies, sounding rather like anthropologists of the Pacific, remark on the astonishing ease with which children are moved from parent to parent, for shorter or longer stays (Guemple 1979). Several of these studies inquire into the impact of this movement on the affective as well as the structural and functional domains of social life.

The frequency of adoption in large-scale, complex societies has also piqued anthropological interest, though without major impact on the discipline. In 1980, for instance, [Arthur] Wolf and [Chieh-shan] Huang published an exhaustive study of adoption in China whose importance has mainly been acknowledged by other Sinologists. *Marriage and Adoption in China 1845–1945* traces trends in the transactions of women and of children as these reflect social and political changes. With a century's worth of historical records, Wolf and Huang had data other anthropologists might envy. Yet their analysis remains conventional, assuming that the meaning of adoption can be transferred from "us" to "them" and describing the social to the exclusion of the psychological ramifications of the phenomenon.

The silence accorded to full-scale studies of adoption continues. To take a final example: Esther Goody's pioneering analysis of "child exchange" in West African societies and among West Africans in London recognizes the range of meanings and functions moving a child may have (Goody 1982). Discussing numerous particular cases in which parenthood is delegated, Goody reminds her readers that words like *adoption* and *fosterage* are culturally and historically relative as well as individually negotiated. Her book speaks a quiet warning against assuming that the meaning of adoption holds from group to group, time to time, or even person to person.

One cannot, of course, leave the subject of adoption and kinship without referring to the work of Jack Goody—especially his under-appreciated article, "Adoption in Cross Cultural Perspective." The point he made in this 1969 piece remains all too appropriate: "For I know of no attempt to do a systematic survey of the distribution of this phenomenon, which is not for example included in the data recorded in the Ethnographic Atlas (1967) nor mentioned in Goody's study of changing family patterns (1963)" (Goody 1969:56). As far as we know, his agenda for the comparative study of adoption has not been followed. Nor have the issues raised in the ethnographic writings cited above been taken as far as they might.

If anthropologists embrace the goal of examining rather than imposing meanings of core concepts on others—or, for that matter, our own society—then adoption would seem to be a crucial area of study. For it is here that the multivocal meanings of personhood and identity, of kinship and social bonds, can be thoroughly explored—and from the point of view of those who "make" these kinds of relationships. Existing writings on adoption suggest there is more to be said about the self-conscious gesture involved in creating kin and its diverse manifestations. Virtually everywhere it occurs, adoption inscribes and perpetuates understandings of birth, blood, and belonging, of essence and accident or choice. In the late 19th century, the British jurist Sir Henry Maine articulated the premise of his own culture's understanding of adoption: fictive kinship, he wrote, replicates "real" kinship; the bond of law "imitates" the bond of birth and the child is "as if begotten" (Maine 1861). The ramifications of this premise in Western society, and the import of transferring it to other societies, have too rarely been seen as problematic.

The treatment of adoption in anthropological literature perpetuates a sense that the concept is nonproblematic. The transaction of a child, evidently, is not considered either a major social event or a key cultural text; rather, child exchange is analyzed as "only" an aspect of kinship, form of social solidarity, or response to demographic conditions. The neglect also speaks to a conservatism about our methods and categories of analysis, despite (or perhaps because of) the popularity of postmodernist writings in the discipline. Further confirming this is the modest reception given to several recently published radical reexaminations of kinship, of kinship and gender, and of theories of identity and ethnicity (e.g., Collier and Yanagisako 1987; Linnekin and Poyer 1990a; Schneider 1984; Weston 1991). These studies do show, however, that at least some anthropologists are drastically rethinking the context and meaning of fundamental aspects of social life.

Kinship and Adoption

Adoption as a category of meaning, like adoption as social practice, is problematic. Western common sense says the distinction between kin and non-kin is self-evident, a distinction that allows for the concept of "*as if* begotten." Adoption is thus a phenomenological category betwixt categories, a category that straddles the fence, a category in our society that dooms those who fall within it to be both kin and non-kin—real and "fictive." As Schneider has demonstrated through his brilliant analysis of the cultural unit on Yap called *tabinau*, there is much to be gained by recognizing how considerably varied and flexible the meanings of words can be (Schneider 1984:21).

Although Western ideas about kinship and adoption assume the primacy of blood ties and biological inheritance and see people as discrete and bounded individuals (Linnekin and Poyer 1990b:2, 7), anthropologists know that these presuppositions are not universal. Pomponio, for example, notes that while children on Mandok Island, Papua New Guinea, are thought to share the substance of their parents and other kin, "substance" means more than it does in Western thought: not just shared biogenetic endowment but the combination of blood, food, and work. "The transubstantial nature of Mandok personhood is evidenced by their belief that firstborns can be 'created' through adoption, and adoption is not limited to married couples." Many children (13 of 81, or 16 percent of her sample), in fact, are adopted specifically for this purpose. She concludes, "The important substance here is not contained in blood or semen, but food and work (i.e., caretaking). By feeding and caring for a child, the substance of the adult is transferred to that child" (Pomponio 1990:54).

Lieber argues that what Pomponio observes about the nature of kinship and adoption on Mandok may be true of Oceanic societies generally. What it means to be a person in many Pacific Island societies is structured, he says, by local theories of ontogeny (Lieber 1990:71) in which what a person becomes is not "in their blood," but is credited instead to the nurturing social and physical environment within which they mature. In other words, as Howard has summarized the argument, kinship in Oceania is considered to be contingent rather than absolute.

> Thus, on the one hand, kinship has to be validated by social action to be recognized; on the other, kinship status can be achieved through social action (i.e., by consistently acting as kinsmen even though genealogical linkages may be questionable or unknown). [Howard 1990:266]

A similar argument made by Sahlins chastens anthropologists for separating adoption—and kinship—from all aspects of culture and social structure. In Hawaii, where belonging comes from action and relationships are contingent,

Sahlins claims: "From family to state, the arrangements of society were in constant flux, a set of relationships constructed on the shifting sands of love" (Sahlins 1985:20). The civil state, he might have added, rests upon chosen attachments much like the relationship between parents and child.

Anthropology and the Public

The process of rethinking theories of the person, of kinship, and of social and cultural life that is essential to our discipline also bears on current debates about multiculturalism occurring throughout the American university environment. Anthropologists have expressed amazement that scholars from across the disciplinary spectrum have discovered "the other," "multivocality," and "multiculturalism" without discovering anthropology (Perry 1992). But it is equally fair to argue that anthropologists have not actively guided the debate or introduced an anthropological vocabulary to a public that will feel the effects of such debate.

Anthropologists—or at least anthropologists who read the *Anthropology Newsletter*—do not need to be told that it is important to be "public or perish" (Givens 1992). Nevertheless—all too often, it seems—anthropologists focus on what their colleagues will say about their work and overlook opportunities to be heard and appreciated by others. Even when they cannot grab newspaper headlines with startling news about lost tribes, missing links, or the oldest potsherds in the world, they need to ask themselves: who might be interested to know what I know?

Thanks to anthropologists such as Schneider, it may no longer be intellectually strategic to study adoption simply to refute the conventional wisdom that the bonds of kinship are genealogical—given by "birth" (Schneider 1984: 169–177). Studying adoption can also be a way of discovering the meanings and implications of aspects of culture and social order that remain problematic for both anthropologists and the public. Adoption not only belies what Schneider has called "biologistic" ways of marking and defining human character, human nature, and human behavior (Schneider 1984:175), it also reveals interpretations of concepts like identity, family, and ethnicity.

Thus, for instance, a study of adoption can shed light on definitions of and criteria for "citizenship": What does it mean to belong to a group or nation, and is this linked with ideas about what it means to belong to a family? Nor is adoption irrelevant to larger concerns about assimilation, "true" cultural identity, and ethnic purity, raising as it does the problem of being *"as if begotten"* when contract has been the mode of entry. At core, adoption is about who belongs and how—a subject of immense political as well as disciplinary significance. It is also, and increasingly, about power, privilege, and poverty. Concerns are properly raised about babies moving from the poor to the rich, or, a new version of the old "baby-selling" cry, about residents of impoverished nations and regions putting their babies on the international market. But anthropologists have not addressed those concerns. Moreover, these are issues that touch the lives of a general public, well beyond those who may experience, or know about, an adoptive relationship.

Conclusion

In societies such as ours where caring for children who are not one's own by birth is seen as risky, painful, and unnatural, learning through anthropology's eyes that what adoption does to people is not written in stone would undoubtedly be beneficial to birth parents, adoptive parents, and adoptees. It seems equally apparent that studying adoption in different societies can be a window through which anthropologists may learn about other facets of life.

Our own interest in adoption (beyond the powerful consideration that we are both adoptive parents) lies in both these directions. We are interested in adoption as an empirical question. What are the meanings, values, and contexts of caring for children "other than your own" in different societies? What determines the place and popularity (or lack thereof) of adoption in different societies? The agenda Jack Goody set over twenty years ago can benefit from recent literature on reflexivity and multivocalism, so that adoption is considered not only a social transaction but also a cultural text. The comparative task, then, will involve analyzing the forms of attachment and the representations of experience constituted by adoption—or, broadly, "child exchange"—as practiced by diverse cultural groups.

A study of adoption becomes an inquiry into fundamental beliefs about the person and personal connections as these intertwine with political, economic, and historical developments. Taking the perspective of constructed kinship and making the most of the "construction" it entails, so that adoption is not assumed to be univocal or universal in meaning, can advance theories of culture creativity, human agency, and identity formation. Ideally, studying adoption will preserve the centrality of individual experiences in the composition of social worlds and cultural texts.

We also want to strengthen public awareness of the diverse ways that people in different parts of the world—and in different ethnic communities here in North America—build and value human relationships and family ties and obligations. In the process we should demonstrate that anthropology importantly is, as it historically has been, a "way of seeing" for those other than its practitioners.

References

Adamec, Christine, and William Peirce, 1991, The Encyclopedia of Adoption. New York: Facts on File.

Bartholet, Elizabeth, 1993, Family Bonds. Adoption and the Politics of Parenting. Boston: Houghton Mifflin.

Bates, J. Douglas, 1993, Gift Children. A Story of Race, Family, and Adoption in a Divided America. New York: Ticknor and Fields.

Brady, Ivan, ed., 1976, Transactions in Kinship: Adoption and Fosterage in Oceania. Honolulu: University of Hawaii Press.

Brodzinsky, David M., Marshall D. Schechter, and Robin Marantz Henig, 1992, Being Adopted. The Lifelong Search for Self. New York: Doubleday.

Carrol, Vern, ed., 1970, Adoption in Eastern Oceania. Honolulu: University of Hawaii Press.

Collier, Jane Fishburne, and Sylvia Junko Yanagisako, eds., 1987, Gender and Kinship. Essays toward a Unified Analysis. Stanford: Stanford University Press.

Givens, David B., 1992, Public or Perish. Anthropology Newsletter 33(5):1, 58.

Goody, Esther, 1982, Parenthood and Social Reproduction. New York: Cambridge University Press.

Goody, Jack, 1969, Adoption in Cross-Cultural Perspective. Comparative Studies in Society and History 2:55–78.

Guemple, D. L., 1979, Inuit Adoption. Ottawa: National Museums of Canada.

Howard, Alan, 1990, Cultural Paradigms, History, and the Search for Identity in Oceania, *In* Cultural Identity and Ethnicity in the Pacific. Jocelyn Linnekin and Lin Poyer, eds. Pp. 259–279. Honolulu: University of Hawaii Press.

Kirk, H. David, 1984, Shared Fate. A Theory and Method of Adoptive Relationships. Port Angeles, WA: Ben-Simon Publications.

Levy, Robert, 1973, The Tahitians: Mind and Experience in the Society Islands. Chicago: University of Chicago Press.

Lieber, Michael D., 1990, Lamarckian Definitions of Identity on Kapingamarangi and Pohnpei. *In* Cultural Identity and Ethnicity in the Pacific. Jocelyn Linnekin and Lin Poyer, eds. Pp. 71–101. Honolulu: University of Hawaii Press.

Liliuokalani, 1990, Hawaii's Story by Hawaii's Queen. Honolulu: Mutual Publishing.

Linnekin, Jocelyn, and Lin Poyer, 1990a, [eds.] Cultural Identity and Ethnicity in the Pacific. Honolulu: University of Hawaii Press.

———, 1990b, Introduction. *In* Cultural Identity and Ethnicity in the Pacific. Jocelyn Linnekin and Lin Poyer, eds. Pp. 1–16. Honolulu: University of Hawaii Press.

Lowie, Robert, 1933, Adoption. *In* Encyclopedia of the Social Sciences. E. A. Seligman and A. Johnson, eds. Pp. 459–460. New York: Macmillan and Company.

Maine, Sir Henry, 1861, Ancient Law. London: Macmillan.

Mandeville, Elizabeth, 1981, Kamano Adoption. Ethnology 20:229–244.

Marshall, Mac, 1977, The Nature of Nurture. American Ethnologist 4(4):643–662.

Melina, Lois Ruskai, 1986, Raising Adopted Children. A Manual for Adoptive Parents. New York: Harper and Row.

Modell, Judith, 1994a, Nowadays Everyone Is *Hanai:* Child Exchange and the Construction of Hawaiian Urban Culture. *In* Urban Cultures in the Pacific. C. Jourdan and J. M. Philibert, eds. Forthcoming.

———, 1994b, Kenship with Strangers: Adoption and Interpretations of Kinship in American Culture. Berkeley: University of California Press.

Perry, Richard J., 1992, Why Do Multiculturalists Ignore Anthropologists? Chronicle of Higher Education 38(26):A52.

Pomponio, Alice, 1990, Seagulls Don't Fly into the Bush: Cultural Identity and the Negotiations of Development on Mandok Island, Papua New Guinea. *In* Cultural Identity and Ethnicity in the Pacific. Jocelyn Linnekin and Lin Poyer, eds. Pp. 43–70. Honolulu: University of Hawaii Press.

Register, Cheri, 1991, "Are Those Kids Yours?" American Families with Children Adopted from Other Countries. New York: Free Press.

Sahlins, Marshall, 1985, Islands of History. Chicago: University of Chicago Press.

Samuels, Shirley C., 1990, Ideal Adoption: A Comprehensive Guide to Forming an Adoptive Family. New York: Plenum.

Schaffer, Judith, and Christina Lindstrom, 1989, How to Raise an Adopted Child. A Guide to Help Your Child Flourish from Infancy through Adolescence. New York: Penguin Books.

Schneider, David M., 1984, A Critique of the Study of Kinship. Ann Arbor: University of Michigan Press.

Silk, Joan, 1980, Adoption and Kinship in Oceania. American Anthropologist 82(4): 799–820.

Webster, Steven, 1975, Cognatic Descent Groups and the Contemporary Maori: A Preliminary Reassessment. Journal of the Polynesian Society 84:121–152.

Weston, Kath, 1991, Families We Choose: Lesbians, Gays, Kinship. New York: Columbia University Press.

Wolf, Arthur, and Chieh-shan Huang, 1980, Marriage and Adoption in China, 1845–1945. Stanford: Stanford University Press.

POSTSCRIPT

Is It Natural for Adopted Children to Want to Find Out About Their Birth Parents?

Lifton's argument is clearly situated within the adoption rights movement and draws upon her personal experiences as much as on the experiences of those she has interviewed. She and her American informants clearly have a burning need to know who their birth parents are, and she concludes that it is unnatural for anyone to be deprived of this information. She and her informants feel a certain amount of psychic pain and emptiness, as well as lack of wholeness.

Terrell and Modell, on the other hand, argue that however real such feelings may be, they are cultural constructs rather than natural, biological ones. They cite examples from Pacific Island societies to show that such feelings are not human universals but culturally specific responses to a particular normative kinship structure.

This issue raises questions about just how "natural" are kinship systems in different societies. American society has long placed emphasis on biological families, just as Americans have long accepted biologically or physiologically based illnesses as more real than psychological ones. As Terrell and Modell note, some anthropologists have not found it easy to ignore their own culture's views on adoption. Nevertheless, they argue that anthropologist David Schneider was essentially correct in his description of American kinship. In *American Kinship: A Cultural Account* (Prentice-Hall, 1968), he argues that while Americans contend that kinship is about biological relatedness, in practice it is those who "act" like close kin who are accepted as one's closest kinsmen. Thus, it is the social behavior rather than the genetic relationship that is most important in shaping our social worlds.

To what extent do significantly higher rates of adoption in Oceania or other parts of the world challenge American views that biologically based parent-child relationships are inherently more "real" than socially constructed relationship created by adoption? How are we to explain the strongly held views of Lifton and other adoption rights advocates, who clearly feel something lacking in their own lives if they do not and cannot know who their birth parents are?

Some of Lifton's other books include *Twice Born: Memoirs of an Adopted Daughter* (Penguin, 1977) and *Lost and Found: The Adoption Experience* (HarperCollins, 1988). Somewhat earlier versions of the same argument are provided by John Triseliotis's *In Search of Origins: The Experiences of Adopted People* (Routledge & Kegan Paul, 1973) and H. David Kirk's *Adoptive Kinship: A*

Modern Institution in Need of Reform (Butterworths, 1981), as well as his *Shared Fate: A Theory and Method of Adoptive Relationships* (Ben-Simon Publications, 1984). See also David M. Brodzinsky, Marshall D. Schechter, and Robin M. Henig's *Being Adopted: The Lifelong Search for Self* (Doubleday, 1992).

Modell has written a more extended view of the cultural construction of American adoption in *Kinship With Strangers: Adoption and Interpretations of Kinship in American Culture* (University of California Press, 1994). For similar perspectives, see Karen March's *The Stranger Who Bore Me: Adoptee–Birth Mother Relationships* (University of Toronto Press, 1995) and Katarina Wegar's *Adoption, Identity and Kinship: The Debate Over Sealed Birth Records* (Yale University Press, 1997). For a survey of current views of the problems of modern adoption, readers should consult a special issue of *Family Relations* (vol. 49, no. 4, October 2000), edited by Karen March and Charlene Miall.

For discussions of adoption in Pacific Island cultures, see *Adoption in Eastern Oceania* (University of Hawaii Press, 1970), edited by Vern Carroll. See also Jocelyn Linnekin and Lin Poyer's collection, *Cultural Identity and Ethnicity in the Pacific* (University of Hawaii Press, 1990), and Mac Marshall's essay "The Nature of Nurture," *American Ethnologist* (vol. 4, 1977).

ISSUE 13

Are San Hunter-Gatherers Basically Pastoralists Who Have Lost Their Herds?

YES: James R. Denbow and Edwin N. Wilmsen, from "Advent and Course of Pastoralism in the Kalahari," *Science* (December 19, 1986)

NO: Richard B. Lee, from *The Dobe Ju/'hoansi,* 3rd ed. (Wadsworth Thomson Learning, 2003)

ISSUE SUMMARY

YES: Archaeologists James R. Denbow and Edwin N. Wilmsen argue that the San of the Kalahari Desert in southern Africa have been involved in pastoralism, agriculture, and regional trade networks since at least A.D. 800. They imply that the San, who were hunting and gathering in the twentieth century, were descendants of pastoralists who lost their herds due to subjugation by outsiders, drought, and livestock disease.

NO: Cultural anthropologist Richard B. Lee counters that evidence from oral history, archaeology, and ethnohistory shows that the Ju/'hoansi group of San living in the isolated Nyae Nyae-Dobe area of the Kalahari Desert were autonomous hunter-gatherers until the twentieth century. Although they carried on some trade with outsiders before then, it had minimal impact on their culture.

Can hunter-gatherers (also called "foragers") be economically self-sufficient and politically autonomous even when in contact with more powerful food-producing peoples? This is the basic question behind the "Great Kalahari Debate," which is illustrated by the following selections.

Even in the late nineteenth century, hunting-and-gathering peoples living outside the disruptive influence of complex societies and colonialism were scarce. By then most Native American hunter-gatherers were on reservations or incorporated into the fur trade, and others, like the Veddas of Sri Lanka, had been absorbed and transformed by the dominant societies that surrounded them. The most striking exception was the Australian Aborigines, who were still nomadic hunter-gatherers using stone tools at the time of European contact. Aborigines became the model of the earliest stage of cultural evolution as discussed by Emile Durkheim in *The Elementary Forms of the Religious Life* (George Allen and Unwin Ltd., 1915) and Sigmund Freud in *Totem and Taboo* (Moffat, Yard, 1918). By the 1950s, however, most Aborigines, too, had been settled on ranches, missions, or government settlements, and their cultures had been radically disrupted. Anthropologists' waning hopes of studying other "pristine" foragers were suddenly raised when an American family, the Marshalls, found and studied a group of Ju/'hoansi (!Kung) San living by independent foraging in the Kalahari Desert of Southwest Africa (now Namibia). Lorna Marshall's scholarly articles (later collected in her book *The !Kung of Nyae Nyae* [Harvard University Press, 1976]), her daughter Elizabeth Marshall Thomas's popular book *The Harmless People* (Knopf, 1959) and her son John's films (e.g., *The Hunters*) attracted great attention to the San.

In 1963 then–graduate student Richard B. Lee went to northwestern Bechuanaland (now Botswana) in search of an independent foraging San group. He found such a group in the Ju/'hoansi at Dobe waterhole. Although he recognized that they interacted with Bantu-speaking herding people in the region, his research focused on their adaptation to the natural environment. His findings led to a radically new image of the San and, eventually, of foragers in general. Once thought to live in a precarious struggle for survival, he found that the Ju/'hoansi actually needed to work less than 22 hours a week to get an adequate amount of food. The key to their success was their dependence on plant foods, mostly gathered by women, rather than meat, and the emphasis placed on food sharing.

By the early 1970s, however, some anthropologists had begun to question the popular image of San as isolated people with a continuous history of independent foraging since preagricultural times. In their selection, James R. Denbow and Edwin N. Wilmsen make the case that the Kalahari San have long participated in the regional economy and political system. They argue that the Ju/'hoansi and other inhabitants of the Kalahari Desert were agropastoralists (farmer-herders) and commodity traders until the late nineteenth century, when dominating outsiders, drying climate, and livestock diseases caused some of them to lose their herds and revert (temporarily) to full-time foraging.

Richard B. Lee responds that some San groups—such as the Ju/'hoansi of the Nyae Nyae-Dobe area—were quite isolated from outsiders until the late nineteenth century, when Europeans and Bantu-speaking Africans began to make occasional journeys into their homeland. Thus, his research suggests that foraging societies can live in contact with food-producers without being economically or politically subjugated by them.

This debate raises a number of important questions. Can small-scale, politically weak societies have economic and political ties with powerful outsiders without being dominated and fundamentally changed? Can one generalize from one case like the Dobe Ju/'hoansi to other foraging peoples? If foragers were herders or farmers in the past, can they still tell us something about the hunting-and-gathering way of life before the advent of agriculture?

James R. Denbow and
Edwin N. Wilmsen

 **YES**

Advent and Course of Pastoralism in the Kalahari

It has long been thought that farming and herding were comparatively recent introductions into the Kalahari and that it has been a preserve of foraging "Bushmen" for thousands of years. Agropastoral Bantu-speakers were thought to have entered this region only within the last two centuries. However, fully developed pastoralism and metallurgy are now shown to have been established in the Kalahari from A.D. 500, with extensive grain agriculture and intracontinental trade added by A.D. 800. Archeological, linguistic, and historical evidence delineates the continuation of mixed economies in the region into the present. Consequences of this revised view for anthropological theory and for policy planning concerning contemporary Kalahari peoples are indicated.

When the principal ethnographic studies of southern African peoples, then called "Bushmen" (1), were undertaken in the 1950's and 1960's, very little was known of their prehistory or of the history of their association with herding and farming peoples; a similar lack of historic depth characterized earlier southern Bantu studies (2). At the time, it was universally assumed that Bantu-speaking farming-herding peoples had intruded into the Kalahari no more than two or three centuries ago. The region was presumed to have been peopled previously only by San-speaking foragers who had, until then, remained isolated from external influences.

Before the mid-1970's, only two systematic archeological investigations had been carried out in Botswana, an area approximately the size of Texas (575,000 square kilometers); only one attempt had been made to integrate the history of relations among hunting and herding Kalahari peoples. In addition, the climatic history of the Kalahari and its potential influence on local economies was entirely unknown. Likewise, linguistic studies, with their implications for revealing the history of social interaction and diversification in the region, were in their infancy. The assumption that pastoralism and social heterogeneity in the Kalahari were very recently introduced appeared to be correct.

Current work in archeology, geology, linguistics, and anthropology renders that assumption untenable. Since 1975, excavations have been carried

From James R. Denbow and Edwin N. Wilmsen, "Advent and Course of Pastoralism in the Kalahari," *Science*, vol. 234 (December 19, 1986). Copyright © 1986 by The American Association for the Advancement of Science. Reprinted by permission. Some notes omitted.

out at 34 archeological sites in Botswana as well as at other sites in Zimbabwe and Namibia. Seventy-nine radiocarbon dates now delineate the chronology of domesticated food production in Botswana during the past 2000 years. These investigations indicate that cattle (*Bos taurus*) and ovicaprids were introduced along with ceramics into the northern Kalahari in the final centuries B.C. and first centuries A.D. Slightly later, grain cultivation and metallurgy were part of the economic repertoire of Early Iron Age (EIA) pastoralists in the region. By the ninth century, these peoples were engaged in trade networks that brought exotic goods such as glass beads and marine shells from the Indian Ocean into the Kalahari.

Geologic evidence suggests that significantly higher rainfall may have created an environment that encouraged the initial establishment of pastoral economies in the region. Linguistic evidence points to the diversification of Khoisan and southern Bantu languages coincident with this agropastoral expansion. Archival sources from the 18th and 19th centuries as well as oral histories document varying conjunctions of pastoralism and foraging in the economies of both Khoisan and Bantu-speakers that existed in precolonial time and characterize the region to this day. These sources also confirm the continued involvement of these peoples in ancient intracontinental trade networks that were not dominated by European colonial merchants until the second half of the 19th century. As a result of these studies, relations among hunters and herders in the Kalahari are shown to be both of longer duration and more integrated than has been thought.

The Context of Initial Pastoralism

Excavations of Late Stone Age (LSA) sites in the Kalahari reveal forager subsistence patterns differing from those recorded ethnographically among San in the region. Brooks and Helgren report that, in at least some LSA sites in the Makgadikgadi Pans area, fish and other aquatic resources complemented land animals in the subsistence of foragers between 4000 and 2000 years ago. At Lotshitshi, on the southeastern edge of the Okavango Delta, a LSA stratum dating within this period was found to contain fish, bullfrogs, and turtles along with large land mammals. Reconnaissance in the Makgadikgadi complex located over 50 additional LSA sites; two of these include small quantities of Bambata ceramics in their assemblages; eight others contain somewhat later EIA Gokomere or Kumadzulo pottery types. At Bambata Cave, in Zimbabwe, ceramics with remains of domesticated sheep are dated tentatively as early as the second century B.C. Maunatlala, in eastern Botswana, has ceramics and pole-and-clay hut remains at the end of the fourth century A.D.

The middle LSA level of Lotshitshi dates in the third century A.D. Faunal remains from this component indicate a broadly based economy including cattle (*B. taurus*) along with zebra, wildebeest, duiker, warthog, smaller game, and fish. Ceramics from this site are too fragmented for accurate identification, but their thin, charcoal-tempered fabric and finely incised decoration are compatible with Bambata types. Farther westward, in Namibia, ceramics (not Bambata ware) were present before A.D. 400 at Mirabib (with domestic sheep) and Falls Rock. Of the sites mentioned thus far, only Maunatlala has yielded evidence of metal use.

Radiocarbon dates placing sheep, and possibly cattle, but not metal, as far south as the Cape of Good Hope in the first century A.D. have been available for some years, consequently, a gap in data existed between these very early pastoralist manifestations in the far south and older centers north of the Okavango and Zambezi Rivers. The early pastoralist sites in the Kalahari and its margins begin to fill that gap. Consistent association of ceramics and domestic animals with LSA assemblages and their early dates indicate that pastoralist elements were introduced from the north into indigenous foraging economies here before the currently documented beginning of the Iron Age in southern Africa.

Recently acquired geomorphological evidence for fluctuating climates in the region has implications for these changes in LSA economies. At the Cwihaba caverns in western Ngamiland, periodically more humid climatic conditions are indicated by episodes of rapid sinter formation. In order to account for these episodes, Cooke suggests that rainfall in western Ngamiland reached 300 percent of the present annual mean between 2500 and 2000 years ago and again around 750 years ago. In general, these dates parallel those obtained for the sequence of beach levels found around the Makgadikgadi, Ngami, and Mababe basins where a number of higher lake levels with intervening regressions are indicated between 3000 and 1500 years ago.

Although it cannot be assumed that these high lake levels were caused solely by increased rainfall, Shaw argues for generally wetter conditions over the delta at dates congruent with those of Cwihaba. He estimates that rainfall over the Okavango increased between 160 and 225 percent. Under such a regime, many currently ephemeral pans and springs would also have contained more constant supplies of available water. Brain and Brain found evidence, in the form of microfaunal proportions, for episodes of climatic amelioration between about 4000 and 500 years ago at Mirabib in Namibia. Thus, several independent studies indicate higher rainfall during the millennium embracing the initial spread of agropastoral economies through the region 2500 to 1500 years ago.

In recent years, studies of Khoe (Central Khoisan) languages have proliferated in the Kalahari; all lead to an estimate that Khoe diversification in this region began about 2000 years ago. Vossen finds words for cattle and milking with apparent Proto-Khoe roots in the Khoe languages of north central Botswana. Köhler finds such words, along with a Khoe crop vocabulary, among the Kxoe (Khoe-speakers of northern Namibia). Both conclude that pastoralism must have been familiar to these peoples for a long time.

Ehret also argues that the basic separation of Khoi and Central Khoisan languages took place in the Botswana-Angola border region shortly after 500 B.C. He proposed further, from lexical evidence, that the basic pastoralist vocabulary of southern Bantu is derived through a Khoisan intermediary in this area, implying that these Bantu-speakers, but not others farther north, acquired cattle and sheep from Khoisan-speaking peoples. Pfouts suggests diversification of the Bantu languages of Namibia and southern Angola beginning about 1500 to 2000 years ago, whereas Ehret and Kinsman specifically place diversification of Proto-southeast Bantu in the EIA of this time frame. These authors suggest that economic factors contributed to this process of linguistic differentiation; their conclusions are compatible with the archeological evidence regarding initiation of pastoralism and socioeconomic heterogeneity in southern Africa. Elphick reconstructs historical data to reach a similar conclusion.

The Early Iron Age

The western sandveld. The presence of Iron Age agropastoral communities in the Kalahari by the middle of the first millennium is now attested for Ngamiland as well as for eastern Botswana. At Tsodilo Hills, in the sandveld, 70 kilometers west of the Okavango, extensive excavations have uncovered settlements that span the period from the 6th to the 11th centuries A.D. Ceramics from the earliest (A.D. 550–730) of these sites, Divuyu, indicate that it belongs to an EIA variant, the distribution of which appears to extend northward into Angola. There are no close parallels in known EIA assemblages to the south, either in Zimbabwe or South Africa. Common decoration motifs consist of multiple parallel bands of combstamping separated by spaces that are either blank or filled-in with incised motifs. Divuyu ceramics are charcoal tempered but have substantial inclusions of calcrete.

A wide variety of iron and copper implements and ornaments were recovered from Divuyu but only a single stone tool. The presence of slag and bloomery waste indicates that metal working took place on the site. An amorphous scatter of friable burned clay fragments with stick impressions marks the probable location of a pole-and-clay hut. Fragments of perforated ceramic strainers indicate that salt was extracted from local sources. Unidentified marine shells provide firm evidence for coastal links, possibly through Angolan sites. Local trade with peoples of the Okavango system is indicated by the presence of fish bones and river mollusk shells (*Unio* sp. or *Aspartharin* sp.). Domesticated ovicaprids made up a large portion of the diet at Divuyu; domesticated *Bos* was rare. Large quantities of carbonized mongongo nut shells (*Ricinodendron rautanenii*) attest to the importance of foraging in the economy.

In the second Iron Age site at Tsodilo, Nqoma, a lower stratum contains Divuyu ceramics contemporary with the final dates at Divuyu itself. The major components at Nqoma stratigraphically overlie this material and are dated in the ninth and tenth centuries. Ceramics from these later components are uniformly charcoal tempered with few inclusions of other materials; decoration is most often applied as bands of interlocking triangles or in pendent triangles filled with hatching, combstamping, or linear punctuating. False-relief chevron designs occur frequently. Only a few dated sites are presently available for comparison. We see affinities with Sioma, in southwestern Zambia, and Dundo, in northeastern Angola, dated to the sixth through eighth centuries in the range of Divuyu and the beginning of

Nqoma occupations at Tsodilo, but systematic ceramic comparisons of these sites have yet to be undertaken. Nqoma ceramics are similar to those from the ninth century site at Kapako on the Okavango River in Namibia; charcoal-tempered ceramics have been dated to the same period far out in the sandveld at NxaiNxai and are found in adjacent parts of Botswana and Namibia.

Evidence for metal working is attested at Nqoma by the presence of tuyeres as well as slag and bloom. Iron and copper ornaments are common and include finely made chains and necklaces with alternating links of copper and iron as well as bracelets with designs sometimes preserved by rust and oxidation. Moderate numbers of stone tools of LSA types are present. Dense areas of burned clay with pole and stick impressions mark the locations of substantial house structures.

Cattle (*Bos taurus*) were paramount in the pastoral economy of Nqoma; preliminary analysis suggests they outnumber ovicaprids by a factor of 2. Bifid thoracic vertebrae indicate that at least some of these cattle were of a hump-backed variety. Carbonized seeds of sorghum (*Sorghum bicolor* caffra), pearl millet (*Pennisetum americannum* thyphoides), and perhaps melons (*Cucurbita* sp.) provide direct evidence for cultivation. Remains of wild game along with carbonized mongongo nuts and *Grewia* seeds indicate that foraging continued to form an important part of the diet of this Iron Age population. Fish bones and river mollusk shells document continuing trade connections with the Okavango to the north and east.

Many glass beads and marine shells, primarily cowrie, along with worked ivory, one piece in the shape of a conus shell, provide evidence that Nqoma was an important local center in an intracontinental trade network extending to the Indian Ocean in the ninth century.

The river systems.   Although the origins of the EIA communities at Tsodilo point consistently northward to Angola, contemporary agropastoralist sites on the eastern margins of the Okavango Delta as well as on the Chobe River belong firmly within the Kumadzulo-Dambwa complex documented by Vogel for the Victoria Falls area. This complex forms a regional facies of the widespread Gokomere tradition of western Zimbabwe and northeastern Botswana. Kumadzulo-Dambwa complex ceramics and small clay figurines of hump-backed cattle were found at the eighth century site of Serondela, on the Chobe River, and cattle bones along with LSA lithics and similar ceramics were recovered at Hippo Tooth on the Botletle River dating to the early ninth century. At the island site of Qugana, in the eastern delta, the same ceramic complex with burned, reed-impressed clay hut remains dates to the eighth century; as yet, no domestic fauna have been recovered from this site.

Matlhapaneng, on the southeastern Okavango, is an extensive site dated between the late seventh and tenth centuries, contemporary with the Nqoma sequence at Tsodilo. Ceramics are charcoal tempered with Kumadzulo-Dambwa decoration motifs. Pole-and-clay structures, iron, copper, and ivory ornaments, slag, and bloomery waste mark this as a fully formed EIA community. LSA stone tools are also present. Although this site is not as rich as Nqoma, long-distance trade connections are attested by the presence of cowrie shells and glass beads. Carbonized remains of sorghum (*S. bicolor caffra*), millet (*P. americanum* typhoides), and cow peas (*Vigna unguiculata*) provide evidence for agriculture; cattle and ovicaprids dominate faunal remains. Foraging was important here as it was at Tsodilo; carbonized marula (*Sclerocarya caffra*) and *Grewin* seeds are present and wild animal remains are common.

The eastern hardveld. Similar developments took place simultaneously in the eastern hardveld where thick kraal dung deposits vitrified by burning have been found at more than 200 sites, indicating that large herds were kept in the region. The same EIA suite of materials already described is present, although ceramics are of Gokomere-Zhizo types with affinities eastward to Zimbabwe and northern Transvaal. East coast trade, documented by glass beads and marine shells, is dated in the late first millennium at a number of these sites as well as at contemporary sites in Zimbabwe and the Transvaal.

Major chiefdoms developed along this eastern margin of the Kalahari at the end of the first millennium, marking a transition to later centralized state development. A tripartite hierarchy of settlement size and complexity is discernible at this time. Large towns of approximately 100,000 square meters, Toutswe, K2, and Mapungubwe, dominated extensive hinterlands containing smaller villages and many small hamlets. Rulers of these chiefdoms succeeded in controlling the Indian Ocean trade into the Kalahari; it is possible that a system supplying valued goods in tribute to these chiefdoms from the western sandveld was instituted at this time, displacing previous exchange relations in which foreign imports as well as local exports had circulated widely.

Supporting evidence for changes in social relations of economic production is found in a comparison of age distributions of cattle and ovicaprid remains at the middle-order sites, Nqoma, Matlhapaneng and Taukome, with those at the capital towns, Mapungubwe and K2. At the first set of sites, a bimodal culling pattern is found similar to that of present-day cattle posts in Botswana, where slaughter is highest in nonreproductive age classes. Such a strategy conserves breeding stock and emphasizes rates of herd growth rather than meat production. Producers and consumers of herd products at these sites probably belonged to the same local social units.

In contrast, at Mapungubwe and K2, both primary centers, the majority of cattle slaughtered were in prime age classes; offtake appears not to have followed the conservative strategy found at the secondary sites. In other studies, this form of distribution has been associated with differential social stratification among occupants of a site. This appears to be the most plausible explanation for the contrasting culling patterns observed in our study. Elites at primary centers appear to have been selective consumers of prime rather than very old animals, many of which would have been produced elsewhere.

The Kalahari in the Second Millennium

These eastern Kalahari chiefdoms collapsed around the beginning of the 13th century. Great Zimbabwe emerged at this time, supplanting the political role played earlier at Toutswe, K2, and Mapungubwe. The extent of this new hegemony is indicated by stone-walled Zimbabwe-Khami outposts found far out in the Kalahari on the margins of the Makgadikgadi Pans. Control of trade became the prerogative of this kingdom. The final component at Toutswe (A.D. 1500) is devoid of exotic goods and no long-distance trade items have been recovered from two rock shelters, Qomqoisi and Depression, excavated at Tsodilo and dated to the 16th and 17th centuries, nor in an upper stratum at Lotshitshi, which, though undated, probably falls in this period.

Glass beads reappear at Xaro in Ngamiland at the beginning of the 17th century. These and cowrie shells are abundant at the 18th century site, Kgwebe, as well as in a probably contemporary (though not yet dated) upper stratum at Nqoma. Portuguese, through their Atlantic trade into the Kongo and Angola, were the probable source of these beads, which reached the interior along trade routes that had functioned since the Early Iron Age. Many of the first Europeans to enter the region from the Cape record that this trade in Portuguese goods was active south of the Orange River and to the east at least as far as the Zambezi by the 18th century. Native peoples including San-speakers, not Portuguese themselves, are specified in these records as the interior agents of this trade.

Archival records as well as oral histories testify to the importance of pastoralism throughout the Kalahari long before Europeans arrived. Every European who first observed the region from the 18th century on reports the presence of peoples of different languages, appearance, and group designation—Bantu and Khoissan—everywhere they went. Virtually every one of these Europeans remarks on the importance of pastoralism in all parts of the region and on the involvement of San-speakers in herding; several specifically mention San owners of livestock. Indeed, the herds of subsequently subjugated peoples were one inducement for Tswana expansion into Ngamiland in 1795. So rich in cattle was the northwestern Kalahari that 12,000 head were exported annually from it alone to the Cape during the 1860's through the 1880's, while unknown but apparently large numbers of interior cattle had been supplied to the Atlantic trade since the late 18th century.

In addition to cattle, 100,000 pounds of ivory along with many bales of ostrich feathers and hides are recorded to have been exported annually from the region as a whole during those decades in exchange for guns, tobacco, sugar, coffee, tea, cloth, beads, and other European goods. These were newly developed markets, but the trade networks they followed were continuations of Iron Age systems. Both Khoisan- and Bantu-speakers are reliably recorded by many observers to have been thoroughly involved in production for precolonial regional exchange networks. When first seen by Europeans in the 19th century, the copper mines and salt pans of northern

Namibia were exclusively under San control; 50 to 60 tons of ore were estimated to be taken annually from those mines and traded to Bantu smiths. Trade routes were linked to wider subcontinental networks. Salt, manufactured into loaves, was traded far into the interior and is reported to have been at least as important an exchange commodity as copper.

In extension of this economic activity, San are credited with producing the bulk of ivory and ostrich feathers exported through Bantu and Nama middlemen during the 19th century. Relations of production and exchange were thus not strictly bounded by ethnic or linguistic divisions but cut across them. More than anything else, it is this negotiable lattice of relations among peoples and production that characterizes the last two millennia in the Kalahari.

Discussion

We have summarized a large body of data pertaining to prehistoric and historic economies of Kalahari peoples, and those surrounding them, which has been accumulated by a number of investigators. . . . We have concentrated on the early introduction and subsequent local transformations of agropastoralism in the region because these have been the least known aspects of those economies. Pastoralism has been treated in the ethnographies cited at the beginning of this article as if its history in and adjacent to the Kalahari has been recent and separate from that of indigenous foraging. A guiding assumption of these anthropological studies was that 20th-century foraging there is a way of life that has remained unchanged for millennia. Practitioners of these segregated economies have been rather strictly supposed to have had distinct ethnic and racial origins, in contact only for the last two centuries or less. This position can no longer be supported.

Many problems remain to be investigated. Much of the central Kalahari is unexplored archeologically, and the extent to which Iron Age pastoralism penetrated this area is unknown. A hiatus exists in our knowledge of the entire region between the 12th and 16th centuries. While large centralized states with many satellite communities flourished in the east, few if any sites are presently known for this period in the entire western half of southern Africa, with some possible exceptions at the Cape. Drier conditions may have led to shifts in settlement size and location, making detection of sites in the Kalahari difficult under present conditions. A reasonable hypothesis posits a concentration of population along the river systems and permanent springs leaving less densely peopled the drier hinterland, where foraging may have waxed and waned in accordance with changing environmental and regional economic conditions, particularly after European influence penetrated the region. It is unlikely that herders withdrew entirely from the sandveld; more likely, they at least continued to exploit seasonal surface water and grazing. At present, there is no evidence either to support or refute these propositions.

All of the peoples of the Kalahari during the past two millennia have been linked by extensive social and economic networks; thus, during this period of time, the Kalahari was never the isolated refuge of foragers it has been thought to be. It was the vastly intensified extraction of commoditized animal products in the colonial period, abetted by a drying climatic trend and stock diseases, especially rinderpest, which killed 75 percent of all cattle and antelope in southern Africa at the end of the 19th century, that combined to pauperize the region. These forces became factors leading to increased labor migration to the newly opened South African mines. In the process, the dues and privileges of earlier native states became increasingly translated into private family fortunes of a colonially favored aristocracy, while previously flexible relations among Khoisan and Bantu-speakers were transformed into ethnic categories defined by criteria of race, language, and economic class. The resultant divisions gave, to anthropological observers in the 20th century, the false impression of a Kalahari eternally empty, its peoples long segregated and isolated from each other.

An unresolved problem concerns the presence of Bantu-speakers in the western half of the subcontinent, a presence that now appears to have been more pervasive and much earlier than previously assumed. There is no doubt that the introduction of EIA economies from central Africa brought with it a complex interdigitation of people south of the Zambezi-Okavango-Cunene Rivers. In the eastern half of the subcontinent, it is well established that Iron Age Bantu agropastoralists gained a dominant position over indigenous foragers and pastoralists, ultimately subjugating, absorbing, or eliminating them. This did not happen in the west where, in fact, Khoi-speaking (Nama) herders dominated a large part of the area when first encountered by Europeans. It has been thought that a major reason for this difference lay in the short history of association of these peoples in the west. The perceived isolating severity of the Kalahari environment has been seen as a primary factor protecting San foragers from Bantu pastoralist domination. Neither supposition finds support in the research reported here.

This research has profound implications for understanding relations among contemporary southern African peoples. In particular, those relegated to the ethnographic categories "Bushman" and "hunter-gatherers" are seen to have a history radically different from that hitherto assumed. It is clear that, rather than being static, uniform relics of an ancient way of life, San societies and cultures have undergone transformations in the past 2000 years that have varied in place and time in association with local economic and political alterations involving a variety of peoples.

Two important consequences flow from this new understanding. The first forces reevaluation of models of social evolution based on assumptions brought to the anthropological study of these peoples. At the very least, ethnographic analogies formulated on modern San "foragers" and applied to studies of evolving social forms must be modified to take into account the millennia-long association of these peoples with both pastoralism and Bantu-speakers. Following on this, and more immediately important, is the need to bring the results of this research into the arena of policy planning. In this arena, San are routinely dismissed as rootless "nomads," without legitimate claim to full participation in modern national politics because they are conceived to be unprepared by history to cope with complex decisions involving economic and political alternatives. That this is no more true of them than of any other peoples should be clear in even this brief account of their recent past.

Notes

1. Etymologies of the terms "Bushmen" and "San" are debated; a long-standing derogatory connotation is acknowledged for the first of these, but San, as also "Bantu," has acquired segregating racial and ethnic overtones. To avoid such implications, we use Khoisan and Bantu as adjectives to designate speakers of two different language families, retaining San only where necessary to specify peoples so labeled in ethnographies. We use Setswana spelling, in which c and x represent the front clicks and q the back clicks of Khoisan words.
2. L. Marshall, *The !Kung of NyaeNyae* (Harvard Univ. Press, Cambridge, MA, 1976); R. Lee, *The !Kung San* (Harvard Univ. Press, Cambridge, MA, 1979); J. Tanaka, *The San* (Univ of Tokyo Press, Tokyo, 1980); G. Silberbauer, *Hunter and Habitat in the Central Kalahari Desert* (Cambridge Univ. Press, Cambridge, 1981); I. Schapera, *The Bantu-Speaking Tribes of Southern Africa* (Routledge, London, 1937); W. Hammond-Tooke, Ed., *The Bantu-Speaking Peoples of Southern Africa* (Routledge, London, 1974).

The Kalahari Debate: Ju/'hoan Images of the Colonial Encounter

The Kalahari Debate, also known as Kalahari revisionism, sprung up in the late 1980s and early 1990s, and has been a topic of discussion among anthropologists ever since. What is at stake in the Kalahari Debate is the question of who the San peoples are historically—autonomous foragers or dependent serfs. The position taken [here] is that the Ju/'hoansi of the Dobe area, despite recent changes, show an unbroken history as independent hunters and gatherers that can be traced back far into the past. The "revisionists" argue that the Nyae Nyae and Dobe area Ju/'hoansi have been bound into regional trade networks and dominated by distant power holders for centuries. In this view they were not even hunters in the past but cattle-keepers, or servants of cattle people, raising the possibility that the Ju/'hoansi's unique cultural features of sharing and egalitarianism come not from their hunting and gathering traditions, but rather from being outcasts, at the bottom of a social hierarchy.

Curiously, until recently, neither the revisionists or their opponents had bothered to systematically ask the Ju people themselves for their views of their own history. How do the Ju/'hoansi interpret their past and how does that picture square with the evidence from archaeology and history? . . .

Beginning in 1986–1987 when the revisionist debate began to heat up, I started to ask Botswana Ju elders focused questions about the time they refer to as *n//a k'aishe* or "first time." The goal was to elicit collective memories of their pre-colonial past, a time we could date historically to the pre-1870s. Subsequently I returned for two more periods of interviewing, in 1995 and 1997, with informants from the Nyae Nyae and Cho/ana areas of Namibia. Now there are five major areas of Ju settlement represented in the oral history accounts. In this discussion, I will draw on three bodies of evidence on the Nyae Nyae-Dobe area Ju/'hoansi: their own oral histories, archaeology, and ethnohistory. . . .

Oral Histories

During my fieldwork in the Dobe area starting in the 1960s, the Ju/'hoansi were acutely aware that they were living under the gaze and control of the Tawana chiefdom and, beyond it, the British colonial authority. However in speaking of the area's past, Ju/'hoansi informants spoke of their own autonomy in the nineteenth century as a given: they were foragers who lived entirely on their own without agriculture or domesticated animals.

The existence of many Later Stone Age archeological sites in the Dobe area with thousands of stone artifacts and debris supports this view. But left unexplained is the presence on these same sites of small quantities of pottery and iron, indicating Iron Age presence or contact with Iron Age cultures. The Ju/'hoansi themselves explain the presence of these goods in terms of their long-standing trade relations with riverine peoples. On the other hand, Kalahari revisionists have argued that these archeological traces are proof positive of domination of the Dobe area by Iron Age peoples and the incorporation of the Ju/'hoansi into a regional polity. Wilmsen has further argued that people labeled Bushmen had raised cattle in centuries past:

> [I]n this century . . . an overwhelming majority of peoples so labeled have pursued a substantially pastoral way of life in symbiosis with, employed by, or enserfed to Bantu-speaking cattle owners . . . this is equally true of earlier centuries.

Remarkably, in all the voluminous writings on the Kalahari Debate . . . , neither side had systematically investigated how the Ju/'hoansi themselves articulate their own history.

An Interview With Kumsa N≠whin

Kumsa n≠whin, a 70-year-old Dobe man, was a former tribal policeman and famous healer I interviewed in 1987. I began by asking him if long ago his ancestors had lived with cattle.

"No," he replied. "My father's father saw them for the first time. My father's father's father did not know them. The first non-San to come to the region were Europeans, not Blacks. We worked for them, got money and obtained our first cattle from the Tswana with that money. The Whites first came to !Kubi [south of Dobe], killed elephants and pulled their teeth [i.e., ivory]. In the old days the Ju/'hoansi also killed elephants with spears for the meat. At least 15 men were required for a hunt. They dumped the tusks [they didn't have a use for them].

"The Whites came by ≠dwa-/twe [lit. "giraffe-horse" [i.e., camels]. The Whites had no cattle, they had horses and camels. 'Janny' came from the south. Another one made a well at Qangwa [also called Lewisfontein]. My father said 'Oh, can water come out of there?' They used metal tools but not engines. This well is not used today. They spoke Burusi [Afrikaans]."

I asked, "Before the Whites came did you know 'Ju sa jo' [Black people] here?" His response was unequivocal: "No. We only knew ourselves. Ju/'hoansi exclusively."

"But when the Blacks did come, who was first?"

"The first Black was Mutibele, a Tswana, and his older brother, Mokgomphata. They came from the east following the paths made by the Whites going in the opposite direction. They were shown the waterholes by Ju/'hoansi including my father/Twi. They were shown the killing sites of the elephants, where the bones lay, the sites where Whites killed. And they said 'Oh, the Whites have already got the n!ore [territory] from us.' Then [Mutibele's] father claimed the land and all the Ju/'hoansi on it, but he deceived us."

"How did he deceive you? When the Tswana claims he is master of you all, do you agree?"

"If he was the master, he didn't give us anything, neither clothes nor pots, or even one calf. The Europeans had given the Ju/'hoansi guns. When the Tswana saw this they decided to give guns to other Ju/'hoansi, so that they could hunt eland and giraffe."

Later in the conversation I explored the nature of San-Black interactions in the precolonial period. What had they received from the Blacks?

"When I was young," Kumsa replied, "we had no iron pots. We used the clay pots of the Goba. We couldn't make them ourselves."

"Then how do you account for the fact that there are many potsherds on old Ju/'hoansi sites around here?"

"Our fathers' fathers and their fathers' fathers got them from the Gobas. They would trade for them with skins. The Gobas didn't come up here. They stayed where they were [on the rivers] and we went to them. This went on for a very long time [so that is why there are so many potsherds]."

"We [always] got two things from them: iron and pots. If you go to Danega today you will find the right earth. But the Gobas didn't come here. We always went to them."

⚫⚫⚫

Kumsa's statements are congruent with a model of autonomy. Others had also made the point that a long-standing trade existed with riverine peoples *in which the Ju did the travelling*. It would be hard to argue that the Blacks could dominate the Dobe area without any physical presence, but I suppose it is not impossible. The trading trips made by the Ju to the east and elsewhere would certainly account for the presence of Iron Age materials on the Dobe area sites. In fact Polly Wiessner has argued that the levels of iron and pottery found on Dobe area Later Stone Age (LSA) sites can be accounted for by *hxaro* trade, a traditional form of delayed exchange still practiced by the Ju/'hoansi that historically has been a vehicle for long-distance trade.

One suggestive point was Kumsa's intriguing statement that the precolonial Ju hunted elephant but discarded the tusks; remarkable because it indicates that the Dobe Ju/'hoansi were hunting elephant for subsistence and were not part of a mercantile *or* a tributary network, since in either case elephant ivory would have been a prime valuable item.

Also interesting is Kumsa's rather dismissive view of the Tswana as overlords. For Kumsa the criterion for being a chief [lit. in San, "wealthperson"] is giving away in this context, not exercising power *per se*. The Europeans were chiefs because they gave guns, the Tswana were "deceivers" because in Kumsa's terms they claimed chiefly status but gave nothing.

A !Goshe Commentary on the Early Days of Contact

/Ti!kai-n!a, aged 80 at the time of the interview (1987), and /Ti!kai-tsau ("tooth") age 63, were two of the leading men of !Goshe, 16 kilometers east of Qangwa, and the easternmost and most economically "progressive" of the Dobe area villages. !Goshe is the jumping-off point for travel to the east, and the village has kept Tswana cattle since the 1910s. With their strong ties to the east where most Blacks reside, !Goshe people, by reason of history and geography, are the most attuned to links to "Iron Age" peoples.

"Certain Europeans in Gaborone," I began, "argue that long ago you Ju/'hoansi, [that is] your fathers' fathers' fathers' fathers had cattle. Do you agree?"

"No! Not a bit!" was the younger /Ti!kai's emphatic answer. "Long ago our fathers' fathers' fathers' fathers, the only meat *they* had was what they could shoot with arrows. We only got cows from the Tswana."

I persisted. "But when you dig holes deep down beneath where you live, you find pieces of pottery. Where did they come from?"

"Oh those pots were our own work!" replied the elder /Ti!kai. "Our ancestors made them. They would put them on the fire and cook with them. But since we got iron pots from you Europeans we lost the knowledge of pottery making."

Shifting the topic, I asked, "What about iron?"

"We got that from the Mbukushu," said /Ti!kai. "But we learned how to work it ourselves. . . . You stick it in the fire, heat it up, and hammer it. . . . We did it ourselves. We saw how the Gobas did it and we learned from them."

"Where did you get the iron itself from?"

Their answer surprised me. "The Europeans," said /Ti!kai. "The Tswana and Gobas didn't have it. They also got it from the Europeans."

I had to disagree. "But," I said, "in the oldest abandoned villages of the Gobas, iron is there. Long before the Europeans came."

At this point the older /Ti!kai intervened. "Yes! /Tontah is right. Long ago the Mbukushu had the pieces of iron that they worked."

The younger /Ti!kai turned to the older and asked, incredulously, "Well, where did they get the iron from?"

Matter-of-factly, the older man replied, "From the earth."

Much discussion followed on this point. The younger man was unconvinced that the Gobas had iron before the Europeans, but old /Ti!kai stuck to his story.

Shifting topic again, I asked, "Long long ago, did your fathers' fathers' fathers' fathers practice //*hara* [farming]?"

There was no disagreement on this point. "No, we didn't. We just ate the food that we collected from the bush."

The older /Ti!kai added, "When I was a boy we had learned about //*hara* from the Tswanas. They showed us how [to do it]."

The !Goshe interviews corroborate the account of Kumsa on the absence of cattle and agriculture before the twentieth-century arrival of the Tswana.

They add detail on Ju/'hoan understandings of the history of pottery and iron use. In the first case they spoke of Ju manufacture of pottery, whereas other informants spoke of it as only imported. In the second case there was an intriguing difference of opinion. There was agreement that iron was imported from the Gobas but only in the recent past, but some believed that iron was so recent that the Gobas only obtained iron *after* the arrival of the Europeans, a view that we were to encounter elsewhere.

N!ae and /Kunta at Cho/ana

Another round of oral history interviews took place in 1995 at Cho/ana, a former Ju/'hoan waterhole, 65 kilometers northwest of Dobe, now located in Namibia's Kaudom Game Reserve. The informants were N!ae and her husband /Kunta (/Tontah) one of my namesakes. Cho/ana has long been known to historians as a meeting point for Ju/'hoansi from several regions. It was a convenient water hole for Ju/'hoan parties engaged in *hxaro* trade to meet.

In tracing the earliest history of the place, /Kunta saw the original owners as Ju/'hoansi, not Blacks or any other ethnic group. In the beginning, asserted /Kunta, only Ju/'hoansi lived here; there were no Gobas. Ju people would come from Nyae Nyae and from the north, to do *hxaro* here. It was a waterhole that always held water. People from the South (Nyae Nyae) would bring /*do* (ostrich eggshell beads). People from the North brought /*an* (glass beads). In /Kunta's words, "*Hxaro* brought them together."

A point of emphasis in our interviews was the question of whether the Gobas made trips to the interior to trade or to make their presence felt. /Kunta was emphatic: "No, [they didn't come to us] we went to them. We saw pots on their fires and wanted them, so they gave us some."

"And what did you give them in return?"

"We gave Gobas /*do* in exchange for pots."

The interior Ju/'hoansis' proximity to Iron Age peoples on their periphery and the use of iron as a marker of Iron Age overlordship has been a particular point of emphasis for the revisionists. I was anxious to hear /Kunta and N!ae's views of the pre-colonial use of iron and its source.

"Did your ancestors have !*ga* (iron)?"

"Are you joking? We didn't know !*ga*. If we needed arrows we used ≠*dwa* (giraffe) or *n!n* (eland) bones."

"Who gave Ju/'hoansi the iron?"

"We visited north and east and saw this wonderful stuff for arrows and knives; we asked Gobas for it and got some. It was very valuable; when others saw it their hearts were sad because they didn't have it; they wanted it so badly they would even fight other Ju for it. Parties went north to seek it; Gobas gave it to them in exchange for steenbok and duiker skins and other things."

"Where did Goba get iron from?"

Without hesitation /Kunta replied, "From the European."

"Are you saying that before Europeans came Gobas had no iron?"

"Yes, they had no iron."

●◦◉◦●

It is interesting that informants see iron coming ultimately from Europeans; they saw the appearance of iron and Europeans in their areas as so close in time that iron was associated with Europeans. While it is true that the amount of iron on Nyae Nyae-Dobe LSA sites is miniscule, it is striking that the long history of Iron Age occupation on their periphery, for example at the Tsodilo Hills with radiocarbon dates as early as 500 A.D., doesn't have much resonance with the Ju/'hoansi informants. When they did obtain iron from the Gobas, it was clearly an item of trade and not a marker of overlordship. In any event the very (post-European) regency of the trade in iron challenges the revisionist view of a deep antiquity of Ju/'hoan subservience.

Discussion

In all interviews there was repeated insistence that no Gobas or any other Blacks occupied their area or even visited prior to the late nineteenth century; several spoke of the Gobas' preference for staying on the river and avoiding the dry interior. All these accounts illuminate the pragmatic and matter-of-fact approach of Dobe and Nyae Nyae area people to questions of history. These, after all, are questions of the most general nature and the accounts agree closely, not only about the autonomy of the area from outside domination but also about the absence of cattle and agriculture in pre-colonial times (though not of pottery and iron). There are interesting divergences of opinion on whether pottery was imported or locally made, and on whether the Gobas had iron before the Europeans. Taken together these accounts along with others . . . constitute a fair representation of mid and late twentieth-century Ju/'hoan views of their forebearers' nineteenth-century history of autonomy.

One other indication of the Ju sense of their history is the largely positive self-image of their past. They see themselves as actors, not victims, and this contrasts with the negative self-imagery expressed by other San people, (such as Hai//om or Nharo views of their present and past).

Archaeological Tie-ins

The oral history interviews in both 1995 and 1997 accompanied archaeological excavation, designed to link archaeology with the knowledge that was part of the living tradition of the Ju/'hoansi. Professor Andrew Smith of the University of Cape Town started excavating a rich Later Stone Age archaeological site at Cho/ana, which provided a continual stimulus for oral history as new and interesting materials came to light in the excavations. The Ju informants' comments provided a valuable adjunct to the archaeological work (and vice versa). They identified plant remains, made tentative suggestions regarding fragmentary bone materials, and provided a social context in which the material could be interpreted. For example, the elders described a kind of white glass bead as one of the earliest of the European trade goods obtained through intermediaries to the north. A few days after the interview, precisely such a bead was found in a sealed level in association with an LSA industry.

But the most stunning confirmation of the direct late nineteenth-century encounter between people with advanced stone-working skills and colonialists was a piece of bottle glass (mouth and neck) showing signs of delicate micro-retouching that the South African Later Stone Age is famous for. This gave a further indication of the persistence of LSA stone-working techniques into the colonial contact period.

The oral history's insistence on the absence of cattle and Blacks in the interior was confirmed by the complete lack in the archaeological record of the presence of domesticated animals or of non-Ju/'hoan people in the area prior to the latter part of the nineteenth century. . . .

Colonial Constructions of the Ju/'hoansi

Turning to the third body of evidence, what light do ethnohistoric documents shed on these Ju accounts of their own past? Do they support or contradict Ju accounts of relative autonomy? In general, the few historical accounts we do have support the Ju/'hoansi view of autonomy. . . .

One of the earliest detailed accounts of the Nyae Nyae-Dobe Ju/'hoansi comes relatively late when Hauptman Müller, a German colonial officer, traveled through the Nyae Nyae area in 1911. Müller offers some unusually detailed observations on the situation of the Nyae Nyae-Dobe area Ju/'hoansi some 30 years after colonial trade had been established. In Müller's account (1912) the area remained remote and inaccessible. His visit was the first to the interior from the west in five years.

Most telling is Müller's ethnographic description of the bushman inhabitants of this stretch of land he calls "virginal" [jungfräulich]. He depicts their state as "noch uberuhrt von aller Zivilisation, in alter Ursprunglichkeit" [still untouched by all civilization in their old pristine state]. He reports with amusement how European objects such as matches and mirrors were unknown to them, as well as the camels of his troopers, which startled them and caused the women to grab their children and scatter into the bush. However, he did find them using such things as wooden bowls, glass and iron beads, cooper rings, and "Ovambo knives," all obtained through trade with Black neighbors.

Of particular interest is Müller's descriptions of the Bushman themselves. In his account they were well nourished and relatively tall, thanks to an ample diet of meat (hunted with bone-tipped arrows) and a variety of wild plants. There is no mention in Müller's account of any resident cattle or Bantu-speaking overlords, though BaTswana were visiting the area during his stay. For Müller the association of the Nyae Nyae Bushmen with the BaTswana was not ancient; it was of recent date and was based on trade and assistance rendered at the latters' hunting expeditions. The Bushmen were rewarded with gifts for their services and the relationship with the hunter/herders is described as equitable and friendly:

> The Bushmen seem, however, to be good friends with the BaTswanas. When I asked a Bushman if it didn't bother him that the BaTswanas were killing off so much game every year he said "Yes, but we are getting presents!" . . .

Müller's is one of the earliest accounts to be based on actual reports of what he observed, as distinguished from second-hand accounts at a distance. And the preceding short quotation is among the very first to cite the actual words of a Ju/'hoan person.

⚜

To sum up this section, both German and Ju/'hoan testimony are consistent and mutually supportive. The detail presented by Müller and the others (such as Hans Schinz and James Chapman) attests to five propositions that accord closely with statements made by the Ju/'hoansi themselves:

1. The relative isolation of the Nyae Nyae-Dobe area from the West and the low volume of European traffic, 1880–1911
2. The absence of cattle in pre-colonial Ju subsistence
3. The absence of Bantu overlords or tributary relations
4. The relatively favorable terms of trade between Blacks and San
5. The relatively good foraging subsistence base and nutritional status of the San

These lines of evidence argue the case that the views of the Ju/'hoansi about their historical autonomy are not sharply at odds with the ethnohistoric sources.

Hunter-Gatherer Discourse and Agrarian Discourse

Both the Ju oral histories and the German and other historical texts are cultural constructions, and yet, how are we to account for the correspondences between these two bodies of evidence? Why do they corroborate one another? To argue that both are careful fabrications still leaves open the question of why they agree so closely. One would have to invoke conspiracy or coincidence, in either case a tough sell. Surely it would be more reasonable to assume that they agree because they are describing the same reality. If Kumsa's, the two /Ti!kai's, N!ae and /Kunta's and others' collective accounts of the Ju/'hoansi autonomous past gibe so closely with those of European eyewitnesses such as Müller, then on what grounds rests the view of the historic Ju/'hoansi as enserfed pastoralists? And why has this view gained such currency in anthropological circles?

A more fruitful approach to understanding the recent debates is to attempt to place them in the context of the intellectual currents of the late twentieth century. How does the current conjuncture shape our perceptions of the situation of indigenous "others"?

Obviously, by the 1990s, the processes affecting the Dobe Ju/'hoansi had brought them to becoming clients, laborers, and rural proletarians, subject to and dependent on regional and world economies. Their current predicament is well understood by recourse to theories arising from political economy, dependency theory, or colonial discourse. Current theorizing is much weaker, however, in understanding the antecedent conditions. Part of the inability of contemporary theory to encompass hunters and gatherers as historical subjects is the lack of attention to the *differences* between discourses about hunters and gatherers and the discourses concerning agrarian societies and the emerging world system.

In agrarian discourse the presence of structures of domination are taken as given; it is the *forms* of domination and the modes of exploitation and surplus extraction that are problematic. In the literature on the agrarian societies of the Third World, stratification, class and class struggle, patriarchy, accumulation, and immiseration constitute the basic descriptive and analytical vocabulary.

In hunter-gatherer discourse it is not the forms and modes of domination that are at issue; rather the prior question to be asked is whether domination is *present*. I have been struck by the eagerness of otherwise competent analysts to gloss over, sidestep, or ignore this question.

There is no great mystery about what separates hunter-gatherer from agrarian societies. The former usually live lightly on the land at low densities; they can move and still survive, an escape route not available to sedentary farmers. The latter, with high densities and fixed assets, can no longer reproduce themselves outside the system, and are rendered far more vulnerable to domination.

In the recent debate some analysts seem to have taken the world systems/ political economy position so literally that every culture is seen as nothing more than the sum total of its external relations. But surely there is more to a culture than its links of trade, tribute, domination, and subordination. There is the internal dynamic of the means by which a social group reproduces itself ecologically, socially, and in terms of its collective consciousness. . . .

An historically informed ethnography can offer an alternative to the totalizing discourses of world systems theory. The unself-conscious sense of their own nineteenth- and early twentieth-century autonomy expressed by Ju/'hoan hunter-gatherers and its corroboration by contemporaneous colonial observers is one example of how these powerful assumptions can be challenged. They bear testimony that in the not very distant past other ways of being were possible.

That said, autonomy should not be taken as an article of faith, nor is it an all-or-nothing proposition. It is, or should be, an empirical question, and each society may exhibit a complex array of more or less autonomy at stages in its history. Even in agrarian societies spaces are opened up, however small, for the expression of autonomous thought and behavior. Thus it need not be the exclusive preserve of non-hierarchical or noncolonized societies. . . .

With reference to the latter though, a final point: What is desperately needed is to theorize the communal mode of production and its accompanying world view. Without it there is a theoretical vacuum filled far too facilely by imputing capitalist relations of production, bourgeois subjectivity, or "culture of poverty" frameworks to hunter-gatherer peoples.

POSTSCRIPT

Are San Hunter-Gatherers Basically Pastoralists Who Have Lost Their Herds?

These selections express two radically different worldviews. Denbow and Wilmsen's view—which has been called the "revisionist" view—emphasizes the interconnectedness of societies and the tendency for powerful polities to exert control over their less powerful neighbors. On the other hand, Lee's view—called the "traditionalist" view—emphasizes the people's adaptation to their natural environment and sees their relations with outsiders as variable, depending on local circumstances. Most anthropologists recognize that all cultures are influenced by local conditions and by the larger social environment, including, to some extent, the entire "world system." The question is, How much weight should one give to these two types of influence?

The disagreement between these scholars and their supporters is not merely a matter of theoretical emphasis. They also disagree about the facts and their proper interpretation. In subsequent publications Wilmsen and Lee, in particular, have argued over such matters as the precise locations of groups and trade routes mentioned in travelers' journals and whether or not the presence of cattle bones, for example, in an archaeological site indicates trade or outside domination. For elaboration of Wilmsen and Denbow's views see "Paradigmatic History of San-Speaking Peoples and Current Attempts at Revision," *Current Anthropology* (vol. 31, no. 5, 1990) and Wilmsen's book *Land Filled With Flies: A Political Economy of the Kalahari* (University of Chicago Press, 1989). For Lee's critique of these sources see his and Mathias Guenther's "Problems in Kalahari Historical Ethnography and the Tolerance of Error," *History in Africa* (vol. 20, 1993) and "Oxen or Onions? The Search for Trade (and Truth) in the Kalahari," *Current Anthropology* (vol. 32, 1991).

The literature on the San is voluminous. Alan Barnard's book *Hunters and Herders of Southern Africa: A Comparative Ethnography of the Khoisan Peoples* (Cambridge University Press, 1992) is an excellent overview of the various San and Khoi (formerly called "Hottentot") peoples. Important expressions of the revisionist view include Carmel Schrire's article "An Inquiry Into the Evolutionary Status and Apparent Identity of San Hunter-Gatherers," *Human Ecology* (vol. 8, no. 1, 1980) and her chapter entitled "Wild Surmises on Savage Thoughts," in her edited volume *Past and Present in Hunter Gatherer Studies* (Academic Press, 1984). A crucial source on the history of the San is Robert Gordon's *The Bushman Myth: The Making of a Namibian Underclass* (Westview Press, 1992). Works supporting the traditionalist view include Susan Kent's "The Current Forager Controversy: Real vs. Ideal Views of Hunter-Gatherers," *Man* [n.s.] (vol. 27, 1992).

ISSUE 14

Do Some Illnesses Exist Only Among Members of a Particular Culture?

YES: Sangun Suwanlert, from *"Phii Pob:* Spirit Possession in Rural Thailand," in William Lebra, ed., *Culture-Bound Syndromes, Ethnopsychiatry, and Alternate Therapies,* vol. 4 of *Mental Health Research in Asia and the Pacific* (The University Press of Hawaii, 1976)

NO: Robert A. Hahn, from *Sickness and Healing: An Anthropological Perspective* (Yale University Press, 1995)

ISSUE SUMMARY

YES: Physician Sangun Suwanlert from Thailand asks whether or not one particular illness he observed in northern Thai villages, called *phii pob,* corresponds to Western diagnostic categories or is restricted to Thailand. After documenting how this condition does not fit standard psychiatric diagnoses, he concludes that *phii pob* is indeed a "culture-bound syndrome" that can only occur among people who share rural Thai cultural values and beliefs.

NO: Medical anthropologist Robert A. Hahn counters that the very idea of the so-called culture-bound syndrome is flawed. He contends that culture-bound syndromes are reductionist explanations for certain complex illness conditions—that is, explanations that reduce complex phenomena to a single variable. Hahn suggests that such conditions are like any illness condition; they are not so much peculiar diseases but distinctive local cultural expressions of much more common illness conditions that can be found in any culture.

For most of a century, anthropologists have observed that people in many tribal societies suffer from peculiar health complaints that seemed to occur only among members of particular cultures. Most of these illnesses were psychiatric in nature, including various kinds of "wild man" behaviors, such as *amok* in Malaysia, the *witiko* (or *windigo*) psychosis of the Ojibwa, the "Arctic hysterias" of some Eskimo and Siberian groups, startle reactions like *latah* in Indonesia and Malaysia, and various panic reactions found among certain Australian aboriginal groups. In some Australian tribes, observers have reported that people have died of no apparent physiological cause after learning that they were victims of sorcery performed against them by an enemy. These diverse conditions appeared quite different from mental illnesses observed in Western countries, and some seemed to have physiological symptoms that were not seen in industrial countries. Such cases raised the possibility that some illnesses might be rooted in a specific culture or even caused by aspects of the cultures themselves. Thus, the idea of the culture-bound syndrome was born.

For medical anthropologists, these culture-bound syndromes seemed to define a special niche in the medical world where anthropologists could contribute valuable insights that physicians, psychologists, and psychiatrists could not provide. Most anthropologists accepted the premise that anthropology could offer few new insights about such conditions like pneumonia, malaria, gastrointestinal diseases, and cancer. But if psychological conditions in different cultures were profoundly shaped by culture or even caused by aspects of a particular culture, then anthropology seemed to have a special role to play in medicine.

For these medical anthropologists, the question that confronted them was, How different are these syndromes from Western psychiatric conditions and neuroses? How can such different symptomatologies be explained? How do the details of local cultural traditions actually influence the symptoms of a particular condition, or alternatively, how does culture actually cause such illnesses?

These are some of the questions that Sangun Suwanlert addresses in the following selection. He focuses attention on a particular syndrome called *phii pob,* which he observed in northern Thailand. Rural Thai explain *phii pob* as a kind of spirit possession, which most typically affects married women. Symptoms of possession include numbness of limbs, falling down (sometimes with convulsions), rigid limbs, clenched fists, and sometimes shaking. While each of these symptoms has been observed in Western cultural contexts, the specific configuration observed in Thailand does not readily map onto any specific Western diagnosis. Suwanlert concludes that *phii pob* represents a syndrome that is culture-bound and can only emerge among rural Thai.

Robert A. Hahn challenges the very notion that any specific syndrome is so closely linked to any particular culture that it would justify the label "culture-bound syndrome." All illnesses, he argues, are shaped by the local cultures in which they occur. These illnesses would include psychological and psychiatric conditions as well as those we ordinarily assume to be strictly physiological, such as infections, diabetes, chronic pain, and so on. Thus, for Hahn, *phii pob, amok,* Arctic hysteria, and the *witiko* psychosis are merely distinctive local symptomatic expressions of conditions that are found in industrialized nations.

Phii Pob: Spirit Possession in Rural Thailand

In Thailand, as in all other countries, there are many people who seem to believe in spirits and ghosts. The Thais refer to the spirits and ghosts in general as *phii*. From my experience in treating psychiatric patients, I have found that the patients and their relatives are very much concerned with spirits and ghosts. *Phii* (evil spirit) possession is often found to be a basic cause in mental disease, both functional and organic, and we can divide them into three types:

- Ghosts of the dead: *phii* of grandparents, father, mother, ancestors, or spirits of important and respected people.
- Spirits of sacred things, not emanating from human beings.
- Spirits of the living, such as *phii pong, phii pob, phii ka*, and *phii krasu*.

My paper will be on the spirits of the living, the third type, or *phii pob*, with special emphasis on the psychiatric study of the *phii pob*. The first two kinds of *phii* mentioned above, those that originate from the dead and sacred things, are found to possess people more often than the third kind. . . .

Phii pob . . . is a common spirit in the northeast, north, and some provinces of the central plain of Thailand. Some say that *phii pob* is nonsubstantial; that nobody can definitely describe its shape. Some say that it is in the shape of a black dog; others say it is shaped more like a monkey. . . .

Phii pob originates in a living person, conceals itself in the body of that person, who is called the originating host, and comes and goes at any time. There are three ways in which a person can become a source of *phii pob:* it may originate in the person himself; he may inherit it from his ancestors; or he may possess an object said to bring good fortune to its owner, and the *phii pob* dwelling in this object may transfer itself to the owner.

Origination within the host. *Phii pob* seems to originate in people who study magic arts and spells, such as the spell for prosperous trading, the spell enabling one to talk cleverly, and the magical love arts, to make a person desire sexual intercourse with the opposite sex or to make one's sexual organs attractive. After a person completes his study, he becomes a teacher in his special field of magic.

From CULTURAL-BOUND SYNDROMES, ETHNOPSYCHIATRY, AND ALTERNATE THERAPIES, edited by William P. Lebra. Copyright © 1976 by University of Hawai'i Press. Reprinted by permission.

Almost every teacher of magic observes certain restrictions against doing certain things. . . . These restrictions may proscribe eating certain kinds of food, accepting fees for treatment and teaching, or going underneath a clothesline. As time passes and such a person forgets these restrictions, the *phii pob* originates automatically within him, although the host may not be aware of it. Since it is believed that the *phii pob* hiding within a person can leave the body of that person to possess another, the new possessed host can discover and make known who the originating host of the *phii pob* is. Usually a person hosts only one *phii pob* of the same sex as himself, but many informants confirm that it is possible for a person to host many and possess both males and females.

Inherited from the host's ancestors.   Although the host grows old and eventually dies, the *phii pob* does not. It goes on hiding in the children of the host, usually the eldest child of the same sex; that is, the father's *phii pob* will transfer to the eldest son and the mother's to the eldest daughter. If the host has no children, the *phii pob* will hide in a close relative and is called *pob chue.*

Origination in objects.   One can become host of *phii pob* by possessing commodities such as *wan krachai* and *wan phii pob,* a tuberous plant, or *see poeng sanei,* a wax charm, which are said to bring good fortune to the possessor. Some believe that *phii pob* dwell in these things and may transfer themselves to the owner.

A person will be possessed by a *phii pob* when he has had an argument with its host, but this is not necessarily the only time. A person or animal can be possessed in four ways:

1. Possession can occur in time of sickness, causing complications, during menopause or at the age of involution, or during the transition from adolescence to adulthood. It is believed that the spirit will eat away at the viscera (kidney, intestines, liver, et cetera) until the individual finally dies.
2. A *phii pob* can possess a boy or a girl under ten years of age and make the child talk irrelevantly. It is believed that most children thus possessed will eventually die.
3. Large domestic animals such as cows, buffalo, and horses can be possessed and die suddenly.
4. A *phii pob* can enter people who have had no previous symptoms, generally women between the ages of 18 and 40, men, less frequently. The possessed host will usually identify the originating host; this is called *ook pak* ("to speak out") in Northeastern Thai.

The Study

At various times from 1967 to 1971, I conducted a study of *phii pob* possession in north and northeast Thailand. My research had the following aims:

- To study the nature of *phii pob* in the upper regions of Thailand, where people believe that *phii pob* is the cause of some illness.

- To study the relationship between the possession syndrome and the environment, the local culture, and the reaction of the people toward this syndrome.
- To determine whether this is a psychiatric syndrome and, if so, how to classify it.
- To study folk treatment for the possessed host and originating host.

This paper reports on sixty-two cases of possessed hosts; six cases of originating hosts; and ten cases of possessed hosts whose *phii pob* refused to leave them. . . .

Symptoms of Possession

The earliest sign of the onset of possession is a numbness of limbs, followed by falling, with or without convulsions. Most who are possessed become unconscious; some become rigid, clench their fists, and must be forced to lie down or sit. After being in this condition for a while, some can answer questions, although somewhat confusedly. There are five categories of symptoms that appear after a person has been possessed:

1. Making noises like *"phii,"* shouting out, screaming, weeping.
2. Tensing, clenched fists, or short spasms.
3. Shaking following spasms, (not in all cases).
4. Timidity or shyness, manifested by an inability to speak to or face others. Sometimes facial expressions are similar to those of the originating host.
5. Identifying or speaking out the host's name (*ook pak*).

The fifth is the most important symptom, for it reveals not only the host's name but also the purpose of the possession, whether it is good or bad and whether it is merely passing through the village. Whether this symptom appears depends largely on the ability of the shaman; if he is skillful, he will have the victim talking relevantly.

Possessed Host: Case Illustrations

For illustration, I would like to describe the two cases of possession occurring at the health station that I was able to observe from the onset. . . .

Case 1.   A young, unmarried girl, 16 years of age, a Buddhist, with a primary-school education, from the Amnatcharoen District, and of low economic status was admitted to the Class I health station complaining of abdominal pain in the umbilical region. A physical examination revealed no abnormality, and she was referred to me for observation.

In an interview with the girl's mother, it was learned that, although she was very cooperative, the mother knew very little about her daughter because since the age of two the girl had been under her grandmother's care and had lived in another district. When the mother was in her sixth month of pregnancy, the girl's father left home and never returned. After the birth of the child, the mother struggled to make a living for both of them; when the girl was two, the mother remarried, and the child was sent off to her grand-mother's. At the age of 15 the girl went to Bangkok with relatives and worked as a servant for six months, but she was unable to cope with her job so went back to live with her mother and stepfather.

Two days after witnessing her drunken stepfather slap her mother during an argument, the girl was possessed by a *phii pob*. The possession, according to the mother, lasted for about an hour. The originating host seemed to be one of the stepfather's friends who lived in the next village, because during possession the girl's general bearing was masculine when she described the kind of husband her stepfather was and when she threatened him with punishment by his ancestors' spirits.

The patient, with decorative cotton strings tied around her neck and wrists, was an attractive girl with sad eyes and a low, soft manner of speaking. During the interview she repeatedly said, "I don't know what my problem is, but I'm anxious about it." Crying, she complained of severe abdominal pain while continually asking her stepfather to do things for her.

The second night after being admitted, about 11:00 P.M., the patient was again possessed by a *phii pob*. When I went to the ward, the relatives, fearful of her falling off the bed, had her lying on the floor, and her mother was massaging her legs. I spoke to her but there was no recognition on her part. However, when she heard me, she sat up immediately in a cross-legged position. Her face became flushed and her eyes widened but did not focus. She raised her hand and said coherently, "I'm Mr. ——— (stepfather's friend). I was angry when I heard that my friend did something wrong in the village. I'm here for a visit only." The mother cried out, "Please, go." "No," replied the girl. To the other relatives' suggestion of calling a shaman, the possessed girl answered, "I don't care." Then a relative asked, "Why don't you? This is a government office." (It is a common belief that *phii pob* are afraid of government offices.) The reply was, "I want my friend to behave. I want to let him know that if he doesn't, the ancestors' spirits will break his neck." After the stepfather promised that he would behave, the other relatives asked many questions; an hour later the spirit departed via the mouth, without the help of a shaman.

The patient was treated for ten days with a mild tranquilizer and super-ficial psychotherapy. She was discharged when she stopped complaining of abdominal pain, and she returned home to her grandmother.

Case 2. A 32-year-old Buddhist woman, wife of a peasant, with a primary-school education, and of low-income status, was admitted to the health station because of manifest muscle twitching in both arms, insomnia, and loss of appetite. A physical examination did not reveal any abnormality.

According to her husband, they had been married for several years. Before their marriage he had been a bachelor and she a divorcée with no children. About a year before admission, the wife was informed that the husband had had a long talk with a girl. Subsequently she began to nag, asking about his relationship with the girl. The more he denied, the more she nagged. A few days later the woman was possessed twice in one day. Ten days before her hospitalization, the husband went to see the girl in question on a business matter. When the wife learned of it she became hysterical, swore at her husband, cried, and ultimately fell into depression. Two days later the muscles in her arms began to twitch.

I visited the patient an hour every morning during her hospitalization because she was on a mild tranquilizer and superficial psychotherapy under my care. Whenever I started talking to her, her husband had to hold on to her arms to prevent them from twitching. Although the patient was pale, she looked younger than her years. She seemed to understand me well enough to make me think that she was not confused. However, she often said, "I'm quite worried about my future."

On the fourth night after admission, she became possessed by a female *phii pob.* The spirit claimed that it had come for a visit and asked the husband how things were going at home and how he had been behaving lately. Approximately fifteen minutes later the patient became silent and fell into depression, indicating that the spirit had departed. After ten days at the health station, the patient felt much better and the muscle twitching disappeared; she was discharged.

I consider the two cases cited above simple cases, but only when the precipitating cause of possession is taken into consideration. The cause was a kind of wish-fulfillment for people living in a noncomplex society. . . .

Originating Hosts

Case 1. Mrs. S., age 65, was from Amphur Wapee Patum, Mahasarakam Province. She looked slightly younger than her age, was dressed neatly in a long-sleeved blouse and a local type of skirt and wore the Northeastern type of earrings. Throughout the interview she sat properly and was very cooperative.

According to her, about five years ago in 1963, one of her sons who was working at Amphur Barn Pai in Kohnkaen Province befriended a man who had fallen off a car and broken his leg. The man had run out of money and wanted to sell a box containing a small image of Buddha on one side and a closely knitted gold fabric on the other. The man wanted 100 baht (US$5) for it but took the 20 baht offered. The man told him to take good care of it since it was valuable. When her son returned home, he placed the object on the shelf for worship. About a month later Mrs. S. began to have headaches and insomnia, so she consulted a shaman. He advised her that the object was the cause of the ailment and to get rid of it. One neighbor suggested that she throw it away but another asked for it so she gave it to the latter. Her headaches and insomnia soon disappeared.

After she disposed of the object in 1967, three of her neighbors, girls aged 14–15, were entered by *phii pob.* All of them claimed that it was a *phii pob* from Mrs. S. Mrs. S. felt very uneasy and asked the head of the village to find an expert who could expel the *phii pob* from her. She was referred to someone and paid over 1,000 baht (US$50) for his service. Because she feared that she might not be completely cured, she continued to receive a treatment of "holy water" at least once a month.

When asked how she felt after the shaman had beaten her with a stick and the *phii pob* had supposedly left, although the neighbors still accused her of being a *phii pob*, Mrs. S. said that she felt no pain nor anything else but shame and worry. She did not want to see anybody. She was worried about her seven sons who would have to bear the accusation for a long time. This is why she made her way to Wat Dhat Panom for the expulsion of *phii pob* from her. The person she consulted told her that if she would gather together a small Buddhist image, holy thread, and a fallen fragment of a pagoda, she would be protected from *phii pob*. She replied that she had spent all her money and could not purchase the necessary articles. I bought and gave them to her, and it seemed to lift up her spirits.

Case 2. A 36-year-old man, Mr. B., married and living in Amphur Boor Kaw, Kalasinthu Province, came to Wat Dhat Panom to have *phii pob* driven out of his body. He was told that he had two *phii pob*, both in the shape of monkeys, perched on his shoulder. In our interview, Mr. B. reported that about five years before, when he was unmarried, he bought a wax charm to attract women and make them fall in love with him. He did not think much more about it until he discovered that his *phii pob* was going around possessing the neighborhood women.

When asked how he felt when the *phii pob* left his body to enter into another, he said that he trembled with no apparent cause, but did not feel anything leave his body. He was not concerned that his neighbors would do any harm to him. Whenever he thought about it, he said, he felt sad and worried, but he strongly denied having any illness.

I then asked him about his wife's and children's reaction to his being called the host. He said they were all ashamed and worried about it, especially when one of his children overheard the villagers talking about him.

About a month before he came for treatment at Wat Pra Dhat, someone in the village became possessed again. At that time a villager fired a shot into the sky, and Mr. B. began to fear for his life. Until then, he was sad and worried about the situation he was in, but he never thought anyone would do him any harm. (The probable reason for this was that he had a relative in a monastery who was highly respected by the villagers.) After this incident, he was unable to sleep well and often dreamed of monkeys and black dogs. Finally he decided to seek help at Wat Pra Dhat since the two spirit doctors who had treated him did not help him feel better.

I studied the symptoms of depression in the six cases of originating hosts to see whether illness such as depression existed in the distant villages. A questionnaire based on Cleghorn and Curtis' depression study was used. Results suggested that the patients came for treatment out of worry over bodily harm that they might receive and out of depression manifested by the symptoms such as sadness, insomnia, and loss of appetite. These symptoms lead one to conclude that villagers do become depressed and try to avoid other people when they are accused of being a *phii pob*. . . .

Villagers' Attitude toward *Phii Pob*

Belief in spirits has become a part of village tradition. The spirits, both good and bad, are perceived as superhuman beings, so good spirits are worshipped or respected and the bad ones are driven away as quickly as possible. The modernization introduced by education and communication has not changed these beliefs much. The villagers justify their belief in spirits by declaring that it is not harmful to anyone.

Actually there are three groups of people with respect to belief in spirits. (1) Nonbelievers include persons who have had some training in Buddhism, those who have been educated in cities or towns, and those whose families were troubled by spirits and have become good Buddhists. (2) Partial believers usually have a little more formal education than the average villager and often talk about true and false spirit possession and have tried to prove it. (3) Full believers include those who have lived only in the village, those who have experienced spirit possession, and those persuaded by others to believe in spirits. In actual number there are more full believers than nonbelievers and partial believers put together.

One may conclude that *phii pob* are considered suprahuman but bad spirits that should not be dwelling inside a human being. The method of driving out the bad spirit is either by physical punishment, beating the possessed with a cane, or by luring the bad spirits with the good because if the spirit is in a person too long the person can die or become mentally ill (*phii ba'*). Once a person's spirit has been expelled, he is considered cured and can continue to live in the village without prejudice. . . .

Analysis

Possessed host group 1.   Working in the health station and in the villages, I was soon able to recognize a person who had been possessed by a *phii pob*. A possessed woman was usually distinguished in her beauty, dramatic in manner, and charmingly seductive. It was common to see her with cotton strings tied around her neck and wrists. While being interviewed, I noted, the possessed hosts were sensitive and easily stimulated, quick-tempered, self-centered, and susceptible to suggestions. These characteristics may be classified as belonging to a "hysterical personality," which is generally found more in women than in men. Perhaps this could be one of the reasons for the predominance of women among the 50 possessed hosts whom I studied in 1967. Fully 96 per cent of them were women, and only 4 per cent were men; 38 per cent were 21–30 years old; 76 per cent were married. They may have had problems before being possessed. It seems that the mechanism of *phii pob* possession is a socially accepted way of solving social and internal conflicts.

The feeling of numbness prior to possession experienced by 42 per cent of the possessed was, I feel, a result of emotional tension rather than malnutrition, because most of the possessed hosts were physically healthy (see Table 1). After exhibiting other symptoms, such as depression and visual and auditory hallucinations, they went through a state of which they had no recollection.

Table 1

Pre- and Post-Possession Symptoms (ranked by frequency)

Pre-Possession Symptoms (frequency rate = 42-2)*	Post-Possession Symptoms (frequency rate = 41-2)**
1. Felt numbness throughout the body and limbs.	1. Felt quite well.
2. Felt like crying.	2. Felt aches and pains all over the body.
3. Felt dizzy.	3. Felt weary.
4. Had vision of round shapes.	4. Became frightened and worried.
5. Felt sick at heart.	5. Developed insomnia.
6. Had headaches and chills.	6. Felt heart palpitations.
7. Had vision of a monkey.	7. Became groggy and befuddled.
8. Had vision of a man.	
9. Had vision of a dog or a cat.	
10. Heard voices calling.	
11. Felt stiffness in chest.	
12. Had vision of a chicken.	
13. Heard a dog barking.	
14. None.	

*Some symptoms appeared in combination, e.g., numbness and having vision of a monkey, but here they are listed separately.
**Most of the possessed could not remember what they said or did while being possessed, but some felt pains as though beaten with a cane, although very vaguely. Their gestures were similar to those of the originating host.

This syndrome should without question be considered psychiatric, although there was not much content to their hallucination. Mainly they saw round objects, monkeys, cats, men, or dogs, suggesting toxic psychosis. But the symptom that makes it different from toxic psychosis is the state of trance, during which the patients could talk relevantly.

While being possessed, the patients seemed to take on a "double personality" for a short period, not more than an hour (see Table 2). At this time the possessed seemed to be in a state of trance as if hypnotized, which I would classify as "dissociative reaction". *Phii pob* possession may be a type of hysteria, but I feel that it is a kind of "dissociative reaction" that occurs only in specific Thai cultural groups but has not yet been geographically localized or classified, unlike *amok* or *latah*.

An originating host is considered a clever person who practices many kinds of spells and is respected by the villagers. Because he is considered a clever person, the possessed identifies with the host and does not feel that any harm will come about. Identification is said to be an important mental mechanism in hysteria and it occurs in people who have had a previous relationship with each other. Characterization appears to be on the conscious level.

The villagers feel that *phii pob* possession is a genuine occurrence—everyone in my investigation believed in it. They might be smiling and giggling, but when asked about *phii pob*, their facial expression at once becomes solemn. They also believe that the *phii pob* or the hosts have their central location in

Table 2

Characteristics of Possession Episode (Group 1, 1957: N = 50)

Characteristic	Number	Percent
Duration:		
Momentary	13	26
1 hour	16	32
2 hours	7	14
3 hours	5	10
8 hours	2	4
48 hours	1	2
Undetermined	6	12
Departure Point:		
Unknown	16	32
Mouth (vomiting)	9	18
Bladder (urinating)	7	14
Another part of the body	18	36
Number of times Possessed:		
1	22	44
2	6	12
3	10	20
> 3	12	24

Baan Chyak, Tambon Nacik, which perhaps accounts for the fact that more patients come from south of Amnat Charoen than from north of it.

Possessed host group 2.   Group 2 includes ten possessed hosts, whose *phii pob* refused to depart after 48 hours, whom I studied in 1969–1971. After receiving treatment at the hospital for about a week, these persons felt much better. In their case, the diagnosis might be hysterical psychosis and the mechanism of *phii pob* is more complicated and difficult to generalize than for group 1.

Originating hosts.   It was very difficult to get information from originating hosts at the beginning of the study, because I presumed that my clients would resent inquiries from a total stranger. In addition, there were always others around when I conducted the interviews, and I felt that harm might result. However, through the cooperation of the Buddhist monks, I was able to interview six originating hosts (*phii pob*).

Through the interviews it was established that one could become a *phii pob* by three means: through inheritance, incantation study, and possession of "sacred" things. Although the *phii pob* accepted the causes, they could not see how the spirits in their bodies could go and possess others. They admitted to worrying and feeling depressed and ashamed about what had happened, but they had no other feelings or reactions.

Being a *phii pob* seemed to last from one to five years. All of those affected earnestly sought to expel the spirits in them. I felt that the only time the villagers noticed that one of them was a *phii pob* was when the *pob* possessed another and "spoke." On the other hand, such identification could have been a vindictive fabrication. Once identified, though, the only way out for the accused was to announce that he was going to have treatments to expel the *phii pob*.

Judging from the six cases I studied, the mental health of the accused was poor, affecting the immediate family members and other relatives. I often wonder what was the basic cause of the one case where the healing process was completed and the *phii pob* was supposedly buried only to have the woman go and dig it up. Was it the power over others that she enjoyed, or was she really overpowered by the spirits, as claimed? These questions still remain unanswered.

Some people are sympathetic toward *phii pob* but will not live under the same roof with them and will try to exile them. Tolo Village in Roi-Et Province seemed to accept the exiles; no one in that village seemed possessed, although the majority of the villagers were known to be *phii pobs*.

Phii pob possession is both good and bad. It may be a socially acceptable way of solving social and interpersonal conflicts. On the other hand, it is quite simple for a person to falsely accuse another of being *phii pob,* with disastrous consequences. Usually the only way out for the accused is to admit that he is a *phii pob* and to promise to undergo treatment to drive out the spirit, or move to another place. I believe that public reaction profoundly affects a person's mental health.

Conclusion

. . . Sixty-two cases of possessed hosts were studied in the villages of two provinces in Northeast Thailand; ten were admitted by relatives for treatment at Srithunya Hospital, Nondhaburi, because shamans could not drive the spirits off.

With group 1, 50 cases studied in 1967, *phii pob* possession occurred in the village, and the duration of possession was momentary to 48 hours. After the spirit was driven off, the possessed hosts became their former selves and felt quite well. The personalities of hosts who were repeatedly possessed were hysterical, precipitating various kinds of causes for illness. During the period of possession, the symptoms were similar to hysterical trance or a dissociative phenomenon. The diagnosis might be a hysterical neurosis that occurs only in specific Thai cultural groups. It seemed that the mechanism of *phii pob* possession was a socially accepted way of solving social and internal conflicts.

Group 2, studied in 1969–1971, comprised ten cases of *phii pob* who refused to depart from their possessed hosts within 48 hours. The possessed hosts were brought into the psychiatric hospital as psychotics. After receiving treatment for about a week, they felt much better. The diagnosis might be hysterical psychosis. The mechanism of *phii pob* possession for this group is more complicated than for group 1. . . .

 **NO**

Culture-Bound Syndromes Unbound

One of the jumpers while sitting in his chair with a knife in his hand was told to throw it, and he threw it quickly, so that it stuck in a beam opposite; at the same time he repeated the order to throw it, with cry or utterance of alarm resembling that of hysteria or epilepsy. He also threw away his pipe when filling it with tobacco when he was slapped upon the shoulder. . . . They [the jumpers] could not help repeating the word or sound that came from the person that ordered them any more than they could help striking, dropping, throwing, jumping, or starting; all of these phenomena were indeed but parts of the general condition known as jumping. . . . All of the jumpers agree that it tires them to be jumped and they dread it, but they were constantly annoyed by their companions.

— "Jumpers," Moosehead Lake, Maine, described by Beard

E. A. B. at the time of the event was 20 years old, unmarried, the third of four siblings and an Iban. At the time he ran amok *he had been uprooted from his normal surrounding, a longhouse in one of the upper reaches of the Batang Lupar river. He was working in an oil drilling camp, approximately 200 miles from home with no direct communication. One night, while living on a barge near the camp, he grabbed a knife and slashed five of his fellow workers, three Malay and two Chinese.*

— A man with *amok* in Malaysia, described [by] Schmidt

A man, about age 45, with wife and children, took a second wife. Afraid of the first wife's jealousy, he tried to keep the new relationship secret, but in time the second marriage became known. One evening, he came home tired and fatigued. He got the shivers, broke out in a cold sweat, and felt that his penis was shrinking. At his cry for help, the neighbors came running. Only men helped him. One man tightly held the patient's penis while another went for a sanro, *a native healer. The* sanro *performed one ritual and after a while the anxiety disappeared, ending the day's attack.*

— An Indonesian man with *koro*, reported [by] Chabot

Observers of seemingly strange behavior have distinguished a variety of behavioral syndromes that, because of their apparent uniqueness and fit to local cultural conditions, are described as culture-bound. The observers of such behavior have most often been from Western settings, the behavior observed principally in non-Western ones. In this [selection], I examine the logic by which the generic diagnostic label "culture-bound syndrome" is ascribed to some conditions and not to others. I claim that the idea of culture-bound syndromes is a conceptual mistake, confusing rather than clarifying our understanding of the role of culture in sickness and fostering a false dichotomy of events and the disciplines in which they are studied. All conditions of sickness are affected in many ways, and none is exhaustively determined by its cultural setting. Physiology, medicine, psychology, and anthropology are complementary rather than contrary and exclusive; all are relevant and necessary to the comprehensive understanding of human phenomena of sickness and healing. . . .

The very notion of a culture-bound syndrome indicates a form of reductionism—the explanation of a given phenomenon by a single principle or body of knowledge. Other explanatory principles are thus denied relevance. Reductionists may claim that they have fully explained a culture-bound syndrome and that, in consequence, this phenomenon falls exclusively within their domain of inquiry. This mistaken effort is apparent in versions of anthropology as well as in Western medicine, psychiatry, psychoanalysis, and psychology. I argue that such claims fragment human function and its study into falsely opposed divisions.

Although anthropologists may believe that they have established a firm position by appropriating culture-bound syndromes to their own domain of explanation, their claims are at once excessive and too modest, claiming too much for culture-bound syndromes and too little for the diseases staked out by Biomedicine. I argue that full explanation requires an opening of the inner sanctum of Biomedicine to anthropological review and a concomitant recognition of pervasive physiological constraint in the workings of culture. Humans are bound by their cultures—but not rigidly. Nor is culture the only binding principle; body, mind, society, and the broader environment also bind. An exploration of culture-bound syndromes thus reaches the variety of forms of sickness and the range of human disciplinary approaches.

To assess the notion of culture-bound syndrome, I briefly define *syndrome* and *culture* and suggest how syndromes might be *bound* by culture. I distinguish three ways in which culture-bound syndromes have been understood. . . . I propose that we discard the misleading concept of culture-bound syndrome in favor of a broader study of the role of human mind, physiology, culture, and society in pathology and its relief.

Syndromes, Cultures, and Binds

A *syndrome* (from the Latin "things that run together") is a group of conditions, generally pathological, that may be physical and/or mental, signs and/or symptoms, and that is thought to constitute a discrete entity. One syndrome, AIDS (acquired immunodeficiency syndrome), has gained recent attention; it is defined by a complex set of signs and symptoms that has evolved with changing knowledge as well as political-economic circumstances. Numerous other syndromes are named in Biomedicine, some after their discoverer, others after their symptoms. Syndromes are distinguished from other events that co-occur in that their co-occurrence is thought to be not simply coincidental; a syndrome is a part of a unifying phenomenon—for example, a recognized biological process. The constituents of a syndrome may reflect a group of similar causes. What makes AIDS a syndrome is the acquisition of a specific virus, the human immunodeficiency virus, which causes a range of outcomes constituting AIDS.

The specificity with which a syndrome is defined will substantially affect what can validly be said about it—its distribution by nation and ethnic group, and other characteristics. . . .

A culture, in the anthropological sense, is the set of beliefs, rules of behavior, and customary behaviors maintained, practiced, and transmitted in a given society. Different cultures may be found in a society as a whole or in its segments—for example, in its ethnic groups or social classes.

A syndrome may be regarded as culture-bound if particular cultural conditions are *necessary* for the occurrence of that syndrome; thus the culture-bound syndrome is thought not to occur in the absence of these cultural conditions. Some analysts of culture-bound syndromes may regard specific cultural conditions as *sufficient* for the syndrome's occurrence; in this view, no conditions other than these cultural ones (for example, other cultural conditions or noncultural ones) are necessary to provoke the occurrence of the culture-bound syndrome.

A Hypothetical Ethnography of the Diagnosis Culture-Bound Syndrome

Some of the dilemmas inherent in the notion of culture-bound syndrome are apparent in the ethnographic sources of this diagnosis. The history of specific terms and interpretations of these conditions is most often lost in the memories and notes of colonial settlers. Winzeler provides a rare historical account of the development of notions of latah. Edwards formulates the history of another condition, koro, its multiple names, and purported cases; as in the example of koro described at the outset of this [selection], a person who experiences koro is usually under great stress or anxiety, suffers a retraction of the genitals, and may fear death.

In general, we may guess that the application of the generic label culture-bound syndrome and of terms for specific conditions, such as latah, and "wildman behavior," occurs in a sequence approximating the following:

1. Observers, most often trained in Western medicine, psychiatry, or psychoanalysis, or in anthropology or psychology, visit a foreign setting or an ethnic setting at home. Most often, ethnic settings are those that differ in their culture from the observers' own. Most often, though not always, the observers are white Americans or Europeans.
2. The observers notice behavior that seems strange (that is, unusual by their standards of normality) and indicative of deviance and disturbance. According to their interpretive bent, the observers are likely to take the observed behavior as pathological in some way—medically,

psychiatrically, psychodynamically, behaviorally, and so on. Yet they may not know how to diagnose this pathology since it does not fit the familiar criteria of Western nosology. The culture-bound syndromes were early described as "exotic," a term that may tell us more about its users than about its intended referent.

3. The people among whom the strange behavior occur may offer a solution to the diagnostic dilemma. They may distinguish and label the observed behavior, although recognition of such labels in an unfamiliar setting is problematic. A response to an observer's question (such as, "What and I observing, and what is it called?"), which perhaps is not well understood, may not truly indicate what nevertheless comes to be accepted as an indigenous label for the observed condition. Vallee, for example, suggests that the term for one such condition, *pibloqtoq* (also referred to as "Arctic hysteria"), is the fabrication of early explorers rather than a usual term of Eskimo usage. . . .

4. The observers return home with their prized possession: a new syndrome that, because it seems to be found only in the cultural setting from which they have returned, is labeled culture-bound. Culture-bound syndromes are residual; they are conditions that do not fit the nosological scheme of a Western observer. Rather than questioning the completeness or validity of the Western nosology, the new syndrome is set apart as an oddity from another culture.

5. The observers now face the ambiguous challenge of showing how this culture-bound syndrome actually fits into their own explanatory paradigm. The dilemma here is that, as the phenomenon is encompassed by the observers' explanatory system, it may lose its uniqueness and become a version of the broader phenomenon. Explanatory gain may be culture-specific loss. Analysts of culture-bound syndromes have attempted to keep their syndrome while reducing it also, by showing how social, cultural, and psychological conditions—general elements of their own scheme—are so distinctively configured in the local scene as to make this particular syndrome unlikely to occur elsewhere. Their reductions combine the universal principles of their own discipline—for example, the learning theories of psychology—with the unique cultural peculiarities of the local setting—for example, the specifics of who teaches, what is taught, and how. The local fit and indigenous label appear to give these conditions an immunity from spreading elsewhere; they may *look* like the "xyz" syndrome found elsewhere, but they are really different.

6. Having established a new condition, often distinguished by an ascribed indigenous term, the "discoverer" of this syndrome (or other observers) may then find further instances of similar conditions in new settings, applying the established term, but now crossing cultural boundaries. Amok is the most notorious condition to be exported. . . .

Understanding Culture-Bound Syndromes

Three alternative understandings of culture-bound phenomena are plausible. One may be described as "exclusionist," the other two as "inclusionist." I refer to one inclusionist position as "nature-culture continuum," to the second as "multiple-aspect."

The exclusionist interpretation of culture-bound syndromes is suggested by the phrase "culture-bound syndrome" itself. The phrase implies or assumes that some conditions are culture-bound and others are not. Conditions that are not culture-bound may be regarded as culture-free, culture-blind; perhaps they are thought of as nature-, physiology-, or materiality-bound. In the exclusionist view, that a condition falls in one-half of this divide implies that it does not fall in the other, and vice versa. Latah and amok are culture-bound syndromes; measles and lung cancer are not. This division is held to correspond to disciplinary divisions as well, so that culture-bound syndromes are the concern of anthropological and/or psychological or psychiatric expertise and culture-free syndromes are the subject of medical or physiological examination.

Kenny provides an excellent example of the exclusionist position in his analysis of latah. In Kenny's work, some conditions are regarded as clearly culture-bound and others as clearly universal (though universal conditions may be differently interpreted in different settings).

> Measles or smallpox, for example, are clearly identifiable disease entities, but receive very different cultural interpretations. Is this also true for "latah," "amok," and other ostensibly culture-bound syndromes? In short, are latahlike startle responses better considered [quoting Simons 1980] as the "exploitation of a neurophysiological potential," *or* are they themselves more plausibly considered as the outcome of social *rather than* biological factors? (emphasis added)

Kenny's "or" and "rather than" are exclusive connections. "Disease entities" are regarded as universal phenomena, the results of biological factors; culture-bound syndromes, in contrast, are not diseaselike and result from social factors. Kenny claims that cultural patterns "fully explain" latah; it would thus seem that biological explanation has no room. . . .

Kenny believes the "true" nature of latah to be dramaturgic, an arena he believes unrelated or exclusive of human biology. . . . Kenny writes: "If this is the case, then the latah performance is taken out of the province of biomedical reductionism and is seen in what I take to be its true light—as theater." Kenny here replaces biomedical reductionism with theatrical reductionism.

Psychologist John Carr's interpretation of another Southeast Asian condition, amok, represents a version of the exclusionist position distinct from Kenny's. Though Carr writes that some syndromes are culture-bound, he goes on to formulate a plausible interpretation of amok behavior based on a theory of learning from Western psychology. Carr applies universal principles to the Malay setting, asserting that amok is a learned behavior response to a highly ambiguous yet demanding culture situation. Langness claims that similar cultural conditions—"contradictory demands and discontinuities"—account for "wildman behavior" in New Guinea.

Yet although Carr relates this culture-bound syndrome to universal principles of learning, like Kenny, he explicitly dissociates it from universal processes of disease, as formulated in Biomedicine: "The notion that culture-bound syndromes share underlying common disease forms is rejected. Instead, the ethno-behavioral model postulates that culture-bound syndromes consist of culturally specific behavioral repertoires legitimated by culturally sanctioned norms and concepts, but with both behavior and norms acquired in accordance with basic principles of human learning universal to all cultures."

Using notions of disease and illness developed by Kleinman, Carr associates culture-bound syndromes with illness behavior, which, "as distinct from the disease process, is always culturally determined." He concludes that a culture-bound syndrome is "a distinct repertoire of behaviors that (1) have evolved as the result of a social learning process in which the conceptual and value systems, and the social structural forms that mediate their effects, have served to define the conditions under which such behavior is an appropriate response, and (2) have been legitimated within the indigenous system as *illness* primarily in terms of extreme deviation from the behavioral norm as defined by preeminent culturally-specific conceptual dimensions governing social behavior."

This description of culture-bound syndromes parallels Kleinman's distinction between disease and illness and corresponds to disciplines appropriate to each [as seen in Table 3].

Carr notes, however, that culture-bound syndromes "may be precipitated by any number of etiological factors, among them physical, as well as sociocultural determinants." Thus, the basic cause of amok is thought to be psychological; the particular elements that are psychologically incorporated are culturally specific, and given this established syndrome, a number of precipitants, including physical ones, may elicit this behavior. Carr regards diseases as phenomena that appear universally, in "inviolate" form, and that are the legitimate concern of medicine and psychiatry, whereas illnesses are "always culturally determined" and are thus the legitimate concern of psychology and anthropology. . . .

The inclusionist nature-culture continuum position maintains that all human events, including the supposed culture-bound ones, have cultural *and* biological *and* cognitive *and* psychodynamic aspects, though some events are more profoundly shaped by one of these aspects than by others. Thus, although no conditions are exclusively culture-bound or culture-free, some may be largely culturally shaped and others principally determined by universal physiology. In this conception, the notion of culture-bound syndrome remains a

Table 3

Explanatory Principle

	Culture	Nature
Condition	Culture-bound syndrome Illness	Culture-free syndrome Disease
Discipline	Psychology Anthropology	Physiology Medicine Psychiatry

valid one. An example of the nature-culture continuum position is the work of Leighton and Murphy:

> So far as the total process in the development of psychiatric disorder is concerned, it would seem best to assume that heredity, biological, and psychological factors are all three engaged. To claim dominance for one, or for any subarea within one, *as a matter of general theory,* is to express a linear conception of cause and effect which is out of keeping with what we know about all the processes in the world around us. More germane is an approach to the topic that aims to discover and map out the interrelated factors and the nature of their interrelationships.

The recommendation that the relative importance of heredity, biology, and psychology cannot be theoretically determined in advance but must be empirically analyzed suggests that these factors may have more or less weight for different sicknesses.

The continuum understanding would make the extent to which a condition is culture-bound a matter of degree. It might be possible, at least theoretically, to quantify the proportions in which different factors contribute to given outcome conditions. Measles might occupy the natural, physiological end of this spectrum, the culture-bound syndromes the other; it is not clear what sorts of conditions might fall between—perhaps depression and alcoholism. . . .

Anthropological Queries and Logical Doubts . . .

Defining Syndromes: Category and Context

The prevailing view of culture-bound syndromes is that these behaviors are distinctive of their cultural circumstances. Taken to its extreme, this view has implications that make scientific comparison impossible. All phenomena and events are unique, each differentiable from all others by some or, more likely, by many characteristics: each screw produced in a factory, every case of depression and tuberculosis, every episode of latah. The variations of each occurrence of a phenomenon are explicable, though perhaps not by current knowledge, in terms of the context of that occurrence. Indeed, such explanation is what we mean by "context"—a phenomenon's context is its circumstance, its environment. It is the explanatory power of a phenomenon rather than its simple physical contiguity that constitutes the context of something to be explained. Because one phenomenon is significant in the explanation of another, however, does not bind the two to the exclusion of other explanatory principles. Occurrences of latah may well be different in large and small communities, as manifested by older and younger performers, by one person and another, even by an individual person at different times or in different circumstances. Do we then talk of community-bound, age-bound, person-bound, person-time-circumstance-bound syndromes?

By contextualizing in this way, we end up with a list of occurrences-for-persons-at-times-in-circumstances, and so on, ad infinitum. . . .

In Search of the Whole: Interpretive and Causal Explanation

The exclusionist claim that some behavioral complexes are culture-bound and that others are not, and that the latter fit into some universal scheme, suggests that the culture-bound phenomena are so distinctive that they are beyond comparison. The explanation of such phenomena, exclusionists assume, connects them with other local phenomena and patterns of meaning, rather than with phenomena and patterns elsewhere. This perspective parallels one of two radically different positions that divide anthropology as well as literary studies, historiography, and psychology: interpretive and causal. Culture-bound syndromes provide a perfect example of the interpretive school, since they are thought to be explicable only by their local context.

According to the interpretive understanding, a position also called hermeneutic and phenomenological and sometimes associated with the philosopher Ludwig Wittgenstein, social and cultural phenomena are fully explained when they are shown to fit with their local phenomena in a system that "makes sense." In this view, questions about the causes of the phenomena of interest are regarded as misconceived or tangential. Thus, Kenny objects to attempts to explain culture-bound syndromes by universal, causal principles: "These medical or pseudo-medical labels evoke the notion that there is some kind of causal process underlying *latah*. The interpreters of *latah* seek to identify factors in the life experience of the victim which make her condition inevitable." It is implied that no kind of causality underlies latah. In a more general vein, Geertz writes, "Believing, with Max Weber, that man is an animal suspended in webs or significance he himself has spun, I take culture to be those webs, and the analysis of it to be therefore not an experimental science in search of law but an interpretive one in search of meaning."

Although it is obvious that anthropology is not an experimental science, Geertz goes further to assert that a search for law, presumably causal, excludes a search for interpretation. Interpretation is deemed appropriate only in the study of the workings of culture. Thus Geertz distinguishes blinks, which may be causally analyzed by science, from winks, which are intentional acts shaped by cultural systems to be analyzed by an interpretation of meaning in society and the circumstances of the winker. Yet, at some level, human biology is the mechanism of winks and may be involved in their motivation as well, and blinks, too, may express a symbolic meaning; these two forms of eye movement are not as distinctive as Geertz claims them to be.

. . . [I]f comprehensive explanation rests with those who perform an action, we become ensnared in webs of meaning that lead logically to solipsism [a theory holding that the self can know nothing but its own modifications and that the self is the only existent thing]. If local phenomena and labels for them can be understood only in terms of other local phenomena and their labels, then research across localities, as in much of anthropology, becomes impossible. Anthropologists may pursue their own tales, but not those of others.

Anthropology, Sibling Disciplines, and the Spectrum of Sickness

A conceptual and theoretical solution to the troubles of the exclusionist position might be founded in four principles:

1. A cross-cultural theory of sickness should begin, though not necessarily end, with the indigenous and personal understandings of the sufferer. Forms of suffering that do not fit the Biomedical mold will not be excluded as culture-bound. Patients at home will not be rejected as superstitious or as "crocks" because they fail to fall into Biomedical diagnostics. Pathology would be defined by the experience of the patient rather than by principles that seem a priori universal because they work fairly well among some groups at home and because they can be significantly explained by physiology, also apparently universal. Although a person may be (asymptomatically) unaware of the conditions that might later affect his or her well-being, still the state of well-being itself, and thus the sources of threat to it, are defined by the thought world of the patient him- or herself.

2. Interpreting a human act or syndrome—that is, showing its fit to the understandings and to the local circumstances in which it occurs—may be necessary, but it is not sufficient for full understanding. Minimally, an explanation that some phenomenon occurs in one place because of such-and-such conditions must also show that it does not occur elsewhere, where these conditions are not met. Comparison is a necessity and requires the development of comparative categories so that we may say that this is found here but not there, and that that is found there but not here. Even interpretation itself requires comparative categories; without them, the terms of one language and culture (say, the interpreter's) could not apply to those of another; translation would be impossible; and interpretation could thus be made only in local terms and only for local consumption. Exclusionism, by insisting on the exclusive local fit of all cultural phenomena, thereby precludes comparison; indeed it precludes communication across cultural boundaries.

   The difficulties of causal explanation are notorious, though perhaps better recognized than the hazards of interpretation. Nevertheless causal explanation, however systematic and nonlinear, must be pursued. In this way a universal scheme will come to take local meaning into account.

3. The course of human events is inevitably many-leveled, so that neither our disciplines—such as anthropology, physiology, psychology—nor their central concepts—culture, biochemical exchanges, human experience—can exclusively appropriate any event. That is, human events are not simply cultural or psychological, but inevitably bear these aspects and others.

4. . . . [T]here are several ways in which the organization and culture of societies affect their processes of pathogenesis and healing. Societies inform their members about how the world is divided up and put together. With regard to pathogenic and healthful processes I have recommended three forms of understanding: *disease* models, *illness*

models, and *disorder* models. Societies also engage in the production of sickness because of the ways in which they organize cultural beliefs and social relations. Carr's psychosocial analysis of amok illustrates the pathogenic powers of the social environment.

Such a sociocultural framework applies not only to conditions that are obviously affected, but to the purportedly hard-core diseases as well. The Biomedical model has obscured rather than enlightened such effects. Yet the history of tuberculosis, as brilliantly portrayed by René and Jean Dubos forty years ago, illustrates sociocultural effects in this condition whose biological characteristics appear to be clearly defined. The variety and power of ideology in tuberculosis-like conditions in European society are visible in a great range of attitudes toward this former (and reemerging) "captain of the men of death," its victims sometimes believed to manifest intensified creative powers as they were "consumed." Ideologies continue to be modified. The Duboses suggest that the term *tuberculosis,* already bearing a denotation not directly indicative of contemporary etiological conceptions, could be modified to fit current knowledge. The bacterium itself was then being shown to be neither necessary nor sufficient to the symptomatic complex that we call tuberculosis. The Duboses insisted on the causative importance of the host's sociocultural and natural environment. They also noted that though psychological factors were likely to be of importance, their extent and workings were unknown. A great variety of remedial efforts have also followed beliefs about this condition and about the broader order of social life. Tubercular patients have been revered and isolated, placed in dry climates and wet ones, required to rest and to exercise exhaustively.

Culture, nature, and the human mind between play central roles in diseases commonly thought of in terms of microorganisms and toxins as well as in apparently strange behavioral complexes. Only an inclusionist framework can encompass the range of pathological (and healthy) forms.

Culture-bound syndromes constitute an important frontier between anthropology, Biomedicine, and the medical systems of other societies. Built in premises different from our own, they challenge our standard divisions of things. In striking fashion they have reminded us that our own forms of sickness and of reacting to events do not cover the spectrum of the humanly possible. A comprehensive theory of human reactions and pathology must take them into account.

I have argued that the exclusionist understanding of culture-bound syndromes, implicit in the term, yet not intended by early proponents, distorts the role of culture and of physiology in human affairs. It claims too much of culture at the margin of our nosological scheme and too little of culture at medicine's core. Medical professionals, anthropologists, and others have conspired in a false division of labor. False divisions obstruct understanding. The abandonment of the erroneous category, culture-bound syndrome, might serve to redirect our attention to the formulation of a theory of human sickness in which culture, psychology, and physiology were regarded as mutually relevant across cultural and nosological boundaries.

POSTSCRIPT

Do Some Illnesses Exist Only Among Members of a Particular Culture?

In discussing *phii pob,* Suwanlert accepts this condition as a medical problem that he believes occurs only among rural Thai people. As he outlines the syndrome, he links its occurrence to cultural factors specific to rural communities in transition that are not found in industrial societies. He does not find any systematic correspondence between *phii pob* and psychological diagnoses in the West, and thus he concludes that *phii pob* is a culture-bound syndrome. Hahn, in contrast, steps back from the details of specific conditions described as culture-bound syndromes to ask what they all have in common rather than focus simply on one condition like *phii pob.* He asks, In what sense can these syndromes be seen as distinct from Western diagnostic categories? Hahn concludes that authors like Suwanlert have typically reduced what must be complex illness experiences to a single set of cultural factors. He concludes that there are no culture-bound syndromes; all illness conditions are rooted in the biology and psychology of individual patients but shaped by the cultures in which they live. Thus, culture plays no more important role in *phii pob* than in malaria, pneumonia, cancer, or depression.

Suwanlert and Hahn differ on whether or not conditions like *phii pob* are really so different that they cannot be explained as manifestations or local cultural expressions of more common psychological problems. Suwanlert argues that *phii pob* is unlike anything described in the standard reference manual, *Diagnostic and Statistical Manual of Mental Disorders (DSM-IV),* (American Psychiatric Association, 1994). Hahn contends that the symptoms associated with conditions such as *phii pob* are typically so vague and ambiguous that they only seem to not fit *DSM-IV.* In this instance, patients with *phii pob* may have any subset of the symptoms that include numbness, falling down, convulsions, tensing, clenched fists, short spasms, timidity, and a distinctive kind of vocalizations. None of these symptoms by itself is sufficient to define the condition as *phii pob,* and no particular set of these symptoms are required for the case to be defined as spirit possession.

A similar issue concerns whether or not we could actually compare culture-bound syndromes if they genuinely were bound to particular cultures. Hahn argues that if they were truly culture-bound, comparisons among different kinds of hysterias, wild man behaviors, startle reactions, spirit possessions, and the like would be impossible. Such syndromes would have no common basis for comparison since it is the distinctive cultures, not something in the bodies and psyches of patients, that are causing the conditions. Hahn suggests that comparison among different conditions, such as the comparison Suwanlert provides in his selection, would be impossible.

Ronald C. Simons and Charles C. Hughes edited *The Culture-Bound Syndromes: Folk Illnesses of Psychiatric and Anthropological Interest* (D. Reidel, 1985), which surveys the various syndromes and attempts to sort them into general patterns. This volume has an exhaustive bibliography of primary sources about most of the documented conditions that have been labeled as culture-bound syndromes. Although Simons and Hughes accept the premise of the culture-bound syndrome, they conclude that some conditions probably should not be considered culture-bound, while others, such as Arctic hysteria, *amok,* and *latah,* probably should be accepted as legitimate culture-bound syndromes. Despite the fact that this volume accepts some culture-bound syndromes as distinctive, Hughes challenges the suitability of using this terminology, since many of the conditions can be related to conditions described in the *DSM-IV.*

Suwanlert's selection comes from one of the first collections to document many of the culture-bound syndromes: *Culture-Bound Syndromes, Ethnopsychiatry, and Alternate Therapies,* William P. Lebra, ed. (University Press of Hawaii, 1976). The collection contains detailed discussions of *latah, amok, witiko* psychosis, Arctic hysteria, and other syndromes mentioned here. Another volume of interest to psychological anthropologists and students interested in the relationship between culture and mental health is *Cultural Conceptions of Mental Health and Therapy,* edited by Anthony J. Marsella and Geoffrey M. White (D. Reidel, 1982). For a good discussion of *latah,* see Robert L. Winzeler's *Latah in Southeast Asia: The History and Ethnography of a Culture-Bound Syndrome* (Cambridge University Press, 1995).

ISSUE 15

Is Ethnic Conflict Inevitable?

YES: Sudhir Kakar, from "Some Unconscious Aspects of Ethnic Violence in India," in Veena Das, ed., *Mirrors of Violence: Communities, Riots and Survivors in South Asia* (Oxford University Press, 1990)

NO: Anthony Oberschall, from "The Manipulation of Ethnicity: From Ethnic Cooperation to Violence and War in Yugoslavia," *Ethnic and Racial Studies* (November 2000)

ISSUE SUMMARY

YES: Indian social researcher Sudhir Kakar analyzes the origins of ethnic conflict from a psychological perspective to argue that ethnic differences are deeply held distinctions that from time to time will inevitably erupt as ethnic conflicts. He maintains that anxiety arises from preconscious fears about cultural differences. In his view, no amount of education or politically correct behavior will eradicate these fears and anxieties about people of differing ethnic backgrounds.

NO: American sociologist Anthony Oberschall considers the ethnic conflicts that have recently emerged in Bosnia and contends that primordial ethnic attachments are insufficient to explain the sudden emergence of violence among Bosnian ethnic groups. He adopts a complex explanation for this violence, identifying circumstances in which fears and anxieties were manipulated by politicians for self-serving ends. It was only in the context of these manipulations that ethnic violence could have erupted, concludes Oberschall.

Since the 1960s anthropologists and other social scientists have debated the causes, origins, and necessary conditions for ethnic differences to erupt into ethnic violence. Such discussions have built on an older debate about the origins of ethnicity. In the earlier debate, two key positions emerged. The first is the *primordialist* view, in which ethnic attachments and sentiments emerge from the fact of being members of the same cultural community. Although cultural in origin, the primordialists see kinship, language, and customary practices as the source of ethnic identity and social bonds between people of the same ethnicity. Ethnicity in this view is something one is born with, or at least born into, because it develops as one learns kinship, language, and culture. A second position, often called the *circumstantialist* perspective, was developed by the Norwegian anthropologist Fredrik Barth in his book *Ethnic Groups and Social Boundaries* (Little, Brown, 1969). For Barth, a person's ethnicity is neither fixed nor a natural condition of his or her birth. One's ethnicity could be (and often was) manipulated under different circumstances. By dressing differently, by learning a different language, and by intermarriage, people in many ethnic groups within a generation or two could become members of another ethnic group and have a different ethnic identity. Later, if it became advantageous to be members of the first ethnic group, these same people could acknowledge their past and become members of the first group.

The following selections shift the ethnicity debate to the problem of whether or not ethnic conflict is inevitable. Sudhir Kakar uses a psychological approach to develop a primordialist argument to explain the frequent and almost continual problems of ethnic violence in India. For Kakar, ethnic sentiments and attachments emerge from deep psychological concerns at the unconscious or even preconscious level. He contends that psychologically there are primordial differences between Indians of different ethnic backgrounds, and such differences lead to conflicts over access to resources, jobs, and the like.

Anthony Oberschall considers possible explanations for the sudden appearance of ethnic conflict in the former Yugoslavia. He acknowledges that the primordialist variables of kinship, religion, and language may play some role in explaining why Serbs, Croats, and Bosnian Muslims behaved as they did once ethnic conflict broke out. Traditional animosities existed for centuries in the Balkans, and they reemerged suddenly after 50 years of peace and cooperation. But such variables cannot explain why these groups started fighting with one another in the first place, says Oberschall, after nearly half a century of living together peacefully, regularly socializing, and even intermarrying with one another; such ties as kinship, language, and religion do not explain why tensions flared up or why neighbors suddenly tried to eliminate people of other ethnic backgrounds from their towns and villages. Drawing on a complex pattern of circumstantial variables, Oberschall develops a circumstantialist model, arguing that politicians were manipulating local sentiments for their own ends. In the context of great uncertainty and crisis, people of all ethnic backgrounds bought into the anxieties suggested by their different leaders.

What leads people to hate people of different ethnic backgrounds? Is it deeply held fears of cultural differences? Or does conflict emerge because individuals fear losing what they have worked hard to obtain? How could people in Yugoslavia live together harmoniously for 50 years and then suddenly participate in the "ethnic cleansing" of their neighborhoods? Could the willingness to commit such acts of violence against neighbors have been suppressed for half a century by a strong central government? What is the source of this kind of group hatred, since differences in skin color and physical features are largely not present in either the Indian or Yugoslavian cases?

Sudhir Kakar

Some Unconscious Aspects of Ethnic Violence in India

T he need to integrate social and psychological theory in the analysis of cultural conflicts, i.e. conflicts between ethnic and religious groups, has long been felt while its absence has been equally long deplored. Though everyone agrees on the theoretical questions involved—how do these conflicts originate, develop, and get resolved; how do they result in violent aggression—a general agreement on the answers or even on how to get these answers moves further and further away.

A large part of the problem in the study of these questions lies with the nature of and the crisis within the social sciences. The declining fortunes of logical positivism, hastened in the last twenty years by the widespread circulation and absorption of the views of such thinkers as Gadamer, Habermas, Derrida, Ricouer and Foucault, has led to a plethora of new models in the sciences of man and society. The dominant model of yesteryears—social science as social physics—is now only one among several clamouring for allegiance and adherents. It incorporates only one view among many on the nature of social reality and of social science knowledge. Anthropology, sociology, political science, psychology and even economics are all becoming more pluralistic and scattering into frameworks. In such a situation, the calls for a general theory of ethnic violence or indeed (as Clifford Geertz has remarked) of anything *social,* sound increasingly hollow, and the claims to have one science seem megalomaniacal. Thus, without taking recourse to other disciplines and even ignoring the grand theories of human aggression in psychology itself—those of animal ethology, sociology, Freudian Thanatos and so on—I would like to present some limited 'local knowledge' observations on ethnic violence in India from a psychoanalytic perspective.

In the manner of a clinician, let me begin with the concrete data on which I base my observations on the first question, namely the origins of ethnic conflict. The data for these observations, and those which follow, come from diverse sources: spirit possession in north India, dreams of psychotherapy patients, eavesdropping on group discussions at the Golden Temple complex in July 1984, and finally, personal participation in large religious assemblies.

The Other in Ethnic Conflict

Some years ago, while studying the phenomenon of possession by spirits in rural north India, I was struck by a curious fact. In a very large number of cases, 15 out of 28, the *bhuta* or malignant spirit possessing Hindu men and women turned out to be a Muslim. When, during the healing ritual, the patient went into a trance and the spirit started expressing its wishes, these wishes invariably turned out to be those which would have been horrifying to the patient's conscious self. In one case, the Muslim spirit possessing an elderly Brahmin priest vigorously insisted on eating kababs. The five women surrounding the man who had engaged the *bhuta* in conversation were distinctly disheartened that he had turned out to be a *Sayyad* and one of them lamented: 'These Mussulmans! They have ruined our *dharma* but they are so strong they can withstand our gods.' In another case, the *bhuta* inhabiting a young married woman not only expressed derogatory sentiments towards her 'lord and master' but also openly stated its intentions of bringing the mother-in-law to a violent and preferably bloody end.

Possession by a Muslim *bhuta,* then, seemed to reflect the afflicted person's desperate efforts to convince himself and others that his hunger for forbidden foods and uncontrolled rage towards those who should be loved and respected, as well as all other imagined transgressions and sins of the heart, belonged to the Muslim destroyer of taboos and were furthest away from his 'good' Hindu self. In that Muslim *bhutas* were universally considered to be the strongest, vilest, the most malignant and the most stubborn of the evil spirits, the Muslim seemed to symbolize the alien and the demonic in the unconscious part of the Hindu mind.

The division of humans into mutually exclusive group identities of tribe, nation, caste, religion and class thus seems to serve two important psychological functions. The first is to increase the feeling of well being in the narcissistic realm by locating one's own group at the centre of the universe, superior to others. The shared grandiose self, maintained by legends, myths and rituals, seems to demand a concomitant conviction that other groups are inferior.

India has not been exempt from this universal rule. Whatever idealizing tendencies we might have in viewing our past history, it is difficult to deny that every social group in its tales, ritual and other literature, has sought to portray itself nearer to a purer, divine state while denigrating and banishing others to the periphery. It is also undeniable that sharing a common ego-ideal and giving one's own group a super-individual significance can inspire valued human attributes of loyalty and heroic self-sacrifice. All this is familiar to students of culture and need not detain us further here.

For the psychoanalyst it is the second function of division into ethnic groups, namely the need to have other groups as containers for one's disavowed aspects, which is of greater significance. These disavowed aspects, or the demonic spirits, take birth during that period of our childhood when the child, made conscious of good and bad, right and wrong, begins to divide himself into two parts, one that is the judge and the other that is being judged. The unacceptable, condemned parts of the self are projected outside, the projective processes being primitive attempts to relieve pain by externalizing it. The expelled parts of the self are then attached to various beings—animals and human—as well as to whole castes, ethnic and religious communities. This early split within our nature, which gives us a future license to view and treat others as if they were no better than the worst in ourselves, is normally completed by the time the child is six to seven years old. The earliest defenses for dealing with the unacceptable aspects of the self—namely their denial, the splitting from awareness and projection onto another group—require the active participation of the members of the child's group-parents and other adults who must support such a denial and projection. They are shared group defenses. The family and extended group of a Hindu upper-caste child, for instance, not only provides him with its myths and rituals which increase his sense of group cohesion and of narcissism in belonging to such an exalted entity, but also help him in elaborating and fleshing out his demonology of other ethnic and religious groups. The *purana* of the Muslim demon, for instance, as elaborated by many Hindu groups, has nothing to do with Sufi saints, the prophet's sayings or the more profound sentiments of Islam. Instead, its stories are of rape and pillage by the legions of Ghazni and Timur as well as other more local accounts of Muslim mayhem.

The Muslim demon is, so to say, the traditional container of Hindu conflicts over aggressive impulses. It is the transgressor of deeply-held taboos, especially over the expression of physical violence. Recent events in Punjab, I am afraid, are creating yet another demon in the Hindu psyche of north India. Over the last few years, tales of [Sikh militant leader] Bhindranwale's dark malevolence and the lore of murderous terrorists has led to a number of reported dreams from patients where Sikhs have appeared as symbols of the patient's own aggressive and sadistic superego. A group of Sikhs with raised swords chasing a patient who has broken into an old woman's shop, a Nihang stabbing a man repeatedly with a spear on the street while another patient as a frightened child looks down upon the scene from an upstairs window—these are two of many such dream images. Leaving aside the role played by these images in the patients' individual dramas, the projection of the feared aggressive parts of the self on the figure of the Sikh is an unhappy portent for the future relationship between the two communities. The fantasy of being overwhelmed by the frightening aggressive strength of the Sikhs can, in periods of upheaval and danger—when widespread regression in ego takes place and the touch with reality is weakened—lead to psychotic delusions about Sikh intentions.

Sikh Militancy

Until this point I have used some psychoanalytic, especially Kleinian, concepts of splitting and projective identification to understand data that bears on the question of ethnic conflict. More specifically, I have outlined the origins of certain pre-conscious attitudes of Hindus towards Muslims and Sikhs. These attitudes reflect the psychological needs of the child, and the adult, to split off his bad impulses, especially those relating to violence, and to attach them to other communities, a process supported and reinforced by other members of the group. Let me now use another set of analytical concepts of group identity and narcissism, narcissistic hurt and rage, to understand the phenomenon of Sikh militancy. To avoid any misunderstanding let me state at the outset that I am primarily talking about the militant Sikh youth of Punjab, not of all Sikh youths, and certainly not of the Sikh community as a whole. Also, the word narcissism in psychoanalysis is not used in a pejorative sense but, together with sexuality and aggression, as the third major and fundamental motivational factor in human beings which is concerned with the maintenance of self-esteem. The data for these observations comes from being an observer of heated and anguished discussions among randomly formed groups which were being spontaneously held all over the Golden Temple complex in Amritsar, five weeks after Operation Blue Star.* said elsewhere, the aftermath of Blue Star, which heightened the awareness of their cultural identity among many Sikhs, also brought out in relief one of its less conscious aspects. I have called it the Khalsa warrior element of Sikh identity which, at least since the tenth guru and at least among the Jats, has expressed itself in images of 'lifting up the sword' against the 'oppression of a tyrannical ruler', and whose associated legends only countenance two possible outcomes—complete victory (*fateh*) or martyrdom (*shaheedi*) of those engaged in the battle. The surrounding society has of course reinforced this identity element over the years by its constant talk of Sikh martial process and valour. The Sikh youth's acceptance of these projections of heroic militancy made by the Hindu can lead to his overestimation of this aspect of his identity as he comes to feel that it is his very essence. All other qualities which may compromise heroic militancy, such as yearnings for passivity, softness and patience, will tend to be denied, split off and projected onto other, despised groups. The damage done to the Akal Takht—as much a symbol of corporate militancy as of religious piety—reinforced the two M's— militance and martyrdom—the inner counterparts of the well-known five K's which constitute the outer markers of the Khalsa warrior identity. The exaggerated value placed on martyrdom is hard to understand for Hindus since oppressors in *their* mythology—the Hindu equivalent of Sikh legendary history—tended to be destroyed by divine intervention rather than by the sacrifice of martyrs.

The army action was then a hurt to Sihk religious sentiments in a very different way from the sense in which a Hindu understands the term. It was an affront to group narcissism, to a shared grandiose self. The consequent feelings were of narcissistic hurt and rage. This was brought home to me again and again as I listened to groups of anguished men and women in front of the ruins of the Akal Takht. Most men stood in attitudes of sullen

---

* [Operation 'Blue Star' was the code name for the army action to clear the Golden Temple of Sikh militants in June 1984, in which Bhindranwale died. The operation resulted in extensive damage to the sacred site.—Ed.]

defeat, scorned and derided by the women with such sentences as 'Where is the starch in your moustache now?'

Given the collective need for the preservation of this core of the group identity, the Golden Temple action automatically completed a circle of associations. The army action to clear Akal Takht from desperadoes became an attack on the Sikh nation by a tyrannical 'Delhi durbar'. It was seen as an assault designed to wipe out all its traces, its *nishan*—since this is how it was in the past. The Sikhs killed in the attack were now defenders of the faith and martyrs—since this too is a pattern from the past. The encounter was viewed as a momentous battle, an oppressive empire's defeat of the forces of the Khalsa. The relatively heavy army losses are not a consequence of its restraint but a testimony to the fighting qualities of the Khalsa warrior. Paradoxically, the terrorist losses were exaggerated to simultaneously show the overwhelming strength of the army and the Khalsa readiness to die in martyrdom when victory is not possible.

Bhindranwale, in dramatically exemplifying the two M's of militancy and martyrdom, has touched deep chords. His status with much of the Sikh youth today is very near that of an eleventh guru. Initially, Bhindranwale may have been one of many *sants,* though more militant than most, who dot the countryside in Punjab. What began the process of his elevation was his successful defiance of the government—echoes, again of Sikh history, of defiant gurus contesting state authority. In setting the date and terms of his arrest ('*Santji* gave arrest', and not 'He was arrested', is how the people at the Temple complex put it), and predicting the day of his release, Bhindranwale began to be transformed from a mortal preacher to a 'realized' saint with miraculous powers. (And the reputation of being able to work miracles is, we know, essential for those aspiring to enter the portals of gurudom in all religious traditions.) His 'martyrdom' has now cemented the transformation and made his elevation into the Sikh militant pantheon irreversible. The tortures and murders in the Temple complex or outside are no longer his responsibility, being seen as the doings of deluded associates, acts of which Santji was, of course, unaware.

It is obvious that after the army action there was a threat to the cultural identity of at least a section of the Jat Sikh youth. This led to regressive transformations in the narcissistic realm, where reality is interpreted only as a balm to narcissistic hurt and as a coolant for narcissistic rage. It needs to be asked what precisely constituted this threat. I would tend to see the threat to the Jat Sikh group identity as part of a universal modernizing process to which many groups all over the world have been and continue to be exposed. This group though has preferred to change a social-psychological issue into a political one. The cultural decay and spiritual disintegration talked of in the Anandpur resolution are then viewed as an aspect of majority-minority relations rather than as an existential condition brought on by the workings of a historical fate. A feeling of inner threat is projected outside as oppression, a conflict around tradition and modernity as a conflict around power.

Narcissistic rage, then, is the core of the militancy of Sikh youth and Sikh terrorism. As Kohut says about this rage: 'The need for revenge, for righting a wrong, for undoing a hurt by whatever means, and a deeply anchored, unrelating compulsion in the pursuit of all these aims, gives no rest to those who have suffered a narcissistic injury.' For the analyst, this becomes paramount in the understanding of youthful militancy, the foreground, while political, social and other issues recede into the background.

Let me now make a few observations on the question of ethnic conflict resulting in violent aggression, i.e on mob violence. My data for these remarks is, paradoxically, personal participation in largely peaceful and loving groups engaged in religious and spiritual endeavours. Yet many of the psychological processes are common to the two kinds of groups. Both emotionally charged religious assemblies and mobs on the rampage bring out in relief the vulnerability of human individual ego functions confronted with the power of group processes. In the face of these, the 'integrity', 'autonomy', and 'independence' of the ego seem to be wishful illusions and hypothetical constructs. Mobs, more than religious congregations, provide striking examples of the massive inducement, by group processes, of individuals towards a new identity and behaviour of the sort that would ordinarily be repudiated by a great majority of the individuals so induced. They illustrate, more clearly than in any other comparable social situation, the evanescence of rational thought, the fragility of internalized behavioural controls, values, and moral and ethical standards.

The most immediate experience in being part of a crowd is the sensual pounding received in the press of other bodies. At first there may be a sense of unease as the body, the container of our individuality and the demarcator of our boundaries in space, is sharply wrenched away from its habitual way of experiencing others. For, as we grow up, the touch of others, once so deliberately courted and responded to with delight, increasingly becomes a problem. Coming from a loved one, touch is deliciously welcomed; with strangers, on the other hand, there is an involuntary shrinking of the body, their touch taking on the menacing air of invasion by the other.

But once the fear of touch disappears in the fierce press of other bodies and the individual lets himself become a part of the crowd's density, the original apprehension is transformed into an expansiveness that stretches to include others. Distances and differences—of class, status, age, caste hierarchy—disappear in an exhilarating feeling that individual boundaries can indeed be transcended and were perhaps illusory in the first place. Of course, touch is only one of the sensual stimuli that hammers at the gate of individual identity. Other excitations, channelled through vision, hearing and smell, are also very much involved. In addition, there are exchanges of body heat, muscle tension and body rhythms which take place in a crowd. In short, the crowd's assault on the sense of individuality, its invitation to transcend one's individual boundaries and its offer of a freedom from personal doubts and anxieties is well nigh irresistible.

The need and search for 'self-transcending' experience, to lose one's self in the group, suspend judgement and reality-testing, is, I believe, the primary motivational factor in both religious assembly and violent mob, even though the stated purpose is spiritual uplift in one and mayhem and murder in the other. Self-transcendence, rooted in the blurring of our body image, not only opens us to the influx of the divine but also heightens our receptivity to the demonic. The surge of love also washes away the defences against the emergence of archaic hates. In psychoanalytic terms, regression in the body image is simultaneous with regression in the superego system. Whether the ego reacts to this regression in a disintegrated fashion with panic that manifests itself (in a mob) in senseless rage and destructive acts—or in a release of love encompassing the group and the world outside—depends on the structure provided to the group. Without the rituals which make tradition palpable and thus extend the group in time by giving assurances of continuity to the beleaguered ego, and without the permanent visibility of leaders whose presence is marked by conspicuous external insignia and who replace the benign and loving functions of the superego, religious crowds can easily turn into marauding mobs. Transcending individuality by merging into a group can generate heroic self-sacrifice but also unimaginable brutality. To get out of one's skin in a devotional assembly is also at the same time to have less regard for saving it in a mob.

Some Implications

The implications of my remark, I know, are not too comforting. The need for communities, our own to take care of our narcissistic needs and of others to serve as recipients for our hostility and destructiveness, are perhaps built into our very ground-plan as human beings. Well meaning educative efforts in classrooms or in national integration seminars are for the most part too late and too little in that they are misdirected. They are too late since most of the evidence indicates that the communal imagination is well entrenched by the time a child enters school. They are misdirected in that they never frankly address the collective—and mostly preconscious—fears and wishes of the various communities. Demons do not much care for 'correct' interpretations of religious texts by scholars, nor are they amenable to humanist pleas of reason to change into good and loving beings. All we can do is accept their existence but reduce their potential for causing actual physical violence and destruction. The routes to this goal, the strategies for struggle with our own inner devils, are many. One strategy strives for the dissolution of small group identities into even large entities. Sikhs and Hindus in Punjab can move towards a group identity around 'Punjabiyyat', in which case the despised demon shifts outside to the *Purubia* or the *Madrasi*. One can go on to progressively larger identities of the nationalist Indian whose *bete-noire* can then be the Pakistani or the Chinese. One can envisage even larger groupings, for instance of the 'Third World', where the sense of narcissistic well being provided by this particular community needs a demonic West as the threatening aggressor.

A second strategy is, in a certain sense, to go the opposite way. By this I mean less the encouragement of various ethnic identities than in ensuring that all manifestations of ethnic group action—assemblies, demonstrations, processions—are given as much religious structure as possible in order to prevent the breakout of archaic hate. Vedic chants and Koranic prayers, *mahants, pujaris* and *mullahs* in their full regalia and conspicuous by their presence, are fully encouraged to be in the forefront of religious processions and demonstrations. Traditional religious standards, flags and other symbols are liberally used to bind the religious assemblies.

Yet another strategy (and let me note that none of these are exclusive) is to concentrate all efforts at the containment of the communal demon on the dominant community. We know that the belief of the dominant party in a relationship often becomes a self-fulfilling prophecy, involuntarily changing the very consciousness of the weaker partner. In India the Hindu image of himself and of other communities is apt to be incorporated in the self image of non-Hindu minorities. Even when consciously accepted, the denigrating part of the image is likely to be a source of intensive unconscious rage in other communities. Their rage is stored up over a period of time, till it explodes in all its violent manifestations whenever historical circumstances sanction such eruptions.

Anthony Oberschall

The Manipulation of Ethnicity: From Ethnic Cooperation to Violence and War in Yugoslavia

Four views on ethnicity and ethnic violence are common. In the 'primordial' view, ethnic attachments and identities are a cultural given and a natural affinity, like kinship sentiments. They have an overpowering emotional and non-rational quality. Applied to the former Yugoslavia, the primordialist believes that despite seemingly cooperative relations between nationalities in Yugoslavia, mistrust, enmity, even hatred were just below the surface, as had long been true in the Balkans. Triggered by fierce competition for political power during the breakup of Yugoslavia and driven by the uncertainties over state boundaries and minority status, these enmities and hatreds, fuelled by fear and retribution, turned neighbour against neighbour, and district against district, in an expanding spiral of aggression and reprisals. Although the primordial account sounds plausible, and it is true that politicians activated and manipulated latent nationalism and ethnic fears, some evidence contradicts it. Ethnic cleansing was more commonly militias and military against civilians than neighbour against neighbour. In seventeen assaults against villages during the ethnic cleansing of Prijedor district in Bosnia in May/June 1992, we found that the aggressors wore military and paramilitary uniforms and insignia. In fourteen assaults, the survivors did not recognize any of the aggressors, who did not bother to wear masks or disguises. These 'weekend warriors' from central Serbia openly bivouacked at the Prijedor police station. The primordial theory omits the fact that ethnic hatreds can subside as a consequence of statecraft and living together. [President Charles] de Gaulle and [Chancellor Konrad] Adenauer managed to reconcile the French and German people. Why no lasting conciliation in Yugoslavia after forty years of ethnic peace?

In the second, 'instrumentalist' view, ethnic sentiments and loyalties are manipulated by political leaders and intellectuals for political ends, such as state creation. For Yugoslavia, the instrumentalist explanation highlights Serb nationalists' goal of a Greater Serbia, and a similar Croat nationalism. Ethnic cleansing resulted from a historical longing by Serbs

From Anthony Oberschall, "The Manipulation of Ethnicity: From Ethnic Cooperation to Violence and War in Yugoslavia," *Ethnic and Racial Studies*, vol. 23, no. 6 (November 2000). Copyright © 2000 by Routledge Journals, Taylor & Francis Ltd. Reprinted by permission of the author and Taylor & Francis Ltd. http://www.tandf.co.uk/journals. Notes and references omitted.

in Croatia at first backed moderate nationalists, for a Greater Serbia, with deep cultural roots. [Slobodan] Milosevic and Serb nationalists tried to implement it when the opportunity arose in the late 1980s and early 1990s. Greater Serbia required ethnic cleansing of non-Serbs from areas inhabited by a majority of Serbs and the corridors linking Serb population clusters. Although there is evidence that ethnic cleansing was a state policy, orchestrated by the highest authorities in Serbia and the Bosnian Serb leadership, this explanation ignores that many Bosnian Serbs did not want secession, that many Serbs in Croatia at first backed moderate nationalists, and that many Serbs evaded the draft. The instrumentalist view assumes an ethnic consensus that initially does not exist. But if many were reluctant to wage war and to participate in ethnic cleansing, how did ethnic extremists prevail over these moderates?

The third 'constructionist' view of ethnicity and ethnic conflict was originally formulated by [Leo] Kuper. It supplements the insights of the primordial and of the instrumentalist views. Religion or ethnicity are very real social facts, but in ordinary times they are only one of several roles and identities that matter. There is a great deal of variance in a population on ethnic attachments and identities. In the words of [Juan J.] Linz and [Alfred] Stepan 'political identities are less primordial and fixed than contingent and changing. They are amenable to being constructed or eroded by political institutions and political choices'. The constructionist view offers insights but is incomplete. How are nationality and ethnicity constructed and eroded by political mobilization and mass media propaganda?

A fourth model of ethnic violence centres on state breakdown, anarchy, and the security dilemma that such conditions pose to ethnic groups who engage in defensive arming to protect their lives and property against ethnic rivals, which then stimulates arming by other ethnic groups like an arms race between states. The driving motivations are not ethnic hatreds but fear and insecurity. In the Yugoslav crisis Michael Ignatieff puts it thus:

> Once the Yugoslav communist state began to split into its constituent national particles the key question soon became: will the local Croat policeman protect me if I am a Serb? Will I keep my job in the soap factory if my new boss is a Serb or a Muslim? The answer to this question was no, because no state remained to enforce the old ethnic bargain.

There is a security dilemma in ethnic conflict, but why so much ethnic violence without state breakdown? Can insecurity and fear be spread by propaganda even when daily experience contradicts the allegations of ethnic hostility and threat? Can the powerful fear the weak?

Building on the four views and mindful of [Rogers] Brubaker and [David] Laitin's criteria for a satisfactory theory of ethnic violence, I use the idea of latent nationalism at the grass roots, and show how it was activated; I highlight ethnic manipulation by political leaders, and explain why manipulation was successful; I take into account the variance in ethnic identities and analyse why extremists prevailed over moderates; I focus on the security dilemma and ethnic fears and insecurity, and show how fears and insecurity grew from lies and propaganda. To this arsenal of concepts and models for generating the dynamics of ethnicization and collective violence, I add 'cognitive frames'. Combining all, I seek to explain how forty years of cooperative ethnic relations ended with collective violence and war.

Prijedor: A Case-Study

To get a sense of what is to be explained about ethnic conflict and violence at the grass roots, consider the Prijedor district in Northwest Bosnia where major ethnic violence took place in the spring of 1992. In the 1991 Census, Prijedor district was 42.5 percent Serb and 44 percent Muslim. It was surrounded by districts that had either a slight Serb majority or were close to even, as Prijedor was. Prijedor Serbs were not an isolated Serb minority island surrounded by a sea of Muslims and Croats.

There had been no Serb complaints of mistreatment, discrimination, or intimidation in Prijedor by non-Serbs, or vice versa. On the contrary, as a bewildered Muslim refugee from Prijedor stated,

> In Prijedor there were no conflicts between nationalities. We didn't make the distinctions. My colleague at work was an Orthodox Serb, we worked together. When we were children we went to the Orthodox church or the mosque together . . . I don't understand. Before there were never any problems between us. We lived together. My sister is married to a Serb, and a brother of my wife is married to a Croat.

According to the [United Nations] Bassiouni Report, Serbs held the leading positions in Prijedor in 1991, as they had done for decades. . . . In the 1991 elections, the predominantly Muslim SDA [Party of Democratic Union in Bosnia] won thirty seats; the Serb SDS [Serbian Democratic Party] twenty-eight, and thirty-two went to other parties. The Muslims refrained from taking over a number of leading posts to which their electoral victory entitled them because they believed in power-sharing. Even so, the SDS blocked the work of the Prijodor Assembly and organized a parallel governance for Serbs, in alliance with the SDS leaders in nearby Banja Luka. In Bosnia as a whole, the Serbs shared political power and controlled the most important military forces.

As in other towns and cities in Bosnia, the SDS in Prijedor organized a successful Serb plebiscite for Greater Serbia. A parallel Serb governance, called the 'Crisis Committee', secretly created an armed force of Serbs with weapons obtained from Serbia. Serb crisis committees were also formed among Serbs in some of Prijedor district's towns and villages. On the night of 29 April 1992, without any provocation or a shot being fired, 1,775 well-armed Serbs seized the city of Prijedor in a *coup d'état*. By this time the Prijedor local government had completely lost power to various Serb groups. Paramilitaries had seized the radio and television transmitters and cut off all but Serb transmissions. The Serb *coup d'état* in Prijedor is similar to what happened elsewhere in Northern Bosnia.

Non-Serb leaders were arrested and shortly afterwards disappeared, presumed executed. The Muslim police and other officials were fired from their posts. Schools closed; the newspaper ceased publication, and a Serb paper was started. Non-Serbs were harassed, intimidated, fired from their jobs. Amid incessant house searches, weapons, mostly hunting guns, belonging to non-Serbs, were rounded up. After the attempt on 30 May by the Patriotic League of Croats and Muslims—an armed formation of 150 fighters—to retake the old city, many non-Serb inhabitants were arrested and sent to the infamous Omarskca camp. At Omarska, prisoners were tortured, brutalized, starved and killed. The guards were rural Serbs from nearby villages; the interrogators were Prijedor police inspectors. . . . People were rounded up and some were executed: those shot were Muslim leaders whose names appeared on a list. Atrocities took place elsewhere in the district.

Several observations should be made about the events in Prijedor. Muslims and Serbs had lived in peace before the conflict erupted. The Serbs were neither a numerical minority, nor discriminated against. They not only had a share of power, but they had the biggest share, and they were well armed. Why, then, did Serbs fear their fellow citizens in Prijedor? A cartoon from this period expresses the puzzle well. It shows a bearded Serb paramilitary, armed to the teeth, with guns, hand-granades, ammunition belts, knives, waving a machine gun, looking worried, and yelling at the top of his voice, 'I am being threatened!' There was no anarchy, no state breakdown in Prijedor. The Serbs used the police and military of a functioning government to subdue the non-Serbs. Serbs may have been apprehensive about their future in an independent Bosnia, but even in Bosnia they had a big presence—numerical, military, political, economic. There was no spontaneous violence initiated by Serb civilians against non-Serbs, nor vice-versa. Instead, there was a highly organized, secretly prepared *coup d'état,* like the 1917 Bolshevik seizure of power in Russia. . . . As in the Russian revolution with the Soviets, the Serb parallel government was not only an instrument for seizing power from non-Serbs but of stripping the moderate Serbs of any influence and authority.

What was the reaction of ordinary Serbs to these events? Though there is no information on Prijedor itself, one can learn from what observers recorded in nearby Banja Luka. Peter Maas reports that a Serb lawyer there estimated that 30 percent of Serbs oppose such things [ethnic cleansing], 60 percent agree or are confused and go along with the 10 percent who 'have the guns and control the television tower'. . . . An armed, organized 10 percent who control mass communications can have its way when the majority supports it overtly or tacitly or is confused, and when the opposition is unorganized, divided, and scared. One has to explain how it was that 60 percent were supportive of or confused on ethnic cleansing, since their support and quiescence were necessary for the success of the extremist 10 percent.

Was Violent Conflict Inevitable?

In a multinational state such as Yugoslavia, nationality will be a salient dimension of political contention, and there will be leaders and intellectuals with a nationalist ideology and agenda. The Yugoslav constitution and its political institutions were delicately balanced and crafted to deal with nationality.

A nationalist challenge would inevitably zero in on stateness, minority rights and power-sharing: if accepted boundaries of political units are renegotiated or remade, who decides which peoples and territories belong to new and old political entities? Will all peoples in the new units be equal citizens for governance, or will majority ethnonational affiliation become the admission ticket for full citizenship?

Once unleashed, nationalism in Yugoslavia set on a collision course the two largest nationalities, the Serbs and the Croats. With a quarter of Serbs living outside Serbia; a centralized Yugoslav state was a guarantor of Serb security. For Croats and their history of opposition to Hapsburg rule, a decentralized state and weak federation meant control of their own destinies, unencumbered by inefficient state agencies and enterprises staffed and controlled by Serbs. Nevertheless, nationality issues could have been sorted out with democratic institutions in a confederation, with collective rights for minorities, and with systems of political representation in elections and collective decision rules in assemblies that would protect minority voice and favour coalitions rather than majority domination. With these reforms, nationalist leaders would have found it difficult to rally the citizenry to their cause.

In a country with great differences in economic development and standards of living between the Republics, there will be disagreements over economic policies, taxation, transfer, subsidies across regions, and abandoning socialism for a market economy. All Republics had experienced dramatic economic gains since World War II. Yugoslavia was not beyond economic repair.

As in other communist states in the late 1980s, the Yugoslav communist leaders wanted to remain in power. Some reprogrammed as reform communists, and hoped to move into European-style social democracy. Others chose ethnonationalism as the issue that would carry them to power and create a new principle of legitimacy for the post-communist regime. Moderate nationalists stood for conciliation among nationalities; extremists were willing to pursue their goals with force and violence. The defeat of the moderates was not inevitable. Why did xenophobic nationalism resonate with the citizenry? How is it that when the media unleashed the war of words and symbols before the war of bullets, so many believed the exaggerations, distortions and fabrications that belied their personal experiences?

Ethnic Relations Before the Crisis

Survey research on ethnic relations in mid-1990 found that in a national sample of 4,232 Yugoslavs, only 17 percent believed that the country would break up into separate states, and 62 percent reported that the 'Yugoslav' affiliation was very or quite important for them. On ethnonational relations, in workplaces, 36 percent characterized them as 'good', 28 percent as 'satisfactory', and only 6 percent said 'bad' and 'very bad'. For ethnonational relations in neighborhoods, 57 percent answered 'good', 28 percent 'satisfactory', and only 12 percent chose 'bad' and 'very bad'. For the majority of Yuogoslavs, on the eve of the Yugoslav wars, nationalist contention in the public arena did not translate into hostile interpersonal ethnic relations. . . .

Ignatieff is puzzled, 'What is difficult to understand about the Balkan tragedy is how . . . nationalist lies ever managed to take root in the soil of shared village existence. . . . In order for war to occur, nationalists had to convince neighbors and friends that in reality they had been massacring each other since time immemorial.'

The Manipulation of Ethnicity

For explaining ethnic manipulation one needs the concept of a cognitive frame. A cognitive frame is a mental structure which situates and connects events, people and groups into a meaningful narrative in which the social world that one inhabits makes sense and can be communicated and shared with others. Yugoslavs experienced ethnic relations through two frames: a normal frame and a crisis frame. People possessed both frames in their minds: in peaceful times the crisis frame was dormant, and in crisis and war the normal frame was suppressed. Both frames were anchored in private and family experiences, in culture and in public life. In the normal frame, which prevailed in [Josip Broz] Tito's Yugoslavia, ethnic relations were cooperative and neighbourly. Colleagues and workers, schoolmates and teammates transacted routinely across nationality. Some did not even know or bother to know another's nationality. Intermarriage was accepted. Holidays were spent in each others' Republics. Except in Kosovo, the normal frame prevailed for most Yugoslavs throughout the 1980s.

The crisis frame was grounded in the experiences and memories of the Balkan wars, the first and second world wars—and other wars before that. In these crises, civilians were not distinguished from combatants. Old people, children, women, priests were not spared. Atrocities, massacres, torture, ethnic cleansing, a scorched-earth policy were the rule. Everyone was held collectively responsible for their nationality and religion, and became a target of revenge and reprisals. . . .

Tito had wanted to eradicate the crisis frame, but it simmered in the memories of older people, the families of victims, intellectuals and religious leaders. Milosevic, Tudjman and other nationalists did not invent the crisis frame; they activated and amplified it. . . .

If the normal frame prevailed in the 1980s as shown by . . . survey findings, how did nationalists activate and amplify the crisis frame after decades of dormancy? The emotion that poisons ethnic relations is fear: fear of extinction as a group, fear of assimilation, fear of domination by another group, fear for one's life and property, fear of being a victim once more. After fear comes hate. The threatening others are demonized and dehumanized. The means of awakening and spreading such fears in Yugoslavia were through the newsmedia, politics, education, popular culture, literature, history and the arts.

The crisis frame in Yugoslavia was first resurrected by Serb intellectuals over the plight of the Kosovo Serbs. . . .

Fear of extinction was spread with highly inflated figures on the ethnic killings in World War II. . . .

In my interview with a Serb refugee one can trace how the atrocities discourse switched on the crisis frame: 'We were afraid because nationalists revived the memory of World War II atrocities . . . nationalist graffiti on walls awakened fears of past memories; it was a sign that minorities [Serbs in Croatia] would not be respected and safe'.

Fears of domination, oppression and demographic shrinkage were roused by the incessant rape and genocide discourse. . . .

Ordinary people echo the intellectuals' and the media crisis discourse. . . . Peter Maas asks a Serb refugee couple why they had fled their village. Their answer: Muslims planned to take over, a list of names had been drawn up, Serb women were to be assigned to Muslim harems after the men had been killed. They had heard about it on the radio; the Serb military had uncovered the plan. The journalist probes: 'Did any Muslims in the village ever harm you?' They reply, 'Oh no, our relations with the Muslims in the village were always good, they were decent people'. In the minds of the Serb couple, the crisis frame had eclipsed the normal frame. What under peaceful circumstances were totally implausible events—young women become sexual slaves in harems for breeding janissaries; a fifteenth- and sixteenth-century style Turkish/Islamic invasion of Europe—become credible narratives of ethnic annihilation and domination within the crisis frame.

Fear and the crisis frame provided opportunities for nationalists to mobilize a huge ethnic constituency, get themselves elected to office, and organize aggressive actions against moderates and other ethnics. . . .

Populist nationalism worked. The Vojvodina and Montenegro party leaderships resigned and were replaced by Milosevic loyalists. Abolishing the autonomous provinces of Kosovo and Vojvodina precipitated a constitutional crisis. . . . The nationality balance in Yugoslav politics was thus disturbed. Serbia gained control of over half the votes in all federal bodies and institutions. Slovenes and Croats reacted with their own nationalism.

There was grass-roots resistance to nationalism and to activation of the crisis frame. A content analysis of news stories in *Oslobodjenje* for 1990 indicates that municipalities, youth and veterans' organizations, and trade unions repeatedly protested against ethnic polarization and hatreds. . . . Important as this opposition was, it was countered by the spread of populist nationalism. *Oslobodjenje* in 1990 is full of affirmations of national symbols and identities: the renaming of localities; the reburial of bones of atrocity victims from World War II; nationalist graffiti on churches, mosques, monuments and in cemeteries; fights over flags, ethnic insults, nationalist songs, ethnic vandalism. To many, these were signs that normal times were sliding into crisis, and the authorities had lost control.

Mass communications and propaganda research help to explain why ethnic manipulation worked and why the crisis frame eclipsed the normal frame. First, . . . fear arousing appeals, originating in a threat, were powerful and effective in changing opinion and belief. Furthermore, the most important reaction to fear is removing the source of threat, precisely what nationalists were promising to do in Yugoslavia. Second, studies of propaganda routinely find that repetition is the single most effective technique of persuasion. It does not matter how big the lie is, so long as it keeps being repeated.

Third, much of what we know is vicarious knowledge and not based on personal experience. We accept the truths of authorities and experts whom we respect and who have socially recognized positions and titles. Who could really tell or check how many Serbs had been massacred by Ustasha? Fourth, outright falsehoods were common and intentional. According to a media analyst, 'In Serbia and Croatia, TV fabricated and shamelessly circulated war crime stories . . . the same victims would be identified on Zagreb screens as Croat, on Belgrade screens as Serb'. . . .

Fifth, mass communications studies of the two-step flow of communication show that in ordinary circumstances crude propaganda from 'patriotic journalism' is discounted because people are exposed to a variety of broadcast messages and because they check media messages against the beliefs and opinions in their social milieus in interpersonal relationships and conversations. Ethnic crisis politics breaks down the two-step flow. . . .

Nationalists Win the 1990 Elections

Second only to the mass media wars for the revival of the crisis frame were the 1990 elections. Every town and city experienced the founding of political parties, often at a huge rally in a public building or a sports stadium, during which speaker after speaker gave vent to exaggerated nationalist rhetoric and hostile pronouncements and attacks against other nationalities. . . .

Nationalists persuaded voters not to 'split the ethnic vote' but to vote as a bloc for the nationalists because the other nationalities would bloc-vote and gain power. Bloc-voting became a self-fulfilling prophecy. . . . The politicians elected were more nationalist than their voters. . . .

Repression of Minorities and Moderates

The demise of the moderates was due to a combination of electoral defeats, loss of credibility about being effective in a crisis, and intimidation and threats from extremists. . . .

The nationalist winners purged their ethnic opponents and moderates of their own nationality from party and state positions. The targets were sent anonymous threat letters, were fired from their jobs, forced into military service, charged with treason, subversion and plotting armed rebellion, and subject to office and house searches for weapons, radio transmitters and 'subversive' literature. . . . In a Bosnian example reported by [Tadeusz] Mazowiecki, 'According to a witness [from Bosanska Dubica], the elected authorities who were moderates and who tried to prevent acts of violence were dismissed or replaced by Serbian extremists'.

Other methods were cruder. . . . Ordinary people could not escape ethnic polarization. In an interview a Serb taxi driver explained: 'No one wanted the coming war, but if I don't fight, someone from my side [Serb] will kill me, and if my Muslim friends don't fight, other Muslims will kill them'.

The overthrow of moderates by extremists or radicals is well known in the great revolutions: Girondins were overthrown by the Jacobins in the French revolution and all groups were overthrown by the Bolsheviks in the Russian revolution. The means of seizing power are similar. The radicals create parallel governance to the state and come to exercise *de facto* authority in many institutions, and militias and mutineers execute a *coup d'état*. Then the remaining moderates are purged. It happens in ethnic violence as well. It did so in the mixed ethnic districts of Croatia and Bosnia, and it happened in Prijedor.

Militias Take Over

Militias and paramilitaries roamed far and wide and perpetrated ethnic cleansing, massacres, atrocities and other war crimes, as in the Prijedor district. . . .

Militiamen were not necessarily fanatics filled with hatred to start with. [Tim] Judah described how a Serb militiaman got recruited by his peers from the local SDS who pressured him for weeks: 'We've all got to take up arms, or we'll disappear from here'. He had Muslim and Croat friends. Would they protect him against extremists of all nationalities? Not likely, if it got violent. So he 'took out a gun'. Peer pressure, fear, not only of Muslims but of extremist Serbs who might finger him as a 'traitor', were the major reasons for joining a militia. Some of these men were unemployed and expected a job in the coming Serb government as militia or police.

Once the young man 'took out a gun' he became encapsulated in a quasimilitary unit subject to peer solidarity and ethnic loyalty. He was trained in weapons and indoctrinated with the beliefs and norms of the crisis frame about other ethnics:

   a. *Collective guilt:* 'They' act in unison; children grow into adults; women give birth to future warriors; even old people stab you from behind; 'they' will never change.
   b. *Revenge and retaliation:* 'They' massacred 'us' in the past, and are about to do it again, in fact they have already started. A setting of scores is justified; an eye for an eye.
   c. *Deterrence/first strike:* Disable them before they strike, which is what they are about to do, despite appearances, because they are secretive and treacherous.
   d. *Danger/survival:* These are extraordinary times, one's entire nationality is threatened, and extreme measures are justified.
   e. *Legitimacy:* Ordinary people and militias are justified in taking extreme measures because the constituted authorities have not come to the defence of our people.

These are the rationalization and the justifying norms for unrestrained, collective, ethnic violence. Other motives for collective violence were economic gain, peer pressure and lack of accountability. From being an ordinary man in normal times the militiaman changed into being a killer at crisis times.

The Bassiouni report (UN Security Council 1994) counted eighty-three paramilitaries in Bosnia alone operating between June 1991 and late 1993, fifty-three for Serbs, with an estimated 20,000–40,000 members, thirteen for Croats, with 12,000–20,000, and fourteen for Bosniac, with 4,000–6,000 men. In view of 700,000 Bosnian Serb men aged fifteen to thirty-five, militiamen were 10–20 percent of the Serb men of military age in Bosnia. Ten to 20 percent of adult males in militias, added to the military and police, are more than enough for death and destruction against civilians on a massive scale.

Conclusion

My account is not a narrative of events but an analytic explanation for the breakup of Yugoslavia amid collective violence. . . . On the eve of the wars, Yugoslavs reported cooperative interpersonal ethnic relations and opposed a breakup of the state. Nationalist leaders succeeded in manipulating ethnicity by spreading fear, insecurity and hatred, which advanced their political agenda of separate national states.

To explain their success I draw on elements from the primordialist, instrumentalist and constructionist views on ethnicity and on the theory of ethnic violence originating in fear and insecurity. To these I add the concept of a cognitive frame which clarifies élite-grass-roots linkage and ethnic manipulation. Nationalism, ethnic identity and attachment alone, however intense, do not explain grass-roots ethnic actions. Yugoslavs possessed two frames on ethnic relations: a cooperative frame for normal, peaceful times, as in the decades of the fifties to the eighties. They also possessed a dormant crisis frame anchored in family history and collective memory of wars, ethnic atrocities and brutality. Threats and lies that were implausible and dismissed in the normal frame could resonate when the crisis frame was switched on: they became persuasive, were believed, and inspired fear.

In the waning days of Communism, nationalists activated the crisis frame on ethnicity by playing on fears of ethnic annihilation and oppression in the mass media, in popular culture, in social movements, and in election campaigns. Élite crisis discourse resonated at the grass roots, made for ethnic polarization, and got nationalists elected. Once in office, nationalists suppressed and purged both moderates in their own ethnic group and other ethnics. They organized militias who perpetrated acts of extreme violence against innocent civilians. They conducted war according to the crisis script. Without the tacit, overt or confused support of the majority, the nationalist leaders could not have escalated ethnic rivalry and conflict into massive collective violence.

POSTSCRIPT

Is Ethnic Conflict Inevitable?

Although Kakar's argument draws heavily on psychology, he clearly adopts a primordialist perspective that ethnic differences are inherently threatening; such differences lead to tension and will ultimately emerge as conflict. Individuals may keep their fears and anxieties in check for a time, but preconscious fears and anxiety will eventually emerge. For Kakar, no amount of education or politically correct training will eliminate these anxieties or permanently overcome them.

Oberschall's argument accepts the reality of primordialist variables such as kinship, language, and religion as more important than did Barth in his original formulation of the circumstantialist perspective. But for Oberschall, such variables must be triggered by circumstantialist factors before they can be aroused. The Balkans case is a particularly apt one, as ethnicity in Bosnia is largely based on religious differences. All three "ethnic" communities have emerged from essentially the same pool of genetic material. The language spoken by all three groups is essentially the same language, often called Serbo-Croatian by linguists, though the Serbs use a Cyrillic alphabet and the Croats use a Roman one. The main "ethnic" differences emerge from their three different religions: Eastern Orthodox, Roman Catholic, and Islam. Religious differences in Bosnia correspond to traditional political alliances, but, as in the conflict in Northern Ireland, they are not fundamentally based on significant biological or linguistic differences. In Bosnia, unlike Northern Ireland, people of all three ethnicities had lived and worked side by side; they socialized together and had even intermarried. The primordialist variables are, in Oberschall's view, insufficient to trigger the ethnic violence and brutality that erupted in Bosnia. Ethnic violence, massacres, and ethnic cleansing could only have emerged if people in the towns and villages were manipulated into fearing their neighbors, concludes Oberschall.

Anthropologists and sociologists have long recognized that racial and ethnic tensions in the United States and other countries are linked to issues about access to jobs, land, resources, and opportunities. But it is not clear whether or not such circumstantialist variables are sufficient to explain why social conflict so often allows ethnic affiliations to become so central.

For further reading on genocide and ethnic cleansing, see Alexander L. Hinton's edited volume *Annihilating Difference: The Anthropology of Genocide* (University of California Press, 2002). For another view on ethnic conflict in India, see Ashutosh Varshney's *Ethnic Conflict and Civic Life: Hindus and Muslims in India* (Yale University Press, 2002). For a recent perspective about ethnicity, see André Burguière and Raymond Grew's edited volume *The Construction of Minorities: Cases for Comparison Across Time and Around the World*

(University of Michigan Press, 2001). For more circumstantialist discussions of ethnic conflict, see Jack Eller's *From Culture to Ethnicity to Conflict* (University of Michigan Press, 1999) and *The Myth of "Ethnic Conflict": Politics, Economics, and "Cultural" Violence,* edited by Beverly Crawford and Ronnie D. Lipschutz (International Area Studies, University of California at Berkeley, 1998).

American Anthropological Association Code of Ethics

Created by the American Anthropological Association, the largest organization of anthropologists in the world, this American Anthropological Association Code of Ethics Web site provides a code of ethics for its members and a handbook on ethical issues faced by anthropologists.

```
http://www.aaanet.org/committees/ethics/
                   ethcode.html
```

Kennewick Man

This site contains an article on the controversy following the discovery of the bones of a 8,400-year-old man, now called Kennewick Man. The article discusses whether the bones, which do not appear to be Native American, should be protected under the Native American Graves Protection and Repatriation Act (NAGPRA) and therefore be reburied. Links are provided to previous articles, which give further information from both sides of the debate on Kennewick Man.

```
http://www.archaeology.org/9701/etc/
                 specialreport.html
```

The Yanomamö

Created by Brian Schwimmer, this Yanomamö (also spelled *Yanomami*) Web site explores intergroup relations, alliances, and the role of warfare among the Yanomamö. This site also provides links to additional sites on the subject.

```
http://www.umanitoba.ca/anthropology/tutor/
               case_studies/yanomamo/
```

Exhibitions at the Smithsonian: National Museum of the American Indian

This Web site of the National Museum of the American Indian was created by the Smithsonian Institution and provides images of current and recent exhibits about Native American art and society. The links provided on this site allow students to evaluate how this museum represents the Native American community.

```
http://www.nmai.si.edu/exhibits/index.html
```

PART 5

Ethics in Anthropology

*T*he ethical treatment of other peoples has come to play an increasingly important role in contemporary anthropology. Ethical issues directly affect how cultural anthropologists should treat their living human subjects. But similar issues also affect archaeologists and biological anthropologists because the artifacts of past communities often represent the ancestors of living communities. Here the interests of anthropologists and native peoples diverge, and we ask whether such bones should be reburied to respect the dead or if they should be studied for science. Similarly, we may ask what the ethical responsibilites of Western anthropologists should be when they find certain cultural practices abhorrent or unjust. Should anthropologists work to change these practices? All of these issues raise questions about how involved anthropologists should become with the peoples with whom they work. Should anthropologists take a passive, objective, and even scientific position or should they use what they know to support or change these native communities?

- Should the Remains of Prehistoric Native Americans Be Reburied Rather Than Studied?

- Did Napolean Chagnon's Research Methods and Publications Harm the Yanomami Indians?

- Do Museums Misrepresent Ethnic Communities Around the World?

ISSUE 16

Should the Remains of Prehistoric Native Americans Be Reburied Rather Than Studied?

YES: James Riding In, from "Repatriation: A Pawnee's Perspective," *American Indian Quarterly* (Spring 1996)

NO: Clement W. Meighan, from "Some Scholars' Views on Reburial," *American Antiquity* (October 1992)

ISSUE SUMMARY

YES: Assistant professor of justice studies and member of the Pawnee tribe James Riding In argues that holding Native American skeletons in museums and other repositories represents a sacrilege against Native American dead and, thus, all Indian remains should be reburied.

NO: Professor of anthropology and archaeologist Clement W. Meighan believes that archaeologists have a moral and professional obligation to the archaeological data with which they work. Such data are held in the public good and must be protected from destruction, he concludes.

From the beginning, the relationship between Native Americans and anthropologists in the United States has been an uncertain one, ranging from mutually cooperative to overtly hostile in which Native Americans deeply mistrust anthropologists and feel that Native American culture is exploited.

Native American activitists have invoked concerns about religious freedom, arguing that the excavation of bones is a desecration, a violation of native rights, and a sacrilege against Native American religion. These individuals and organizations demanded the immediate return and reburial of all Native American skeletons currently held in public museums and other repositories. They objected both to the exhibition of the remains and to research on remains by physical anthropologists. Many Native Americans have pointed out that the same museums that exhibit Native American skeletons do not simultaneously display the bones of white Americans.

Responding to the concerns of Native Americans, in 1990 the U.S. Congress enacted the Native American Graves Protection and Registration Act (NAGPRA), which mandates that all public collections of Native American remains must be returned to relatives or descendants for reburial. The return of bones and material culture has come to be called "repatriation."

James Riding In, himself a Pawnee, argues that anthropologists and archaeologists have consistently desecrated graves by excavating and studying the bones of Native Americans. He begins his discussion by outlining the history of many public museum collections of Native American skulls. Many of these, he maintains, were war dead from the Indian Wars of the 1870s, and they should have been reburied on the spot. Riding In says that Native Americans believe that the bodies of the dead must be reunited with "Mother Earth."

Clement W. Meighan counters that the debate over what should be done with bones from archaeological excavations is a conflict between science and religion. In the case of very early prehistoric sites, there is usually no evidence that links living tribes inhabiting the surrounding areas with the early community; many of these groups would either be unrelated to living tribal members or might even be the remains of enemy groups.

For Meighan the requirements of science must be defended, and the unraveling of humankind's prehistory in the New World is of public interest to all Americans, whether Native or not. He contends that the public's right to know about the past is important, and any reburial of archaeological material represents the destruction of scientific data that can never be recovered. Arguing that political motives are at the heart of Native American claims to religious interest in archaeological remains, Meighan views reburial as an attempt to censor archaeological and anthropological findings that conflict with Native American legends and myths.

Although NAGPRA has been the official law of the land for a decade, there remain many contentious concerns about just which bones should be repatriated and how they should be treated both legally and professionally. Riding In and Meighan raise a number of questions about the interests of science and Native American religions. Are Native American religious beliefs more important than those of secular scientists? Do archaeologists desecrate Native American sacred sites whenever they excavate? Should the religious concerns of one ethnic or cultural community override either the professional concerns of another group or the intellectual rights of the general public? Who should control information about the past? Who should control depictions of any ethnic group's past?

James Riding In

 **YES**

Repatriation: A Pawnee's Perspective

My opposition to scientific grave looting developed partially through the birth of the American Indian repatriation movement during the late 1960s. Like other American Indians of the time (and now), I viewed archaeology as an oppressive and sacrilegious profession that claimed ownership over many of our deceased relatives, suppressed our religious freedom, and denied our ancestors a lasting burial. My first encounter with an archaeologist occurred at a party in New Mexico in the late 1970s. After hearing him rant incessantly about the knowledge he had obtained by studying Indian remains, burial offerings, and cemeteries, I suggested that if he wanted to serve Indians he should spend his time excavating latrines and leave the graves alone. Of course, he took umbrage at the tone of my suggestion, and broke off the conversation. While studying history at the University of California, Los Angles [UCLA] in the mid-1980s, I became committed to pursuing the goals of the repatriation movement, which was gaining momentum. Like other reburial proponents, I advocated the reburial of all Indian remains warehoused across the nation in museums, universities, and federal agencies. I also promoted the extension or enactment of laws to protect Indian cemeteries from grave looters, including archaeologists.

While working to elevate the consciousness of the UCLA campus about the troubled relationship between archaeologists and Indians, a few of us, including students, staff, faculty, and community members, took advantage of opportunities to engage in dialogue with the anti-repatriation forces. During these exchanges, tempers on both sides often flared. Basically, the archaeologists were functioning on metaphysical and intellectual planes that differed from ours. We saw their professional activities as sacrilege and destructive, while they professed a legal and scientific right to study Indian remains and burial goods. We wanted the university to voluntarily return the human remains in its collections to the next-of-kin for proper reburial. They desired to protect excavation, research, and curatorial practices. Asserting profound respect for Indian concerns, beliefs, and values, members of the archaeology group offered a host of patronizing excuses for refusing to endorse our calls for repatriation. In this sense, the UCLA struggle mirrored the conflict over human remains ensuing throughout much of the country. In 1989, as the UCLA battle ensued, I accepted an offer to assist the Pawnee government in its efforts as a sovereign nation to reclaim the remains of its ancestors held at the

Smithsonian Institution. Being a citizen of this small and impoverished nation of Indians, I welcomed the opportunity to join other Pawnee activists in the repatriation quest. Earlier that year, Congress had enacted a repatriation bill that provided a legal mechanism for Indian governments to reclaim ancestral remains and burial offerings held at the Smithsonian.

Despite the law, obdurate Smithsonian personnel sought to frustrate Indian repatriation efforts with such tactics as stonewalling, deceit, and misinformation. Although Smithsonian personnel claimed that the true identities of six skulls classified as Pawnee could not be positively established, subsequent research on my part uncovered a preponderance of evidence confirming the authenticity of the accession records. This research also showed that, after U.S. soldiers and Kansas settlers had massacred a party of Pawnee men who had been recently discharged from the U.S. army, a Fort Harker surgeon had collected some of the victims' skulls in compliance with army policy and shipped them to the Army Medical Museum for craniometric study.

Since that report, I have written articles, given presentations, and, in conjunction with others, conducted research on behalf of Pawnee repatriation initiatives at Chicago's Field Museum of Natural History. I also have written a report from information found in the Native American Graves Protection and Repatriation Act (NAGPRA) summary letters showing the location of additional Pawnee remains, sacred objects, objects of cultural patrimony, and cultural artifacts.

This essay offers some of my views concerning the reburial aspect of the repatriation struggle. It seeks to show the intellectual and spiritual foundations behind the movement as a means for understanding the complexity of the controversy. It also attempts to demonstrate how repatriation advocates managed to effect discriminatory laws and practices. Finally, it conveys a message that, although old attitudes continue to function within the archaeology and museum communities, a concerted effort brought to bear by people who espouse cooperative relations is in place to bring Indian spiritual beliefs in conformity with non-Indian secular values.

At another level, I write with the intent of creating awareness about a pressing need to disestablish racial, institutional, and societal barriers that impede this country's movement toward a place that celebrates cultural diversity as a cherished and indispensable component of its social, political, and economic fabric. Despite the tone of skepticism, caution, and pessimism found within this study, I envision a society where people can interact freely, respecting one another without regard to race, color, ethnicity, or religious creed. Before this dream becomes a reality, however, America has to find ways to dissolve its racial, gender, cultural, and class barriers.

Pawnee Beliefs, Critical Scholarship, and Oppression

The acts committed against deceased Indians have had profound, even harmful, effects on the living. Therefore, as an activist and historian, I have had to develop a conceptual framework for giving meaning and order to the conflict.

The foundation of my perspective concerning repatriation is derived from a combination of cultural, personal, and academic experiences. An understanding of Pawnee religious and philosophical beliefs about death, gained through oral tradition, dreams, and research, informs my view that repatriation is a social justice movement, supported by native spirituality and sovereignty, committed to the amelioration of the twin evils of oppression and scientific racism. Yet, I am neither a religious fundamentalist nor a left- or right-wing reactionary. Concerning repatriation, I simply advocate that American Indians receive what virtually every other group of Americans enjoys; that is, the right to religious freedom and a lasting burial.

My training as critical scholar provides another cornerstone of my beliefs about the nature of "imperial archaeology." My writings cast the legacy of scientific body snatching within the realm of oppression. Oppression occurs when a set or sets of individuals within the dominant population behave in ways that infringe on the beliefs, cultures, and political structures of other groups of people. Acts of stealing bodies, infringing on spirituality, and resisting repatriation efforts represent classic examples of oppression.

Although exposed to years of secular interpretations about the nature of the world and the significance of archaeology for understanding the past through formal Euroamerican education, I have continued to accept Pawnee beliefs about the afterlife. To adopt any other perspective regarding this matter would deny my cultural heritage. I cannot reconcile archaeology with tradition because of the secular orientation of the former as well as its intrusive practices. Unlike archaeologists who see Native remains as specimens for study, my people view the bodies of deceased loved ones as representing human life with sacred qualities. Death merely marks the passage of the human spirit to another state of being. In a 1988 statement, then Pawnee President Lawrence Goodfox Jr. expressed a common perspective stressing the negative consequences of grave desecration on our dead: "When our people die and go on to the spirit world, sacred rituals and ceremonies are performed. We believe that if the body is disturbed, the spirit becomes restless and cannot be at peace."

Wandering spirits often beset the living with psychological and health problems. Since time immemorial, Pawnees have ceremoniously buried our dead within Mother Earth. Disinterment can occur only for a compelling religious reason. Equally critical to our perspective are cultural norms that stressed that those who tampered with the dead did so with profane, evil, or demented intentions. From this vantage point, the study of stolen remains constitutes abominable acts of sacrilege, desecration, and depravity. But racist attitudes, complete with such axioms as "The only good Indian is a dead Indian," have long conditioned white society to view Indians (as other non-whites) as intellectually inferior subhumans who lacked a right to equal treatment under legal and moral codes. Complicating matters, value judgments about the alleged superiority of the white race became interlocked with scientific thought, leading to the development of oppressive practices and policies.

Consequently, orgies of grave looting occurred without remorse. After the Pawnees removed from Nebraska to Oklahoma during the 1870s, local settlers, followed by amateur and professional archaeologists, looted virtually every

Pawnee cemetery they could find, taking remains and burial offerings. Much of the "booty" was placed in an array of institutions including the Nebraska State Historical Society (NSHS) and the Smithsonian Institution.

We have a right to be angry at those who dug our dead from the ground, those who established and maintained curatorial policies, and those who denied our repatriation requests. Last year, my elderly grandmother chastised white society in her typically reserved, but direct fashion for its treatment of our dead. After pointing to an Oklahoma bluff where many Pawnee relatives are buried, she declared, "It is not right, that they dug up all of those bodies in Nebraska." What she referred to can be labeled a spiritual holocaust. When anyone denies us our fundamental human rights, we cannot sit idly by and wait for America to reform itself. It will never happen. We have a duty not only to ourselves, but also to our relatives, our unborn generations, and our ancestors to act. Concerning repatriation, we had no choice but to work for retrieval of our ancestral remains for proper reburial and for legislation that provided penalties for those who disrupted the graves of our relatives.

Yet our initiatives sought redress in a peaceful manner. In 1988, Lawrence Goodfox expressed our goals, declaring "All we want is [the] reburial of the remains of our ancestors and to let them finally rest in peace and for all people in Nebraska to refrain from, forever, any excavation of any Native American graves or burial sites." In our view, reburying the disturbed spirits within Mother Earth equalizes the imbalance between the spiritual and physical worlds caused by the desecration.

National Challenges to Imperial Archaeology and Oppression

The Pawnee reburial struggle occurred within the context of a worldwide indigenous movement. What beset my people had affected Natives everywhere. In this country, few Indian nations escaped the piercing blades of the archaeologists' shovels or the slashes of the headhunters' knives. These operations infringed on Indian beliefs, burial rights, and sovereignty. The notion that this type of research had validity was so ingrained in the psyche of many non-Indians that rarely did anyone question the morality, ethics, or legality of these practices; that is, until the repatriation movement surfaced in the late 1960s. This movement stands on a paramount footing with the valiant struggles of African-Americans for civil rights and women for equality. Taking a leading role during the early stages of the repatriation movement, organizations such as the American Indian Movement (AIM), International Indian Treaty Council, and American Indians Against Desecration (AIAD) expressed in dramatic fashion Indian concerns about the excesses of archaeology and oppression. Committed to the causes of reburying all disinterred Indians and stopping grave disruptions, these groups often employed confrontational strategies. Near Welch, Minnesota, in 1972, for example, AIM members risked arrest by disturbing a dig site. In addition to burning field notes and tools, they confiscated unearthed artifacts and exposed photographic film. Throughout the 1970s and 1980s, AIAD challenged the human remains collections and curatorial policies of government agencies, museums, and universities. As time progressed, many college campuses saw a dramatic increase in tensions between Indians and archaeologists. These actions catapulted the repatriation movement into the consciousness of sympathetic politicians, newspaper editors, and members of the general public. Increased knowledge of the issues subsequently spawned unprecedented levels of non-Indian backing of repatriation.

As the 1980s progressed, more conciliatory Indians, often coming from the professions of law and politics, surfaced as leading figures in the movement. Unlike the universal reburial advocates, these moderates tended to see compromise as the most expedient means available to acquire the desired legislation. They often sought a balance between scientific study of Native remains and the need for Indians to gain religious, burial, and repatriation rights under the law. Organizations such as the National Congress of American Indians and the Native American Rights Fund espoused the moderate cause. Realizing that public sentiments increasingly favored the Indians' views, some archaeologists and museum administrators endorsed compromise as a means of cutting their losses and saving face. With common ground beneath their feet, individuals and organizations waged a series of intense political battles at the state and federal levels.

With moderates in control, reform transpired relatively swiftly. By 1992, more than thirty states had placed laws on the books extending protection to Indian cemeteries, including several with repatriation provisions. Congress passed two pieces of legislation, the National Museum of the American Indian Act in 1989 and NAGPRA the following year. Collectively, these national laws provided Indian nations a means to obtain human remains linked to them by a "preponderance of evidence" and associated funerary offerings held by institutions that received federal funding. NAGPRA also provides penalties for individuals convicted of trafficking in human remains.

Ongoing Reburial Initiatives

With legal avenues now open for Indian governments to reclaim stolen ancestral remains and associated burial objects, some of the old repressive policies fell by the wayside. The change enabled relatives to begin the task of reclaiming stolen bodies and grave offerings for reburial. Collectively, Indian nations thus far have interred thousands of stolen remains. To date (summer 1995), the Pawnees alone have placed nearly a thousand bodies back in Mother Earth. The total number of recovered bodies will surely reach the tens of thousands within a few years.

Reinterment ceremonies, along with funeral feasts, evoke a gamut of emotional expressions ranging from sorrow to joy. When conducting reburials, people rejoice at the fact that the repatriated remains are finally being returned to Mother Earth, but, like modern funerals, an air of sadness pervades the ceremonies. In particular, reinterring the remains of young children causes grieving and weeping. Mourning is part of the healing process in that reburials seek to restore harmony between the living and dead by putting restless spirits to rest. At another level, reburials bring closure to bitterly contested struggles.

Future Concerns

Legislation emanating from the repatriation movement has changed the customary ways that archaeologists and museums operate. Most notably, Indian governments now have established a sovereign right to reclaim the bodies of their ancestors from offending museums, universities, and federal agencies. In this capacity, they have the power to grant and deny access to their dead. Additionally, the new laws make face-to-face interaction routine between museums and Indian nations in certain repatriation matters. Several observers have proclaimed that the common ground signals the dawning of a new era of cooperative relations between Indians and museums. Despite changing attitudes and practices, it is too soon to assess the long-term ramifications of the reburial controversy. Six problematic areas cause me concern about the future of repatriation:

First, the laws do not provide for the reinterment of ancient, unclaimed, or unidentified remains. In other words, the fate of tens of thousands of bodies, along with associated funerary offerings, is uncertain. Will those with authority take steps to provide for a proper reburial for these bodies or will they allow the continuance of old practices and policies?

Second, the absence of legislation and aggressive enforcement of burial protection laws in some states may send a message that grave looting can resume without fear of arrest, prosecution, or punishment.

Third, NAGPRA's graves protection stipulations apply only to federal lands and entities that receive federal funding. In states without both progressive reburial legislation and a substantial Indian populace, large-scale acts of grave desecration may continue. . . .

Fourth, and perhaps most significant a pervasive attitude among elements of the archaeology and museum communities keeps repressive and archaic ideas alive. In fact, members of these groups have consistently disavowed any wrongdoing by themselves and their predecessors. Rather, some present their work to the public as neutral, impartial, and objective interpretations of distant Native American cultures. To counter claims that the digging and study is disrespectful, others assert that taking remains for study shows respect for Indian people and culture. In a twisted logic, still others insist that they are the "true spiritual descendants of the original Indians and the contemporary Indians [are] foreigners who had no right to complain about their activities." Like most other repatriation advocates, I reject these pleas as condescending and duplicitous acts of misguided people and lost souls. . . .

Anti-repatriation advocates echoed a common refrain. They viewed their pursuits as being under attack by narrow-minded and anti-intellectual radicals who sought to destroy archaeology. Equating repatriation with book burning, some alarmists often charged falsely that Indians would not rest until they had stripped museums and universities of their Indian collections. These strategies contain elements of self-delusion, arrogance, and racism. A tacit message found in these paternalistic defenses of imperial archaeology was that Indians must, for their own good, learn to respect the work of archaeology. Equally disturbing is the notion that Indians need archaeology. However, the exact opposite is true. Beneath the self-serving rhetoric lay a deceptive ambiance of cultural imperialism that masked the stark reality of how archaeology and museums infringed on Indian religion and burial rights.

Fifth, imperial archaeologists have had substantial levels of support from real and pretend Indians. The phenomena of co-optation and self-interest reverberates loudly here. Usually found working in museums, universities, and government agencies, some of these individuals claim a heritage complete with a Cherokee princess, but they embrace the secular views and values of Western science. Others belonging to this camp clearly have significant amounts of Indian blood, but they rely heavily on the goodwill of their non-Indian colleagues to promote and maintain their careers. Non-institutional advocacy surfaced from some grassroots Indians. At meetings, conferences, and confrontations, archaeologists rarely failed to produce a reservation Indian or two who spoke passionately against reburial in an effort to convince the public and policy makers that Native communities lacked unanimity on the subject. Whatever their motive, degree of Indian blood, or cultural orientation, their willingness to endorse oppressive archaeological practices marks a radical departure from traditional Indian philosophy.

Collectively, "wannabes" and misguided Indians may be able to damage reburial efforts. As the movement pushed for national repatriation legislation in the late 1980s, we found them sitting on committees convened by anthropology and museum associations that issued reports condemning repatriation. In a worst-case scenario, NAGPRA and other committees stacked with them and imperial archaeologists could conceivably frustrate or undermine repatriation requests.

Finally, it seems that archaeologists have launched a campaign to convince the public, tribal leaders, and others that skeletal investigations are necessary for a variety of reasons. According to a recent *Chronicle of Higher Education* article, "More and more of those kinds of opportunities will occur, many scholars agree, when researchers learn to persuade American Indians and others that skeletal remains and artifacts represent something other than a publication toward a faculty member's promotion and tenure." In other words, we are seeing archaeologists adopt less abrasive tactics to get their hands on our dead. Succumbing to subtle pressure, aimed at convincing us to accept a secular view of the dead as research objects, will erode a cherished part of our belief systems and cultures. In any event, some Indian nations have allowed the creation of archaeology programs on their reservations.

Clearly, the repatriation movement has won some major victories, but the war is unfinished. United States history teaches the lesson that individuals who face the threat of losing a privileged status often will devise rationalizations and strategies to resist change. Southern slave owners, for example, argued against abolitionism by making the outlandish claim that involuntary servitude was a benevolent institution that saved millions of blacks from the savagery of Africa. Historians repeated this claim well into the twentieth century.

It is conceivable that at some point someone will challenge the constitutionality of NAGPRA. If this occurs, will the courts respect Indian beliefs and burial rights? America's long history concerning issues of Indian religious freedom and political rights makes the possibility of a legal suit a scary thought. The Supreme Court has occasionally protected Indian sovereignty, as well as hunting, fishing, and water rights, but it also has incorporated such imperialistic notions as the doctrine of discovery and the plenary power doctrine into U.S. law. Its decisions also have eroded the power of Indian self-government by allowing the imposition of federal jurisdiction over certain crimes committed on Indian lands.

In recent years, conservative justices appointed by President Ronald Reagan have endangered Indian religious freedom. In *Lyng v. Northwest Indian Cemetery Protective Association* (108 S. Ct. 1319 (1988)) Justice Sandra Day O'Connor wrote the majority decision stating that the U.S. government had the right to build a road through an area on federal lands sacred to Yurok, Karok, and Tolowa Indians even if such a construction project would destroy the ability of those people to worship. In *Employment Division Department of Human Resources of Oregon v. Smith* (110 S. Ct. 1595 (1990)) the court held that a state could abridge expressions of religious freedom if the state had a compelling reason to do so. In this case, the court paved the way for states to deprive Native American Church (NAC) members of the right to use peyote in connection with their worship. Fortunately, in 1994, Congress addressed the religious crisis caused by the court by enacting a law that sanctioned peyote use for NAC services.

History demonstrates that promises made by white America to help Indians have not always materialized. The administrative branch of the federal government has entered into 371 treaties with Indian nations and systematically violated each of them. The legislative record is another cause of concern. The Indian Reorganization Act of 1934 authorized Indian nations to restructure themselves politically but only in accordance with models and terms acceptable to Department of Interior officials. During the 1970s, Congress declared that Indian government could exercise more powers of self-government. Federal bureaucratic controls over Indian governments, however, actually became more stringent, if not suffocating, in this era. During that decade, Congress also enacted the American Indian Religious Freedom Act of 1978 in a half-hearted effort to encourage federal agencies to accommodate customary Indian worship practices at off-reservation sites. The act provided virtually no protection because federal agencies and the Supreme Court, as we have seen, have followed a tradition that sees nothing wrong with suppressing Indian religious freedom. Although Indians are pursing a legislative remedy to resolve these problems, Congress has yet to enact a true religious freedom law for them.

Conclusion

Facing overwhelming odds, the repatriation movement has achieved many noteworthy successes. United States society, including a growing number of sympathetic archaeologists and museum curators, has finally recognized that Indians are not disappearing, and that Indians are entitled to burial rights and religious freedom. Nevertheless, under the new repatriation laws, many non-Indian entities still "legally" hold thousands of Indians remains and burial offerings. With many archaeologists and museum curators committed to upholding oppressive operational principles, values, and beliefs, the fate of these bodies remains in question. Moreover, others, perhaps best described as wolves in sheeps' clothing, are seeking to gain our cooperation, a euphemism meaning the delivery of another blow to our revered philosophies about the dead.

Given the durability of imperialist archaeology and the new approaches being used to gain access to the remains of our beloved ancestors, we must remain vigilant and monitor their operations. Protecting our dead must remain a moral and spiritual obligation we cannot callously abandon for we cannot allow further erosions of our beliefs and traditions. Thus a need still exists for maintaining the cultural traditions that inspired the repatriation movement.

NO

Clement W. Meighan

Some Scholars' Views on Reburial

[T]here is something inherently distasteful and unseemly in secreting either the fruits or seeds of scientific endeavors.

— Judge Bruce S. Jenkins

Destruction of archaelogical collections through the demands for reburial presents a serious conflict between religion and science. Archaeologists should not deal with these matters by "compromise" alone, but must sustain their rights and duties as scholars.

The above quotation is from a court case having nothing to do with archaeology, yet if we believe that archaeology is a scientific endeavor we must agree that this statement applies to archaeology as well as medicine, chemistry, or other fields of scholarship. The recent increased attention given to the ethics of scientists and scientific organizations, with news accounts almost weekly in such journals as *Science,* requires archaeologists to examine their basic assumptions about the nature of science and their obligations to scholarship. This is brought forward most forcefully in the debate over the past 20 years about the problems of reburial of archaeological and museum collections.

The discussion by Goldstein and Kintigh (1990) is a valiant effort to unravel some of the strands of conflict inherent in the controversy over the destruction of museum collections in the name of Indian religious beliefs. They seek some sort of middle ground in which scholarly and ethnic concerns can coexist in a constructive way. However, in view of the massive losses of scientific data now legislated by the federal government and some of the states, it needs to be made clear that many archaeologists do not agree with some aspects of the philosophical position taken by Goldstein and Kintigh. In particular, their statement that "We must change the way we do business" (Goldstein and Kintigh 1990:589) is not justified, particularly since their suggestions for change involve the abandonment of scholarly imperatives and the adoption of an "ethical" position that accepts the right of nonscholars to demand the destruction of archaeological evidence and the concealment of archaeological data. Of course, changes in the way archaeology is done will inevitably take place, for both internal (professional) and external (social/legal) reasons. This does not mean that the basic rules of scholarly obligations to one's data should change as well.

From Clement W. Meighan, "Some Scholars' Views on Reburial," *American Antiquity,* vol. 57, no. 4 (October 1992). Copyright © 1992 by The Society for American Archaeology. Reprinted by permission. Some references omitted.

Goldstein and Kintigh fall into the anthropological trap of cultural relativism. In asserting that we must balance our concerns for knowledge with "our professional ethic of cultural relativism," they argue that our values are not the only values or ethics, but only one legitimate belief system. The implication is that all belief systems are of equal legitimacy, therefore one cannot make a clear commitment to any particular values as a guide to action. However, most individuals do make a commitment to the values that will guide their personal action. Recognizing that other people may have other values does not mean that one must accept those values or compromise his/her own ethical standards. Indeed, the dictionary has a word for believing one way and acting another—it is "hypocrisy."

Those who affiliate with organized groups, whether the Church of the Rising Light or the Society for American Archaeology (SAA), supposedly accept the beliefs and goals of the organization as stated in their by-laws or scriptures. The SAA, as an organization dedicated to scholarly research in archaeology, is bound by the general rules of scholarship that require *honest reporting and preservation of the evidence.* If the research data are subject to censorship, how can there be honest reporting? If the evidence (collections) is not preserved, who can challenge the statements of the researcher? Who can check for misinterpretations, inaccuracies, or bias? Once the collection is destroyed, we have only an affidavit from the researcher; we can believe it or not, but there is no way that additional investigation or new laboratory techniques can be applied to the collection to gain a better understanding of the evidence. The astounding new methods for medical and genetic research on ancient populations require a piece of the bone—pictures and notes won't do. Similarly, laboratory advances in dating and determining the source of artifact materials require that the relevant objects be available for study. Since we commonly proclaim that archaeological collections are unique and irreplaceable, how can we ever justify the conscious and acquiescent destruction of our data?

The suggestion of Goldstein and Kintigh that we balance our own values with the professional ethic of cultural relativism by "compromise and mutual respect" is not realistic. Many archaeologists are not going to compromise away their most fundamental scholarly beliefs. Similarly, many Indian activists are not going to compromise away their beliefs (however unsupported by evidence) that every Indian bone of the past 12,000 years belongs to one of their ancestors. There are some instances in which compromise and mutual respect have led to satisfactory results for both sides; there are many more instances in which these valued qualities have been insufficient to prevent or postpone destruction of important archaeological finds.

Those who want to do away with archaeology and archaeological collections are of course entitled to their beliefs, and they are also entitled to use whatever political and legal machinery they can to bring about their stated goals. Originally, the goals were modest, but they have escalated every year since this discussion began more than 20 years ago, as reviewed by me in an earlier article (Meighan 1984). The present-day goals have repeatedly been made clear. For example, Christopher Quayle, an attorney for the Three Affiliated Tribes, stated in *Harpers* (Preston 1989:68–69): "It's conceivable that some time in the not-so-distant future there won't be a single Indian skeleton in any museum in the country. We're going to put them out of business." The "them" refers in this statement to physical anthropologists, but it is also extended to archaeologists. For example, the recent agreement between state officials in West Virginia and a committee representing Indian viewpoints (a committee which, incidentally, includes non-Indians) states that everything in an ongoing study of a 2,000-year-old Adena mound must be given up for reburial within a year—"everything" includes not only the bones of the mythical "ancestors" of the claimants, but also all the artifacts, the chipping waste, the food refuse, the pollen samples, the soil samples, and whatever else may be removed for purposes of scientific study. While the tax-payers are expected to pay for a 1.8-million-dollar excavation on the grounds that it is in the public interest for archaeological data to be preserved, *nothing* of the tangible archaeological evidence is to be preserved. Meanwhile, Indian activists are paid to "monitor" the excavation, and they were given the right to censor the final report and prevent any objectionable photographs or data from appearing.

If there is any doubt about the goals of the anti-archaeology contingent, consider the case of Dr. David Van Horn, charged with a felony in California for conducting an environmental impact study required by law, and being honest enough to report what he found in the site, including some small bits of cremated bone, which required hours of study by physical anthropologists to identify as human. Is the reporting of a legally mandated salvage excavation a felony? It can be in California, and there are many who would like to make archaeology a crime throughout the United States. Archaeologists who accept these situations or treat them as merely local concerns (apparently the position of most scholarly organizations including the SAA), have not just compromised, they have abandoned scholarly ethics in favor of being "respectful and sensitive" to nonscholars and anti-intellectuals. When the current round of controversy is over, this loss of scientific integrity will be heavily condemned.

So there are some situations in which compromise is not necessarily the best approach, and this is one of them. Archaeologists may well be legislated out of business, and museums may well lose all their American Indian collections, and indeed the Indians have been far more successful than the archaeologists in the political arena. Many archaeologists believe, however, that this should not occur with the happy connivance of the scholarly profession of archaeology. Over 600 of them are members of the American Committee for Preservation of Archaeological Collections (ACPAC), which has argued for over 10 years that archaeology is a legitimate, moral, and even useful profession, and that collections that were legally made should remain in museums as an important part of the heritage of the nation. Bahn may have had this group in mind in his news report on the "first international congress on the reburial of human remains," in his reference to "the extremists, who unfortunately did not attend the congress to put the case for rejecting the whole notion of reburial." Who are these extremists? Neither ACPAC nor any individual known to me has stated that no reburial of any kind should take place; everyone agrees that bones of known relatives should be returned to demonstrable descendants. The disagreement is over remains to which no living person can demonstrate any relationship.

Museum materials 5,000 years old are claimed by people who imagine themselves to be somehow related to the collections in question, but such a belief has
no basis in evidence and is mysticism. Indeed, it is not unlikely that Indians
who have acquired such collections for reburial are venerating the bones of
alien groups and traditional enemies rather than distant relatives.

If the present attacks on archaeological data were happening in engineering, medicine, or chemistry, they would not be accepted by the general public
since destruction or concealment of the facts in those areas of scientific knowledge can lead to disastrous results for many living people. The general lack of
public concern about the attack on archaeology arises from the perception that
archaeological conclusions really do not matter—if someone's reconstruction
of the ancient past is ridiculous or unsupported by evidence, who cares? It will
not affect the daily lives of anyone now alive, no matter what we believe about
what happened thousands of years ago. However, the principles of scholarship
and scientific evidence are the same in all scholarly research, including archaeology and anthropology, and credibility of conclusions is an essential consideration for any field of scholarship, whether or not there are immediate practical
effects of the conclusions that are reached.

In one of the polemics put forward by Indian spokesmen in the student
newspaper at the University of California (Los Angeles), those of us on the
archaeological faculty were accused of participating in an activity that was
comparable to the "killing fields of Cambodia." Even allowing for the juvenile
rhetoric characteristic of student newspapers, I was dumbfounded at such a
statement. How could I harm any person who had already been dead for
thousands of years? How could anything that my studies did with the bones of
these ancient people harm any living person? The condemnation seems
extreme for a "crime" that is merely a failure to invite mythical descendants to
control my research and destroy museum collections held in the public interest. When issues of respect and sensitivity are raised, it needs to be pointed out
that these work both ways.

Some Legal Issues: Constitutional Requirements

The first amendment states that Congress shall make no laws respecting an
establishment of religion. Most state constitutions have similar clauses; that of
California says the state will *never* pass such laws. Yet California, other states,
and the federal government have numerous laws on the books that are specifically written to favor aboriginal tribal religious beliefs and compel others to act
in accordance with them. Religious infringement also occurs when archaeologists are excluded from evaluating claims regarding repatriation because they
do not hold particular religious beliefs. Until these statutes are challenged and
overturned, they remain an opening for other groups to seek similar legislation
making their religious beliefs enforceable by law. Creationists, for example,
have been trying for over 60 years to outlaw the teaching of evolution because
it is in conflict with their religious tenets.

That there is a science vs. religion aspect is clear in the religious justification
for the claiming of bones and "sacred" artifacts, as well as the proclamation of

many activists that archaeologists and museums are committing sacrilege in obtaining, storing, and studying archaeological remains. I discuss bone worship elsewhere (Meighan 1990). Tonetti (1990) provides a case study of the situation in Ohio, documenting the religious roots of the anti-archaeology movement. He also reports a survey of Ohio legislators that reveals a frightening ignorance of science in general and archaeology in particular: "As Zimmerman so dramatically stated in his op ed piece in the Columbus Dispatch, he does not want the General Assembly making law dealing with science issues when over 75% do not know what his 5 year old son has known for years—that dinosaurs and humans did not coexist" (Zimmerman [1989], as quoted in Tonetti [1990:22]; recent news reports state that some Indians are now claiming dinosaur bones recovered by paleontologists).

Some Legal Issues: Cultural-Resource Laws

There is a serious conflict between the laws mandating return and destruction of archaeological material (not just bones but also artifacts and anything deemed "ceremonial" by the claimants), and those laws mandating cultural-resource management and the study and conservation of archaeological sites and remains. The Van Horn case previously mentioned put Van Horn in the position of doing an environmental-impact report required by law, only to find himself spending thousands of dollars defending himself against a felony charge for violating laws based on Indian religious beliefs about cremated bones. The judge agreed with defense witnesses that there was no basis for a trial, but the state made its point that archaeologists will be heavily punished if "Indians" request it, regardless of the validity of their complaint.

The legal dichotomy between science and religion as it pertains to archaeology may be related, as Goldstein and Kintigh (1990:589) point out, to the fact that public perception does not include Indian history as part of the history of the United States, even though they recognize that public policy and law include the non-European past as an integral part of the history of the nation. That part of American history that is Indian history is largely the contribution of archaeology; *all* of it prior to 1492 is the contribution of archaeology. This has been recognized and supported by the government since the Antiquities Act of 1906, and it is the basis for all the environmental-impact laws dealing with archaeological remains.

Many opponents of archaeological-resource laws believe that since archaeology has no effect on public health or safety, it ought to be excluded from environmental impact laws. They are given considerable ammunition by laws that state that it is in the public interest to spend a lot of money to get archaeological materials, and then state that such materials are not worth preservation but are to be reburied as soon as possible after they are dug up, in some cases within a few days or weeks of the fieldwork. Further, the belief that archaeology belongs to Indians removes it from the heritage of all of the citizens and makes it less likely that the public will be interested in supporting activities not seen to be in the broad public interest. In these times of stringent budgets, it is hard enough to convince the taxpayers that they should finance archaeological excavations without having to convince them that they should also finance the reburial of the items recovered.

There are major negative results for archaeology in the present situation where not only the federal government, but states, counties, cities, and a plethora of political agencies believe that they should pass regulations controlling archaeological research. These laws and regulations conflict with one another and vary from jurisdiction to jurisdiction. In some states the conduct of archaeological research is a risky business. The smart archaeologist in California does not find certain things. If they are found, they are either thrown away or not mentioned in his/her reports. Field classes are also careful not to expose students or teachers to criminal charges, meaning that students in those classes will never expose a burial or deal with any "controversial" finds. Chipping waste is still a safe area for study.

This chilling effect on research is creating an underground archaeology of ill-trained students, dishonest researchers, and intimidated teachers who are afraid to show a picture of a burial to their classes, let alone an actual human bone. Students, who are often more perceptive than their professors, rapidly catch on and change their major or move their archaeological interests to parts of the world where they will be allowed to practice their scholarly profession. There is an increasing loss to American archaeology, and of course to the Indians whose history is dependent on it.

Some Museum Issues

A negative effect of the ongoing shift to tribalism and the right of anyone to claim anything in museums is already happening. In the past, most of the support for museums came from private donors, who contributed not only money but collections. Donors of collections had the tacit (and sometimes written) agreement that their materials would be preserved in the public interest. Who would contribute anything to a museum if they thought the museum was going to give their material away for reburial or destruction? When even Stanford University and other respected repositories of scientific collections decide that their first obligation is to whatever Indian claimant comes along, the donor who wants his/her material *preserved* will seek a repository in a state or country that is dedicated to that aim. It is a paradox that the National Park Service is busily developing new standards of curation for government collections at the same time the new National Museum of the American Indian is declaring that it will not keep anything that Indian claimants declare that they want.

Reviewers of this article believe that only a very small part of archaeological collections will be taken away from museums and archaeologists. This is a pious hope in view of the escalation of claims previously noted, reaching the apex in the West Virginia case in which *everything* recovered by archaeologists is to be given up for reburial. There are numerous cases in which archaeologists or museum employees have given up entire collections rather than negotiate with Indian claimants; for example, one prominent California case (the Encino excavation) included reburial of a number of dog skeletons, not required by any statute. It is true that the Smithsonian and some other museums now have committees to evaluate claims against their collections; perhaps these will protect scholarly and public interests, but it remains to be seen whether they can withstand the political pressures brought to bear. While I am sure that not all collections will entirely disappear, under current legislation all physical remains, all mortuary associations, and all items claimed to have religious or ceremonial significance are at risk—these are the major sources of information in many archaeological studies. When claimants can get museum specimens merely by using the word "sacred," it should be apparent that anything can be claimed by someone. It does happen, it has happened, and scholars can only hope that it will not happen in the future.

Conclusions

When scholarly classes in United States archaeology and ethnology are no longer taught in academic departments (they are diminishing rapidly), when the existing collections have been selectively destroyed or concealed, and when all new field archaeology in the United States is a political exercise rather than a scientific investigation, will the world be a better place? Certainly the leadership in archaeological research, which has been characteristic of the last 50 years of American archaeology, will be lost, and it will be left to other nations to make future advances in archaeological methods, techniques, and scholarly investigations into the ancient past.

One reviewer of this paper commented that I am engaged in a "futile attempt to resurrect a bankrupt status quo." In this view, not only can nothing be done to improve the present situation, but nothing *should* be done, and we should all meekly accept the regulations, limitations, and restrictions of academic freedom that are brought forward by politicians and pressure groups. For the last 20 years, those who have attempted to change these restrictions in favor of scholarly ethics and the preservation of collections have been dismissed as a small group of outmoded discontents who cannot adapt to a changing world. This is a mistake; I may represent a minority view, but it is not confined to a small number and is growing rapidly as archaeologists see more and more of their basic data destroyed through reburial. ACPAC's 600 members (in 44 states) include a sizeable fraction of the leading archaeologists in the United States as well as physical anthropologists, museum workers, and yes, Indians.

I am, however, triggered by the accusation that my comments lead to nothing but intransigence to offer a few suggestions for action other than "compromise," which so far has mostly meant giving in to political demands. My suggestions:

1. Archaeologists negotiating with Indians or other groups should make an effort to be sure that *all* factions of the affected group are heard, not merely the group of activists who are first in the door. Many archaeologists have been doing this for years, and nearly all of us can report that we had little difficulty in finding Indians who would work with us in a mutually agreeable and often rewarding relationship that respected Indian interests but at the same time preserved the archaeological

collections. Unfortunately, numerous instances can be cited of savage personal attacks on those Indians who agreed to share the archaeologists' task, with attempts to force the archaeologist to use other consultants and claims that the one chosen was not a real Indian (see an example in Tonetti [1990:21]). When money is involved, this is probably inevitable. However, there is no reason for archaeologists to be controlled by enemies of their discipline when they can work with friends. The existence of Indian physical anthropologists, archaeologists, and museum workers, as well as the increasing number of Indian-owned museums with scientific objectives and high standards of curation, should offer opportunities for real collaboration that do not require the destruction of evidence nor the censorship of scientific reporting.

2. Professional organizations should work to amend the legislation dealing with archaeology to get a time cut-off inserted: Remains older than a certain age should not be subject to reburial. The present laws, which ignore time and assume that everything, regardless of age, is directly related to living people, are not scientifically valid, and the scientific organizations are in a position to make this clear, if necessary in court. The recent reburial of an Idaho skeleton dated at 10,600 years ago should never have happened, but as reported by the State Historic Preservation Office of that state, Idaho law requires *no* demonstration of any relationship between Indians and archaeological remains.

3. Professional organizations should point out the disagreements between "preservation" laws and "religion" laws and should try to strengthen the former and eliminate the conflicts. If they are unable to resolve the issue by negotiation, they should support court cases that address the matter.

4. If scholarly organizations are unwilling or unable to make a clear statement of their position with respect to the giving up of archaeological collections and data, it is left to the individual archaeologist to decide his or her own professional ethics in this matter. A clear review of the moral issues is given by Del Bene (1990). This should be considered, particularly by young archaeologists entering the profession, so that they are consciously aware of the decisions they are making and the consequences for their professional future.

References

Del Bene T.A. 1990. Take the Moral Ground: An Essay on the "Reburial" Issue. *West Virginia Archeologist* 42(2):11–19.

Goldstein, L., and K. Kintigh. 1990. Ethics and the Reburial Controversy. *American Antiquity* 55:585–591.

Meighan, C.W. 1984. Archaeology: Science or Sacrilege? In *Ethics and Values in Archaeology,* edited by E.L. Green, pp. 203–233. Free Press, New York.

1990. Bone Worship. *West Virginia Archeologist* 42(2):40–43.

Preston, D.J. 1989. Skeletons in Our Museums' Closets. *Harpers.* February: 66–75.

Tonetti, A.C. 1990. Ghost Dancing in the Nineties: Research, Reburial and Resurrection Among the Dead in Ohio. *West Virginia Archeologist* 42(2):20–22.

POSTSCRIPT

Should the Remains of Prehistoric Native Americans Be Reburied Rather Than Studied?

Since these two selections were written, many Native American groups have requested the return of human remains from museums, and these bones have been reburied. Other groups have expressed little interest in recovering the remains of ancestors or skeletons excavated from their lands because they do not share the same cultural beliefs as those expressed by Riding In. A number of museum curators and archaeologists have taken a much more tempered and conciliatory approach to dealing with these issues than the position expressed by Meighan.

Such possibilities suggest that there are a variety of alternative approaches to the issue of reburial besides the diametrically opposed positions expressed here. Many groups, both from museums and universities, have urged compromise. A number of Native American groups have also tried to find ways to accommodate anthropological interests without sacrificing their own rights. Several contentious issues remain. What should be done with the remains of prehistoric Native Americans who have no known living descendants or cultural groups? Should the religious beliefs of one group of Native Americans stand for the rights of all groups? Should modern Native American communities have rights to rebury any human remains found on their lands? What should happen to the remains of the very earliest settlers in North America who are unlikely to be biologically related to modern tribes?

One recent incident arose in 1996 when a prehistoric skeleton was found along the banks of the Columbia River near Kennewick, Washington. Kennewick Man, as this individual has been called, appears to have lived 9,000 years ago and has been the center of an intense academic, political, and legal debate.

At first the bones were thought to be a white settler's, but carbon-14 dating suggests a much earlier date, which has ruled out ancestry from some early-nineteenth-century settler. When forensic anthropologist James Chatters examined the bones he concluded that the bones were Caucasoid rather than Native American. If true, such a finding would require a revision of North American prehistory. Although archaeologists wanted to examine these bones more carefully, local Native American groups claimed the right to rebury this individual, and the courts have generally supported their motions. These legal wranglings have led some archaeologists to complain that the Native Americans simply want to rebury the evidence that Europeans may have reached the New World at some early prehistoric period and may have predated the arrival of Native American groups coming from Asia. Evidence that Kennewick Man is

Caucasoid is slim at best, but without examination by physical anthropologists we will never know.

For a discussion of the Kennewick Man debate, see David Hurst Thomas's recent *Skull Wars: Kennewick Man, Archeology, and the Battle for Native American Identity* (Basic Books, 2000). Other sources on this controversy include Douglas Preston's "The Lost Man: Umatilla Indians' Plan to Rebury 9,300 Year Old Kennewick Man With Caucasoid Features," *The New Yorker* (June 16, 1997) and two articles in *Archaeology,* "A Battle Over Bones: Ancestry of Kennewick Man" (January/February 1997) and "Kennewick Update: Nondestructive Lab Tests on Controversial Skeleton to Begin" (November/December 1998).

For an excellent summary of anthropological interest in Native American remains, see Robert Bieder's *A Brief Historical Survey of the Expropriation of American Indian Remains* (Native American Rights Fund, 1990). J. C. Rose, T. J. Green, and V. D. Green's "NAGPRA Is Forever: Osteology and the Repatriation of Skeletons," *Annual Review of Anthropology* (vol. 25, 1996) provides a useful summary of NAGPRA.

Riding In has also explored the issue of repatriation and the imperialist nature of archaeology in "Without Ethics and Morality: A Historical Overview of Imperial Archaeology and American Indians," *Arizona State Law Journal* (vol. 24, Spring 1992).

Several essays in Karen D. Vitelli, ed., *Archaeological Ethics* (Altamira Press, 1996) are relevant to this debate. For an example of a more moderate approach that urges compromise, see Lynne Goldstein and Keith Kintigh's "Ethnics and the Reburial Controversy," *American Antiquity* (vol. 55, 1990).

ISSUE 17

Did Napoleon Chagnon's Research Methods and Publications Harm the Yanomami Indians?

YES: Terence Turner, from *The Yanomami and the Ethics of Anthropological Practice* (Cornell University Latin American Studies Program, 2001)

NO: Edward H. Hagen, Michael E. Price, and John Tooby, from *Preliminary Report,* http://www.anth.ucsb.edu/ucsbpreliminaryreport.pdf (Department of Anthropology, University of California Santa Barbara, 2001)

ISSUE SUMMARY

YES: Anthropologist Terence Turner contends that journalist Patrick Tierney's book *Darkness in El Dorado* accurately depicts how anthropologist Napoleon Chagnon's research among the Yanomami Indians caused conflict between groups and how Chagnon's portrayal of the Yanomami as extremely violent aided gold miners trying to take over Yanomami land.

NO: Anthropologists Edward Hagen, Michael Price, and John Tooby counter that Tierney systematically distorts Chagnon's views on Yanomami violence and exaggerates the amount of disruption caused by Chagnon's activities compared to those of others such as missionaries and gold miners.

In September 2000 a startling message flew around the e-mail lists of the world's anthropologists. It was a letter from Cornell University anthropologist Terry Turner and University of Hawaii anthropologist Leslie Sponsel to the president and president-elect of the American Anthropological Association (AAA), with copies to a few other officers, warning them of the imminent publication of a book that they said would "affect the American Anthropological profession as a whole in the eyes of the public, and arouse intense indignation and calls for action among members of the Association." The book in question, which they had read in galley proofs, was Patrick Tierney's *Darkness in*

El Dorado: How Scientists and Journalists Devastated the Amazon (W.W. Norton and Company, 2000). The letter summarized some of Tierney's charges that medical researcher James Neel, anthropologist Napoleon Chagnon, and others seriously harmed the Yanomami Indians of Venezuela, even causing a measles epidemic that killed hundreds.

The leaking of the letter and the subsequent publication of an article by Tierney in *The New Yorker* caused great excitement at the annual meeting of the AAA in San Francisco in mid-November 2000. Discussion climaxed at a panel discussion that filled a double ballroom at the Hilton Hotel with several thousand anthropologists and media representatives from around the world. The panel included Tierney, anthropologist William Irons (representing Chagnon, who declined to attend), and experts on the history of science, epidemiology, and South American Indians. (Neel could not defend himself, as he had died earlier that year.) Numerous members of the audience also spoke. During and after the meeting a consensus developed that Tierney was wrong in his claim that the measles epidemic in 1968 was caused by Neel's and Chagnon's inoculations, since measles vaccines are incapable of causing the actual disease. However, Tierney's accusations that Chagnon had treated the Yanomami in an unethical manner during his research and had distorted his findings were not so easily dismissed. Later, the Executive Board of the AAA established a task force to examine the allegations in Tierney's book. The 300-page Task Force Final Report was completed on May 18, 2002 and is now posted on the AAA Web site.

Why would a book about researchers' treatment of a small Amazonian tribe have caused such an uproar? The reason is that, due to the enormous sales of Chagnon's book *The Yanomamö* (now in its fifth edition) and the prize-winning films he made with Timothy Asch, the Yanomami (as most scholars spell their name) are probably the world's best-known tribal people and Chagnon one of the most famous ethnographers since Margaret Mead. Chagnon's use of his Yanomami data to support his sociobiological explanation of human behavior has also had influence outside anthropology (for example, in evolutionary psychology). The idea that the most aggressive men win the most wives and have the most children, thus passing their aggressive genes on to future generations more abundantly than the peaceful genes of their nonaggressive brethren, is a cornerstone of the popular view that humans are innately violent (see Issue 2). Thus, Tierney's attack on Chagnon's credibility sent shock waves through the scholarly community.

In this selection, Turner argues that Tierney is correct in claiming that Chagnon failed to object when gold miners used his portrayal of the Yanomami as violent to hinder the establishment of a Yanomami reserve in Brazil, that Chagnon manipulated his demographic data to support his hypothesis that more violent Yanomami men have more wives and children than less violent ones, and that his fieldwork practices caused conflict between Yanomami groups. Hagen, Price, and Tooby counter that Tierney deliberately misrepresents evidence in claiming that Chagnon violated Yanomami taboos in his fieldwork and that he manipulated his data to support his claim that killers have more offspring than nonkillers.

YES

Terence Turner

The Yanomami and the Ethics of Anthropological Practice

Controversy over the mistreatment of the Yanomami, an indigenous people of Venezuela and northern Brazil, by scientific researchers and anthropologists had smoldered for over a decade before it burst into flame [in 2001] with the publication of Patrick Tierney's *Darkness in El Dorado*. The controversy over the issues raised in the book, and more broadly over what has been done to the Yanomami by anthropologists and other researchers, confronts the discipline of anthropology, as represented by it professional society, the American Anthropological Association, and several universities and learned societies with which some of the principals in the case were connected, with ethically fraught issues. How these issues are dealt may well set significant precedents for the ethical and scientific standards of the institutions and professions involved, particularly in regard to the responsibilities of professional associations for the conduct of their members, and of researchers in the field for their human subjects. . . .

My work as head of the AAA Special Commission to Investigate the Situation of the Brazilian Yanomami in 1990–91 was the original reason for my involvement in Yanomami affairs. Together with subsequent work with NGOs and anthropologists engaged in the struggle to support and defend the Yanomami, it remains the basis of my appraisal of much of Tierney's account of Chagnon's activities among the Yanomami, including his attacks on Yanomami-support NGOs and Yanomami leaders. I was appointed to head the Special AAA Commission on the Brazilian Yanomami by the then President of the AAA, Annette Weiner, on the basis of my work as an activist with Brazilian indigenous groups and indigenous support NGOs and my personal acquaintance, based on long-standing cooperation, with many actors and groups involved in the Yanomami struggle. My mission was to report back to the President and Executive Board of the Association on what if any action the Association should take on behalf of the Yanomami of Brazil. The context of this unusual appointment was the desperate, and at the time apparently losing battle to save the huge Yanomami Reserve. After a ten year struggle led by the Brazilian NGO, the CCPY (Committee to Create a Yanomami Park), the area had been studied, surveyed and tentatively demarcated by an official Brazilian governmental team, only to be invaded by 40,000 illegal gold miners in 1988. . . .

My investigation of the situation created by the multiple Yanomami crises of 1988 to 1991 for the AAA involved me in new or renewed contacts with Brazilian NGO workers, indigenous rights activists, medical doctors and health workers from governmental and private agencies, personnel of FUNAI, missionaries, progressive journalists, lawyers, politicians, and anthropologists (including officers of the Brazilian Anthropological Association, ABA). These encounters and consultations, together with further contacts and collaborations on subsequent visits to Brazil, comprise the basis of my published responses to Chagnon's unfounded calumnies against NGOs, Missions and the Yanomami leader Davi Kopenawa at the time of the gold miners' invasions and the campaign to dissolve the Yanomami Reserve from 1988 to 1991, his untruthful statements on the responsibility of the Salesians and the Yanomami themselves for the massacre at Haximu in December 1993, and his renewed diatribes against Davi Kopenawa at the 1994 AAA Meetings and on more recent occasions. They are also the basis of my evaluation of Tierney's account of the same events in his book, which I find substantially correct. . . .

The great majority of contemporary researchers who have worked with the Yanomami, or who have studied the effects of Chagnon's representations of the Yanomami in both Brazil and Venezuela, have critically challenged many of Chagnon's ethnographic and theoretical claims, his methods and actions in the field, and a number of his statements in popular media. . . .

The interdependence of ethical and empirical issues is unavoidable in dealing with Chagnon's work, in which factual claims of Yanomami aggressiveness and the link between killing and reproductive success are adduced, explicitly or implicitly, as "scientific" evidence for the sorts of statements he has made in the media that have been decried on ethical grounds. The issue becomes even more complex when one confronts the criticisms of Chagnon's data and analysis summarized and extended by Tierney. These criticisms, notably in Tierney's Chapter 10 that deals with Chagnon's 1988 article in *Science*, seriously imply the manipulation and withholding of data to support unsound but theoretically and ideologically desired conclusions. . . .

I will organize my discussion under five general headings [excerpt: from two are included here], designating general types of ethically problematic behavior, comprising representative instances from Tierney's text that seem to me to be sufficiently well documented and analyzed, and/or attested from other sources, to be considered "well founded". . . .

I. Statements and Silences by Chagnon Damaging to the Yanomami

I.A. Statements About "Fierceness" or Violent Aggressiveness as a Dominant Feature of Yanomami Society, and Silences (Failure to Speak Out Against Misuses of These Statements Damaging to the Yanomami)

Chagnon stood by virtually without demur during the drive to dismantle the Brazilian Yanomami reserve in 1988–92, while politicians, military leaders and journalists allied with mining interests employed his portrayal of the Yanomami as ferocious savages involved in chronic warfare over women, to justify the dismemberment of Yanomami territory. Their argument ran that Yanomami communities needed for their own safety to be isolated from one another by "corridors" of open land, which would incidentally be accessible to gold miners. Chagnon's refusal to disown this use of his work in Brazilian media, where it might have had some effect, became understood by both sides in the struggle over the Yanomami reserve from 1988 to 1992 as a statement by omission in support of the miners and their political allies. This had a serious enough impact that the Brazilian Anthropological Association formally appealed to the American Anthropological Association in 1989 demanding that the U.S. Association investigate the ethics of its member's tacit support of those who were exploiting his statements. The American Association failed to take action, and this failure has come back to haunt it. . . .

The issue, as the Brazilian Association's new statement forcefully put it, is not simply that third parties exploited Chagnon's statements and silences for their own purposes. Anthropological researchers, its statement acknowledges, have an obligation to speak the truth about their research findings, and cannot control the uses to which others may put their findings. They do, however, have an ethical responsibility to speak out against the misuse of their findings by third parties, especially when such misuse directly damages the people referred to and most especially when these people were the subjects of the anthropologist's research. . . .

I.B. Repeated and Untruthful Attacks on NGOs, Anthropological Activists and Yanomami Leaders

I.B.1. Attacks on NGOs, Anthropological Activists
. . . Tierney . . . accurately reports Chagnon's shocking charge "that the very people who posed as defenders of the Indians were actually destroying them". This was Chagnon's allegation, which he repeated in the *Times Literary Supplement* and the *New York Times,* that the medical clinics and outreach programs instituted by missionaries and NGOs were not actually helping but rather "killing" the Indians ("killing by kindness", in his words). Although primarily directed against the Salesians in Venezuela, this allegation was phrased so as implicitly to include missions and secular NGOs in Brazil. He further asserted that the Salesian missionaries, as well as unnamed Protestant missionaries at Mucajaí, were promoting warfare among Yanomami villages by giving or selling shotguns to the Indians on their mission stations. Yanomami leaders like Davi Kopenawa, he claimed, were not authentic leaders but "pawns" or "parrots", mindlessly repeating what their NGO and missionary manipulators told them to say. . . .

I.B.3. Chagnon's Attacks on Yanomami Leaders: (1) Davi Kopenawa
Chagnon has publicly charged on several occasions, beginning in the late 1980's and early 1990's, that the Brazilian Yanomami leader Davi Kopenawa was a mere "parrot" of NGOs, mouthing lines he was fed by the do-gooder organizations that supposedly kept him as a useful symbol for self-serving

fund-raising campaigns (again, he never cited specific statements or texts). Davi Kopenawa was a major asset in these struggles, as virtually the only Yanomami leader capable of speaking out for Yanomami interests in the Brazilian and international political arenas, who at the same time commanded genuine support among the Yanomami of his own and other communities. Kopenawa was and remains the most important spokesman for the Brazilian Yanomami: he is a dynamic, effective, and independent person and leader. Chagnon's gratuitous and untruthful attacks damaged (or were clearly intended to damage) him. Chagnon is still at it: A CNN TV crew that interviewed Chagnon in November 2000 was startled to hear him call Kopenawa "a cigar store Indian"). . . .

I.C. Ethnographic Misrepresentation as an Ethical Issue

Tierney analyzes a number of Chagnon's texts and statements that appear to involve possible manipulations of statistical data to support theoretical conclusions that would otherwise not follow, and the use of the same kinds of manipulations to implicate political enemies in causing the deaths of (or, in Chagnon's blunter term, "killing") Yanomami. Cases of the first kind may be considered to constitute a grey area between incorrect statistical analysis and deliberate manipulation. There seems little doubt, however, about the ethics of the much graver charges in the second category. . . .

Chagnon's article, "Life Histories, Blood revenge, and warfare in a tribal population", published in *Science* in 1988, has been taken by his critics and sociobiological supporters alike as the quintessential formulation of his theoretical claim that violent competition (fierceness) among males is driven by competition for sexual access to females, and that success in this competition, as measured by killing other men, therefore leads to increased reproductive success. Sociobiologists seized upon the Yanomami, as represented by Chagnon, as living examples of the evolutionary past of the race: the most direct links between the human present and the supposed primate heritage of Alpha male-centered harems and dominance hierarchies. . . . Tierney correctly points out that this notoriety, and the central misconception on which it was based, was overtly cultivated by Chagnon in public statements such as his presidential address to the Human Behavior and Evolutionary Society:

> I demonstrated that Yanomamo men in my 25 year study who had participated in the killing of other men had approximately three times as many children and more than two times as many wives as men their own ages who had not.

As Tierney also correctly says, this statement is thoroughly false. . . .

Tierney, relying partly on Lizot, somewhat more on Albert and most heavily on Ferguson, and contributing some findings of his own, provides a reasonably accurate summary of the criticisms of Chagnon's analysis. He reviews three fundamental criticisms of Chagnon's statistical manipulation of his data. Firstly, Chagnon's statistical comparison of the number of wives and children of "killers" (defined as "unokai", on the basis of their having undergone the ritual of purification for those who have participated in the killing of a person, *unokaimou*) to those of non-killers has been criticized as skewed by his inclusion of a large number of young men between 20–25 and 25–30 as members of the statistically relevant population. Very few Yanomami men of this age had killed anyone and almost none had wives or children. The result was to inflate the relative advantage of the killers, almost all of whom were older men, some over 30 and most over 40. When killers were compared with men of their own age-bracket, "the reproductive success of killers was not nearly as impressive— ranging between 40 to 67 percent, a fraction of the 208 percent advantage that Chagnon had broadcast to the press". In other words, age was a factor that accounted for much of the variation, and Chagnon had not taken it properly into account.

Another variable Chagnon left out of account, according to critics like Ferguson and Albert, was headman status (and the additional, partly overlapping status of shaman). In his 1988 paper, he simply classed all headmen as killers, "*unokai*", but as Tierney says, that is a confusion of categories. Most Yanomami headmen have several wives, because of their status as headmen rather than their status as "killers" ("*unokai*", in Chagnon's translation). Headman status, like age, is thus another variable that must be recognized as accounting for a significant part of the contrast in number of wives and children between men in the killers category and non-killers. Yet another important variable, explicitly excluded by Chagnon in his text, was the death of fathers. For reasons he did not explain, Chagnon excluded the children of dead fathers from his initial analysis. This turns out to have been a strategic point for his whole argument about reproductive success. According to Chagnon and other Yanomami ethnographers, successful killers become themselves the main targets of vengeance raids, and are highly likely to be killed in the midst of their reproductive years. As Brian Ferguson had been the first to point out, if this likelihood of killers to have their reproductive careers cut short were taken into account, the supposed reproductive advantage of killers might actually disappear to become negative. . . .

Tierney also raises a series of questions about manipulations of statistically strategic bits of data. Two young men in their twenties were listed in Chagnon's 1997 *Yanomamo Interactive* CD on The Ax Fight as having four and five children respectively. This was far more than the other men in their age category, and these two men had been identified as violent participants in the ax fight shown in the CD. Tierney checked Chagnon's original census and found that Mohesiwa was listed as born in 1938 and Ruwamowa in 1939, thus making them 33 and 32, respectively, rather than 24 and 27, as Chagnon now claimed, at the time of filming. Tierney "found no other mistakes in the census transfer. And if these were mistakes, they were statistically perfect ones"—as they seemed to show the greater reproductive success of violent men in contrast to their supposed age-mates in the under-30 categories.

There was also the case of the five young men Chagnon listed as killers in the under 25 age group, all of whom had wives. When challenged by Albert, however, Chagnon removed them to the 30-plus category, remarking that since the Yanomami do not count past three, the estimation of age is necessarily approximate. Their removal substantially altered the statistical predominance of killers as husbands and fathers in their age category. In sum, as Tierney remarks, "Minute manipulations in each age category could easily skew all the results"—and apparently had done so in the cases in question. . . .

Tierney also pointed out that although Chagnon had given the impression in his *Science* article that the three raids he described involved communities that were still living in a relatively traditional way, unaffected by the presence of missionaries and government agents that had led to the decline or suppression of warfare in other areas of Yanomami country, this was not the case. Chagnon had identified the villages in his article only by number, which Lizot had complained made them impossible to match up with any known (named) Yanomami communities. Tierney succeeded in identifying 9 of the 12 villages involved, showing that they were the same ones where he had done most of his fieldwork. . . .

Once identified and connected by Tierney to their known historical contexts, the three raids described in abstract terms in the *Science* article assumed different meanings. Pinning down the actual identities and locations of the villages showed that they were actually situated in an area of heavy contact with Venezuelan society and missionary influence. No longer abstract instances of violent competition for reproductive success, in an indigenous world whose essential patterns of warfare had not yet been affected by alien presences such as missionaries or anthropologists, they now appeared as significantly affected by Chagnon's own presence and activities. Chagnon himself, it transpired, had "filmed, transported, and coordinated" two of the three raiding parties over part of the distance to their targets. . . .

I.C. False Accusations Against Missions and NGO's of "killing" Yanomami or Otherwise Being Responsible for Raising Their Death Rate

In an OpEd column in the New York Times of October 1993, Chagnon claimed that Yanomami were dying at missionary posts with medical facilities at four times the rate obtaining in "remote" villages. This was supposedly based on statistics Chagnon had collected and was the key data he cited in support of his shocking allegation that the Salesian missionaries were "killing the Yanomami with kindness". Tierney notes that this has become "one of the most frequently quoted statements in the Yanomami controversy," but shows that it is actually a misleading effect obtained by switching statistical data between categories of the study. He explains,

> Chagnon divided the villages in three categories of mission contact: "remote", "intermediate", and "maximum". The villages with maximum [mission] contact had a thirty percent *lower* mortality rate than remote groups, while the "intermediate" villages suffered four times as many deaths as the missions. Chagnon's data thus confirmed what all other researchers have found, but in the NYT Chagnon converted the "intermediate" villages into "missions", which they are not. . . There is no doubt that the debate about mission mortality has been based on misinformation.

Tierney accurately chronicles Chagnon's attempt to spin the tragic episode of the massacre of twelve Yanomami from the village of Haximu by Brazilian gold miners in July 1993 into a series of spurious charges against the Yanomami from the village of Paapiu for being partly responsible for the massacre and the Salesian missionaries for trying to cover it up. The "cover up", in Chagnon's version, chiefly consisted in a campaign by the missionaries to block his "investigation" of the massacre, in order to prevent him from discovering and disclosing their role in "killing the Yanomami by kindness" at their mission stations (see preceding section). This was tantamount to accusing the Salesians of being accessories after the fact to mass murder.

Chagnon claimed he had the right to investigate the murders as a member of a Venezuelan Presidential Commission on Yanomami affairs. With his ally Brewer-Carias, Chagnon had in fact been appointed to a commission to supervise the projected Yanomami Biosphere Reserve by the transitional President who succeeded Carlos Andres-Perez after the latter's impeachment. This commission, however, lacked any specific investigative powers relevant to the massacre. An unprecedented national outcry, with massive street demonstrations and protests against Brewer's and Chagnon's appointments, specifically including their declared intention to conduct an investigation of the massacre, followed the announcement of these appointments. This historically unprecedented wave of opposition led the President to appoint a different commission specifically to investigate the massacre. The intent was clearly to remove Chagnon and Brewer from any connection with the Haximu investigation, and it was so understood by the Venezuelan media and public, although the President did not get around to formally dissolving the Brewer-Chagnon commission until later. . . . Chagnon, accompanied by Brewer, nevertheless attempted to go to Haximu to "investigate", regardless of the fact that the new Presidential investigating commission was already en route to the spot, and they lacked the necessary authorization to go to the area, let alone to conduct an investigation. When they landed at the village airstrip, two miles from the massacre site, they were summarily ordered to leave by the judge who headed the legitimate investigative commission. She gave Brewer and Chagnon a choice: get out of Haximu immediately or face arrest. The air force pilot who had flown them to the spot sided with the judge. He flew Chagnon straight to Caracas, confiscated his notes and told him to get out of Venezuela within twenty-four hours. Chagnon did so. . . .

Another of Chagnon's attempts to implicate missionaries in fomenting Yanomami killings by distributing shotguns was his attack, in the fourth edition of his book, on the Protestant Missionaries of the Evangelical Mission of Amazonia, supposedly stationed at Mucajaí. Tierney shows that this account is a fictional pastiche, combining aspects of the geography, personnel and history of the distant, and long-abandoned, mission station of Surucucu with those of Mucajaí, and adding elements of fantasy and distorted and displaced versions of actual actions. Indians lugging a washing machine over the mountain by the mission station at Surucucu becomes a single Missionary carrying a refrigerator on his back over a non-existent mountain at Mucajaí. The refusal of missionaries at Surucucu to sell shotguns to the Indians, and their abandonment of the mission post there rather than be obliged to do so, becomes the provision of shotguns by the Mucajaí missionaries to the Yanomami, their guilt supposedly redoubled by their subsequent refusal to inquire if the guns they had provided had been those used in an attack on a "remote" village (Chagnon suggests that if they found out that the guns they had provided had been the ones used, they would have to confiscate them, which would have made the Yanomami forsake the mission. As Tierney reports, everyone with any knowledge of these events, including the missionaries in question and others familiar with the different posts and mission families Chagnon had conflated, denounces Chagnon's account as fictional. . . .

II. Field Methods Disruptive of Yanomami Society

Drawing heavily on the writings of Brian Ferguson and his own data, Tierney documents charges that Chagnon's methods of obtaining the names of dead relatives, by exploiting enmities between factions and hostile communities, and above all by giving massive amounts of steel goods as presents, destabilized Yanomami communities and inter-communal relations, giving rise to conflicts, raids and wars. He also documents that Chagnon took a limited part in raids by transporting raiding parties in his motor launch. The issues here centrally involve the scale of operations and the time-pressure under which Chagnon was obliged to collect his pedigree data. Whether working for James Neel or on his own, his commitment to surveying the maximum possible numbers of villages in relatively minimal periods of time precluded normal anthropological methods of building rapport and finding culturally appropriate ways of obtaining culturally taboo information that have been used successfully by other anthropologists who have worked among the Yanomami. This forced him to resort to bullying and intimidation, including shooting off firearms and performing shamanic rituals of magical child-killing. It also led him to resort to bribery on a massive scale, using huge amounts of steel tools, pots, etc. These hoards of otherwise rare and highly valued items became foci of conflict between rival factions and villages, which on a number of documented occasions led to raids and wars in which people were killed.

As his work continued over the years, Chagnon, rather than modifying his modus operandi to diminish its destabilizing effects, continued to raise the ante, becoming a player in the regional system of conflicts and the struggle for dominance that were set off in part by quarrels over the wealth he brought with him. There began to be wars between "Chagnon's" village, containing Yanomami dependent on him for steel goods, and villages associated with other sources of goods, such as the anthropologist Lizot, and the independent Yanomami cooperative SUYAO. All of this, Tierney, Ferguson, Albert, and others have argued, represented a massive disruption of Yanomami social peace consequent upon Chagnon's field methods. If so, it may be considered to constitute a violation of clause III.A.2 of the AAA Code of Ethics: "Anthropological researchers must do everything in their power to ensure that their research does not harm the safety, dignity, or privacy of the people with whom they work . . .".

The sheer scale of Chagnon's operations thus came to constitute a sui generis factor with ethical effects and implications not anticipated by the existing AAA Code of Ethics. Over a period of thirty years, according to anthropologist Brian Ferguson and others familiar with the political and historical aspects of his research, Chagnon has used methods to extract culturally sensitive data and biological specimens from Yanomami that have involved the violation of Yanomami cultural norms and caused dissension, and occasionally conflict, between communities and between factions of the same community. These conflicts, according to Ferguson, seconded by Tierney, have sometimes led to the breakup of communities and to inter-village raiding. Chagnon's tactics reportedly included giving large amounts of steel tools, the most esteemed presents, to certain villages or factions, thus inevitably destabilizing relations with non-recipients groups. The[se] also included, by his own account, deliberately lying to a village or faction that he had obtained the taboo names of their dead relatives from another village or faction, thus arousing anger and resentment that he could exploit to get the village or faction in question to give up the names of the deceased ancestors of the other group. After Chagnon got his data and departed, the villagers were left with bitter resentments that could aggravate existing tensions and provoke open conflicts. Chagnon seems also to have employed bullying and intimidation, brandishing weapons and shooting off firearms to make the Yanomami (who are usually the opposite of "fierce" in relations with non-Yanomami such as Venezuelans and Euro-North Americans) willing to give him information, if only to get rid of him.

The effectiveness of these tactics owed much to Chagnon's dramatic exploitation of the great discrepancy between his resources of wealth and power and those of the Yanomami as leverage to extract information, without regard to the ways this disrupted the social relations, stability and political peace of the communities of the people among whom he worked. The main authority for these allegations are the writings and public statements of Chagnon himself. One does not need to be a "left wing academic" or an "anti-science culturologist" to agree that these tactics raise questions of research ethics. . . .

IV.B. What Is to Be Done?

I believe that we as anthropologists owe it to the Yanomami, and to ourselves, to speak the truth publicly about what has been done to the Yanomami. In this sense, the role of the Association and its Task Force may be compared to that of truth commissions in places like South Africa or Guatemala: not to punish individuals, but to make principled public statements about what has been done, by whom, and in what ways the actions and statements in question may have violated the collective ethical standards of the profession. . . .

Anthropology as a discipline and as a profession can learn valuable lessons from analyzing what went wrong in Neel's and Chagnon's work, and why. I have suggested that a common thread connecting the ethical problems of both researchers is that concern with large-scale data collection under high time pressure, exacerbated in some cases by the institutional pressures of big scientific research projects, led both to make inadequate allowance for ethical and cultural standards, and in some cases, the social and physical well-being of the individual persons and communities comprising their subject populations. For anthropology, the lesson is that the pursuit of large amounts of quantitative data in abstraction from the cultural and social forms of life of the local people may become an end in itself that leads researchers to lose sight of or ignore the social standards and needs of the people they study. Such data, no matter how scientifically valuable, must never be pursued to the point of disruption of local social relations and cultural standards, or allowed to take priority over the well being of persons and communities. . . .

NO

Edward H. Hagen, Michael E. Price, and John Tooby

Preliminary Report

Introduction

As we will begin to show in this report, *Darkness in El Dorado* is essentially a work of fiction. Its author, Patrick Tierney, has very selectively quoted hundreds of sources in order to, first, caricature anthropologist Napoleon Chagnon's work on the Yanomamö, and second, to discredit what he claims is "Chagnon's ethnographic image of the ferocious Yanomami" by instead portraying them as meek, peaceful, helpless, and, ultimately, victims of Chagnon himself. Tierney's creative use of primary sources in this venture begins almost immediately. After a brief introductory chapter, Tierney wastes little time attempting to undermine Chagnon's portrayal of Yanomamö males as relatively healthy and frequently engaged in war:

> Before going into the jungle, I had read and admired The Fierce People. So it was surprising to see that the Yanomami—so terrifying and "burly" in Chagnon's text—were, in fact, among the tiniest, scrawniest people in the world. Adults averaged four feet seven inches in height, and children had among the lowest weight-height ratios on the planet.

References are supposed to support, not refute, the claims one is making. Tierney's reference above cites a relatively short paper by Rebecca Holmes on Yanomamö health. Although the paper does confirm the widely known fact that Yanomamö are short, it does not support one of Tierney's major themes: that Chagnon has exaggerated the frequency of Yanomamö warfare. What Tierney fails to mention here or anywhere else in his book is what Holmes says in her paper about Yanomamö war:

> Raids resulting in serious wounds and death occur *several times a year* in spite of missionary pressure to restrict warfare. About 20 warriors from Parima A, a two-day walk through the jungle from Parima B, raided one of the settlements in Parima B during our fieldwork. There were no injuries, although a study of the nurse's recent medical records indicates that these raids not uncommonly result in wounds from poison arrows. (Holmes 1985, p. 249; emphasis added).

Tierney cites Holmes' paper four times but he fails to mention her evidence on war and violence on any of these occasions, evidence which is directly relevant to one of the major themes of his book. This failure is obviously deliberate. . . .

Preliminary Evaluation of Chapter 3

Naming the Dead

Tierney, in Chapter 3 (The Napoleonic Wars) and elsewhere in his book, fingers Chagnon's method of obtaining accurate genealogies as a source of conflict between individuals and villages, and, more generally, as an affront to Yanomamö dignity (Chagnon's recent statement on this issue can be found in Appendix XIV). What we will show below is that Tierney's account is substantially undermined by the very sources he cites.

First, however, it may be useful to note that most societies, including the US, have a 'name taboo.' In the US, for example, it is not wrong to mention one person's first name or nickname to another person who does not know it, but it is often considered rude to *use* the nickname or first name of someone if you do not know them well. For example, even if Judith Smith's friends call her 'Judy', she might be offended if a stranger used that name instead of 'Judith' or Ms. Smith. How many news articles on *Darkness* have referred to 'Pat' or even 'Patrick' instead of 'Patrick Tierney' or 'Mr. Tierney'? None. In professional contexts, it is also rude to use someone's first name instead of their title and last name (e.g., Dr. Smith). In court rooms, we do not even use the judge's name, but instead address him or her as 'your honor' even though it is perfectly OK to know the judge's name, or ask someone what his or her name is. So, Americans have a rather elaborate name taboo.

The Yanomamö 'name taboo' is quite similar to the American 'name taboo.' Names are *not* 'scared [sic] secrets' (almost everyone knows them, in fact), but their *use* in particular social contexts is considered rude and insulting, just as, for Americans, *knowing* someone's first name or nickname is not insulting or wrong, but the *use* of nicknames and first names is rude and insulting in certain social contexts. (For the Yanomamö, the improper use of names is much more insulting than for Americans, however.) Here is Chagnon explaining the name taboo:

> The taboo is maintained even for the living, for one mark of prestige is the courtesy others show you by not using your name publicly. This is particularly true for men, who are much more competitive for status than women in this culture, and it is fascinating to watch boys grow into young men, demanding to be called either by a kinship term in public, or by a teknonymous reference such as 'brother of Himotoma' (see Glossary). The more effective they are at getting others to avoid using their names, the more public acknowledgment there is that they are of high esteem and social standing. Helena Valero, a Brazilian woman who was captured as a child by a Yanomamö raiding party, was married for many years to a Yanomamö headman before she discovered what his name was. The sanctions behind the taboo are more complex than just this, for they involve a combination of fear, respect, admiration, political deference, and honor.

The Yanomamö were understandably concerned that if the stranger in their midst (Chagnon) learned their names, he might *use* them disrespectfully. Chagnon *never* did this. Chagnon *always* addressed individuals in the proper manner, and he never intentionally used names disrespectfully (nor does Tierney present any evidence that Chagnon used names disrespectfully). Chagnon always used the Yanomamö equivalent of 'Judith' when that was appropriate, 'Ms. Smith' when that was appropriate, and 'Your Honor' when that was appropriate. Because he was struggling with a foreign culture, Chagnon occasionally but *unintentionally* offended individuals. Unlike academics, the Yanomamö are forgiving; they knew his missteps were accidental, and took no lasting offence.

Chagnon also found that it was easier to obtain a person's name from non-kin or enemies. In the US, Judith Smith's friends might be reluctant to reveal Judith's nickname to a stranger—not because *knowing* the nickname is taboo, but because its improper *use* might offend their friend—but people who were not close friends of Judith's would feel no such reluctance, nor would they violate any taboo by revealing the nickname. The same applies to the Yanomamö—asking non-kin and enemies about names is *not* taboo (remember, these names are widely known, and there is no taboo against outsiders knowing these names).

Contrary to Tierney's claims, Chagnon did *not* play enemies or villages off one another to obtain names. Notice that in Tierney's account of Chagnon's method, these claims have no supporting citations:

> Chagnon found himself in a difficult predicament, having to collect genea-logical trees going back several generations. This was frustrating for him because the Yanomami do not speak personal names out loud. And the names of the dead are the most taboo subject in their culture.
>
> "To name the dead, among the Yanomami, is a grave insult, a motive of division, fights, and wars," wrote the Salesian Juan Finkers, who has lived among the Yanomami villages on the Mavaca River for twenty-five years.
>
> Chagnon found out that the Yanomami "were unable to understand why a complete stranger should want to possess such knowledge [of per-sonal names] unless it were for harmful magical purposes." So Chagnon had to parcel out "gifts" in exchange for these names. [Anthropologists have 'to parcel out gifts' for most interviews with most informants on most topics. Giving gifts in exchange for extensive genealogical information is common practice in anthropology] One Yanomami man threatened to kill Chagnon when he mentioned a relative who had recently died. Others lied to him and set him back five months with phony genealogies [both these events are discussed in detail by Chagnon]. But he kept doggedly pursuing his goal.
>
> Finally, he invented a system, as ingenious as it was divisive [no citation], to get around the name taboo [Chagnon was not trying to 'get around the name taboo,' a claim that makes no sense ('getting around the name taboo' would entail *using* names disrespectfully—something he never did, nor had any desire to do). Chagnon was trying, not only get information necessary to his research, but also to integrate himself into Yanomamö society by learning what was common knowledge: everyone's name, including those of ancestors]. Within groups, he sought out "informants who might be considered 'aberrant' or 'abnormal,' outcasts in their own society," people he could bribe and

isolate more easily. These pariahs resented other members of society, so they more willingly betrayed sacred secrets [names are not 'sacred secrets'—they are public knowledge] at others' expense and for their own profit. [son-in-laws doing bride service—who are therefore not living with their kin—are a common example of what Tierney terms 'pariahs'] He resorted to "tactics such as 'bribing' children when their elders were not around, or capitalizing on animosities between individuals." [using children as informants is, again, common practice among anthropologists—usually because they have the patience for the all the tedious questions that anthropologists ask]

Chagnon was most successful at gathering data, however, when he started playing one village off against another. "I began traveling to other villages to check the genealogies, picking villages that were on strained terms with the people about whom I wanted information. I would then return to my base camp and check with local informants the accuracy of the new information. If the informants became angry when I mentioned the new names I acquired from the unfriendly group, I was almost certain that the information was accurate." [see below for the material that Tierney has omitted from this quote]

When one group became angry on hearing that Chagnon had gotten their names, he covered for his real informants but gave the name of another village nearby as the source of betrayal [no citation]. It showed the kind of dilemmas Chagnon's work posed. In spite of the ugly scenes he both witnessed and created, Chagnon concluded, "There is, in fact, no better way to get an accurate, reliable start on genealogy than to collect it from the enemies."

His divide-and-conquer information gathering exacerbated individual animosities [no citation], sparking mutual accusations of betrayal [no citation]. Nevertheless, Chagnon had become a prized political asset of the group with whom he was living, the Bisaasi-teri.

As usual, Tierney deliberately omits critical evidence that readers need to fairly evaluate his accusations and insinuations. With the exception of the quote from the Salesian missionary Juan Finkers, all of the cited information in the above quote comes from Chagnon's publications.

Tierney also conveniently fails to mention that Kaobawa, a Yanomamö headman, *demanded* that Chagnon learn the truth, even though he knew that would involve Chagnon learning the names of his dead kinsmen:

[Kaobawa's] knowledge of details was almost encyclopedic, his memory almost photographic. More than that, he was enthusiastic about making sure I learned the truth, and he encouraged me, indeed, *demanded* that I learn all details I might otherwise have ignored. . . . With the information provided by Kaobawa, and Rerebawa [another informant], I made enormous gains in understanding village interrelationships based on common ancestors and political histories and became lifelong friends with both. And both men knew that I had to learn about his recently deceased kin from the other one. It was one of those quiet understandings we all had but none of us could mention.

This information is in Chagnon's popular monograph, *Yanomamö* (which Tierney cites numerous times).

When Chagnon began his fieldwork with a Yanomamö village in the sixties, the Yanomamö did not know why Chagnon wanted to know their names, and were understandably quite reluctant to reveal this information to an outsider who might use it disrespectfully. Chagnon recounts the humorous and ingenious tactics the villagers used to deceive him about their real names during his initial stint in the field, and his own equally ingenious method of penetrating this deception by getting the information from other Yanomamö in enemy villages (see Appendix XIII for the monograph excerpt). Indeed, this is one of the major flaws in Tierney's account: he conveniently fails to mention that the methods that Chagnon discusses are those he used during the first six months or so of his fieldwork, before the Yanomamö had come to trust that Chagnon was not going to use the information disrespectfully. That Chagnon made strenuous attempts to avoid offending anyone while collecting names is clear from sentences that immediately follow those Tierney chooses to cite (material in bold not cited by Tierney):

> I began traveling to other villages to check the genealogies, picking villages that were on strained terms with the people about whom I wanted information. I would then return to my base camp and check with local informants the accuracy of the new information. If the informants became angry when I mentioned the new names I acquired from the unfriendly group, I was almost certain that the information was accurate. **For this kind of checking I had to use informants whose genealogies I knew rather well: they had to be distantly enough related to the dead person that they would not go into a rage when I mentioned the name, but not so remotely related that they would be uncertain of the accuracy of the information. Thus, I had to make a list of names that I dared not use in the presence of each and every informant. Despite the precautions, I occasionally hit a name that put the informant into a rage, such as that of a dead brother or sister that other informants had not reported. This always terminated the day's work with that informant, for he would be too touchy to continue any further, and I would be reluctant to take a chance on a accidentally discovering another dead kinsman so soon after the first.**
>
> **These were always unpleasant experiences, and occasionally dangerous ones, depending on the temperament of the informant.**

Chagnon stresses his efforts to avoid mentioning the names of the dead to close kin in all five editions of his monograph, yet Tierney *deliberately* fails to mention this. . . .

However history may judge Chagnon's method of obtaining accurate genealogies (Native North Americans rely heavily on accurate genealogies in laying claim to valuable government benefits, etc.) it is important to properly represent what he did. Tierney instead deliberately omits key evidence that would allow the reader to evaluate his claims and improperly characterizes names as "sacred secrets" of the Yanomamö as a group; instead, their public *use* reflects the status and respect accorded to particular individuals. Using the same sources cited by Tierney, it is clear that Chagnon never used names disrespectfully, and soon came to be trusted on this matter by the Yanomamö. . . .

Detailed Evaluation of Chapter 10:
To Murder and to Multiply

Brief Introduction

Chapter 10 of *Darkness in El Dorado* by Patrick Tierney is an extended attack on a well-known 1988 paper published by Chagnon in *Science* entitled "Life Histories, Blood Revenge, and Warfare in a Tribal Population." In this paper, Chagnon argues that warfare among the Yanomamö is characterized by blood revenge: an attack on one group by another prompts a retaliatory attack, which itself prompts retaliation, *ad infinitum*. In other words, Yanomamö war is quite similar to the patterns of conflict we see in the Balkans, the Middle East, Africa— anywhere ethnic groups come into armed conflict. In order to understand this pattern among the Yanomamö (and thus, perhaps, everywhere else), Chagnon presents data which suggest that successful Yanomamö warriors (unokai—men who have killed) are rewarded for their bravery and success. Among the Yanomamö, these rewards take the form of wives. Chagnon showed that unokai have more wives, and consequently more offspring, than non-unokai. Chagnon argued that if, over evolutionary time, cultural success lead [sic] to reproductive success, individuals would be selected to strive for cultural success. He further argued that cultural success is often achieved by engaging in successful military actions against enemies. Perhaps, then, the cycles of violence suffered by countless groups worldwide are driven, in part, by men who seek status and prestige by successfully attacking enemies.

This entire thesis has been assailed by Chagnon's critics, and Tierney hopes to bury it by demonstrating that Chagnon's research was shoddy, dishonest, and contradicted by other studies. In fact, whether or not Chagnon's theory is correct, *many* studies have demonstrated that, in small-scale societies, cultural success does lead to reproductive success, that cultural success is frequently associated with military success, and conflicts are often caused by conflicts over women. Tierney reviews almost none of these studies, and when he does, he omits key evidence that supports Chagnon's thesis.

Before we begin our analysis of Tierney's efforts in this chapter, we note that people often misconstrue Chagnon's work to mean that the Yanomamö are exceptionally violent, unlike other groups. Nothing could be further from the truth. In fact, we now know that most non-state societies have (or had) high rates of violence compared to state societies. Chagnon was one of the first to document in detail the profound impact of intergroup violence on a non-state society. . . .

Chagnon has also famously claimed that Yanomamö wars often start with conflicts over women. Tierney implies or states several times that this is either unimportant, "secondary," or a fabrication of Chagnon's. For example:

> Yet the popular image of the Yanomami waging war for women persisted. Chagnon deftly *created it* by repeatedly claiming that men went on raids, captured women, and raped them at will afterward.

If Chagnon had created this image, then there should be no independent reports of Yanomamö raiding for women, and there should especially be no such reports predating Chagnon's. There are, however, many accounts of Yanomamö raiding for women that predate Chagnon's, accounts that place more emphasis on wife-capture than Chagnon does (Chagnon has stated several times that it is often not the principle [sic] motivation for a raid). . . .

Selective Omission of Data Which Support Chagnon's Findings

Claim   Tierney argues against Chagnon's claim that warriorship and reproductive success are correlated in tribal societies, citing a study of the Waorani:

> Among the Waorani of the Ecuadorian Amazon, a tribe with the world's highest known rate of attrition of war, every known male has killed at least once. But warriors who killed more than twice were more than twice as likely to be killed themselves—and their wives were killed at three times the rate of other, more peaceful men. Most prolific killers lost their wives and had to remarry—which made it look as if they had more wives if they survived.

Misrepresentation   Here, Tierney omits important information which supports the validity of Chagnon's result. Tierney refers to a recent ethnography of the Waorani in which the authors actually went out and collected the data to test Chagnon's model. The problem was, since all Waorani males had participated in a killing, they could not separate killers from non-killers. Instead they categorized men based on how many killings they had participated in: 1–5, 6–10, and 11+. Then they compared the numbers of wives and offspring among men in each of these categories. They found that killers of 1–5 people averaged 1.35 wives and 4.37 offspring, killers of 6–10 people averaged 2.00 wives and 6.08 offspring, and killers of 11+ people averaged 2.25 wives and 8.25 offspring. Thus, these data are highly consistent with those of Chagnon. The Robarcheks have essentially replicated Chagnon's finding, although they have a different interpretation of this result. They go on to present data showing that more prolific killers are more likely to get killed themselves and to lose a wife to violence; the latter are the only data that Tierney chooses to report. Tierney thus omits what is both the crux of the Robarcheks' study, and also the most useful element for evaluating the reliability of Chagnon's result: the successful replication of that result. . . .

Insinuates That Chagnon Dishonestly Confounded Unokais and Headmen

Claim   Tierney insinuates that Chagnon dishonestly includes headmen, in addition to unokais, in his sample and that the presence of headmen somehow skewed his results:

> "In his *Science* piece all headmen were also included as "killers," a confusion of categories; when the headmen were factored out, the study's statistical significance in one of its major age categories collapsed, Chagnon admitted. He would not say which category it was. . . . Again, Chagnon maintained a tenacious silence in the face of public challenge, this time by the anthropologist Brian Ferguson."

Misrepresentation Chagnon does indeed include headmen in his sample of unokais, but only because these headmen are unokai, as Chagnon states clearly: "All headmen in this study are unokai." Tierney seems to suggest that Chagnon includes some headmen that he knows not to be unokai. Brian Ferguson, in *American Ethnologist,* did challenge Chagnon's inclusion of headmen in his study, saying that since headmen usually have more wives and children, and since all headmen in the study were unokai, the inclusion of headmen might increase the correlation between unokainess and reproductive success. Ferguson's point is actually misguided: the fact that all headmen were unokai is highly consistent with Chagnon's theory that in tribal societies "cultural success leads to biological success," i.e. good warriorship leads to high social status, which in turn leads to high reproductive success, and it is absurd to suggest that the presence of unokai headmen somehow contradicts a theory which it in fact strongly supports. Nevertheless, in a piece entitled "Response to Ferguson" which immediately followed Ferguson's challenge in the same issue of *American Ethnologist,* Chagnon agreed to reanalyze the data with headmen removed. Even with headmen removed, unokais (compared to non-unokais) had significantly more offspring in all four age categories, and more wives in three of four age categories ($ps < .05$). In one age category (ages 31–40), the difference between unokai and non-unokai wives was just barely not significant ($p = .07$). The statistical "collapse" to which Tierney refers is apparently the fact that $p = .07$ rather than $<.05$ for the 31–40 category, an extremely minor discrepancy misleadingly referred to as a "collapse." And there was no "tenacious silence" by Chagnon with regard to which age category was affected by the removal of headmen: Chagnon states clearly in his *American Ethnologist* piece that the category is "31–40." Tierney is clearly aware of this article (he cites it and it appears in his bibliography), so it is odd that he seems to overlook it here. . . .

Misrepresents Chagnon's Explanation for Unokai Reproductive Success

Claim Tierney suggests that Chagnon claims that the link between killing and reproductive success is due solely to the fact that Yanomamö killers are more successful in abducting women in raids. Tierney notes that this link is "tenuous" because only a "low" number of women are actually abducted in raids:

> Nor was there anything but the most tenuous connection between killing, raiding, and the capture of women. The number of women captured in the warfare of the Yanomami is low, despite their reputation. . . . Yet the popular image of the Yanomami waging war for women persisted. Chagnon deftly created it by repeatedly claiming that men went on raids, captured women, and raped them at will afterwards.

Misrepresentation In fact, Chagnon has stated repeatedly that when he says the Yanomamö "fight over women," he does not mean that they usually initiate raids for the purpose of abducting women. He simply means that most conflicts begin as some kind of sexual dispute, and he makes this clear in the target article: "most fights begin over sexual issues: infidelity and suspicion of infidelity, attempts to seduce another man's wife, sexual jealousy, forcible appropriation of women from visiting groups, failure to give a promised girl in marriage, and (rarely) rape." On the same page he is clear that most wars are perpetuated by revenge, not the desire to abduct women: "The most common explanation given for raids (warfare) is revenge for a previous killing, and the most common explanation for the initial cause of the fighting is 'women'." In his famous ethnography—cited extensively by Tierney—Chagnon says "although few raids are initiated solely with the intention of capturing women, this is always a desired side benefit" and "Generally, however, the desire to abduct women does not lead to the initiation of hostilities between groups that have no history of mutual raiding in the past." Tierney completely ignores that Chagnon downplays the significance of abduction as a motivation to raid and then claims that Chagnon "deftly created" the image of the Yanomamö waging war in order to abduct women.

Further, by concentrating exclusively on abduction as the only explanation for the high reproductive success of unokais, Tierney ignores what Chagnon claims might be "the most promising avenue of investigation to account for the high reproductive success of unokais," the fact that "cultural success leads to biological success." Chagnon explains that unokais, because of their prowess and willingness to take risks in military matters, are regarded as more valuable allies than non-unokais: "in short, military achievements are valued and associated with high esteem." This high status of unokais makes them more attractive as mates. In a published response to criticism about the target article, Chagnon goes into even greater detail about how unokai status makes men more attractive as mates.

Why Has Tierney Been So Dishonest?

To conclude our preliminary report, we ask the obvious question, "Why has Tierney been so dishonest?" The short answer is, we don't know. We offer the following two speculations [one included here]—but we must stress that these are only speculations, speculations we ourselves find less than satisfying. . . .

The field of anthropology has been riven for at least the last two decades by a debate between 'scientifically oriented' anthropologists and 'humanistically oriented' anthropologists. The former tend to believe that there is an objective human reality and that scientific methods will help us discover it. The latter tend to believe that realities are relative, and socially or culturally constructed, and they are often extremely skeptical and critical of Western science. The debate between these two camps has frequently been so bitter that it has caused prominent anthropology departments, like Stanford's, to split in two (http://www.stanford.edu/group/anthro). The debate is not confined to anthropology. It is widespread in the humanities and social sciences, and has come to be known as the Science Wars.

Tierney clearly hoped to successfully indict two of the most famous scientists to work with indigenous people in the Amazon, Chagnon and Neel, with serious crimes and breaches of ethics, and thus strike a blow against scientific, and particularly evolutionary, anthropology. For students and others, we provide our perspective on this issue, and how it may account, in part, for Tierney's dishonesty.

There are three fundamental aspects of Chagnon's career that place him at ground zero in the debate between 'scientific' anthropologists and 'humanistic' anthropologists. First, Chagnon has been a staunch and vocal proponent and practitioner of scientific anthropology, one whose books and films are widely assigned in anthropology courses around the world. Second, and even more galling to 'humanistically' oriented anthropologists (and disconcerting to many 'scientific' anthropologists as well) is Chagnon's use of sociobiological theory. Sociobiology is a set of theories and general principles about animal social behavior that derive from Darwin's theory of evolution by natural selection. Although biologists were excited by the sociobiological theories that appeared in the 1960's and 1970's, there was an immediate outcry by some biologists (e.g., Stephen J. Gould) and many social scientists when E. O. Wilson suggested that sociobiology might be useful for understanding *human* social behavior. It was 'obvious' to both sides in the sociobiology debate that the other side was motivated entirely by politics. In the ensuing war of words between supporters and critics of sociobiology, the field became stigmatized. Few social scientists are willing to use the theory, and even the many biologists employing sociobiology in their study of non-human animals avoid mentioning the word 'sociobiology.' Despite this, sociobiology is a standard part of the theoretical toolkit used by biologists in virtually every biology department in the world. It is, without doubt, the theory most widely used to study and understand the social behavior of all (non-human) living things. The world's most prestigious scientific journals, Science and Nature, routinely publish research articles using sociobiology, and hundreds of research articles using sociobiology are published every year in major biology journals. Applying sociobiology to humans, however, remains strictly taboo. Chagnon has openly violated this taboo by interpreting his data in light of sociobiological theories.

Finally, Chagnon has focused his career on one of the most contentious issues in anthropology: violence and aggression in small-scale, 'primitive' societies. Critiquing Western culture has been a popular topic in anthropology since the 1920's. (In fact, a widely used cultural anthropology text is titled *Anthropology as Cultural Critique.*) In order to critique Western culture, anthropologists often feel they must find non-Western cultures that do things better. Because violence and aggression in Western societies are well deserving of critique, anthropologists hoped to discover societies with little aggression or violence that could serve as examples of a better way of living. Chagnon, by contrast, argues that violence and aggression are common in most non-Western societies—even small-scale societies like the Yanomamö—and that violence and aggression are probably part of human nature. This has infuriated the many anthropologists who prefer practicing anthropology as cultural critique. The favorite alternative to Chagnon's interpretation of Yanomamö war is that of Brian Ferguson. Ferguson, unsurprisingly, blames Yanomamö war on the influence of Western culture.

By taking aim at Chagnon, Tierney has charged into the middle of this debate on the side of the humanists against the scientists, particularly against the tiny minority who apply Darwinian theory to people. The subtitle of his book is "How Scientists and Journalists Devastated the Amazon." The very first words in the book, in the frontpiece, are from Daniel Dennett: "It is important to recognize that Darwinism has always had an unfortunate power to attract the most unwelcome enthusiasts—demagogues and psychopaths and misanthropes and other abusers of Darwin's dangerous idea." (Although Tierney doesn't mention it, Dennett is actually a strong advocate of Darwinian approaches to social science, and has written in defense of Chagnon.) And much of the book is a muddled attempt to attack Chagnon's sociobiological approach to Yanomamö warfare. Tierney constantly inserts comments like "Chagnon picked up where Social Darwinists left off" (Ch. 2), and he is even willing to make unsupported accusations of murder: "the incredible faith the sociobiologists had in their theories was admirable. Like the old Marxist missionaries, these zealots of biological determinism sacrificed everything— including the lives of their subjects—to spread their gospel." (Ch. 2).

Maybe Tierney thought that if he could destroy Chagnon, arch-enemy of many humanistic anthropologists and culture critics, he would be a hero in the Science Wars. And maybe he really thought a victory in the Science Wars would help the Amazon and its peoples. But the Amazon is not being devastated by scientists. Or journalists. Or sociobiologists. It is being devastated by logging, mining, road building, and slash-and-burn farming by the region's burgeoning population. Character assassination will do precisely nothing to change this.

POSTSCRIPT

Did Napoleon Chagnon's Research Methods and Publications Harm the Yanomami Indians?

Turner agrees with journalist Patrick Tierney that Chagnon callously refused to disavow the image he created of the Yanomami as violent when gold miners and their supporters used that image against them. He also blames Chagnon for manipulating his data to contend that Yanomami are genetically programmed to be violent, due to violent males having more children than nonviolent ones, and for actually causing violence by his gift giving and violations of taboos. Hagen, Price, and Tooby retort that Tierney systematically selects and distorts his evidence to portray Chagnon in the worst possible light, and they argue that the amount of harm Chagnon did to the Yanomami pales compared to that caused by missionaries, gold miners, and other intruders into their territory.

This controversy exposed a deep rift in the anthropological community. The rift has been variously defined as between those who see anthropology as a science and those who consider it a humanistic discipline, between sociobiologists and cultural determinists, and, at the basest level, between scholars who personally like or dislike Neel and Chagnon. The battle lines are sharply drawn, and few anthropologists have remained neutral. The antagonists are pulling no punches in their charges and countercharges.

The El Dorado Task Force of the American Anthropological Association (AAA), which investigated Tierney's accusations, concluded, among other things, that Neel and his associates should be praised, not condemned, for vaccinating Yanomami against measles, an action that "unquestionably . . . saved many lives" (see the Final Report on the AAA Web site at http://www.aaanet.org). However, it criticized Chagnon on ethical and professional grounds for working with a group of wealthy and corrupt Venezuelans to gain access to the Yanomami in 1990, despite having been denied a research permit by the Venezuelan government. It also criticized him for misrepresenting the Yanomami as the "fierce people," a view used by others to justify violence against them, and for not correcting that image or supporting their human rights. Not surprisingly, the report has been criticized by Chagnon's supporters as too harsh and by his enemies as too lenient.

This controversy has generated a huge literature in a short time, the speed being due in large part to the widespread use of the Internet. The literature includes articles and book reviews in newspapers, popular magazines, and scholarly newsletters and journals; radio programs; and numerous documents and opinions posted on Web sites. The most comprehensive and balanced guide to sources is the Web site of Douglas Hume, a graduate student at the University of Connecticut (http://members.aol.com/archeodog/darkness_in_el_dorado/index.htm). It includes a comprehensive bibliography of materials published from September 2000 to the present and links to relevant Web sites and documents. The Web site for Public Anthropology (http://www.publicanthropology.org) contains papers from a round table discussion among several scholars with varying points of view. The Department of Anthropology at the University of California at Santa Barbara Web site (http://www.anth.ucsb.edu/chagnon.html) provides a number of documents and statements supporting Chagnon. The paperback edition of Tierney's book contains an eleven-page postscript responding to his critics. Other printed publications include the *Current Anthropology* Forum entitled "Reflections on Darkness in El Dorado," which presents comments by six scholars (*Current Anthropology*, vol. 42, no. 2, pp. 265–76, 2001). A relevant earlier source is Leslie Sponsel's article "Yanomami: An Arena of Conflict and Aggression in the Amazon" (*Aggressive Behavior*, vol. 24, no. 2, pp. 97–122, 1998).

ISSUE 18

Do Museums Misrepresent Ethnic Communities Around the World?

YES: James Clifford, from *The Predicament of Culture: Twentieth-Century Ethnography, Literature, and Art* (Harvard University Press, 1988)

NO: Denis Dutton, from "Mythologies of Tribal Art," *African Arts* (Summer 1995)

ISSUE SUMMARY

YES: Postmodernist anthropologist James Clifford argues that the very act of removing objects from their ethnographic contexts distorts the meaning of objects held in museums. He contends that whether these objects are displayed in art museums or anthropological museums, exhibitions misrepresent ethnic communities by omitting important aspects of contemporary life, especially involvement with the colonial or Western world.

NO: Anthropologist Denis Dutton asserts that no exhibition can provide a complete context for ethnographic objects, but that does not mean that museum exhibitions are fundamentally flawed. Dutton suggests that postmodernists misunderstand traditional approaches to interpreting museum collections, and what they offer as a replacement actually minimizes what we can understand of ethnic communities from museum collections.

In the late nineteenth and early twentieth centuries, museums were a major focus of anthropological research. In the United States, for example, until after the First World War more anthropologists were employed in museums than in universities. By 1940 cultural anthropologists had largely moved out of museums as they focused on intensive fieldwork. This change was directly related to a shift in paradigms from cultural evolution to functionalism, which happened in the 1920s and 1930s.

As anthropologists later began to focus on functional questions about how societies and their institutions worked, museum collections became increasingly unimportant. Many anthropologists believed that differences in the bindings of stone axes have little to say about how marriages were contracted or how clans were linked together; objects cannot explain how leadership worked or what role religious ideas might have had in maintaining social order.

The following selections deal with the question of how museums should exhibit and interpret ethnographic collections that were obtained during the "museum period" of anthropology. Both authors are critical of certain exhibitions, particularly art historian William Rubin's "Primitivism" show from 1984, and both feel that a good exhibition should contextualize museum objects historically. But the authors differ profoundly in their approach to the study of museum objects.

James Clifford surveys several different kinds of museum exhibits in New York and asks, Do any of them do justice to the peoples who made and used these objects? For Clifford, objects and the cultures from which they come have histories. He questions how much of these histories are present in the several exhibitions he visited. By definition, each and every non-Western object in a Western museum has been removed from its original ethnographic context, a process often referred to as "decontextualization."

Clifford explains in his selection how museums offer a "representation" of tribal peoples as if these societies were timeless and without history. By focusing on particular features of tribal culture, each exhibition makes statements about the relationship between modern Americans and "primitive" peoples. For him, these are fundamentally misleading representations.

Denis Dutton accepts that exhibitions such as those discussed by Clifford are inevitably incomplete, but the lack of a full context does not completely invalidate the exercise of exhibiting objects from tribal societies. He argues that Clifford and the other postmodernist critics of museum exhibitions go too far in their criticisms and that they, too, have an agenda that is itself misleading. Referring to this postmodernist agenda as a "new mythology" about tribal art, Dutton contends that the new mythologists have exaggerated their interpretations of museum exhibitions.

Dutton argues that museums can never offer complete representations of ethnic communities; but this does not mean that exhibitions cannot be both informative and enlightening even if they are incomplete. He asserts that Clifford's analysis leads us away from any understanding of museum objects; instead Clifford prefers to present his understandings of the culture through museum curators in our own modern culture. For Dutton, the goal should be to discover the meanings and significance of objects from the point of view of their original communities, and such meanings will never emerge from critiques of museum exhibitions like Clifford's.

How serious are the inevitable distortions of a museum exhibit? Does the omission of the current historical and global economic context misinform the public? How much context can a museum exhibition realistically provide? If such misrepresentations do occur, would it be better not to exhibit "primitive" art at all? What solutions to the problem of distortion do Clifford and Dutton propose?

James Clifford

 **YES**

Histories of the Tribal
and the Modern

During the winter of 1984–85 one could encounter tribal objects in an unusual number of locations around New York City. This [selection] surveys a half-dozen, focusing on the most controversial: the major exhibition held at the Museum of Modern Art (MOMA), "'Primitivism' in 20th Century Art: Affinity of the Tribal and the Modern." The . . . "ethnographic present" is late December 1984.

The "tribal" objects gathered on West Fifty-third Street have been around. They are travelers—some arriving from folklore and ethnographic museums in Europe, others from art galleries and private collections. They have traveled first class to the Museum of Modern Art, elaborately crated and insured for important sums. Previous accommodations have been less luxurious: some were stolen, others "purchased" for a song by colonial administrators, travelers, anthropologists, missionaries, sailors in African ports. These non-Western objects have been by turns curiosities, ethnographic specimens, major art creations. After 1900 they began to turn up in European flea markets, thereafter moving between avant-garde studios and collectors' apartments. Some came to rest in the unheated basements or "laboratories" of anthropology museums, surrounded by objects made in the same region of the world. Others encountered odd fellow travelers, lighted and labeled in strange display cases. Now on West Fifty-third Street they intermingle with works by European masters— Picasso, Giacometti, Brancusi, and others. A three-dimensional Eskimo mask with twelve arms and a number of holes hangs beside a canvas on which Joan Miró has painted colored shapes. The people in New York look at the two objects and see that they are alike.

Travelers tell different stories in different places, and on West Fifty-third Street an origin story of modernism is featured. Around 1910 Picasso and his cohort suddenly, intuitively recognize that "primitive" objects are in fact powerful "art." They collect, imitate, and are affected by these objects. Their own work, even when not directly influenced, seems oddly reminiscent of non-Western forms. The modern and the primitive converse across the centuries and continents. At the Museum of Modern Art an exact history is

From James Clifford, *The Predicament of Culture: Twentieth-Century Ethnography, Literature, and Art* (Harvard University Press, 1988). Originally published as "Histories of the Tribal and the Modern" in *Art in America* (April 1985). Copyright © 1985 by Brant Publications, Inc. Reprinted by permission of *Art in America*. Notes and references omitted.

told featuring individual artists and objects, their encounters in specific studios at precise moments. Photographs document the crucial influences of non-Western artifacts on the pioneer modernists. This focused story is surrounded and infused with another—a loose allegory of relationship centering on the word *affinity*. The word is a kinship term, suggesting a deeper or more natural relationship than mere resemblance or juxtaposition. It connotes a common quality or essence joining the tribal to the modern. A Family of Art is brought together, global, diverse, richly inventive, and miraculously unified, for every object displayed on West Fifty-third Street looks modern.

The exhibition at MOMA is historical and didactic. It is complemented by a comprehensive, scholarly catalogue, which includes divergent views of its topic and in which the show's organizers, William Rubin and Kirk Varnedoe, argue at length its underlying premises. One of the virtues of an exhibition that blatantly makes a case or tells a story is that it encourages debate and makes possible the suggestion of other stories. Thus in what follows different histories of the tribal and the modern will be proposed in response to the sharply focused history on display at the Museum of Modern Art. But before that history can be seen for what it is, however—a specific story that excludes other stories—the universalizing allegory of affinity must be cleared away.

This allegory, the story of the Modernist Family of Art, is not rigorously argued at MOMA. (That would require some explicit form of either an archetypal or structural analysis.) The allegory is, rather, built into the exhibition's form, featured suggestively in its publicity, left uncontradicted, repetitiously asserted—"Affinity of the Tribal and the Modern." The allegory has a hero, whose virtuoso work, an exhibit caption tells us, contains more affinities with the tribal than that of any other pioneer modernist. These affinities "measure the depth of Picasso's grasp of the informing principles of tribal sculpture, and reflect his profound identity of spirit with the tribal peoples." Modernism is thus presented as a search for "informing principles" that transcend culture, politics, and history. Beneath this generous umbrella the tribal is modern and the modern more richly, more diversely human.

⋅◈⋅

The power of the affinity idea is such (it becomes almost self-evident in the MOMA juxtapositions) that it is worth reviewing the major objections to it. Anthropologists, long familiar with the issue of cultural diffusion versus independent invention, are not likely to find anything special in the similarities between selected tribal and modern objects. An established principle of anthropological comparative method asserts that the greater the range of cultures, the more likely one is to find similar traits. MOMA's sample is very large, embracing African, Oceanian, North American, and Arctic "tribal" groups. A second principle, that of the "limitation of possibilities," recognizes that invention, while highly diverse, is not infinite. The human body, for example, with its two eyes, four limbs, bilateral arrangement of features, front and back, and so on, will be represented and stylized in a limited number of ways. There is thus a priori no reason to claim evidence for affinity (rather than mere resemblance or coincidence) because an exhibition of tribal works that seem impressively "modern" in style can be gathered. An equally striking collection could be made demonstrating sharp dissimilarities between tribal and modern objects.

The qualities most often said to link these objects are their "conceptualism" and "abstraction" (but a very long and ultimately incoherent list of shared traits, including "magic," "ritualism," "environmentalism," use of "natural" materials, and so on, can be derived from the show and especially from its catalogue). Actually the tribal and modern artifacts are similar only in that they do *not* feature the pictorial illusionism or sculptural naturalism that came to dominate Western European art after the Renaissance. Abstraction and conceptualism are, of course, pervasive in the arts of the non-Western World. To say that they share with modernism a rejection of certain naturalist projects is not to show anything like an affinity. Indeed the "tribalism" selected in the exhibition to resemble modernism is itself a construction designed to accomplish the task of resemblance. Ife and Benin sculptures, highly naturalistic in style, are excluded from the "tribal" and placed in a somewhat arbitrary category of "court" society (which does not, however, include large chieftainships). Moreover, pre-Columbian works, though they have a place in the catalogue, are largely omitted from the exhibition. One can question other selections and exclusions that result in a collection of only "modern"-looking tribal objects. Why, for example, are there relatively few "impure" objects constructed from the debris of colonial culture contacts? And is there not an overall bias toward clean, abstract forms as against rough or crude work?

The "Affinities" room of the exhibition is an intriguing but entirely problematic exercise in formal mix-and-match. The short introductory text begins well: "AFFINITIES presents a group of tribal objects notable for their appeal to modern taste." Indeed this is all that can rigorously be said of the objects in this room. The text continues, however, "Selected pairings of modern and tribal objects demonstrate common denominators of these arts that are independent of direct influence." The phrase *common denominators* implies something more systematic than intriguing resemblance. What can it possibly mean? . . . The affinity idea itself is wide-ranging and promiscuous, as are allusions to universal human capacities retrieved in the encounter between modern and tribal or invocations of the expansive human mind—the healthy capacity of modernist consciousness to question its limits and engage otherness.

. . . The affinities shown at MOMA are all on modernist terms. The great modernist "pioneers" (and their museum) are shown promoting formerly despised tribal "fetishes" or mere ethnographic "specimens" to the status of high art and in the process discovering new dimensions of their ("our") creative potential. The capacity of art to transcend its cultural and historical context is asserted repeatedly. . . .

At West Fifth-third Street modernist primitivism is a going Western concern. . . .

Indeed an unintended effect of the exhibition's comprehensive catalogue is to show once and for all the incoherence of the modern Rorschach of "the primitive." . . . [T]he catalogue succeeds in demonstrating not any essential affinity between tribal and modern or even a coherent modernist attitude toward the primitive but rather the restless desire and power of the modern West to collect the world.

⋅◈⋅

. . . If we ignore the "Affinities" room at MOMA, however, and focus on the "serious" historical part of the exhibition, new critical questions emerge. What is excluded by the specific focus of the history? Isn't this factual narration still infused with the affinity allegory, since it is cast as a story of creative genius recognizing the greatness of tribal works, discovering common artistic "informing principles"? Could the story of this intercultural encounter be told differently? It is worth making the effort to extract another story from the materials in the exhibition—a history not of redemption or of discovery but of reclassification. This other history assumes that "art" is not universal but is a changing Western cultural category. The fact that rather abruptly, in the space of a few decades, a large class of non-Western artifacts came to be redefined as art is a taxonomic shift that requires critical historical discussion, not celebration. That this construction of a generous category of art pitched at a global scale occurred just as the planet's tribal peoples came massively under European political, economic, and evangelical dominion cannot be irrelevant. But there is no room for such complexities at the MOMA show. Obviously the modernist appropriation of tribal productions as art is not simply imperialist. The project involves too many strong critiques of colonialist, evolutionist assumptions. As we shall see, though, the scope and underlying logic of the "discovery" of tribal art reproduces hegemonic Western assumptions rooted in the colonial and neocolonial epoch.

Picasso, Léger, Apollinaire, and many others came to recognize the elemental, "magical" power of African sculptures in a period of growing *négrophilie,* a context that would see the irruption onto the European scene of other evocative black figures: the jazzman, the boxer (Al Brown), the *sauvage* Josephine Baker. To tell the history of modernism's recognition of African "art" in this broader context would raise ambiguous and disturbing questions about aesthetic appropriation of non-Western others, issues of race, gender, and power. This other story is largely invisible at MOMA. . . . Overall one would be hard pressed to deduce from the exhibition that all the enthusiasm for things *nègre,* for the "magic" of African art, had anything to do with race. Art in this focused history has no essential link with coded perceptions of black bodies—their vitalism, rhythm, magic, erotic power, etc.—as seen by whites. The modernism represented here is concerned only with artistic invention, a positive category separable from a negative primitivism of the irrational, the savage, the base, the flight from civilization.

A different historical focus might bring a photograph of Josephine Baker into the vicinity of the African statues that were exciting the Parisian avant-garde in the 1910s and 1920s; but such a juxtaposition would be unthinkable in the MOMA history, for it evokes different affinities from those contributing to the category of great art. The black body in Paris of the twenties was an ideological artifact. Archaic Africa (which came to Paris by way of the future—that is, America) was sexed, gendered, and invested with "magic" in specific ways. Standard poses adopted by "La Bakaire," like Léger's designs and costumes, evoked a recognizable "Africanity"—the naked form emphasizing pelvis and buttocks, a segmented stylization suggesting a strangely mechanical vitality. The inclusion of so ideologically loaded a form as the body of Josephine Baker among the figures classified as art on West Fifty-third Street would suggest a different account of modernist primitivism, a different analysis of the category *nègre* in *l'art nègre* and an exploration of the "taste" that was something more than just a backdrop for the discovery of tribal art in the opening decades of this century.

Such a focus would treat art as a category defined and redefined in specific historical contexts and relations of power. . . .

Since 1900 non-Western objects have generally been classified as either primitive art *or* ethnographic specimens. Before the modernist revolution associated with Picasso and the simultaneous rise of cultural anthropology associated with Boas and Malinowski, these objects were differently sorted—as antiquities, exotic curiosities, orientalia, the remains of early man, and so on. With the emergence of twentieth-century modernism and anthropology figures formerly called "fetishes" (to take just one class of object) became works either of "sculpture" or of "material culture." The distinction between the aesthetic and the anthropological was soon institutionally reinforced. In art galleries non-Western objects were displayed for their formal and aesthetic qualities; in ethnographic museums they were represented in a "cultural" context. In the latter an African statue was a ritual object belonging to a distinct group; it was displayed in ways that elucidated its use, symbolism, and function. The institutionalized distinction between aesthetic and anthropological discourses took form during the years documented at MOMA, years that saw the complementary discovery of primitive "art" and of an anthropological concept of culture." . . .

Cultural background is not essential to correct aesthetic appreciation and analysis: good art, the masterpiece, is universally recognizable. The pioneer modernists themselves knew little or nothing of these objects' ethnographic meaning. What was good enough for Picasso is good enough for MOMA. Indeed an ignorance of cultural context seems almost a precondition for artistic appreciation. In this object system a tribal piece is detached from one milieu in order to circulate freely in another, a world of art—of museums, markets, and connoisseurship.

Since the early years of modernism and cultural anthropology non-Western objects have found a "home" either within the discourses and institutions of art or within those of anthropology. . . . Both discourses assume a primitive world in need of preservation, redemption, and representation. The concrete, inventive existence of tribal cultures and artists is suppressed in the process of either constituting authentic, "traditional" worlds or appreciating their products in the timeless category of "art."

⁂

Nothing on West Fifty-third Street suggests that good tribal art is being produced in the 1980s. The non-Western artifacts on display are located either in a vague past (reminiscent of the label "nineteenth-twentieth century" that accompanies African and Oceanian pieces in the Metropolitan Museum's Rockefeller Wing) or in a purely conceptual space defined by "primitive" qualities: magic, ritualism, closeness to nature, mythic or cosmological aims. In this relegation of the tribal or primitive to either a vanishing past or an ahistorical, conceptual present, modernist appreciation reproduces common ethnographic categories.

The same structure can be seen in the Hall of Pacific Peoples, dedicated to Margaret Mead, at the American Museum of Natural History. This new permanent hall is a superbly refurbished anthropological stopping place for non-Western objects. In *Rotunda* (December 1984), the museum's publication, an article announcing the installation contains the following paragraph:

> Margaret Mead once referred to the cultures of Pacific peoples as "a world that once was and now is no more." Prior to her death in 1978 she approved the basic plans for the new *Hall of Pacific Peoples*. (p. 1)

We are offered treasures saved from a destructive history, relics of a vanishing world. Visitors to the installation (and especially members of *present* Pacific cultures) may find a "world that is no more" more appropriately evoked in two charming display cases just outside the hall. It is the world of a dated anthropology. Here one finds a neatly typed page of notes from Mead's much-disputed Samoan research, a picture of the fieldworker interacting "closely" with Melanesians (she is carrying a child on her back), a box of brightly colored discs and triangles once used for psychological testing, a copy of Mead's column in *Redbook*. In the Hall of Pacific Peoples artifacts suggesting change and syncretism are set apart in a small display entitled "Culture Contact." It is noted that Western influence and indigenous response have been active in the Pacific since the eighteenth century. Yet few signs of this involvement appear anywhere else in the large hall, despite the fact that many of the objects were made in the past 150 years in situations of contact, and despite the fact that the museum's ethnographic explanations reflect quite recent research on the cultures of the Pacific. The historical contacts and impurities that are part of ethnographic work—and that may signal the life, not the death, of societies—are systematically excluded.

The tenses of the hall's explanatory captions are revealing. A recent color photograph of a Samoan *kava* ceremony is accompanied by the words: "STATUS and RANK were [sic] important features of Samoan society," a statement that will seem strange to anyone who knows how important they remain in Samoa today. Elsewhere in the hall a black-and-white photograph of an Australian Arunta woman and child, taken around 1900 by the pioneer ethnographers Spencer and Gillen, is captioned in the *present* tense. Aboriginals apparently must always inhabit a mythic time. Many other examples of temporal incoherence could be cited—old Sepik objects described in the present, recent Trobriand photos labeled in the past, and so forth.

The point is not simply that the image of Samoan *kava* drinking and status society presented here is a distortion or that in most of the Hall of Pacific Peoples history has been airbrushed out. (No Samoan men at the *kava* ceremony are wearing wristwatches; Trobriand face painting is shown without noting that it is worn at cricket matches.) Beyond such questions of accuracy is an issue of systematic ideological coding. To locate "tribal" peoples in a nonhistorical time and ourselves in a different, historical time is clearly tendentious and no longer credible (Fabian 1983). This recognition throws doubt on the perception of a vanishing tribal world, rescued, made valuable and meaningful, either as ethnographic "culture" or as primitive/modern "art." . . .

At the Hall of Pacific Peoples or the Rockefeller Wing the actual ongoing-life and "impure" inventions of tribal peoples are erased in the name of cultural or artistic "authenticity." Similarly at MOMA the production of tribal "art" is entirely in the past. Turning up in the flea markets and museums of late nineteenth-century Europe, these objects are destined to be aesthetically redeemed, given new value in the object system of a generous modernism.

⠀⠀✦⠀⠀

The story retold at MOMA, the struggle to gain recognition for tribal art, for its capacity "like all great art . . . to show images of man that transcend the particular lives and times of their creators," is taken for granted at another stopping place for tribal travelers in Manhattan, the Center for African Art on East Sixty-eighth Street. Susan Vogel, the executive director, proclaims in her introduction to the catalogue of its inaugural exhibition, "African Master-pieces from the Musee de l'Homme," that the "aesthetic-anthropological debate" has been resolved. It is now widely accepted that "ethnographic specimens" can be distinguished from "works of art" and that within the latter category a limited number of "masterpieces" are to be found. Vogel correctly notes that the aesthetic recognition of tribal objects depends on changes in Western taste. For example it took the work of Francis Bacon, Lucas Samaras, and others to make it possible to exhibit as art "rough and horrifying [African] works as well as refined and lyrical ones." Once recognized, though, art is apparently art. Thus the selection at the Center is made on aesthetic criteria alone. A prominent plac-ard affirms that the ability of these objects "to transcend the limitations of time and place, to speak to us across time and culture . . . places them among the highest points of human achievement. It is as works of art that we regard them here and as a testament to the greatness of their creators."

There could be no clearer statement of one side of the aesthetic anthro-pological "debate" (or better, *system*). On the other (anthropological) side, across town, the Hall of Pacific Peoples presents collective rather than indi-vidual productions—the work of "cultures." At the American Museum of Natural History ethnographic exhibits have come increasingly to resemble art shows. Indeed the Hall of Pacific Peoples represents the latest in aestheti-cized scientism. Objects are displayed in ways that highlight their formal properties. . . . While these artistically displayed artifacts are scientifically explained, an older, functionalist attempt to present an integrated picture of specific societies or culture areas is no longer seriously pursued. There is an almost dadaist quality to the labels on eight cases devoted to Australian aboriginal society (I cite the complete series in order): "CEREMONY, SPIRIT FIGURE, MAGICIANS AND SORCERERS, SACRED ART, SPEAR THROWERS, STONE AXES AND KNIVES, WOMEN, BOOMERANGS." Elsewhere the hall's pieces of culture have been recontextualized within a new cybernetic, anthropological discourse. For instance flutes and stringed instruments are captioned: "MUSIC is a system of organized sound in man's [sic] aural environment" or nearby: "COMMUNICATION is an important function of organized sound."

In the anthropological Hall of Pacific Peoples non-Western objects still have primarily scientific value. They are in addition beautiful. Conversely, at the Center for African Art artifacts are essentially defined as "masterpieces," their makers as great artists. The discourse of connoisseurship reigns. Yet once the story of art told at MOMA becomes dogma, it is possible to reintroduce and co-opt the discourse of ethnography. At the Center tribal contexts and functions are described along with individual histories of the objects on display. Now firmly classified as masterpieces, African objects escape the vague, ahistorical location of the "tribal" or the "primitive." The catalogue, a sort of *catalogue raisonné,* discusses each work intensively. The category of the masterpiece individuates: the pieces on display are not typical; some are one of a kind. The famous Fon god of war or the Abomey shark-man lend themselves to precise histories of individual creation and appropriation in visible colonial situations. Captions specify *which* Griaule expedition to West Africa in the 1930s acquired each Dogon statue. . . . We learn in the catalogue that a superb Bamileke mother and child was carved by an artist named Kwayep, that the statue was bought by the colonial administrator and anthropologist Henri Labouret from King N'Jike. While tribal names predominate at MOMA, the Rockefeller Wing, and the American Museum of Natural History, here personal names make their appearance.

In the "African Masterpieces" catalogue we learn of an ethnographer's excitement on finding a Dogon hermaphrodite figure that would later become famous. The letter recording this excitement, written by Denise Paulme in 1935, serves as evidence of the aesthetic concerns of many early ethnographic collectors. These individuals, we are told, could intuitively distinguish masterpieces from mere art or ethnographic specimens. (Actually many of the individual ethnographers behind the Musée de l'Homme collection, such as Paulme, Michel Leiris, Marcel Griaule, and André Schaeffner, were friends and collaborators of the same "pioneer modernist" artists who, in the story told at MOMA, constructed the category of primitive art. Thus the intuitive aesthetic sense in question is the product of a historically specific milieu.) The "African Masterpieces" catalogue insists that the founders of the Musée de l'Homme were art connoisseurs, that this great anthropological museum never treated all its contents as "ethnographic specimens." The Musee de l'Homme was and is secretly an art museum. The taxonomic split between art and artifact is thus healed, at least for self-evident "masterpieces," entirely in terms of the aesthetic code. Art is art in any museum. . . .

The non-Western objects that excited Picasso, Derain, and Léger broke into the realm of official Western art from outside. They were quickly integrated, recognized as masterpieces, given homes within an anthropological-aesthetic object system. By now this process has been sufficiently celebrated. We need exhibitions that question the boundaries of art and of the art world, an influx of truly indigestible "outside" artifacts. The relations of power whereby one portion of humanity can select, value, and collect the pure products of others need to be criticized and transformed. This is no small task. In the meantime one can at least imagine shows that feature the impure, "inauthentic" productions of past and present tribal life; exhibitions radically heterogeneous in their global mix of styles; exhibitions that locate themselves in specific multicultural junctures; exhibitions in which nature remains "unnatural"; exhibitions whose principles of incorporation are openly questionable. The following would be my contribution to a different show on "affinities of the tribal and the postmodern." I offer just the first paragraph from Barbara Tedlock's superb description of the Zuni Shalako ceremony, a festival that is only part of a complex, living tradition.

> Imagine a small western New Mexican village, its snow-lit streets lined with white Mercedes, quarter-ton pickups and Dodge vans. Villagers wrapped in black blankets and flowered shawls are standing next to visitors in blue velveteen blouses with rows of dime buttons and voluminous satin skirts. Their men are in black Stetson silver-banded hats, pressed jeans, Tony Lama boots and multicolored Pendleton blankets. Strangers dressed in dayglo orange, pink and green ski jackets, stocking caps, hiking boots and mittens. All crowded together they are looking into newly constructed houses illuminated by bare light bulbs dangling from raw rafters edged with Woolworth's red fabric and flowered blue print calico. Cinderblock and plasterboard white walls are layered with striped serapes, Chimayó blankets, Navajo rugs, flowered fringed embroidered shawls, black silk from Mexico and purple, red and blue rayon from Czechoslovakia. Rows of Hopi cotton dance kilts and rain sashes; Isleta woven red and green belts; Navajo and Zuni silver concha belts and black mantas covered with silver brooches set with carved lapidary, rainbow mosaic, channel inlay, turquoise needlepoint, pink agate, alabaster, black cannel coal and bakelite from old '78s, coral, abalone shell, mother-of-pearl and horned oyster hang from poles suspended from the ceiling. Mule and white-tailed deer trophy-heads wearing squash-blossom, coral and chunk-turquoise necklaces are hammered up around the room over rearing buckskins above Arabian tapestries of Martin Luther King and the Kennedy brothers, The Last Supper, a herd of sheep with a haloed herder, horses, peacocks.

Mythologies of Tribal Art

Forty years ago Roland Barthes defined a mythology as those "falsely obvious" ideas which an age so takes for granted that it is unaware of its own belief. An example of what he means can be seen in his 1957 critique of Edward Steichen's celebrated photographic assemblage "The Family of Man." Barthes declares that the myth this exhibition promotes first seems to stress exoticism, projecting a Babel of human diversity over the globe. From this picture of diversity, however, a pluralistic humanism "is magically produced: man is born, works, laughs and dies everywhere in the same way. . . ." The implicit mythological background of the show postulates "a human essence."

Barthes is exactly on target about the philosophic intentions of "The Family of Man." In his introduction to the published version of the exhibition, Steichen had written that the show was "conceived as a mirror of the universal elements and emotions in the everydayness of life—as a mirror of the essential oneness of mankind throughout the world." Such juxtapositions as that which places Nina Leen's *Life* magazine image of an American farm family next to a family in Bechuanaland (now Botswana), photographed by another *Life* photographer, Nat Farbman, are therefore meant to convey the idea that despite all differences of exterior form, of cultural surface, the underlying nature of all families and peoples is essentially the same. This position is what Barthes views as the sentimentalized mythology of "classic humanism," and he contrasts it with his own "progressive humanism," which must try "constantly to scour nature, its 'laws' and its 'limits' in order to discover History there, and at last to establish Nature itself as historical." While classic humanism regards the American and African families as embodying, beneath culture and skin color, abiding natural relationships of kin and affection, progressive humanism would insist that these bourgeois conceptions of the natural are themselves historically determined. Barthes claims that such imperialistic juxtapositions ignore the political and economic roots of diversity.

Although "The Family of Man" had a potently relevant message for the generation that had witnessed the genocidal horrors of the Second World War, it was also worth paying attention to Barthes's claim that Steichen's collection, for all its antiracism and humanist charms, conveyed an implicit

Excerpted from Denis Dutton, "Mythologies of Tribal Art," *African Arts*, vol. 28, no. 3 (Summer 1995). Copyright © 1995 by The Regents of the University of California. Reprinted by permission of *African Arts* and the author. Notes and references omitted.

illusion of equality of power among the cultures it portrayed. It is now two generations later, however, and critics who accept the importance of exposing cultural mythologies and covert ideologies have new work to do. One area of criticism that especially stands in need of fresh examination is the shell-pocked field where battles have raged over the status and understanding of ethnographic arts. Barthes's reaction to MOMA's "The Family of Man" is particularly pertinent in this regard, because much of what he says adumbrates reactions to another exhibition, " 'Primitivism' in 20th Century Art," which took place over a quarter of a century later in that same museum. That show displayed side-by-side images of Africa and Europe, not photographs of people, but works of art. And it too was denounced as complacently positing, without regard to cultural difference, a specious universalism—aesthetic instead of moral.

But a sea change in academic thinking separates Barthes's critique of "The Family of Man" from the more strident critics of the "Primitivism" show. In the middle 1950s, Barthes was nearly alone in his dissent against a much loved and widely praised exhibition. The generation of critics who questioned (or denounced) "Primitivism" represented a manner of thinking that had become a virtual academic fashion. Some of these later critics were arguing from a set of ideas that had themselves come to embody a virtual mythology in precisely the Barthesian sense. Their views presuppose and constitute, in point of fact, a New Mythology of tribal arts—a prevailing set of presuppositions, prejudices, and articles of political and philosophical faith which govern many discussions of these arts and their relations to European criticism, art, and aesthetics. A contemporary Africanist art historian [Sidney Kasfir] for example, writes in a recent *African Arts* article on the authenticity of African masks and carvings: "That from an African perspective, these objects are *not* art in the current Western sense is too well known to discuss here." The phrase "too well known to discuss here" is symptomatic of a mythology. Barthes claimed his intention to unmask "the mystification which transforms petit-bourgeois culture into universal nature." Today we should be just as willing to deal with those mystifications that transform prevailing conventions of academic culture into validated truth.

This vigorous New Mythology of tribal arts takes on its life against the backdrop of what it posits as the Old Mythology. As with other ideologies, the New Mythology would no more describe its precepts as "mythology" than would the Old: both operate according to the familiar adage "Your views are so much mythology; mine speak the truth." Nevertheless, much contemporary theorizing and criticism about tribal arts are founded on a complacent acceptance of a substrate of givens and unsupported hypotheses which constitute the central tenets of the New Mythology. To be sure, not all of the theses are false. On the other hand, not all of the beliefs the New Mythologists stigmatize as Old Mythology are false either. Independent, critical thinkers should want to choose the component ideas of these mythologies that are worth rejecting, preserving, or reviving.

Providing a disinterested assessment of these ideas is not easy in the present ideologically charged and factious atmosphere. This indeed is part of the problem: so many contemporary theorists of tribal arts posit enemies who have it all wrong, in contrast to themselves, who have it right. This lack of any generosity whatsoever toward one's perceived (or invented) opposition increasingly stultifies writing in this area. The New Mythology finds itself expressed by a wide range of writers, including, for example, the more vociferous critics of the "Primitivism" show such as Thomas McEvilley and Hal Foster; James Clifford in his treatment of museums and ethnographic art; Arnold Krupat in *Ethnocriticism;* Sidney Kasfir in her article "African Art and Authenticity," published in this journal; Sally Price in *Primitive Art in Civilized Places;* Marianna Torgovnick in *Gone Primitive;* and Christopher B. Steiner in *African Art in Transit.*

Mythologies, Old and New

There are actually two phases of the Old Mythology to which these writers tend to react. What I will call *premodernist* or *colonialist* Old Mythology includes the elements of nineteenth-century imperialism—racism, contempt for "childish" artifacts, and regard for "primitive" art as representing a lower evolutionary stage of human development, with missionaries burning "fetishes" and the wholesale looting of indigenous art, as in Benin. The later, more enlightened, *modernist* Old Mythology, exemplified by such figures as Picasso, Roger Fry, and the "Primitivism" exhibition itself, is, from a New Mythological perspective, perhaps even more insidious, because while it pretends to valorize these arts, it perpetuates acts of imperialism, appropriation, and ethnocentric insensitivity toward Third World peoples—all in the name of enlightened, magnanimous liberalism. The grounds for my three-fold distinction—between premodernist/colonialist Old Mythology, modernist Old Mythology, and the New Mythology—can be usefully developed in terms of the following key ideas. Again, some of these notions included within these mythologies are entirely valid, some constitute half-truths, and some are plainly false; no one of these sets of ideas has a monopoly on truth.

> *(1) According to the premodernist Old Mythology, at least as the New Mythology likes to imagine it, tribal artifacts weren't works of art at all, but merely "fetishes," "idols," "fertility symbols," "ancestor figures," and the like, which colonialists collected as they might botanical specimens. The later, post-Picasso modernist version of the Old Mythology insists, on the contrary, that they are works of art, embodying universal aesthetic values.*

Curiously, the New Mythology frequently sides with the colonialist Old Mythology by aggressively questioning the status of tribal artifacts as works of art: in the New Mythological view, the Old Mythology at least acknowledged difference. This convergence of opinion, however, is complicated. Philistine colonialists often regarded artifacts as demonstrating little skill and no sense of form: the colonialists were applying nineteenth-century European aesthetic criteria to genres of work they did not begin to comprehend, and so were reluctant to call them "art." The New Mythologists' reluctance to identify tribal artifact genres as "art" is based on the notion that this would be hegemonic or imperialistic. Such reluctance is frequently supported by unthinking repetition of the folk legend that pretechnological peoples have no art because they have no word that refers to what Europeans call "art." Patrick R. McNaughton recognizes another aspect of this New Mythologists' doctrine and has stressed the importance of challenging it, "because so many scholars still recite what has become a kind of maxim asserted by outsiders about Africans, that they unlike us treat what we call art as a functional part of life" rather than something for aesthetic contemplation.

(2) The Old Mythology essentialized the primitive, subsuming the endless variety of tribal cultures under a few crude stereotypes.

The New Mythology, on the other hand, while eager to recognize the diverse and frequently unique characteristics that distinguish tribal societies, essentializes "the West," creating, in an inversion of Edward Said's familiar formulation, a kind of Occidentalism. Thus, in the example cited earlier, Kasfir qualifies her discussion of authenticity with the remark that the artifacts in question should not be considered art "in the current Western sense." The quaintness of this last phrase should not go unnoticed: among Praxiteles, Donatello, Rembrandt, Judy Chicago, Duchamp, and Koons—not to mention the myriad genres of European folk craft and popular art—there is no "current Western sense" of art, but various, radically different, and rival senses of the concept, each partially implicated in competing social practices and theories of art. In fact, in its crudity, the very phrase "the West" is the New Mythologists' answer to "the Primitive" as that term might have been used a century ago. The latter was a lazy and misleading way of lumping together such cultures as Hopi, Sepik, Benin, and !Kung—even Aztec, in some understandings of "primitive." In the New Mythology, "the West" refers to twelfth-century French villages, horror movies, the Industrial Revolution, the theology of St. Augustine, New Zealand public education, the international banking system, modern toy retailing, medieval concepts of disease, Thanksgiving dinner, electronic mail, Gregorian chants, Linnaean botany, napalm, the Chopin études, and bar codes—as though the values and ideologies found therein can be the subject of useful generalization. The New Mythology replaces one set of stereotypes with another set, equally banal.

(3) In the Old Mythology, precontact tribal societies were seen as largely isolated, unchanging, coherent, and unbroken in their cultural tradition. Colonialism was supposed to have destroyed their structure and belief base. Their Golden Age of aesthetic and cultural achievement, and hence authenticity, predates European contact. Postcolonial culture and artifacts are culturally "inauthentic."

The New Mythology asserts to the contrary that these societies never were isolated, were not necessarily "unified" or "coherent," and underwent profound breaks in their traditions before European contact. The Old Mythology's " people without a history" view was a convenient colonialist construction. The New Mythology responds to claims of "inauthenticity" by variously claiming (a) indigenous belief systems were not destroyed but only occulted during the colonial period, and are now coming again into flower; (b) what is truly authentic is now found in the process of mutual appropriation by indigenous and colonial cultures; and in any event, (c) authentic cultural values must always be defined by the people who hold them: therefore, whatever indigenous people claim as authentic is, *ipso facto,* authentic, whether traditional, postcolonial, or merely imported.

Old and New Mythologists for the most part agree that small-scale indigenous societies have been permanently altered or obliterated by the encounter with the West's political systems, media, missionaries, technology, commerce, wage labor, and so forth. New Mythologists, however, are especially keen to emphasize that this has involved imperialist domination and exploitation. What is awkward for them is the fact that less desirable elements of culture change have been enthusiastically (and voluntarily) embraced by many indigenous peoples: cigarettes, soft drinks, movies, pop music, and Jack Daniels. By stressing that tribal cultures were always borrowing and in a state of flux, the New Mythology places in benign perspective the obliteration (or active abandonment) of traditional indigenous values: all cultures, it seems, are in the process of being altered by history.

> *(4) The Old Mythology, especially in its colonial form, held it unproblematic that traders or travelers might buy or barter for artifacts. Alternatively, artifacts might be accepted as gifts. None of this disturbs their meanings in the Old Mythology, and if anything the native should be thankful for receiving payment for the work before the termites got to it.*

The New Mythology sees buying, selling, and trading as essentially Western concepts. Even to accept these objects as gifts is to become, as Kasfir puts it, implicated in "the web of conflicting interests that surround them." There is hence no "noninterventionist" way of obtaining these artifacts, since somewhere in the scheme power relations will obtrude, leading to the exploitation of the indigenous maker or owner of the object. In other words, the native always gets cheated. The New Mythology seems to impute to precontact tribal societies a premercantile edenic state, as though trade and barter (not to mention theft or conquest) of ritual or other valuable artifacts did not occur among these peoples until Europeans came along.

> *(5) The only reason to collect primitive artifacts, according to premodernist Old Mythology, was as curiosities, examples perhaps of an early stage of Social Darwinist development: they were to be placed in a cabinet alongside fossils and tropical insects. After Picasso & Co., the Old Mythology proclaimed that primitive art embodied the aesthetic sensibilities found in all art, and therefore was as much worth collecting as Constables or Utamaros, and for precisely the same reasons.*

The New Mythology displays an oddly ambivalent attitude toward collecting. On the one hand, collecting is persistently disparaged, for instance as a "hegemonic activity, an act of appropriation . . . a largely colonial enterprise . . . the logical outcome of a social-evolutionary view of the Other." McEvilley speaks of "captured" tribal objects, a trope suggesting they exist in Western collections as prisoners or slaves. Given the reprehensible nature of collecting, one would expect New Mythologists to demand that the trade in ethnographic art cease, but I have not encountered any such suggestions (except, of course, for the criminal trade in looted antiquities). Even those writers who take moral satisfaction from criticizing collecting appear themselves to have "captured" the occasional artifact.

(6) On puritanical grounds the Old Mythology often forbade taking pleasure in works of tribal art: the sexual element in carvings offended missionary and nineteenth-century colonial sensibilities. In New Zealand, as elsewhere, genitals were hacked off Maori figures, and some overtly sexual carvings were simply burned, lest prurient pleasure be aroused.

The New Mythology replaces this attitude with a new and asexual form of puritanism. Enjoyment of any sort derived from the experience of ethnographic art is considered a cultural mistake at best, a form of visual imperialism at worst: "the colonialist gaze." Angst-ridden New Mythologists are reluctant to record appreciation or enthusiastic emotional reactions to artifacts. Thus Torgovnick heaps contempt on Roger Fry, among many others, for his "insensitive" and "racist" readings in praise of African art, but she never provides, in her own voice, nonracist, sensitive readings to instruct us on how to do it right. Nicholas Thomas is simply bemused: of the museums crammed with indigenous artifacts—"carved bowls, clubs, spears, baskets, pots," etc.—he honestly admits that "I have never understood why people want to look at such things (although I often look at them myself)." Christopher B. Steiner makes the bizarre claim that the objects are valued by Westerners as a way to "celebrate" the loss of the utility they had in their original cultural contexts. Other New Mythologists, such as James Clifford and James Boon (whose article title "Why Museums Make Me Sad" is clear enough), write about ethnographic arts with such a brooding sense of guilt about the historical treatment of conquered cultures that no sense of joy or love for the art is ever allowed to emerge.

(7) Colonialist Old Mythology held that though primitive cultures were to some degree capable of adopting Western technologies and manufactured articles, they could not possibly understand Western culture. In fact, having no adequate comparative perspective, the primitives could not even fully understand their own cultures. Their simple little societies were, however, transparent to the educated, sophisticated Westerner.

The New Mythology, on the contrary, contends that it is the "educated" West which fails to grasp the vast subtleties offered by these cultures, ranging from ethnobotany and folk medicines to spiritual wisdom. Instead, the West ethnocentrically imposes on them its own categories, such as "individual," "religion," or "work of art," when in actuality these concepts have no place in the cultural landscape of the Other. In the matter of borrowing, the New Mythology holds that indigenous artists are, in its preferred parlance, free to appropriate from European culture, infusing their new work with "transformed meanings," fresh associations given to foreign elements introduced into a new cultural context. The reverse—Europeans borrowing from indigenous arts—is to be discouraged. This inversion of the Old Mythology means that an innovative Sepik dancer who incorporates cigarette wrappers in an elaborate headdress is participating in an exciting fusion of cultures, while a Swedish office-worker who wears a New Guinea dog-tooth necklace is implicated in hegemonic, colonialist appropriation.

As a frontispiece for *Gone Primitive,* Torgovnick presents a heavily ironic, not to say sneering, painting (by Ed Rihacek) of a stylish European woman wearing sunglasses and sitting before a zebra skin, surrounded by a collection of "primitive art." In his derisory essay on the "Primitivism" exhibition, Clifford reproduces a 1929 photograph of Mrs. Pierre Loeb, seated in her Paris apartment filled with Melanesian and African carvings. Clifford labels this as an "appropriation" which was "not included in the 'Primitivism' Show" (a curious observation inasmuch as this very photograph appears in the show's catalogue). Both of these images suggest a kind of disapproval of European cultural appropriation that it would be unthinkable to direct toward their cultural inversion—for example, the 1970s posed village photograph Susan Vogel has published showing a Côte d'Ivoire man seated before a wrinkled, painted backdrop of an airplane, a cassette radio proudly displayed on his lap.

> *(8) The Old Mythology at its colonialist worst posited an ethnocentric aesthetic absolutism: advanced, naturalistic European art forms were seen, especially because of their naturalism, as demonstrating a higher stage in the evolution of art. Modernist Old Mythology retained the idea of universal aesthetic standards, but argued that tribal arts fully met these criteria for excellence, which were formalist rather than naturalistic.*

In rejecting both these positions, some New Mythologists urge the abandonment of any idea of transcultural aesthetic criteria (which would be implicitly imperialistic) in favor of complete aesthetic relativism. McEvilley imputes to Kant an epistemology which "tacitly supported the violent progress of 19th- and 20th-century imperialisms" and which justified a view of the Western aesthetic sense as superior to that of non-Western cultures. The New Mythology owes its aesthetic relativism entirely to the climate of poststructural thought rather than to any empirical study of ethnographic and other world arts.

> *(9) More generally, both colonialist and modernist Old Mythologies imply or presuppose an epistemic realism: they both presume to describe the actual, existent characteristics of tribal societies and their arts.*

Under the influence of poststructuralism, the New Mythology often presupposes various forms of constructivism, the idea that categories of human existence are constituted entirely by our own mental activity: we "invent" or "construct" the "primitive," tribal "art," "religion," and so on. The knots into which theorists become tied in trying to introduce such poststructural rhetoric into the study of indigenous arts is illustrated by Barbara Kirshenblatt-Gimblett who writes: "Ethnographic artifacts are objects of ethnography. They are artifacts created by ethnographers. Objects become ethnographic by virtue of being defined, segmented, detached, and carried away by ethnographers." From her first sentence, a dictionary definition, Kirshenblatt-Gimblett deduces a constructivist howler: the trivial fact that ethnographers define the ethnographic status of artifacts does not entail that *they create the artifacts*. Nor do they create the artifacts' meanings; it is the people being studied who determine that, and this awkward reality gets obviously in the way of attempts by New Mythologists to relativize cultural knowledge and meaning. Constructivism is a strong force among New Mythologists most influenced by literary theory, and is less persistent among those who come from a background of academic anthropology. Despite their tendency to toy with the jargon of literary theory, anthropologists generally acquire a robust respect for the independent existence and integrity of the peoples they study.

> (10) Finally, premodernist Old Mythology, especially in its Victorian colonialist guises, preached the superiority of Western culture. It proposed to bring moral enlightenment to people it viewed as savages, mainly through Christianity, but also with science and modern medicine. In this, it stands starkly apart from modernist Old Mythology, and even from some eighteenth-century explorers of the South Pacific, who claimed that the moral sense and intellectual capacities of "primitive man" were at least equal to those of Europeans.

The air of smug moral superiority has returned with a vengeance with the arrival of the New Mythology, whose champions patronize, censure, and jeer at any Old Mythology text they find wanting. The New Mythology of tribal arts displays a sense of righteous certitude that would fit the most zealous Victorian missionary.

At Play in the Fields of the Text

In some respects, the New Mythology's frequent borrowing from poststructuralism and the general intellectual climate of postmodernism is healthy and appropriate. For example, the approach to tribal arts must necessarily involve "blurred genres" and fused disciplines, bringing together ethnography, art history, philosophical aesthetics, and general cultural, including literary, criticism. This is fully in the poststructural/postmodern spirit, as is calling into question the peculiarly European distinction between the so-called fine arts and the popular and folk arts and crafts, which normally has no clear application in understanding tribal arts. But there are other aspects of poststructuralism which sit uneasily with the study of tribal arts.

One such notion is the pervasive poststructuralist attack on the authority of the artist or author in aesthetic interpretation. Barthes, whose thinking was again seminal in this regard, proclaimed the death of the god-author, along with the end of the ideologies of objectivity and truth, insisting that the meaning of a literary text is a critical construction instead of a discovered fact. In the theory of literature and the practice of criticism, such constructivist ideas have had their uses, liberating criticism from traditional demands to invoke authorial intention as a validating principle for critical interpretation.

However, the poststructural abandonment of the notion that texts contain meanings placed there by their authors (which it is criticism's job to determine) is only possible in a cultural landscape in which there is enough prior agreement on meanings to allow criticism to become thus freely creative. The poststructural death of the author could only take hold in literary theory because there was already in place an extensive tradition of interpretation of, say, *Madame Bovary* or *Moby Dick*. These novels enjoy a canonical status as works of literary art: they observe the conventions of established genres and were written in European languages by recognized literary artists. The cultural conditions that form the context of their creation and reception are solid enough to enable a generation of critics—notably Barthes, Foucault, and Derrida, but also the New Critics of the Anglo-American world—to declare the hypothetical death of the author and advocate a liberated, creative criticism of *jouissance*.

But do these doctrines and strategies of contemporary theory provide useful models for the critical ethnography of indigenous arts? Hardly. Poststructuralism's image of the free-spirited critic at play in textual fields goes counter to one of the most strongly held (indeed, in my opinion, indispensable) principles of the New Mythology: respect for the autonomous existence of tribal artists, including respect for their intentions and cultural values. Declaring the death of the (European) author may be jolly sport for jaded literary theorists, but an analogous ideological death of the tribal artist is not nearly so welcome in the New Mythology, nor should it be in any anthropology department. The study of tribal arts—indeed, all non-Western arts—cannot presuppose a sufficiently stable, shared background understanding against which one might declare artists' intentions irrelevant or passé. Moreover, the New Mythology gains its sense of identity by pitting itself against what it takes to be the Old Mythology's ethnocentric disregard not only for the intentions of tribal artists but for their very names as well. (Price calls this "the anonymization of Primitive Art," and it was a major complaint lodged against the "'Primitivism' in 20th Century Art" exhibition. If such ethnocentrism is not to be actively encouraged, the tribal artist's interpretations *must* enjoy special status, defining in the first instance the object of study. In order to respect the cultures and people from which tribal works of art are drawn, the New Mythology must treat indigenous intentions—ascertained or, where unavailable, at least postulated—as constituting the beginning of all interpretation, if not its exhaustive or validating end.

This deep conflict between doctrines of the New Mythology and the poststructuralism it seems so eager to appropriate keeps breaking out despite efforts to paper it over. McEvilley and Clifford enthusiastically adopt the discourse of constructivism, so long as they are talking about how "we," or "the West," or the "omniscient" curatorial mind, construct the generalized primitive, but New Mythologists are not nearly so keen to revert to constructivist parlance when it comes to discussing the actual meanings of works of tribal art. Thus Kasfir asks, "Who creates meaning for African art?," where "for" indicates "on behalf of," implying that Western collectors and exhibitors make a meaning for African art to satisfy the Western eye and mind.

This, however, avoids the more obvious wording of the question "Who creates the meaning *of* African art?" If there is any answer at all to this question, it must begin with the artists and cultures that produce the art. The West can "construct" in the poststructuralist manner to its heart's content, but its understandings will always be about the indigenous constructions of the cultures from which African works derive. It is indigenous intentions, values, descriptions, and constructions which must be awarded theoretical primacy. If an African carving is intended by its maker to embody a spirit, and that is an ascertainable fact about it, then any ethnography that constructs its meaning in contradiction to that fact is false. Of course, ethnography need not culminate with indigenous meanings and intentions, any more than literary criticism comes to an end when an author's intended meaning for a work of fiction has been determined. But ethnography has no choice except to begin with indigenous meanings, which it does not construct, but discovers.

POSTSCRIPT

Do Museums Misrepresent Ethnic Communities Around the World?

Clifford, like many critical theorists, is deeply suspicious of all representations of others. Dutton, in contrast, seems to question both the motives and the logic of this suspicion. He is especially critical of Clifford's lack of historical accuracy when describing the goals and motivations of museums and their curators. Are Clifford's postmodernist conclusions guilty of misrepresenting the museum world in ways that parallel his critique of particular exhibits? Does Dutton's critique of the postmodernists solve the historical problems that are present in both museums and the writings of their critics? Is there a middle ground that would allow for exhibitions with more sensitive context?

Clifford has also dealt with museum exhibits in his book *Routes: Travel and Translation in the Late Twentieth Century* (Harvard University Press, 1997). Related approaches to the problem of representation in museums include Sally Price's *Primitive Art in Civilized Places* (University of Chicago Press, 1989) and Shelly Errington's *The Death of Authentic Primitive Art and Other Tales of Progress* (University of California Press, 1998).

Nicholas Thomas's *Entangled Objects: Exchange, Material Culture and Colonialism in the Pacific* (Harvard University Press, 1991) considers the problem of representation among ethnographic objects in the Pacific. Enid Schildkraut and Curtis A. Keim's *The Scramble for Art in Central Africa* (Cambridge University Press, 1998), Ruth B. Phillips and Christopher B. Steiner's *Unpacking Culture: Art and Commodity in Colonial and Post Colonial Worlds* (University of California Press, 1999), and Michael O'Hanlon and Robert L. Welsch's *Hunting the Gatherers: Ethnographic Collectors, Agents, and Agency in Melanesia* (Berghahn, 2000) provide examples of the rich historical context of museum collections of the sort Dutton seeks.

Both Clifford and Dutton build their arguments on the premise that objects have complex histories, an idea that was originally developed in slightly different ways by anthropological historian George W. Stocking, Jr.'s *Objects and Others: Essays on Museums and Material Culture* (University of Wisconsin Press, 1985) and by anthropologist Arjun Appadurai's *The Social Life of Things: Commodities in Cultural Perspective* (Cambridge University Press, 1986). Both books make two crucial points: objects have histories, and the meanings of objects change when the objects themselves move from one context to another. Also, both argue that objects can take on many different meanings depending on context and viewpoint. Together these books have redefined museological studies and transformed what had been an anthropological backwater into a thriving specialization within the discipline.

Contributors to This Volume

EDITORS

KIRK M. ENDICOTT is a professor and the chairman of the Department of Anthropology at Dartmouth College. He received a B.A. in anthropology from Reed College in 1965, a Ph.D. in anthropology from Harvard University in 1974, and a D.Phil. in social anthropology from the University of Oxford in 1976. He has repeatedly conducted field research among the Batek people of Malaysia. He is the author of *An Analysis of Malay Magic* (Clarendon Press, 1970) and *Batek Negrito Religion: The World-view and Rituals of a Hunting and Gathering People of Peninsular Malaysia* (Clarendon Press, 1979), and is coauthor, with Robert K. Dentan, Alberto G. Gomez, and M. Barry Hooker, of *Malaysia and the "Original People": A Case Study of the Impact of Development on Indigenous Peoples* (Allyn and Bacon, 1997).

ROBERT L. WELSCH is a visiting professor of anthropology at Dartmouth College and adjunct curator of anthropology at The Field Museum in Chicago. He received a B.A. in anthropology from Northwestern University in 1972, an M.A. in anthropology from the University of Washington in 1976, and a Ph.D. from the same department in 1982. He has conducted field research among the Ningerum people of Papua New Guinea, the Mandar people of South Sulawesi, Indonesia, and the diverse peoples of the Sepik Coast of Papua New Guinea. He is the author of *An American Anthropologist in Melanesia* (University of Hawaii Press, 1998) and coeditor, with Michael O'Hanlon, of *Hunting the Gatherers: Ethnographic Collectors, Agents, and Agency in Melanesia* (Berghahn Publishers, 2000).

STAFF

Larry Loeppke	Managing Editor
Jill Peter	Senior Developmental Editor
Nichole Altman	Developmental Editor
Beth Kundert	Production Manager
Jane Mohr	Project Manager
Tara McDermott	Design Coordinator
Bonnie Coakley	Editorial Assistant
Lori Church	Permissions

AUTHORS

BRIAN R. BILLMAN is an associate professor of anthropology at the University of North Carolina. His research has focused on the prehistory of Peru and the American Southwest. His publications include *Settlement Pattern Studies in the Americas: Fifty Years Since Virú* (Smithsonian Institution Press, 1999), which he coauthored with Gary M. Feinman.

JAMES CLIFFORD is a professor of the history of consciousness at the University of California at Santa Cruz. He has written many books and articles about postmodern anthropology, including *Routes: Travel and Translation in the Late Twentieth Century* (Harvard University Press, 1997).

JAMES R. DENBOW is an associate professor of anthropology at the University of Texas at Austin. He has conducted field research in southern Africa and was curator of archaeology at The National Museum of Botswana.

THOMAS D. DILLEHAY is a professor of anthropology at the University of Kentucky. He is best known for his excavations at Monte Verde, Chile, and in the southwestern United States. He is the author of *Monte Verde: A Late Pleistocene Settlement in Chile* (Smithsonian Institution Press, 1997).

KURT E. DONGOSKE is a tribal archaeologist working in the Cultural Preservation Office of the Hopi Tribe. He is coauthor, with Mark S. Aldenderfer, of *Working Together: Native Americans and Archaeologists* (Society for American Archaeology, 2000).

DENIS DUTTON is associate professor of art theory in the School of Fine Arts at the University of Canterbury at Christchurch, New Zealand. He is a specialist on aesthetics and tribal art and is the author of *The Forger's Art: Forgery and the Philosophy of Art* (University of California Press, 1983).

T. J. FERGUSON is a consultant with Heritage Resource Management Consultants in Tucson, Arizona. He is the author of many articles and books, including *Historic Zuni Architecture and Society* (University of Arizona Press, 1996).

STUART J. FIEDEL is an archaeologist working with John Milner Associates in Alexandria, Virginia. He is the author of many books and papers, including *Prehistory of the Americas,* 2d ed. (Cambridge University Press, 1992).

DEREK FREEMAN (1916–2001) was an emeritus professor of anthropology at the Research School of Pacific and Asian Studies at the Australian National University. He conducted field research among the Iban of Borneo and the Samoans of western Samoa. He is author of many books and articles, including *The Fateful Hoaxing of Margaret Mead* (Penguin, 1999).

CLIFFORD GEERTZ is a professor at the Institute for Advanced Study in Princeton, New Jersey. He has conducted field research in Indonesia and Morocco. He is the author of *Works and Lives: The Anthropologist as Author* (Stanford University Press, 1988).

GEORGE W. GILL is a professor of anthropology at the University of Wyoming. He is a forensic anthropologist and has examined human skeletons from Mexico, Peru, Easter Island, and the Great Plains.

MARIJA GIMBUTAS is a late professor of European archaeology at the University of California at Los Angeles. She was the author of seventeen books and some two hundred articles on European prehistory, including *The Civilization of the Goddess* (HarperCollins, 1992).

JOHN J. GUMPERZ is an emeritus professor of anthropology at the University of California at Berkeley. His research interests have concentrated on sociolinguistics and issues of language and culture. He is the author of numerous books and articles, including *Discourse Strategies* (Cambridge University Press, 1982).

EDWARD H. HAGEN is anthropologist in the Institute for Theoretical Biology at Humboldt University in Berlin. His research has focused on evolutionary approaches to depression. He has published several articles about biosocial science and sociobiology.

ROBERT A. HAHN is epidemiologist with the Centers for Disease Control and Prevention and an adjunct professor of anthropology at Emory University. He has published many articles and books on various topics in medical anthropology, including *Anthropology in Public Health: Bridging Differences in Culture and Society* (Oxford University Press, 1999).

MARVIN HARRIS (1927–2001) was a professor of anthropology at Columbia University until 1980, when he was appointed graduate research professor of anthropology at the University of Florida. He was the author of many books on anthropology and anthropological theory, including *Cultural Materialism: The Struggle for a Science of Culture* (Random House, 1979).

ELLEN RHOADS HOLMES has conducted field research in Samoa. She is coauthor, with her husband Lowell D. Holmes, of *Samoan Village: Then and Now* (Harcourt Brace, 1992) and *Other Cultures, Elder Years: An Introduction to Cultural Gerontology* (Sage, 1995).

LOWELL D. HOLMES is an emeritus professor of anthropology at Wichita State University. He has conducted field research in Samoa and in contemporary America. He is the author of many articles and books, including *Quest for the Real Samoa* (Bergin & Garvey, 1986).

JEAN-JACQUES HUBLIN is a professor of anthropology at the University of Bordeaux as well as director of the Dynamics of Human Evolution Laboratory at France's Centre National de la Recherche Scientifique. He is the author of many articles and books on paleoanthropology, including *Les Hommes Préhistoriques* (Hachette, 1995).

SUDHIR KAKAR is widely known as the father of Indian psychoanalysis and has practiced for many years in New Delhi. He has been a visiting professor of psychology at the University of Chicago and is currently a senior fellow at the Center for the Study of World Religions at Harvard University. His books include *The Colors of Violence: Cultural Identities, Religion and Conflict* (University of Chicago Press, 1996).

ROGER M. KEESING (1935–1993) was a professor of anthropology at McGill University. He is best known for his research among the Kwaio people of Malaita in the Solomon Islands and published four books and many articles about them, including *Custom and Confrontation: The Kwaio Struggle for Cultural Autonomy* (University of Chicago Press, 1992).

PATRICIA M. LAMBERT is an associate professor of anthropology at Utah State University. Her research focuses on a variety of topics in North American bioarchaeology. She edited *Bioarchaeological Studies of Life in the Age of Agriculture: A View from the Southeast* (University of Alabama Press, 2000).

RICHARD B. LEE is a professor of anthropology and chair of the African Studies Programme at the University of Toronto. He is best known for his research among the San peoples of the Kalahari Desert. He is senior editor of *The Cambridge Encyclopedia of Hunters and Gatherers* (Cambridge University Press, 1999).

BANKS L. LEONARD is an archaeological consultant with Soils Systems, Inc. in Phoenix, Arizona. He has coauthored a number of articles and book chapters about Southwestern prehistory.

STEPHEN C. LEVINSON is director of the Language and Cognition Group at the Max Plank Institute for Psycholinguistics at Nijmegen in the Netherlands. His research has focused on linguistic anthropology and cognitive anthropology. He is the author of numerous books and articles, including *Presumptive Meanings* (MIT Press, 2000).

BETTY JEAN LIFTON is a therapist, freelance writer, and adoption rights advocate who has published widely on adoption in the United States. Her books include *Twice Born: Memoirs of an Adopted Daughter* (St. Martin's Press, 1998).

JONATHAN MARKS is an anthropology professor in the Department of Sociology and Anthropology at the University of North Carolina at Charlotte. He researches primate and human evolution, race, and molecular biology. He is the author of many books and articles, including *What It Means To Be 98% Chimpanzee* (University of California Press, 2002).

DEBRA L. MARTIN is a professor of biological anthropology at Hampshire College. Her research has focused on skeletal biology and bioarchaeology in North America. She is the author of many articles and books, as well as coeditor of *Harmony and Discord: Bioarchaeology of the La Plata Valley* (Museum of New Mexico Press, 2001).

CLEMENT W. MEIGHAN (1925–1997) was a professor of anthropology at the University of California at Los Angeles (UCLA) and for many years director of UCLA's Archaeological Survey. He excavated numerous archaeological sites in California and Mesoamerica. He was coauthor of *Chronologies in New World Archaeology* (Academic Press, 1978).

LYNN MESKELL is an associate professor of anthropology at Columbia University. Her archaeological research is focused on Egypt and the Mediterranean. She is the author of *Object Worlds from Ancient Egypt* (Berg, 2004).

JUDITH MODELL is a professor of anthropology, history, and art at Carnegie Mellon University in Pittsburgh, Pennsylvania. Best known for her research on adoption, she has written many articles and books, including *A Sealed and Secret Kinship: Policies and Practices in American Adoption* (Berghahn Books, 2001).

ANTHONY OBERSCHALL is professor of sociology at the University of North Carolina at Chapel Hill. He has written many books and articles dealing with social conflict, including *Social Movements: Ideologies, Interests, and Identities* (Transaction Books, 1993).

DALE PETERSON is a professor at Tufts University. He is the author, with Jane Goodall, of *Visions of Caliban: On Chimpanzees and People* (Houghton Mifflin, 1993) and, with Richard Wrangham, *Demonic Males: Apes and the Origins of Human Violence* (Houghton Mifflin, 1996).

STEVEN PINKER is a professor of brain and cognitive sciences at the Massachusetts Institute of Technology. His research has focused on the relationship between language and cognitive function. He has written numerous books, including *Words and Rules: The Ingredients of Language* (Basic Books, 1999).

MICHAEL E. PRICE is an anthropologist and postdoctoral fellow at the University of Indiana, formerly a graduate student at the University of California at Santa Barbara. He has published several articles about biosocial science and sociobiology.

JAMES RIDING IN is an associate professor of Justice Studies and American Indian Studies at Arizona State University. A historian by training, he is also a member of the Pawnee tribe.

E. S. SAVAGE-RUMBAUGH is a professor of biology at Georgia State University. She is the author of many articles and books about apes and their capacity for language, including *Ape Language: From Conditioned Response to Symbol* (Columbia University Press, 1986).

ROBERT W. SUSSMAN is professor of physical anthropology at Washington University in St. Louis and was recently editor of *American Anthropologist*. He is the author many articles and books, and editor of *The Biological Basis of Human Behavior: A Critical Review,* 2nd ed. (Prentice Hall, 1999).

SANGUN SUWANLERT was a physician and psychiatrist at Srithunya Hospital in Nondhaburi, Thailand. His research has focused on the use of psychotropic drugs and other psychological phenomena in Thailand, about which he has published several articles in English.

JOHN TERRELL is curator of oceanic archaeology and ethnology at The Field Museum in Chicago. He has conducted extensive field research in Papua New Guinea as well as in New Zealand, Tonga, Samoa, and Fiji. He has written numerous articles and books, including (with John P. Hart) *Darwin and Archaeology: A Handbook of Key Concepts* (Bergin and Garvey, 2002).

JOHN TOOBY is a professor of anthropology at the University of California at Santa Barbara (UCSB) and codirector of UCSB's Center for Evolutionary Psychology. He is a specialist on the evolution of hominid behavior and cognition. He is coeditor of *The Adapted Mind: Evolutionary Psychology and the Generation of Culture* (Oxford University Press, 1992).

HAUNANI-KAY TRASK is a professor of Hawaiian studies at the University of Hawai'i at Manoa. She is a well-known native Hawaiian activist with Ka Lahui Hawai'i, one of several organizations advocating native Hawaiian sovereignty. She is the author of *From a Native Daughter: Colonialism and Sovereignty in Hawai'i,* rev. ed. (University of Hawai'i Press, 1999).

TERENCE TURNER is a professor of anthropology at Cornell University. He is best known for his research among the Kayapo of the Amazon. His current research focuses on, among other topics, ethics and human rights. He has published many articles and book chapters about the Kayapo.

JOEL WALLMAN is a program officer at the Harry Frank Guggenheim Foundation in New York. In recent years he has studied aggression and linguistic ability. He is the author of *Aping Language* (Cambridge University Press, 1992).

EDWIN N. WILMSEN is a research fellow at the University of Texas at Austin. He has conducted research in Botswana and is the author of *Land Filled With Flies: A Political Economy of the Kalahari* (University of Chicago Press, 1989).

RICHARD WRANGHAM is a professor of anthropology at Harvard University. He studies primate behavior and ecology and evolutionary biology. He is the author, with Dale Peterson, of *Demonic Males: Apes and the Origins of Human Violence* (Houghton Mifflin, 1996).

JOÃO ZILHÃO is the founder and former director of the Archeological Institute of Portugal. His research focused on Neandertals in Paleolithic Iberia. He is a contributor to many academic journals and is the author of *Atomically Archaic, Behaviorally Modern: The Last Neanderthals and Their Destiny* (Oxbow Books, 2001).

Index